THE MIND AND THE MARKET

THE MIND AND THE MARKET

CAPITALISM IN MODERN EUROPEAN THOUGHT

JERRY Z. MULLER

ALFRED A. KNOPF   NEW YORK   2002

All rights reserved under International and Pan-American Copyright
Conventions. Published in the United States by Alfred A. Knopf,
a division of Random House, Inc., New York, and simultaneously in
Canada by Random House of Canada Limited, Toronto. Distributed by
Random House, Inc., New York.
www.aaknopf.com

Knopf, Borzoi Books, and the colophon are registered trademarks of
Random House, Inc.

A portion was originally published in *The Wilson Quarterly*.

Library of Congress Cataloging-in-Publication Data

Muller, Jerry Z., 1954–
The mind and the market : capitalism in modern European thought / by
Jerry Z. Muller.
p. cm.
Includes index.
ISBN 0-375-41411-8
1. Capitalism—History. 2. Capitalism—Europe—History. 3. Economics—
History. 4. Economics—Europe—History. 5. Capitalism—Moral and
ethical aspects. 6. Capitalism—Moral and ethical aspects—Europe.
I. Title.
HB501 .M84 2002
330.12'2—dc21   2002023124

Manufactured in the United States of America
First Edition

For my children,
Eli, Sara, and Seffy

CONTENTS

INTRODUCTION

We live in a world shaped by capitalism. In one or another of its ever-changing forms, capitalism has been with us for three centuries, and it will be with us a long time yet. In twentieth-century Europe, communism and fascism both failed to provide viable alternatives, and their non-European analogues have not proved any more successful. As we try to think through capitalism's present dynamics and future implications, it may help to know the best that has been thought and said on the subject in the past. That is the premise of this book. It is based on the assumption that capitalism is too important and complex a subject to be left to economists. Achieving a critical comprehension of it requires perspectives beyond those characteristic of modern economics. That is why this is a history not of economic ideas, but of ideas about the capitalist economy. After Adam Smith, economics developed as a discipline in part through bracketing off many of the issues central to the thinkers treated here. That has certainly led to gains in analytic precision and in creating a shared disciplinary vocabulary. But in thinking about the market, as in much else, there is no free lunch: the gains in technique and disciplinary cohesion have come at the expense of marginalizing many of the issues about the market that are likely to concern reflective people.

The idea for this book arose in the mid-1980s. During the preceding decade, some of the most penetrating analysts of contemporary society had put the subject of the moral, cultural, and political ramifications of capitalism on the front burner of cultural commentary. Some of these commentators, such as Jürgen Habermas, were on the left; some, like Irving Kristol, were on the right; some, like Daniel Bell and Christopher Lasch, were in between.[1] Their claims were many and diverse: that the familial hearth was being invaded by the forces of commerce; that civic virtue was disappearing; that the willingness to defer gratification upon which capitalism depends was in decline; that individualism and selfishness were destroying any sense of collective purpose; that work was losing its meaning; that men and women were besotted by consumer goods they did not need; that the international market was destroying particular historical cultures, leaving only a colorless syncretism or a hedonistic nihilism; that the spread of market values was eroding the very traditions and institutions on which capitalism depended; that the technological limits of growth had been reached; that the rich were getting richer while the poor were getting poorer—that for all these reasons and more, capitalism was in crisis.

Exploring modern European intellectual history under the stimulus of these present controversies, I found that such apprehensions had been on the minds of intellectuals for a very long time, at least since the eighteenth century. In fact, thinking about the ramifications of capitalism forms one of the great threads running through modern European intellectual history, as I first learned from radical intellectual historians on the anticapitalist left and right who had called attention to the fact.[2] I found that reflections on the cultural, moral, and political effects of capitalism had been central not only to intellectuals often treated as "economists," such as Adam Smith and Joseph Schumpeter, but to figures not usually thought of in connection with the market, from Voltaire through Hegel, from Edmund Burke through Matthew Arnold and beyond. Contemporary commentary often proceeded as if the subject of capitalism and its ramifications were new, with only limited awareness of this rich intellectual past. Commentators thus had a tendency either to reinvent the analytic wheel, to overrate the novelty of contemporary problems and treat as fatal contradictions what were in fact intrinsic but sustainable tensions, or to miss out on potentially useful lines of inquiry suggested in the past but since forgotten. At the same time, even before the demise of the Soviet Union and its empire, it was becoming clear that the world, taken as a whole, was moving toward capitalism, not away from it. At a time when many European intellectuals and their American acolytes were referring to the current age as one of "late capitalism," political and economic forces in what were then known as the First, Second, and Third Worlds were leading nations in each bloc not beyond capitalism, but toward more market-oriented economies and societies.[3] I therefore set out to recover and resuscitate what the best and brightest among European intellectuals—the great and the near great—have thought about the moral, cultural, and political ramifications of capitalism.

Though this is a book about European thinkers, it is not a book for Europeans alone. For while it places each thinker in historical context, it is concerned with arguments about the market that have a logic and validity not necessarily confined to the peculiarities of particular nations. Indeed several of the more recent thinkers wrote their most important works in the United States, not least because they thought that what was going on there had transnational ramifications.

The thinkers discussed in this book come from across western and central Europe, and from across the ideological spectrum. They include analysts who favored capitalism and those who despised it. In fact, as the book will demonstrate, the same analysis could be regarded as an argument for or against capitalism by thinkers who judged capitalism from differing moral premises. Since the evaluation of the moral significance of capitalism depends in no small part on the assessment of its economic effects, the book necessarily deals with what modern European intellectuals thought about how the capitalist economy functions and whom it benefits.

Among the issues that recur throughout this study is the question of poverty and wealth. Does the market make people richer or poorer? If it does tend to make people richer, is that necessarily a good thing? "I've been rich and I've been poor. Believe me, rich is better," declares the heroine of Fritz Lang's film *The Big Heat* (1953). But as we will see, the deeply entrenched traditions of classical republicanism and Christian asceticism claimed otherwise. In one way or another, a variety of modern thinkers from Rousseau through Marcuse have taken issue with the assumption that richer is better than poorer, arguing that material gain comes at the expense of moral loss.

Then there are questions of capitalism and culture. Does the market create a society more oriented to this-worldly rather than other-worldly concerns, and is that a point in its favor or against it? Is there a characteristic mentality associated with the market? If so, does that mentality spill over to other realms, and if it does, is that spillover desirable or lamentable?

What of the relation of the market to what we now call "cultural pluralism"? The term can be used in several distinct senses. Cultural pluralism may be said to exist on the international level when nations are culturally distinct from one another. Such difference *between* nations is compatible with enforced sameness *within* each nation, when a government tries to use its power to create or maintain a single, coherent national culture. Cultural pluralism exists in a second sense when there are a variety of ways of life within a single polity; such differences are compatible with enforced sameness within each community, which may try to use social, cultural, or other sanctions to keep individuals within the community's cultural fold. Cultural pluralism can also be used in a third sense, on the personal level, to designate the development of individuals who combine in themselves elements drawn from a variety of cultures and traditions. Whether pluralism in each of these senses is fostered or destroyed by capitalism is an ongoing theme. As we will see, many of the issues regarding the threat to collective historical identity now discussed under the rubric of "globalization" have been on the minds of European intellectuals for well over two centuries.

How the market economy affects the family has been another long-standing focus among the analysts of capitalism. Whether the spread of market relations is conducive to the liberation of women—by exposing them to new commodities or to new vocational possibilities outside the home—is one such concern, one that has been evaluated differently by conservatives, liberals, and radicals. The effect of the market on fertility has also been a subject of ongoing reflection: under differing circumstances, both rising fertility and declining fertility have been interpreted as destructive of the social order.

The relationship between capitalism and equality is another recurrent theme. Does capitalism foster equality or create new inequalities? And whatever answer one gives, does greater equality or inequality matter? Does capitalism rely on equal contributions from all, or does it depend on successfully harnessing the talents and energies of extraordinary individuals? And might there be a tension between the emphasis on equality fostered by political democracy and successfully harnessing the creative and industrious to the capitalist engine?

A larger theme, uniting several of those mentioned so far, is the effect of the market on premarket institutions—political, religious, cultural, economic, and familial. Does a capitalist society depend for its well-being upon such older institutions? If so, does it support, erode, or reshape them? And is that good, bad, or morally mixed? Much of the evaluation of these issues, as we will see, is linked to prior dispositions to favor either dynamism or stability.

Because the rise of the market to its position of centrality in modern European societies coincided with the rise of intellectuals as a distinct social group, another recurring theme is how the thinkers in question conceived of the role of intellectuals within a capitalist society. Should they be seen as the antithesis of the capitalist entrepreneur, or as his counterpart in the field of cultural life? Should the role of the intellectual be to overthrow capitalism, promote it, improve it, or create institutional counterweights to the values of the market? And how is mindfulness to be cultivated, making individuals more reflective about the market and its effects?

Since the Middle Ages, Jews were associated in the Christian west with the handling of money. It is no surprise then that the intellectual evaluation of an economy in which money played a central role was often intertwined with attitudes toward Jewry or toward Judaism. Jews in Christian Europe were permitted by the Church to engage in the stigmatized activity of lending money at interest precisely because they were regarded as outside the community of shared values. For some of the thinkers examined here, Jews served as a kind of metaphorical embodiment of capitalism. Only a society in which the reality of shared community was dead, it was said, would encourage the self-interested economic activities of which money-lending was the paradigm. The targeting of both Jews and capitalism, in turn, led a salient minority of Jews toward socialism and communism, an identification which was then played upon by antisemites. Thus another theme that recurs intermittently in the book is the connection between conceptions of capitalism and the images and fate of the Jews.

The Mind and the Market moves between practical, concrete capitalism, and intellectual reflection on capitalism—between what the Viennese satirist Karl Kraus, in his *Magical Operetta*, called *"tachles"* and *"shmonzes."*

I have explored those texts that seemed to present the best, most recurrent, and most influential arguments about capitalism. Sometimes I have focused on a single text by a particular author, at other times on an author's work as a whole. I have presented whatever contexts seemed the most useful in illuminating the texts and recapturing what their author had in mind. Sometimes that required explaining political events, sometimes economic developments, sometimes social and demographic changes, sometimes the changing contexts of intellectual life. Usually it required some exploration of the intellectual traditions and contemporary debates to which each author was responding. That is why readers will find themselves learning about matters seemingly far removed from the usual stuff of the history of ideas, including stock bubbles, migrating peasants, consumer revolutions, the East India Company, commodity futures, schemes to reform schooling based on "payment by results," and revolutions socialist and fascist. Michael Oakeshott once defined historical understanding as "the opportunity of seeing a passage of the past in terms of hitherto neglected relationships and of being able to imagine it freshly and more perspicuously. . . ."[4] This book tries to provide fresh and more perspicuous understandings of the debates about capitalism over the last three centuries by exploring some often neglected relationships.

I have attempted to construct the book so that each chapter can be read independently, but also so that reading the chapters consecutively shows the development of central themes and arguments across time and space. Through a series of case studies, the book demonstrates that the capitalist market is now and has ever been a morally complex and ambiguous entity. This has long been recognized both by its strongest critics and its subtlest advocates. We do them wrong—and shortchange ourselves—if we try to reflect on it without taking stock of their wisdom, let alone, as is so often done, by invoking their names with only a faint conception of their reasoning.

Rather than presenting an argument for or against capitalism, this book is meant to show how central the issue of capitalism has been in the intellectual history of the modern world, to re-create the arguments that have been made in the past, and to make critical perspectives on capitalism available to the present.

The fact that the authors are presented more or less chronologically is not meant to imply that the later authors are necessarily wiser or more incisive than those treated earlier. I suspect that there remains something worthwhile to be learned from most of these thinkers, even when they are at odds with one another. One can, for example, read all of the works of the final author treated, Friedrich Hayek, and never come across one of the key insights of the penultimate author, Herbert Marcuse, namely that the market is full of people trying to convince you to buy things that you don't really need and for the sake of which you may end up sacrificing your time, pleasure, and creativity. This is arguably one of the most important lessons that those who must forge a life within capitalist society can learn. On the other hand, one can read through all of Marcuse's works and never encounter Hayek's central insights that the market coordinates the manifold activities of individuals by relaying information not otherwise conveyable, and that it allows men and women with radically conflicting purposes to cooperate by focusing on shared means, thereby minimizing the need for consensus. Those already sympathetic to Marcuse's insight would do well to reflect on Hayek's, and vice versa.

A note on method: This book tries to recover the ideas of past thinkers, on the assumption that they may have something important to tell us when we come to think about the moral, cultural, and political effects of capitalism. My goal in each chapter has been to bring to light what the intellectuals in question thought about the market, how they thought about it, and what the market meant in each instance. How they thought about it meant examining the way in which their thinking about the market fit in with their larger concerns and purposes.

What the market meant to them required tracing the economic institutions to which they responded.

My working assumption (the fruit of several decades of methodological reflection by historians of thought) is that we can understand what was really at issue only by placing arguments in their historical context. To deal with "capitalism" or the "market" (or "liberty" or "the family" or most other broad concepts) in a historical vacuum is rarely a useful exercise, for we end up treating very different phenomena as if they were the same, and words that have meant something quite different over time as if they were of a piece. The premise governing contextual intellectual history of the sort practiced in this book is that the historian must establish what statements made in the past meant to their authors. The significance of their arguments can only be understood by relating those arguments to the larger concerns of the authors in question, and those concerns can only be understood by reference to the cultural, political, economic, and social realities that prompted them.

Yet to call this approach to intellectual history "contextual" leaves open the question of which contexts are worth exploring.[5] For a particular statement or argument, the relevant context may be the remainder of the text in which the statement appears. It may be the other works of the author in question. It may be the intellectual context in which the work was written, either the context provided by contemporary writers or the tradition of argument to which the author feels obliged to respond. It may be one or another economic context—of the author, of the intellectuals in his day, of his class, his ethnic group, his nation—or the political context; or, at times, the cultural and religious context. It may be the sum of the institutional contexts in which the author participated. How to decide which of these contexts to examine?

When I began the book over a decade ago, I imagined that in each chapter I would explore the biographical, political, economic, social, and intellectual context of each of the authors treated. But that turned out to be impractical, not least because it would have confirmed Voltaire's dictum, "If you want to bore the reader, tell him everything." In the end, the relevant contexts were determined in part through trial and error, in part through my evolving sense of which arguments by each author were most worth highlighting.

The authors and texts were chosen for inclusion based on several criteria. First, I wanted to cover what seemed like the most significant and recurrent arguments about capitalism, in their most penetrating formulations. Second, I wanted to follow the development of these arguments over time, to show how their significance could change as they were reformulated in different cultural, economic, and political contexts. If the authors are drawn disproportionately from German-speaking Europe, it may be because that is where the debate on capitalism was conducted most intensely among intellectuals. Some of the figures from German-speaking Europe—such as Hegel, Marx, and Schumpeter—would have to be included in any book such as this. Others who are the focus of chapters (such as Möser, Sombart, and Freyer) had their ideological counterparts elsewhere, who made similar arguments in different national contexts. But I was more interested in the range of arguments than the geographic origins (or, for that matter, the genders) of those who made them.

There is an inevitable tension between striving for present significance and writing contextual history. For what counts as "significant" in choosing subjects for historical research is linked to contemporary concerns in general, and to those of the author in particular. The ways in which the problem to be researched is framed, the criteria of what will be investigated, highlighted, and ignored are all connected to the historian and his or her interests. And if the concerns of the intellectuals to be examined are to be explained partly by their historical contexts, this suggests that their concerns might differ radically from those of our present context. My way of reconciling these seemingly conflicting imperatives is to suggest that while our questions might not always be theirs, we might profit by asking their questions, even in an altered context. In addition, their questions are often close enough to ours that we may profit by reflecting upon their answers.

The cost of treating ideas without adequate reference to their context is to traduce those very ideas. But hypercontextualism also has its costs, for too exclusive a focus on historical context may make the ongoing relevance and continuing power of ideas unintelligible.[6] Whatever this book has lost in terms of either present relevance or historical specificity is compensated for, I hope, by the gains made in understanding the arguments of yesterday and their potential interest today and tomorrow.

"Capitalism" is a term coined by the nineteenth-century enemies of the system it was meant to describe (and defame). But many of the most useful concepts in our collective vocabulary were either coined as invidious terms or came into common usage long after the phenomena they describe came upon the scene. The phenomenon that came to be called capitalism long preceded the term. Before Marx, it was variously known as "commercial society" (Adam Smith's term) or as "civil society" (Hegel's). I have therefore used the terms "capitalism" and "the market" to characterize the object of the analyses in this book, while constantly trying to convey just what it was each author meant by "the market" in his time and place.

A working definition of capitalism is "a system in which the production and distribution of goods is entrusted primarily to the market mechanism, based on private ownership of property, and on exchange between legally free individuals." Notice that this definition is not purely "economic," for "private" property and legally free individuals exist only because there are political mechanisms that protect individuals from having their persons and property seized by others. This definition is an ideal type—an abstract model meant to highlight certain features that exist in reality only in imperfect forms. Almost nowhere, for example, have production and distribution been determined purely by free exchange in the market; capitalism has existed with some degree of unfree labor (as in the antebellum American South); and a market-dominated economy has often existed alongside a government-owned sector.

Humans have been exchanging objects with one another since the Stone Age. But it was only in the eighteenth century that one can begin to speak of an economy in which production for trade became more significant than production for subsistence, and in which the market became central to the production and distribution of goods. Before that, in feudal Europe, the major means of production was land, and control of it was based on political power, which itself was largely a function of military force. Under those circumstances, where land and the people on it were the prize and guarantee of political power, it was unthinkable that land or labor could be sold to just anyone with the means to pay for them, regardless of their origins.[7] The erosion of this feudal organization of society had of course been going on for some time by 1700, and in the economically most advanced parts of Europe it was already becoming outmoded or extinct. Most historical "beginnings" have an element of arbitrariness, but one has to begin somewhere, and by the beginning of the eighteenth century the institutions that came to be identified with capitalism were sufficiently established to form an object of sustained intellectual reflection. But that reflection took place against a backdrop of earlier traditions, which is why we must begin before this beginning.

THE MIND AND THE MARKET

CHAPTER ONE

HISTORICAL BACKDROP:
RIGHTS, RIGHTEOUSNESS, AND VIRTUE

*Those who accumulate possessions without end and without
measure, those who are constantly adding new fields and new
houses to their heritage; those who hoard huge quantities of wheat
in order to sell at what to them is the opportune moment; those
who lend at interest to poor and rich alike, think they are doing
nothing against reason, against equity, and finally against divine
law, because, as they imagine, they do no harm to anyone and indeed benefit those who would otherwise fall into great necessity. . . . [Yet] if no one acquired or possessed more than he needed
for his maintenance and that of his family, there would be no des-
titute in the world at all. It is thus this urge to acquire more and
more which brings so many poor people to penury. Can this immense greed for acquisition be innocent, or only slightly criminal?[1]*

—FATHER THOMASSIN, *TRAITÉ DE NÉGOCE ET DE L'USURE,* 1697

*Trade, without doubt, is in its nature a pernicious thing; it brings
in that wealth which introduces luxury; it gives rise to fraud and
avarice, and extinguishes virtue and simplicity of manners; it
depraves a people, and makes way for that corruption which never
fails to end in slavery, foreign or domestic. Lycurgus, in the most
perfect model of government that was ever framed, did banish it
from his commonwealth.[2]*

—CHARLES DAVENANT, "ESSAY UPON THE PROBABLE METHODS OF
MAKING A PEOPLE GAINERS IN THE BALANCE OF TRADE," 1699

To distinguish the novel from the perennial in modern debates
about the moral worth of a society organized around the market,
we must recall the characteristic attitudes of the great traditions of

European thought toward commerce and the systematic pursuit of material gain through trade. For they made up the backdrop of concepts and images against which modern intellectuals would write. Even when these traditional arguments were no longer advanced explicitly, they lingered on as residues, influencing popular perceptions and more articulate debate.

There was no room—or little room—for commerce and the pursuit of gain in the portrait of the good society conveyed by the traditions of classical Greece and of Christianity, traditions that continued to influence intellectual life through the eighteenth century and beyond. Yet when discussion turned from outlining an ideal society to regulating real men and women through law, accommodating commerce and the pursuit of gain inevitably played a larger role. Roman civil law, with its origins in the empire and its emphasis on the protection of property, served as a reservoir of more favorable attitudes toward the safeguarding and accumulation of wealth. The hot and cold wars of religion that marked the early modern period were a turning point in the relations between these traditions. For as men judged the cost of imposing a unified vision of the common good too high, they increasingly took their bearings from the Roman civil tradition, which focused upon giving each his own, without subordinating all to some vision of the common good that they no longer shared.

The two quotations that open this chapter, written on the threshold of the eighteenth century, capture the hostility toward trade and moneymaking within two of the most venerable traditions of European thought. The statement by the Catholic cleric expresses the predominant view of commerce in the Christian tradition. The second, by an English political economist, reflects the tradition of civic republicanism. Both positions drew upon and modified classical Greek and Roman thought. Both traditions were suspicious of commerce, regarding it as inimical to the pursuit of virtue.

The moral disparagement of commerce reached back to the classical roots of western thought. In the city-states of ancient Greece, virtue meant devotion to the well-being of the city and above all to its military defense, in a society in which preparation for war or actual combat was a near constant of political life.[3] "The more men value moneymaking, the less they value virtue," Socrates tells his interlocutor in Plato's *Republic*.[4] Aristotle articulated a widespread Greek conception of freedom, according to which the well-governed city was one in which participation was shared among free men, who were each the head of an economically self-sufficient household. Material needs were provided by household slaves or by independent craftsmen, who were not deemed worthy of citizenship.[5] Possessing substantial wealth was a prerequisite for engaging in the higher activities of civic deliberation and participation, as well as for the exercise of the virtues of magnanimity and liberality. For Aristotle it is desirable to be rich, but morally hazardous to engage in the active pursuit of riches through trade. Thus, those who engaged in trade for their livelihood were to play no political role in the best possible regime, one which was ruled by its best citizens and rewarded virtue. "In the city that is most finely governed," he wrote, "the citizens should not live a vulgar or a merchant's way of life, for this sort of way of life is ignoble and contrary to virtue."[6] Even though Aristotle's fellow Athenians were fed by grain purchased from abroad, the ideal polis of the Greeks left no room for internal commerce or external trade.[7] The Greeks might tolerate commerce as a necessity, but they feared it, suspecting that the economic specialization it brought about would lead to a differentiation of interests and destroy the sense of common purpose and willingness to sacrifice upon which the polis depended.[8] There were merchants, bankers, and moneylenders in Athens, but they were seen as outsiders and denied the status of citizens.[9]

Aristotle regarded commerce—the "trafficking in goods" in which money was the means and goal of exchange—not only as inimical to political virtue, but as a hazard to the moral well-being of the individual. Aristotle's moral theory stressed moderation, the mean between the two extremes of excess and defect. Unlike more moral pursuits, he maintained, the pursuit of wealth lacks any natural, intrinsic limit and is hence prone to excess. Those engaged in commerce for money thus have a propensity to *pleonexia* (greediness or overreaching); they tend to devote their lives to gaining more and more without limit or reflective purpose.[10]

Most classical writers also saw no economic justification for deriving income from the merchant's role of buying and selling goods. Since the material wealth of humanity was assumed to be more or less fixed, the gain of some could only be conceived as a loss to others. Profits from trade were therefore regarded as morally illegitimate.

The most suspect form of commerce was the making of money from money. The lending of money for the sake of earning interest was defined as "usury," which Aristotle condemned as unnatural. "While expertise in exchange is justly blamed since it is not according to nature but involves taking from others," wrote Aristotle, "usury is most reasonably hated because one's possessions derive from money itself and not from that for which it was supplied. . . . So of the sorts of business this is the most contrary to nature."[11] The condemnation of usury would come to occupy a central place in the economic writings of Christian theologians and lawyers up through the early modern era.

If classical Greek thought was suspicious of trade and of merchants, the Christian Gospels and the early Fathers of the Church were actively and intensely hostile.[12]

The Gospels warned shrilly and repeatedly that riches were a threat to salvation. "Do not lay up for yourselves treasures on earth," Jesus is reported to have preached in his Sermon on the Mount. "For where your treasure is, there will your heart be also." "You cannot serve God and mammon," he warned (Matthew 6:19–24), and most famously, "It is easier for a camel to go through the eye of a needle than for a rich man to enter the kingdom of God" (Mark 10:25). Paul reiterated these lessons, and added that "the love of money is the root of all evils" (I Timothy 6:10).

Closely intertwined with this disparagement of wealth was the suspicion of merchants and the pursuit of profit. "Jesus entered the temple of God and drove out all who sold and bought in the temple, and he overturned the tables of the moneychangers and the seats of those who sold pigeons. He said to them, 'It is written, "My house shall be called a house of prayers"; but you make it a den of robbers'" (Matthew 21:12–13). Referring to these verses, the early canon *Ejiciens Dominus* declared that the profession of merchant was scarcely ever agreeable to God.[13] It was later incorporated into the *Decretum*, the great collection of canon law compiled by Gratian in the middle of the twelfth century, and encapsulated the Church's view of commerce as expressed in law and ritual. Gratian condemned trade and its profits absolutely.[14] "The man who buys in order that he may gain by selling it again unchanged as he bought it, that man is of the buyers and sellers who are cast forth from God's temple," he declared.[15] In the prayers for the Thursday before Easter (the day before Good Friday) Judas Iscariot was referred to as "that most vile of merchants."[16]

The Fathers of the Church adhered to the classical assumption that since the material wealth of humanity was more or less fixed, the gain of some could only come at a loss to others. St. Jerome found justifiable the Gospels' description of wealth as " 'unjust riches,' for they have no other source than the injustice of men, and no one can possess them except by the loss and ruin of others." St. Augustine was more pithy: "*Si unus non perdit, alter non acquirit*," he claimed—"If one does not lose, the other does not gain."[17] That remained the dominant view, though not the only one of which Christians could conceive. The pagan teacher Libanius of Antioch suggested in the fourth century that commerce was part of a providential design to permit men to enjoy the widely scattered fruits of the earth, a sentiment echoed by his pupils, the early Church Fathers St. Basil and St. John Chrysostom. But that view was fleeting and soon forgotten.[18]

The development of a more dynamic economy in the Late Middle Ages led Christian thinkers to reconsider their conceptions of commerce. In the centuries from about 1100 through 1300, the commercial economy of Europe began to grow, cities to develop, and new financial instruments were invented. The Scholastic theologians of the period formulated a more nuanced and less hostile approach toward trade, distinguishing between legitimate profits derived from sales or from the employment of others and the stigmatized category of usury.[19] Thomas Aquinas, the greatest of the Scholastics, revived and expanded Aristotle's arguments in favor of the social necessity of private property. He set out not only to synthesize the Gospels with the insights of the newly recovered philosophy of Aristotle, but to reconcile the fundamentally anticommercial ethos of both with an appreciation of the place of work and of property in the life of the more commercial towns of the Middle Ages. Private property was treated as legitimate because useful, work as a part of the process of creation. For Thomas—and for subsequent Thomists—the basis of the social order was the family, which served the naturally given and rationally explicable purposes of propagation and the containment of sexual desire (concupiscence). The division of labor characteristic of urban life led "naturally" to a hierarchy of estates and to the organization of professional associations in the form of guilds. Economic life, in this conception, should be ordered to provide the head of the family with enough income to support his family in the customary standard appropriate to their estate. Such an order provided stability, but only when expectations of consumption were limited and oriented by one's place in the social hierarchy.[20] At least as late as the papal encyclicals *Rerum Novarum* of 1891 and *Quadragisimo Anno* four decades later, Catholic social thought tried to fit the critiques and claims of analysts of the modern capitalist economy into the framework bequeathed by the Angelic Doctor.

Thomas and his successors provided a more religiously benign view of commercial life, by distinguishing the evils of dishonesty and fraud in trade from commerce itself. Aquinas, John Duns Scotus (ca. 1266–1308), and San Bernardino of Siena (1380–1444) all recognized that merchants played a positive role in supplying their customers with wares from distant places, and were entitled to some remuneration for their services.[21] Yet this more positive view of commerce remained highly qualified.[22] Although trade was accepted as a permanent institution, commerce for the sake of profit was generally disdained as unworthy of those who pursued a virtuous life, and the motivations of those who engaged in trade continued to meet with mistrust on a variety of grounds.

From Augustine through Aquinas and beyond, the Christian tradition viewed pride as a fundamental human vice.[23] Humility and meekness were the prerequisites for responding to the divine grace that made salvation possible—virtues thought difficult to reconcile with mercantile life. Echoing Aristotle, Aquinas reasserted that justice in the distribution of material goods was fulfilled when someone received in proportion to his status, office, and function within the institutions of an existing, structured community.[24] Hence Aquinas decried as covetousness the accumulation of wealth to improve one's place in the social order.[25] The pursuit of profit remained linked in Christian theology to the cardinal sins of *avaritia* (avarice) and *luxuria* (lechery).[26] Aquinas cited Aristotle in holding that "trade, insofar as it aims at making profits, is most reprehensible, since the desire for gain knows no bounds but reaches into the infinite."[27]

In Catholic thought the providential role of commerce was overshadowed by the hostility to the search for profit that Father Thomassin conveyed in 1697. If Protestant divines were less suspicious of trade, they were no less convinced that the pursuit of riches threatened salvation. Religious polemics against wealth remained a staple of sermonizing among Dutch Calvinists and English Puritans.[28] In the new world, Cotton Mather reflected on the fate of the Plymouth colony and lamented, "Religion begot prosperity, and the daughter devoured the mother"—a recurrent theme of Protestant jeremiads thereafter.[29] In the eighteenth century, John Wesley, the founder of Methodism, feared that "wherever riches have increased, the essence of religion has decreased in the same proportion. Therefore I do not see how it is possible, in the nature of things, for any revival of true religion to continue long. For religion must necessarily produce both industry and frugality, and these cannot but produce riches. But as riches increase, so will pride, anger, and love of the world in all its branches."[30] To pursue profit was to endanger salvation; the search for gain in this world was likely to lead to the loss of the next.

Of all the forms of commerce disdained by the classical authors, the Fathers of the Church, and the medieval theologians, none was so reviled as the lending of money for the sake of earning interest. This practice, which Aristotle had considered blameworthy, Christian theologians found sinful. "You may lend with interest to foreigners, but to your brother you may not lend with interest": this verse from the twenty-third chapter of Deuteronomy had prohibited Jews from lending with interest to one another, but allowed them to lend to non-Jews.

Medieval Christian and Jewish theologians strove to define the terms "brother" and "stranger" and to provide contemporary applications. By the twelfth century, Christian theologians had concluded that "brother" applied to all men, and that the lending of money at interest was always sinful.[31] Usury was expressly forbidden by the second Lateran Council in 1139. The *Decretum* of Gratian discussed the problem of sale under the general heading of usury, and the moral stigma of usury was extended to other types of contracts, especially those connected with the buying and selling of grain.[32] On a more popular level, the fable of the usurer's demise and passage to hell was a stock genre of the Middle Ages and one that appears in Dante's *Inferno*.[33]

Even as theologians partially adapted to the rise of an urban, commercial economy by defending private property and partially legitimating trade, the opposition of the Church to usury intensified.[34] Aquinas cited both Aristotle and Roman precedents to argue that money was sterile by nature. That "money does not beget money" was central to Scholastic economic doctrine. From Aquinas through the eighteenth century, Catholic casuists remained vitally concerned with distinguishing profits that were usurious and hence illicit from licit profits.[35] Indeed, the Church's prohibition on the taking of interest was reasserted in the papal encyclical *Vix Pervenit* of 1745.[36]

The renewed emphasis on the prohibition of usury led to a clash between religious claims and economic developments. From 1050 to 1300, the Church attained a new level of influence over European life. Administrative tasks were becoming more complex and increasingly came into the hands of those with the ability to read and write—which meant the clergy. A series of reforming popes articulated clerical claims to influence the right ordering of the world, and yoked that ideology to a codification of canon law, an elaboraton of Scholastic thought, and the development of administrative structures to enforce Church doctrine. This intensification of Church influence occurred at the very time when new agricultural surpluses made greater commerce possible, and hence made the economic function of lending money more important.[37] The Church struggled against usury by Christians, while moneylending was more necessary than ever to the expanding European economy. A mortal sin of theology became a mortal necessity of commercial life. "Those who engage in usury go to hell; those who fail to engage in usury fall into poverty," wrote the Italian wit

Benvenuti de Rambaldis de Imola, in his fourteenth-century commentary on Dante's *Divine Comedy*.[38]

One method by which the Church resolved this dilemma, beginning in the twelfth century, was to prevent the evil of Christian usury by allowing Jews to engage in that forbidden economic activity. For Jews were not subject to the prohibitions of canon law, and were condemned in any case to perpetual damnation because of their repudiation of Christ. Pope Nicholas V, for example, preferred that "this people should perpetrate usury than that Christians should engage in it with one another."[39]

Thus began an association of moneymaking with the Jews, an association that would further taint attitudes toward commerce among Christians and that, as we shall see, would survive in transmuted forms in the reflections of modern intellectuals. In early medieval iconography money was often connected with excrement and portrayed as filthy and disgusting. Now Jews themselves were often depicted as foul-smelling. Pictorial representations of avarice often bore standard attributes of Jews.[40] In Passion plays, the negotiations between Judas Iscariot and the Jewish leaders of his day were portrayed as the bargaining among typical medieval Jewish moneylenders.[41] So closely was the reviled practice of usury identified with the Jews that St. Bernard of Clairvaux, the leader of the Cistercian order, in the middle of the twelfth century referred to the taking of usury as "jewing" (*iudaizare*), and chastised Christian moneylenders as "baptized Jews."[42] In order to protect Christian moneylenders who provided them with funds, the kings of France and England created the legal fiction that these moneylenders (both lay and clerical) were to be considered Jews for legal purposes, and hence were under exclusive royal authority.[43] In central Europe, Christian moneylenders were disparaged as wielders of the *Judenspiess*, the "Jews' spear" of usury.[44] This symbolic identification as "Jewish" of the forms of capitalism considered most unseemly would have a long life.

The Jews of Europe, who had once earned their livelihood from farming and handicrafts, were transformed by the thirteenth century into an increasingly mercantile population with an emphasis on the lending of money. A series of factors pushed Jews into the money trade and made it comparatively attractive to them. Jews were forced out of landowning by a Church concerned to collect ecclesiastical tithes on land, which might no longer be paid if the land fell into Jewish hands. The growth of guilds in the later Middle Ages pushed Jews out of crafts by exclusionary policies that restricted membership to Christians.

Since Jewish settlements were made insecure by their dependence on the toleration of Christian nobles and monarchs, Jews were attracted to movable property, especially precious metals and gems, which could be easily concealed and transported. Jews were also drawn toward commerce in general and moneylending in particular as an indirect result of their religious beliefs, which put a premium on devotion to the study of Torah. Earning one's living through commerce left more time for such valued pursuits than did an agricultural or artisanal livelihood. Moreover, because Jews were scattered across Europe and Asia but shared a legal code and a language of discourse (Hebrew), they were positioned to act as traders over wide areas.[45]

The special role of moneylender made Jews both indispensable to the political authorities, which tolerated and protected them, and odious to parts of the Christian population. Jews were often brought in to meet economic needs, especially those of the monarch, for whom they were indirect tax collectors. In medieval Europe, the nobility and the clergy were exempt from royal taxation. These groups borrowed money from resident Jews and repaid their loans with high rates of interest. Much of the money that the Jews accumulated in this fashion made its way into the royal treasury, through royal taxes on the Jewish community or various forms of confiscation. The Jewish moneylender thus acted like a sponge, sucking up money from untaxable estates, only to be himself squeezed by the monarch. The interest rates charged by Jews were in keeping with the scarcity of capital in the medieval economy and the high risks incurred by Jewish moneylenders, whose loans were often canceled under public pressure and whose assets were frequently confiscated. High by modern standards, these rates often ranged from 33 to 60 percent annually.[46]

Within western Christendom, then, the image of commerce was closely connected to that of the Jew, who was regarded as avaricious and, as an outsider and wanderer, able to engage in so reviled an activity as moneylending because he was beyond the community of shared faith.

In Catholic countries, usury was condemned in both canon and civil law until well into the eighteenth century, and remained an object of obloquy even later. Pope Benedict XIV reaffirmed the prohibition against lending at interest in his bull *Vix Pervenit* of 1745, and as late as 1891 the papal bull *Rerum Novarum* of Leo XIII condemned "voracious usury" and linked it with greed and avarice. Usury remained an offense under French law until October 1789. To be sure, the lending of money at interest was practiced by Christians nevertheless, often furtively, sometimes with the aid of Scholastic legal rationalizations that defined the transactions as nonusurious; in some places civil and even ecclesiastical courts adopted a distinction between "moderate" and "immoderate" rates of usury unsanctioned by canon law. By the mid-nineteenth century the Vatican advised faithful Catholics who retained qualms about lending at the legal rate of interest not to worry about its effect upon their souls, but left the theoretical basis for this change of heart undecided.[47]

Long after the Reformation, "usury" remained a stigmatized category among Protestant theologians as well. Luther's economic thought, reflected in his *Long Sermon on Usury* of 1520 and his tract *On Trade and Usury* of 1524, was hostile to commerce in general and international trade in particular, and stricter than the canonists in its condemnation of moneylending.[48] John Calvin took issue with the Scholastic view of money as sterile, and permitted the lending of money up to a fixed maximum rate of 5 percent, but he remained hostile to those who lent money by profession, and banished them from Geneva.[49] The Dutch Reformed Church followed a similar policy, sanctioning interest up to a fixed maximum but excluding bankers from communion until the mid-seventeenth century.[50] In Protestant England a similar distinction was drawn in the course of the seventeenth century between illegal usury and usury that was legal up to a fixed maximum rate of interest.[51]

Yet whether the lending of money at interest was illegal in theory and tolerated in practice (as in Catholic countries), or legal in theory and practice up to some limit (as in Protestant countries), the odium of the traditional connotations of usury and its connection to Jewry lingered. Sir Francis Bacon, in his essay *Of Usury* (1612), recommended that all usurers "should have tawny orange bonnets, because they do Judaize." In the Germanic lands, those who engaged in usury were labeled as *Kristenjuden*.[52] Since the Jew was the archetype of the normative outsider, Calvinists or Puritans who lent money at interest were sometimes stigmatized by other Christians as usurers, thereby relegating them to quasi-Jewish status.[53] An anti-Calvinist satire of 1608, *Der Calvinische Judenspiegel* (The Calvinist Jewish Mirror), purported to demonstrate the close resemblance between the Jews and the Calvinists.[54] In the popular mind, "usury" was not merely a matter of lending at interest: it was a term of opprobrium applied to any mercantile transaction regarded as unseemly or inequitable.[55] Usury in turn continued to be identified with Jews and Judaism.

Beneath the condemnation of merchants and moneylenders was the assumption that only those whose labor produced sweat really worked and produced. Most people simply could not imagine that production might be increased by the decision to invest resources in one place rather than another, with one person rather than another, in one commodity rather than another. The economic value of gathering and analyzing information was beyond the mental horizon of most of those who lived off the land or worked with their hands. The notion of trade—and, even more, the notion of moneylending—as unproductive was often expressed in images of parasitism. In *Oceana*, the seventeenth century English political theorist James Harrington warned that Jews were a people that would "suck the nourishment which would sustain a natural and useful member."[56] Unnatural, useless, parasitic: that was the way in which even some intellectuals thought of commerce. As we will see, many continued to do so, retaining and expanding upon the metaphors of parasitism.

That trade was inimical to communal cohesion was a staple of the civic republican assumptions of early modern political thought. When Davenant wrote that trade and wealth extinguish virtue, he was repeating the most hoary of civic republican clichés.

Like the Christian tradition, the civic tradition looked back to Aristotle for its core assumptions regarding virtue and commerce. Aristotle had viewed man as an essentially political being, whose fullest development included intense participation in the political community. Forged in the Greek city-states, which depended on a high degree of military mobilization for their independence and survival, the civic tradition placed the needs of the political community over other moral demands. It was believed that only a shared vision of the public good would hold society together, and the flourishing of man's political nature was viewed as the purpose of collective existence.[57]

Machiavelli recaptured and reforged this pre-Christian tradition into post-Christian form. Christian thinkers had shared Aristotle's assumption that the polity ought to fulfill some shared purpose (telos). But while for Aristotle the vital purpose of the polity was a this-worldly one of civic participation, Christian thought (at least since Augustine) regarded the polity as a way station that ought to prepare the soul for salvation and eternal life with God.[58] Machiavelli and later civic theorists revived the classical, pagan ideal of citizenship. Machiavelli stressed the need for self-sacrifice for the sake of the common good, a virtue most necessary and most promoted in war and the preparation for it. In general the civic tradition identified "virtue" with

devotion to the public good and "liberty" with participation in political life. Republican "liberty" was the freedom to take part in preserving the freedom of the commonwealth from foreign domination.
Virtue and liberty so construed required that the citizen possess
enough property to provide him with independence and the leisure to
participate in politics. To possess property—by which most civic theorists meant land—was a prerequisite of citizenship, because it freed
men from the need to engage in productive activity and thus allowed
them to devote themselves to the fate of the commonwealth. But to
devote oneself to the acquisition of property, according to the civic tradition, was unworthy of the citizen. From Aristotle through the
defenders of slaveholding in the antebellum South, theorists of the
civic tradition assumed that citizenship would be limited to those who
were unencumbered by the need to devote their energies to productive
activity.[59]

Civic republicanism in the seventeenth and eighteenth centuries
was permeated by the imagery of Sparta, the ancient Greek city-state
whose social institutions had fostered a way of life devoted to self-
sacrifice in war. The image of Sparta (which did not quite accord with
historical reality) was of a communal and military way of life, with an
economy based upon equal division of land, an avoidance of commerce
and industry, and an education devoted to fostering the virtues of obedience and courage. The constitution of the city was attributed to
Lycurgus, a lawgiver of the ninth century B.C. who banished luxury,
moneymaking, and even the use of coins. Sparta stood as the mythical
model of a polity in which devotion to the defense of the city was combined with equality, austerity, and a hostility to commerce and moneymaking.[60]

If the specters haunting Christian theorists when they viewed commerce were sin and avarice, those steeped in the civic tradition were
haunted by the specters of corruption and self-interest. Corruption was
a condition that led to the dissolution of the commonwealth through
either internal disintegration or foreign conquest. Corruption arose
when those who ought to devote themselves to public virtue either
chose or were forced by circumstance to pursue private, material interests. Corruption weakened the citizen's identification with the common good, leading to the decay of political institutions. James
Harrington, the seventeenth-century English ideologist of civic republicanism, reiterated this suspicion of commerce, observing that the
culture of "selling"—what he called the "Jewish humour"—was subversive of commonwealths.[61] To be sure, some of Harrington's English

and Dutch contemporaries (like some earlier civic humanists in mercantile Florence) were coming to the very different conclusion that the
wealth and prosperity that followed from commerce served to
strengthen the commonwealth rather than corrode it.[62] Nevertheless,
the civic tradition, with its emphasis on the devotion of citizens to
political institutions, provided a rhetorical arsenal that was repeatedly
deployed against commerce.[63]

Alongside the Christian and civic traditions, and sometimes intertwined with them, was the tradition of civil jurisprudence. It too was
classical in origin, embodied in the Code of Civil Law, a digest compiled by Justinian in the sixth century. The code reflected a Roman
empire that was highly commercial, with a legal system that permitted free bargaining.[64] While the Christian and civic traditions were
intrinsically suspicious of commerce, the Roman civil law was not.
Rediscovered in the revival of learning in the twelfth century, it
became the basis of civil law on the European continent. Freedom of
property and the rule of law were the hallmarks of this tradition, and
the protection of property from arbitrary confiscation by government
was a pivotal freedom.[65] Rather than valuing the liberty to participate
in government, it valued freedom from government as ensured by law.
Its focus was not on virtue—either in the sense of Christian righteous-
ness or civic devotion to the public good—but on rights, intended to
protect the subject from coercion by the holders of political power and
to safeguard his possessions from confiscation.

The civil law tradition did not play the same role in European intellectual life as the Christian or civic republican traditions. While Christian theology and civic rhetoric provided normative ideals of the holy
or virtuous life, civil law provided a practical framework devoted to
what belonged to each individual, rather than offering a vision of the
overall goal of the polity.[66] Within the civil law, with its concern for
subjects and their possessions, was a latent individualism.[67]

The historical upheavals of the early modern era transformed the
values inherent in the tradition of civil law into challengers to the
Christian and civic republican traditions. The unity of western Christendom was shattered in the mid-sixteenth century, inaugurating an
era of religiously motivated civil and international war that was to last
for well over a century. The great historical fact that served as the
moral backdrop for thinking about capitalism was not the factory or
the mill, but war—not war with the foreign invader, but internal war,
civil war, between men with rival views of ultimate salvation, men

who were so sure of their view of salvation that they were prepared to shed the blood of their fellow man in order to save his soul.[68] It was in this setting that intellectuals set themselves the task of developing a political and social theory that would allow those of radically different visions of the good and holy life to live together. Such a theory would also protect intellectual humanists steeped in multiple religious and national cultures from the depredations of religious fanatics.

The Church had once succeeded in using political power to oppress, repress, and suppress rival claimants to religious authority. But the beachhead established by Protestants during the Reformation made it impossible to maintain the undisputed monopoly of Catholic cultural authority. And the division of western Christendom did not end with only two camps. Soon there were Protestant churches and sects arrayed not only against the Catholic Church, but against one another. It was the experience of religious war and religious persecution that led Thomas Hobbes and a host of lesser lights to rethink the relationship between religion and politics. As long as religious factions saw the state as a proper tool for the enforcement of faith, religiously based civil war was a possibility. And as long as the state legitimated itself as guiding its citizens to a single, unified purpose and vision of the good life, the state would be prey to religious civil war. Despite their differences, the greatest political thinkers of the seventeenth century— Hugo Grotius, Hobbes, John Locke, Benedict de Spinoza—agreed on a strategy for preserving the peace and improving the well-being of their fellowmen. They would deflate religious enthusiasm by pointing out the weak basis for the theological differences over which Christians were willing to kill one another. The Bible, they suggested, was far less clear than most believers supposed, and its political claims far more limited than most believers imagined. All saw that if men were willing to persecute, kill, and be killed for the sake of eternal salvation, the issue of salvation had to be defused, first by insisting that it did not depend upon the theological niceties that divided Catholics from Protestants, Protestants from each other, and even Christians from Jews. More radically, they tried to redirect men's fears from their eternal salvation to their earthly well-being, believing that the prospect of improving their worldly well-being would provide broader grounds for consensus, or at least for peace.[69]

These seventeenth-century thinkers envisioned the future as one in which the state would restrict its claims to realize a shared vision of the good life. Much of modern politics has been a revolt against this rejection of the good life as the purpose of politics.[70] As we will see, it was as a means to these liberal goals that the market was most strongly defended. And the market was most frequently attacked by those who viewed its intrinsic purposelessness as leading to an intrinsic purposelessness in human life as such, and who sought radical alternatives on the left and right.

The theorists who developed the tradition of civil law into what became known as "natural jurisprudence" were in search of a more limited core of politically imposed obligations upon which men of differing ultimate commitments might agree.[71] Their political defense of greater cultural pluralism is captured in the words of Grotius, a central figure in the development of natural jurisprudence, whose book, *The Rights of War and Peace* (1620–1625), asserted that "there are several Ways of Living, some better than others, and every one may choose what he pleases of all those Sorts."[72] Grotius thus abandoned the notion that the task of a just polity was to create a society of saints or an aristocracy of politically active citizens. In its place Grotius offered an alternative conception of justice, which stressed the right of individuals to use the world for their private purposes, and saw the role of the state as protecting such rights.[73]

Though Grotius first adumbrated these themes, Thomas Hobbes gave them their sharpest and clearest formulation, in his *Leviathan* of 1651.[74] He sought to undermine religious claims to political dominance by demonstrating the uncertain basis of Christian religious beliefs and by removing the fear of eternal damnation so that men would be more focused on the here and now rather than on the fate of the soul in the afterlife.[75] Hobbes was scornful, too, of the tradition of civic republicanism. Its emphasis on the virtues of courage, command, and military valor was a threat to peaceful existence.[76] Its high evaluation of political participation led men to believe that only regimes based on direct political participation could be just, thus encouraging rebellion and civil war.[77]

In place of the religious life of the pious or the political life of those who fight, command, and govern, Hobbes laid out an alternate vision of the good life, with its own set of virtues. Although textbook accounts stress only his emphasis on self-preservation, the vision of the good life in *Leviathan* is much richer. Instead of religious otherworldliness, its vision is resolutely this-worldly; and the secular world it seeks to forge is not one of warriors and rulers, but of individuals living in peace, prosperity, and intellectual development. The purpose of the state—Leviathan—for Hobbes is to procure "the safety of the people": "But by Safety here, is not meant a bare Preservation, but also all other Contentments of life, which every man by lawfull Industry, without danger or hurt to the Common-wealth, shall acquire to himselfe."[78] Those "Contentments" include the elements of material well-being, as well as the means to pursue the most lasting pleasures, those of the mind.[79]

Hobbes knew that he was undertaking a transvaluation of values, some of which took the form of the redefinition of character traits. Those which had been regarded as virtues in the Christian tradition, such as piety and faith, were redescribed as superstition and credulity. The passion for honor, glory, and command so valued in the civic republican tradition were treated primarily as causes of contention and war.[80] The real virtues, for Hobbes, were those conducive to "peaceable, sociable, and comfortable living"[81]—the sort of prudential behavior previously undervalued in the Christian and civic republican traditions. Parts of *Leviathan*, therefore, take the form of what the rhetoricians of his day (from whom Hobbes learned a great deal) called "paradiastole," the method of rhetorical redescription by which what had been defined as vices could be redescribed as virtues, and vice versa.[82]

At the beginning of the eighteenth century, Bernard de Mandeville, an English writer of Dutch origin, would again make use of the technique of rhetorical redescription, in his satirical poem "The Grumbling Hive" (1714), later expanded into his book, *The Fable of the Bees; or Private Vices, Public Benefits* of 1723. Substituting irony for paradiastole, Mandeville put forth the deliberately startling claim that modern society was founded upon the very self-regarding passions and self-interested character traits that had long been stigmatized as "vices," especially pride, luxury, and vanity. The poem begins by describing the progress of a hive of bees from poverty to riches. Rather than accepting their comfortable circumstances and enjoying them, the bees take traditional moral precepts to heart and begin to deprecate pride, luxury, vanity, and other corruptions. When Jove grants them the elimination of these vices, the bees discover that they were in fact the necessary conditions of prosperity. The restoration of virtue is accompanied by simplicity, poverty, and primitive conditions.

> *Thus Vice nurs'd Ingenuity,*
> *Which joined with Time and Industry,*
> *had carry'd Life's conveniencies,*
> *It's real Pleasures, Comforts, Ease,*
> *To such a Height, the very Poor*
> *Liv'd better than the Rich before.*

Without the quest to satisfy pride and luxury, Mandeville insisted, commerce and innovation would come to a standstill. In the century that followed, both defenders and opponents of the market would echo Mandeville's argument about the linkage of self-interest to luxury, while stripping it of its irony. Advocates of commercial society— from Voltaire through David Hume and Adam Smith—explored the potential collective benefits of self-interest. The foremost critic of commerce within the Enlightenment, Jean-Jacques Rousseau, would endorse Mandeville's analysis of the vicious basis of commerce, while dismissing his praise of prosperity.[83]

CHAPTER TWO

VOLTAIRE:
"A MERCHANT OF A NOBLE KIND"

The Rise of the Intellectual

A study of capitalism in the minds of modern European intellectuals ought to begin with Voltaire, not least because he did so much to create the role of "intellectual." To be sure, there had long been men of learning, professors, and writers. But the independent man of letters who attempted through his writing to mold public opinion was a new phenomenon. Indeed it was only within the course of Voltaire's life—and in no small measure through his example—that the independent man of letters and the phenomenon of "public opinion" came to exist.

The term "intellectual" as a noun with this peculiar connotation did not come into broad usage until the closing years of the nineteenth century. But the thing long preceded the term, or rather, it went under a series of different names. In the course of Voltaire's lifetime, the designation "philosophe" came to have a meaning close to that of intellectual. When Voltaire was born in 1694, during the closing years of Louis XIV's reign, a *philosophe* was a sage who isolated himself from the frivolity and servility of the court. By the time of Voltaire's death in 1778, the word had come to designate a writer who took a critical stance toward existing institutions and sought to influence public opinion accordingly.[1] The term *"publiciste,"* which had designated a learned authority on public law, also acquired its more modern meaning of a writer who sought to mold public opinion by defining the meaning of terms.[2] The rise of the intellectual and the growth of public opinion went hand in hand. Jacques Necker, who became the French minister of finance shortly after Voltaire's death, called public opinion an "invisible power without money, without police, and without an army," which nevertheless exercised a powerful influence on government policy.[3]

As Voltaire wrote to his comrade in arms, Jean d'Alembert: "People clamor against the *philosophes*. They are right; for if opinion is the queen of the world, the *philosophes* govern that queen."[4]

The ability of a writer to mold public opinion depended not only on what he wrote, but on how he wrote it. Both Voltaire's admirers and his critics agreed on the connection between his influence and the delight of his prose. Adam Smith, who admired Voltaire and kept a bust of him in his home, told a French visitor that

> Reason owes him incalculable obligations; the ridicule and sarcasms which he plentifully poured out upon fanatics and hypocrites of all sects, have prepared men's minds for the light of truth, to the search for which every intelligent mind ought to aspire. He has done more in this matter than the books of the gravest philosophers, which everybody does not read; while the writings of Voltaire are in general made for all and read by all.[5]

Edmund Burke, who found Voltaire's influence malign, conceded that he "has the merit of writing agreeably; and nobody has ever united blasphemy and obscenity so happily together."[6]

The rise of the intellectual as an independent man of letters devoted to the formation of public opinion was made possible by two parallel developments in the eighteenth century: the transformation of the economic basis of literary life from patronage to the market, and the growth of a new form of politics based upon an informed public rather than upon direct appeal to the royal sovereign. Voltaire's career promoted and benefited from both processes.

Until the eighteenth century, writers had depended primarily on the largesse of the rich and powerful to provide them with a living. Voltaire too relied on patronage during the early part of his career, as did Edmund Burke and, to some degree, Adam Smith as well. Patronage took a variety of forms, from public offices and pensions through free room and board. The success of the young Voltaire's epic poem *Oedipe*, for example, was rewarded by a pension from the French regent, and then a second pension awarded by the queen of France in 1725. Two decades later, the publication of his book *The Century of Louis XIV* and his flattery of the reigning monarch, Louis XV, led to his appointment as a "gentleman of the chamber" and then as royal historiographer, a public office with a sizable annual income. Voltaire's many patrons included King Frederick II of Prussia and the wealthy English merchant Everard Fawkener. Patronage was a highly personal relationship between the patron and the object of his or her largesse. To creative intellects like Voltaire and Burke, it provided status and income, and to their patrons the reward of reflected glory.

Voltaire profited from some of his literary works, such as his epic poem *The Henriade,* by sales through subscriptions, an intermediary form between patronage and the book market, by which first editions of a book were sold to a limited number of wealthy subscribers. As the century progressed, books increasingly traveled from author to readers through publishers and booksellers who marketed them. For the first time it became possible to reach a large number of readers and to make a living (usually a rather meager one) through the market for books. The rise of the market loosened the author's direct dependence on powerful patrons, even while it increased his dependence on the tastes of the reading public.[7]

"Public opinion" was a product of new institutions through which a mass of citizens could become familiar with questions of government. These included reading clubs, where men who could not afford to buy many books could gather to read and discuss new works. Coffeehouses played a similar function. Stocked with newspapers and journals, they provided another setting where new ideas were disseminated. Higher up in the social scale were the masonic lodges, which brought together nobles and even royalty with the more elite members of the middle class. Among the most important new forms of expression was the journal of opinion, which popularized ideas and reported on matters of public interest. The first such journal, *The Spectator,* was founded in England in 1711, with the aim of bringing "philosophy out of closets and libraries to dwell in clubs and assemblies."[8] As a result of these developments the model of political influence changed during the course of the century, from the traditional direct appeal to the absolute monarch to the new appeal to the tribunal of "the public."[9]

Voltaire's great talent was as a popularizer of ideas developed by others rather than as an original or systematic thinker. The new reading public and the new institutions of the public sphere put a premium on just such talents. Despite his suspicion of the "spirit of system," Voltaire's major concerns were remarkably consistent through the course of his long career. He championed the pursuit of happiness, the expansion of individual freedom, the rule of law, and the use of human reason modeled on the methods of the natural sciences to challenge the nonrational claims of religious faith. Closely related to these concerns was Voltaire's long campaign against the

Catholic Church and his antipathy toward the political claims of institutionalized religion.

Voltaire's significance for our topic comes from his popularization of two important themes: the legitimization on political grounds of the *pursuit* of wealth through market activity, and the moral legitimization of the *consumption* of wealth. It was the former theme that he developed in the *Philosophical Letters,* a work of social and political criticism that marked the beginning of the French Enlightenment as a public force.

Exchange and Toleration: The Political Argument

Voltaire's defense of the market in the *Letters* and later in his *Philosophical Dictionary* was political rather than economic. Market activity was valued not because it made society wealthier, but because the pursuit of economic self-interest was less dangerous than the pursuit of other goals, above all religious zealotry.

Voltaire was drawn to England by commercial, intellectual, and personal motives. The attack on the established Catholic Church in the *Henriade* made it a target of government censorship in France. The book was published clandestinely, which ensured that almost all of the book's profits would accrue to the publisher rather than to the author. In England, where censorship was much less rigorous, the book could be published openly. Voltaire went to England in part to publish a revised, deluxe edition of his poem, which was sold by subscription to powerful and wealthy patrons. The considerable proceeds went to Voltaire himself.

Though the purpose of Voltaire's visit was commercial, its timing was delayed by his arrest in France. At the Paris Opera he had responded sharply to a slight by the Chevalier de Rohan, a scion of one of the most prestigious families of the French nobility. To teach the insolent commoner a lesson, the chevalier dispatched two of his servants, who beat the poet while the nobleman shouted instructions from his nearby carriage. In search of revenge, Voltaire turned for help to his acquaintances in the nobility and even at Versailles. When they turned him down, he took matters into his own hands. He began fencing lessons, with the intention of challenging Rohan to a duel, and purchased pistols. As rumors of Voltaire's intentions circulated in

Paris, the government ordered his imprisonment in the Bastille. After his arrest Voltaire worked out an agreement with the authorities that allowed him to leave for England instead.[10]

Voltaire's perceptions of England and the image of England which he chose to convey to his French readers in the *Philosophical Letters* were bound up with his intellectual concerns and his political philosophy. What Voltaire most valued about contemporary European civilization was the growing liberty of the individual from coercion, through greater government toleration of intellectual differences and above all through the rule of law. By this standard, England was a model for the rest of Europe.

The argument of the *Philosophical Letters* can only be understood against the historical backdrop of religious persecution and religious war that had dominated the concerns of western and central Europeans in the two centuries that separated Luther from Voltaire. When all European Christians shared a common faith, the use of the power of the state to enforce religious obligations had been taken for granted, as expressed by the formula "one faith, one law, one king."[11] The only tolerated outsiders from the political community of Christendom were members of the small Jewish minority, who were burdened with civic and economic disabilities as a mark of their inferior status.

In the sixteenth century the unity of western European Christendom had been shattered by the rise of Protestantism in its various strands (Lutheran, Calvinist, and Anglican). While the state was regarded as part of the body of Christ, the concept of sharing a political community with those of differing doctrinal commitments was unthinkable. And so it remained at first. Protestant reformers and their Catholic adversaries all insisted that one of the main aims of government was to maintain "true religion." They disagreed, of course, as to which brand of Christianity was true. Thus European history in the sixteenth and seventeenth centuries became a chronicle of civil war, of massacre, and of the expulsions of religious minorities. The notion of religious toleration grew less out of any particular brand of Christianity than out of the fear and frustration of protracted civil war. It was first articulated in France in the late sixteenth century by a group of thinkers known as the *politiques*. Their key innovation was to elevate the preservation of civil peace above the demands of religious orthodoxy, and to suggest that peace could only be preserved by relieving the state of the duty to uphold any particular faith.[12] That argument was further developed by the great thinkers of the seventeenth century, most notably Spinoza and Locke.

The problem of how men of differing faiths could live together without oppressing one another absorbed Voltaire when he arrived in England in 1726. The hero of his epic poem, the *Henriade*, Henry IV of France, had in 1598 brought a temporary halt to the religious wars through the Edict of Nantes, which extended a measure of civic equality to the French Calvinists, the Huguenots. Henry was assassinated in 1610 by a fanatic who believed him to be a menace to the Catholic faith. Voltaire's tale conveyed the political and human costs of religious militance, which he contrasted with the benefits of religious toleration under secular supremacy.

To prepare his English readers for his forthcoming poem, Voltaire preceded it with the publication of *An Essay upon the Civil Wars*. It concluded with an "Advertisement to the Reader" in which he explained the purpose of the work on which he was then engaged, which would first be published as *Letters Concerning the English Nation* and would come to be known under its French title, the *Lettres philosophiques*. It was to be a book by a French traveler in England, intended for his countrymen. As Voltaire put it in his newly acquired English:

> The true aim of a Relation is to instruct Men, not to gratify their Malice. We should be busied chiefly in giving faithful Accounts of all the useful Things and of the extraordinary Persons, whom to know, and imitate, would be a Benefit to our Countrymen. A Traveller who writes in that Spirit, is a Merchant of a noble Kind, who imports into his Country the Arts and Virtues of other Nations.[13]

Voltaire here foreshadows the high moral status he was to assign to commerce in his book. He portrays the enlightened intellectual, like the merchant, as contributing to the welfare of his countrymen through beneficial imports from abroad: his goods are only less tangible. The whole passage bristles with references to trade. The intellectual traveler offers "Accounts," he is concerned with "useful Things" and with potential "Benefits." Voltaire's high estimate of merchants in his works was reflected in his life. He spent much of his English sojourn at Wandsworth, the country estate of Everard Fawkener, a member of a wealthy British merchant family involved in international trade and the Bank of England. The new class of wealthy London merchants provided much of his company. Merchants and bankers were conspicuous among the subscribers to the luxury edition of the

Henriade. Among them was Peter Delmé, the greatest British exporter of woolen goods.[14]

Voltaire's literary portrait of the Royal Exchange (the precursor of the London Stock Exchange) in his *Letters* helped popularize one of the most important and lasting arguments in favor of capitalism. Thanks to the availability of Voltaire's notebooks and letters, we can trace the way his art transformed his experience in Britain to fit his own intellectual priorities.[15] Far from the report of a casual observation, Voltaire's portrait of the exchange is staged to present an argument for the politically beneficial effects of capitalism in general, and a recent and controversial form of financial capitalism in particular.

The scene appears in the sixth of a series of letters devoted to the various religious denominations, entitled "On the Presbyterians." Although no letters are explicitly devoted to Roman Catholicism, the four letters on the Quakers are intended to ridicule the rituals of Catholicism, while in the fifth letter, on the Anglicans, Voltaire observes: "The Anglican clergy have maintained many Catholic ceremonies, particularly that of gathering tithes with the most scrupulous attention." Voltaire's greatest lifelong passion, anticlericalism, is much in evidence, though with greater subtlety than in his *Philosophical Dictionary,* written some four decades later. Yet alongside his anticlerical barbs is a more political theme: Voltaire claimed that religious enthusiasm was a primary source of discord, which led at best to injustice, at worst to civil war.

To the prosperity and liberty of contemporary England, Voltaire contrasted the destruction wrought by the religious wars of the seventeenth century, "at the time when three or four sects were tearing Great Britain asunder with civil wars undertaken in the name of God" (letter 3). After the struggles of the English in the seventeenth century, Voltaire writes, "everybody is sick and tired of sectarian disputes"(letter 7). "I cannot see them at all anxious to kill each other henceforth for the sake of syllogisms" (letter 8). No opportunity is lost to hammer home his contention that religious wars are senseless, since they are rooted in theological questions to which no definitive or even plausible answers can be given. More often religious differences are not so much explored as trivialized, as when Voltaire describes "a doctor named Prynne, scrupulous in the extreme, who would have thought himself damned for ever if he had worn a cassock instead of a short coat, and would have liked one half of the human race to massacre the other for the glory of God and *propaganda fide . . .*" (letter 23). The *Philosophical Letters* record and applaud the passing of religious fanaticism and its replacement by an atmosphere of religious toleration. "An Englishman, as a free man, goes to heaven by whatever route he likes" (letter 5). That was Voltaire's epigrammatic summation of the doctrine of religious toleration.

Religious toleration was one of the "useful Things" about which the *Philosophical Letters* intended to instruct Voltaire's countrymen, by setting out the conditions that advanced the peaceful acceptance of religious difference in England and might do so in France.

It seemed to Voltaire that the very multiplicity of religious sects in England promoted religious toleration. "If there were only one religion in England there would be danger of despotism, if there were two they would cut each other's throats, but there are thirty, and they live in peace and happiness" (letter 6). He thought so highly of this insight that he repeated it late in life in the article on "Toleration" in his *Philosophical Dictionary*. Here was a theme that Adam Smith would pursue in *The Wealth of Nations*.

At least as important, Voltaire thought, was the displacement of religious concerns by the pursuit of wealth and happiness. "Man is born for action, as fire tends to rise and a stone to sink . . . The whole difference lies in the occupations being gentle or fierce, dangerous or useful," he wrote in "On the *Pensées* of Pascal," which he appended to the *Letters*. According to Voltaire, religious enthusiasm made men fierce and dangerous. In contrast to the Christian and civic traditions, Voltaire affirmed self-interest as more likely to promote social peace than ideological commitment.[16] The quest for economic gain, he showed in his description of the stock exchange, made men more gentle.

Voltaire was not the first man of letters to comment upon the stock exchange. *The Spectator*, the English journal of opinion that became the model for similar endeavors across the continent, had devoted an article to the Royal Exchange in 1711; it appeared in a French translation in 1722. The article, by Joseph Addison, described the Royal Exchange as "an assembly of countrymen and foreigners, consulting together upon the private business of mankind, and making this metropolis a kind of *emporium* for the whole earth," and noted the presence of merchants from a variety of nations.[17]

Four years before his trip to England, Voltaire visited Holland, the other great commercial center of the age. He was much impressed by the Hague, which, echoing Addison, he called "the storehouse of the universe." "The opera here is detestable," he wrote to a friend in Paris, "but in its stead I watch Calvinist ministers, Arminians, Socinians, rabbis, and Anabaptists who talk together quite miraculously, and with every reason."[18] The thought echoes Addison's description, but with a new emphasis on the coexistence of diverse faiths.

England brought similar thoughts to mind. "England is the meeting of all religions, as the Royal exchange is the rendez vous of all foreigners," wrote Voltaire in his notebook early in his visit. A crucial development of his thoughts on capitalism occurred when he concluded that there was a link between religious toleration and the forms of behavior engendered by the market. It appears in his notebook under the heading "Tale of a Tub," an allusion to Jonathan Swift's satire on both Roman Catholicism and Protestant religious enthusiasm. As he confided to his notebook in his imperfect English:

> Where there is not liberty of conscience, there is seldom liberty of trade, the same tyranny encroaching upon the commerce as upon Religion. In the Commonwealths and other free contrys one may see in a see port, as many relligions as shipps. The same god is there differently whorship'd by jews, mahometans, heathens, catholiques, quackers, anabaptistes, which write strenuously one against another, but deal together freely and with trust and peace; like good players who after having humour'd their parts and fought one against another upon the stage, spend the rest of their time in drinking together.[19]

Voltaire would spell out the connection between freedom of belief and commerce at greater length in the *Philosophical Letters*. He would refine and expand upon Swift's contention that men of radically different beliefs who might otherwise be enemies could live "together freely in trust and peace" when they were "dealing," that is, engaging in commerce. There is a hint in the final sentence that their amity rests on the implicit belief that their commercial activity is more real to them than their professed religious convictions; their relationship to their religious professions is that of the actor to his lines, which he knows to be merely a diverting fiction.

The connection between commerce and toleration was not new. It had been made earlier, often by those who condemned both because they believed that political stability was linked to government enforcement of religious uniformity. In 1651 Andrew Marvell had looked across the channel at Holland and scoffed:

> *Hence Amsterdam, Turk-Christian-Pagan-Jew,*
> *Staple of sects and mint of schism grew;*

> *That bank of conscience, where not one so strange*
> *Opinion but finds credit, and exchange.*[20]

Voltaire took Marvell's analysis and reversed its moral conclusion. For Marvell, the scene in Amsterdam was a threat. For the advocate of religious toleration, commerce was to be applauded.

Voltaire's decision to shift the locale of his argument for the political benefits of commerce from the harbor to the Royal Exchange was significant. For the London exchange was the embodiment of a new form of financial capitalism, closely linked to the rise of the modern state and to international transoceanic commerce.

> Although the Episcopalian and the Presbyterian are the two main sects in Great Britain, all the others are welcome and live quite well together, while most of their preachers detest each other with about as much cordiality as a Jansenist damns a Jesuit.
>
> Come into the London Exchange, a place more respectable than many a court. You will see assembled representatives of every nation for the benefit of mankind. Here the Jew, the Mohametan and the Christian deal with one another as if they were of the same religion, and reserve the name "infidel" for those who go bankrupt. Here the Presbyterian puts his trust in the Anabaptist, and the Anglican accepts the Quaker's promissory note. Upon leaving these peaceful and free assemblies, one goes to the synogogue, the other for a drink; yet another goes to have himself baptized in a large tub in the name of the Father through the Son to the Holy Ghost; another has his son's foreskin cut off, and over the infant he has muttered some Hebrew words that he doesn't understand at all: Some others go to their church to await divine inspiration with their hat on their head. And all are content. (letter 6)

Before coming to the stock exchange scene, the *Letters* are replete with reminders that when religious differences become the prime objects of the emotions, the result is often the coercion of those regarded as infidels. The stock exchange, by contrast, brings together believers in diverse faiths into "peaceful and free assemblies." The source of their comity is their common pursuit of a common object: wealth. While religious enthusiasm might lead them to damn each other as infidels, the quest for wealth creates a new consensus, for all agree that the bankrupt, and he alone, is "unfaithful." Here Voltaire is the prophet of the profit motive: compared to the competitive quest for salvation, the quest for wealth is more likely to make men "peaceful" and "content." Compared to the altruistic crusade of forcibly saving one's neighbor's soul, even if it leaves his body in ruins, the pursuit of wealth is a potentially more peaceable pursuit, and one that leaves one's neighbor content.

What were these merchants buying and selling? To what portion of "the private business of mankind" were they attending?

The trading on the London exchange was mainly in government securities and shares of the so-called "monied companies," the East India Company and the Bank of England, the two pivots, at home and abroad, upon which English mercantile policy turned.[21] The joint market for government securities and shares of "monied companies" reflected the interdependence of the expansion of government power and of commercial activity.

As their names indicated, companies such as the South Sea and the East India sent ships across the globe, ships that returned to Europe laden with spices, silks, porcelains, sugar, tobacco, coffee, and tea, all of which were regarded as "luxuries" suitable only for the well-to-do. Such companies mixed politics and economics. They were owned in part by royal investors, in part by private shareholders who shared the risks and hoped to share the profits. They were chartered by the government and granted the exclusive right to import goods from their designated region. Within that region they were mandated to perform governmental functions and empowered to collect taxes to defray the costs of ruling. Transoceanic trade demanded the investment of large amounts of capital in risk-laden enterprise, with a long period before profits could be expected. Given these circumstances, the monopoly granted by the Crown played a crucial role by raising the potential profits of overseas trade to a level that would make such risks worthwhile to those with money to invest.[22] Though the evidence is sketchy, Voltaire himself appears to have invested in the French India Company.[23] He may have put his money where his mouth was.

The founding of the Bank of England in 1694 was an important prerequisite for the rise of Britain's naval power and its economic growth in the eighteenth century. Before states had access to the market for capital, war was often decided by whichever government was first to run out of money to pay and supply its troops. The British Crown chartered the Bank of England for political, not economic, reasons. William III's government needed money to continue its war against the French in Flanders. Like most European governments of the day, its expenditures usually exceeded its revenues. Until the late seventeenth century, the government of England had raised its revenues in the French manner: Private moneylenders lent money to the Crown to cover government expenses. Then, to repay its debts, the government sold to "tax farmers" the right to collect some form of tax, such as excise taxes on sweet wine. A stipulated amount was to be paid to the government, and whatever the tax farmer extracted beyond that belonged to him. These tax farmers also played the role of financiers, lending money to the government to cover its short-term deficits. This dependence on tax farmers and financiers was expensive, for the government borrowed money at the same rate of interest as private individuals.[24]

In the late seventeenth century, the government of Britain decided to imitate a method of funding government debt pioneered by the Italians and the Dutch by establishing a chartered national bank. The Bank of England began by providing the government with £1,200,000, in return for which the government promised to pay an annual sum of £100,000 in perpetuity and permitted the bank to receive deposits, make loans, and issue notes. The stockholders included not only investors from the City of London, but the king and queen, Dutch investors, Huguenots, and Jews. It soon functioned as the leading purchaser of interest-bearing bonds, which covered the national debt.

Traded on the London exchange were shares in the Bank of England and the great mercantile companies, and bonds and other financial instruments through which the government borrowed from the private money market. These included army debentures, navy bills, and Exchequer (i.e., Treasury) bills.[25] In each case the government promised to pay some face amount at a future date, and a fixed annual interest until the bill became due. The government's ability to borrow was contingent upon the belief among its creditors that it had the capacity to meet its payments. Confidence in the government's ability to pay was warranted by the development of an effective tax system. This provided a substantial and regular flow into government coffers, which in turn ensured a private market for state debt.[26] The emergence of this stable, public market for state debt was the most politically significant economic innovation of the age. It allowed the British government to borrow funds at a far lower rate than had been the case when it depended on moneylenders and tax farmers—the system that remained in force in France.

While the role of the profits of overseas trade in British economic development has been exaggerated,[27] the role of men and institutions involved in the buying, selling, transport, and lending of money was long overlooked by historians of capitalism, or treated as an unproductive, parasitic growth on the body of the "real" economy of production and distribution. But the increasing circulation of capital in London led to a rapid fall in interest rates, providing a further stimulus to commerce.[28] The development of reliable means of transferring funds, the existence of currency markets that made possible trade across political borders, the expansion of credit through bills of exchange, and the channeling of existing capital to productive purposes, were all a result of developments in finance that were under way in Voltaire's day, and in which he participated.[29]

The advantages to English power and English commerce brought by this "financial revolution" are now widely acknowledged by historians. But at the time, the public reacted to the new institutions of finance with suspicion and even hostility.[30] Especially suspect was the speculative nature of some of the buying and selling on the exchange. For the value of government securities rose and fell with the fortunes—or rumored fortunes—of the British Navy and the British Exchequer. The value of company stock oscillated with the fate of ships on high seas, or the possibility that a company would not have its monopoly renewed.[31] Most of those on the floor of the exchange both traded stock on their own account and acted as stockbrokers, buying and selling stock on behalf of clients for a commission. By the 1720s trading on margin and the trading of stock options had already been developed.[32] This combination of factors created unprecedented possibilities for speculation.

In 1720, the stock of the new South Sea Company shot up almost tenfold when the government accepted the company's proposal to take over the national debt in return for the monopoly on trade to the South Pacific. That set off a speculative boom on the London exchange. Money poured in from Amsterdam, Paris, and Dublin, and the stocks of new companies created for ever more dubious purposes were promoted on the exchange. Parliament passed an act, known to posterity as the Bubble Act, in an attempt to halt such activity. The unanticipated effect of the act was to bring about a collapse of South Sea Company stock, which coincided with the end of speculative fever in Amsterdam and Paris. The boom and bust on the exchange led to a wave of public moralizing, blaming the "South Sea Bubble" and its collapse on avarice and the love of luxury.[33]

The speculative activity that reached its height in the South Sea Bubble was the froth on the wave of the financial revolution. But it was the froth that caught the attention of moralists. Spokesmen for those whose wealth rested upon landed property interpreted events through the filter of civic republicanism to decry the new "monied interests," whose wealth was held to rest upon "fantasy" rather than the solid basis of land.[34]

Written while the South Sea Bubble (and its counterparts in Paris and Amsterdam) was a recent memory, Voltaire's London exchange scene was not just a political defense of capitalism. It was a vindication of financial capitalism at its most speculative. Voltaire defended what to moralists seemed the Achilles' heel of the new world of finance. By moving his observation from the harbor to the exchange, Voltaire focused not on the entrepreneur, not on the hardworking merchant, but rather on those trying to profit by trading in stock, bills of exchange, and national debt.

Those who owned land—the traditional source of wealth—had little need to engage in the more risk-laden economic activities represented on the exchange. Hence, those most active in exchange included few aristocrats, but a disproportionate number of social and religious outsiders: Huguenots, Quakers, Dissenters, and Jews.[35]

Banished from England in 1290, the Jews had only recently been readmitted, and the small Jewish community of London was made up in good part of Sephardim. These were Jews who had left Spain and Portugal in the late fifteenth century to escape religious persecution, many of whom had moved to Amsterdam (when it was a Spanish possession) and thence to England. With their international contacts, London's Jewish merchants specialized in international trade and in stock transactions. They were especially active in handling foreign bills of exchange, through which the buyer of goods in one country could pay the seller in another country, thus smoothing international trade. These Jewish merchants in London, wrote Addison, were "like the pegs and nails in a great building, which though they are but little valued in themselves, are absolutely necessary to keep the whole frame together."[36]

One such "peg" was the Mendes da Costa family, a prominent family of Portuguese origin, with branches in London and Holland, whom Voltaire came to know shortly after his arrival in England. John Mendes da Costa, the patriarch of the clan, owned sizable blocks of stock in the Bank of England and the East India Company.[37] In preparation for his trip to England, Voltaire bought a bill of exchange, drawn upon John's son, Anthony Mendes da Costa. But Voltaire's trip was delayed by the Rohan affair, and by the time he reached England,

Anthony had fled the country and been declared bankrupt, leaving his father as the court-appointed creditor. "At my coming to London I found my damned Jew was broken," wrote Voltaire to his friend Thieriot. Voltaire's curse would make its way into the published version of the *Philosophical Letters*.[38]

The entire exchange scene was written so as to upset the reader's expectations by inverting the accustomed hierarchy of values. In the very first line, Voltaire compares the exchange—a frequent object of snide disdain—favorably with the court, the peak of the existing social hierarchy. Though the stock jobbing on the exchange was often depicted as the depth of self-seeking, Voltaire regards those engaged in trading as pursuing "the benefit of mankind." The key inversion of the accepted hierarchy of values, of course, concerns business and religion, or the pursuit of wealth and the quest for salvation. We expect to be told that the latter is more noble than the former. Yet in Voltaire's portrait, religion is made to seem ridiculous, commerce respectable. Here we have an outstanding example of Voltaire's art—the art of the propagandist of Enlightenment, the art of the persuader of public opinion. There is no logical presentation, which might expose his premises to criticism and possible rejection. Instead, the entire scene is an argument, constructed so that the desired solution is contained in the very way in which the problem is posed, and spiced with a touch of humor, which makes it palatable and memorable. As James Beattie, a Scottish critic, noted: "The admirers of Voltaire will not easily be brought to reason, for they cannot give up an argument without losing a joke."[39]

The premise that religious differences are ridiculous is insinuated through what the literary critic Erich Auerbach termed "the search-light device." Out of the intellectual and symbolic complexity of each religious tradition, Voltaire calls our attention only to one ceremonial custom. The ritual in question—baptism, circumcision, wearing a hat—is highlighted, but the larger complex of ideas and practices from which the ceremony derives its meaning is purposely left in the dark, making the rituals appear arbitrary. The religious rituals are juxtaposed with the mundane consumption of alcohol, an equation by which they are devalued.[40]

Voltaire's scene is meant to suggest that the market mechanism permits the existence of pluralism—in this case, religious pluralism. Yet there is also an insinuation that the mechanism functions so well because it tends to devalue, at least comparatively, all of the religious cultures, because the pursuit of wealth is actually more real to those on the exchange than their pursuit of salvation. Religious observance,

as described by Voltaire, has become formalistic, as in the instance of
the Catholic, who garbles the formula of the Trinity, and the Jew,
whose incomprehension of Hebrew is emphasized. Voltaire, whose
concern is the containment of religious strife but also the promotion of
worldly happiness as an ultimate goal, applauds these consequences.
The suggestion that the pursuit of wealth is actually more real to those
on the exchange than their pursuit of salvation reappears here in a
form more muted than Voltaire's original treatment of the theme in his
notebooks. For as his description of the various sects made clear, the
English lived in peace not because they did not take religious belief
seriously but in spite of the fact that they did.[41]

Two notions mooted in the London exchange scene are pursued at
greater length elsewhere in the *Philosophical Letters*. The market is
referred to as a "peaceful and free assembly," that is, a voluntary form
of association. Commerce is thus pictured as a basis of peaceful coexistence. In his critical remarks on Pascal, Voltaire took issue with Pascal's reiteration of the commonsense view of social order as founded
upon altruism. "Each of us tends toward himself. That is against all
order. We must tend toward the whole; and the tendency toward self-
interest is the beginning of all disorder in war, in government, in economy etc.," Pascal had written. Voltaire's response prefigured much of
the argument of later thinkers from Smith to Hayek, who held that the
individual's self-regarding propensities were the basis of social order,
rather than the threat to it that Christian and civic moralists imagined:

> It is as impossible for a society to be formed and lasting
> without self-interest as it would be to produce children
> without carnal desire or to think of eating without appetite,
> etc. It is love of self that encourages love of others, it is
> through our mutual needs that we are useful to the human
> race. That is the foundation of all commerce, the eternal
> link between men. Without it not a single art would have
> been invented, no society of ten people formed. It is this self-
> love, that every animal has received from nature, which
> warns us to respect that of others. The law controls this self-
> love and religion perfects it. It is quite true that God might
> have created beings solely concerned with the good of oth-
> ers. In that case merchants would have gone to the Indies
> out of charity and the mason would have cut stone to give
> pleasure to his neighbour. But God has ordained things dif-
> ferently. Let us not condemn the instinct He has given us,

and let us put it to the use He commands. ("On the *Pensées* of Pascal")

Voltaire did not use the term "invisible hand," but the notion is there in embryo.

In Letter 10, "On Commerce," Voltaire returned to the links between England's national power, its commerce, and its liberty. "Commerce, which has enriched English citizens, has helped to make them free, and this freedom in turn has extended commerce, and that has made the greatness of the nation.... A small island which has no resources of its own except a little lead, some tin, some fuller's earth and coarse wool has through its commerce become powerful enough to send, in 1723, at one and same time, three fleets to the extremities of the world..." He contrasted the disdain felt by continental aristocrats toward men of commerce to the willingness of the younger siblings of distinguished English aristocrats to engage in trade. "I wonder which is the more useful to a nation," he asked rhetorically, "a well-powdered nobleman who knows exactly at what minute the King gets up and goes to bed, and who gives himself grand airs while playing the part of a slave in some Minister's antechamber, or a business man who enriches his country, issues orders from his office to Surat or Cairo, and contributes to the well-being of the world." Here Voltaire was indeed acting as a merchant of ideas, attempting to sell his French audience on what was rapidly becoming a standard theme in English letters, namely that the merchant was a new sort of hero.[42]

This preference for the merchant over the aristocrat provided the backdrop against which Voltaire championed one of the central themes of the enlightenment: the need for equality before the law. In his letter "On the Government," he contrasted the notion of "freedom" as a privilege with the enlightened notion of freedom as applying to all. The fact that the Magna Carta mentioned "free men of England," he wrote, was "a sorry demonstration that some existed who were not free. We see in Article 32 that these so-called free men owed services to their overlord. Such freedom still had much of slavery about it." Voltaire thus championed a political structure in which no man lived in direct dependence upon a legal master. Voltaire's description of the British government emphasized that, in contrast to France, all were subject to taxation. "Everyone gives, not according to his rank (which is absurd) but according to his income." It took the French Revolution to eliminate the legal privileges and taxation by rank that Voltaire regarded as a fundamental injustice of the old regime.

Intellectual Speculation

The villains of the *Philosophical Letters* were the priest, the warrior, and the aristocrat. Its heroes were the merchant—and the intellectual. The man of letters as the agent of progress and enlightenment was to become a favorite theme of Voltaire and of the *philosophes* in general.[43] The paragon of intellectual life for Voltaire and many later intellectuals of the Enlightenment was Isaac Newton. They set out to discover laws of the social world as Newton had discovered those of the natural world. To compare the value of the intellectual with that of the man of arms, Voltaire contrasted Newton with Cromwell: "It is to the man who rules over minds by the power of truth, not to those who enslave men by violence, it is to the man who understands the universe and not to those who disfigure it, that we owe our respect" (Letter 12). Bacon, Locke, and Newton are the real heroes of the *Letters*, the "philosophers who should be the teachers of the human race" (Letter 22).[44] Among the lessons that Voltaire hoped the French would learn from the English was how to treat "philosophers." In England, intellectual talent and merit were rewarded not just honorifically, but in hard cash. He noted that Alexander Pope's translation of Homer had earned him two hundred thousand francs: "Such is the respect this nation has for talent that a man of parts always makes his fortune there." He offered a list of distinguished intellectuals who had been rewarded by lucrative government sinecures. Had he written his *Letters* some decades later, his list might have included Adam Smith, who was rewarded with the post of commissioner of customs.

Voltaire's *Philosophical Letters* were intended to teach the French how to reward men of intellectual merit. But Voltaire did not sit back and wait to be rewarded by his countrymen. "I saw so many poor and despised men of letters that I decided long ago not to add to their number," he wrote in his memoirs. "There is always one way or another by which a private individual can profit without incurring any obligation to anyone; and nothing is so agreeable as to make one's own fortune."[45]

Voltaire was far wealthier at the end of his stay in England than at its beginning. Some of his new wealth came from the profits of his *Henriade,* but most of Voltaire's monetary gains came from a series of financial speculations that he did not make known and that many of the merchants with whom he associated considered shady and dishonest. Those who knew him in England accused him of forging banknotes, altering contracts, and reneging on his debts. Voltaire departed from England with widespread animosity toward him, due largely to his financial misconduct.[46] As we shall see, similar behavior led to his departure in disgrace from the court of Frederick the Great two decades later, and Voltaire would repeatedly be judged by his associates and even loved ones as avaricious.[47]

What was the "one way or another" by which a writer could make a fortune? The characteristics of curiosity, unorthodoxy, and audacity that shine through Voltaire's writings were reflected in his financial activity as well. There were few contemporary avenues of economic advance at which he did not try his hand. Royal patronage, sales of his books, the international grain market, moneylending, land development, and financial speculation: Voltaire tried all of these routes on his road to fortune. Voltaire's financial activities, like his literary works, often skirted the bounds of propriety.

One path was through the patronage of the wealthy and powerful. No one was as wealthy and powerful as monarchs, so Voltaire consistently cultivated them. As we have seen, he enjoyed the patronage of the French royal house before his English sojourn. Early in 1727, he was received at court by the king of England. Voltaire dedicated the British edition of his *Philosophical Letters* to the queen, who found herself described in Letter 11 as "a delightful philosopher on the throne," and praised lavishly for her patronage. A second and more modern source of fortune was profit from the sale of books, either by subscription or through booksellers.

But Voltaire first made his fortune through the institution that tied together monarchs and merchants: the public debt. In their desperation to raise money to cover public debt, eighteenth-century governments frequently resorted to lotteries. They are usually regarded as the most speculative form of financial activity, in which the possibility of gain is governed wholly by chance. Voltaire's breakthrough to real wealth came by way of a lottery. But it was a lottery in which he maximized his chances of success through the use of reason.

The government of France had raised money from the public by issuing bonds. To disguise the government's indebtedness, the bonds were issued through the Paris city hall. Voltaire had apparently owned some of these government bonds before his departure for England. By the time he returned to France in 1728, the government's financial straits had caused the bonds to lose their value. In an attempt to restore the confidence of bondholders, the government decided to reimburse them in stages by means of a monthly lottery. Tickets were available, at a cost of one franc, only to those who held the bonds; for every thousand francs of bonds held, one ticket could be purchased for each drawing. The monthly prize of 600,000 francs came mostly from the government itself.

Voltaire collaborated with Charles de la Condamine, a noted mathematician, to calculate the resources required to purchase all the tickets for selected drawings and hence ensure success. Together they organized a syndicate that cornered all the tickets for a given drawing and split the prize money. In 1729–1730, Voltaire's syndicate won six to seven million francs, of which his share was half a million. A few months later Voltaire took advantage of a loophole in an issue of bonds in Lorraine to make another killing.[48]

The chief stimulant of the state's growing need for funds was the need to raise and maintain armies. Provisioning these armies—providing them with food, clothing, weapons, and transport—was a most complex organizational task. Since the state possessed only the most rudimentary of bureaucracies, such tasks were left to individual entrepreneurs. For these feats of coordination there were large profits to be made. Among Voltaire's admirers were the brothers Paris, merchants who became the provisioners of the French army in the 1730s and 1740s. Voltaire admired their entrepreneurial skill; they in turn made the *philosophe* into a silent but grateful partner.[49]

The Defense of Luxury

Overseas trade was the fastest growing area of the French economy in Voltaire's day, and a key element in the expansion of the capitalist economy in Europe. Much of this trade was in what were regarded as "luxury" goods, grown or manufactured beyond Europe's shores.[50] Voltaire too was involved in international commerce. In 1730 he became part of a company that imported grain from North Africa to the French port of Marseilles, and then re-exported it to Italy and Spain. The company also imported cocoa, sugar, tobacco, and indigo from America to France. Voltaire was no silent partner here; he was forever soliciting the information on prices, markets, and currencies required for success in international trade.[51]

Voltaire thus had a financial interest in the importation of "luxuries." But he had an intellectual interest in it as well. For in his day, when such goods played so central a role in international trade, debate about the moral ramifications of the burgeoning capitalist economy was centered on the concept of "luxury."

In the *Philosophical Letters*, published in 1734, Voltaire defended the market as an antidote to religious fanaticism because of its promotion of the peaceable virtue of self-interested cooperation. In two poems published a few years thereafter, he set forth a second defense of commerce: that it promoted material wealth and comfort.

To us, the argument for material well-being might seem uncontroversial. But in the eighteenth century, material prosperity was frequently condemned as "luxury" by religious and civic moralists.[52] It was not a morally neutral word but a pejorative one, connoting not comfort but excess, the possession of nonnecessities. The notion of luxury was intricately connected with the existence of a recognized social hierarchy: what was necessary for those of high status was regarded as excessive for those of low status. Luxury meant the enjoyment of material goods not appropriate to one's station in life. Critics of luxury saw it as confounding social ranks.

Moralists in the civic tradition saw luxury as leading to national decline. English critics pointed to ancient Sparta as the model of a republic that preserved its independence through martial virtues and frugality. In France, it was the ancient Roman republic that served as the exemplar of these virtues. Polybius' account of the decline of Rome was read as a warning of the corrupting effects of luxury. The richer the commonwealth became, the greater would be the pursuit of individual material satisfactions at the expense of the common good. Material comfort, it was alleged, made men soft and effeminate; nations that pursued luxury would thus be defeated by the armies of more austere, virtuous, and warlike nations.

Christian moralists portrayed luxury as distracting men from the pursuit of salvation. In *The City of God,* Augustine had warned that prosperity begets luxury and then avarice. Subsequent Christian thinkers warned that luxury bound the flesh to the world and to the devil.[53] There was a long Christian tradition of interpreting virtue in ascetic terms: abstinence, privation, and humility were qualities of character to be cultivated.

Both the civic and the Christian tradition condemned the pursuit of material wealth, but for different reasons. The civic tradition saw it as corrupting the virtuous citizen, who ought to be prepared to sacrifice his private concerns for the state, bringing himself glory by defending the commonwealth in war. The Christian tradition saw it as a temptation to sin, leading away from the imitation of God and the divine virtues of abstinence, humility, and love. That the civic and the Christian virtues were to a considerable degree incompatible with one another did not stop moralists from amalgamating the two traditions in their condemnation of luxury as an invitation to both sin and corruption.[54]

Voltaire and other leading thinkers of the moderate Enlightenment reacted against a political culture based on manliness and warfare and a religious culture that emphasized piety. In its place they endorsed an emerging secular culture, one that valued gentler relations of sociability and looked for guidance not to religion but to philosophy, science, literature, and the arts. David Hume scorned what he called "the monkish virtues" of ascetic self-denial, which contributed nothing to social cooperation, while Voltaire, in his *Philosophical Dictionary*, wrote, "We live in society; therefore nothing is truly good for us that isn't good for society."[55] As the peoples of Europe became more civilized, they would come to share this common morality, Voltaire asserted.[56] By the mid-eighteenth century, this new basket of values had come to be known in England as "refinement" and in France as "civilization."[57]

Reversing the connotations of "luxury" was key to the attempt of enlightened intellectuals to legitimate the pursuit of happiness as a worthy political goal. Between Mandeville's *Fable of the Bees*, published in 1714, and Hume's essay "On Luxury" of 1742 came Voltaire's poetic contributions to the moral rehabilitation of luxury.

Voltaire entered the debate in 1734, with the distribution of his poem "The Worldling." "I thank wise nature which for my benefit caused me to be born in this age, so decried by our poor Doctors [of the Church]," the poem began. It combined its praise of contemporary worldly joys with ridicule of the Christian and civic myths of past golden ages, and coupled a paean to urban luxury with an attack on the Christian virtue of self-denial and the civic virtue of frugality.

Given the poem's iconoclastic anticlericalism, Voltaire feared that its appearance in print would bring down the wrath of the Catholic authorities. Rather than publishing it, Voltaire sent copies to friends in Paris. But when one recipient died, the poem was found among his effects, and several hundred copies were published without Voltaire's permission. It soon came under attack as a scandalous apology for vice. Fearing clerical persecution, Voltaire left France for Prussia. There he penned a second poem, "The Defense of the Worldling," in which he reiterated his previous arguments for luxury and added new ones, drawing upon recent economic arguments from *The Fable of the Bees*

and from Jean-Francois Melon's *Political Essay on Commerce* (1734).
For our purposes, the two poems and related writings by Voltaire can
be treated together.

"Abundance is the mother of the arts," wrote Voltaire in "The
Worldling."[58] The argument that material prosperity was the prerequisite for the development of higher civilization would henceforth be
repeated by virtually every advocate of capitalist economic growth.
Voltaire usually made this argument in negative form, by casting
aspersions upon the purportedly nobler past. The state of nature, he
wrote, was far from edenic. He pictured Adam and Eve in their
primeval garden: their faces burned by the sun, their hands scaly, their
uncut nails long, cracked, black, and hooked.[59] He insisted that the life
of the ancient Romans was characterized not by the vaunted virtue of
frugality, but by poverty, discomfort, and ignorance, which had nothing admirable about them.[60] Voltaire thus ridiculed the civic and the
Christian visions of the good old days, unspoiled by decadent luxury.
The garden he wanted to cultivate was no longer in Eden. "The terrestial paradise is in Paris," he concluded in the first version of his poem,
which he later revised to read "The terrestial paradise is where I am."
Because it was richer, modern urban life could be more civilized. To
make poverty seem not noble but sordid was central to Voltaire's rever-
sal of the terms of Christian and civic discourse.

Like Mandeville and Melon, Voltaire defended luxury against its
moralist detractors by trying to relativize the notion and to show that
much of what his contemporaries considered basic necessities had
once been quite extraordinary. "If one went back to a time when men
wore no shirts, if someone had told them that they ought to wear light,
fine, shirts of the most elegant material, and white as snow, they
would have cried, 'What luxury! What effeminacy! Such magnificence
is scarcely suitable for kings! You want to corrupt our morals and
destroy the state!' "[61] He developed this critique of the notion of luxury
as excess in his *Philosophical Dictionary*:

> When scissors, which surely do not date from remote antiq-
> uity, were invented, what wasn't said against the first people
> who clipped their nails, and who cut some of the hair that
> fell down over their noses? They were doubtless called
> dandies and squanderers, who bought an expensive instru-
> ment of vanity to mar the work of the Creator.[62]

Voltaire also suggested several *economic* arguments for luxury that
had been developed at length by Mandeville and Melon. Material con-

sumption by the rich—traditionally denounced as a vice—gave rise to the demand for the labor of the poor, who in time profited from the creation of greater wealth. The spending of the rich thus allowed the poor to accumulate, and the taste for luxury goods was already growing among the lower echelons of society in England and in France.[63] It was the desire for luxuries that had led to transoceanic commerce, and which increasingly tied together the inhabitants of the earth.[64] Voltaire praised Louis XIV's first minister, Colbert, for having promoted the production of luxuries. He thus enriched the state and "expanded the source of all our arts."[65] By ultimately improving the lot of the poor, enriching the state, and increasing international contacts, the taste for luxury was a source of public benefit.

Not only were the critics of luxury mistaken, Voltaire suggested, they were also hypocrites, who took the finery of their own lives for granted while condemning the comforts of others as "luxury." "The Defense of the Worldling" develops as a dialogue between the author and "Maître Cafard"—Master Hypocrite—a priest who serves as Voltaire's foil. Into Cafard's mouth Voltaire placed the standard religious condemnations of luxury and comfort. The poet responds by pointing out to Cafard the sources of the coffee he sips out of his porcelain cup. "Does it not have to be ravished by human industry from the fields of Arabia? The porcelain and the fragile beauty of this enamel coated in China, was made for you by a thousand hands, baked and rebaked, and painted and decorated. This fine silver, chased and fluted, whether flat or made into vessels or saucers, was torn from the deep earth in Potosa, from the heart of a new world. The whole universe has worked for you, so that in your complacent rage, with pious acrimony, you can insult the whole world, exhausted to give you pleasure."[66] The poet concluded that this high-living critic of luxury was himself a "worldling."

Among Voltaire's pecuniary pursuits was moneylending. The direct lending of money for interest remained legally forbidden as usury, but there were many subterfuges through which the prohibition could be overcome. Voltaire loaned large sums of money to members of the royalty, in return for a lifelong annual payment. In 1752 he donated 150,000 livres to Prince Charles-Eugene of Württemberg, in return for a lifelong annuity of 15,750 francs; in case of his death, 7,500 per year would be paid to his niece and mistress, Mme. Denis. He made a similar loan to the elector of the Palatinate. Voltaire's famed hypochondria has been attributed in part to these economic pursuits. He lived for eighty-four years, and throughout the last four decades of his life, he spoke of illness and his imminent demise. Since his debtors had to make the full annual payments only as long as the original lender was alive, those to whom Voltaire loaned funds were more likely to agree to a higher annual rate if they had reason to believe that his life would be short.[67]

Having made and augmented his fortune through lotteries, financial speculation, merchant activity, and moneylending, Voltaire in 1759 bought a chateau at Ferney, where he lived out the last two decades of his life. During these years he turned a virtual wilderness into a thriving village, of which he was the owner and seigneur. At the time of his death in 1778, the annual rents he collected made him one of the twenty greatest landlords in France.[68] He was not only the most fêted man of letters of his age, but one of the richest commoners in Europe.

Avarice and the Jews: The Limits of Enlightenment

As we have seen, Voltaire was actively involved in those commercial activities that had been most suspect in the Christian tradition: merchant activity and the lending of money. Despite his antipathy to Christianity, his principled defense of the pursuit of wealth, and his success in capitalist endeavors, Voltaire felt defensive about his interest in making money. Perhaps the first reference to financial activity in his surviving correspondence comes in a letter of April 1722 to the Marquise de Bernières, an aristocrat with whose husband Voltaire had recently formed a company. The poet protests repeatedly that he would prefer to spend his time in *her* company rather than with this *"caisse de juifrerie"* or "fund for jewing."[69] Through this disparaging link of commerce to Jews, Voltaire distanced himself from his commercial engagements. It was a technique that he would use frequently in the years to come.

Voltaire moved to Potsdam, on the outskirts of Berlin in 1750, at the invitation of Frederick II. A devotee of French culture, the Prussian king began to correspond with the leading French man of letters in 1736. The intellectual influence of Voltaire is evident in Frederick's early work *Anti-Machiavel*, which advocated the rule of law, in enlightened fashion. There was a more direct influence as well: Voltaire edited the book before its first publication and eliminated some ideas with which he disagreed, such as Frederick's argument in favor of just wars.[70] Though the young Frederick shared the Enlightenment goals of equal justice before the law and the promotion of the happiness of his subjects, his priorities as a ruler were the expansion of his kingdom and the enhancement of state power through rationalizing the bureaucratic and military apparatus and promoting economic growth to fund them.[71]

To realize the Enlightenment ideals of formal equality, the rule of law, freedom of commerce, and religious toleration, Voltaire and many of the other *philosophes* looked to absolutist monarchs, whose policies they hoped to influence. The support of the *philosophes* for the expansion of the monarch's sovereign power was tactical. It arose not out of a principled belief in the throne, but out of the recognition that only a strong monarchy had the power to override the resistance to enlightened legislation by the privileged churches, estates, and corporations that made up continental European society.[72]

The extent of his differences with the monarch was not yet clear to Voltaire when he accepted Frederick's invitation to settle in Prussia. Frederick hoped to gain prestige by his association with the most renowned intellectual of his day. It could be very useful to have such a shaper of public opinion at one's side. Yet Frederick did not seek Voltaire's political counsel: he valued Voltaire's advice on poetry, not policy. Voltaire came to Potsdam to find a respite from the clerical persecution that dogged him in France, in the company of a like-minded opponent of *"l'infame."* He hoped to increase his prestige through his close association with a reigning monarch, and hoped to influence the man whom he praised as a philosopher-king. It was not the last time an intellectual and a despot would enter into a marriage of mutual convenience.

Among the events that led Voltaire to depart from Prussia in ignominy was his illegal speculation in government bonds.[73] He had earlier exhibited his knack for turning legal anomalies into financial opportunities. In Paris and Lorraine, he had enriched himself and his associates by thwarting government policy. In Potsdam, Voltaire tried to skirt the law in order to profit from public debt. But this time the law had been issued by Frederick, Voltaire's host and patron. In the process, Voltaire blackened his reputation among his supporters, as he had two decades earlier in England.

Like most governments of the day, the state of Saxony covered its debts in part through government bonds. During the Wars of Austrian Succession, Saxony had joined with Austria against Prussia. Defeated by Frederick, the Saxons agreed to a peace treaty in 1745 that included heavy financial payments to the Prussians. The loss of the war against Prussia led to a decline in confidence in Saxon bonds, which sank drastically in value. Among the owners of Saxon bonds were Prussian subjects. Concerned about the wealth of his kingdom, Frederick included in the treaty a clause that required the Saxon government to redeem these Prussian-owned bonds at their original face value.

Within months of Voltaire's arrival in Potsdam, he sized up the situation and recognized that there was a great profit to be made if a Prussian subject could buy devalued Saxon bonds in nearby Saxony and redeem them at their face value. He was not the first to identify this opportunity: earlier attempts had led Frederick to issue a decree in 1748 explicitly banning such speculation, since the Saxons cited such abuses and threatened to back out of the treaty's financial provision.

In late 1750 Voltaire found Prussian subjects whom he could use as a front to buy Saxon bonds on his behalf and redeem them at their original value. The subjects were Abraham Hirschel and his son, both of whom were among Frederick's "court Jews." While most Jews were excluded from citizenship and even residence within German cities, "court Jews" were granted special privileges in return for their services to the court. There they played a number of roles: they loaned money to the prince, helped collect taxes, and acted as factors who obtained provisions for the court and the army. Like the medieval Jewish moneylenders, the court Jews of the early modern era were tolerated in an otherwise hostile society because their economic functions were indispensable.[74]

In September 1750, Voltaire arranged for the Hirschels to buy Saxon bonds on his behalf, to be redeemed at their full value. He gave Hirschel a bill of exchange for some 40,000 francs, drawn on a notary in Paris. Hirschel traveled to the Saxon capital of Dresden to purchase the bonds, and through a string of intermediaries sent the bill of exchange to Paris. In November, while Hirschel was in Dresden, Frederick learned of Voltaire's plans and expressed his disgust. Voltaire tried to end the arrangement in December, and sent word to his Paris notary that the bill was not to be redeemed. Hirschel returned from Dresden and reported to Voltaire that he could not acquire the Saxon bonds. The Hirschels agreed to repay Voltaire his 40,000 francs as soon as the money for Voltaire's bill of exchange arrived from Paris. Shortly thereafter Hirschel learned that the Paris notary had refused to transfer the money.

For his part, Voltaire sought to cancel his black mark with Frederick, and to ensure that Hirschel would not wind up with his money. He asked Hirschel to lend him jewelry for use in the plays he staged at court. To remain in the king's good graces, Voltaire had Hirschel write up a false contract, which he planned to show to the monarch to make it appear that Voltaire's payment had been for the jewels rather than bonds. In the meantime, Voltaire planned to keep the jewels he had borrowed from Hirschel until his bill of exchange was returned. When he took them to be evaluated, however, he discovered they were worth considerably less than the money he had deposited with the Hirschels. When Hirschel visited Voltaire in late December and reported that the bill of exchange had not yet been returned from Paris, Voltaire called him a swindler, then pulled a ring off Hirschel's finger and kept it.

Fearful of losing his money to the Hirschels, Voltaire sued. He applied to Frederick, who created a special commission to hear the case, headed by Samuel von Cocceji, a noted jurist who had drafted the new Prussian law code, the Codex Fredericianus. The younger Hirschel—who had arranged with Voltaire to purchase the Saxon bonds and lent him the jewelry—was imprisoned. He was bailed out by his father, who put up his house, his jewels, and his own certificate of Jewish privilege as collateral. The upcoming trial became the talk of Berlin. The talk about Voltaire was typified by the remark of Frederick, who wrote to his sister that it was "the affair of a scoundrel who wants to cheat a rogue."[75] While the trial was in session during January and February, the king cut off all contact with his guest.

At the trial, Voltaire claimed that he had given Hirschel the money in order to buy diamonds and furs. To cover his tracks, Voltaire apparently destroyed the original contract by which he paid the Hirschels to acquire the bonds. He then insisted that Hirschel's testimony was not admissible as evidence, and resorted to a litany of traditional anti-Jewish charges. It was well known that Jews engaged in perjury, Voltaire maintained; their secret dogmas held that an oath made to a Christian authority was not binding on conscience, since on the Day of Atonement Jews were absolved of all oaths.

Neither Voltaire nor Hirschel emerged from the trial unscathed. The younger Hirschel at first denied that he had signed a contract with Voltaire, then changed his testimony when the contract was presented in evidence. Between the trial and the verdict, the senior Hirschel died of grief. The court's decision did not absolve either man: Hirschel was commanded to return the bill of exchange (which had only recently returned from Paris) and pay a small fine for not doing so earlier; Voltaire was required to return to Hirschel most of the jewels he had "borrowed."

Trying to put the best face on the result, Voltaire wrote to Frederick immediately of his "victory." But Frederick was not taken in, informing Voltaire that though he was welcome to remain in Berlin, he would have to "live like a *philosophe*." The judgment of the Berlin public was expressed in a 1753 poem about the affair by Gotthold Lessing, who had served as Voltaire's translator during the trial and had seen most of the relevant documents. Lessing described Hirschel as a rogue, and Voltaire as a greater rogue. Voltaire wrote to a friend in Paris that he was finally finished with his "trade with the Old Testament."[76]

The response of Lessing and Voltaire to Voltaire's confrontation with Hirschel epitomizes a repeated pattern in Voltaire's relationship to capitalist activity and to the suspicion of trade and the pursuit of wealth within the Christian tradition.

Time and time again Voltaire was accused by those who knew him of just those negative attributes that the Christian tradition had associated with mercantile activity: dishonesty and avarice. In England, he was accused of shady business practices, and his banker there concluded that "Voltaire is very avaricious and dishonest." Frederick and Lessing termed his financial practices those of a scoundrel. His lover, Mme. Denis, wrote to him that he was "pierced by avarice." "Your heart makes you the lowest of men," she wrote, "but I will hide the vices of your heart as best I can."[77]

Voltaire reacted by denouncing the Jews as the embodiment of the vices of which he was so frequently accused—a classic case of projection. He did so often, in letters and in print. Though it might be tempting to regard his anti-Jewish sentiments as a product of his dealings with Jews such as Mendes da Costa and Hirschel, his antisemitism in fact preceded these encounters. In 1722, not long after he joined in the "fund for jewing," Voltaire wrote to the French king's principal minister, Cardinal Dubois, that "a Jew belongs to no country other than the one where he makes money," thus repeating the traditional Christian view of the Jew as wanderer and outsider.[78]

Voltaire's reference to Hirschel as the "Old Testament" was typical of the way in which Jews and Judaism would be characterized in his books.[79] In his historical writings and in historical references scattered throughout his works, Voltaire not only characterized contemporary Jews as avaricious usurers but attributed these characteristics to Jews throughout the ages, beginning with the biblical Hebrews. According to Voltaire, Abraham was so avaricious that he prostituted his wife for money; David slew Goliath not to protect his people but for economic gain; Herod did not complete the rebuilding of the temple because the Jews, though they loved their sanctuary, loved their money more.[80]

Jewish avarice and usury thus appeared as ongoing racial characteristics. The *Philosophical Dictionary* is replete with references to the inherently usurious nature of the Jews. Of the biblical Hebrews, he wrote in the article entitled "The Heaven of the Ancients" that "their only science was the trade of jobbery and usury."[81] In his treatment of the expulsion of the Jews from Spain in his *Essay on Manners*, Voltaire wrote: "At the end of the fifteenth century, in searching for the source of Spain's misery, it was found that the Jews drew to themselves all the money of the country by commerce and usury . . ."[82] In addition to picturing Jews as avaricious usurers, Voltaire frequently portrayed them as dishonest in their economic dealings. To reach these conclusions, Voltaire took whatever sources were at hand. If they were anti-Jewish, he accepted them at face value. If they were not, he gave the facts an anti-Jewish twist.[83] The Jew as avaricious usurer and economic parasite remained a recurring theme among those Enlightenment thinkers who followed Voltaire's lead.[84]

Of course Voltaire's antipathy to Jews and Judaism had other sources as well. He hated Judaism as the progenitor of Christianity, and in order to evade censorship he sometimes criticized Christianity by allusion through his direct attacks on Judaism. Though Voltaire was vehement in his antipathy to Christianity, one of the few elements of his Christian heritage which he managed to preserve was the link between the stigmatization of commerce and of the Jews. Perhaps this reflected a psychological need to deflect the traditional accusations against commerce hurled—with good cause—against himself. In any event, it revived a much older pattern, by which those aspects of economic activity deemed most threatening were attributed to the Jews.

Voltaire also criticized Jews, ancient and modern, for the tenacity with which they clung to their faith and to a separate and distinct identity. If reason was universal and its use entwined with the growth of civilization, the continued existence of Jews as a particular group was an affront to reason and civilization. Jews who continued to identify themselves as such stood apart from the vision of a cosmopolitan world.[85] Voltaire chastized the Jews for the preservation of their particularity and their pursuit of economic gain. Voltaire did not link the two charges, and the latter charge, as we have seen, was anomalous given Voltaire's intellectual defense of capitalism and his own economic activity. Karl Marx, who shared Voltaire's cosmopolitan abhorrence of particularity, would link it to the Christian tradition's suspicion of commerce, producing a more potent synthesis of antisemitism and anticapitalism.

And what of Voltaire's character and its influence upon later intellectuals? It is difficult to dissent from the final judgment of Adam Smith, who classified Voltaire among those men of "splendid talents and virtues" who "have often distinguished themselves by the most improper and even insolent contempt of all the ordinary decorums of life and conversation. They have thereby set the most pernicious example to those who wish to resemble them, and who too often content themselves with imitating their follies, without even attempting to attain their perfections."[86]

CHAPTER THREE

ADAM SMITH:
MORAL PHILOSOPHY AND
POLITICAL ECONOMY

"This Smith is an excellent man!" wrote Voltaire after meeting the Scottish philosopher. "We have nothing to compare with him, and I am embarrassed for my dear compatriots."[1] *An Inquiry into the Nature and Causes of the Wealth of Nations*, which Smith published in 1776, is the most important book ever written about capitalism and its moral ramifications. Though *The Wealth of Nations* is in good part about commerce, it was not written for businessmen or merchants. A book focused on the analysis of market processes motivated by self-interest, it was written by one of the most admired philosophers of the Enlightenment, a former professor of logic, rhetoric, jurisprudence, and moral philosophy, in order to influence politicians and rouse them to pursue the common good. As a moral philosopher, Smith was concerned about the nature of moral excellence, but like many enlightened intellectuals, he tried to begin by describing humanity as it really *is*. His project was to take man as he actually is and to make him more like what he should be, by discovering the institutions that made men tolerably decent and might make them more so. Smith drew upon more than a century of reflection on the possible social benefits of the individual's propensities to self-love, egotism, self-interest, pride, and approbativeness, when these were properly channeled by social institutions.[2] Josiah Tucker, an Anglican divine who was the foremost British advocate of free trade before Adam Smith, summed up this approach: "The main point to be aimed at is neither to extinguish nor enfeeble self-love, but to give it such a direction, that it may promote the public interest by pursuing its own."[3]

The most important argument of *The Wealth of Nations* is that a market economy is best able to improve the standard of living of the vast majority of the populace—that it can lead to what Smith called "universal opulence." The book built on the Enlightenment assumption that worldly happiness was a good thing, and sought to show that material well-being need not be confined to "luxuries" available only to a thin stratum at the top. On the contrary, Smith made the purchasing power of consumers the measure of "the wealth of the nation." The book also argued that under the right institutional conditions, the spread of "commercial society" would lead to greater individual liberty and more peaceful relations among nations.

For Smith, the promotion of national wealth through the market was a goal worthy of the attention of moral philosophers because of its place in his larger moral vision. Smith valued commercial society not only for the wealth it produced but also for the character it fostered. He valued the market in part because it promoted the development of cooperative modes of behavior, making men more gentle because more self-controlled, more likely to subordinate their potentially asocial passions to the needs of others. In its own way, *The Wealth of Nations*, like Smith's *The Theory of Moral Sentiments* (1759), was intended to make men better, not just better off.

Smith's Life and Milieu

An awareness of Smith's milieu and career explains his stated intention in *The Wealth of Nations* to contribute to "the science of a statesman or legislator."[4] The political philosopher as the teacher of legislators was one of the oldest conceptions of the man of learning, reaching back to Plato and Aristotle.[5] Revived by Renaissance Italian humanists and their northern European successors,[6] it remained the self-conception of many Enlightenment thinkers, who sought to influence the holders of power. Nowhere was this conception more plausible than among the top rank of Scottish intellectuals, who were closely connected to the ruling elites of Scotland and England, and often enough worked in the emerging state bureaucracy.

Smith spent most of his life in Scotland, a great incubator of British intellectual innovation in the middle of the eighteenth century. He was raised in a milieu in which property, patronage, education, and government service were closely linked; these coordinates continued to chart his social course thereafter.[7] Born in 1723, sixteen years after the Act of Union ended Scotland's existence as a separate political entity, he spent his boyhood in the small port town of Kirkcaldy on the east coast of Scotland. As a result of the Union of 1707, Scotland relinquished its sovereignty and independence. In return, its landowning elite gained seats in both Houses of Parliament in London, and its merchants and manufacturers gained access to the British market through a customs union. The budding economic prosperity of Scotland was due in good part to its free trade with England, as its merchants and improving landlords were well aware.

Scotland was largely a rural society, at a comparatively low level of commercial and industrial development. The main industries in the Kirkcaldy region—coal mining and salt panning—were conducted by unfree laborers, legally bound for a period of time to their place of work. Another industry was nail making, and it is a measure of the primitive level of commercial development that some nail makers paid their workers in nails, which local shopkeepers were willing to accept in place of currency.

At the age of fourteen, Smith was sent to the University of Glasgow. An outstanding student, he won a scholarship to Oxford, where he spent half a dozen years. In 1748 Smith began to make his name in the intellectual world, through a series of lectures in Edinburgh. To an audience made up of students as well as prominent citizens of the town, Smith lectured on rhetoric, belles lettres, and jurisprudence. The success of his lectures led him to a professorship at the University of Glasgow, where in 1751, at the age of twenty-eight, he was appointed to the chair of logic and rhetoric, and then to the chair of moral philosophy. Smith's lectures on ethics formed the basis of *The Theory of Moral Sentiments*. Even before completing that book, he had begun to lecture on "jurisprudence," a topic that included not only the principles of law but those of government and political economy as well. The portions of Smith's lectures dealing with political economy and with defense were eventually to find their way, in modified form, into *The Wealth of Nations*. Smith never managed to complete the material on government and law to his own satisfaction, and his notes for a book on that topic were consigned to the flames by his executors. Fortunately, copies of student notes on those lectures, as well as on his lectures about the history of rhetoric and literature, have come to light, rounding out our portrait of one of the most wide-ranging minds of the Enlightenment.

The Theory of Moral Sentiments was published in 1759 to great acclaim in Scotland and England, as well as on the Continent. The book attracted the attention of Charles Townshend, a leading member of Parliament, who in 1755 had married Lady Dalkeith, a dowager who presided over the Earldom of Dalkeith, one of Scotland's grandest estates.[8] In 1763 Townshend lured Smith away from Glasgow to become the tutor of his stepson, Henry Scott, the Duke of Buccleuch, by offering Smith a handsome sum and a generous lifetime pension. For two years, Smith accompanied the young duke on his Grand Tour of the Continent, using the opportunity to visit Voltaire in Geneva and to confer with many of the leading French thinkers in Paris. He also gathered materials on duties and taxation in Europe for his book on political economy. Returning to England late in 1766, Smith set about writing *The Wealth of Nations*, which was published a decade later.

Even before its publication, Smith's advice was sought by leading political figures in London. The esteem of Townshend and Buccleuch strengthened Smith's links to the highest levels of British politics. After the publication of *The Wealth of Nations* in 1776, Smith's star rose even higher. He was appointed a commissioner of customs for Scotland, in part because the prime minister and leading figures at the Treasury were impressed by his writings.[9]

Smith spent the last decade of life in Edinburgh, devoting most of his time to his job as commissioner of customs. He began new intellectual projects, but completed none of them to his satisfaction. Though his days were filled with the concerns of trade and revenue, his mind seems to have turned back to the questions of ethics and the social formation of character central to *The Theory of Moral Sentiments*, a book he revised substantially for its sixth edition of 1790. Smith appears to have conducted himself according to the dictates of benevolence that *The Theory of Moral Sentiments* tried to evoke in its readers. He lived modestly, despite the considerable income from his pension from the duke, from his salary as commissioner of customs, and from royalties from his books. Yet upon his death in 1790 his estate was minimal, since Smith had given away most of his income in acts of charity, which he took care to conceal.[10]

Though Smith was born in Scotland and spent most of his life there, he was a cosmopolitan thinker. He did not regard himself as a Scottish thinker in the sense of reflecting primarily upon Scottish experience or writing for a Scottish audience. Smith wrote for a British audience, and more broadly for a European and transcontinental one. Smith, like his friend David Hume and many of the other great figures of the Scottish Enlightenment, tended to be more cosmopolitan than their English counterparts. This provincial cosmopolitanism freed the Scottish intellectuals from a narrow fixation on their own institutions. It made them particularly sensitive to the variety of social and political arrangements, and drew them toward comparative and historical inquiry into the origins and effects of institutions.

Within Scotland itself there were regions at very different stages of social and economic development.[11] Through the early decades of the eighteenth century, the society of the Gaelic-speaking Highlands, which remained beyond the reach of the central government, was still based upon the clan. In the absence of centralized government control, self-protection came from membership in a clan. Each clan's hereditary chieftain was the highest political and military authority, with the power of life and death over his subjects. In 1745, the Highland clans sided with the Jacobite revolt against the British throne and threatened the more economically developed and English-speaking Lowlands. After the revolt was crushed, the Highlands were "pacified" by the permanent stationing of government troops, and the clans disrupted by the exile of their chiefs. Even more important for the dissolution of the clan system was the gradual integration of the region into the market economy of the Lowlands. The role of central government power and the spread of commerce in the development of civilization would figure prominently in Smith's writings.

In the more advanced Lowlands, social relations based upon the market and legally free labor existed alongside forms of domination that were more direct and all-encompassing. Feudal relations, in which the landlord exercised political and judicial control over his tenants, were abolished in the countryside only in the 1740s, and rural tenants were obliged to offer feudal services to their superiors until well into the second half of the century. Landlords often served as justices of the peace, who were empowered to control wage rates—a power they used to keep wages down. Beyond the more cosmopolitan and mercantile port cities of the south of Scotland lay a hinterland in which older and more direct forms of political and cultural control still predominated. It was in comparison with them that Smith judged the newer forms of human relationship developing in the more politically and economically advanced regions of Europe.

The Consumer Revolution

Most people in the Great Britain of Smith's day lived in what most of us would regard as poverty. Hundreds of thousands were willing to risk the possibility of death in transit and years in indentured servitude for the chance to escape to the New World. Yet the population of Britain was probably better off economically than that of any major nation on the globe. To put relative poverty and wealth in perspective, let us take the standards of apparel considered necessary by ordinary day laborers, the lowest of the working poor, as recounted in *The Wealth of Nations*. In England, Smith reports, the poorest day laborer of either sex would be ashamed to appear in public without leather shoes. In Scotland, a rung lower on the ladder of national wealth, it was considered inappropriate for men of this class to appear without shoes, but not for women. In France, a rung lower still, custom held that both men and women laborers could appear shoeless in public.[12] Below France there were many rungs in Europe. And below Europe there were many more rungs still.

The Wealth of Nations grew out of Smith's reflections upon the real successes of eighteenth-century Britain in producing economic growth. The gradual but unmistakable rise in the standard of living not only of the rich but of the working poor was real enough. But it was hampered, in Smith's eyes, by some of the protectionist restrictions to which his countrymen attributed their growing riches, and it could be speeded up by expanding the greater market freedom already visible in parts of the economy. The old system of economic regulation of domestic trade— in which the price of goods was set by guilds, and the rate of wages set by justices of the peace—was being increasingly abandoned by the middle of the eighteenth century. But the regulation of foreign trade was actually increasing.[13] Much of Smith's book was an argument for expanding the freer market regime already dominant in internal trade to the realm of international commerce.

Trade with other European powers was generally viewed by policy makers as a form of undeclared warfare, with the object of maximizing benefits to England while minimizing those to rival nations. The prime weapon in this war was the duty on imported goods. These customs duties were originally levied to provide the national government with revenue, but by Smith's day they were increasingly seen as a means of protecting British producers by raising the prices that consumers had to pay for imported goods. In its efforts to protect British industries from foreign competition, Parliament went so far as to prohibit some foreign imports entirely, including calico cotton, silk, leather gloves, stockings, velvet, and even some types of paper.[14] Even more elaborate were the restrictions on transcontinental trade, which was becoming an ever more important facet of the British economy. By Smith's day most parliamentary activity revolved around endorsing, enforcing, or curbing economic interests. Lobbying by commercial interest groups became a highly organized affair: they raised funds, set up committees, tried to elect their representatives to the House of Commons and to influence current members of Parliament. Any attempt to alter existing tariffs ran up against a wall of well-organized parliamentary opposition.

Yet despite these barriers and prohibitions, the most important economic fact of Smith's day was that the nation was becoming wealthier—not only its elite, but its laboring masses as well. For perhaps the first time in history, a basic minimum of food, shelter, and clothing was a nearly universal expectation.[15] Contemporary observers were struck by the relative ease with which an ordinary laborer could provide the means of subsistence for himself and for his family.[16] Wage rates increased gradually for most of the century, growing most rapidly in the 1760s and 1770s, when Smith was at work on *The Wealth of Nations*.[17] New manufacturing technologies made it possible to employ women and even children—whose labor had usually been confined in the past to the farm or the home—in remunerative jobs. As a result, total family wages rose to the point where a substantial portion of the laboring classes could reasonably hope to purchase goods once beyond their aspirations.[18] As wages moved upward and as the costs of production fell in agriculture and in the manufacture of basic necessities such as textiles for clothing, the standard of living rose. What had once been regarded as "luxuries" came to be seen as mere "decencies," what had been "decencies" became "necessities," and the very definition of "necessities" changed. Tea, a luxury beverage of the upper classes when the century began, was a daily drink of road workers by midcentury, as the per capita consumption increased fifteenfold in the course of the century.[19] Objects once reserved for the rich came within the reach of a large part of society; a river of new blankets, linens, pillows, rugs, curtains, pewter, glass, china, brass, copper, and ironware flowed into English homes. Many of the fortunes, small and large, of eighteenth-century entrepreneurs were made by producing more cheaply goods that could appeal to a mass market: nails and buttons, buckles and pots, candlesticks, cutlery, crockery, and saucepans.

This British consumer revolution was both the stimulus and the beneficiary of an industrial revolution then in its earliest stages. Items that were formerly purchased once in a lifetime could now be bought several times over, not because the goods were less durable, but because they were so much less expensive. Goods once produced laboriously at home, such as clothes, beer, candles, cutlery, and furniture, could now be purchased instead. Another side of the consumer revolution was the transformation of marketing, as goods that had formerly been available only at weekly markets, occasional fairs, or from roving peddlers could increasingly be purchased any day of the week but Sunday. It was in the eighteenth century that England became what Smith called "a nation of shopkeepers"—to the convenience of their customers. Advertisements for novel products or new fashions made their first appearance and soon filled much of the newspapers. Fueling and channeling this new ability to buy was social emulation, the desire to resemble those who were one rung up on the ladder of society. The middling orders sought to simulate the manners, morals, and merchandise of the gentry, the maid those of her mistress. What was new was not the *desire* to consume: it was the *ability* to consume that was unprecedented, made possible by the increase in national wealth and the declining cost of goods.[20]

The most frequent response of elite writers to the visible rise in the standard of living of the laboring classes was consternation. To the traditional moralistic denunciation of "luxury" as promoting sin and undermining civic virtue, new economic arguments were added. Rising wages, it was said, would undermine the will to work, since workers would only labor long enough to meet their traditional requirements, after which they would prefer more leisure to more income.[21] There is in fact some (not very reliable) evidence of just this pattern in England in the first half of the eighteenth century, but by the second half of the century wage earners were willing to work longer and harder to earn more, perhaps because of the increasing availability of new commodities at prices they could afford.[22] Writers on economic matters also warned that the high level of Britain's wages would raise the price of its manufactured goods, making them uncompetitive in the international economy.[23]

Smith took precisely the opposite position. While he was not the first to challenge the utility-of-poverty theory, his book clinched the argument against it.[24] He described Britain as a nation in which real wages had risen consistently during the century as a result of falling food prices and the improved quality and variety of basic subsistence goods. For Smith, high and rising real wages—what he called "the liberal reward of labour"—were to be welcomed. "To complain of it is to lament the necessary effect and cause of the greatest public prosperity," he wrote.[25] Smith shared Voltaire's assumption that it was better to be rich than to be poor, but he focused on making a decent life possible for all.

Smith's science of the legislator took from the civic republican tradition the need for the virtuous man to concern himself with the common good. But his view also developed out of a dissatisfaction with the legacy of that tradition. In its focus on the virtue of participation in government, the civic tradition had confined its concern to a narrow, propertied elite capable of participating in government, while neglecting the effects of the political system on "all the different members of the community." Smith's concern was to ensure that the political process contributed to the welfare of the nation as a whole. This well-being extended beyond the political elite, and was defined primarily in terms of improving the quality of life in the private realms of the family and of production and consumption. Smith's emphasis reflected an upward evaluation of the importance of "ordinary life," as well as the transformation of the Christian virtue of charity into the Enlightenment virtue of practical benevolence. Thus while Smith continued the civic republican concern for the common good, his understanding of that good placed greater weight on the moral and material well-being of men and women in their daily lives.[26]

Early in *The Wealth of Nations*, Smith called to the attention of his readers the material circumstances ("accommodation" in the language of his day) of "the most common artificer or day labourer in a civilized and thriving country":

> Compared . . . with the more extravagant luxury of the great, his accommodation must no doubt appear extremely simple and easy; and yet it may be true, perhaps, that the accommodation of an European prince does not always so much exceed that of an industrious and frugal peasant, as the accommodation of the latter exceeds that of many an African king, the absolute master of the lives and liberties of ten thousand naked savages.

Smith traced the superior material welfare of the common European to the fact that in a wealthy country like Britain or Holland, even the common laborer had thousands of people working to provide his needs:

> The woolen coat, for example, which covers the day labourer, as coarse and rough as it may appear, is the produce of the joint labour of a great multitude of workmen. The shepherd, the sorter of the wool, the wool-comber or carder, the dyer, the scribbler, the spinner, the weaver, the fuller, the dresser, with many others, must all join their different arts in order to complete even this homely production. How many merchants and carriers, besides, must have been employed in transporting the materials from some of those workmen to others who often live in a very distant part of

the country! How much commerce and navigation in particular, how many ship-builders, sailors, sail-makers, rope-makers, must have been employed in order to bring together the different drugs made use of by the dyer, which often come from the remotest corners of the world! . . . If we examine, I say, all these things, and consider what a variety of labour is employed about each of them, we shall be sensible that without the assistance and co-operation of many thousands, the very meanest person in a civilized country could not be provided, even according to, what we very falsely imagine, the easy and simple manner in which he is commonly accommodated.[27]

The material advantages of the lowly laborer over the powerful chief was the riddle which *The Wealth of Nations* set out to explain.

Explaining the Market

The first principle in Smith's systematic chain of explanation was the uniquely human propensity to exchange goods in search of self-interest. The second principle was the division of labor. Smith tried to demonstrate to the potential legislator that with properly structured institutions, these two common and well-known principles could be channeled to move the nation toward what he called "universal opulence."

The division of labor, Smith maintained, was the great mechanism which increased human productivity and made universal opulence possible.[28] He illustrated its advantages by describing a pin-making factory, in which an assembly line of ten persons, each specialized in a particular function, could produce 48,000 pins per day. Working individually, he reckoned, they might each produce twenty pins a day at most, for a total of two hundred pins. The division of labor had in this case increased production by two hundred and forty times. In using the pin factory to make his point (an example frequently cited in the eighteenth century), Smith was not touting the advantages of the factory form of manufacture, in which the entire production process took place under one roof. The factory was merely the form in which the division of labor was most immediately visible, and Smith was using it to represent a larger process, in which the division of labor was spread over many sites.

There were several factors to which Smith attributed the tremendous expansion of productivity brought about by the division of labor. The division of labor, he explained, makes workers more proficient in performing specialized tasks. It saves time that would otherwise be lost in switching from one task to another. And by breaking up the process of production into discrete parts, it favors "the invention of a great number of machines which facilitate and abridge labour, and enable one man to do the work of many."[29] He cited as a contemporary example the "fire-engine"—better known to us as the steam engine, the most important prime mover of the industrial revolution.

The division of labor was made possible by the ability of men to *exchange* their labor or the products of their labor, Smith explained, and the greater the extent of exchange, the more labor could be divided. The systematic exchange of labor and the products of labor Smith termed "the market." Thus the greater the extent of the market, the greater the possible gains in production.[30]

The principle that set the market in motion and kept it going was the inclination to satisfy self-interest through exchange. Smith's basic model of the links between human propensities and the wealth of nations is now complete: *self-interest leads to market exchange, leading to the greater division of labor, leading in turn to specialization, expertise, dexterity, and invention, and, as a result, to greater wealth.*

Smith believed that "the propensity to truck, barter, and exchange one thing for another" was innate in human nature.[31] But its ascendancy in economic relations had come about slowly, gradually, unintentionally, and as yet imperfectly. As market exchange became the basis of economic life, society reached a stage at which "every man thus lives by exchanging, or becomes in some measure a merchant, and the society itself grows to be what is properly a commercial society."[32]

If we recall the stigmatization of the merchant so frequent in the traditions of classical republicanism and of Christian thought, we can appreciate the reevaluation of values that Smith proclaimed. For Smith, progress lay in becoming a more mercantile society, in which the commodity that most men had to sell was their labor. The classical republican tradition regarded the occupation of buying and selling as disqualifying one for citizenship. In the Christian tradition, the pursuit of self-interest was a passion and hence part of man's bodily, animal nature. For Smith, it was the pursuit of self-interest through exchange that set man off from the animals and gave him his specifically human dignity. "Nobody ever saw a dog make a fair and deliberate exchange of one bone for another with another dog," Smith wrote. "Nobody ever saw one animal by its gestures and natural cries signify to another, this is mine, that is yours; I am willing to give this for that." This capacity for exchange is what makes the human species uniquely capable of progress, Smith believed. It "encourages every man to apply himself to a particular occupation, and to cultivate and bring to perfection whatever talent or genius he may possess for that particular species of business." Without the opportunity for exchange, men are doomed to remain unspecialized and unable to make use of their different natural talents. It is the possibility of exchange that makes the *differences* between individuals *useful* to one another.[33]

Man was by his very nature dependent upon others, and in a "civilized," "commercial" society man depended on a vast array of anonymous others to make most of what he needed. He was unlikely to meet his needs if he relied solely upon the altruism of the many people upon whom he depended:

> It is not from the benevolence of the butcher, the brewer, or the baker, that we expect our dinner, but from their regard to their own interest. We address ourselves, not to their humanity but to their self-love, and never talk to them of our own necessities but of their advantages. Nobody but a beggar chuses to depend chiefly upon the benevolence of his fellow-citizens.[34]

In this passage, perhaps the most quoted in *The Wealth of Nations,* Smith was not denigrating benevolence or an altruistic concern for others ("humanity"). Nor was he antipathetic toward friendship—on the contrary, for him friendship was so valuable because it implied an intimacy that was rarely achieved in human relations. His claim is that an economic system cannot be *based* on benevolence, which is a limited sentiment not easily extended beyond those one knows.[35] An economic system with an extensive division of labor, in which millions of individuals depend on the production of others to meet their needs, cannot be founded upon sentiments that are morally admirable but necessarily limited.

The first pillar of Smith's argument was the increase in total productivity brought about by the market. The second pillar was his explanation of how the market reconciles supply and demand in a manner that brings about the spread of that wealth by making commodities ever cheaper and ever more available. He tried to show that without restrictions on labor, on prices, and on supply, the natural human propensity of self-interest would lead commodities to be sold at the lowest price possible at the existing level of economic development. Since it was in the interests of all in their capacity as consumers to be able to buy the most with their money, this arrangement redounded to the benefit of all. None of those involved in the production of commodities—workers who provided their labor, landlords who leased their land, "undertakers" who invested their capital—were primarily motivated by a concern for the welfare of the consumer. They each pursued their self-interest, motivated by the desire to better their condition.[36] But by pursuing their self-interest through the market, they ended up benefiting the consumer.

As a social scientist, Smith could explain the logic of the mechanism that transformed the quest for self-interest into universal opulence. Once that logic was understood, it could be put in place by politicians who were now in a position to anticipate the beneficent social effect of the market mechanism, fueled though it might be by self-interest.

The average price of labor, the average level of profits, and the average rent of land across an entire economy varied with the general level of economic development, Smith reasoned. At each level of development, the price of a commodity had to reflect the average cost of labor, the average profits to be gained by capital (money set aside for investment), and the average cost paid to landlords for using their land. Smith called this the "natural price"—the lowest price at which that commodity could be produced without losing money, and hence the lowest price at which it could be available for an extended period of time.[37] The natural price, in other words, represented the price most beneficial to consumers—and in a commercial society, all men and women were consumers, whatever else they might be.

The actual price at which a commodity was sold Smith called the "market price." The market price of the commodity was determined by the relationship between the quantity *offered* by producers and the amount of that commodity *desired* by those with the ability to pay for it—between the supply and effective demand for the commodity in question. At any given time, the market price might be above or below the natural price. But if the market price went *below* the natural price, those who produced the commodity would be motivated by self-interest to move their capital or labor to produce some other commodity where they could make a larger profit or a higher wage. This would lead to a decreased supply of the original commodity, and if effective demand remained the same, the market price would rise. If the market price of a commodity were *above* the natural price, those with capital or labor would be attracted to move their resources toward producing it, since it provided a higher-than-average profit or wage. In time, therefore, the supply of the commodity would go up, and if effective demand remained the same, its market price would go down, making that commodity more available to consumers. The market price therefore was a signal, informing producers of the relationship between supply and demand.[38]

The moral of Smith's analysis was that if the market was structured to operate along the lines of his model, the market prices of all commodities would continually gravitate toward their natural price. Actual prices would tend toward the cheapest prices at which commodities could be produced, given the availability of land, labor, and capital. In this sense, the market would provide the greatest possible benefit to all consumers.[39] Moreover, by allowing capital to flow to where the greatest profits were to be made, the market channeled resources toward those commodities for which there was more demand than existing supply. The market, therefore, was the most efficient institutional mechanism by which to channel self-interest toward the wealth of the nation, and to promote the well-being of the bulk of its citizens.

The majority of any society comprised, Smith knew, not landlords or merchants, but "servants, laborers, and workmen of different kinds," who derived their income from wages. Their welfare was the prime concern of economic policy, as Smith conceived it. "No society can surely be flourishing and happy, of which the far greater part of the members are poor and miserable," he wrote. "It is but equity, besides, that they who feed, clothe and lodge the whole body of the people, should have such a share of the produce of their own labour as to be themselves tolerably well fed, clothed and lodged."[40] The chief economic concern of the legislator, in Smith's view, ought to be the purchasing power of wages, since that was the measure of the material well-being of the bulk of the population.

Self-interest then, if channeled into the market, would lead to the division of labor and make possible a society of universal opulence. This emphasis on the difference between intentions and ultimate results constituted an implicit critique of the Christian and civic republican traditions, and continues to make moralists queasy. Both traditions had stressed the importance of good and benevolent intentions. By unlinking consequences from intentions, Smith called into question the necessity and possibility of elevating the economic behavior of individuals through preaching and propaganda.

Yet just as he transmuted the Christian virtue of charity into the secular virtue of benevolence, on another level Smith preserved the classic republican concern for the common good. Those who could be motivated to devote themselves to promoting the public interest were in need of "superior reason and understanding, by which we are capable of discerning the remote consequences of all our actions, and of foreseeing the advantage or detriment which is likely to result from them."[41] Cultivating that understanding was the responsibility of intellectuals like the author of *The Wealth of Nations*. The legislator for whom the book was written was the politician who could be motivated to promote the public interest. The "science of the legislator" that Smith set out to provide was intended to improve the politician's ability to foresee the consequences, both positive and negative, of laws and policies.

The theme of the unintended and unanticipated consequences of human action appears with many variations in *The Wealth of Nations*, and in additional mutations in *The Theory of Moral Sentiments*. Smith explores the many ways in which the outcomes of intentional actions are different from those anticipated, in directions sometimes positive and sometimes negative, or positive from the perspective of society but not from that of the actor.

Smith is perhaps best known for his explication of unintended consequences that are beneficial for the actor and for society at large. The most striking version of this theme comes in Smith's critique of the arguments made by manufacturers who favored government duties and prohibitions on the importation of goods that could be made in Britain. They argued that such protectionist measures would benefit the nation at large by providing both employment and economic growth. Smith's analysis was that while such measures might indeed help the growth of particular industries, they would do so at the expense of investment in other industries where such investment would be more productive. Government attempts to direct investment might not only be counterproductive, he argued, they were also unnecessary, since by and large individuals were most inclined to invest close to home, where they could keep an eye on their investments. He concluded:

> Every individual is continually exerting himself to find out the most advantageous employment for whatever capital he can command. It is his own advantage, indeed, and not that of the society, which he has in view. But the study of his

own advantage naturally, or rather necessarily leads him to prefer that employment which is the most advantageous to the society. . . .

He generally, indeed, neither intends to promote the public interest, nor knows how much he is promoting it. By preferring the support of domestic to that of foreign industry, he intends only his own security; and by directing that industry in such a manner as its produce may be of the greatest value, he intends only his own gain, and he is in this, as in many other cases, led by an invisible hand to promote an end which was no part of his intention. Nor is it always the worse for the society that it was no part of it. By pursuing his own interest he frequently promotes that of the society more effectually than when he really intends to promote it.[42]

The image of the "invisible hand" in this passage (the only place in *The Wealth of Nations* where the phrase appears) is a metaphor for the socially positive, unintended consequences of the institution of the market, which through the profit motive and the price mechanism channels the self-interest of individuals into collective benefits. Notice that Smith does not dismiss the possibility of deliberately promoting the public interest—he does not believe in some "law of unintended negative consequences." Nor does he believe that the pursuit of self-interest always and inevitably leads to socially positive outcomes. What he does assert is that under the proper institutional conditions, actions motivated by individual self-interest may lead to outcomes that are positive for society, in a way that the social scientist can explain and help the legislator to anticipate.

There is nothing mysterious about the "invisible hand," at least once its functions have been made manifest by social science. And yet, because of the gap between the explicit intentions of the actor and the ultimate result of his action, the notion that the social outcome of the market process is beneficial is counterintuitive, or contrary to common sense. The customer knows from his experience that the merchant sells him a commodity for more than the merchant paid for it. Not only that, but after having tried to purchase it as cheaply as possible, the merchant tries to sell it for the most he can get! How the customer may benefit from a system made up of many such merchants he is at a loss to explain. The legislator knows from his experience that merchants, manufacturers, and laborers are typically self-seeking, at

least in their economic relations. Smith's claim that the ultimate outcome of all this self-seeking can further the common good is, at first,
puzzling. Yet in the very next paragraph, Smith goes on to offer his
most important justification for the superiority of the market in allo-
cating resources:

> What is the species of domestic industry which his capital
> can employ, and of which the produce is likely to be of the
> greatest value, every individual, it is evident, can, in his
> local situation, judge much better than any statesman or
> lawgiver can do for him. The statesman who should attempt
> to direct private people in what manner they ought to
> employ their capitals, would not only load himself with a
> most unnecessary attention, but assume an authority which
> could safely be trusted, not only to no single person, but to
> no council or senate whatever, and which would nowhere be
> so dangerous as in the hands of a man who had folly and pre-
> sumption enough to fancy himself fit to exercise it.[43]

The legislator, then, is not in a position to have adequate knowledge of
the myriad interactions of supply and demand that occur in a sophisticated economy. Nor does anyone else. But individuals have both the
motive (of economic gain) and the ability to gather knowledge of the
supply and demand for any single commodity in a particular market.
Thus the legislator concerned with the common economic good
should, in general, refrain from exercising direct control over prices
and production. Much of that can be left to the "invisible hand" of the
market—even if, as we shall see, maintaining, perfecting, and protecting the market, and compensating for its negative effects, will require
the visible hand of government.

The Legislator and the Merchant

The market would produce the best possible outcome for consumers
under conditions of what Smith called "free competition" or "perfect
liberty." For the market to function most effectively, everyone had to
be able to sell labor, invest capital, or rent land with minimal restriction. But as *The Wealth of Nations* showed, much of European society

and government was structured to impede the free movement of labor, capital, land, and goods. Some of these barriers to free competition were attributable to antiquated institutions, but they were due primarily to the effects of self-interest. Smith did not believe that there was a natural harmony of interests in society. He believed that the public interest would be best served if every man channeled his self-interest through the market. But he realized that from the point of view of the individual producer or group of producers, it was most beneficial to circumvent the competitive market with its attendant risks, and use all available means to prevent competition, in order to obtain the highest possible price for their wares. Those with political clout would try to use it to short-circuit the market.

Smith took elements of contemporary economic life and generalized them into a model of how the economy might function under conditions of free competition. The task, as he saw it, was to leave the individual producer no alternative but to pursue his economic interests in a way that would advance the public good.[44] For it was the force of market competition that led producers, merchants, and laborers to "an unremitting exertion of vigilance and attention."[45] The Sisyphean task of the legislator dedicated to the public interest was to prevent them from bypassing the market, to keep it humming at full speed despite the efforts of organized economic interests to protect themselves from market competition.[46]

Both workers and employers, for example, tried to circumvent the labor market—the workers in an effort to raise their wages beyond what free competition would allow, employers in an effort to keep wages low. Each group tried to organize to pursue its self-interest, but under existing conditions the contest was unequal. The law prohibited workers from combining in order to raise wages, but did not prohibit employers from combining in order to keep wages low. And the employers had more political influence than the workers. "Whenever the legislature attempts to regulate the differences between masters and their workmen, its counsellors are always the masters," Smith noted. This differential in political power was due in part to the fact that most of the "masters" had the vote while few of the "workmen" did.[47] The employers had other advantages: in case of a strike they could hold out longer than the workers, who depended on wages for their daily sustenance. Because employers were fewer in number, it was easier for them to connive without calling attention to themselves.[48]

The most effective means of circumventing the competition of the market was through legal restrictions on the freedom to sell commodities or labor. Legal monopolies gave an individual or a trading company the sole right to sell certain products. That gave the monopolists the power to keep supply below demand, thus keeping the market price above the natural price.[49] Guilds and related "corporations" had a legal right to limit the supply of labor to specific occupations, thus keeping wages above the competitive level. They also had the right to limit output, which kept the profits of producers above the natural price.[50]

Wherever and whenever individuals or groups could promote their own interests at the expense of the public by bypassing the free market, they would. *The Wealth of Nations* is a great compendium of such attempts.[51] "People of the same trade seldom meet together, even for merriment and diversion, but the conversation ends in a conspiracy against the public, or in some contrivance to raise prices," Smith wrote.[52] The citizens of the towns, Smith showed, contrived to keep up the price of urban-made goods, at the expense of the inhabitants of the countryside.[53] Manufacturers were the most successful in pressing their private interests because of their disproportionate influence over members of Parliament.[54] Merchants too were well positioned to persuade those in power that what they wanted was identical to the general interest. They were few in number, they were located in large cities, and they had economic means at their disposal, making their "sophistry and clamour" more effective than that of rival groups.[55] Long accustomed to limiting competition in the towns, merchants had in more recent decades learned to limit competition in international trade.[56] Domestic manufacturers and merchants profited from high duties on imported goods, at the expense of landlords, farmers, and laborers.

For Smith, most of the existing regulation of foreign commerce was motivated by one or another group of merchants or manufacturers trying to limit competition for their goods. Sometimes they did so by prohibiting foreign imports or placing heavy duties upon them.[57] Such duties had been growing in the decades preceding the publication of *The Wealth of Nations*. Smith showed that they were inimical to the public interest, not only because they raised the price of goods to consumers, but also because raising profits in such industries led capital and labor to flow into them, resources which would otherwise have gone into industries where actual demand was greatest.[58]

Most of book 4 of *The Wealth of Nations* is devoted to an attack on the policies of international trade then dominant in Europe. Smith dubbed this policy "the mercantile system." The term was polemical, meant to encapsulate Smith's critique of the existing policies in international trade and international relations. Those policies were based on a view of international economic relations as a "zero-sum game" in which one nation's gain must be another's loss. International trade was perceived as a tacit war against rival nations, a view congenial to the civic republican conception of relations between polities. This tacit struggle often led to actual military confrontation in an attempt to secure trade privileges, trade routes, or colonies. Its logic led to violence and war.[59]

Smith provided a more cosmopolitan and pacific model of international economic and power relations. The growing prosperity and proficiency of other nations, he proclaimed, "are all proper objects of national emulation, not of national prejudice or envy. . . . Mankind are benefited, human nature is ennobled by them. In such improvements each nation ought, not only to endeavour itself to excel, but from the love of mankind, to promote, instead of obstructing the excellence of its neighbours."[60] The function of the intellectual was to counteract national prejudices and a conception of economic life that led to international conflict.

Smith coined the term "the mercantile system" to describe the dominant economic doctrine because he believed that it reflected both the *interests* and the *mentality* of merchants and manufacturers, whose quest for monopoly had been expanded into a view of international commerce that taught that each nation's interest "consisted in beggaring all their neighbours." "Each nation has been made to look with an invidious eye upon the property of all the nations with which it trades, and to consider their gain as its own loss. Commerce, which ought naturally to be, among nations, as among individuals, a bond of union and friendship, has become the most fertile source of discord and animosity," Smith lamented. The trade policy of Europe had been led by "the interested sophistry of merchants and manufacturers" from the recognition that "a nation that would enrich itself by foreign trade is certainly most likely to do so when its neighbours are all rich, industrious, and commercial nations."[61] This was the great pacific and beneficent potential of the market not as it *was* but as it *might be*, were the mutual benefits of competitive free trade more fully understood. The market could be made to serve the national and the international interest if policy makers were guided by the science of political economy developed by Smith and other intellectuals devoted to the commonweal, rather than by the partisan advice of merchants.

Smith made the same point in regard to colonies. They were good for the nation insofar as they extended the market, making a more productive division of labor possible. But to grant British merchants a monopoly on trade with the colonies benefited merchants at the expense of the nation, an expense that was aggravated by the military costs of maintaining such monopolies by force.[62]

The conduct of international commerce by privileged companies with a monopoly on trade with foreign regions was even more destructive. The growth of European trade with China, India, Japan, and the East Indies, Smith reasoned, ought to have been of great benefit to the consumers of Europe. But it had been of only limited advantage because it was conducted exclusively by monopolies, such as the East India Companies of Holland, England, and France.[63] Such companies, which established military control over foreign regions in order to maintain their own trade monopoly, were detrimental to the home country and ruinous to the subject nations, Smith maintained. The consumers of the home country suffered all the disadvantages that came from an exclusive supplier unrestrained by the forces of competition and free to undersupply the market and thus raise prices for imported goods.

If mercantilist policies had kept Europe from gaining the full potential benefits of transcontinental trade, the consequences for some of its colonies were downright negative, Smith showed. In an attempt to restrict the supply of Indian goods to be exported to Europe, the East India Company had deliberately limited their production and had wastefully destroyed the excess. Officials of the company used their power to establish private monopolies on the export of goods from India and even on the flow of goods within the subcontinent. A true sovereign understood that his own revenue depended upon the wealth of the nation, which he would try to promote through freer trade. But a company of merchants that had become the sovereign of a territory seemed incapable of grasping such considerations, and used its political power only to buy more cheaply in India in order to increase company profits. The effect of company rule, Smith concluded, was to stunt the growth of the Indian economy.[64] In the East and West Indies the effect of two to three centuries of European colonial expansion on the native population had been similarly detrimental.

Smith's analysis of colonial expansion provided a striking example of how mercantile self-interest could result in vast harm when not properly channeled by institutions, a theme explored at length in one of the monuments of Enlightenment criticism, the *Philosophical and Political History of the Establishment and Commerce of the Europeans in the Two Indies* (first published in 1772, with many subsequent expanded editions) by the Abbé Raynal and Denis Diderot. It was a theme to which Edmund Burke would return a few years later.

The Moral Balance Sheet of Commercial Society

The conceptual common denominator of Smith's major works was the analysis of the ways in which social institutions tend to pattern character through their appeal to human passions. Some passions were dangerous, others were benign, and still others could lead beyond the benign to the morally noble. Depending upon the incentives provided by institutions, human passions could be channeled to morally laudable and socially beneficent forms of behavior. In addition to the material benefits of "universal opulence," Smith saw the market as an effective institutional mechanism for the encouragement of self-control and the channeling of the passions in directions that benefited society.

Smith was not the first to suggest that commerce promoted the development of more "civilized" behavior: that was almost a commonplace of Enlightenment thought.[65] But perhaps no other thinker devoted so much attention to describing how the market and commercial society could be structured to develop that constellation of qualities of self-control, industry, and gentleness that previous moralists, from the humanists through David Hume, had valued. A good deal of virtuous behavior, Smith wrote, was actually prompted by self-interest, such as the worthy habits of "economy, industry, discretion, attention, and application of thought," and related "inferior virtues" such as "prudence, vigilance, circumspection, temperance, constancy, firmness."[66] These virtues commercial society was best suited to promote.

In commercial society based upon exchange, every man "becomes in some measure a merchant."[67] (Notice the qualification: Smith never imagined that man becomes a *homo economicus*.) The pursuit of self-interest in the market, with its division of labor and his resulting dependence on others, leads him to adapt his behavior to the expectations of others. The market itself is therefore a disciplining institution. This disciplining process occurs among those who sell their labor, and in a different form among those who sell more tangible goods. "The real and effectual discipline which is exercised over a workman, is not that of his corporation [guild]," Smith wrote, "but that of his customers. It is the fear of losing their employment which restrains his frauds and corrects his negligence."[68] In order to become successful in his economic exchanges with others, the individual is led to develop the moderate level of self-command which Smith calls "propriety."[69] The character that the market promotes includes prudence, the disciplined pursuit of self-interest, and the ability to defer short-term gratification for long-term benefits.[70]

At the root of the attempt to "better our condition," Smith speculated, lay the desire "to be observed, to be attended to, to be taken notice of with sympathy . . . and approbation." The better off men appear, the more likely they are to get the attention and approbation of others.[71] The dominant motive for economic activity—once the basic bodily necessities are obtained—was the eminently impalpable desire for social status. Smith observed that "moralists in all ages" had complained of the undeniable fact that "the great mob of mankind are the admirers and worshippers . . . of wealth and greatness."[72] That human failing, Smith knew, did not begin with commercial society and remained a problem within it. But a moral advantage of commercial society, he believed, lay in the fact that those "in the middling and inferior stations of life" who were neither rich and powerful nor wise and of superior virtue—that is, most people—were compelled by social institutions to channel their desires for wealth and distinction into decent forms of behavior. For them, "the road to virtue and that to fortune . . . are, happily in most cases, very nearly the same." For their success depended on "solid professional abilities, joined to prudent, just, firm, and temperate conduct," and on "the favour and good opinion of their neighbours and equals," which demanded such conduct of them.[73] The greatest achievement of the invisible hand of social institutions in commercial society was to convert the potentially base desire for status and approbation into relatively virtuous forms of conduct, at least among most of the populace.

Smith contrasts these relatively virtuous forms of conduct with the modes of conduct promoted by premarket sources of wealth and power, "the courts of princes" and "the drawing-rooms of the great." There, success depends less upon "the esteem of intelligent and well-informed equals" than upon "the fanciful and foolish favour of ignorant, presumptuous, and proud superiors." While for the middling and working classes, promotion is based upon "merit and abilities," in the upper reaches of aristocratic and royal society it is based upon flattery and "the abilities to please."[74] A moral advantage of commercial society, therefore, was that it channeled self-interest into less morally corrupt forms than the society that preceded it. Compared to feudal society, which was based upon direct domination, or court society, in which success depended upon flattery, fawning, or deceit, success in commercial society was linked to honesty, industry, merit, and ability. It was thus less likely to promote the corruption of moral sentiments of which moralists had always complained.[75]

For Smith, the most liberating effect of the rise of commercial society was its replacement of direct and open-ended personal dependency with the cash nexus, the contractual relations that limit the entitlement of men to dominate one another. To the extent that every man became a merchant, rather than a slave, retainer, serf, or servant, society became more interdependent, while direct, personal dependence declined. This was one of many senses in which commercial society provided a greater degree of freedom than previous social systems. For Smith, the fact that commercial society provided greater freedom was another important moral argument on its behalf.

His abhorrence of relations of direct personal dependency made him loathe slavery past and present. He described slave traders and slave owners as "the refuse of the jails of Europe, . . . wretches who possess the virtues neither of the countries which they come from, nor of those which they go to, and whose levity, brutality, and baseness so justly expose them to the contempt of the vanquished."[76] Smith maintained that slavery, as practiced for example in the British colonies in the West Indies and in North America, was actually less economically efficient than the use of free wage labor. Both the slave and the poorest free laborer, he reasoned, had to live and reproduce. The cost of maintaining the slave was managed by his master, the cost of maintaining the free laborer by the laborer himself. The rich slave owner, Smith thought, was less likely to develop the habits of frugal attentiveness in expenditure that the free laborer was forced to learn by his economic situation. The free laborer, therefore, actually cost less to maintain than the slave. The institution of slavery continued into his own day, Smith reasoned, because "the pride of man makes him love to domineer . . . Wherever the law allows it, and the nature of the work can afford it . . . he will generally prefer the services of slaves to that of freemen."[77] Slavery could be found where profits were high not because human bondage was intrinsically more profitable, but because only under extraordinarily profitable conditions could proprietors afford so uneconomical a form of cultivation. Smith's economic argument against slavery became a staple of abolitionist literature in Europe and in the colonies.

For Smith, then, the bottom line of the moral balance sheet of commercial society was positive. But that did not mean that it made everyone happy. Indeed, he suggested that those who were most exclusively devoted to increasing their wealth might do so at the expense of their personal happiness, the real sources of which they failed to comprehend. In *The Theory of Moral Sentiments,* he offers his parable of the Ambitious Poor Man's Son, who, born into poverty, "admires the condition of the rich" and imagines that a palatial home and a retinue of servants will bring him happiness and tranquility. To attain them, he "devotes himself forever to the pursuit of wealth and greatness." In order to acquire his imagined goals of ease and social esteem, he finds that he must drive his body to fatigue and his mind to anxiety, exert himself continuously to be better than his competitors, and serve those he hates.

Were this the end of Smith's parable, its lesson would be a Stoic reiteration of the worthlessness of worldly wealth and power. But Smith gives the parable a different gloss. The real benefits of power and riches may not be what the ambitious imagine them to be. But, Smith asserts, "it is well that nature imposes upon us in this manner," since

> [i]t is this deception which rouses and keeps in continual motion the industry of mankind. It is this which first prompted them to cultivate the ground, to build houses, to found cities and commonwealths, and to invent and improve all the sciences and arts, which ennoble and embellish human life; which have entirely changed the whole face of the globe, have turned the rude forests of nature into agreeable and fertile plains, and made the trackless and barren ocean a new fund of subsistence, and the great high road of communication to the different nations of the earth. The earth by these labors of mankind has been obliged to redouble her natural fertility, and to maintain a greater multitude of inhabitants.[78]

The pursuit of ease, riches, and social status, though perhaps motivated by a misapprehension of their ultimate worth, redounds to the benefit of society. It makes possible that accumulation of wealth and productive power upon which the higher satisfactions of culture rest. It provides an incentive for nations to come to know one another, thus contributing to cosmopolitanism. And, last but not least, it makes it possible for more people to live decently, to acquire the "necessaries of life" that allow men to escape the moral degradation of absolute poverty.

The Visible Hand of the State

Commercial society made it possible, for the first time in history, for most people to live a morally decent existence. They could live according to the rules of propriety and prudence, deferring gratification, controlling their appetites. Their search to better their condition would lead them toward frugality and industriousness.[79] Commercial society, in Smith's portrait, did not make most men highly virtuous and noble—but then no society could. It did, however, hold out the possibility of a society in which most of its members would be decent, gentle, prudent, and free. Yet that possibility was threatened by forces within commercial society itself.

Because Smith argued so persuasively against direct government involvement in the economy, the crucial significance of the state in his thought is often overlooked. Smith believed that the state ought to relinquish its direct economic role in enforcing tariffs, wage rates, and other restrictions on trade. But he thought that the size and functions of the state would actually grow with the development of commercial society. "Government in a civilized country is much more expensive than in a barbarous one," he told his students, for a civilized country required armies and fleets for collective defense, public facilities, a judicial system to prevent internal disorder, and a tax system to support it all.[80] The benefits of commercial society required a larger state, but the wealth generated by a well-functioning market economy would make the economic burden of the state bearable.

For Smith, the state was the most important institution on which commercial society depended; the authority and security of civil government, he wrote, is a necessary condition for the flourishing of "liberty, reason, and the happiness of mankind . . ."[81] It was to the security of property provided and enforced by law that Smith attributed much of his nation's increasing wealth, since that security made it worthwhile for every individual to make "the natural effort . . . to better his own condition."[82] The cost of administering justice increased as society became more commercial. Another function of government that was bound to expand with the advance of commercial society was the provision of what Smith called "institutions for facilitating the commerce of society," or what we have come to call "infrastructure": roads, canals, bridges, and harbors that benefit society as a whole but are too expensive or unprofitable to be undertaken by individuals. No wonder *The Wealth of Nations* devotes hundreds of pages to analyzing the functions of government and how to pay for them.

Smith's views on the functions of the modern state followed from his analysis of the predictable *negative* consequences of the central institutions of modern commercial society. That diagnosis took into account forewarnings provided by the history of civilized societies. The spread of the market and the resulting intensification of the division of labor was the source, or at least the precondition, for much of what was best about modern civilized society; it was also the root of a number of intrinsic dangers, which it was the role of the legislator to obviate.

The need for national defense grew more urgent with the progress of economic development. History showed that as a society grew richer, it became a more attractive object of attack for its poorer neighbors. Moreover the division of labor upon which the wealth of the nation depended left most men less fit to be soldiers. In the most advanced stage of history—that of commercial society, characterized by a market economy, urbanization, and an intensive division of labor—the likelihood of being attacked increased. So too did the difficulty and expense of waging war. Moreover, the art of war, like other human activities, became more complex with the division of labor, and its mastery required the same specialization as other fields. Yet it could not be in the interest of private individuals to devote themselves fully to the art of war, which brought no profit in time of peace. Fortunately, the division of labor and the growth of affluence that exacerbated the problem of national defense also provided its potential solution—if legislators put the proper mechanisms into place, at increasing expense to the state.

It was only the wise policy of the state that could attract some individuals to devote themselves fully to military matters—a wisdom often lacking in past advanced societies.[83] Here was yet another case in which the legislator, aided by a social scientific attempt to generalize on the basis of past experience, could foresee and forestall the negative consequences of social developments. An opulent society can afford to devote a portion of its wealth to the cost of maintaining a professional army. The development of modern firearms had made preparation for warfare increasingly expensive, giving wealthy nations an additional advantage over poor nations in preparing for conflict.

By providing for defense, justice, and infrastructure, government created the preconditions for a market economy and for "that universal opulence which extends itself to the lowest ranks of the people."[84] Yet the very process that brought about an increase in national wealth was fraught with negative cultural consequences, which it was up to the intellectual to anticipate and the legislator to mitigate.

Foremost among these was the debilitating cultural effect of the division of labor upon manual workers. Smith began with the premise that the intellect of most men was formed largely by their work. Writing at a time when there was no general education and when the hours of work in manufacturing left little leisure time, Smith provided a harrowing portrait of the development of the great mass of the populace:

> The man whose whole life is spent in performing a few simple operations . . . has no occasion to exert his understanding. . . . He naturally loses, therefore, the habit of such exertion, and generally becomes as stupid and ignorant as it is possible for a human creature to become. The torpor of his mind renders him, not only incapable of relishing or bearing a part in any conversation, but of conceiving any generous, noble, or tender sentiment, and consequently of forming any just judgement concerning many even of the ordinary duties of private life. Of the great and extensive interests of his country he is altogether incapable of judging; and unless very particular pains have been taken to render him otherwise, he is equally incapable of defending his country in war. The uniformity of his stationary life naturally corrupts the courage of his mind. . . . It corrupts even the activity of his body, and renders him incapable of exerting his strength with vigour and perseverance, in any other employment than that to which he has been bred. His dexterity at his own particular trade seems, in this manner, to be acquired at the expence of his intellectual, social, and martial virtues. But in every improved and civilized society this is the state into which the labouring poor, that is, the great body of the people, must necessarily fall, unless government takes some pains to prevent it.[85]

Had Smith believed that this was the inevitable cultural effect of commercial society on the majority of the population, his verdict on capitalism would certainly have been that its gains were outweighed by its losses. Yet the passage is deceptive when isolated from its place in *The Wealth of Nations*. For here Smith is writing what he called rhetorical discourse, which, in order to persuade, "magnifies all the arguments on the one side, and diminishes or conceals those that might be brought on the side contrary to that which it is designed that we should favour."[86] The key to Smith's purposes in this dark portrait lies in the last phrase: "unless government takes some pains to prevent it." For Smith then proceeded to suggest the most extensive and expensive recommendations for new public expenditures in *The Wealth of Nations*. Having alarmed his readers, he suggests the means of dispelling their anxiety.

As an antidote to the mental degradation caused by the division of labor Smith recommended the encouragement of universal public schooling, largely at government expense, so that even those in the lower ranks of society could acquire the essential skills of reading, writing, and arithmetic. This suggestion contradicted the advice of enlightened intellectuals like Voltaire, and was deeply at odds with the prevailing wisdom of the dominant classes in Britain, who feared it would discourage deference.[87] Smith did not suggest making schooling compulsory, but offered a plan to make it more accessible and more useful, and to provide incentives for parents to educate their children. Such incentives were necessary because, as Smith knew, the spread of manufacture based upon the division of labor, by making it possible for children to be employed at income-generating tasks, often led parents to send even very young children out to work.[88] The division of labor therefore not only stunted intellectual abilities by narrowing the horizons of the worker, but also created economic incentives for the neglect of any formal education.[89] Hence the need for the public to "facilitate . . . encourage, and . . . even impose upon almost the whole body of the people the necessity of acquiring those most essential parts of education."[90]

Smith suggested a system of public incentives to prevent a characteristically modern form of degradation, "the gross ignorance and stupidity which, in a civilized society, seem so frequently to benumb the understandings of all the inferior ranks of people. A man without the proper use of the intellectual faculties of a man is, if possible, more contemptible than even a coward, and seems to be mutilated and deformed in a still more essential part of the character of human nature." The benefits of education were not only important to the *individual*, Smith maintained; they were also a prime political consideration for the *state*. The more educated the population, Smith believed, the less they would be prone to "the delusions of enthusiasm and superstition" and hence to being stirred up by priests and preachers to religious civil war. The populace would also be "more disposed to examine, and more capable of seeing through, the interested complaints of faction and sedition" and hence better citizens. In addition,

Smith thought, an educated population would be more decent and orderly.

The market, then, did not necessarily promote the use of mind. The visible hand of the state might be required to rectify the potentially stultifying effects of the invisible hand of the market. Smith did not make the mistake of believing that everyone could become an intellectual or an artist, or that society should be found wanting to the extent that they failed to do so. But he did believe in encouraging the use of the mind by exposing people to knowledge that they might not otherwise pursue. He advocated the spread of schooling not only to provide basic literacy and numeracy for all, but to encourage learning among the middle and upper classes: he suggested that those who aspired to enter the liberal professions or hold public office be required to demonstrate a knowledge of science and philosophy.

Virtues Inferior and Superior

The great strength of commercial society, as Smith describes it, is its tendency to promote the "inferior virtues" typically associated with striving for rank and fortune and with the prudent pursuit of self-interest. The virtues of these prudent men "who are contented to walk in the humble paths of private and peaceable life" are "temperance, decency, modesty, and moderation . . . industry and frugality."[91] The prudent man is characteristic of commercial society. He is so concerned with the undisturbed enjoyment of his private tranquility that he eschews the quest for nobility and great ambition and leaves "the public business" to be managed by others.[92]

Smith appreciated the prudent man, without lionizing him. The prudent man's pursuit of his own health, fortune, rank, and reputation produces a character worthy of our "cold esteem," Smith writes, but these virtues are neither very ennobling nor endearing.[93] It would be only slightly anachronistic to see in Smith's description of the prudent man the image of the "bourgeois" who was to become the foil of so much of European cultural criticism.[94] Yet Smith did not characterize the bourgeois as without virtue. To do so would have been to disdain the qualities of prudence, deferred gratification, and self-control that made social relations more gentle and produced the universal opulence that made possible a decent life for the many. It was this disdain, so characteristic of the civic republican tradition and of aristocratic mores, that he sought to dispel.

Yet he also believed that society required other human types if it was to flourish, people who possessed virtues not readily promoted by the market. Another role for the intellectual, as Smith understood it, was to encourage character traits beyond prudence: the superior virtues of wisdom, benevolence, self-sacrifice, and public-spiritedness. "The wise and the virtuous," Smith believed, were inevitably a "small party."[95] Yet the members of that party played a number of crucial roles in promoting the moral and economic wealth of the nation. Like much of Enlightenment thought, Smith's work was designed not merely to convince people to regard commercial society as the best regime, but to dramatize the personal qualities of courage, patriotism, and refinement that needed to be cultivated in opposition to the very same regime.[96] Time and again Smith insists that the survival and prosperity of society depends upon the cultivation of the superior virtues, at least in some men. He devotes little explicit attention to the institutional means by which this can be achieved. But implicit in Smith's works is his assumption that superior virtue, insofar as it is susceptible to active cultivation, can be enhanced by exposure to works like *The Wealth of Nations*—which encourages the legislator to pursue the public interest—and *The Theory of Moral Sentiments*.

Smith thought that philosophy had a role to play in the cultivation of virtue and the refinement of morality. For while prudent self-interest may be conducive to the development of the inferior virtues, it is far from the whole story. *The Theory of Moral Sentiments* begins with a challenge to those who try to explain all of human action through an appeal to self-interest. "How selfish soever man be supposed, there are evidently some principles in his nature, which interest him in the fortunes of others, and render their happiness necessary to him, though he derives nothing from it except the pleasure of seeing it." The book not only offers a social-scientific explanation of how moral conscience develops, it explains to the careful reader why virtuous action brings happiness—and all without recourse to unresolvable metaphysical and theological premises.

For Smith, the source of morality did not lie in some specific revelation by God (a matter both unprovable and open to endless dispute and strife), nor did it flow from some innate "moral sense," nor was it a function of philosophic reason. Instead, he sought to account for morality through an analysis of ordinary experience. Central to Smith's account of how we become moral is not reason, or the soul, but the imagination, combined with our desire for approbation.[97] It is our ability to imagine ourselves in the place of others, combined with the fact that we desire to be in harmony with them, that leads us beyond selfishness. In our search for the approbation of those with whom we interact, we use our imagination to try to see the world as they see it. We begin to adopt the perspective of an impartial spectator, someone who is biased neither toward us nor toward those who are the objects of our actions. It is this process of internal reflection that accounts for what we usually call "conscience" and that makes it possible to act in ways that are at odds with our selfish urges. This "impartial spectator" within, Smith thought, made it possible for men and women to act justly (in the sense of impartially) and even benevolently.

It is through this ongoing process of imaginatively placing ourselves in the minds of others that we learn moral rules. Such rules, Smith thought, have their origin in demonstrated utility, and are continually modified and reinterpreted over time as society changes, changing with it the rules necessary for survival. They come neither from God nor from nature, though it is our God-given natural desire for the approbation of others that makes us able to learn such rules and act upon them. The person of developed moral sensibility seeks not the approval of others, but the self-approval that comes from knowing that one has lived up to proper moral standards, even when one's actions go unrecognized by others. Thus virtue brings happiness, not necessarily in the form of recognition from others, and not in the afterlife, but through the self-approbation that comes from knowing that one has tried to do the right thing.

Works of moral philosophy, such as *The Theory of Moral Sentiments*, remind us that there are valuable activities that may go unrewarded by the market and by the quest for social status. But for the man of developed moral sensibility, such activities provide their own reward. They include the pleasures of scientific knowledge, of artistic refinement, of cultivated moral sensibility, and of devotion to the public weal.

For Smith, one public role of the intellectual was to influence men of power: to encourage their public-spiritedness and to provide them with the concepts and information through which the probable consequences of governmental action could be better anticipated.[98] It was to such men that *The Wealth of Nations* was addressed, and Smith adapted his rhetoric to reach them. Its effectiveness was best captured by Walter Bagehot's reflections on the centennial of the book's publication. Smith, Bagehot wrote, was one of those rare intellectuals with the ability to "describe practical matters in such a way as to fasten them on the imagination, and not only get what they say read, but get it remembered and make it part of the substance of the reader's mind ever afterwards." By his style, Smith "carried political economy far beyond the bounds of those who care for abstract science, or who understand exactly what it means. He has popularized it in the only sense in which it can be popularized without being spoiled; that is, he has put certain broad conclusions into the minds of hard-headed men, which are all which they need know and all which they for the most part will ever care for, and he has put those conclusions there ineradicably."[99]

But Smith's rhetorical strategy skewed the influence of his book, the ultimate fate of which Smith might have regarded with ambivalence. For if the great persuasive power of the book lay in its display of the "system of natural liberty," the price of this oft-repeated apothegm was to lead many readers to overlook the complexity of Smith's conception of the moral life and to conclude that liberty, in itself, was always a good thing. That was a proposition against which Edmund Burke, Hegel, and Matthew Arnold would take up cudgels. And the analytic insight with which Smith expounded the unintended beneficial workings of the market mechanism and the imaginative power of his metaphor of the invisible hand led many readers to overlook the subtleties of his arguments, and to assert that the market was the solution to every economic problem.

For Adam Smith, the creation of an open market across national borders was a source of hope, leading to more peaceful relations between nations, to liberation from inherited servility, to a rising standard of living, and to a more decent society. But other European intellectuals looked at the spread of the market and saw the ruin of all they cherished and all that gave life meaning. One of them was Smith's German contemporary, Justus Möser.

CHAPTER FOUR

JUSTUS MÖSER:
THE MARKET AS DESTROYER OF CULTURE

The Virtues of Knowing One's Place

In his *Philosophical Letters*, Voltaire endorsed market exchange as a mechanism that allowed those of differing ways of life to live together. In *The Wealth of Nations* Smith put forward a cosmopolitan vision of peace among nations mutually enriched by international trade. But to others, the spread of the market looked like a threat to the very existence of their culture and society. Justus Möser (1720–1794) was an early progenitor of the argument that the market *destroys* pluralism by striking at the economic basis of local cultural particularity. One might say that Möser was one of the earliest critics of "globalization."

Möser was born and lived most of his life in Osnabrück, an area where some 125,000 inhabitants occupied less than fifty square miles in western Germany, not far from the Dutch border. From the age of twenty-four almost until his death in 1794 he was the central figure in the tiny state. The political and economic institutions of Osnabrück that Möser defended in his writings were medieval in origin and feudal in conception, the remnants of a world in which property, power, and honor were indissolubly linked. That institutional world was in the process of being destabilized by the market economy.[1]

Justus Möser saw the international market as pernicious for destroying the particular culture of Osnabrück. It did so, first, by creating new needs that could not be fulfilled by the traditional economy of the region. Second, competition from commodities that could be produced more cheaply abroad was destroying the traditional guild-based modes of production, and the social and political structures with which they were intertwined. The market was thus destroying cultural particularity and hence pluralism. In the subsequent development of capitalism, the fear (often well-grounded) that local cultures and social structures faced destruction by more wide-ranging markets would often be repeated: towns by province-wide markets, provinces by national markets, nations by international markets.

The *philosophes* were cosmopolitan not only in the range of their interests, but in the substance of their moral and political thought. According to Voltaire, Europe was becoming "a kind of great republic divided between the various states" and would be governed in accordance with certain universal principles.[2] It was ridiculous, Voltaire observed elsewhere, that someone might lose a lawsuit by the rules of one village that he would win by those of a neighboring one.[3] Behind his cosmopolitanism lay the premise that since men everywhere were fundamentally the same, it must be possible to discover universal goals and universally valid institutions for pursuing them. As local institutions were reformed in the light of universal reason, they would become more uniform.

This quest for uniform, standardized law was central to the economic policy of eighteenth-century enlightened absolutism, and was articulated by the cameralists, the bureaucrats of German-speaking Europe charged with enhancing national wealth and thereby increasing tax revenue. The state and its citizens, they reasoned, could become richer if men were allowed to follow their "natural" self-interest. The enlightened German theorists of Möser's day regarded the market as a tool that encouraged economic growth. The cameralist writer Johann Heinrich Gottlob von Justi, for example, regarded merchants, peddlers, and financiers as "exchangers" whose activities harmonized the creations of the productive groups of society. The role of government policy, in his view, was to assure "exchangers" the freedom to perform this integrative function.[4] Like Adam Smith and his contemporary in France, Turgot, Justi believed that the task of law was to create the "natural" free conditions that would allow the economy to grow. "If we wish to regulate the nature of economic movement correctly," wrote Justi in 1760, "then we must imagine how it would be if it perfectly followed its natural processes and found not the slightest hindrance from the state."[5]

Creating those conditions meant doing away with much of existing historical law and custom. Only through an extension of the power of the central bureaucracy could existing barriers to exchange be eliminated, creating the greater economic freedom that it was thought would ultimately redound to the commonweal. This was the formula of the theorists of enlightened absolutism in the area of economic policy, or what the eighteenth century called "police science."[6]

To Justus Möser, by contrast, the existence of differing laws in neighboring villages was laudable and indeed natural, despite the fact that they were inconvenient for those bureaucrats of the centralizing monarchy "who would like to derive everything from simple principles," and scandalous to those "who wish the state to be governed according to the prescriptions of some academic theory." To comply with such demands for universal, standardized law, Möser argued, would be to "depart from the true plan of nature, which reveals its wealth through its multiplicity, and would clear the path to despotism, which seeks to coerce all according to a few rules and so loses the richness that comes with variety." According to Möser, economic ordinances promulgated by the central bureaucracy were for the most part "arrogant interference in human reason, destructive of private property and violations of freedom."[7] "Human reason," "private property," "freedom"—these were all values that enlightened philosophers and enlightened government officials also held dear. But Möser used these terms to mean something quite different from the enlightened principles he attacked.

The notion of "property" that Möser sought to conserve was neither "private" nor strictly "economic" in the modern sense. Before the absolutist state set out to monopolize political power, there was no clear division between the public and the private, between the realm of the state and that of the economy. The ownership of property itself conferred power.[8] The lord of the estate had the power to restrict the movements of those serfs who lived on it. The guilds' legal privileges (their liberties) gave them the power to control production of some goods. Membership in the guild also gave one an indirect role in the decisions of the town estate. In the traditional corporatist society of ranks (*Ständestaat*) that Möser set out to defend, honor, property, livelihood, and political participation were intertwined. Möser defended this medieval conception of property as including power and responsibility against nascent legal and economic developments that made property "private" and divorced it from political power.

To the Enlightenment's critical weapons of universal reason, humanitarianism, and the rights of the individual, Möser countered with the logic of historical development, regional particularity, and the rights of collective, corporate institutions. Möser emphasized the benefits of knowing one's place, the importance of belonging to an existing collectivity, and hence the need to cultivate loyalty to the real, existing institutions that provided the individual with a firm sense of place. In contrast to the Enlightenment's emphasis on individual opportunity and autonomy, Möser valued those institutions that circumscribed the individual, if in doing so they provided a firm sense of identity. This concern for the welfare of existing corporate institutions he called "patriotism."[9] The purpose of his journalistic writings was to cultivate this sense of virtue. He titled the collected volumes of his essays *Patriotische Phantasien,* which might best be translated as "Visions of Local Virtue." By Möser's time, however, new forms of capitalist economic activity were transforming the social basis on which his vision of virtue rested.

His vision of society was a corporatist and inegalitarian one, in which inequality rested largely on inherited status, and status included honor, property, and power. Only the existence of a hierarchy of ranks allowed one to know one's place. Belonging to a rank brought with it a sense of equality to those of equal rank, a sense of deference to those of higher rank, and a sense of superiority combined with responsibility toward those of lower rank. For Möser the expansion of the market was primarily a challenge, which was coupled with and promoted by the spread of enlightened absolutism. In tandem, cameralism and capitalism threatened to erode the existing corporate institutions that he so valued. He was willing to countenance a limited role for the market in economic life. But he sought to use the market to preserve existing institutions and hierarchies under changing economic conditions. Like many subsequent conservatives, he sought to buttress an institutional order that he regarded as already corroded by the social and cultural impact of the spreading market economy.

Möser argued against the Enlightenment on its own ground. It was his ability to challenge the Enlightenment according to its own criteria—by the standards of happiness and utility—that earned him the attention of his contemporaries and his later reputation as a precursor of modern conservatism. Möser represented the conservative side of the German Enlightenment. He published in the leading journals of the German Enlightenment and founded a local newspaper designed to spread knowledge of public affairs and create an informed public opinion. To reach a broad readership, he deliberately wrote about questions of public policy in a homey and accessible style, often developing his views in dialogues between stock figures. His journal articles, written between 1766 and 1782, were collected by his daughter and published in four volumes from 1774 to 1786. These collections, as well as his multivolume *History of Osnabrück,* were widely read by the new enlightened German public, members of clubs and lodges who gathered to discuss matters of public interest. Yet Möser usually sought to rally nascent public opinion against what he called "our century, so pregnant with all sorts of books of general laws."[10]

The intellectual as a distinct social type appeared in Möser's work in a variety of guises—all of them negative. At times he appeared as the adviser to the enlightened monarch, rich in Latin learning but poor in the experience of the world and hence lacking "healthy understanding" (*gesunde Vernunft*), which left him prey to the snare of humanitarianism.[11] In another guise he was the learned fool, like the sacristan who proclaimed grand ideas for economic improvement based on foreign models and dismissed the wisdom of the past as "prejudice," but whose knowledge of the real world was so scanty that he barely knew how to set the church sundial. In his skeptical portrait of the intellectual as the noble-minded advocate of universal principles who had an inadequate appreciation of the consequences of their implementation, Möser was a precursor of much of modern conservative thought.[12]

Time and again he contrasted the claims of rationalist theory with the deeper rationality of local, historical experience. If the intellectual was the voice of the former, Möser was implicitly the voice of the latter. He was the paradigm of a "rooted" intellectual: a man deeply enmeshed in the controlling political and social institutions of his homeland. The general lawgivers whom Möser criticized were the bureaucrats of the enlightened absolute monarchs of Prussia and the Habsburg Empire. Osnabrück was an independent state, but it was virtually surrounded by Prussia. The Habsburg monarch's reach was indirect, as emperor of the Holy Roman Empire of the German People, a loose political structure to which Osnabrück belonged. The ultimate sovereign of Osnabrück during Möser's adult years was the House of Hanover. It too had attempted to develop a centralized bureaucracy, but by Möser's day the head of the House of Hanover was more interested in his role as monarch of Britain, and left the control of his German possessions largely in the hands of local patrician administrators, like Möser himself.

The institutional world in which Justus Möser spent almost his entire life, the world he set out to defend with his pen, was a small world in which he was close to the center of real power. Most of the political and economic institutions of Osnabrück still retained their medieval structure. It was a world on the margins of the growing Atlantic economy and beyond the direct control of the absolutist state—but it was subtly being undermined by both forces.

The state of Osnabrück was a "prince-bishopric," a quirky product of the religious struggles of the early modern era.[13] At the top of the political hierarchy of Osnabrück was its ruler, either a Catholic bishop or a Protestant prince-bishop of the Hanoverian line. But these nominal rulers were rarely present in the bishopric. In times of Catholic dominance, major decision-making power was vested in the cathedral council, made up largely of Catholic nobles, and in time of Protestant dominance in the estate of the nobility, which was restricted to those who could demonstrate their descent from sixteen noble ancestors. In addition, the towns within the bishopric had their own estates, with the right to ratify laws relating to them. As the son of a leading official in Osnabrück, Möser participated in the governance of Osnabrück from 1744 until his death in 1794. For the last three decades of his life he was the leading government official in the bishopric.

Since medieval times, the residents of the countryside had been a handful of noble lords and a mass of serfs and peasants who supported themselves by farming. The nobles owned most of the arable land in the bishopric. They lived on their rural estates, deriving much of their income from feudal dues paid by their serfs or by the rents paid by legally independent peasants. By custom it was considered unsuitable for a noble to work as hard, as long, or for the same remuneration as a commoner, and unlike the commoner the noble was exempt from taxation. The lord's holdings were passed on to his descendants and could not be bought and sold. The serf was not free to own land, and could not move without the permission of his lord. The peasant acquired his land through hereditary leasehold. Lordship and servile status were hereditary, and the prospects of the legally free peasant were circumscribed by the lease to the land that he inherited from his ancestors. Nobles, serfs, and independent peasants lived their lives barely aware of the market economy.

Of course, the market—exchange of goods mediated by money—had played a role even in the traditional society of Osnabrück. But for most lords, serfs, peasants, and artisans, it was marginal to their existence. The peasant household produced much of what it consumed, and consumed most of what it produced. The peasant went to the town market occasionally to sell eggs, butter, poultry, or vegetables, and used the money so earned to pay taxes and buy the products of the guilded artisans in the towns, who sold what they themselves produced, without the intermediary of the merchant. More exotic items not produced locally could be purchased only sporadically, at annual market fairs. Merchants and their commodities had traditionally played a small role in the life of Osnabrück, and indeed of most of European society.[14]

That institutional world was in the process of being undermined by the market economy, which was beginning to transform even an economic backwater like Osnabrück.

The town dwellers of Osnabrück had their own privileges and were represented in their own estate and town council. The ruling town council was dominated by an oligarchy of urban commoners—merchants, lawyers, Protestant clergymen, and government officials— most of whom were related by blood. Within this inbred oligarchy, as within every stratum of this society, vocation and economic status were largely determined by birth rather than achievement.

Artisans, who made up the backbone of the urban economy, were also represented in the town estate, not as individuals but through membership in one of the Osnabrück guilds. There were separate guilds for blacksmiths, cobblers, bakers, tanners, butchers, furriers, jewelers, carpenters, coopers, wig makers, bookbinders, surgeons, cloth makers, and linen weavers. The members of each guild elected a guildmaster, who represented them on the town estate, which in turn elected the town council.[15] Guilded artisans were thus *Bürger*, a term that meant both "citizen" and "townsman." In addition to the citizens of the town, who were represented in this constitutional framework, there was a growing number of "inhabitants" who were not citizens and not represented in its guilds or councils: day laborers, servants, and vagrants. Membership in a guild thus conferred both economic privileges and the right to political participation.

The policy of the guilds and of the town estates they dominated was to restrict admission to their trades and to press for exclusive rights to sell their respective products in the town and the surrounding countryside. Each guild had the right to enforce its monopoly by confiscating products from outside the town if the guild produced them locally. Guild regulations specified the conditions for the acceptance of new apprentices, including that they be of good character and honorable birth. After years of working with a guildmaster, the apprentice became a journeyman, and eventually rose to become a master himself, after demonstrating his skill by producing a "masterpiece." As in other parts of Osnabrück society, a man's lineage largely determined his own vocation. In admitting new apprentices, the sons of masters were advantaged: their tuition was minimal, and they were required to spend fewer years as apprentices.

Central to Möser's view of the human world was "honor," a notion that was as important to corporatist society as the notion of dignity would be for the more individualistic society that succeeded it.[16] In

Möser's view, a person acquired his identity from his place in the institutional structure of society, a society in which economic, social, and political institutions were not distinguished from one another. His status (as a guildsman, noble landowner, serf, or independent peasant cottager) determined not only how he earned his living, but his sense of who he was, of what his duties and obligations were, of those to whom he ought to defer and those who ought to defer to him. (In the language of modern sociology, Möser's society was one in which almost all of the individual's roles derived from a single status.) Who one was was largely a continuation of what one's forebears had been. For Möser the real self was the socially encumbered self, the self based on status, on historical and regional particularity, and on property. It was a self whose prime virtue was honor. Status and the honor that attached to it were inherited, though they could be lost if one failed to live up to the duties of one's rank. This hereditary and institutional conception of honor permeates Möser's view of society and of the corrosive effects of enlightened absolutism and the market upon it.

The guilds had once been the bulwark of Osnabrück society, and it was in their defense that Möser best articulated his social thought and his fears regarding the spread of the market.

Möser's principled opposition to the social and economic policies of enlightened absolutism comes through most jarringly in his writings on bastards. At the instigation of the Prussian monarch, the enlightened Habsburg emperors promulgated an ordinance in 1731 intended "To Remedy Abuses Among the Guilds." In addition to submitting the guilds to greater control by the government authorities, the decree sought to eliminate certain practices that inhibited the guilds' economic efficiency. It sought, for example, to force the guilds to admit to their ranks the children of parents whose occupations were regarded as lacking in sufficient honor to qualify their descendants for guild membership.[17] The decree forbade the exclusion of the children of jail keepers, gravediggers, watchmen, beadles, street sweepers, ditch clearers, shepherds, and other folk regarded as socially repugnant. It went on to forbid the guilds to discriminate against "children illegitimately conceived and born before or after priestly legitimation."

The stipulation that applicants for guild membership be "conceived by honorable parents under pure circumstances" (*ehrliche Eltern aus reinem Bett erzeuget*) had become increasingly common in the course of the seventeenth and eighteenth centuries.[18] In terms of economic efficiency or of individual responsibility, the stipulation made no sense. Yet the abolition of such stipulations was fought tooth and nail by many guildsmen, and, thanks to the limited power of the empire to actually enforce its rulings, the guildsmen sometimes retained their right to decide the relationship between ancestry and guild membership.

Möser reflected upon the ordinance in two essays written in 1772. As was so often the case, the titles of the essays telegraphed their conclusion: "Were the Authors of the Imperial Ordinance of 1731 Right in Making Honorable Many People Who Were Not?" and "On the Diminished Shame of Whores and Their Children in Our Day."[19] Möser characterized the ordinance as demanding that the guilds accept "almost any creature with two legs and no feathers" and as an example of "the contemporary fad of humanitarianism." The love of one's fellow man was a noble sentiment, Möser wrote, but it was no basis for government social policy.

"The unpolitical philosophy of our century," Möser complained, elevated humanitarianism over civic sense—"*Menschenliebe*" over "*Bürgerliebe*." Marriage was an important political institution. The family household was of greater value to the state than was bachelorhood, not only because marriages produced more children than did a series of illicit sexual liaisons, but because the institution of the family helped to control vice and nurture virtue. Should its power decline, one could anticipate an increase of vice and the need for government to punish crimes more harshly as a deterrent. Yet marriage had its burdens and discomforts and bachelorhood its attractions: hence it was politically wise for the state to create incentives to marriage and disincentives to bachelorhood and illicit sex. By giving illegitimate children equal status with those honorably born, Möser argued, the law diminished the common disdain against women who engaged in illicit sex and against their children; that eliminated one of the strongest incentives to marriage. Policies that diminished the disgrace of loose women and their children therefore did so at the expense of the institution of marriage, a key constituent of civic life.

The enlightened ordinance was thus "unpolitical," Möser claimed. By deducing the civic rights of bastards from abstract human rights or from the state of nature, it ignored the function of popular prejudice against the offspring of extramarital sex in maintaining the institution of marriage, an institution that filled a variety of political functions. "Our ancestors, who always demanded a certificate of honorable birth before they admitted someone into their guilds," Möser wrote, "were guided by experience rather than by theories." This contrast was repeated often by Möser, and it became a staple of later conservative thought. "Experience" embodied a wisdom that could not be matched by conclusions deduced from abstract premises of justice and efficiency. For the wisdom of experience took into account that the functions of existing institutions, of guilds and of the family, were interlinked, and that the beliefs associated with them—such as the common disdain for bastards—embodied a wisdom that those who held them could not necessarily articulate. Möser often saw his role as discovering and making explicit the tacit wisdom of existing institutions and practices.

The forced admission of bastards into the guilds, Möser reasoned, by diminishing the honor of the guilds, had caused guild membership to decline in value. It became unrespectable to join a guild once its honor had been destroyed by such an admissions policy. Men no longer aspired to guild status, and as a result the guilds had begun to decline. The enlightened bureaucrats who promulgated the ordinance had thus dispossessed guildsmen of their property, Möser argued, and by diminishing their traditional privileges without consulting them, had robbed the guildsmen of their liberty as well.

To Möser, such an ordinance was an attack on the guildsmen's honor, on their liberty, and on their property by government officials who failed to understand the consequences of their actions because of their generalized disdain for those below them. Their attempt to make bastards honorable revealed a lack of comprehension of the *meaning* of honor and dishonor. Honor was the right to be treated as an equal by those who shared one's rank, in a society composed of a hierarchy of ranks, classes, and estates. The "dishonorable" also had their rank: they were assigned to the lowest of the traditional ranks of society. The ordinance made it seem intolerable to belong to this lowest rank. Once this was accepted, Möser asked, would not each rank come to resent the inferiority of its honor to that of the rank above it? For Möser, the officials of the absolutist monarchy, by weakening the concept of honor, were striking at the very principle by which society was structured. Without a firm sense of rank—each with its own privileges, duties, and honor—how would men know their place?

Möser scandalized enlightened intellectuals by defending the institution of serfdom, the traditional paternalistic relationship between lord and serf in which the serf was the lord's legal property (*Leibeigentum*). He pointed out that the conception held by many intellectuals of the serf as lacking in all rights and property and at the total mercy of his master did not correspond to the reality of serfdom in Westphalia, where for historical reasons it had developed in a much milder form.[20] In fact, he claimed, serfdom as it existed in Westphalia was superior to economic relationships based upon the legal freedom of both partners. He argued that once the serf had "redeemed" himself by buying his legal freedom through a cash payment, the lord lost the interest in him and in his welfare. A serf, he wrote, is like a carriage horse, which it behooves its owner to maintain, while a peasant farmer who rents his land from the landowner is like a rented horse, which one exploits as much as possible without concern for his future welfare.[21]

The replacement of paternalist economic relations by capitalist attitudes toward landed property alarmed Möser. In the countryside around Osnabrück, landowners were evicting legally free peasants who were unable to pay their debts from their ancestral plots of land, and replacing them by renters. The effect of this, he warned, was a decline in the peasant's feeling of attachment to his "ancestral legacy" (väterliches Erbe), and of the connection between property ownership and civic responsibility. Möser tried to stem the peasant's indebtedness by legally limiting his ability to borrow, and by making it more difficult for creditors to appropriate the possessions of those who fell into debt.[22]

Though Möser was suspicious of the market, he was not opposed to commerce as such. Instead he tried to restrict and accommodate it to his essentially noncommercial vision of society. Möser favored some forms of economic development, and preferred that they be controlled by government. He liked the market more the less free it was. Möser was enough of a mercantilist to applaud merchants who exported locally manufactured goods and thereby enriched his state. As the administrator of a region whose economy had been damaged by the Seven Years' War, Möser used his state's funds and monopoly powers to encourage economic development. He offered financial support to craftsmen to settle in Osnabrück to supply essential needs, founded government-run pottery and basket factories (both failed), and developed plans for a local bank to make better use of funds held by individuals and government offices in Osnabrück.[23] Like Voltaire, Möser was himself active in economic affairs, lending money to the local nobility and participating in a local mining venture.[24]

On occasion Möser could even urge a market-based economic policy because of its utility and practicality. He did so on the most sensitive question of economic policy in the eighteenth century, namely the government's role in policing the supply of grain.[25] He argued against the existing policy of providing grain from government storehouses at times of shortage. The grain trade, he explained, was so constituted that merchants often sustained losses for nine years while grain was cheap, for which they were compensated in the occasional years when a shortage of grain raised the price of their stock. No merchant, Möser argued, would assume the risks of the nine cheap years knowing that prices would not be allowed to rise in the tenth. A government that attempted to fix the price of grain would have to reckon with the fact that it could not rely on commerce to ensure supply, and hence would have to provide grain on its own, which it was not capable of doing adequately. "In this instance," he wrote, "one can rely completely on the appetite for gain, which is placed in all men, and not without purpose."[26]

Destroying Local Culture

Yet despite these accommodations with commerce, Möser regarded the market primarily as a threat—to the artisanal citizens of the town, to the traditional wants of the peasantry, and to the political structure of society, since it created a growing class of people outside the traditional paternalistic relations of the countryside. Möser's conception of contemporary political and economic trends in Osnabrück was essentially tragic and tinged with that idealization of the past that would later be called romantic.[27] Möser's heroes were the artisan-citizen and the independent peasant, his villains the shopkeeper and the peddler.

The artisan was pivotal to Osnabrück's political institutions, as Möser conceived of them, for he was a citizen (Bürger) who provided the taxes upon which the state depended, and who in time of war could be called to arms or offer quarter for professional soldiers. He provided the traditional products to meet the customary needs of the people of his region. Economic privileges and political duties had been neatly intertwined within a static and stable economy.

The status of the artisan, Möser believed, was now being undermined by the international market and its local agent, the shopkeeper (Krämer).[28] The shopkeeper imported goods from beyond Osnabrück and sold them in his shop. These goods came from London, Paris, and big cities in Germany, where they were produced by a process of division of labor that Möser called "simplification" and that historians have come to call "concentrated manufacture."[29] In place of the guilded master artisan who worked with a few apprentices and journeymen, this new style of production involved a master who employed thirty or forty wage laborers. The process of production was broken down into steps, each of which was performed by a worker who specialized in that phase. Möser referred to the system as "simplification" because each worker mastered only one step in the process of production. While the journeyman learned to make the entire product and might eventually become an independent master, each wage laborer in a "simplified" industry learned only a small part of the production process, and hence was permanently dependent. Goods produced by this process could be sold more cheaply, Möser recognized, though—unlike Adam Smith—he failed to recognize the economic rationale by which costs were reduced. Production in the big cities also had other economic advantages, which Möser enumerated: raw materials were easier to obtain, the city had a large market of its own, and the new factories were in a position to use new machines powered by wind and water that were beyond the means of the artisan. It was the shopkeeper who imported these city-made, manufactured goods into towns like Osnabrück. The products of "simplification," Möser recognized, were often better and less expensive than those produced by the hometown artisan. And so the artisan was increasingly displaced by the shopkeeper. Möser estimated that in the last century the number of artisans in Osnabrück had fallen by half, while the number of shopkeepers had tripled. The independent artisanry was thus in economic decline, and with it the urban institutions of corporatist society.

Time and again Möser condemned the growing taste for new, imported commodities, especially among the lower ranks. Even a beggar now considered coffee, tea, and sugar among his basic needs, Möser wrote with polemical exaggeration.[30] He shared the common mercantilist concern with the balance of trade, and sought to discourage the growing taste for imports while attempting to increase exports and the consumption of locally made goods.[31] By encouraging the consumption of foreign goods at the expense of those produced locally, the shopkeeper enriched foreigners while impoverishing his fellow citizens, Möser claimed. In keeping with these mercantilist assumptions, Möser distinguished the shopkeeper from the merchant (Kaufmann), who made his living by exporting locally made goods to foreign markets, or who imported raw materials for local processing and eventual export. The merchant was a boon to the state, while the shopkeeper was a bane. The merchant's honor was of the first rank, Möser wrote, but the shopkeeper's status ought to be below that of the artisan.[32]

Imported foreign goods had another quality that disturbed Möser: their novelty. In the great cities, he wrote, tastes and styles were constantly changing, while the town artisan made his goods in the traditional way. The shopkeeper thrived by encouraging the taste for fashion and for luxury (Wohllust), by stimulating new desires. "Lead us not into temptation," the Lord's Prayer urged. Yet according to Möser, that was the role of the shopkeeper, the local agent of the new international economy who robbed the artisan of his customers and of his livelihood. "Fashion" thus became "the great pillager of provincial towns."[33]

Möser thus condemned capitalism on the grounds that it *created* new needs, which disrupted customary expectations and unbalanced society—a judgment common in the eighteenth century, and one revived periodically by moralists thereafter.[34] He railed against the replacement of indigenous tastes by international ones.[35]

While Möser was suspicious of the urban shopkeeper as the agent of change in the city, he reserved his greatest hostility for the peddler, the agent of the market economy in the countryside. In the primitive economy of rural Westphalia, the contact of most peasants with the world market and the goods it made available was limited. Since poor roads made travel difficult and hazardous, the peasant rarely visited the towns and their shops. Fairs at which foreign goods could be purchased were few and far between. In such economically backward regions, the main source of foreign goods was the peddler, a man who carried his stock on his back and marched off through the paths and byways to the homes of the peasants. The peasants had little to spend and were hard to reach. But to the peddler, a would-be merchant with little capital and no inherited status, they represented an untapped market. The peddler carried items produced outside the region and sold them in small quantities to people largely outside the market economy.[36] Such peddlers were often Jews.

To Möser, the activities of the peddler ruined "the good morals" of the rural population by awakening new needs and desires. Once the peasants had been satisfied with indigenous products, Möser claimed, and did not aspire to foreign-made goods that were above their station. It was the peddler who led them astray, by encouraging them to buy items they would never have thought about on their own:

> Our ancestors did not tolerate these rural shopkeepers; they were spare in dispensing market freedoms; they banned the Jews from our diocese; why this severity? Certainly in order that the rural inhabitants not be daily stimulated, tempted, led astray and deceived. They stuck to the practical rule: that which one does not see will not lead one astray.[37]

The peddler led people to buy what Möser thought they did not really *need*; what they did need, Möser assumed, was what they had traditionally needed. It was the aim of government policy makers like himself to protect the public from the temptation of buying products which Möser knew they did not really need.[38]

What were these pernicious but tempting goods to which the peddler exposed unsuspecting peasants and their wives? Silk kerchiefs, linen from Flanders, leather gloves, wool stockings, metal buttons, mirrors, cotton caps, knives, and needles. These are what the defenders of customary consumption regarded as luxuries. Möser was particularly leery of the peddlers because so many of them were foreigners carrying foreign goods. To his mercantilist mind, they were primarily a conduit drawing wealth out of Osnabrück. Since they paid no taxes and competed with local artisans, their effect was to impoverish the state. They were the fiscal equivalent of smugglers.[39]

Möser also saw the market and its agents as despoiling morals, because they drew women away from the protected confines of the household and the supervision of their husbands. He was dismayed by the fact that the peddler appeared at the peasant woman's door and appealed directly to her, without the steadying presence of her spouse.[40] He argued against weekly local markets on the grounds that they would draw women and children away from the "bourgeois tranquility" (*bürgerlichen Bequemlichkeit*) of the home and into the marketplace, where they would chat and waste money on snacks and pleasantries, while ignoring their household duties.[41] Once again, the market was portrayed as the destroyer of custom and tradition.

As we have seen in our discussion of Möser's views on the grain trade, he did grasp the positive role of the market. This applied even to peddlers. Möser acknowledged that they did keep local shopkeepers from overcharging. And so he recommended that peddlers be tolerated, but only to sell "necessary" foreign goods and only at fairs, which were infrequent and where female customers would be properly accompanied.[42]

Creating the Poor

Yet the greatest threat to the institutional structure of Osnabrück came from the spread of new capitalist forms of manufacture to the countryside. By Möser's time, this transformation was sufficiently advanced that he was obliged to support it, while trying to ignore its disruptive political effects.

Möser conceived of the rights of citizenship as tied to the ownership of property. The ancient Germanic tribes, in Möser's description, had maintained their political virtue and the purity of their morals by restricting residence and citizenship to those who owned and worked their own land.[43] Like Locke, he believed that the polity was based on some original contract. But in Möser's conception, the shares of this original contract were based on the ownership of property, especially land. Not everyone's share was the same size: the nobles had large shares, the peasants small shares, and some had no shares at all.[44] In this scheme of things, there was no room for the unpropertied, whose income derived from wage labor.[45] Those who were propertyless and lacking in citizenship rights he referred to as Nebenwohner, resident aliens or sojourners. The essential dilemma that Möser faced was that the growth of new forms of production in the countryside created an ever larger population that lacked the property requirements of citizenship, and had no place within the traditional institutions of Osnabrück.[46]

Möser thus faced a predicament that was to confront policy makers in many developing economies: how to accommodate a new situation in which changes in economic opportunity (along with nutrition) made it possible for many more people to be maintained by the economy, but at a level barely above subsistence. The size of the peasant family had traditionally been limited by the economic constraints of land scarcity. The typical male peasant would only marry when he could afford to maintain a family, which meant when he took possession of his own plot of land, usually inherited at the death of his father. Traditionally, most peasant men married at about the age of thirty, and only then did they begin to raise children. By Möser's time, however, the opportunities for peasants had been altered by migrant agricultural labor and domestic industry.

In Osnabrück most peasants worked their small plots of land with their own labor. But the quality of the soil was low and the population density high. The independent farmers of nearby Holland, a more advanced economy less than fifty miles to the west, required hired labor to harvest their crops. And so, by Möser's day, some six thousand men of Osnabrück made their way to Holland each summer, to work as hired farm laborers.[47]

A second new source of economic opportunity was rural, home-based manufacture. It was through this—"cottage industry" or "the putting-out system"—that many residents of Möser's bishopric became most closely tied to the growing international market economy. Under this system of dispersed manufacture, cloth was produced in steps by peasants in their cottages, usually in the winter, when there was less need for agricultural work. Within their homes some peasants would spin, others would weave, and others might dye the resulting cloth. The system was created and held together by merchant entrepreneurs who advanced the peasant the raw materials and often the necessary equipment, moved the product on through the various steps, and finally marketed the finished product.[48] In some parts of Europe, Möser's Osnabrück among them, a rapid rise in population was made possible by the growth of cottage industry.

Möser was keenly aware of the impact of these new economic opportunities on the economy and society. Linen manufactured under the domestic system of production was Osnabrück's most important export, and hence a key concern to a mercantilist-minded administrator. For only a growing economy could support a growing population and keep its members off the public rolls. Much of that linen was produced in households that only remained economically viable because their menfolk migrated to Holland each summer. For these reasons, Möser tried to encourage and develop the linen industry, and supported the summer migrations to Holland.[49]

Yet the social effects of these new economic patterns worried Möser. Among those peasants whose income derived from their own plot of land, Möser noted, men did not marry until almost the age of thirty, when they inherited the family plot. Once a man could earn a living as a hired laborer, however, he could afford to marry at twenty. Thus the rate of population growth among wage laborers (who supplemented their income through domestic industry) was one-third higher than among traditional peasants.[50] A whole new class of people arose, known to Möser variously as *Heuerleuten* (people for hire) or *Hollandgänger* (Holland goers) or *Nebenwohner* (sojourners), because they lacked the property that was a prerequisite of citizenship.

Many of the unpropertied lived on the edge of subsistence. Unable to accumulate wealth for themselves, some even preferred to become serfs in order to obtain a plot of land that they could call their own and hand on to their children.[51] Not everyone was suited to the strenuous nature of this new form of labor, Möser warned, and many would be prone to escape it by thievery or beggary. He perceived them above all as a potential drain on the public coffers and hence on the resources of the landed and propertied citizens of Osnabrück.[52] To keep this new population from swamping the bishopric required a harshness and an abandonment of the communal sentiments traditionally applied to citizens.

To keep this new mass of handworkers on the straight and narrow path, the legislator must stand over them with cudgel in hand so to speak. He must deter potential beggars among them by workhouses, he must forbid almsgiving, he must assign this mass a very different worth from the peasant proprietor. He must no longer let ten guilty go free to protect one innocent; large goals require large sacrifices. . . . Only rarely can a considerable population be made up of handworkers, without letting half of them die under the cudgels of hunger and distress. A state made up of 10,000 farms and 200,000 *Heurleute* cannot treat all of the poor and sick equally. . . . It is an often abused rule, that people must be pressed if they are to be industrious; but it retains its core of truth, namely that distress is the best disciplinarian, and it is fallacious to ease this distress if charity creates loafers, which is always to be feared among the handworkers. The demands of distress are stricter than those of law. . . .[53]

Möser held that policies motivated by Christian charity or humanitarianism would only encourage the poor to live off the public purse; only if poverty was seen as wretched would there be sufficient incentive for the new class to work.[54]

To Möser, the new population of unpropertied, politically disenfranchised workers was an object not of sympathy but of suspicion. Unlike the guilded artisans of the towns or the free peasants and dependent serfs of the countryside, the handworkers did not fit into Möser's vision of Osnabrück society. To him they represented a threat to its very foundations. His strategy was not to accommodate them, but to keep them from becoming a crushing burden on the other classes of Osnabrück, a strategy that included expelling some of the "useless maws" before they became a "plague."[55]

Voltaire devoted *Candide*, his most famous tale, to satirizing the view that this was the best of possible worlds. Möser had his own way of explaining the beneficent role of collective pain and misfortune, but his was a far darker theodicy than that of Dr. Pangloss. For Möser, periods of privation and desperate need, such as those in which agricultural plagues brought about a rise in the price of food, served their own providential purpose, by activating human virtues that otherwise lay dormant. To the poor, the scourge of hunger encouraged their appetite for work; to the rich, viewing the deprivation of the poor opened the heart to sympathy; to both, scarcity taught the virtues of moderation and thrift.[56] It is his acceptance of the plight of the poor as both ineradicable and morally unproblematic that distinguishes Möser most dramatically from Adam Smith.

Commerce and the Eclipse of Virtue

Möser was only one voice among the eighteenth-century cultural critics of capitalist civilization.[57] The lament for the purported eclipse of civic virtue by the quest for monetary gain was a common complaint among eighteenth-century intellectuals. By the time Möser raised it in the 1770s, it had already been voiced by Rousseau and by Adam Ferguson. Thereafter it would be repeated in endless variations and modulations. Representatives of the civic virtue tradition were always at hand to warn that a political culture dominated by the values of self-interest was in danger of collapse. Möser decried the fact that the quest for money had displaced the quest for public honor; the values of the market were crowding out that readiness to sacrifice for the sake of the common good that was the core of civic virtue:

> Without a quick remedy, all will be lost. Honor, that power-
> ful motive of human actions, will no longer be there to serve
> us; the noble love of property will vanish; the reward for all
> public services will have to paid in cash (to the state's detri-
> ment). . . . The crown of laurels which the citizens of Rome
> valued as their greatest reward would satisfy no one today;
> knightly honors no longer lead to knightly deeds; the nobil-
> ity itself has become lazy. Money and paid service decide all,
> and both have shamefully extinguished the economy of pub-
> lic honor which were the nonmonetary means by which
> patriots were rewarded. The economy of public honor led in
> a certain and orderly fashion to the commonweal; it func-
> tioned on the basis of duties rather than punishments, it
> created patriots willing to sacrifice for the sake of their fel-
> low citizens and become involved in undertakings for the
> sake of the state and renown. Now the rich in their gilded
> coaches trample the common citizen into the dust, and the
> paid servant laughs at the man who once sought as his

reward for voluntary and grand service nothing but the
honor of wearing the black coat of public office.[58]

But the tide of the money economy, Möser knew, was too powerful
to be turned back; at best one could mitigate its negative effects.[59] Yet
his suggestions about how to do so carried little conviction, for he recognized their impracticality. To restore the prestige of artisans and
peasants—and to further distinguish them from wage workers and
sojourners—he recommended allowing them to bear arms, since the
Germans had long been accustomed to connecting honor with that
right.[60] Möser's suggestion of a citizen militia as a tool for the re-
creation of civic virtue was another oft-echoed theme in the mid-
eighteenth century. Möser also proposed (with tongue only partly in
cheek) the creation of a hierarchy of uniforms, to be worn as a symbol
of honorable status by those who had demonstrably contributed to the
common good. The chance to don such a symbol of respect would
serve as an incentive to public service, while the possibility of losing
the right to a uniform would discourage crime. Yet the article in which
these suggestions appeared, "The Advantages of a General National
Uniform, Declaimed by a Citizen," ended on an ironic note: "He [the
citizen] wanted to go on speaking; but when his wife became concerned that he was about to suggest a uniform for the female sex, she
commanded him to shut up."[61] Möser's irony indicated that the measures required to re-create "the economy of public honor" had little
chance of public acceptance.

Möser was thus among the first of many critics to state the dilemma
of the cultural effects of the rise of the market: how was one to restore
honor, virtue, a quest for the commonweal in a population in which
such qualities were lacking? Despite the occasional radicalism of his
criticism, his prudence and deep entanglement with existing institutions made him loath to suggest radical solutions. Future intellectuals,
less at home with the political institutions of their societies, would
echo Möser's criticisms. Their search for solutions would be more desperate and more radical.

But the fear that commerce would undermine the institutional
order was not confined to conservative critics of the market in economic backwaters like Osnabrück. It was soon to be echoed by
Edmund Burke, an advocate of the market in London, the center of the
late-eighteenth-century economy. Anxiety about the cultural effects of
the market was to become perhaps the most consistent tension within
conservative social and political thought.

CHAPTER FIVE

EDMUND BURKE:
COMMERCE, CONSERVATISM,
AND THE INTELLECTUALS

Edmund Burke's *Reflections on the Revolution in France* (1790) is the single most influential work of conservative thought published from his day to ours. It struck every chord of conservative sentiment, rang every chime of conservative analysis, and enunciated virtually every subsequent theme of conservative ideology.[1] Along with Burke's arguments for the continuity of established institutions as conducive to human happiness, the *Reflections* is best known for its critique of the pernicious role of intellectuals in political life. Less well known is the book's sustained contention that "men of money" were undermining the institutions of the state and the Church. Yet Burke, who emerged as a scourge of politicized men of letters and men of money, was among the most important intellectuals in European politics before 1789, and indeed formulated the rationale for a more intellectualist conception of political life. And Burke championed capitalist economic development from his earliest published writings until his last days, advocating a reliance on the profit motive and the market as the coordinating mechanism of economic life, as did Adam Smith. Why then did the foremost intellectual in politics and the advocate of the market pen one of the most biting critiques of both intellectuals and entrepreneurs?

Unraveling this seeming paradox will lead us into the tensions between capitalism and conservatism in a commercial society. Justus Möser's brand of conservatism had been hostile to capitalism, since Möser rightly saw the spread of the market as a threat to a society he sought to conserve. The society Burke sought to conserve, by contrast, was already highly commercial, dominated by a landed aristocracy that was itself commercially minded.[2] Burke shared the preference of Voltaire and Smith for commercial society over its historical alternatives. But he concluded that Smith had overlooked the institutional and cultural prerequisites of a commercial society, and that Voltaire and his successors presented a threat to the foundations upon which modern commercial society rested. The problem, as Burke formulated it, was not with intellectuals or with the market. It was with intellectuals who had an unreasonable conception of reason and of men of money whose self-interest was unrestrained by legal or cultural rules.

Understanding how Burke arrived at that position requires a journey through his career, focused on his conception of the proper role of the intellectual in politics and his own and others' experiences of profit seeking. That turned Burke into the scourge of the largest corporation of his day, the British East India Company, and anticipated his analysis of the French Revolution.

The Intellectual in Politics

Like his friend Adam Smith, Burke began on the periphery of Britain, and advanced toward the center of the British establishment through a combination of ability and patronage. An outsider turned insider, Burke maintained a critical distance that left him attuned to the latent functions and frailties of established institutions, which those born into the establishment rarely understood.

Burke was born in Dublin in 1729, which made him nine years younger than Justus Möser and six years younger than Smith.[3] He was educated in a fine provincial university: Trinity College, Dublin. There he edited a journal aimed at the local reformation of manners—a project that echoes the reformist societies with which Smith and Hume were involved in Scotland.[4] Yet here the circumstances of Smith and Burke diverge. Scotland was in the midst of an economic efflorescence, led by a class of improving native landowners linked to London by a customs union and by political preferment. Burke's Irish homeland, by contrast, suffered under less propitious political and economic circumstances. It was a country comprised largely of Catholic peasants, dominated by landowners who were English and often absentee; its populace was restricted from many forms of commerce and manufacture by legislation designed to subordinate the Irish economy to English needs. Burke's Ireland lacked a politically connected, native elite devoted to economic growth. In one of his earliest articles, Burke lamented Ireland's economic backwardness, which he attributed to its domination by landowners who, instead of setting an example of economic improvement, were bent on impoverishing a land they despised.[5] The theme of capitalist economic growth was on Burke's mind from his earliest days as a writer.

Young Burke moved to London and burst onto the intellectual and then the political stage in several leaps, beginning with the publication in 1756 of *A Vindication of Natural Society*, a spoof and critique of exaggerated rationalism. The next year Burke published his *Philosophical Enquiry into the Origin of Our Ideas of the Sublime and the Beautiful*, regarded at the time and since as one of the most important eighteenth-century works on aesthetics. Like Smith's *Theory of Moral Sentiments*, which appeared two years later, Burke's book argued that "a consideration of the rationale of our passions seems to me very necessary for all who would affect them upon solid and sure principles."[6] The book was well received in England and Germany, and led Smith to declare that its author deserved a university chair. In 1758, Burke launched the *Annual Register*, a summary of the major European political, literary, social, and artistic events of the preceding year. Through 1763, he wrote much of the volume himself and turned the project into a commercial success.

By his mid-thirties, Burke had achieved the recognition of his fellow men of letters. He was an early member of "The Club," which included such intellectual luminaries as Samuel Johnson and (when he was in London) Adam Smith. Joshua Reynolds, the Club's founder, provided Burke with moral and monetary support in the decades that followed. But the intellectual and cultural stage was not large enough to hold Burke. He made his way into politics through the only gate open to a man of large talent but modest means: patronage.

Burke began his political involvement in 1759, when he became personal assistant to William Gerard Hamilton, a member of Parliament. Hamilton was soon elevated to Chancellor of the Exchequer for Ireland, a sinecure, and conferred on Burke an annual pension from the Irish Treasury. But Burke soon gave up his pension and broke with his patron when he felt that Hamilton aimed to tie him to "a settled servitude," a situation intolerable, as Burke put it, to a "gentleman, a freeman, a man of education, and one pretending to literature."[7] In 1765, through a connection with Charles Townshend—who had, two years earlier, hired Smith away from Glasgow to tutor his stepson, and who surely ranks as one of the supreme talent spotters of the age—Burke became private secretary to the Marquis of Rockingham. A great landowner and rising politician, the marquis was appointed prime minister later that year and presided over a short-lived administration. The marquis became Burke's major source of political and financial support, while Burke formulated the ideals and rationale upon which Rockingham attempted to forge a diverse group of members of Parliament into a political party, capable of taking power or acting as an effective opposition.[8] After Rockingham's death in 1782, his nephew and political heir, the Earl Fitzwilliam, became Burke's patron.

The party that Burke helped to forge aimed at government led by a landed aristocracy, open to mercantile and commercial interests, and dedicated to conserving the place of the House of Commons within the British constitution. Burke and the Rockingham Whigs sought to preserve Parliament not only from royal encroachment but also from the undue influence of the unpropertied many, whether expressed through more equal and democratic representation or through the pressure of mob action. During much of his long career in Parliament, which stretched from 1766 through 1794, Burke owed his seat to aristocratic patronage.

It was no mean trick for a man of letters without money, and hampered in his adopted English environment by a Dublin accent and Catholic origins (though Burke, like his father, was a Protestant), to attain some measure of political influence. It was Burke's achievement to exercise considerable sway over public affairs, even though he spent most of his career in the parliamentary opposition. It was as an intellectual that Burke exerted his political influence, and he regarded the attempt to influence public affairs as an honorable calling for a man of letters. "To study only for its own sake is a fruitless labour; to learn only to be learned is moving in a strange Circle," he wrote in his youthful notebooks. "The End of learning is not knowledge but virtue; as the End of all speculation should be practice of one sort or another."[9]

Burke's *Thoughts on the Cause of the Present Discontents* (1770), most famous for its intellectual legitimation of political parties, also includes Burke's eloquent justification for the involvement of the intellectual in politics. The core of Burke's argument in favor of coherent parties lay in his claim that "no men could act with effect, who did not act in concert; that no men act in concert, who did not act with confidence; that no men could act with confidence, who were not bound together by common opinions, common affections, and common interests."[10] That common interests and common affections were a source of political coherence was a commonplace of Georgian politics. The significance of Burke's *Thoughts* was that it presented not only an intellectual legitimation of party, but a theory of party that put a new premium on mind in politics. For Burke defined party as "a body of men united for promoting by their joint endeavors the national interest upon some *particular principle* in which they are all agreed."[11] And he insisted that "the greater part of the measures which arise in the course of public business are related to, or dependent on, some great, *leading, general principles in government* . . ."[12] A view of party which emphasized common principles and common opinions placed a premium on those who articulated principle and created shared opinions.

Against men of letters who saw such activity as soiling their souls, Burke's *Thoughts* offered a justification for the intellectual to become involved in politics. "For my part," he wrote, "I find it impossible to conceive, that any one believes in his own politics, or thinks them to be of any weight, who refuses to adopt the means of having them reduced into practice. It is the business of the speculative philosopher to mark the proper ends of government. It is the business of the politician, who is the philosopher in action, to find out proper means towards those ends, and to employ them with effect."[13] Burke scorned those who guarded their intellectual purity through political celibacy. The very definition of intellectual virtue, he maintained, was linked to realizing ideals in action. There was a need, he wrote, "to model our principles to our duties and our situation. To be fully persuaded, that all virtue which is impracticable is spurious; and rather to run the risk of falling into faults in a course which leads us to act with effect and energy, than to loiter out our days without blame, and without use. Public life is a situation of power and energy; he trespasses against his duty who sleeps upon his watch, as well as he that goes over to the enemy."[14]

Even after decades in Parliament, Burke was regarded by the most vital intellectuals in the kingdom as one of their own. In November 1783, he was elected to the honorary post of rector of the University of Glasgow. He stopped first in Edinburgh, where he visited with Smith and the illuminati of the Scottish Enlightenment. Smith accompanied Burke to his inauguration in Glasgow, and shortly thereafter nominated Burke to the Royal Society of Edinburgh, which Smith had recently helped to found.[15]

The predilections that came so naturally to Burke by virtue of his role as intellectual also influenced his theory of political representation. In his "Speech at the Conclusion of the Poll in Bristol" of 1774, Burke told his constituents that "Parliament is not a *congress* of ambassadors from different and hostile interests, which interests each must maintain, as an agent and advocate, against other agents and advocates; but Parliament is a *deliberative* assembly of *one* nation, with *one* interest, that of the whole . . ."[16] This conception of Parliament not as a group of delegates pledged to assert the interests of their constituents but as a deliberative body in which consensus emerges through argument implicitly places a high value on speech and reason. Not surprisingly, it has remained a favorite of intellectuals in politics, reiterated a century later by John Stuart Mill in his *Essay on Representative Government* (1861) and resuscitated a century after that by Jürgen Habermas in his *Structural Transformation of the Public Sphere* (1962).

As the intellectual engine of the Rockingham faction, Burke's function was to enunciate principles, to influence Parliament through his speeches and reports, and to influence extraparliamentary opinion through the reports of his speeches in the press and through his own publications.

Burke often served as the spokesman in Parliament for the Rockingham faction, and used his parliamentary speeches to erect a coherent set of principles for his party.[17] Part of Burke's effectiveness as an intellectual in politics lay in his eloquence. That, in turn, was related to his learning, which impressed opponents as well as admirers. His great polemical works brim with well-chosen allusions and quotations from the Bible, the classics of Greek and Latin literature, and the great works of English poetry and drama. He combined his learning and his fund of contemporary information with rhetorical prowess. At a time when the great majority of MPs spoke rarely if at all, Burke's oratorical powers and his ingenuity as a debater made a deep impression on his contemporaries.[18] When he made his first appearance as a member of Parliament (in a series of orations in favor of Rockingham's motion to repeal the Grenville Stamp Act), his debut, according to Samuel Johnson, "filled the town with wonder" and gained Burke "more reputation than perhaps any man . . . before."[19] Later, Burke was the director and star of the impeachment of Warren Hastings, an event which brought London society into Westminster for the longest-running show of the decade.[20]

Burke's standing also derived from the facility with which he could condense and analyze information. He was a one-man think tank: contributing to the *Annual Review*,[21] composing detailed refutations of published accounts that tarnished (and Burke claimed, traduced) the record of his party in *Observations on a Late Publication, Intitled "The Present State of the Nation"* (1769), and offering a book-length study of the politics and economics of India.

The Market for "Intelligence" and "Public Opinion"

But Burke's greatest influence was exerted via the new means of cultural production through which "public opinion" was created: the commerce in books, pamphlets, and newspapers that appealed to an educated public concerned with parliamentary affairs. Burke presented the Rockinghams as practicing a new and superior politics accessible to public discussion.[22] Political discourse was increasingly public, conducted in good part through the newspaper press. It was an age of increasing information, or, as it was called at the time, "intelligence."[23] It was the expansion of the market for "intelligence" that created a market niche for an intellectual in politics. In an age when Parliament was gaining in importance in the life of the nation, Burke addressed the Commons knowing that his words would reach a wider audience, the political nation "out of doors."[24]

It was Burke's combination of the roles of member of Parliament and man of letters that led him to devote so much of his energy to the printed parliamentary speech, a relatively new literary genre devoted to influencing public opinion. In the two decades that separated *Thoughts on the Cause of the Present Discontents* (1770) from *Reflections on the Revolution in France* (1790), most of Burke's publications took this form. His published speeches were the result of a careful, three-step process. Burke would first write extensive notes in preparation for the speech; these he would use in Parliament, adding, subtracting, and editing his text as he went along; finally, he would make use of the transcripts of his speech in reworking the material for publication.[25] The "Ninth Report of the Select Committee on India," which Burke wrote in its entirety, was published by Debrett soon after its presentation to Parliament. He published his great "Speech on the Nabob of Arcot's Debts" of 1785 after circulating earlier drafts to knowledgeable parties for correction, with a full complement of footnotes and a series of appendices.[26] Such speeches-cum-books became an important source of educating both MPs and a wider public about national issues. Burke's political influence came in no small part from the extraparliamentary effects of his speeches.

In England, politicians and newspapers of the 1780s increasingly invoked the power of "public opinion," which was equated with the vox populi and linked to the virtues of a free press assuring open discussion of public issues.[27] In France, as we have seen, enlightened intellectuals increasingly touted the role of "public opinion"—founded upon the new printed mass media of pamphlets, newspapers, and books—as a court of judgment in which issues of public policy were exposed to the criteria of rationality and objectivity.[28]

Burke, too, was very conscious of the fact that the spread of commercially distributed means of information had made "public opinion" into an ever more important factor in politics, and that what counted as "public opinion" was heavily influenced by intellectuals. What distinguishes Burke's treatment of the subject is his awareness—which he shared with Voltaire—that the "public opinion" often hailed as the voice of public reason and good sense was in fact the voice of men of letters. "Public opinion" in other words, was increasingly coming to mean *published opinion*, which endowed men of letters with a new, and possibly ominous, significance, as he stressed in his writings after 1789.[29] In his analysis of the origins of the French Revolution, Burke would maintain that the principal actors included "monied men" and "men of letters." "[A]s money increases and circulates, and as the circulation of news, in politicks and letters, becomes more and more diffused, the persons who diffuse this money, and this intelligence, become more and more important," he observed.[30] The circulation of newspapers was "infinitely more efficacious and extensive than ever they were. And they are a more important instrument than generally is imagined. They are a part of the reading of all, they are the whole of the reading of the far greater number. . . . Let us only suffer any person to tell us his story, morning and evening, but for one twelvemonth, and he will become our master."[31]

In one of his last publications, the "Second Letter on a Regicide Peace," Burke responded to those practical men of affairs who were inclined to downplay the importance of "opinion" and of those who create it. "Opinions are of infinite consequence," he wrote. "They make the manners—in fact, they make the laws: they make the Legislator. They are, therefore, of all things, those to which provident Government ought to look most to in their beginnings. After a time they may look to them in vain. When, therefore, I am told that a war is a war of opinions, I am told that it is the most important of all wars."[32]

The Critique of Abstract Reason

It was as a combatant in the war of opinions that Burke made his initial appearance on the London intellectual scene, when in 1756 he published *A Vindication of Natural Society*. From the beginning of his public career to its end, Burke warned of the potentially disastrous social and political results of intellect gone astray. In his first book, he focused on the snares of abstract rationalism, a frame of mind that demanded a rational justification of every institution, rejected every institution that did not meet the standards set by speculative theories of justice, and demanded that human society be reconstructed to conform to such criteria.

Burke's doubts about the claims of rationalism, both as motivation and as guide to worldly affairs, is evident in his youthful essays, written when he was still in his early twenties and left unpublished in his lifetime. Those who have gone through a long course of study and have mastered the principles of most sciences, he noted, "find how weak and fallacious the Grounds of many are, and how uncertain the very best."[33] "Perhaps the bottom of most things is unintelligible; and our surest reasoning, when we come to a certain point, is involved not only in obscurity but contradiction," he speculated.[34] For the young Burke, as for Möser, an awareness of the limits of human reasoning led to a principled respect for custom. "There is some general principle operating to produce Customs, that is a more sure guide than our Theories. They are followed indeed often on odd motives, but that does not make them less reasonable or useful."[35] Not only was the usefulness of a custom or institution not always immediately understood, the young Burke thought, but the attempt to subject all institutions to rational scrutiny could have its own negative consequences. "It is not easily conceived what use funeral ceremonies . . . are to mankind. Trifling as they may seem, they nourish humanity, they soften in some measure the rigour of Death, and they inspire humble, sober and becoming thought. They throw a decent Veil over the weak and dishonourable circumstances of our Nature. What shall we say to that philosophy, that would strip it naked? Of such sort is the wisdom of those who talk of the Love, the sentiment, and the thousand little dalliances that pass between the Sexes, in the gross way of mere procreation. They value themselves as having made a mighty discovery; and turn all pretences to delicacy into ridicule."[36]

The image of inherited culture as a veil, without which we are left with "the weak and dishonorable circumstances of our Nature," would furnish the master metaphor of Burke's reflections on the revolution in France almost four decades later. But his attack on those who would strip away the veil are found in his first book, *A Vindication of Natural Society or, A View of the Miseries and Evils Arising to Mankind from Every Species of Artificial Society. In a Letter to Lord* **** *by A Late Noble Writer*, which he published anonymously in 1756 at the age of twenty-seven. The book was a parody. Its strategy was to combat an increasingly popular mode of thought that Burke regarded as fundamentally mistaken, and which he tried to discredit by displaying its logical consequences.

The book takes the form of a letter from a young philosopher to an older aristocrat. The philosopher argues in favor of a rationalistic and universal "natural religion" and "natural society" free of any historical or nonrational accretions. He condemns all existing social, political, and cultural institutions for their departures from this rationalist standard. Since all of human history has been based upon such irrational institutions, the philosopher argues, it is a tale of unremitting woe, and he adduces copious (if specious) evidence to show that this has been the case.

So adept was Burke in entering into the mind-set of this new species of critical intellectual, and in recapturing this characteristic mode of thought and argument, that many readers failed to recognize his ironic and satirical intentions. He was obliged to begin the second edition, of 1757, with a new preface, in which he laid out his true assumptions and intentions. The tract, Burke explained, was about "the Abuse of Reason": "The Editor is satisfied that a Mind which has no Restraint from a Sense of its own Weakness, of its subordinate Rank in the Creation, and of the extreme Danger of letting the Imagination loose upon some Subjects, may very plausibly attack every thing the most excellent and venerable."[37] "What would become of the World if the Practice of all moral Duties, and the Foundations of Society, rested upon having their Reasons made clear and demonstrative to every Individual?" he asked rhetorically. The danger of open criticism of existing, taken-for-granted truth, he warned, lay in the fact that what was true was often difficult to demonstrate and what was easy to demonstrate was often not true, yet even a mistaken critique of existing institutions could have negative consequences.

From the earliest to the latest stages of his career, Burke was an intellectual on guard against what he regarded as the epistemologically pretentious and socially pernicious style of rationalist social criticism that led to "the Fairy Land of Philosophy."[38] For if government increasingly rested upon "public opinion," which was increasingly influenced by published opinion, then such criticism might destroy the hold of custom and habit that made institutions stable.

Burke as Supporter of Commerce

Burke became an active politician at a time when parliamentary activity was becoming ever more commercialized, a process in which he and his party were active. During the Rockingham ministry of 1766, Burke played a key role in linking merchants with the ministry, which encouraged them to consult with government.[39] When the Rockingham Whigs went into opposition, Burke was involved in soliciting support from the bankers and financiers of the City of London.[40] Diverse commercial interests were becoming ever more skilled at lobbying Parliament, and much parliamentary activity centered on the conflicting claims of rival commercial constituencies. Commercial considerations played a dominant role in international relations in ways that Smith had criticized.[41]

Burke's interest in matters economic went back as far as his student years in Dublin. In response to the moral and material degradation of the Irish peasantry, the nineteen-year-old lamented the absence of a commercially minded, improving landed class. "The Riches of a Nation are not to be estimated by the splendid appearances or luxurious lives of its Gentry," he declared; "it is the uniform Plenty diffused through a People, of which the meanest as well as greatest partake, that makes them happy, and the Nation powerful."[42] If this early sentiment of 1748 recalls the concerns of Smith's *Wealth of Nations*, so does much of Burke's subsequent writing on economic subjects. Toward the end of his life, Burke noted in his "Letter to a Noble Lord" (1796) that he had "made political economy an object of my humble studies, from my very early youth to near the end of my service in parliament, even before (at least to any knowledge of mine) it had employed the thoughts of speculative men in other parts of Europe. . . . Great and learned men thought my studies were not wholly thrown away, and deigned to communicate with me now and then on some particulars of their immortal works."[43] The reference was to Smith himself.[44] Both before the publication of Smith's "immortal work" and after, Burke was in substantial agreement with him on acquisitiveness as an engine of public utility, the importance of free international trade, and reliance on the market mechanism in economic affairs.

Burke emphasized the potential public benefits of what Smith called "the desire to improve our condition." In his "Tract on the Popery Laws," composed in the early 1760s, Burke wrote of "that laudable avarice, which every wise State has cherished as one of the first principles of its greatness."[45] Late in his life, when the question arose whether the British government ought to finance the war against revolutionary France by means of a forced loan or through government borrowing on the financial market, Burke penned this remarkably Smithian passage in favor of relying on the market:

> The love of lucre, though sometimes carried to a ridiculous, sometimes to a vicious excess, is the grand cause of prosperity to all States. In this natural, this reasonable, this powerful, this prolifick principle, it is for the satyrist to expose the ridiculous; it is for the moralist to censure the vicious; it is for the sympathetick heart to reprobate the hard and cruel; it is for the Judge to animadvert on the fraud, the extortion, and the oppression: but it is for the Statesman to employ it as he finds it, with all its concomitant excellencies, and with all its imperfections on its head. It is his part, in this case, as it is in all other cases, where he is to make use of the general energies of nature, to take them as he finds them.[46]

To "make use" of the energy provided by avarice and the love of lucre, Burke believed, meant to channel that energy into market relations, not only domestically but internationally. "It is the interest of the commercial world that wealth should be found everywhere,"[47] he wrote, but he recognized that most people, and certainly most merchants, found it natural to assume that trade was a zero-sum game. "I know that it is but too natural for us to see our own *certain* ruin in the *possible* prosperity of other people. It is hard to persuade us that every thing which is *got* by another is not *taken* from ourselves. . . . Trade is not a limited thing; as if the objects of mutual demand and consumption could not stretch beyond the bounds of our Jealousies."[48] Burke maintained that a liberal policy, which left each part of the empire free to make the best use of its resources, would promote the welfare of the empire as a whole. Commerce and manufacture in Burke's native Ireland were restricted for the sake of corresponding interests in England, and Irish manufactures and exports that might compete with British goods were prohibited by law. While sitting in Parliament as a representative of the mercantile town of Bristol, Burke fought for the elimination of such restraints on Irish trade. Burke's position was opposed by the merchants of Bristol and, despite a brilliant defense of his position in his *Two Letters from Mr. Burke to Gentlemen in the City of Bristol* (1778) and "Letter to Thomas Burgh" (1780), at the next election, Burke paid with his parliamentary seat for his commitment to free trade.[49]

Burke championed the market as the most effective means of economic growth in internal trade as well. In 1772, he moved the repeal by Parliament of statutes against forestalling, engrossing, and regrating, all terms for merchants who bought up supplies of foodstuffs with an eye to selling them at a profit in markets where grain was scarce. Fifteen years later, when an attempt was made to ban such practices once again, Burke rose again in opposition. He was convinced, as he told the agricultural expert Arthur Young, that laws intended to lower the price of agricultural goods actually led to a rise in their prices.[50]

Burke's most extensive defense of the free market as the most effective means of allocation came at the very end of his life. In 1794 and 1795, poor harvests led to a rise in food prices and to rural unrest. The result was a series of proposals for government intervention to lower the price of food or to raise the wages of laborers. In Speenhamland, not far from Burke's home at Beaconsfield, the justices of the peace initiated a policy of supplementing the market wages of the poor with funds raised by local taxation, determining need by the price of bread and by family size. In Suffolk, the justices decided that the wages of laborers should be adjusted in proportion to the price of grain.[51] In Parliament, a bill was proposed that would have established by law the minimum wages that employers would be required to pay.[52] It was under these conditions that Burke penned a memorandum to the prime minister, William Pitt, which was later published as "Thoughts and Details on Scarcity,"[53] a most forceful argument for allowing wages and prices to be determined by market forces.

Burke maintained that the functioning of the market for basic foodstuffs was poorly understood by most people, and those who traded in such goods were the objects of great prejudice. The role of government under these circumstances was to inform the public and, when that was inadequate, to protect traders in foodstuffs by providing "timely coercion" against those whose violence blocked the trading of grain.[54]

The argument of "Thoughts and Details" conveys Burke's conviction that one role of the intellectual in politics is to combat popular prejudices in matters economic, and to advise legislators to stand up to short-term political and moral pressures when they threaten long-term national economic interests. Experience indicated—and the study of political economy confirmed—that the market in grain and in labor had been good for the population at large. The standards of food consumption by the poor had risen in recent decades, he maintained, in part because workers worked more—as Smith had predicted they would—and in part because real wages had risen.[55]

"The statesman who should attempt to direct private people in what manner they ought to employ their capitals," Smith had written, "would not only load himself with a most unnecessary attention, but assume an authority which could safely be trusted, not only to no single person, but to no council or senate whatever, and which would nowhere be so dangerous as in the hands of a man who had folly and presumption enough to fancy himself fit to exercise it."[56] Burke described the proposals to set wages as just such folly and presumption. To have wages set by justices of the peace, rather than through negotiations between employers and employees, he maintained, amounted to placing crucial decisions about the agricultural economy into the hands of those who lacked either knowledge of or interest in agriculture. It was foolish for politicians to heed the cries of urban dwellers who demanded government intervention to lower food prices. Agriculture, Burke argued, ought to operate according to the common principles of commerce, namely that all involved should be expected to be on the lookout for the highest profit. It was the task of government to protect middlemen, such as the "factor, jobber, salesman, or speculator, in the markets of grain," from the ignorance and envy of farmers and consumers.[57]

Time and again in "Thoughts and Details on Scarcity," Burke argued that the foreseeable consequences of the proposed government interventions would be the opposite of their intended results—another example of the overreaching of abstract reason. The attempt by Parliament or by local justices of the peace to set higher wage rates, he claimed, would lead to a diminished demand for labor, or would increase the price of provisions by increasing labor costs. The net effect, in either case, would be different from the intentions of those who sought to alleviate the problems of the poor by such measures.[58] Raising wages beyond their market price would be of small and short-term gain to wage earners, Burke argued, and would come at the expense of profits to employers. The long-term effect would be to slow down or reverse the process of capital accumulation that made sustained wage growth possible. The result would be an equality of poverty.[59]

"Thoughts and Details on Scarcity" makes explicit a theme that was implicit in *The Wealth of Nations:* Popular incomprehension of the conditions that led to the improvement of the standard of living in a commercial society could pose a threat to the development of "universal opulence." Burke warned that the long-term beneficent effects of acquisitiveness channeled through the competitive market were counterintuitive and often poorly understood. It was the role of the intellectual, he thought, to warn politicians, who, under the influence of the ignorant poor or the misguided powerful, were tempted to tamper with the free market. Against those who objected to large-scale middlemen in the grain trade, Burke argued that their larger capital made it possible for them to operate with lower profit margins, and hence ultimately benefited the producer and consumer.[60] The poor, Burke complained, envy and resent the rich without understanding the function of the rich in accumulating capital, and so were apt to act against their own interests. "But the throats of the rich ought not to be cut, nor their magazines plundered; because, in their persons they are trustees for those who labour, and their hoards are the banking-houses of these latter. . . . When the poor rise to destroy the rich, they act as wisely for their own purposes as when they burn mills, and throw corn into the river, to make bread cheap."[61] Urban tradesmen and manufacturers who sought to influence government policy to lower the price of food "are in a state of utter ignorance of the means by which they are to be fed. . . . [O]n any thing that relates to agriculture, they are to be listened to with the same reverence which we pay to the dogmas of other ignorant and presumptuous men."[62] Burke concluded his memorandum with a warning against "breaking the laws of commerce, which are the laws of nature, and consequently the laws of God"—an instance of his propensity to embellish utilitarian arguments with a theological sheen.[63]

Here as elsewhere in his writings, Burke conveys a disposition more conservative than Smith's and even less inclined to government intervention in economic relations. In his *Reflections on the Revolution in France*, for example, Burke laments "the innumerable servile, degrading, unseemly, unmanly, and often most unwholesome and pestiferous occupations, to which by the social economy so many wretches are inevitably doomed." But he concludes that it is "generally pernicious to disturb the natural course of things, and to impede, in any degree, the great wheel of circulation which is turned by the strangely directed labour of these unhappy people."[64]

In the context of legislative attempts to alter the workings of the market, Burke pointed to the positive uses of avarice, the love of lucre, and to "the benign and wise disposer of all things, who obliges men, whether they will or not, in pursuing their own selfish interests, to connect the general good with their own individual success."[65] Yet Burke devoted his longest crusade against the largest and most powerful commercial enterprise of his day, the British East India Company, and against what he saw as the pernicious effects of avarice and the love of lucre when not properly restrained and channeled.

Burke and the British East India Company

In his *Vindication of Natural Society* Burke focused upon the dangers of unbridled intellectual "speculation," which he knew from his immersion in the writings of the French *philosophes* and their English fellow travelers. But Burke also knew the temptations of commercial speculation, from experiences closer at hand.

Burke was able to ponder the economic affairs of the nation in part because others took care of his household economy. Burke's will revealed that, from the time of his marriage in 1757, his business affairs had been managed by his wife, which left him free for other pursuits. Thanks to the patronage of Rockingham and other peers, and to generous gifts from friends such as Joshua Reynolds and the actor David Garrick, Burke was able to acquire and maintain a six-hundred-acre estate at Gregories, near Beaconsfield in Buckinghamshire.[66] Burke, in turn, shared his household with three men whose finances were so intertwined with his own that they sometimes referred to their "common purse." One was his brother, Richard Burke; the second was a close friend from London, William Burke; the third was Edmund Burke's son, Richard. In the mid-1760s, it was William Burke who acted as their common man of business and brought the trio of Burkes into contact with the East India Company.

The British East India Company was the largest commercial enterprise in Britain. Begun as a trading company, by the mid-eighteenth century the EIC was becoming a territorial power in India. From 1744 to 1761, the British company struggled with its French counterpart (in which Voltaire appears to have invested) for control of the south Indian coast, which ended in a complete British victory. Thereafter the company came to dominate large portions of India indirectly, through native rulers who won control with the aid of the company and its troops. In 1756 the EIC's settlement at Calcutta was captured and sacked by the nawab of Bengal. It was recaptured by Colonel Robert Clive, who substituted a nawab of his own choosing as ruler of the region. A decade later, when other Bengalese rulers resisted the demands the company made on its clients, Clive was sent back to India. As governor of Bengal, Clive took control of the "diwan," the territorial revenue traditionally collected by the Mughal emperor from the cultivators of the land through a host of intermediaries. He hoped that this extracted revenue would allow him to maintain order in Bengal, while providing a huge surplus to be sent to England.[67]

In England, Clive's move set off a wave of speculation in EIC stock. As young, talented, and relatively impecunious men, both Edmund and William had acquired seats in Parliament through the patronage of Rockingham's associate, Lord Verney. An Irish peer with an income of £10,000 a year, Verney was an influential landowner in Buckinghamshire. He saw the rising fortunes of the EIC as a way to make himself wealthier yet and to make his protégés William and Edmund Burke financially independent. Verney and William Burke formed a partnership in 1766 to buy a large chunk of East India stock on margin, though most of William's share was purchased with money loaned by Verney himself. In May 1767, the company raised its dividend for the second time in eight months, and the stock continued to rise. William Burke and Edmund's brother Richard, together with Verney and twenty others, now entered a new partnership to buy additional EIC stock from Dutch investors.[68]

Then, in 1769, the speculative bubble burst. News came from India that the Moslem commander Hyder Ali of Mysore was ravaging the Karnatic region of southern India, and reports of the massing of the French fleet off Mauritius led to a fear of French resurgence in the area. With Verney and the Burkes heavily invested in stock purchased on margin in London and Amsterdam, the value of EIC stock suddenly dropped by 13 percent. Verney was ruined, and he threatened to take all the Burkes down with him. It was Verney's understanding that he had made his loan to William and Edmund, so he sued Edmund in court for his share of the loan. Edmund, it appears, took no direct part in these speculative attempts to strike it rich, and seems to have had little grasp of their nature.[69] So the court decided, and Verney lost his lawsuit. But William Burke, who had lost his shirt, went off to India and later to the East Indies in unsuccessful attempts to recoup his fortune and repay his English creditors.

Edmund Burke's first encounter with the East India Company, then, brought home to him the possibility that the love of lucre could lead to economically irresponsible behavior. This personal experience set the stage for his great public campaign against the morally pernicious consequences to which avarice might lead when unrestrained by political limits or inherited cultural codes.

The boom and bust of East India Company stock led Parliament to intervene. The company was compelled to restrict its dividend and discourage speculative investment; it was also required to make an annual contribution of £400,000 to the Exchequer in return for its commercial privileges.[70] In 1772, the company, threatened by bankruptcy, turned to the government for a loan; in return, the company was subject to a new Regulating Act in 1773.[71] The same years, beginning with the election of 1768, saw the parliamentary rise of the "nabobs"—men who had made a fortune in India and returned to England to buy land and parliamentary seats in the "rotten boroughs," constituencies with only a handful of voters, controlled by whoever owned the land.[72] The Court and Parliament became ever more involved in the affairs of the East India Company,[73] while those who had made their fortunes through the company became ever better represented in Parliament.

As the place of Indian affairs in British political life grew, so did Burke's interest, and the more he learned of the company's doings in India, the more outraged he became. For he concluded that the employees of the EIC were driven by avarice into exploiting and impoverishing India, and that only Parliament could restrain their rapacity.

The intrinsic flaw with the EIC of his day, as Burke saw it, was not that it was a commercial company driven by the profit motive, but that it was *not* a commercial company in the ordinary sense: profit was not the motivating force of the company's activities. In his book-length "Ninth Report of the Select Committee on India" and in his extensive published speeches, he argued that the EIC was impoverishing India while moving toward bankruptcy—a phenomenon hard to reconcile with the profit motive. Burke's investigations led him to conclude that it was the company's managers and administrators who grew rich from the company's exactions from the Indian population. They made their fortunes oppressing the Indians while swindling the stockholders, then returned to England to buy controlling shares of the company in order to cover up their own misdeeds, fostering the practices that had given rise to their own wealth.[74]

The problem with the East India Company, Burke believed, was that while it was nominally a commercial company, it did not operate as a profit-making enterprise according to the laws of supply and demand. Instead, it used its military power to prevent the operation of a free market in India. The relations between Britain and India were not those of commerce, but of extraction based on the use of force, carried out by a nominally commercial corporation. The Indian goods that flowed into Britain, Burke showed, were not acquired through market transactions. The company used native rulers to extract the "territorial revenue" from the Indian population by force, then used that revenue to buy commodities in India and ship them to England.[75] The goods that the company imported from Britain to India were not primarily commodities purchased by the Indian population; they were military supplies for the armed forces of the EIC, together with goods consumed by Europeans residing in India. To increase its profits the company had engaged in an "endless Chain of Wars" to dominate ever larger portions of India, Burke charged. "At Home," he wrote, "these Measures were sometimes countenanced, sometimes winked at, sometimes censured, but always with an Acceptance of whatever Profit they afforded," because the government and the directors of the company both had an interest in increasing its revenue.[76]

The EIC, in other words, was in Burke's analysis managed as a vehicle for tribute. "The main Spring of the Commercial Machine, the *Principles of Profit and Loss*" had been abandoned.[77] The merchants and artisans of India were being devastated by the company's monopoly over commodities, its fixing of prices, and its use of forced labor in the textile industry. The policy of the EIC, Burke wrote, ensured that India would be "radically and irretrievably ruined."[78]

Yet despite its use of violence in support of avarice, the EIC remained unprofitable, Burke charged, not least because the servants of the company used it to trade on their own, making private fortunes in the process.[79] But the very wealth accumulated by the employees of the EIC made it difficult to reform the company, for wealth was translated into political influence. "He that goes out an insignificant boy, in a few years returns a great Nabob. . . . One of these gentlemen, suppose, returns hither, loaded with odium and with riches. . . . That man's whole fortune, half a million perhaps, becomes an instrument of influence . . . and the influx of fortunes which stand in need of this protection is continual. It works both ways; it influences the delinquent, and it may corrupt the minister."[80] Burke's prime example of this process was Paul Benfield, the archetype of the new nabobs who used corrupt means to enrich themselves in India, then used their wealth to corrupt the British government itself by buying their way into Parliament.

The son of a land surveyor, with little formal education, Benfield first went to India as an architect in 1763 at age twenty-two, under the patronage of one of the company's directors. He began as a "writer," a minor bureaucratic post within the company, soon becoming a private merchant and then a banker, in which capacity he lent funds to the Raja of Tanjore to enable him to fend off an attack on his realm in 1771. Benfield then began to provide similar services to the raja's enemy, the Nawab of the Karnatic, who made use of the funds he borrowed from Benfield to conquer Tanjore. Benfield gathered funds from wealthy Indian merchants, from British officers stationed in India, and from EIC officials. These funds were lent at very high interest to the nawab, who could borrow with confidence that the EIC would not interfere with him, since the fortunes of some of its officials had been loaned to him through Benfield. Following his victory, the nawab assigned much of the tax revenue of Tanjore to Benfield, in order to repay the loans that had allowed him to conquer the territory. When the newly appointed governor of Madras, Lord Pigot, restored Tanjore to the raja in 1776, Benfield became one of the moving spirits in a plot that led to the removal and arrest of Pigot, who died in captivity a year later. Recalled by the directors of EIC to Britain in 1779 to answer for his role in the Pigot affair, Benfield used part of the fortune he had acquired in India to buy himself a seat in Parliament and to establish connections with the governments of Lord North and then of Pitt.[81]

In hot pursuit of Benfield, Burke went so far as to acquire £1,000 worth of EIC stock, the minimum required for a vote in the company's governing Court of Proprietors. At its meeting of January 1781, Burke accused Benfield not only of having violated the order of the company's directors, but also of harming the revenues of the company, and "the trade, prosperity, and safety" of the population of Madras. The immense magnitude of the sums that Benfield claimed were due to him for loans to the nawab could only have been acquired by unlawful means, Burke charged. The board of the EIC decided to put Benfield's fate to a vote of its shareholders. The government of Lord North urged its supporters to vote in favor of Benfield. As a result, a majority voted to reinstate Benfield and send him back to India.[82]

Defeated in his attempt to eliminate the exploitative practices of a nominally private corporation deeply entwined with the government,

Burke turned to parliamentary inquiry as a means of reform. He joined the newly created Select Committee of the House on Bengal, authoring its most significant document, the famous "Ninth Report," as well as its "Eleventh Report" of November 1783. That same month, Burke's ally, Charles James Fox, introduced his "East India Bill," the principles of which came from Burke himself.[83] The bill sought to bring the company under government supervision by placing ultimate control in the hands of a commission appointed by Parliament. In his "Speech on Fox's India Bill," Burke argued that the company was no longer controlled by investors in any conventional sense. Normal investors, interested primarily in their dividends, would be concerned with the peculations of the company's servants. "Such a body would not easily have left their trade as a spoil to the avarice of those who received their wages. But now things are totally reversed," he asserted. Shares of the company were purchased so that shareholders or those close to them could be sent off to make "an obnoxious fortune in India"; in other cases shareholders became the beneficiaries of patronage from those who had already made such fortunes.[84] The EIC, he concluded, had thus become utterly incorrigible, and ought to have power removed from its hands. Burke's legislative proposals redefined the relationship between the British state and the global enterprise it had fostered, asserting the priority of human rights over commercial rights. The bill was passed by the Commons, but was defeated in the Lords thanks to pressure from the Crown.

In 1784 Pitt asked the king to dissolve Parliament, and the resulting elections were a disaster for Burke's parliamentary allies. The EIC was active in the campaign against Burke and his friends, and a press campaign paid for in good part by Paul Benfield portrayed Burke's East India bill as aimed at getting the loot of India into the hands of the dominant coalition.[85] When the election was over, at least fifty "company men" had been elected, seventeen of them for the first time, including Benfield.[86] At least two other MPs owed their seats directly to Benfield's patronage, though Burke credited him with controlling eight seats. That influence was used to shape the Pitt government's India policy. Benfield became a director of the EIC and an alderman of London.

Back in India, the nawab, his territory shattered by the war against Mysore, found himself unable to pay off his debt to Benfield's consortium. Among Pitt's supporters in the Commons sat seventeen of the nawab's creditors. The Board of Control of the EIC, dominated by Pitt's appointees, now decreed that the debts to the nawab's creditors should be paid in full out of the revenues that the company collected from the

Indian population. When Burke's party asked for the relevant documents, the request for information was denied.[87] It was under these circumstances that, in 1785, Burke rose to deliver his "Speech on the Nabob of Arcot's Debts," a four-hour-long performance.

Burke charged that the debts had arisen primarily through corrupt bargains between the nawab and the Europeans, headed by Benfield; that the decision to pay the debt out of EIC funds represented a corrupt deal between Pitt and the creditors who had used their wealth to help him win the elections of 1784; and that the burden of these corrupt practices would fall on the impoverished peasantry of the Karnatic, from whom it would be squeezed in "territorial revenue." He provided details on how company servants conspired with the nawab to increase their own fortunes. Circumventing EIC regulations, they had encouraged the nawab to conquer additional territory and had provided him with loans to raise armies provisioned by EIC.[88] Burke deemed their scheme a "magnificent plan of universal plunder, worthy of the heroic avarice of the projectors."[89] The annual interest on the nawab's debts, Burke pointed out, amounted to more than double the entire annual dividend of the EIC![90] The nawab had no assets other than his power over his impoverished subjects, from whom the debt was to be collected. "It is therefore not from treasuries and mines," Burke declaimed, "but from the food of your unpaid armies, from the blood withheld from the veins, and whipt out of the backs of the most miserable of men, that we are to pamper extortion, usury, and peculation, under the false names of debtors and creditors of state."[91]

The result, in Burke's words, was to transfer "public revenues to the private emolument of certain servants of the East India Company, without the enquiry into the origin and justice of their claims."[92] The unwillingness of the government to furnish information was evidence of the beginnings of "a grand revolution," a revolution without principle, driven by "a corrupt, private interest . . . set up in direct opposition to the necessities of the nation." Benfield, Burke concluded sarcastically, was typical of "the new and pure aristocracy" being created by Pitt "as the support of the crown and constitution" against the "natural interests of this kingdom" represented by the Rockingham Whigs.[93]

Delivered to a parliamentary audience made up in good part of this new elite, Burke's speech was received with great hostility.[94] But with an eye to publicizing his case, he published the speech, along with supporting documents. Shortly thereafter, Burke initiated his long crusade to impeach the former governor-general of Bengal, Warren Hastings, before the House of Lords. At a time when the reform of the EIC was a low priority for the Rockingham Whigs, Burke's crusade left him increasingly marginalized within Parliament.[95] Though the impeachment campaign was ultimately unsuccessful, it went on for almost a decade and provided Burke with another public forum in which to expose the company's depredations. Through these actions, Burke more than anyone else was responsible for making the EIC accountable for its treatment of the Indian population, and for bringing to an end the system of exaction and exploitation that had characterized the company in its earlier phase.[96]

A recurrent theme of Burke's speeches and writings on Indian affairs was that a great and venerable civilization was being destroyed by a group of moneylenders who were motivated by avarice unrestrained by political or cultural controls. India, he wrote, was inhabited by "a people for ages civilized and cultivated; cultivated by all the arts of polished life, whilst we were yet in the woods." It had its own princes, "an ancient and venerable priesthood, the depository of their laws, learning, and history, the guides of the people whilst living, and their consolation in death," as well as "a nobility of great antiquity and renown."[97] This civilization was being devastated by Britons whose greed was unrestrained by civilized codes. "Young men (boys almost) govern there," Burke declared. "Animated with all the avarice of age, and with all the impetuosity of youth, they roll in one after another. . . ."[98] This image, of a new elite unsocialized into the cultural legacy of the nation and acquiring political power on the basis of dubiously acquired wealth, was to recur in Burke's analysis of the French Revolution.

Burke's language repeatedly connected the excesses of avarice with sexual excess, an association that recalled the traditional Christian link between the sins of avarice (*avaritia*) and lechery (*luxuria*).[99] He depicted the exorbitant interest that the EIC's servants sought from the public purse to pay off the Nawab of Arcot's debts as "the unbridled debauchery and licentious lewdness of usury and distortion." The nawab himself, now without military or political substance, was a tool in the hands of Benfield and his supporters, "carefully kept alive as an independent and sovereign power for the purpose of rapine and distortion."[100]

It was against the background of this decade-long investigation into the destructive effects of unbridled avarice on the venerable civilization of India that Burke came to analyze the revolution that broke out in France in 1789.

Burke's Analysis of the French Revolution

In November of 1790 Burke published a work of contemporary polemic on which he had labored for almost a year, *Reflections on the Revolution in France*. The book was nominally a letter to a young French correspondent as well as a response to a sermon by the Reverend Richard Price, a Unitarian minister and writer on philosophical, mathematical, and political subjects who had delivered a sermon praising the French Revolution. After his extended crusade against the corrupting effects of the East India Company, Burke was better known as a critic than as a defender of the existing British administration. With the coming of the revolution in France, and in the face of widespread support for the revolution within the British intelligentsia and within his own party, he devoted himself to a critique of the theory and practice of the French revolutionaries, and to a principled defense of British institutions. At the conclusion of the *Reflections,* he explained his altered stance as a change of emphasis prompted by changing circumstances but reflecting a basic consistency.[101] In offering a critical analysis of the origins and dynamics of the revolution and a pessimistic prognosis of its likely course, Burke challenged the dominant prorevolutionary sentiment among the makers of British public opinion.

Burke attributed the revolution in France to the combined influence of men of letters and financiers of government debt, who together were subverting the intellectual and institutional basis of a civilized society of manners. By stripping away the veil of culture, and by undermining the traditional institutions of the aristocracy and the Church that had supported that veil, Burke argued, the intellectual and financial speculators were leading France into disaster. The result, he feared, would be a return of man to his "natural" state, a state not elevated and benign, but brutish and barbaric.

The question of public revenue looms large in Burke's analysis, as it did in the revolution itself. From its earliest meetings, the revolutionary National Assembly was faced with the problem of France's enormous debts. In September, a dramatic suggestion was advanced by Dupont, the deputy for Nemours and a close associate of Turgot and the Physiocrats. Dupont proposed that the government begin collecting the revenues on Church property, while at the same time taking responsibility for Church expenses.[102] On November 2, 1789, the

Assembly approved a bill that declared that "all ecclesiastical properties are at the disposal of the Nation, which undertakes to provide in an appropriate manner funds to meet the expenses of the Church, stipends for its ministers, and relief for the poor." These properties were to provide the backing for a new form of government paper, the "*assignat*," which the revolutionary government used to pay the holders of government debt.

The principal opponent of the proposal to expropriate the property of the Church was the king's chaplain, the abbé Maury. "To reestablish credit, you have proposed putting the capitalists in place of the holders of benefices, and the holders of benefices in place of the capitalists," he declared. By using the Church's property to pay off the state's debts, he charged, the Assembly was transferring the Church's legacy to the holders of state debt (*créanciers*), many of whom (his listeners knew) were foreigners.[103] And in expropriating the Church's holdings, Maury claimed, the Assembly was destroying the basic right of property.

Burke, who appears to have consulted the published proceedings of the National Assembly, adopted this analysis, and it figures centrally in his characterization of the revolution.[104] The fact that the Assembly had nullified all laws of the old royal government except for the public debt could only be explained, he thought, by "the description of the persons to whom it [the debt] was engaged."[105] Unlike the British Parliament, which was composed in good part of the "natural landed interest of the country," the French National Assembly was disproportionately made up of minor lawyers and "the dealers in stocks and funds, who must be eager, at any expence, to change their ideal paper wealth for the more solid substance of land."[106] By compelling the use of the *assignats* in commerce, the Assembly had forced all Frenchmen to accept "the symbols of their speculations on a projected sale of their plunder."[107] The rate at which Church lands were sold would affect the price at which the *assignats* were traded. Thus land, once a basis of social stability, would be transformed by "the spirit of money-jobbing and speculation."[108] The value of land, like the value of the new paper currency, would become unstable and subject to the whims of financial speculators.[109] It was, he wrote, as if "the Jews in Change Alley" had acquired "a mortgage on the revenues belonging to the see of Canterbury."[110]

In reconstructing Burke's intentions, it is worth comparing his language here with his policy statements elsewhere. From the evidence of Burke's "Third Letter on a Regicide Peace," written some six years later, we see that he had no principled objections to high interest ("usury") or to financing the public debt through the money market ("stockjobbing").[111] Burke's frequent verbal linkage of the holders of public debt to the Jews—a linguistic identification heightened by the fact that his antagonist, Richard Price, preached at a chapel in the "Old Jewry" and was an expert on compound interest—is meant to suggest that the expropriation of Church lands had strengthened the power of social and cultural outsiders. He stressed that in France, power had fallen into the hands of those who owned the public debt, and that these men were incapable of governing.

Burke's contention was based upon his own sociology of knowledge. There was a mentality inherent in the way of life of each class, Burke thought, and the mentality that led to success in finance was, in isolation, disastrous for government. "The monied interest is in its nature more ready for any adventure; and its possessors more disposed to new enterprizes of any kind. Being of a recent acquisition, it falls in more naturally with any novelties. It is therefore the kind of wealth which will be resorted to by all who wish for change."[112]

Men of finance, according to Burke, shared this propensity to innovation with "a new description of men . . . the political Men of Letters" with whom they had become allied.[113] These political men of letters, Burke wrote, sought to increase their influence through a variety of strategies, from cultivating despots such as Frederick II of Prussia (an allusion to Voltaire) to forging an alliance with the new monied men. Through their connections, "they carefully occupied all the avenues to opinion."[114] Politicized French intellectuals, Burke maintained, were motivated by the desire to destroy the Christian religion, and he predicted, quite accurately, that they would soon attempt to eliminate the established Church entirely.[115] Burke noted that of all the obligations of the previous government, it was holders of the debt that were to be paid off, while of all the possible sources of property that might have been nationalized by the new regime, it was that of the Church which was expropriated. These priorities, Burke claimed, reflected the anti-Christian animus of the political men of letters, together with the interest of money men in collecting their loans to the previous government.

In contrast to the composition of the French National Assembly, Burke argued that the governing bodies of the state ought to include both men of "ability" inclined to innovation, and their opposite—men of inherited large-scale property, who tended toward conservatism. Burke's argument in favor of the representation in government of these men of hereditary wealth was based not on their inherent superiority or merit, but on grounds of public utility. The preservation of property, he reasoned, was among the most important functions of government, because the desire for the transgenerational transfer of familial wealth was crucial to social order. "The power of perpetuating our property in our families is one of the most valuable and interesting circumstances belonging to it, and that which tends the most to the perpetuation of society itself. It makes our weakness subservient to our virtue; it grafts benevolence even upon avarice." One key role of government was therefore to secure property from the envy and resentment of those who owned less. Those least inclined to use government to redistribute wealth in this manner were men of large-scale inherited property, who thus formed "a natural rampart about the lesser properties in all their gradations" and acted as "the ballast in the vessel of the commonwealth."[116]

In his early *Vindication of Natural Society*, Burke had ridiculed the propensity of some enlightened intellectuals to judge institutions by abstract principles, and had insisted that the attempt to do so would delegitimate all existing institutions without being able to create better ones in their place. His critical initial response to news of the revolution in France reflected these earlier assumptions, which served as the leitmotif of his analysis. *Reflections on the Revolution in France* is a critique of the revolutionary mentality that attempts to create entirely new structures on the basis of rational, abstract principles, a mentality that Burke contrasted unfavorably to his own conception of legitimate reform as building upon existing, historical institutions.

To Burke, it seemed that the French intelligentsia had, in 1788 and 1789, done everything he had warned against three decades earlier. They had engaged in a wholesale critique of all the premises of their major institutions, and they had done so publicly. Although their critique was radically exaggerated, Burke thought, its effectiveness did not depend on its accuracy. For, as Burke had noted in the *Vindication*, even a mistaken critique of existing institutions could have negative consequences by leading to their delegitimation in weak minds. Now the French would live with the results of the fairyland of philosophy, results that they had not anticipated, but that he could. The French men of letters had delegitimated the monarchy, the aristocracy, and the taxing powers of the state in the eyes of the larger public.[117] As a result, they were left with a government drained of authority and no longer capable of collecting taxes or conducting commerce. The result, he predicted, would be ongoing instability and the threat of anarchy, which would be controlled only by the massive use of force, and eventually, military rule.[118] Burke made these predictions long before the execution of Louis XVI, the Terror, the massacre of thousands of civilians in the Vendée, or the rise of Napoleon.

The task of reform, Burke maintained, could not be based upon a priori or abstract reasoning about human rights and the institutions that would guarantee them. The science of reform was an "experimental science" that ought to be based on experience and proceed cautiously. It was in this context that Burke laid out the arguments for caution in reform, which would make *Reflections on the Revolution in France* an arsenal of conservative thought. Burke pointed out the difficulty of anticipating the consequences of a particular reform, especially because institutions had functions that were not evident, and became apparent only when the institution was disrupted and its positive functions lost.[119] Societies are complex entities, he stressed, answering, however imperfectly, a multiplicity of needs, and their institutions are interconnected in ways not always apparent. Most important, perhaps, innovation must be slow because a good deal of the effectiveness of institutions comes from the reverence that develops for them over time. It is this reverence that creates voluntary submission to laws and mores, in the absence of which submission must depend either on rational reflection (an undependable source, as Burke had noted in his *Vindication of Natural Society*) or on the threat of force.[120] To destroy inherited institutions is therefore irresponsible, he argued, especially since new institutions, no matter how well conceived, cannot command the same degree of loyalty and commitment as old institutions rooted in experience.[121]

For Burke, almost everything that makes life worthwhile is a result of society, its inherited codes, knowledge, and institutions. These goods are fragile, and when they are destroyed, the result is human misery. "The restraints on men, as well as their liberties, are to be reckoned among their rights," Burke wrote. Among the greatest of men's needs, according to Burke, was the need for society and government to provide "a sufficient restraint upon their passions."[122] As far back as his *Vindication of Natural Society*, Burke had argued that the destruction of inherited institutions and cultural practices would result not in natural harmony, but in barbarism. For Burke, as for Adam Smith, man is preeminently social man, who realizes himself morally only under the tutelage of society. In *The Theory of Moral Sentiments*, Smith described the process of becoming moral as a social process.[123] In his unpublished *Lectures on Jurisprudence*, Smith provided an account of the institutionalization of moral standards as a historical process.[124] That theme was pursued at greater length in the intervening years by the Scottish historians William Robertson and John Millar. For them, "chivalry" denoted a revolution in manners within the feudal world, which restrained the will of barbarian warriors toward the weak, toward the female sex, and toward one another. It was a revolution in which men of power came to subordinate themselves, in part at least, to the moral demands of Christianity as expressed in canon law and as interpreted by men of learning. The result was a society in which the will of the powerful was restrained by cultural codes of conduct, which had their origin in the Church and were reinforced by it.[125] Burke drew upon a theme in Montesquieu and these historians of the Scottish Enlightenment in stressing what he called "the spirit of our old manners and opinions."[126]

Burke now returned to his early metaphor of culture as a "veil," a fabric of understandings that hides the direct object of the natural passions. Culture, in other words, is a means of sublimation, of diverting the passions to more elevated goals, and of creating restrictions on the expression of the passions of domination and self-gratification. The most important metaphor in the *Reflections* is that of veiling and drapery, which functions as an implicit attack on the metaphors of light and transparency so dominant in the discourse of the age.[127] Burke ridicules the "great acquisitions of light" of the Enlightenment, the "new conquering empire of light and reason" and of "naked reason"— the last perhaps a reference to a nude statue of Voltaire, commissioned by a group of *philosophes* from the sculptor Pigalle at the suggestion of Diderot.[128]

For Burke, the revolution's attack on the institutional bases of the Church and the aristocracy threatened to destroy the "manners" on which a decent commercial society depended. Having spent over a decade lamenting the impact upon the population of India of domination by young Britons whose avarice was unrestrained by either the laws or the cultural codes of their native land, he now interpreted the French Revolution through this prism. The destruction of the power of the aristocracy and of the economic basis of the institutional influence of the Church, he claimed, would unleash avarice and the will to exploit others for one's own pleasure—to "rapine" and to "rape." The words were not only related etymologically: in Burke's day "rape" meant the seizure both of property and of the object of sexual desire.

A central scene in the *Reflections*, in which Burke describes the invasion of the queen's bedchamber by a revolutionary mob, must be understood in this context. We can now unpack Burke's famous lament that the attack of the mob on the queen's bedchamber was evidence that the "age of chivalry is gone.—That of sophisters, oeconomists, and calculators, has succeeded; and the glory of Europe is extinguished for ever." It was the "mixed system of opinion and sentiment," Burke claimed, with its origins in medieval chivalry, which had "without force, or opposition . . . subdued the fierceness of pride and power" and allowed "domination . . . to be subdued by manners."[129] It was this cultural heritage, he maintained, that gave modern European civilization a moral advantage over the civilizations of Asia and of the ancient world. Burke focused on the invasion of the bedchamber of the Queen of France, Marie Antoinette, because of her sex and her rank. The fact that even the most distinguished woman in France was open to assault, he suggests, is evidence that inherited cultural codes were eroding, and that this erosion marked a descent into barbarism.[130]

"Sophisters" is Burke's term of opprobrium for the French *philosophes*, especially Voltaire and Rousseau; the reference to "oeconomists" is probably meant to recall the Physiocrats in general and Turgot in particular, whose disciple Dupont de Nemours had suggested the nationalization of Church property; and the term "calculators" may allude to the Reverend Richard Price, who had written works on actuarial science and on the calculation of debt. Burke's specific referents are less important than his general message, namely that those who believe that commerce is a civilizing agent forget that commercial society itself depends upon institutions and modes of behavior that have their origin outside of commerce. The mentality of self-interest, unrestrained by cultural codes transmitted and enforced by precommercial institutions, threatens to degenerate into a condition of material and sexual assault—of rapine and rape. For Burke, the influence of "calculators" who portray all human relations in terms of individual profit and loss, together with that of sophisters who eliminate the hold of past cultural codes that restrain individual conduct, is to create an invitation to use one another for direct individual gratification. To use later terms that perfectly capture Burke's meaning: by delegitimating culture, the *philosophes* have opened the door to massive desublimation.

According to Burke, the effect of the *philosophes'* relentless critique of inherited beliefs and institutions is not only to delegitimate all existing political authority, it is to tear away the veil of culture that leads men to restrain themselves, and so to leave them open to act on their animal urges:

> All the pleasing illusions, which made power gentle, and obedience liberal . . . are to be dissolved by this new conquering empire of light and reason. All the decent drapery of life is to be rudely torn off. All the superadded ideas, furnished from the wardrobe of a moral imagination, which the heart owns, and the understanding ratifies, as necessary to

cover the defects of our naked shivering nature, and to raise
it to dignity in our own estimation, are to be exploded as
ridiculous, absurd, and antiquated fashion. On this scheme
of things, a king is but a man; a queen is but a woman; a
woman is but an animal; and an animal not of the highest
order. All homage paid to the sex in general as such, and
without distinct views, is to be regarded as romance and
folly. . . . On the scheme of this barbarous philosophy . . .
laws are to be supported only by their own terrors, and by
the concern, which each individual may find in them, from
his own private speculations, or can spare to them from his
own private interests. In the groves of *their* academy, at the
end of every vista, you see nothing but the gallows. Nothing
is left which engages the affections on the part of the commonwealth.[131]

Burke valued both commerce and intellectuals—"men of learning."
His argument in the *Reflections* was that the French financiers and
political intellectuals were cutting away the cultural and institutional
supports upon which modern commerce and learning rested. The
patronage of the nobility and the profession of the clergy, he argued,
had kept classical learning alive in the Middle Ages. That learning had
been developed by modern men of letters in a way that had been beneficial to both religion and government. "Learning paid back what it
received to nobility and to priesthood; and paid it with usury, by
enlarging their ideas and by furnishing their minds."[132] The problem,
as Burke saw it, was that the new men of letters were overstepping
their institutional bounds. Religion was also indispensable in keeping
men moral. Like many other thinkers before and after him, Burke
maintained that belief in divine reward and punishment, whether or
not philosophically tenable, provided most men and women with a
necessary motive for moral behavior.[133] By freeing themselves from the
patronage of the nobility and by turning their intellectual armor
against the Church, the intellectuals were unwittingly preparing the
way for their own destruction at the hands of the mob. "Happy if learning, not debauched by ambition, had been satisfied to continue the
instructor, and not aspired to be the master! Along with its natural pro-
tectors and guardians, learning will be cast into the mire, and trodden
down under the hoofs of a swinish multitude."[134] The proper role of
intellectuals was as instructors of the rulers—not so different from
Burke's role, or Smith's.

Men of finance, like men of letters, were cutting off the branches on which they sat, Burke warned. For by contributing to the destruction of the nobility and the clergy, they were unwittingly sapping the institutional sources of "manners," the veil of culture that led to the self-restraint on which the social stability of commercial society depended. "If, as I suspect, modern letters owe more than they are always willing to own to ancient manners, so do other interests which we value.... Even commerce, and trade, and manufacture, the gods of our oeconomical politicians, are themselves perhaps but creatures; are themselves certainly but effects, which, as first causes, we choose to worship. They certainly grew under the same shade in which learning flourished. They too may decay with their natural protecting principles."[135] It was characteristic of men of finance, Burke thought, to overlook the role of institutions like the church, which provided "the foundations of public order."[136]

The revolution, for Burke, marked the triumph of "the spirit of ambition, now for the first time connected with the spirit of speculation."[137] In the *Reflections*, and more explicitly in his later writings, Burke suggested that it took an intellectual like himself to understand the mentality and motivations of the intellectuals who played so prominent a role in the French Revolution. In "Letter to a Noble Lord" (1796), Burke writes that he is "better able to enter into the character of this description of men than the noble Duke can be.... I can form a tolerable estimate of what is likely to happen from a character, chiefly dependent for fame and fortune, on knowledge and talent, as well in its morbid and perverted state, as in that which is sound and natural."[138] It was this empathic understanding that allowed him to predict a far more radical trajectory of developments than most members of the British establishment could imagine. The new political men of letters, freed from the patronage of the aristocracy and the church, had a particular mentality that was prone to imprudence, Burke contended. Without a stake in the existing social order (or without an *awareness* of their stake in that order), intellectuals in power were disposed to treat the country as an object for intellectual experimentation. "In these gentlemen there is nothing of the tender parental solicitude which fears to cut up the infant for the sake of an experiment,"[139] he wrote in the *Reflections*. He continued the metaphor in his "Letter to a Noble Lord": "These philosophers are fanatics; independent of any interest, which if it operated alone would make them much more tractable, they are carried with such an headlong rage towards every desperate trial, that they would sacrifice the whole human race to the slightest of their experiments."[140] Regarding humanity as a fit object for experiment in order to prove their a priori theories, they are willing to disregard the short-term suffering of their victims on the grounds that it will lead to long-term improvement. "Nothing can be conceived more hard than the heart of a thorough-bred metaphysician," Burke wrote. "These philosophers consider men in their experiments, no more than they do mice in an air pump."[141]

If, in Burke's analysis, the revolution in its early stages was driven by men of financial and intellectual speculation, the destruction of the political and religious order led to the radicalization of the revolution as politicized intellectuals came to dominate men of property. After jettisoning the ballast first of landed gentlemen and then of the new monied financiers, the state was left in the hands of men of letters who had nothing to lose but their theories, and who for the first time mobilized society as a whole for the purpose of spreading their "armed doctrine." Their lack of a rooted profession made them particularly dangerous. France, he wrote in 1796, was controlled by a government in which "property is in complete subjection, and where nothing rules but the mind of desperate men. . . . They have every thing to gain, and they have nothing to lose. They have a boundless inheritance in hope; and there is no medium for them, betwixt the highest elevation, and death with infamy. Never can they who from the miserable servitude of the desk have been raised to Empire, again submit to the bondage of a starving bureau, or the profit of copying music, or writing plaidoyers by the sheet."[142]

For Burke, the French Revolution represented an upset of the balance between the sluggish, prudential influence of inherited, landed wealth and status on one hand, and the dynamic, innovating influence of men of financial and intellectual speculation on the other. By putting the boot to the institutional bases of the aristocracy and the established church, the financiers and intellectuals of the revolutionary government had kicked away the supports of both property and culture.

The Noncontractual Basis of Commercial Society

Burke not only insisted upon the noncommercial bases of commercial society, he also underscored the limits of the commercial mentality in understanding the nature of social and political obligation. The central metaphor of society as a contract, Burke believed, was fundamentally misleading. For a contract was, in its essence, a voluntary agreement, entered into willingly, and subject to dissolution by the voluntary withdrawal of any of the parties. But some of our most profound obligations and duties, Burke maintained, were not of this sort. "The state ought not to be considered as nothing better than a partnership agreement in a trade of pepper and coffee, callico or tobacco, or some other such low concern, to be taken up for a little temporary interest, and to be dissolved by the fancy of the parties," he wrote in his *Reflections*. The state was an essential element of social order, and men needed social order and inherited culture in order to develop their capacities. "As the ends of such a partnership cannot be obtained in many generations, it becomes a partnership not only between those who are living, but between those who are living, those who are dead, and those who are to be born."[143] Because the dissolution of the social order would mean the end of those social institutions through which men's passions are guided, restrained, and perfected, the individual has no right to opt out of the "social contract" with the state. "Men without their choice derive benefits from that association; without their choice they are subjected to duties in consequence of these benefits; and without their choice they enter into a virtual obligation as binding as any that is actual."[144]

This noncontractual basis of commercial society, Burke wrote, was evident in other social relations as well. Marriage was a matter of choice, but the duties attendant upon marriage were not. Parents and children were bound by duties that were involuntary.[145] While liberalism was to emphasize the voluntary basis of social order, Burke's deflation of the notion that binding duties and obligations can only be the result of voluntary agreement would become a characteristic conservative theme.

In the generations after Burke, even some of those who found his description of the actual practice of the aristocracy and the Church idealized and implausible (as they certainly were) were to agree on the need for institutions that preserved the culture of the past and offered guidance in the present. That guidance included reminders of the limits of the commercial mentality and the hazards of regarding choice as an end in itself. They recognized that the aristocracy was an unreliable sponsor of intellectual activity, and found the Church too theologically constraining for the cultural message they sought to impart. Some, such as Coleridge or Matthew Arnold, would look to the state itself to provide an institutional home to men of letters, and to provide a counterweight to an overly commercial view of human capacities and obligations.[146]

But it was in the work of Hegel that the model of contract as the paradigm of human relations would find its most sophisticated critique, and the need for institutional safeguards of the noncommercial prerequisites of commercial society its most thorough elaboration.

CHAPTER SIX

HEGEL:
A LIFE WORTH CHOOSING

Feeling at Home in the Modern World

In 1820, at the age of fifty, Georg Wilhelm Friedrich Hegel published his *Philosophy of Right* (*Grundlinien der Philosophie des Rechts*). That book, together with the accompanying lectures that he gave to students, presents a comprehensive attempt to explain the place of the market in history and its significance for mankind. For Hegel, the market was the central and most distinctive feature of the modern world, a world he affirmed and sought to explain to his contemporaries. His understanding of the market reflects his reading of *The Wealth of Nations*, and draws together strands of analysis that we have seen in Voltaire, Möser, and Burke.

Today we are in some ways better equipped than ever before to recapture Hegel's views on the market. For the book in which he explored the theme most directly, *The Philosophy of Right*, was in many respects an abstract of ideas that were expressed more fully, concretely, and accessibly in his lectures to students. Hegel began lecturing on the subject matter of the book while he was a professor in Heidelberg, in 1817–1818; when he moved to Berlin a year later, he lectured on it again.[1] In the autumn of 1820 he published his book, largely to aid his students in following his lectures, and he continued the lecture series annually through 1825. Fortunately, Hegel spoke slowly, and students copied down virtually every word. Excerpts and paraphrases of some of these lecture notes were published in the decade after his death in 1831. But only in recent years have scholars transcribed and published these notes in their entirety, which now present us with a much fuller picture of Hegel's views.[2]

That Hegel devoted so much of his attention to the market, and that his attitude toward it was primarily affirmative, may come as a surprise to those who identify Hegel with philosophical abstraction and with the deification of the state. But beneath his often recondite and idiosyncratic vocabulary lies a focus on *institutions*. In fact, it is in his writings that the study of institutions and their historical development becomes central to formal philosophy. For not only did Hegel believe that history had to be understood philosophically, he also thought that philosophy could only be understood historically. And by historically he meant in relationship not only to the great texts of the past, but to the past's social and political institutions. Hegel's reputation as a philosopher of the state makes it difficult for those who assume a necessary antagonism between state and market to appreciate the positive role of the market in Hegel's interpretation of the modern world.[3] But the perspective changes if Hegel is put in the context of his time. Then we see why it made sense to believe that only a powerful state could create the preconditions for the market and for a liberal society. And when we reconstruct Hegel's analysis of the defects of a market-oriented society, we see why it was plausible for him to believe that the state was required to remedy those defects.[4]

Hegel's *Philosophy of Right* is in some ways a synthesis of the concerns of all three of Smith's books. The word "right" in the title, as Hegel uses it, goes far beyond civil law to include morality, institutional analysis, and world history.[5] Hegel draws directly on *The Wealth of Nations* in explaining how, in a market economy, self-interest can create a system of interdependence and lead to the common welfare. As in *The Theory of Moral Sentiments*, Hegel is interested in the way in which human character is formed by institutional settings. And like Smith in his *Lectures on Jurisprudence*, Hegel is vitally concerned with the role of the family and the law in the institutional order of the modern world. But, as in Burke's *Reflections on the Revolution in France*, Hegel emphasizes that the contractual model of human relations is not appropriate for understanding all relationships in the modern world.[6] Hegel shares Burke's fear that those who focus myopically on liberty may lose sight of its institutional and moral preconditions, and that the self-interested mentality of "calculators," if it comes to dominate all areas of life, will threaten the family and the state.[7]

Hegel believed that the experience of the French Revolution demonstrated that unless modern men rationally understood the institutions they most valued and their continuity with the past, they would lack loyalty toward those institutions. Burke was content to discover the hidden rationality of historically developed institutions, yet loath to expose those institutions to analysis based on rational first principles. Hegel, one might say, is a Burke without veils. He thought that it was characteristic of the modern mentality to demand that men give their assent to institutions they could affirm, and to do so because they understood how those institutions promoted their own well-being. Hegel insisted that institutions were historically legitimate only when they were based upon rational principles. That meant condemning some institutions as superannuated, but affirming others by explaining how they functioned to create both freedom and personal purpose.

Hegel looked forward to a society that allowed for far more individuality and more choice than the traditional society that Möser had defended a generation earlier. Yet like Möser, Hegel believed that it was essential to have a sense of one's place in the world, and as we will see, he hoped that a liberalized version of the guilds and estates might help provide that sense of place and purpose, along with the family and the state. But Hegel thought that to regard choice itself as the highest and only value was a characteristic mistake—perhaps *the* characteristic mistake—of members of a liberal, market-oriented society. That was why he devoted so much of his work to a critique of freedom understood only as "doing as one likes." "The ordinary man," he wrote, "believes he is free when he is permitted to act arbitrarily, but in this very arbitrariness lies the fact that he is unfree."[8] For Hegel, the great challenge of the modern world is not only to provide us with a sense of *individuality* and *subjectivity*, but also to link us to a series of institutions with which we *identify* and which give us the sense of *belonging* to a reliable world. In Hegel's interpretation of the modern world, there was room for choosing arbitrarily—for choosing without good reasons. But Hegel also wanted to show that there were good reasons for individuals to endorse the familial, economic, and political institutions of which they were a part. Hegel's work has been aptly characterized as a "project of reconciliation."[9]

For Hegel, the question of what our social and political institutions ought to be is linked to the philosophical issue of what sort of person it is good to become. And the question of what sort of person it is good to become is based, in part, on the potential for human development created by historical institutions. That is why for Hegel, ethical theory is social and political theory, and all three are tightly linked to historical developments.

If Hegel thought it necessary to justify the capitalist market, it was because influential predecessors and contemporaries insisted that the developing market was irreconcilable with human well-being. Their critiques boil down to three charges: (1) that commercial society leaves men less happy by increasing their wants faster than the means necessary to satisfy them; (2) that it leads to a decline in virtue, understood in the civic republican sense of willingness to sacrifice on behalf of the polity, and to a split between private and public interest; and (3) that the division of labor leads to specialization, and thus fosters one-sided, atrophied personalities.

The first of these charges was leveled in Rousseau's discourses "On the Arts and Sciences" (1750) and "On the Origin and Foundations of Inequality Among Men" (1755). There he insisted that the development of civilization actually diminishes human happiness, because it causes artificial, socially induced needs to grow faster than the means for their satisfaction, leaving men ever more discontented.[10] And in *On the Social Contract*, Rousseau famously distinguished between the virtuous *citizen* of the ancient republics and the modern, self-seeking *bourgeois*.[11] As Adam Ferguson, Smith's younger contemporary, put it in his *Essay on the History of Civil Society* (1767), the ancient Greeks were motivated by "the habit of considering themselves as part of a community" and "had a perpetual view to objects which excite a great ardour in the soul; which led them to act perpetually in the view of their fellow-citizens, and to practice those arts of deliberation, elocution, policy, and war, on which the fortunes of nations, or of men, in their collective body, depend."[12] Under such circumstances, Ferguson maintained, "the interests of society . . . and of its members, are easily reconciled. If the individual owes every degree of consideration to the public, he receives, in paying that very consideration, the greatest happiness of which his nature is capable; and the greatest blessing that the public can bestow on its members, is to keep them attached to itself."[13] But the modern growth of commercial civilization, Ferguson claimed, brings about a decline in concern for the public interest and a specialization of function.[14]

Hegel's German contemporaries focused on another criticism of the modern capitalist world, the theme of specialization as "fragmentation." Its best-known expression was in the sixth of Friedrich Schiller's *Letters on the Aesthetic Education of Mankind*, published in 1795, a book that borrowed from Rousseau as well as Ferguson.[15] In ancient Greece, Schiller claimed, men had developed their faculties in a harmonious manner. But under modern conditions,

> we see not merely individuals, but whole classes of men, developing but one part of their potentialities, while of the rest, as in stunted growths, only vestigial traces remain. . . .

With this confining of our activity to a particular sphere we
have given ourselves a master within, who not infrequently
ends by suppressing the rest of our potentialities . . . enjoyment is separated from labor, the means from the end, exertion from recompense. Everlastingly chained to a single
little fragment of the Whole, man himself develops into
nothing but a fragment; everlastingly in his ear the monotonous sound of the wheel that he turns, he never develops the
harmony of his being, and instead of putting the stamp of
humanity upon his own nature, he becomes nothing more
than the imprint of his occupation, of his specialized knowledge.[16]

Hegel's friend, the poet Friedrich Hölderlin, summed it up in his
poem "The Archipelago" (1800), when he wrote, "Each man is forged
to his labor."[17] Here was a restatement of Smith's scathing description
of the negative effects of the division of labor on the common workman, now extended to all occupations in the name of the suppressed
potential for well-rounded individuals.

As a young man, Hegel too had been entranced by the idealized
image of Greek wholeness and its contrast with the purported fragmentation of modernity, an idea fashionable in the German high culture of his time.[18] But by the time he came to write *The Philosophy of
Right*, his concern was to reconcile his contemporaries to the reality
of the modern world. It was not only the Greeks who felt at home in
their world and could identify with the institutions in which they
lived. That was possible for modern man as well, if only he understood that it was the institutions of his society—and not least the
market—that made possible his sense of himself as an individual.[19]
For Hegel, the market is a key institution, both for the development of
a sense of individual self-worth and for habituating us to regard others
as individuals.

Hegel thought that the role of the philosopher is to reflect not on
abstract or eternal principles, but on the functions of the historically
evolved institutions of his society.[20] The ultimate purpose of his books
and lectures was to reconcile the inquiring individual with present
institutions, by means of a philosophy that would explain the rational
content of historically developed institutions.[21] Men might once have
been content to rely upon faith in the authority of their political or religious superiors. But it was characteristic of modern men, Hegel
thought, to demand a rational justification of the institutions in which
they participated. Only a rational explanation of why such institutions

were good for them would satisfy their sense of themselves as autonomous—as giving the law to themselves.[22]

The Setting of The Philosophy of Right

Hegel was born in 1770 in Stuttgart, the capital of the Duchy of Württemberg (population half a million), into a Lutheran family that had come to Württemberg in the sixteenth century to escape religious persecution. He came from a family of theologians, jurists, and bureaucrats. Since, in Württemberg, as in many Protestant German states, pastors and professors were paid by the government, his ancestors on both sides had been civil servants.[23] The Hegels belonged to a state service class that included judicial and administrative officials, the hierarchy of the Protestant state church, and teachers and professors in the state-controlled schools and universities. Hegel regarded himself as part of a cultural elite that looked out for the general welfare of society and was responsible for articulating and transmitting its cultural values.[24] Entrance into that elite was based on educational achievement, and the universities of late-eighteenth-century Germany were its training ground. Its claim to leadership on the basis of education and insight was a challenge to those who believed that leadership should be based upon noble origins or the ownership of large-scale property.[25]

The educated middle class from which Hegel sprang made up the core of the "literary public," whose mental horizons extended beyond their local social world. Those capable of reading books, journals, and newspapers made up perhaps 5 percent of the population.[26] At a time when most people did not venture far from home, physically or mentally, the educated class of which Hegel was a part was exceptional in its geographical mobility and in its expansive intellectual vistas. Not only did its members frequently travel away from home to attend university, they moved about in search of appropriate work. Hegel was typical in this respect. He studied at the University of Tübingen; became the house tutor to a wealthy family in Bern, Switzerland; and moved to Frankfurt and then to Jena, in Saxony, at a time when that university was the center of German intellectual life. When, in 1806, the march of Napoleon's army into Jena disrupted university life there, Hegel moved to Bavaria, becoming first a newspaper editor, then principal of a classically oriented high school (Gymnasium) in Bamberg.

When a university professorship opened up at Heidelberg, he moved to the state of Baden. When, finally, he moved to Berlin in 1818, he had lived in most of the major polities of German-speaking Europe. Hegel also followed developments beyond the German-speaking lands: he studied closely the progress of the French Revolution and the development of commerce in Britain.

During the second half of the eighteenth century, in Württemberg as elsewhere in the German-speaking lands, the civil service bureaucracy had developed from mere administrators of the ruler's fortune into a force for social and economic modernization. Rulers interested in expanding the taxable wealth of their subjects and hence their own power turned to their bureaucrats to create a more productive society, a more orderly society, a more industrious society.[27] Members of the civil service came to regard themselves as servants not of the king but of the state, from which their authority derived and through which they sought to advance the common good. Reading Smith confirmed and systematized what leading advocates of reform already knew: that a market, fueled by the profit motive, was the most likely road to increasing the wealth of the nation.[28] They became the movers and shakers, bent on transforming the social order.[29] The civil service class shared an ethic of pride in achievement (as opposed to lineage) with the small class of merchants engaged in translocal trade and in manufacture, using the putting-out system. In Germany, where outside of a few independent cities the merchant class was small and weak, the major stimulus to the development of the market came from the civil service class. As an administrative official in the government of the Duchy of Old Württemberg, Hegel's father had participated in the duke's attempts at economic reform. It was a goal that Hegel shared.

But as Hegel reached his thirtieth year at the turn of the century, these attempts at bureaucratically led modernization had not advanced much, because the power of rulers like the Duke of Württemberg and the King of Prussia was circumscribed. Effective power in the countryside lay in the hands of the landed nobility. In return for military service (including providing troops from their peasants) and some tax payments, they were allowed to wield political, judicial, and legal power over the peasants who worked or rented their lands. In the towns, the guilds and other privileged corporations controlled much of daily life. They kept social and religious outsiders out of the town's economy, and even outside the town's borders. Among those so excluded were Jews, who could not enter most professions or live in many towns. The "representative" political bodies, the estates, represented the entrenched interests of those who profited from existing arrangements. And by and large they were successful in resisting the policies of rulers and enlightened civil servants who wanted to shake things up to create a freer and more dynamic society.[30]

It was Napoleon's victories over the German princes that gave the bureaucratic reformers a new chance. Most of the three hundred politically fragmented and decentralized polities that made up the Holy Roman Empire of the German People proved too weak to defy the new mass armies of postrevolutionary France. Much of German-speaking Europe was conquered by Napoleon, who created a number of new client states under French tutelage. They adopted the *Code Napoléon*, a uniform legal system that included, for the first time, equality before the law (for men, that is) regardless of religion or ancestral status. It was in this form that the liberal ideals of the French Revolution were first realized on German soil, providing civil equality, not political participation. The rulers of the remaining German states recognized that they would have to take radical steps to transform their polities if they were to hold out against Napoleon and reconquer lost territories. As so often happens in history, the threat of foreign conquest provided a stimulus to defensive modernization.

The war against Napoleon brought the kingdom of Prussia to the brink of extinction as a major power. Shortly after the German defeat at Jena in 1806—a battle which Hegel witnessed while he was putting the final touches on his first great work, *The Phenomenology of Spirit*—Friedrich von Hardenberg, a stymied reformer, drafted a memorandum to the King of Prussia with a program of radical reform. He advocated "a revolution in a positive sense, one leading to the ennoblement of mankind, to be made not through violent impulses from below or outside, but through the wisdom of the government."[31] The king invited Hardenberg, together with another bureaucratic reformer, Baron von Stein, to reorganize his state along the lines long advocated by progressive administrators. Their task was to make Prussia capable of withstanding the French challenge.

Under their leadership, what had once been an absolute monarchy was transformed into a bureaucratic monarchy, in which ministers, not the king, presided over the formulation and execution of policy. Entrance into the civil service bureaucracy and promotion within its ranks increasingly depended upon examinations, and the prestige of the bureaucracy was enhanced by pension rights and special tax status.[32] They set about trying to bring Prussian reality closer to their ideal of a more free and more productive society, by creating greater civil equality, social mobility, and economic freedom. In 1807, peasants were freed from hereditary serfdom. Compulsory labor services and payments in kind to their lords were ended as well, though peasants were required to compensate their lord for the loss of these seignorial dues. Restrictions on the buying and selling of noble estates were eliminated, in an attempt to put agriculture on a more commercial footing so that land would be owned by those who could use it most efficiently. All occupations were opened to nobles and commoners alike. Within German-speaking Europe, Prussia thus became a pioneer in the dissolution of the feudal agrarian order and its replacement by a society in which property was divorced from political domination (*Herrschaft*). In the years immediately thereafter, the Hardenberg regime enacted legislation to remove the nobles' exemption from taxation, to weaken the power of the guilds, and to otherwise ease restrictions on commercial activity. Jews were declared to be "natives and citizens," and restrictions on their social and economic activity were partially lifted, though they were still excluded from political participation and from the civil service.[33]

The Prussia to which Hegel was invited in 1818 was in many ways a new state. It comprised regions scattered across northern Germany, which had been consolidated into a single kingdom only a few years earlier. Its collective identity was yet to be formed.

To aid in carrying out their reform program, Hardenberg and Stein brought to Prussia a cadre of administrators and intellectuals from across Germany. Part of their effort at regeneration was the founding of a new university in the Prussian capital, Berlin, until then a military and administrative rather than an academic or cultural center. They drew upon the best and brightest of German intellectual life. The new university, as conceived by Friedrich Schleiermacher, was to unite within its precincts all of the faculties of learning, centered around the philosophical faculty, which was to integrate the various realms of knowledge into a comprehensive whole.[34] To fill the chair of philosophy, they recruited Hegel.

Hardenberg tried to concentrate power in the bureaucratic state in order to diminish the local domination of the Prussian nobility, the Junkers. In 1812 he proposed a major reform, which would have put justice and administration on the local level in the hands of administrators chosen by the state rather than by the local nobility. His program was one of increasing the power of the state, and especially its bureaucracy, in order to provide personal freedom. Though that may sound self-contradictory, it was not. Civil freedom—to move, to marry, to engage in any trade—would become possible for most Germans only if the power of the central government could be used to break the power of the intermediary power holders, the nobility and the guilds.

The heady transformation envisioned by the Prussian reformers was realized only in part. After Waterloo the external stimulus to reform ended. Within Prussia, resistance from aristocratic forces and from local governments increased. Outside of Prussia, the forces of reaction, led by the Austrian chancellor, Metternich, were strengthened. Among the foremost ideologists of the reaction was the Romantic philosopher Adam Müller, whose *Elemente der Staatskunst* (Elements of State-craft) of 1809 provided arguments against the Hardenberg reforms. Müller articulated a conception of politics based not on legally free and equal participants in a market society, but on noble paternalism. His model for political relations was the family, and the noble lord was to relate to his subjects as a father to his children. He opposed the "universal despotism of money" as a depersonalization of human relations.[35] Another leading theorist of the reaction, the Swiss jurist Carl Ludwig von Haller, devoted five volumes to the "restoration of political science," premised on the notion that the "artificial, bourgeois" state advocated by the reformers was a "chimera."[36] He attacked the notion that power and property should be divorced. For Haller, society was a web of private relationships; property created a domain in which authority could be legitimately exercised. The head of the familial household, the lord of the manor, and the monarch of the state each ruled the realm of their property. Müller, Haller, and the noble landowners who were attracted to their doctrines objected to the very notion of a political realm, in which laws were applied equally and impersonally by state officials, and where property would be "private" and distinct from political power. On the contrary, they insisted, *Herrschaft* was personal, and property should remain indissolubly linked to political authority.[37]

The Junkers, who sought to continue their direct economic and political domination, cloaked that domination in the language of paternalism. It is in that light that Hegel's emphasis on the distinctions between political, economic, and familial relations acquires its significance. And it is against this background that Hegel's conception of the state and its bureaucracy must be understood.

It was a close associate of Hardenberg who in 1818 attracted Hegel to the recently founded University of Berlin. Baron Karl Sigmund von Altenstein was the Prussian minister of education, and an advocate of compulsory elementary education for all.[38] When, in his inaugural address as professor of philosophy in Berlin, Hegel praised Prussia as a state that had attained world-historical stature by institutionalizing the demands of reason, he was referring to the recent attempts by the reformers to use the power of the Prussian state to create universal equality before the law.[39] His commitment to Prussia was not a matter of ethnic particularism, still less of German nationalism: it was a commitment to the program of the embattled bureaucratic class of a great power that, Hegel thought, was doing its best to reshape society in line with the best understanding of the age. To that understanding we must now turn.

Individuality and Universality

Hegel's emphasis on the philosophy of history was stimulated by the French Revolution. For while he supported its ideals—especially the principle of equality before the law—like many of his generation he was struck by the failure of the revolution to establish a stable set of institutions that were accepted as legitimate by the French people. Hegel attributed that failure to the faulty understanding of the nature of liberty among the French revolutionaries. By regarding every institution as a barrier to individual freedom, they made it impossible to establish any institutional order.[40] And by regarding their revolutionary project as cut off from the cultural legacy of the past, they drained it of an important source of legitimacy. If Hegel devoted so much attention to history, it was because he agreed with Burke's observation in *Reflections on the Revolution in France* that the British had benefited "from considering our liberties in the light of an inheritance. . . . This idea of a liberal descent inspires us with a sense of habitual native dignity . . ."

Hegel wanted to explain to his contemporaries that the notion of viewing everyone as a subject, as someone capable of deciding for themselves, did not emerge from the Enlightenment ex nihilo. Nor had it emerged universally. It was the result of the historical development of European culture, with roots in ancient Greece and the Christian tradition of spirituality. But it had not become a reality even in Europe, as long as there was slavery or serfdom, and as long as property and economic relationships were bound by feudal fetters. The Protestant Reformation, as he interpreted it, was an essential milestone along the road to modern freedom. The rise of the modern secular state had made it possible to leave behind the notion that the polity belonged to an individual or to a family, and that the state should be under the control of a single religion or devoted to a single way of life. For Hegel, the

French Revolution, despite its failures in France, inaugurated a new era, in which modern freedom and subjectivity—still confined to a sliver of the European world and its offshoots—would become universal.[41] Much of his philosophy of history was devoted to demonstrating to his contemporaries that the institutions that he and they valued did, indeed, have a liberal descent.

Contemporary institutions, Hegel thought, were made possible by a set of implicit norms, which were themselves the product of historical development. Long before Matthew Arnold or Max Weber, Hegel interpreted the modern, liberal, capitalist world as an outgrowth of Protestantism. But unlike Weber, Hegel believed that the modern post-Protestant world had its own ethical nature, an ethic embodied in its institutions, what Hegel called "*Sittlichkeit.*"

Hegel sought to explain that, rightly understood, the institutions of the modern world were worth affirming, for modern institutions have their own ethical dimension. By his use of "*Sittlichkeit,*" which has its root in the word for custom (*Sitte*), Hegel meant to suggest that ethical life is only a worldly reality when it is experienced by individuals as an integral part of the institutions in which they live.[42] Though the term "*Sittlichkeit*" is often translated as "ethics" or "ethical life," it is better rendered as "normative institutions."

For Hegel, Protestant *Sittlichkeit* marked a crucial advance over the Catholic emphasis on *Heiligkeit* (saintliness), in that it represented a sanctification of the world through a redirection of spiritual energies away from other-worldly monasticism and into worldly institutions. Catholic saintliness was the ethic of a small clerical elite, Protestant *Sittlichkeit* that of society as a whole. In place of the Catholic vow of chastity, Protestantism substituted a glorification of marriage and the family. Protestantism replaced the Catholic vow of poverty with "the *Sittlichkeit* of bourgeois society," namely a commitment to "the activity of supporting oneself through reason and industriousness, and rectitude in economic relations and in the use of one's fortune."[43] Finally, in place of the Catholic vow of obedience (what Hegel calls "the enslavement of conscience"), Protestantism substituted the virtue of obedience to the law as embodied in legal institutions, "the *Sittlichkeit* of the state."[44]

One task of the philosopher, as Hegel understood it, was to bring to light the rational and ethical content of those institutions, to conceptualize their implicit ethic, so that self-conscious individuals could become more aware of the meaning of the institutions in which they participated—a step toward feeling at home in those institutions.

Hegel was of the same generation as the founders of German Romanticism. The shared lament of German Romantic poetry, polemic, theology, and politics was that the modern secular world left the individual alienated—internally divided, lacking a sense of community or a feeling of transcendence. The Romantics' solutions to the problem amounted to variations on a common theme. On the one hand, they stressed the creative power and particularity of the individual; on the other, the need for the individual to connect with some higher force through intuition or a leap of the imagination. That higher force could be nature, the nation, the *Volk*, the Catholic Church, or God. But the link between the individual and the larger "whole" was, for the Romantics, an essentially nonrational one, a surrender of the rational self to a higher force, which endowed life with meaning.[45]

Like the Romantics, some of whom he had counted among his friends, Hegel was concerned that individuals feel themselves to be part of some larger whole. Indeed, for Hegel, that whole (or "totality") included the relationship of the individual to God and to history. If Hegel stemmed from a long line of civil servants, he was also the descendant of theologians, and he began his higher education as a student of theology. His work was implicitly and sometimes explicitly an attempt to provide a rational theodicy—to explain the ways of God to man, by explaining human history as the progressive development of man's potential to lead a free and rational existence. But, unlike the Romantics, Hegel claimed that the relationship of the individual to the larger institutions of which he was a part could be grasped by reason and must be objectively communicable. He insisted that the individual got a sense of himself as part of something larger not through an irrational surrender to some other-worldly source, but through a series of institutional links—what Hegel called "mediations"—between the individual and the wider world. His task as a philosopher was to explain those links: how they had come about, and how they functioned to give the individual a sense of himself both as an autonomous subject and as a part of some larger project that he could rationally affirm.

Hegel's philosophical project is to reconcile men to the world, a world in which modern men pride themselves on their individual subjectivity and particularity. Hegel knew that to most people "freedom" meant the possibility of doing what one liked, without institutional restrictions. Limitations on our activity, in this conception, are barriers to freedom. Freedom so understood is *negative* freedom. Taken seriously, Hegel says, it becomes destructive of every institutional order, since it views every institution as an intolerable limitation.[46] It was that flawed understanding that had doomed the French Revolution.

Hegel's conception is perhaps best understood by contrasting it with the contemporary belief, widespread in his day as in ours, that a person's good can be defined simply as what he or she in fact desires or prefers, and that those desires are most authentic when they reflect the distinctive particularities of the individual. In this Romantic conception, freedom is measured by "the extent to which it *diverges from what is universally acknowledged and valid* and manages to invent something *particular* for itself."[47] The alternative views (with many variations) assert that it is the role of social institutions to shape our preferences and direct our desires. The need for institutions to direct the passions was the implicit premise behind Smith's work,[48] but in Hegel that purpose is explicit and articulated.

The first problem for those who believe that "the good" is to be identified with our idiosyncratic desires is that they can offer little guidance as to how preferences are to be formed. The process of preference formation—or, in other words, the direction of desire—is central to Hegel's social, political, ethical, and pedagogic thought. For the sort of person we become depends, in large part, on the sort of institutions in which we find ourselves, and the moral norms to which we are exposed.[49] Hegel's whole view of life is pedagogic: a good life, he asserts, is one in which we are formed by institutions into self-conscious individuals, and into responsible members of institutions that we value because we understand that in the long run they function to make us into the sort of people we want to be.

For Hegel, the fundamental fact about man is that he is capable of being free. That does not mean that he is born free—quite the contrary. To the extent that men act spontaneously upon their natural instincts and drives, Hegel thinks, they are the opposite of free, for they are slaves to their passions. They are liberated from the unfreedom of natural drives by social and cultural institutions, which transform the individual so that he acts in a way that is good for him, and in that sense reflects his rational will. Ethical life, for Hegel, involves the reorientation of natural drives by a higher self that is the product of culture and institutions: it is the replacement of nature by "second nature." It is his emphasis on the fact that ethical behavior *ought* to become habitual that distinguishes Hegel's thought from that of Kant and many other thinkers. Institutions, for Hegel, are habit-forming—and that is what he values about them.[50]

For Kant, moral action is free because it is determined by our reason, rather than by our emotions, which are part of our natural selves.

Hegel criticized Kant's conception of ethics for this separation of reason and feeling. Hegel's thought is distinguished by its unremitting
focus on "second nature"—that is, the transformation of the natural
self by the historically developed social and political institutions
through which cultural norms are conveyed to individuals and inter-
nalized by them. An ethical order, Hegel thought, was an institutional
order that created in its members the habitual disposition to act ethically toward one another, so that their feelings corresponded to their
duties.

But Hegel did not think that good people were created only by institutions that socialized them into good habits. The point of his philosophical reflection was to provide rational "insight into the good" so
that they could rationally affirm the duties and obligations imposed on
them by institutions.[51] His purpose was to provide "insight grounded
on reasons" (eine Einsicht durch Gründe).[52]

Hegel believed that one great error of Romanticism and of certain
varieties of liberalism was to regard binding duties only as limitations
on the real self. On the contrary, he thought, knowing and accepting
one's duties frees the individual. Institutions give our potentially tur-
bulent inner life a sense of direction, which is why Hegel refers to
them as "Einrichtungen" (from "Richtung," the German word for
"direction").[53] Duties free us from becoming a slave to our biological
urges. They free us from "unoriented subjectivity," from constantly
having to ask "What should I do now?" And they make it possible for
us to have an impact on the real world, rather than remaining trapped
in our subjective musings.[54] Hegel was bitingly critical of the notion
that to be moral is to stand out or to adhere to some individual conception of virtue. In an ethical society, Hegel writes, to be virtuous is to
live up to one's institutionally imposed duties. "In an ethical community, it is easy to say *what* someone must do and *what* the duties are
which he has to fulfill in order to be virtuous. He must simply do what
is prescribed, expressly stated, and known to him within his situation."[55] Those rules connect one to the larger constellations of people
of which one is a part: to the family, professional peers, the state, and
mankind. In that sense, they provide "mediations" between the individual and the universal.[56]

Civil Society and Its Discontents

The existence of individuals with a strong sense of their own interests, their own inner subjective life, and their own particularity may have been a symptom of corruption in the ancient polis, Hegel suggests. But it gives the modern state its tensile strength, by means of institutions that allow for the reconciliation of particularity and the common interest.[57]

What most distinguishes the modern condition is what Hegel calls *"die bürgerliche Gesellschaft."* The phrase can be translated as either "bourgeois society" or "civil society"—Hegel probably intended both connotations. "Civil society" is the realm in which everyone is treated as a self-sufficient individual. Their persons and property are protected by law. Their relations to one another are based on interaction through the market for the satisfaction of their wants (*Bedürfnisse*).[58]

Traditionally, the English term "civil society," like its Greek and Latin equivalents, had essentially meant "government," or the sort of society in which government exists. Hegel introduces "civil society" as that realm or set of relationships that lie between the family and the state. Its central institutions are property and the market. But it also includes certain key governmental functions, including the judiciary and the police who enforce the law.[59] Why does Hegel regard the government's law-protecting function as part of "civil society," together with the market?

One of Hegel's central contentions is that the notion of "natural rights"—including the idiom of "natural liberty" in which Adam Smith speaks of freedom of persons and property—is confused and misleading. Smith, like so many eighteenth-century authors, had used the term "nature" to express both what was factual and what was normative: the world as it really is, and the way things ought to be.[60] Rights to control one's person and property are morally desirable, Hegel insists; indeed, they are crucial to what makes modernity so valuable. But they are not *natural*. They are the product of the historical evolution of cultural understandings, of "second nature," and their reality is only made possible by the modern state.[61] He refers to them as "abstract rights," in part to bring out the fact that such rights have a reality only in the concrete embodiment of the modern state.[62] For without the state, which makes rights into laws, there are no protections of person and property in the real world. Yet citizens in the modern state typically lose sight of the fact that their particular interests are dependent on the more universal structure of the state. Hegel mentions the disinclination of individuals to pay taxes to the state as evidence of this lack of recognition of the realities that make civil society possible.[63] His purpose was to make his fellow citizens conscious of those realities, so that they would regard the state not as something alien and external, but as an institution that they identified with their own goals.

Private property, for Hegel, is a product of the historical development of the modern state. The idea of *private* property implies that owning property does not convey political power over other individuals. It was precisely the opposite of the sort of patriarchal relations favored by the Junkers and their apologists.

Property is so morally important, Hegel explains, because of the possibilities it creates for the expression of our individuality. One of the constants of his philosophy is that states of mind are only stable when they are concretized in the external world: in things, in institutional rules, in the patterns by which people relate to one another. (That is why the love between a man and a woman is made more stable when it is publicly recognized through the institution of marriage, Hegel says.) It is all very well to have some internal sense of oneself as an individual, but that sense must correspond to an external reality. Part of that external reality is property. The fact that something belongs to me and not to everyone increases my sense of myself as someone in particular.[64] For Hegel, that sense of individual particularity is intrinsic to the modern moral order.[65] Indeed "the right of the subject's *particularity* to find satisfaction, or—to put it differently—the right of *subjective freedom*, is the pivotal and focal point in the difference between *antiquity* and the *modern age*."[66] The fact that others do not take my property—that they regard it as *mine*—is also a way in which they recognize me as an individual. It is precisely this recognition that the slave, the bondsman, and the serf lack. That the right to own private property, to control some corner of the world, is universal in the modern state is for Hegel part of its glory. This understanding of modernity leads him to conclude that one goal of government policy should be to encourage widespread ownership of property.

Property also expresses and externalizes our individuality in another sense. Our property is a part of the natural world that we have worked on, that we have transformed in accordance with our will.[67] In that sense it is part of the humanization of nature, the infusion of the human spirit into the world, which is one of the central themes of Hegel's theory of historical development.

Together with property, it is the market that is central to civil society. It was in discussions of the market and of economic life, Hegel wrote, that moralists of superficial understanding were most likely to "vent dissatisfaction and irritation" by treating the market as an anarchy of caprice and chance.[68] To provide a more accurate understanding of the market, Hegel looked to *The Wealth of Nations*, along with Smith's leading English and French successors, David Ricardo and Jean-Baptiste Say.[69] Their great virtue, Hegel thought, was to show that what appears on the surface to be anarchic is in fact a *system* for the mutual satisfaction of wants. But what Hegel thought they had failed to adequately explain was the institutional underpinnings and philosophical implications of the market, which he tried to provide in *The Philosophy of Right*.[70] The market, Hegel took pains to point out, was a social institution that made men more social. Because the individual's needs can only be met through the production of others, he must orient himself to other people, and take an interest in what they think.[71] He must bend his own will to the requirements of others.

The market is based on the relations that grow out of the attempt to satisfy the wants of individuals. Those wants, Hegel emphasizes, are not "natural." But while past moralists had denounced the attempted satisfaction of "unnatural" wants as "luxury," Hegel takes a very different tack. *Most* human wants, he insists, are not fixed by nature: they are a result of the imagination. Rather than using this as a stick with which to condemn the growth of wants, Hegel explains that it is this ability to want the products of our imagination that distinguishes humans from animals. Our perception of "necessities" is a product not of nature but of second nature—of historically evolved culture. The development of civilization creates ever more differentiated wants, which are experienced subjectively as "needs."[72] And this process of ever-greater refinement of needs is open-ended. Those in a crude state of society (or uncultured people), Hegel says, do not make distinctions: culture is the process in which more and more distinctions are made.[73] Here Hegel provides a grounding for Voltaire's defense of luxury, through an interpretation of human nature that undercut the basic premises of the critics of material expansion.

Hegel was discussing a process already well developed among the German middle classes. By the late eighteenth century, one of the most widely read magazines was the *Journal of Luxury and Fashion*, which instructed the new "bourgeois man of the middle estate" (*der bürgerliche Mann vom Mittelstande*) on how he and his family ought to live, dress, and furnish their homes. A single, all-purpose living room would no longer do, it advised. In an age of increased written communication, contracts, and correspondence there was a need for a proper office in the house, which afforded the proper concentration, free of the household distractions of the old family common room (*Wohnstube*). And since one did not want small children around when company came to call, the house needed a playroom. And for the older children, yet another room, to which they could repair with the household tutors.[74]

Perhaps because he had read Say, who suggested that "it is production which creates a demand for products," Hegel recognized (as Smith had not) that entrepreneurs were a major force in the expansion of the imagined wants of consumers. The market, that is to say, did not just *satisfy* wants, it *created* them. Wants arose from the manufacturers who sought to profit by their emergence. They called attention to the discomfort of the consumer, in order to provide a solution to that discomfort, in the process awakening a sense of discomfort where it had not previously existed.[75]

It was the quest for individual recognition through consumption that led to the modern cycle of fashion, Hegel explained. The desire to demonstrate equality with others (to show that others were not better than themselves) led individuals to imitate the consumer goods of those above them. Then the desire for individuality led to the creation of new products, in order to express one's individuality by standing out from the crowd. The result was a never-ending cycle of imitation and innovation.[76]

The pressures of competition, Hegel noted, gave market societies an outward thrust. The search for markets in which to sell those products for which supply now exceeded demand led entrepreneurs to push on into areas that were relatively backward economically, both internally and beyond the nation's borders. Indeed it was the impetus of trade that often brought cultures separated by oceans into contact with one another, and that made it possible for them to learn from one another. In that sense, Hegel told his students, the development of civil society contributed to the educational process of mankind.[77]

Hegel's Romantic contemporaries portrayed the world of work and of market activity as a threat to individuality. Wrong, Hegel insisted: supporting themselves by earning a living is one of the most important ways in which men get a sense of themselves as individuals. (Here the term "men" is used advisedly. For women, in Hegel's conception, functioned largely in the family, outside the sphere of civil society.)[78] The fact that labor was legally free gave it an essential dignity that it did not have under conditions of slavery or serfdom, when one worked at the command and for the sake of one's legal and political superiors.[79] Those who lament the need to restrict themselves to a particular activity in the division of labor misunderstand the conditions under which the individual and the universal can be related in the modern world. It is an error of youth, Hegel thought, to perceive the need to choose an occupation, and hence restrict one's possibilities, as a great constraint on the self. For it is only by accepting the need for limitation that we become an effective link in the chain of civil society.[80] True individuality under modern conditions, then, includes identifying with our professional place in the inevitable division of labor. And modern virtue consists, for the most part, not in extraordinary political actions beyond civil society, but in professional rectitude (*Rechtschaffenheit*), in living up to the duties of one's professional station (*Stand*).[81] One becomes part of some larger whole by accepting the need to limit oneself to a particular occupation within civil society.

"Subjective particularity is the principle which activates civil society."[82] The market is where we express our particularity and individuality through the possibility of choosing. There are higher and lower forms of choice, for Hegel, and the higher form occurs when we make our choices for good, rational reasons. Perhaps the most important choice that one can make in civil society is the choice of profession.[83] (The other is the choice of a marriage partner.)[84] But there is also some value, he thought, to the possibility of making arbitrary choices, that is to say choices made for no good reason, that are merely a matter of taste and even whim. The possibility of choosing among thirty flavors of ice cream is not the highest form of choice, but it is a choice nonetheless that expresses something of our individuality. For Hegel, the problem arises when we come to believe that this is the only form of choice.[85]

As we have seen, Hegel saw the market as creating new wants that are perceived by the individual as "needs." Indeed, the market was a want-creating machine. On the one hand, it created possibilities for the expression of individuality and universality through consumption. But it also presented a hazard to the individual, when desire (*Begierde*) remained unrestrained. When the individual has no life plan that includes a sense of an appropriate level of consumption, he becomes a plaything of wills other than his own, tossed to and fro by the capricious stream of fashion and wants induced by others. The result could degenerate into the continual, irritable search for more and more, without satisfaction in any level of attainment—psychic misery in the midst of material excess.[86] When consumer goods are chosen merely on the basis of ever new induced wants, rather than because they fit in with a rational life plan, the result would be what Hegel called a "bad infinity." It was the latest guise of what Aristotle had called *"pleonexia."*

Hegel's solution to the problem of unbounded wants lies in part, as we shall see, in the family, in part in the state, and in part in professional associations, which for Hegel are an essential element of civil society. For it is in professional associations (what he calls "corporations") that the individual gets a sense of what level of wants is appropriate to the way of life of the profession he has chosen. Like Möser, Hegel wanted individuals to have a sense of their place in society. Möser had looked to the guilds and the estates to provide such a sense of place. Hegel hoped for similar, legally constituted organizations, which would regulate entry into urban trades and educate members to the demands of their profession. But unlike the guilds and the estates that Möser had championed—and which still existed in much of Germany in the 1820s—entry into such professions was to be voluntary, based on individual choice and talents. Hegel hoped that such organizations could form an essential intermediary source of commitment between the individual and the state. They would provide a forum for mutual assistance, and draw the individual into a concern with interests wider than his own. Indeed, Hegel wanted political representation to occur through these professional corporations. The individual would come to identify with the welfare of his profession. And he, in turn, would acquire a sense of worth and identity through the honor that accrued to him as a member of the profession. Like the guilds, the corporations would provide honor (*Ehre*) and a sense of place in the world (*Stand*). Recognition from his professional peers, Hegel hoped, would save the individual from the temptation to seek recognition through the display of wealth, and from the "bad infinity" of unlimited wants.[87]

Hegel recognized that these corporations would pursue the group interests of their members. He thought it the role of state authorities to intervene when this occurred to an excessive degree, when, for example, they engaged in price-fixing. Though such corporations were at odds with the principle of freedom of trade, Hegel was willing to part with some of the advantages of freedom of trade for the sake of the social stability that he hoped the corporations would provide.[88]

Another problem that Hegel thought intrinsic to civil society was a new form of poverty. By that he did not mean only the existence of people who lacked means of material support. They had been around before market society. But there were two novel aspects of poverty: the systematic creation of groups in the population whose skills left them jobless, and the sense of grievance and resentment that those without work harbored against society as a whole.

It was the inherent dynamism of the market that created unemployment. The division of labor created by the market meant that many workers had work-related skills that were highly specialized, and hence suited for a narrow range of jobs. Because the market was defined by shifting and ever-refined wants, Hegel reasoned, the demand for new products meant a decline in the market for older products. That left workers whose whole working lives had been devoted to their role in the production of the old product without a job, and without the training that would allow them to find new work. In addition, the mechanization of production led to a loss of jobs.[89] The market thus created unemployment, and did so among men who could not easily adapt to new trades.[90] (Hegel also noted that the development of the capitalist economy had been accompanied by a rise in population, though he did not develop the point—an important oversight.)[91]

A second problem arose from the fact that a sense of self-worth in civil society was linked to having work, which gave one a place in society. Those who were without work were nevertheless a part of the same society, and felt entitled to its benefits, including a right to subsistence. "In England," he noted, "even the poorest believe that they have rights; this is different from what satisfies the poor in other countries."[92] The poor were thus resentful of those who were part of civil society. And because those outside of civil society did not partake in its civilizing institutions, they failed to develop the character traits that made them suitable for work. They thus became not only unemployed but unemployable.

Modern poverty thus presented the hazard of what Hegel calls "pauperism," distinguishable from poverty understood as absolute material deprivation. Not all paupers are poor. They are characterized by their state of mind. They lack a sense of honor and reliability. They trust to luck, avoid work, and are capricious. Unaccustomed to regular work, they lack the habits of industriousness. Yet in a society in which most people do have the means of subsistence, they feel entitled to support. "The evil of the paupers (*Pöbel*) is that they do not have sufficient honor to gain their livelihood through their work, yet claim that they have a right to receive that livelihood."[93] They form a group that is constantly aggrieved, and a danger to civil society.[94]

The problem of providing subsistence even to those of the poor who had not been reduced to pauperism was difficult in civil society, and Hegel pointed to England as an example. Actually giving work to the poor created its own problems, by increasing the production of goods for which there was not enough effective demand. Providing the means of subsistence through charity did not solve the problem that those without work lacked a fundamental prerequisite of self-worth in a bourgeois society: a job. Charity developed the pauper's belief in entitlement. In some cases, Hegel noted with resignation, it was better to allow the poor to beg, since that at least kept alive the desire to work.[95]

Hegel's comments on poverty and pauperism were drawn less from observation of conditions in Germany than from reading about Great Britain, where commercial society was most advanced. Well informed about the seeming intractability of the problems of British poverty, he hoped to avoid them in Germany, in part at least, through governmental measures. But he also thought that overseas colonization might be the best bet for the poor in commercial society.[96]

By and large, the roles that Hegel assigned to government were what Smith also specified: maintaining the rule of law and the preservation of property; the provision of physical infrastructure and public goods such as bridges, roads, and public health; and the education of children.[97] But Hegel favored a government that went beyond these to carry out functions that would help to alleviate what he had identified as the intrinsic problems created by the market. Government authorities, he indicated, should intervene to counter the effects of the disruption of international trade and to moderate and, if possible, shorten the ups and downs of the market. They should inspect foodstuffs and medicines, and in time of emergency actually set the price of basic provisions.[98] For Hegel, these governmental functions—which he refers to as the public policy *(Polizei)* or administration *(Regierung)*—should be thought of as a part of civil society, in that they provide the framework that makes possible the pursuit of self-interest through the market.[99]

Beyond Civil Society

If it was in civil society that men acquired a sense of themselves as free individuals,[100] it was below and above the realm of civil society that relationships of love and altruism were to be found. It was in the realm of the family and the realm of the state that individuals became part of a unity beyond themselves, a community important enough to sacrifice on its behalf. Those were realms beyond contractual relations, in which the calculation of individual self-interest should not hold sway.

For Hegel, the family was a realm of relationships based upon emotional altruism. There we learn to become ethical beings in an immediate, emotional form, in the relationship of love between men and women, and in the relations of love and obedience between parents and children.[101] He was critical of those who conceived of marriage merely as a civil contract. Marriage, he thought, begins from the point of view of contract, but only to supersede that point of view.[102] It reverts to the contractual point of view only when it is dissolving.[103] Marriage is an ethical institution, based upon "love, trust, and the sharing of the whole of individual existence" such that we ultimately put the interests of other family members above our own.[104] He was critical of the romantic conception of love as a deep, irrational outburst of emotion, and of conceptions of marriage as based solely on love. Marriage, Hegel explained, is an ethical institution, in which natural drives become part of an ethical order. Love itself is only one element of the marriage: other essential elements are the sharing of wealth, the sharing of worries, and the raising of children.[105]

In the family, then, the self-interested actors of civil society become members of a collectivity to which they are emotionally attached. It is this collective interest that gives property and self-interest a very different meaning. It is the desire to form a family that makes it necessary to acquire a continuous stream of income in civil society, so that "the self-interestedness of desires becomes a communally beneficial concern for something held in common."[106] For the external and public reality of the family is its wealth, its family fortune (*Vermögen*), which is the basis for the survival of its members. One way in which the love and deep obligation that characterize the family are expressed is by earning a living in the marketplace. In the search for familial wealth, Hegel said, self-interest and selfishness are transformed into concern for something shared.[107] One's concerns are broadened: "It is no longer the satisfaction of needs as the satisfaction of *Begierde* (selfish and passionate desire), for that is broken. It is a condition of concern for one's self along with others, and the others along with oneself; it is here that self-seeking (*Eigensucht*) vanishes."[108]

But while bourgeois society requires the family for human flourishing, it also transforms the scope of familial relationships. Before modern government and the market, obligations were primarily determined by blood. Under modern conditions, blood ties lose their all-encompassing nature, while professional ties and ties of friendship increase in importance. It is only because of the rise of bourgeois society that family members are no longer subordinated to the "patriarchal whole" of the family. If the family is essential to moral well-being in bourgeois society, it is that very structure of society that puts a limit on the claims of familial identity and allows for identity as an individual.[109] Family and civil society, then, are in tension: drawing us, on the one hand, toward subordinating ourselves to the interests of those we love, and on the other to asserting ourselves as individuals beyond the mark of blood and descent.

If the family is characterized by relationships beyond those of individual self-interest, so too, for Hegel, is the state. Hegel thought that the state was misconceived in liberal thought when it was regarded only as an agency for the self-interested protection of individual rights and property. It was also the institutional embodiment of the collective identity of its populace. The limits of the liberal conception of the state were most evident, he thought, in the phenomena of taxes and of war.[110] For the state required taxes, the payment of which would not necessarily redound to the self-interest of individual taxpayers.[111] And, in time of war, the modern post-Napoleonic state required that its citizens be willing to risk their lives—a calculation impossible to justify on grounds of self-interest. A state whose citizens were not disposed to pay taxes could not prosper in peacetime, and without the additional willingness of citizens to fight on its behalf in time of war, the state would ultimately disappear. War reminds individuals in civil society of what they ordinarily forget: that without the state, their person and property have no security.[112]

Patriotism in its modern sense comes from identifying with the state. That identification may be habitual or emotional, but Hegel's overriding purpose in *The Philosophy of Right* is to make it *rational*, by explaining how the modern state serves the needs of individuals to satisfy both their particularity and their universality as members of communities.[113] For Hegel, representative political bodies are most significant not for allowing citizens some measure of control over government, but because they create a degree of participation in the state, and hence increase knowledge of it and identification with it.[114] Their function is primarily educational, to develop an informed and politically conscious citizenry, mindful of the principles on which the political life of the community is based. Indeed, for Hegel this function of representative institutions is more important than their efficiency in decision making, which he believed would be limited.[115]

The General Estate and the Role of the Philosopher

In Hegel's view, an essential counterweight and complement to the forces of the market is the civil service. For in a society where most people, most of the time, have in mind the particular interests of themselves, their families, or their professional associations, it is essential that there be a group devoted to the general interest of society. That is why Hegel refers to the civil service as "the general estate." Recruitment into the civil service, he stressed, should be open to all on the basis of demonstrated knowledge and proof of ability[116]—still an unrealized goal of semireformed Prussia, but more advanced there than elsewhere. To free bureaucrats from the influence of those in civil society, it was essential that government officials receive adequate salaries.[117] The relationship of the civil servant to his work, Hegel wrote, should be "the main interest of his spiritual and particular existence." It was to be not a job, but a vocation.[118]

Civil servants needed of course to be properly trained in administrative procedure, economics, and the rest of what in Germany were known as "the sciences of state."[119] Yet since bureaucratic training and daily operations could be mechanical and mind-numbing, Hegel wanted the members of the general estate to be educated in philosophy—the philosophy developed in *The Philosophy of Right*—in order to properly comprehend their role as guardians of the general interest.[120] One purpose of the university, as Hegel conceived it, was to provide not only specialized knowledge, but a historically and culturally informed perspective on the present, which would allow the members of the general estate to anticipate the larger needs of their society. The university, then, was to be a place in which types of knowledge and orientations quite different from those of the market were to be cultivated.

Individuals became reconciled to modern civil society in part by their participation in its institutions, where they learned the norms and expectations that formed them into responsible and autonomous people. But they became reconciled in a more mindful way through a rational grasp of the functions of those institutions, as laid out in *The Philosophy of Right*. That book was part of Hegel's larger project, to explain to his contemporaries their connection to world history and ultimately to the cosmos, a project that involved distilling all that is valuable in the past—including philosophy, art, and religion—into his own categories. Hegel's writings had tremendous resonance among the upcoming generation of German intellectuals, not least because his works tried to reconcile so many of the characteristic tensions of the age: between Christianity and a rational comprehension of the world, between tradition and revolution, and between the individual, the market, and the state.[121] That project has often been seen as hubristic if not megalomaniacal. Yet even those unsympathetic to and unconvinced by Hegel's total philosophical project may conclude, with Erich Voegelin, that "the systematic works themselves are filled with excellent philosophical and historical analyses which can stand for themselves, unaffected in their integrity by the system into which they are built."[122]

Hegel's influence upon later intellectuals was formidable, and reached well beyond German-speaking Europe. As we will see, Karl Marx cut his philosophical teeth on Hegel, before turning his back on Hegel's reconciliation of the individual with the institutions of the liberal and capitalist world. British intellectuals like Matthew Arnold were attracted to Hegel's critique of freedom as nothing more than "doing as one likes," and to his project of using the universities to create an educated class of civil servants who would help to guide the ship of state through the moral shoals created by the spread of the market.

CHAPTER SEVEN

KARL MARX:
FROM JEWISH USURY TO
UNIVERSAL VAMPIRISM

Karl Marx (1818–1883) and his collaborator, Friedrich Engels (1820–1895), were to become the best-known critics of the market. It is to them that we owe the popularity of the term "capitalism" as a synonym for what Smith had called "commercial society" and Hegel "civil society." Many thinkers more favorably disposed to such societies than Marx and Engels have objected to the very use of the term "capitalism," regarding it as fundamentally pejorative. So it was intended to be, as we will see. But like many an epithet born in political polemic, the term outgrew its origins, and eventually came to be adopted by those who rejected its invidious connotations. If Marxism as a political movement has passed its expiration date, its attractiveness as a source of analysis and as a critique of the market is unlikely to wither entirely. That is because from its earliest days, Marxism has exercised a dual appeal.

The first was grounded in sympathy for an impoverished industrial working class, forced into material privation. Marx not only evoked that poverty and degradation in his writings, but also offered an analysis that explained it as an inevitable and irreversible outcome of the market. And he connected that present suffering to a redemptive future, one of the deepest tropes of the Christian tradition.

This argument was to diminish in appeal whenever the economic and social condition of the working class improved, as it eventually did. But alongside it, and ultimately overtaking it in appeal, was a second set of arguments: the cultural critiques of capitalism that permeated the work of Marx and Engels. They portrayed the competition inherent in the market as morally abhorrent, as reducing human relations to the level of animality. In its place, they posited a society in which there would be no distinction between public and private interest. Above all, Marx expressed the discontent of those who, though not *materially* impoverished by capitalism, felt anguish at the need to fit themselves into the vocational grooves of the market economy, to bend themselves to fit into a particular professional niche.

Marx is frequently regarded as a disciple of Hegel, albeit a radical and critical one. But his critique of the stultifying effects of labor in a capitalist society is a direct continuation of the Romantic conception of the self and its place in society, a conception that Hegel rejected in his mature work. Similarly, Marx's abhorrence of market competition harked back to modes of thought that not only preceded Hegel, but were at odds with the fundamental assumptions of the Enlightenment about the potentially positive, unintended consequences of human activity and the legitimacy of self-interest. Indeed, the fundaments of Marx's economic analysis went back further yet. To a degree rarely appreciated, he merely recast the traditional Christian stigmatization of moneymaking into a new vocabulary and reiterated the ancient suspicion against those who used money to make money. In his concept of capitalism as "exploitation" Marx returned to the very old idea that money is fundamentally unproductive, that only those who live by the sweat of their brow truly produce, and that therefore not only interest, but profit itself, is always ill-gotten.

In his depiction of capitalism as alienation, Marx expressed a notion that many felt implicitly: that the satisfaction of individuals in modern society is sacrificed to forces over which they seem to have no control. And his counterconcept of communism dangled the promise of gaining that control, even though, as we will see, he had remarkably little to say about the institutional mechanisms by which such a society would function.

The hundreds of scholarly studies that stress the development of Marx's theories over the course of his lifetime tend to obscure what the most acute analysts of Marx's thought have discerned, namely that the whole of his later work was an attempt to confirm and elaborate ideas that he had developed by the age of thirty, when he penned *The Communist Manifesto*. Indeed, most had been worked out by 1844, when he was twenty-six.[1]

Marx's Jewish Problem and His Labor Problem

Marx was born in the Rhineland city of Trier in 1818, the year that Hegel accepted the call of the Prussian reformers to the University of Berlin. The family name, Marx, was a recent acquisition, adapted from "Mordechai," the name of Karl's grandfather. Karl's father, Heschel Marx, was the descendant of a central European rabbinic dynasty that had provided the rabbis of Trier since the sixteenth century. Karl's mother, too, was descended from many generations of rabbis.[2]

One of Karl Marx's crucial essays was "On the Question of the Jews," and the issue of Marx's relationship to his Jewish origins has been much discussed and often misunderstood. For there was nothing Jewish about Karl's upbringing, and despite attempts by critics to describe his mind as "Talmudic," he would not have known which end of a Talmudic page was up. For Heschel Marx had as a young man broken with his own family and with Judaism, about which he conveyed nothing to his children.[3] At the time of Karl's birth, Heschel was a lawyer at the High Court of Appeal in Trier. By the time Karl was a teenager, his father was active in the Rhineland's liberal movement, which pressed for a constitutional monarchy with representative institutions. A respected member of bourgeois society, he was president of the association of lawyers in Trier.

That respectability, however, was purchased at the price of any residual Jewish identification. Even after the Hardenberg administration eased many of the discriminatory laws against Jews in Prussia, they were excluded from positions in the service of the state. When the Rhineland came under Prussian control after Waterloo, the Prussian bureaucracy decided that those laws should apply to the Rhineland as well. Heschel Marx appealed his case, asking to be permitted to appear in court while remaining Jewish. When his appeal was rejected, he chose to convert to Christianity in 1817 to retain his livelihood, selecting the official state religion of Prussia, Lutheran Protestantism. At the same time, Heschel changed his name to the more German "Heinrich." His wife deferred her own baptism until the death of her rabbinic father in 1825. A year earlier, when their children were old enough to begin school, the Marxes had their children baptized, including their eldest son, Karl.

Of the content of Judaism, Karl Marx learned little. His father was steeped in the rationalism of the French and German Enlightenment; he was more of a morally focused deist than a theological Protestant. His favorite authors were Voltaire and Rousseau, and it was not the Bible but Voltaire that Heinrich read to his son.[4] Karl was raised in a town in which his uncle (Heinrich's brother) was the rabbi. But by converting, Heinrich had cut off relations with his Jewish relatives. Thus, Karl grew up with an awareness of his family's Jewish origins, but no positive attachments to Jews or Judaism.[5] His knowledge of things Jewish came almost entirely from non-Jewish sources, and his evaluation of the Jews came mostly from their enemies. Yet he was regarded as Jewish by others, who dubbed him "the Moor" because of his swarthy complexion, a tacit reference to his Semitic origins.

The most important source of Marx's cultural ideal lay in the culture of the German educated middle classes (Bildungsbürgertum), among whom a new style of life and a new mode of self-understanding had been developing since the late eighteenth century. It reflected a new conception of self-worth in which respect derived less from inherited social position (Stand) or from doing one's religiously and socially prescribed duties than from an individual identity carved out for oneself. The new ideal was the cultivation of a multifaceted individuality, expressed in philosophy and literature, in theater, in music, and in the visual arts. Culture was not to be merely a matter of passive reception. Reading became a means of developing one's mind, and of interacting with other minds on the written page. The educated Bürger was expected to express himself by writing poetry (or at least keeping a diary), by playing a musical instrument, and by drawing. Art, released from its liturgical and ornamental functions, came to be prized as a value in itself. Self-development through the cultivation of aesthetic sensibilities in a variety of cultural realms became the mark of the educated person. It was an ideal that contemporaries called "dilettantism."[6]

Marx imbibed this cultural ideal less from his parents than from Baron Ludwig von Westphalen, a neighbor of higher social status who took the young Karl under his wing and exposed him to Homer, Shakespeare, and Romantic poetry.[7] The taste for drama and for literature remained with Marx throughout his life. (Decades later, even though he and his family were on the edge of bankruptcy, Marx sent his children to a private school where they studied languages and literature, had them tutored in music and singing, and so cultivated their love of the theater that all three daughters considered becoming actresses.) When Karl went off to university, he considered a career as a poet, and then as a dramatist or theater critic. Many of his poems were dedicated to von Westphalen's daughter, Jenny, whom he eventually married.

Marx's Romantically inspired poems included attacks on "philistines," those who followed utilitarian professions based on an ordered and rational approach to life. His youthful writings, from his final year at the *Gymnasium* through the early years of university, vacillate between the ideal of self-sacrifice for the benefit of humanity and the cult of the isolated genius at war with the philistinism of his age.[8]

The perils of dilettantism were evident in Marx's vocational dilemma. Heinrich Marx was able to provide the accoutrements of bourgeois life for his family, including a university education for his son. But he was not rich enough to provide for Karl indefinitely. He was concerned that Karl be able to earn a living of his own, and wanted him to focus his education accordingly. In a letter of late 1837, he chastised his son for "meandering in all the fields of knowledge"—for dilettantism.[9] He tried to steer his son away from uncertain career prospects toward the safe haven of the legal profession. Karl was more interested in philosophy, but acceded to his father's wishes and took up the study of law. Yet as soon as Heinrich died, Karl abandoned the study of law for philosophy. Karl's mother, too, worried about her son's ability to earn a living, and this conflict strained their relationship. "If only Karl had made some capital instead of writing about it!" he remembered her exclaiming.[10]

Multifacetedness may be an admirable ideal, but it carries with it the danger of carrying nothing to completion. Many of Karl's erstwhile friends (he almost always ended up quarreling with them) commented on his inability to get anything finished. As a student at the University of Berlin, Marx tried to write a comprehensive philosophy of law: he stopped after three hundred pages to try his hand at a "new metaphysical system," which he never completed either.[11] In 1842 and 1843, he did research for a critical history of religious art. Before it was completed, he turned to writing a history of the French Revolution; though he gathered material for the project, it too remained unwritten. In 1844, his then collaborator, Arnold Ruge, noted that Marx "always wants to write on what he has read last, yet continues to read incessantly, making fresh excerpts."[12] From 1844 until the end of his life, Marx would labor on a comprehensive explanation of modern market society—another work that he never completed to his own satisfaction.[13]

These aspects of Marx's background and personality help account for fundamental elements of his social theory. His origin as a member of a minority, stigmatized for its religion, regarded as a separate nationality, and disdained for its economic role, led him to a posit a society in which religious and national differences would be obliterated and moneymaking abolished. His normative image of man is steeped in the Romantic ethos of the artist as a creator of reality, an image that Marx democratized and universalized. Behind his vision of the socialist future lay the new bourgeois cultural ideal of personal expression through creativity and all-roundedness. All of this was at odds with Hegel's emphasis on mediating institutions such as the family and the corporation, which lay between the individual and the larger whole, not to speak of his conception of maturity as coming to terms with one's place in the division of labor.[14] Marx's social vision owed less to Hegel than to Hölderlin.

Yet it was reading Hegel that inspired Marx to pursue a university career as a philosopher. After receiving his doctorate, he began lecturing at the University of Bonn, while collaborating with a lecturer in the faculty of theology, Bruno Bauer, on a journal to be titled the *Archive of Atheism* as well as on a book-length critique of religion. Not surprisingly, the Prussian authorities decided that the faculty of theology was no place for atheists. Bauer lost his post, and Marx, recognizing that philosophical radicals like himself had no prospect of a university career, turned to journalism. He began to write for, and soon to edit, the *Rheinische Zeitung*, a newspaper that stood "for politics, commerce, and industry" and represented the interests of the Rhineland's middle classes and entrepreneurs. On their behalf, Marx attacked the reactionary policy of the new king, Frederick William IV, and his administration, which aimed at a re-Christianized and paternalistic state. Marx's perspective at the time was Hegelian; he conceived of the state as "the great organism in which juridical, moral and political liberties must be realized and in which each citizen, by obeying the laws of the state, only obeys the natural laws of his own reason, human reason." From this perspective, the king's attempts to re-Christianize the state and to diminish freedom of the press were steps backward. The role of the press, as Marx then envisioned it, was to educate the public, including those in the civil service, about the shortcomings of the regime as judged by Hegel's conception of the modern state.[15] These issues interested the liberal owners of the newspaper, but they and other middle-class Germans were increasingly concerned with "the social question." Soon Marx was as well.

The Social Question

As early as the 1780s, Justus Möser had been alarmed by the wave of impoverished people who were migrating to the towns from the countryside yet who could not be absorbed into the guilds. Economically dependent and politically disenfranchised, they were a menace to the stability of the social order. Their number continued to grow, and during the 1820s, as we have seen, Hegel pointed to the seeming intractability of the problem of "pauperism." The number of those bereft of a stable source of income continued to rise during the 1830s, and by the early 1840s the problem of pauperism became a focus of public concern, giving rise to anxieties about the inevitability of revolution if it was not remedied.[16] The term "proletariat" was imported from France to designate those who, lacking land, capital, and a stable profession, lived in persistent insecurity and represented a threat to the existing social order.[17]

Some intellectuals and politicians attributed the increase in the army of the impoverished to the rise of industrial manufacture. Such was the view of one young conservative politician, Otto von Bismarck, who proclaimed in 1848 that "the factories enrich individuals, but they create a mass of poorly nourished proletarians, who by virtue of the insecurity of their existence have become a threat to the state."[18] Businessmen and supporters of more liberal economic policies were also alarmed by "the social problem," and some of the most farsighted believed that the growth of industry was the solution to the problem of the unemployed, rather than the source of the problem.[19] But that was a minority opinion.

Yet factory workers made up only a tiny percentage of the German workforce before 1848; less than 170,000 souls worked in factories or mines within the boundaries of the German customs union (*Zollverein*), and together with miners they made up only 2¼ percent of the economically active population.[20] By and large, their circumstances were miserable. Even the better-paid skilled workers among them lived in a state of economic uncertainty. Most industrial workers could keep their families housed, clothed, and fed only because their wives and children worked as well. And when accident or disease intervened, as it so often did, even that was not enough. In some branches of industry, especially textiles, women made up half the workforce; 15 percent of the factory workforce were children, some as young as seven. In the factories of the Rhineland, these children worked from five in the morning until dusk. To be sure, these circumstances were exceptional: even at the height of child factory labor, in 1846, only 6.5 percent of children aged nine to fourteen worked in factories, and starting in the late 1830s, German states began to regulate child labor, limiting work hours and requiring school instruction.

But the burden of factory labor was by no means confined to childhood. It took its toll on the men who worked long hours—twelve hours a day was not unusual, and seventeen hours not unknown—under conditions that often included deafening noise, stifling heat, and choking dust in poorly ventilated factories. The toll on the body was exacerbated by the monotony of the required movements. By age forty, a worker who had labored for more than two decades under such conditions was already an old man. If he beat the odds and survived the ever-present possibility of accident leading to injury and invalidism, he could look forward to a middle age of decreasing income and an old age of poverty.[21]

The spread of pauperism and the slow growth of factory labor occurred at a time when German agriculture was becoming more productive as a result of the innovations of the Prussian reformers, and when manufacturing too was on the upswing. Thus although poverty was increasing, so too was the sum total of social wealth.[22]

The source of this paradox lay in demographic growth, which had been rising since the mid-eighteenth century and which quickened during the first half of the nineteenth. The number of people living in the German states (excluding those in the Austrian empire) rose by almost 50 percent in the three decades between Marx's birth and the revolutionary year of 1848, from 22 million in 1816 to 33 million in 1850.[23] That growth was made possible by an agricultural revolution that produced more food and even more jobs. Former serfs, now freed from direct seignorial control by the legal changes of the reform era, could marry earlier—and hence began to have more children. Still in its infancy in Möser's day, cottage industry became the major site of production, alongside older, artisanal production. Cottage industry was a highly decentralized form of production for the market, which reached into the tiniest dwelling and provided an opportunity for the landless to earn a living. Better nutrition led to a decline in mortality: fewer Germans died in infancy, more survived into adulthood.[24]

The result was more people, more than the economy could absorb. The number of artisans doubled, but the demand for artisanal products did not. The result for artisans was declining wages and rising unemployment. By the 1840s, workers in cottage industry faced a crisis of their own. Those in the textile trades—spinners, weavers, and clothiers—confronted competition from industrially produced goods, as machines driven by steam produced items at much lower prices. Most of these factory-made goods came from England, some from Germany itself. To remain competitive, the entrepreneurs who employed the cottage workers cut wages. Not for the last time, a new, more efficient organization of production was coming into being at the expense of older, more traditional forms. To make ends meet, the cottage workers were forced to labor ever longer hours. The result was the death agony of cottage industry, which came to the attention of shocked contemporaries in 1844 when linen weavers in the Prussian province of Silesia revolted against the entrepreneurs who had lowered their incomes to near-starvation level.[25]

Population growth without adequate job creation led to the economic distress that increasingly plagued Germany and other parts of Europe in the decades when Marx and Engels were coming of age. In one of his very first publications—a series of articles about life in his native Wuppertal, which appeared under a pseudonym when he was only nineteen—Engels sketched the themes that were to echo through his subsequent work. The conditions in the newly created factories were robbing workers of their strength and vitality, he wrote. He described grown men and children as young as six working in airless rooms filled with steam and dust, dying of consumption, "destroyed in body and soul." Their travails were temporarily drowned in alcohol, or in enthusiastic religion. The factory owners, pietist Protestants like his own family, came off as hypocrites, for whom religious piety replaced social responsibility, and moneymaking any tincture of higher culture and aspiration.[26] Engels described his native region as "a sea of pietism and philistinism, without an island of aesthetic beauty."[27]

The stresses in the social order were heightened to the breaking point in the years from 1845 to 1847, when the British and French economies took a downturn. First the potato blight and then an extraordinarily hot and dry summer leading to a poor grain crop sent the price of food sky-high. At a time when most people still devoted most of their earnings to buying food, the rise in food prices left consumers with less to spend on other products. That meant a decline in demand for manufactured goods and therefore a drop in prices and in the profits of entrepreneurs. They in turn lowered production and fired workers. The downturn was made still worse by a bank panic. Years of bad harvests had put farmers and landowners into debt, and bankers feared they would never be able to collect on their loans. As businesses ran into trouble, they found banks unwilling or unable to loan them money. Some went under, leaving even more workers without employment. The upshot was widespread distress and discontent.[28]

In retrospect, we know that this was the last great agrarian crisis in the history of western Europe. But to many contemporaries, burgeoning unemployment and the hunger that accompanied higher food prices seemed to augur the collapse of the social order. In 1848, a third of the population of the Rhineland city of Cologne was receiving poverty relief, and a further 40 percent lived in the gray zone of occasional hunger. The swelling lower classes of the cities faced an ongoing struggle to survive, and their numbers and misery struck fear in the hearts of middle-class observers.[29] Revolution did indeed break out in 1848, first in France and then in most of the rest of continental Europe. In the years between 1843, when Marx wrote "On the Question of Jews" and Engels his "Critique of Political Economy," and late 1847, when together they composed *The Communist Manifesto,* their assumption that the capitalist economic order meant the immiserization of the mass of the population was eminently plausible.

"A specter is haunting Europe—the specter of Communism," the *Manifesto* began. The "communism" that Marx and Engels conjured up was indeed spectral. In the German states, socialists were numbered in the hundreds; some of them were intellectuals, others artisans who had gone abroad to look for work and learned their socialism in Paris, Brussels, or London. Socialist ideas were more widespread in France than anywhere else, but even there, on the eve of the 1848 revolution, there were at most tens of thousands who counted themselves socialists, most of them craftsmen and laborers in urban areas. What *did* exist throughout Europe was the fear of the "red menace." Serfs rebelling against their feudal lords, peasants seizing wood from the forests, craftsmen demanding a return of the guilds, artisans and laborers going on strike—all these actions were described, and feared, as communism.[30] Marx and Engels interpreted what was in fact the agony of a declining preindustrial order as the birth pangs of a postcapitalist future.

From Hegelianism to Communism

Hegel had claimed that the modern state could both satisfy the individual's desire to pursue particular interests—as a member of civil society—and yet provide him with a sense of participation in the larger whole of the state through representative institutions, the estates.[31] But ultimately, in Hegel's scheme, it was only the civil service, "the universal estate," that was unequivocally devoted to the common good. Marx knew from his own experience how implausible such claims had become.

It was as a journalist in the Rhineland that Marx came face-to-face with the extent of economic distress and the political obstacles that blocked its alleviation. In 1842 he investigated wood theft in the Moselle valley, near his native city of Trier. Traditionally, peasants had been allowed to gather wood from the forests of the nobility; this wood was their major source of fuel. As the number of peasants grew, and as landowners took a more capitalistic attitude to their property, seeking to maximize its profitability, the customary rights claimed by the peasants came into conflict with newfound conceptions of private property embodied in the law.[32] By Marx's day the theft of wood was far and away the single most prosecuted crime in the German states, the most tangible sign of the struggle between the propertied and the propertyless.

The gap between Hegel's theory of the modern state and the realities of Prussian politics soon dawned on Marx and led him toward ever increasing radicalism. When the subject of the laws defining wood theft came up for debate in the legislative body of the Rhineland, the *Landtag*, Marx saw that not only the administration of the law but the very definition of what constituted theft reflected the interests of the owners of property. The landowners who dominated the *Landtag* ran roughshod over the customary law, which supported the claims of the poor to collect fallen wood in the forests. They gave no thought to the general interest. They did not think in universal terms but merely calculated their own advantage.[33] In their pursuit of their legally guaranteed, calculating interests, Marx wrote, they were no more than modern Shylocks, cutting their pound of flesh from the bodies of the poor.[34] That metaphor would become one of his favorites.

At the same time, the ultraconservative regime of Frederick

William IV was cracking down on liberals in the civil service (many of them Hegelians) and intensifying its censorship of journals and newspapers. Prussia as a whole was becoming ever less hospitable to public debate and open criticism; Marx's journalistic career, like his academic career, was cut short. When his newspaper criticized the Prussian government and bureaucracy too brazenly, censors shut it down.

In his newspaper articles, and then in a lengthy commentary that he wrote on his honeymoon in mid-1843, Marx laid out his critique of Hegel's conception of the state, its representative institutions, and its civil service. The state's bureaucracy, he discovered, did not function to guide the state on behalf of the universal interest. Instead, the government protected its own interests by measures such as censorship, which shielded it from criticism.[35] The estates, rather than aiming at the common interest, used their legislative power to promote the economic interests of the groups represented in them, at the expense of the majority of the population, which had no representation.[36] Marx concluded that neither the civil service nor representative institutions were looking out for the welfare of the poor, who were growing in number and desperation. In contemporary Prussia, he argued, there *was* no representative of the general interest.

In search of greater freedom of expression, he went to Paris, where other German intellectuals had already settled. There he read the works of French and German social critics—some of them socialists— who described the degradation of the working classes under the newly emerging system of factory labor. The notion of a struggle between workers and factory owners—indeed, the language of labor versus capital—was not invented by Marx. As early as 1828, John C. Calhoun, who offered a critique of class relations in the American North in order to defend slavery in the South, had written, "After we [the Southern planters] are exhausted, the contest will be between the capitalists and the operatives [workers]; for into these two classes it must, ultimately, divide society. The issue of the struggle here must be the same as it has been in Europe. Under the operation of the system, wages must sink more rapidly than the prices of the necessaries of life, till the operatives will be reduced to the lowest point,—when the portion of the products of their labor left to them will be barely sufficient to preserve existence."[37] In Europe, the Swiss economist Jean Charles-Léon Simonde de Sismondi had in the 1820s depicted a struggle between the "capitalist" and the "worker," and in 1837 he referred to the worker as "proletarian." In a widely read book of 1842, Lorenz von Stein, a German reformist conservative, described the class of proletarians as those who lacked the worldly goods "which give individual personality its value." He warned that without a social monarchy, class conflict would lead to a "dictatorship" of this new class. Marx, who read Stein's book in 1843, turned this warning into a hope for the future.[38] Most of all, Marx drew upon a graphic 1842 French work, Eugène Buret's *The Misery of the Working Classes in England and France*. Buret argued that because the capitalists sought to depress the wages of the working class, the increase of social wealth was accompanied by an impoverished proletariat.[39] But it was the work of his fellow German radical emigré, Friedrich Engels, that more than any other set the direction of Marx's subsequent critique of market society.

Engels' Critique of Political Economy

Marx first read Engels' work in manuscript, when it was submitted to him for publication in the *Deutsch-Französische Jahrbücher*, a volume he edited in Paris. Entitled "Outlines of a Critique of Political Economy," the article laid out in embryonic form many of the ideas that Marx and Engels were to spend the rest of their lives developing.[40] Here the fundaments of their moral arguments against capitalism were first articulated.

The essence of Engels' critique of political economy was simple. The work of Adam Smith and his disciples obscured what Engels found morally scandalous: capitalism was built on avarice and on selfishness. If the key maneuver of Enlightenment thinkers such as Smith was to call attention to the potential social benefits of what had been previously stigmatized as "greed" and "pride," the first countermaneuver of socialist critics such as Engels was to restigmatize self-interest as greed.[41]

Smith might have been right, Engels wrote, about the fact that trade has a humane aspect: it might bring about more gentle relations between individuals; it might diminish war between nations and "civilize the ends of the earth." But all of that was based upon hypocrisy, for the real motives behind trade were those of self-interest:

> Naturally, it is in the interest of the trader to be on good terms with the one from whom he buys cheap as well as with the other to whom he sells dear. A nation therefore acts very imprudently if it fosters feelings of animosity in its

suppliers and customers. The more friendly, the more advantageous. Such is the humanity of trade. And this hypocritical way of misusing morality for immoral purposes is the pride of the free-trade system. . . . You have brought about the fraternization of the peoples—but the fraternity is the fraternity of thieves. You have reduced the number of wars—to earn all the bigger profits in peace . . . When have you done anything out of pure humanity, from consciousness of the futility of the opposition between the general and the individual interest? When have you been moral without being interested, without harboring at the back of your mind immoral, egoistical motives?[42]

For Engels, trade stood condemned, in the first instance, for the *impurity of motivation* that lay behind it. Morality, by definition, could not be based on self-interest.

The problem with capitalism, for Engels, was that it was based upon competition. Competition, he wrote, "isolates everyone in his own crude solitariness," and by setting each at war with his neighbor, consummates "the immorality of mankind's condition up to now."[43] By pitting self-interested individuals against one another, it created a war of all against all, transforming mankind into "a horde of ravenous beasts (for what else are competitors?) who devour one another."[44]

If Engels' first step was to go back to pre-Enlightenment understandings of self-interest, his second was to go back further yet, to pre-Renaissance condemnations of the interest on loans. Profits from trade, he reasoned, were little different from "interest" and could only be distinguished from it by overly subtle logic chopping. And interest was immoral: "The immorality of lending at interest, of receiving without working . . . has long ago been recognized for what it is by unprejudiced popular consciousness, which in such matters is usually right."[45]

In his analysis, Engels also captured an element of industrial capitalism as seen from the point of view of the merchant or manufacturer: the looming omnipresence of uncertainty. As Smith and other political economists had said, prices reflected the relationship between supply and demand. Because that relationship was constantly changing, prices for commodities went up and down, in a way that was difficult to predict. And yet in order to profit from price fluctuations, everyone had to devote attention to buying and selling at the most advantageous moment. Making a profit, therefore, depended not only on what had gone into manufacturing the product, but also on factors independent of the producer—on chance. Smith had thought that in commercial society everyone to some degree becomes a merchant. Engels now maintained that everyone becomes a speculator, who profits by betting on the misfortune of others. Those who buy grain on speculation, for example, hope that bad harvests will raise the value of their speculative purchase. And speculation, Engels claimed, was little different from gambling. For him, as for critics of capitalism from the early eighteenth century on, the quintessence of capitalist evil was the stock market. "[I]mmorality's culminating point is the speculation on the stock exchange, where history, and with it mankind, is demoted to a means of gratifying the avarice of the calculating or gambling speculator. And let not the honest 'respectable' merchant rise above the gambling on the stock exchange with a Pharisaic 'There but for the Grace of God . . .' He is as bad as the speculators in stocks and shares. He speculates just as much as they do. He has to: competition compels him to. And his trading activity therefore implies the same immorality as theirs."[46] For Engels, then, gambling, speculation, profit, and interest were all part of the same avaricious continuum.

War and market activity had a great deal in common, Engels claimed, since both put men in competition with one another. Competition, for Engels, was a nice word for enmity, and enmity a quality of bestiality. And so, beneath the patina of pacific, cooperative relations praised by Voltaire and Smith, the market meant war by other means.

According to Engels, production under capitalism was "unconscious, thoughtless," and at the mercy of chance. While the theory of political economists maintained that supply and demand would come into balance, in fact there was always a gap between supply and demand for any given commodity—with disastrous consequences for individuals. Those who labored producing goods for which supply was greater than demand found themselves without work, or working for lower wages. A dramatic example was at hand in the Silesian weavers, about whom Engels wrote in a radical British periodical, *The Northern Star*. "It is evident," Engels concluded, "that the consequences of the factory system, of the progress of machinery, etc. for the working classes are quite the same on the continent as they are in England: oppression and toil for the many, riches and wealth for the few."[47] Capitalist competition, he argued, would lead to the centralization of private property, as big producers forced smaller ones out of business. The middle classes would disappear, until the world was divided into "millionaires and paupers"[48]—a Manichean scenario that he and Marx continued to predict for the rest of their lives.

Smith had shown, and Burke and Hegel had accepted, that the market produced consequences that were orderly although unintended. For Engels, by contrast, that which was unplanned was disorderly, anarchic. His alternative was socialism, in which the production of the economy as a whole would be rationally planned and centrally organized.[49] This assumption, that only the planned is rational and that only the intentional is orderly, meant the renunciation of the very foundations of political economy as it had developed since the eighteenth century. "The community will have to calculate what it can produce with the means at its disposal; and in accordance with the relationship of this productive power to the mass of consumers it will determine how far it has to raise or lower production."[50] This too would be repeated by Marx, who in fact said little more about how the socialist economy would be organized.

Marx adopted most of Engels' analysis. In combination with the works he was reading by French socialists, Marx was led by Engels' piece to focus on the plight of the industrial working class, and toward a critique of political economy, filtered through the lens of his own philosophical assumptions and concerns.

Jewdom Transcended

A milestone in the development of Marx's critique of capitalism is his essay "On the Question of the Jews" (*Zur Judenfrage*), published early in 1844 alongside Engels' critique of political economy. In this contribution to a long-simmering controversy among German liberal and radical writers, Marx combined his moral critique of capitalism with traditional anti-Jewish images, not in order to bolster antisemitism but to blacken the moral standing of bourgeois society.

The question of the status of the Jews was much debated among German political writers in the first half of the nineteenth century; by one estimate, 2,500 works were published on the issue between 1815 and 1850, by writers Jewish and non-Jewish.[51] For conservatives, the link between the state and Christianity was indissoluble: the state helped to preserve faith, and religion helped to legitimate government. Given that premise, Jews could be tolerated by the state but not granted equality of political status within it. And since, as in the case of the guilds, religion was an intrinsic part of social and economic life, Jews would remain excluded from many nongovernmental occupations as well.

The theoretical starting point of liberal approaches to the status of the Jews was the premise that the modern state should be neutral on questions of religion, as in Hegel's *Philosophy of Right*. For Hegel, the modern state embodies an understanding of individual freedom that is an outgrowth of historical Protestantism. But the state itself is to be religiously neutral, providing the basis for individuals to choose to belong to particular religious denominations—another way it serves to protect individuality.[52] But even among liberals, there were doubts about granting equal political and civil rights to Jews. Liberals often insisted that the Jews' religion led them to segregate themselves from others. The tendency of Jews to eschew the full range of occupations in favor of commerce and finance was treated as further evidence of this pernicious particularity. For some liberals, therefore, equality of rights was to be offered to the Jews only if they embraced Christianity, or, more moderately, if they radically reformed their religion to eliminate its particularistic elements.[53]

In 1843, the debate on what to do about the Jews was ignited within Marx's own circle with the publication of two works by Bruno Bauer, the radical Hegelian colleague with whom Marx had planned to publish the *Archive of Atheism*. Like other radical Hegelians, such as Ludwig Feuerbach, Bauer decided that Hegel had not gone far enough in his secularization of Christian concepts: Christianity itself was to be transcended by atheism. Yet in his writings on the Jewish question, Bauer used the Hegelian argument that Christianity represented a historical stage beyond Judaism. Judaism was a particularistic religion, which applied only to a delimited group, while Christianity, with its universal conception of religion as applying to all men, represented a higher stage of philosophical consciousness. The current stage called for going beyond Christianity itself, to a worldview that was universal while denying Christian theological premises. But, Bauer argued, the Jews could not jump from tribal particularism to philosophical universalism without going through the change of consciousness brought about by Christianity. The Jew, he wrote, seeks to become the citizen of a universal state, but without giving up his claim to separate identity and particularity.

Bauer combined his philosophical attack on granting Jews civil and political equality with a portrait of Jewry etched in acid. (Later on he would abandon his philosophical radicalism, while maintaining his antipathy to the Jews.)[54] He characterized Judaism as a religion of ego-

ism, a recurrent theme among German philosophical radicals.⁵⁵ The
Jews were uninterested in culture, science, and philosophy, Bauer
claimed.⁵⁶ He attacked them above all for their particularism, evidence
of which he found in the fact that they remained outside the guilds and
instead engaged in usury. It was this link between particularism, egoism, and usury on which Marx would focus.

Marx's response was to insist that, despite his purported radicalism,
Bauer's analysis was not nearly radical enough. Bauer had debated
whether the Jews were fit for political emancipation. But that, Marx
countered, was beside the point. To emancipate them, to give them full
civil and political rights, was to create a state free of religion; it was
"the emancipation of the state from religion."⁵⁷ But political emancipation in the liberal democratic state was not worth much, Marx contended, since it did not bring about real human emancipation. Religion
was a system of therapeutic illusion: like opium, it dulled pain. The
question for radical philosophers was the *source* of this pain, which lay
in the worldly experience that gave rise to the need for religion in the
first place. Marx pointed to the experience of the United States, a liberal, democratic, bourgeois society in which religion and state had
been entirely separated. There religion flourished—proof, for Marx,
that bourgeois society and political democracy did not do away with
the experience of deprivation that gave rise to religion. Political reform
leading to a constitutional order that guaranteed personal and property
rights—the creed of liberals—was worthless, according to Marx. So too
was the democratic franchise for which radicals campaigned. It was
not political reform but social and economic revolution that was
urgently needed, for it was the market and the classes to which it gave
rise that were the real sources of human discontent.

This discontent stemmed from the lack of true solidarity and community, which were impossible in civil society. In the democratic
state, the individual was supposed to act as a citizen, concerned with
the common good. But under contemporary conditions, that solidarity
was a mere illusion. For the real, determinative sphere of life was that
of civil society, and in that sphere one could only be active as *"private
man*, who regards other men as means, and is himself degraded into a
means and a plaything of alien forces."⁵⁸ Here was a world of exclusively private interest, in which the general interest was pursued by no
one.

Were the Jews egoistic, as Bauer had charged? Certainly, Marx
answered. But in bourgeois society, *everyone* was egoistic. Were the
Jews particularistic? Of course, but in bourgeois society, there was no
interest but the particular interest. Was Bauer correct in characterizing

the Jew as a "constrained being" (*beschränkte Wesen*)? Yes, Marx replied, because in bourgeois society, all were constrained. Did the Jews cut themselves off from others? Yes, because that is what "rights" meant in a liberal market society: the right to be particular, to be egoistic, to be constrained and encapsulated. All of these followed from the highest of liberal rights: the right to private property. And the right to private property was, as Hegel had said, the right to be willful (*willkürlich*). For Marx, that meant the right to engage in action "without regard to other people."

Self-interest was the fundamental basis of bourgeois society.[59] And that, Marx thought, made bourgeois society morally abhorrent and (although he did not use the term) inauthentic. For man was fundamentally a "species-being" (*Gattungswesen*) who reached his true purpose only through cooperation with others. Modern civil society was based on the opposite of this communal altruism.

In bringing his argument to its crescendo, Marx played on the multiple meanings of the German word "*Judentum*." It could mean Judaism (the religion), the Jews (as a group), or, like its English equivalent "jewing," bargaining fraught with negative connotations. Marx also used a second term with multiple connotations, "*Schacher*." The word was a colloquialism; it is often translated as "haggling," as retail trading that involves bargaining. But that is to miss its resonance to Marx's contemporaries. Like the English term "huckstering," it was used figuratively to mean "a person ready to make his profit on anything in a mean and petty way."[60] It also was a popular term for "usury." The shared element in these meanings came from the fact that *Schacher* was virtually always associated with Jews.[61] Indeed the word itself is derived from the root of the Hebrew term for trade, "*sachar*."[62] Excluded from many areas of the German economy by law and custom, Jews often eked out a living by peddling, trading in whatever items they could buy and sell, including secondhand goods, and lending money.[63] Especially in rural areas little served by merchants and banks, Jews played all of these roles. In a society of lords and peasants, they were among the few who regularly engaged in calculating the relative value of items, and the chances of making a profit by buying and selling. *Schacher*, therefore, connoted the stigmatized economic activities that were typically associated with Jews, a minority of cultural outsiders. In his "Outlines of a Critique of Political Economy," Engels had, in passing, used the term "*Selbstverschacherung*"—"the making oneself into an object of huckstering"—to express his disdain for the fact that land and labor had become commodities that could be bought and sold for profit.[64] Now Marx made use of the multiple connotations of *Schacher* to lay out his critique of market society:

> Let us seek the secret of the Jew not in his religion, rather let us seek for the secret of religion in the real Jew.
>
> What is the worldly basis of Jewdom? *Practical* need, *self-interest*.
>
> What is the worldly cult of the Jew? *Bargaining (Schacher)*. What is his worldly god? *Money*.
>
> Well, then! The self-emancipation of our age would be emancipation from *bargaining* and from *money*, that is from practical, real Jewdom.
>
> An organization of society that would eliminate the prerequisites of bargaining, that would eliminate the possibility of trade, would make the Jew impossible. His religious consciousness would dissolve like a dull mist in the real vital air of society. On the other hand, when the Jew recognizes his *practical* essence as invalid and works at negating and transcending it, he works to go beyond his previous development, toward general *human emancipation*, and he turns against the *supreme, practical* expression of human self-alienation.
>
> And so, we recognize in Jewdom an antisocial element, which is everywhere today, an evil relationship in which the Jews have participated with enthusiasm, which is now being driven to its highest level, a level at which it must inevitably disintegrate. The ultimate significance of *Jewish emancipation* is the emancipation of humanity from Jewdom. . . .
>
> The Jew has emancipated himself in a Jewish way not only by acquiring financial power, but also because through him and without him, *money* has become a world power and the practical Jewish spirit has become the practical spirit of the Christian peoples. The Jews have emancipated themselves insofar as the Christians have become Jews.[65]

Marx embraces all of the traditional negative characterizations of the Jew that were repeated by Bauer, and for good measure he adds a few of his own. But he does so in order to stigmatize market activity. For Marx's strategy is to endorse every negative characterization of market activity that Christians associated with Jews, but to insist that those qualities have now come to characterize society as a whole, very much including Christians. The Christian tradition of stigmatizing Jews and the economic activities in which they engaged by virtue of their marginality now becomes a stick with which to beat bourgeois society. For Marx, Jew-bashing becomes a tool for bashing the bourgeoisie.

Like Voltaire more than a century earlier, Marx condemns the Jews for their stubborn particularism. But the market, which Voltaire saw as a tool for overcoming particularism, for Marx represents the universalization of particular interests. If in a capitalist society Christians too are egoistic and particularistic, then the fact that Christianity is more universalistic than Judaism ceases to matter. Not only religious difference is to be overcome: all self-interest, individual and group, is to be eliminated.

In the second half of his essay, Marx takes on Bauer's claim that the Jews are devoid of interest in higher culture, in philosophy, in man as an end in himself. True enough, Marx says. But in contemporary bourgeois society, all have taken on the characteristics of the moneyman (*Geldmensch*), who is typically uninterested in anything but getting richer. Though the Jews are narrow and confined, so is all of life in bourgeois society.[66] The nationality of the Jews, Marx asserts, is chimerical, like the nationality of the merchant (*Kaufmann*).[67] He agrees with Smith's proposition that in commercial society, every man becomes a merchant to some degree or another. For Marx, however, that insight has entirely negative implications.

At the end of his essay, Marx takes Bauer's claim that Christianity is a more universal religion than Judaism and gives it an ironic twist. It is under the universalist auspices of Christianity that a truly universalist process is occurring, the spread of the market (bourgeois society). But it is universal in that all collective human ties are torn apart by egoism, by self-interested need (*eigennützige Bedürfnis*), dissolved into a world of atomistic individuals practicing relations of enmity.[68]

The true God of the Jews is money, Marx assures his readers, and like the jealous God of the Bible, who would tolerate no lesser gods before him, money tolerates no other relations: it transforms all natural objects and human relationships into commodities that can be exchanged. Radical Hegelians such as Feuerbach claimed that God ought to be understood as the alienated essence of man, in which human characteristics of love and power are projected onto an illusory master to which men had subordinated themselves. So too, Marx suggests, with money, which "is the alienated essence of man's labor and his being," an alien being that dominates him, and which he reveres.[69]

Voltaire suggested that the pursuit of money on the London exchange was socially useful because it kept men from fighting about God. Marx now protests that men have come to worship money itself. Hence Marx's ironic conclusion, "The *social* emancipation of the Jew is the *emancipation of society from Jewdom.*"

"On the Question of the Jews" is Janus-faced. Read carefully, Marx's argument is clear enough: all of the negative moral evaluations that traditional Christians and modern post-Christians like Voltaire and Bauer applied to Jews should in fact be applied to capitalist society. But because Marx himself reiterated so many negative characterizations of the Jews and their economic role, with a twist of the argument one could suggest that the task was to rescue capitalism from its "Jewish" aspects, and from the Jews themselves. That would be the theme, with variations, of subsequent anti-Jewish authors from Richard Wagner to Werner Sombart and down to the Nazi ideologist Alfred Rosenberg.[70]

In two other essays published in the same volume in which "On the Question of the Jews" appeared, Marx for the first time drew a connection between the cultural plight of intellectuals and the material want of the victims of the market economy. He portrayed their common enemy as the "philistines"—the uncultured, unheroic supporters of the repressive, religiously tinged policy of the Prussian monarchy. They accepted their subjugated status and ignored the economic misery into which so many of their countrymen were falling. "The system of industry and trade, of ownership and exploitation of people," he wrote, "leads to a rupture within present-day society." "[T]he existence of suffering human beings who think, and of thinking human beings who are oppressed, must inevitably become unpalatable and indigestible to the animal world of philistinism which passively and thoughtlessly consumes."[71] In another article he put the issue more concretely, but the trio of forces remained the same. On the one hand there was the "philistine mediocrity" [*philisterhaften Mittel-mäßigkeit*] of German society, reflected in the political pusillanimity of its middle classes, who were too timid to bring about revolution.[72] Revolution would come, however, from contact between critical philosophers like himself and the social class he now referred to as "the proletariat." Their poverty was not the result of nature; it was—as Hegel had noted a generation earlier—an "artificially produced poverty." The process of industrialization, which was just beginning in Germany, was leading to the erosion of the traditional, artisanal middle estates (*Mittelstand*) and thus to the "acute dissolution" of traditional society.[73]

In his essay on the Jewish question, Marx connected particular interest to private property and to the money economy, and decried them all. Now he discovered a group that, he insisted, could have no particular interest because it was absolutely without property: the proletariat. As Marx saw it, this group not only lacked the property that conferred standing in civil society, but was completely unassimilable into that society. It was "a class in civil society that is not of civil society, a class that is the dissolution of all classes, a sphere of society having a universal character because of its universal suffering." And when the proper connection was made between intellectuals like himself, who recognized the radical moral inadequacy of bourgeois society, and the proletariat, which had nothing to lose in that society and everything to gain by its supersession, the eventual result would be revolution.[74]

It would be only a slight exaggeration to say that the rest of Marx's career was an attempt to prove these claims, first set out in 1844. For these essays contain, in embryo, most of the subsequent themes of Marx's critique of capitalism: the labor theory of value, the power of money (e.g., capital), the elimination of cultural particularity through the spread of the market, and the fetishization of commodities. In 1845, when Engels published his book *The Condition of the Working Class in England Based on Personal Observation and Authentic Sources*, he forged the final, lasting conceptual links between Marx's moral critique and the social and economic categories in which their subsequent work was cast.

Most of Engels' book was devoted to the degraded condition of the new working class that had come into being in industrial centers such as Manchester, where Engels lived for over a year while gathering information for his study. But in his concluding chapter, "The Attitude of the Bourgeoisie Toward the Proletariat," he linked the moral critique already put forward by Marx and himself to what were to become their central categories of analysis.

> I have never seen a class so deeply demoralized, so incurably debased by self-interest [*Eigennutz*], so internally corroded and incapable of progress as the English bourgeoisie. . . . For it, nothing exists in the world except for the sake of money, including the bourgeoisie themselves, who live for no purpose but to earn money, who know no bliss other than quick profit, and no pain beyond monetary loss. No human relationship is untainted by this avarice [*Habsucht*] and lust for money [*Geldgier*]. . . .
>
> The English bourgeois could not care less whether his

workers starve or not, as long as he earns money. All conditions of life are measured by profitability [*Gelderwerb*], and
whatever does not produce money is nonsense, impractical,
idealistic. That is why political economy, the science of
money-earning [*Gelderwerb*] is the beloved science of these
Schacherjuden. Every one of them is an economist. The
relationship of the factory owner to the worker is not a
human one, it is purely economic. The factory owner is
"Capital," the worker is "Labor." And if the worker refuses
to be limited by that abstraction, if he asserts that he is not
"labor" but a man, for whom work is one characteristic
among others, if he takes it into his head to believe that he
need not let this "labor" be bought and sold like a commodity in the market—then the bourgeois is totally uncompre-
hending.[75]

By 1845, the linkage in Marx's and Engels' writings between the traditional stigmatization of usury and the new anathematization of
industrial capitalism had been forged. Money, that intrinsically unproductive substance, the use of which to make more money had long
been condemned as immoral usury, was now rechristened "capital."
Like money in the Aristotelian-Christian tradition, capital too is
intrinsically infertile. Those who profit from its use—the bourgeoisie
and their leaders, the factory owners—are as philistine, as calculative,
as *Schacherjuden*. And like Jews, they are beyond the morally legitimate community. The task of the hour, Marx and Engels repeated in
their joint work of 1845, *The Holy Family*, was to supercede "the Jewishness of bourgeois society, the inhumanity of present existence,
which finds its highest embodiment in the system of money."[76]

If Marx's vision was forward-looking, its premises were curiously
archaic. As in the civic republican and Christian traditions, self-inter-
est is the enemy of social cohesion and of morality. In that sense,
Marx's thought is a reversion to a time before Hegel, Smith, or Voltaire.
Marx himself came to recognize how much he shared with the pre-
Enlightenment critique of commerce. In his "Theories of Surplus
Value" (written 1861–63), he quotes from Mandeville's contention in
The Fable of the Bees that all of trade and commerce is based on evil.
"Mandeville," Marx comments, "was of course infinitely more
intrepid and honest than the philistine apologists of bourgeois soci-
ety."[77] Quoting Luther's tirades against moneylenders, Marx noted
that the founder of Protestantism "has really caught the character of
old-fashioned usury, and that of capital as a whole."[78]

In their description of the confrontation of capital and labor, Marx and Engels resurrected the traditional critique of usury. Marx's greatest innovation was to link that theme to the Romantic critique of the division of labor, the effect of which he called "alienated labor." By that, Marx meant above all that under capitalism, men and women worked because they *had* to in order to get the money required to buy the necessities of life. Man was forced to expend himself in order to survive.[79] For Marx, this was itself dehumanizing. Animals expended themselves merely to survive; what distinguished humanity was the ability to create freely. Labor, for Marx, was most human when it was an act of self-expression, a creation through which the world was transformed and stamped by the individuality of its creator. And since men and women were assumed to be multifaceted, their labor ought to allow them to develop all of their potentialities. Marx's model of non-alienated labor was the artist and the dilettante. The model of the individual as creator of the world through self-expression came from the Romantics; the emphasis on multifaceted creation came from the cultural ideals of the educated bourgeoisie.[80]

Marx was hardly the first to note the evils of the division of labor. But he was particularly sensitive to the human costs of the process of specialization because of his Romantic assumption that man was most human when his labor expressed his unique inner self. Speculating on the effects of the division of labor on the English working class, the German Romantic Adam Müller observed in 1816:

> Man needs a many-sided, even an all-rounded, sphere for his activity.... But if the division of labor, as it is now being practiced in the big cities and the manufacturing and mining areas, cuts up free man into wheels, cogs, cylinders and shuttles, imposes on him one sphere of activity in the course of his many-sided search for one object—how can one expect this segmented segment to be adequate to the full and fulfilled life ... ?[81]

This theme resonates not only in Marx's analysis of the nature of work under industrial capitalism but in his image of the communist future. In 1845 he contrasted the alienated capitalist present with the unalienated future that he envisioned under communism:

> The division of labor offers us the first example of how—as long as man remains in natural society, that is, as long as a cleavage exists between the particular and the common

interest, as long, therefore, as activity is not voluntarily, but naturally, divided—man's own deed becomes an alien power opposed to him, which enslaves him instead of being controlled by him. For as soon as the division of labor comes into being, each man has a particular, exclusive sphere of activity, which is forced upon him and from which he cannot escape. He is a hunter, a fisherman, a shepherd, or critic, and must remain so if he does not want to lose his means of livelihood; while in communist society, where nobody has one exclusive sphere of activity but each can become accomplished in any branch he wishes, society regulates the general production and thus makes it possible for me to do one thing today and another tomorrow, to hunt in the morning, fish in the afternoon, rear cattle in the evening, criticize after dinner, as the spirit moves me, without ever becoming a hunter, fisherman, cowherd, or critic. This fixation of social activity, this consolidation of what we ourselves produce into an objective power above us, growing out of our control, thwarting our expectations, bringing to naught our calculations, is one of the chief factors in historical development up till now. . . . [82]

Marx returned to this theme time and again. Toward the end of his life, in his *Critique of the Gotha Program* (1875), he reiterated his vision of the communist society of the future, which would eliminate "the enslaving subordination of the individual to the division of labor." Labor would become "not only a means of life but life's prime want." And the growth and efficient organization of the means of production would make possible "the all-round development of the individual."[83]

If Marx had one big idea, it was that capitalism was the rule of money—which was itself the expression of greed. The rule of capital was fundamentally immoral because it deprived the vast majority in a capitalist society of their humanity, requiring labor that enriched a few capitalists while impoverishing the workers physically and spiritually. Men were thus at the mercy of inimical forces that they felt they could not control. Yet in "bourgeois ideology" these forces were treated as natural and inexorable. This set of ideas was not the *conclusion* of his years of inquiry into the capitalist economy: it was the never-abandoned *premise* of that inquiry.[84] From the mid-1840s through his last works, Marx used a number of concepts and metaphors to convey these ideas in dramatic form.

The notion of "alienation" was taken over from radical Hegelians who had applied it to the sphere of religion. In *The Essence of Christianity*, Feuerbach had suggested that under Christianity, the best characteristics of humanity were projected onto a supernatural deity, encouraging man to see himself as weak and irremediably flawed. The result was that the more God was exalted, the more humanity was diminished. Marx took this model of the demeaning worship of a humanly created superhuman force and applied it to the rule of money. In his "Philosophical Manuscripts" (1844), he emphasized that "the more the worker exerts himself, the more powerful becomes the alien objective world that he shapes against himself, the poorer he and his inner world become, the less it is that belongs to him. It is the same in religion. The more man attributes to God the less he retains in himself."[85] What was the source of capital but the sacrifice of life and its pleasures? The principal thesis of political economy, he wrote, "is the renunciation of life and of human needs. The less you eat, drink, buy books, go to the theater or to balls, or to the public house, and the less you think, love, theorize, sing, paint, fence, etc., the more you will be able to save and the greater will become your treasure that neither moths nor theft can consume—your capital. The less you *are*, the less you express your life, the more you *have*, the greater is your externalized life and the greater is the accumulation from your alienated being."[86]

Marx's rhetoric heightened his readers' sense of the irrationality of this ever-deferred gratification by characterizing capitalism as "fetishization." He picked up the term from Charles de Brosses' eighteenth-century book on ancient Egyptian animal worship (which he read in German translation in 1842), according to which primitive man made little idols and then endowed them with power over the destiny of their human creators.[87] For Marx, this served as a metaphor for the relationship of man to capital. As in the sphere of religion, where man is dominated by the product of his own thought, under capitalism he is controlled by the product of his own efforts.[88]

Beyond Particular Identity: The Communist Manifesto

Marx and Engels spent the years from 1844 to 1848 clarifying their own theory and composing book-length works against fellow German

Hegelians (*The Holy Family* and *The German Ideology*, both written in 1845) and fellow French socialists (*The Poverty of Philosophy*, 1846–47), only the first of which was published during Marx's lifetime. They helped set up the Communist League, a tiny group of German exiles, with branches in London, Paris, and Brussels. Its leadership was made up of intellectuals of middle-class origin, its membership largely of artisans. The document that became *The Communist Manifesto* was written by Marx and Engels on behalf of the league in late 1847 and early 1848. Published in German in London in March 1848, it played no role in the revolutions of that year.[89] But in ringing and resonant rhetoric, it summarized Marx and Engels' arguments about history, the market, and the future.

Two of the best-known phrases of the *Manifesto* were borrowed from French socialists. From Etienne Cabet's *Voyage en Icarie* (1841), they took the formula "To each according to his needs, from each according to his strength," and from Louis Blanc the notion that "each man ... will produce according to his faculties and will consume according to his needs."[90] Like most socialists, Marx and Engels took for granted the assumption that because men had created capitalism, they could rationally and deliberately create an alternative, which would preserve all the advantages of capitalism while jettisoning its central institutions of private property and market competition.

In the *Manifesto*, Marx and Engels described a historical process by which the market, fueled by individual self-interest, breaks down all earlier historically developed identities, including those of hereditary status, nation, and religion. But the result of this liberation is the reduction of most people to the status of commodities, their legal freedom a cover for their real fate as objects of market forces. Freedom under these circumstances means a new slavery, in which the individual has less control over his time and body than ever before—a motif that was to become the central theme of *Capital*.

Yet for Marx, this decomposition of traditional identities by the market was a positive development. It tore away the veils of illusion represented by religious belief and the force of custom, leaving men and women to see their real identities, as members of the class of oppressed workers, the proletariat. The wealth and technology created by capitalism made possible the true liberation of humanity, which would be freedom from the constraints imposed by nature and scarcity.

For Marx it was axiomatic that only the owners of capital, the bourgeoisie, could profit from the market. And as owners of capital, the bourgeoisie was revolutionary, having transformed the world. Marx insisted—and this was, perhaps, his most lasting insight—that capitalism was unlike previous forms of socioeconomic organization. Here was a process of constant transformation, a sort of permanent revolution. As he put it two decades later, in *Capital:*

> Modern industry never views or treats the existing form of a production process as the definitive one. Its technical basis is therefore revolutionary, whereas all earlier modes of production were essentially conservative. By means of machinery, chemical processes and other methods, it is continually transforming not only the technical basis of production but also the functions of the worker and the social combinations of the labor process. At the same time, it thereby also revolutionizes the division of labor within society, and incessantly hurls masses of capital and of workers from one branch of production to another. . . . [It] does away with all repose, all fixity and all security as far as the worker's life-situation is concerned. . . . [91]

But for Marx, the ongoing revolution in the means of production was not only an *economic* fact of prime importance; it was also a social and a cultural transformation of greatest import.

> The bourgeoisie cannot exist without constantly revolutionizing the instruments of production, and thereby the relations of production, and therefore social relations as a whole. By contrast, the prime condition of existence for all previous industrial classes was the unaltered preservation of the old modes of production. The continual upheaval of production, the uninterrupted disturbance of all social conditions, eternal insecurity and movement distinguish the bourgeois epoch from every previous one. All fixed, encrusted relations along with their train of ancient and venerable prejudices and opinions are dissolved, and any new ones are antiquated before they can ossify. All that is solid and established melts into air, all that is holy is profaned, and people are finally forced to view their place in life and their relations to one another with open eyes.[92]

Capitalism, in other words, was the most destabilizing process imaginable. By its rapid and irrevocable transformation of the way in which things were made and consumed, and the sort of people who made and consumed them, it made traditional ways of thinking irrelevant. The emotional hold bestowed upon institutions because of their continuity over time—which conservatives like Burke had so valued—was broken by the constant novelty that capitalism produced. Traditional identities grounded in religion, nationality, estate, gender, and profession would be dissolved by the market.

Marx welcomed this prospect. For he viewed all of these traditional sources of identity as systems of illusion, which hid the real facts of human life. What really counted was the physical and psychic poverty wrought by capitalism, and the need to overcome it. Those who owned the means of production—capitalists, or more broadly "the bourgeoisie"—were the problem. Those who had nothing to gain from capitalism—the proletariat—were the solution. Or rather, the solution lay in bringing the workers to see that they had nothing to gain from the existing system. Communism would come when existing ruling elites lost the legitimation that came from appeals to tradition, religion, and national identity. When workers came to view reality clearly, they would recognize that their real interests were as workers and nothing else. Since by eliminating capitalism they would be taking humanity to a higher level of social organization, their interests were those of humanity at large. Self-interest was legitimate only for the proletariat as a class, because its interest was the general interest.

The communist revolution would be brought about, Marx thought, primarily by the pressure of economic reality, which would demonstrate to men that they had no identity but as proletarians, and that as proletarians they had nothing to gain from capitalism. But there was also a place for intellectuals like himself, "ideologists" of bourgeois origin, "who have raised themselves to the level of comprehending theoretically the movement of history as a whole."[93] Their role, presumably, was to demonstrate to the proletariat that its misery was intrinsic to capitalism, and could only be overcome by the elimination of the capitalist system. If Marx substituted the proletariat for Hegel's civil service as the "universal" estate whose interests were those of the larger society, he nevertheless maintained Hegel's assumption that ultimately there was a role for intellectuals as the tutors of the universal class.

Perhaps Hegel and Marx differed most in their perspectives on the institutions that mediate between the individual and humanity as a whole. For Hegel, the attempt to identify directly with everyone and everything is a romantic illusion. That is why the family, professional associations, representative institutions, nations, religions, and philosophy are central to his conception of human happiness: satisfaction comes from identifying with one's particular roles, and particular interests are inevitable, even if there is a need to transcend them at times. For Marx, by contrast, such intermediate and particular identities block real happiness, which begins with the recognition that man is a "species-being" and that the interests of humanity are one. There is no discussion of legal and political institutions in his mature work because he viewed both law and government as mere protection for private and particular interests, which would be transcended in the communist future.[94] The world he imagined would be free of discrimination against Jews because Judaism, together with other religious and collective identities, would evaporate. It would also be a world without "Jewdom" since the egoism and particularism ascribed to the Jews and central to capitalism would be eliminated. It would be a world of great wealth, but without specie. For money—capital—was evil, and the gaining of money from money unjust.

From Usury to Vampirism: Capital

After playing minor roles in the abortive German revolution of 1848, Marx and Engels were forced to flee abroad, and spent most of the remainder of their lives in England. Engels worked for two decades in the Manchester branch of his family's textile firm, Ermen and Engels. Supported in part by income from Engels, in part by the proceeds of his journalistic writing, Marx devoted his remaining decades to trying to bring his message to working-class audiences throughout Europe through the Working Men's International Association, which he helped found in 1864. The bulk of his time was spent on reformulating the ideas he had developed before 1848—or, more precisely, buttressing his previous claims with additional analysis and data. The product of those decades, *Capital*, expanded upon his earlier ideas without altering them fundamentally.

Thus the chapter of *Capital* entitled "The General Formula of Capital" has one main point: that capital is money that makes money, even if in capitalist society it does so through the intermediary stage of the merchant who buys and sells commodities or the industrialist who buys and sells labor. Or in Marx's resonant image, "The capitalist knows that all commodities—however shabby they may look or bad they may smell—are in faith and in fact money, internally circumcised Jews, and in addition magical means by which to make more money out of money." Here capital is not only identified with the Jews, but is endowed with the "Jewish stench" attributed to Jews in Christian Europe since medieval times.[95] All the traditional prejudices against usury were now reformulated as a critique of the market in the age of industry.

One recurrent image that Marx used to characterize the relationship of capital to labor (and of capitalists to workers) is that of vampirism, of the dead that live off the flesh and blood of the living. The notion of moribund capital first appears in Marx's "Paris Manuscripts" of 1844: "The greater the human contribution to a commodity, the greater the profit of dead capital."[96] In "Wage-Labour and Capital" (published April 1849 and based on lectures originally delivered in December 1847), he described wages as the price in money of labor, "this peculiar commodity which has no other repository than human flesh and blood," and noted that the capitalist "will never want for fresh exploitable flesh and blood."[97] (When Lenin later referred to the necessity of eliminating capitalists because they were "bloodsuckers," he was merely heightening Marx's own metaphor.)

The vampire returns in *Capital,* where the labor theory of value is most fully developed. There capital—money acquired by exploiting workers in the past—is described as nothing but "dead labor," invested by the capitalist to bring about profit, which could only be obtained by the exploitation of "living labor." The capitalist mode of production, therefore, was based upon what the dead drew out of the living. "The capitalist . . . as capitalist is only capital personified. His soul is the soul of capital. But capital has only one vital drive, the drive to increase in value, to create surplus value, to make its constant part, the means of production, suck up the greatest possible amount of surplus labor. Capital is dead labor which, vampire-like, lives only by sucking living labor, and lives the more, the more labor it sucks. The time during which the worker works is the time during which the capitalist consumes the labor-power he has bought from him."[98] Marx sustains the metaphors of vampirism, werewolfism,[99] and cannibalism through much of his discussion of the condition of the worker under capitalism. By virtue of the "voracious hunger for surplus labor,"[100] the capitalist is constantly seeking to increase the number of hours that the worker must toil and thus "the means of production consume the worker as the ferment necessary to their own life-process."[101]

Were Marx's characterizations of capitalism as vampirism a metaphorical rendering of the labor theory of value? Or was the labor theory of value an attempt to put into propositional terms the prereflective response depicted in the images of vampirism? When Marx first came upon the labor theory of value, his response to it was "Eureka." And Marx clung to the labor theory of value after it had been abandoned by virtually all economists.[102]

Marx's adoption of the labor theory of value as the fundamental premise of his analysis of capitalism was most peculiar. He picked it up and adhered to it because of his assumption that the making of money by money was unjust. No major writer on political economy had given the labor theory of value the weight assigned to it by Marx. Smith enunciated the theory in *The Wealth of Nations*, but thought that it applied only at a primitive, barter stage of the economy in which labor was the only scarce factor of production.[103] A generation later, David Ricardo suggested that labor was "really the foundation of the exchangeable value of all things." But his real concern had been the distribution of profit between land and industry, and he offered the labor theory only as a rough approximation, convenient for expounding his model.[104] There were in fact two different theories of profit in *The Wealth of Nations* and three or four in Ricardo. That is because, as Joseph Schumpeter has noted, Smith and Ricardo "had no definite theory [of profit] at all. They simply did not worry about the matter."[105] In any case, the inadequacy of Ricardo's labor theory of value had been demonstrated during the 1820s by English economists, who noted the arbitrariness of the notion that the quantity of labor accounted for economic value.[106] Yet Marx, when he began to read political economy, pounced upon the labor theory of value because it could connect his philosophical premises about human creativity with an explanation of the capitalist economy. As he put it in *The Poverty of Philosophy*, "Ricardo's theory of values is the scientific interpretation of actual economic life . . . labor is the source of value. The measure of labor is time. The relative value of products is determined by the labor time required for their production. Price is the monetary expression of the relative value of a product."[107] This was the fundamental theorem upon which his economic analysis rested.

The labor theory of value (and the romantic conception of the creative individual that lay behind it) was the conceptual center of *Capital*. To flesh out its implications, Marx drew on hundreds of documents, many of them produced by British government commissions and inspectors, known because of the color of their covers as "Blue Books." But the assumptions of the labor theory of value were the sieve through which his sources passed.

The premise and promise of *Capital* is that the price of goods exchanged in the market can be explained by the amount of labor that goes into them. The labor theory of value maintains that the true and

exclusive source of economic value is human labor, and that the value
of commodities (goods exchanged in the market) is equal to the value
of the human labor that has gone into their production. Profit is primarily a result of "surplus value": the difference between the amount that
the capitalist gets for his commodity and the amount that he pays to
the workers by whose labor the commodity has been produced.
Because, according to Marx, the capitalist makes more from selling the
commodity than he pays the workers who have produced it, his relationship to them is one of "exploitation." It is important to note that
"exploitation," as Marx uses it, does not refer to harsh use of the
worker by the employer, but is part of his very definition of the relationship between the two, just as "usury" referred not to the excessive
taking of interest, but to the very fact of making a profit from the lending of money. According to Marx's definition, "exploitation" ceases
only when the whole of current net output of labor goes to the workers
and is used for current consumption. "Exploitation" therefore becomes
the equivalent of what most economists would call positive net investment.[108]

But surely, one might say, the employer has other costs besides
labor: he must pay rent, must pay for machinery, must pay for raw
materials, must pay for money he has borrowed. Marx recognizes this.
But he assumes that all of these are only made possible by the past
human labor required to produce them. "Capital," money available for
investment, is itself a result of past labor, accumulated by not paying
the workers the full value of their labor. Since its source is in human
labor, Marx refers to it as "congealed labor" or "dead labor."

The competitive pressures of the capitalist market force those who
own capital to try to get more surplus value out of their workers. First
they are worked as long as possible. When the limits of the potential
workday are reached, the workers are worked harder and harder. When
that too is not enough to keep his enterprise profitable in the competitive market, the capitalist invests larger and larger sums of capital in
the means of production, so that machinery will increase the output of
each worker and make some workers redundant. Those capitalist firms
with the largest amounts of capital to invest can produce most cheaply,
and in the competition of the market, only they survive: those with
less capital available go bankrupt. Thus capital and, with it, the means
of production are concentrated in fewer and fewer hands. Everyone else
joins the swelling ranks of the "proletariat."

As the capitalists invest more and more of their capital in machinery, an ever-smaller portion of capital goes toward labor.[109] But according to the labor theory of value, only the living labor of the workers

actually produces value. Therefore—by deduction, as it were—the rate
of profit must decline, as the capitalists invest a lower and lower percentage of their total capital on workers rather than machines.[110] This
falling rate of profit, in turn, bankrupts the less profitable firms, which
dismiss their workers, who then become unemployed. Since the supply of workers is greater than the demand for laborers, wages go down,
and keep declining to the level of subsistence, and then below. With
workers unemployed or employed at ever lower wages, the general lack
of purchasing power leads to a decline in consumption and deepens the
crisis of the capitalist economy. The resulting poverty and insecurity
lead the workers to revolution.

It was in his analysis of the effects of the mechanization of production that Marx's premise of human labor as individual life-activity
proved most revealing. His focus was the transformation of production
associated with what came to be called the "industrial revolution,"
that series of technological breakthroughs based upon machines powered by inorganic sources of energy, water, and especially steam.
Because these machines were used to replace and augment the muscle
power of humans (and animals), economists thought of them primarily
as *labor-saving* devices. Marx, by contrast, emphasized the toll taken
by machines on the human body and mind.

From the point of view of the worker, machine production was a
qualitatively new experience. In handicrafts, cottage labor, or unmech-
anized factories, Marx pointed out, workers used tools. But the tempo
and direction of bodily movement were set by the worker who manipulated the tool. In machine production, by contrast, the pace and direction of movement were set by the machine, and the worker was forced
to adapt to its unnatural rhythms and movements: he became "a living
appendage" of the machine.[111] As work became yet more monotonous,
the psychological costs of the division of labor grew greater than
ever.[112] The reduced need for muscle power, far from making work
more pleasant, made it "an instrument of torture, since the machine
does not free the worker from the work, but rather deprives the work
itself of all content."

The machine was the enemy of the working class in other ways as
well. The particular skills in the use of tools which a worker accumulated over a lifetime were often rendered worthless by the advent of
new technology. As his skills became unsalable, the skilled worker
was forced back into the lowest ranks of the unskilled.[113] The development of machinery requiring less muscular strength not only reduced
the economic value of male muscular superiority; it also made it pos-

sible to hire women and children. Declining male wages were thus compensated for only by having the entire family engaged in wage labor.[114]

The chapter of *Capital* on "The Working Day" is devoted to demonstrating that the owners of capital seek to increase their profit by forcing workers of all ages to work for excruciatingly long hours. Citing the evidence of the Blue Books, Marx shows that the owners of factories tried to increase the time worked by their employees, snatching five minutes here and there each day out of mealtimes and breaks, and cumulatively stealing thousands of hours from their employees. And it was not only time that was stolen, but also the physical and intellectual vitality of the working class, who were denied education in youth and then rest, sleep, and stimulation in adulthood. In the Nottingham lace trade, Marx writes, "Children of nine or ten years are dragged from their squalid beds at two, three, or four o'clock in the morning and compelled to work for a bare subsistence until ten, eleven, or twelve at night, their limbs wearing away, their frames dwindling, their faces whitening, and their humanity absolutely sinking into a stone-like torpor, utterly horrible to contemplate."[115] He quotes the testimony of a physician in North Staffordshire to a government commission of 1863: "The potters as a class, both men and women, represent a degenerated population, both physically and morally. They are, as a rule, stunted in growth, ill-shaped, and frequently ill-formed in the chest; they become prematurely old, and are certainly short-lived; they are phlegmatic and bloodless, and exhibit their debility of constitution by obstinate attacks of dyspepsia, and disorders of the liver and kidneys, and by rheumatism. . . . [They] are especially prone to chest disease. . . ."[116] Page after page of *Capital* is filled with graphic descriptions of illness and death from overwork, culled from British government reports and newspaper articles.

This accumulation of evidence was supposed to support the deductive conclusion Marx had reached about the intrinsically exploitative character of capitalism. But in fact the evidence was selected to fit the conclusions. Much of the testimony available to Marx came from government inspectors, who used their positions to call attention to factories that were abusing laws that had already been enacted and were in the process of being enforced. Many of the most egregious examples cited came from industries that were far from typical: the speaker from whom Marx took his evidence about the Nottingham lace trade, for example, asserted that these conditions were "unknown in other parts of the kingdom." And the evidence cited is often from trades that were far from the forefront of capitalist industrialization: they were under-capitalized industries such as lace making and bread baking, which Marx himself recognized as archaic.[117]

Capital presents a searing portrait of the costs of capitalist industrialization. But the picture is entirely one-sided, more like muckraking than balanced analysis.[118] One would never know from Marx's portrait of the British working class of his time that the real wages of factory workers rose by 17 percent between 1850 and 1865,[119] or that the average number of hours worked per week by full-time workers was actually falling.[120] Marx had no explanation for trends that contradicted his warning that the proletariat could look forward to only further misery under capitalism. At the end of *Capital*, he predicted (as he had in the *Communist Manifesto*) that capitalist competition would lead to the concentration of ownership in ever fewer hands. The scale of production would become ever larger, the sweep of capitalism ever more global. "Along with the constant decrease in the number of capitalist magnates, who usurp and monopolize all the advantages of this process of transformation, the mass of misery, oppression, slavery, degradation and exploitation grows; but with this there also grows the revolt of the working class, a class constantly increasing in numbers, and trained, united and organized by the very mechanism of the capitalist process of production."[121] The result would be a revolution that would bring an end to private property.

The gloominess of Marx's portrait of capitalism was relieved only by the prospect of a brighter future made possible by capitalism itself. The explosion of productivity made possible by capitalist mechanization created the potential for a society in which work was more fulfilling and in which the hours of work could decrease, leaving more time for the flowering of human creativity. Like the means of production, the means of reproduction—the family—was also in the process of transformation. There, too, the short-term effects were horrendous, but the long-term prospects encouraging. Capitalism led to the dissolution of the traditional family, as women and children were forced into the workplace, often by their husbands and fathers. But this set the stage for future progress: "However terrible and disgusting the dissolution of the old family ties within the capitalist system may appear, large-scale industry, by assigning an important part in socially organized processes of production—outside the sphere of the domestic economy—to women, young persons, and children of both sexes, does nevertheless create a new economic foundation for a higher form of the family and of relations between the sexes. . . . It is also obvious that the fact that the collective working group is composed of individuals of both sexes and all ages must under the appropriate conditions turn into a source of humane development. . . ."[122] The result, he implied, would be a more egalitarian family and a more humane workplace.

It is difficult to overstate the significance that Marx assigned to the labor theory of value in his analysis of and prognosis for capitalism. He spent much of the rest of his life refining it, and like medieval astronomers trying to preserve Ptolemy's theorem that the sun revolved around the earth, he added ever more emendations in an attempt to preserve a fundamentally fallacious explanatory premise. In *Capital*, the fact that the value of commodities is determined by the labor time that it takes to produce them is characterized melodramatically as "the hidden secret beneath the visible movements of the relative values of commodities."[123] Marx wanted to show that the labor theory of value and the theory of surplus value could ultimately explain price, the conventional term for the value at which commodities are exchanged. Prices, he maintained, are transformed labor values, and the sum total of profit at any given time is equal to the sum total of surplus value. This is what is known in Marxist economics as "the transformation problem," and from Marx's day onward Marxist economists have been trying in vain to solve it.[124] Without such a demonstration, the labor theory of value could not explain the "secret" of which it purported to be the solution.

In the decade following the publication of volume 1 of *Capital*, the very premises of Marx's approach to economic analysis came under more fundamental attack. Throughout Europe, economists associated with the "marginalist revolution"—Carl Menger's *Grundsätze der Volkswirtschaftslehre* (*Fundamentals of Economic Theory*) and Stanley Jevons' *Theory of Political Economy* were published in 1871, and Léon Walras' *Éléments d'économie politique pure* (*Elements of Pure Economics*) in 1874—were coming to the conclusion that attempts to explain prices in a capitalist economy by criteria such as labor or even costs of production were misguided.

Marx insisted on the centrality of the labor theory of value to his analysis of capitalism, and kept reformulating the theory in response to critics who found it unconvincing and to sympathetic allies who found it incomprehensible.[125] Yet his masterwork, *Capital*, remained unfinished not because Marx ran out of time, but because he could not figure out how to salvage his theory. He could demonstrate, he thought, that the pessimistic conclusions of the *Communist Manifesto* could be deduced from his labor theory of value. What he could not demonstrate was that the labor theory of value in fact explained much about the workings of the capitalist economy. At some point he conceded that it could not explain what it at first purported to explain—the movement of prices for individual commodities—while holding out the promise that it could explain the movements of the market as a whole. But the portions of *Capital* that were supposed to clarify how the overall market prices for commodities could be explained by the labor theory of value were never completed to his satisfaction (or anyone else's). That is why he tinkered with these chapters for two decades after they were first composed, but never published them. They were eventually edited and published by Engels as *Capital: Volume 3*. But that volume, which dealt in greatest detail with the "law of the tendency of the rate of profit to fall," was actually written before the final version of *Capital: Volume 1*,[126] and never completed because its author recognized that it was not all that enlightening. In his introductions to volumes 2 and 3 of *Capital*, which he published after Marx's death, Engels noted that in these works Marx had switched from a labor value theory of price to a theory of price based on costs of production, the alternative suggested by Smith a century earlier.[127] Marx's critics were astonished to find that in explaining profits by a cost-of-production theory, Marx now seemed to endorse the very theory that he had set out to expose decades before.[128] Engels himself, in his last published article, concluded that the labor theory of value was applicable before the capitalist era, but not in the era of capitalism proper, which was, by his reckoning, since the fifteenth century.

And that was ironic, for the entire drama of Marx's economic writings took the form of a mysterious puzzle, which he promised to unlock with the aid of the labor theory of value. There are hundreds, perhaps thousands, of books on Marx's economics. But the plain unvarnished fact is that Marx's economics, as a systematic enterprise, does not hold up; undergirded by the labor theory of value, it is undermined by the flaws of that theory.

Another of Marx's fundamental economic assumptions was also disproved by experience. His notion that the relative costs of machinery rose with economic development seemed intuitively correct during the early stage of industrialization, which was based on industries such as textiles and iron making. But that was no longer the case by the late nineteenth century, during a second wave of industrialization focused on chemicals and electricity, in which technological advance led to a decline in the relative costs of technology. In volume 3, Marx himself showed that there was reason to believe that the proportion of capital invested in technology as opposed to labor (what he called "the organic composition of capital") would decrease and hence that the rate of profit would not fall, due to the "cheapening of the elements of constant capital." Engels too recognized that in newer branches of production, such as the chemical industry and in metallurgy, the costs of machinery went down with technological advance, and hence the relative amount spent on labor did not decline.[129] While both Marx and Engels took note of these developments, neither faced up to the fact that they negated the *Communist Manifesto*'s predictions of the inevitable collapse of capitalism.

The Aftermath

The communist revolution did not come about in Marx's day, or during the thirty years after his death. And when it did come about, it was not in advanced capitalist economies, but in predominantly peasant societies in the early stages of capitalist industrialization, most notably Russia and China. Revolution was most plausible not where capitalist institutions were well established, as Marx and Engels had imagined, but where the social and demographic effects of early capitalism most resembled the fragile state of German society in the mid-1840s when Marx and Engels reached their conclusions about the self-destructive nature of capitalism. Even then, successful revolution occurred only when the political structure was weakened by external war, and when there existed a devoted and ruthless cadre of revolutionaries able to make use of the opportunities provided.

The revolution that Marx had longed for and predicted failed to come about in western Europe because of factors that Marx overlooked—even though some were staring him in the face. The most important was the growing ability of the capitalist system to improve the economic condition of the working classes, thanks to technological advance and economic growth. In Great Britain, the most industrially advanced nation, gross domestic product rose during almost every decade of the nineteenth century, averaging between 2 and 2½ percent per annum.[130] Though the interpretation of the evidence about the standard of living of British workers in the first half of the century remains in dispute, there is no doubt that those standards were rising during the very years when Marx was writing *Capital,* and that they were about 50 percent higher in 1895 than in 1865.[131] Life expectancy was rising too; the average Briton born in 1800 could expect to live to his mid-thirties; by 1900, that expectation had reached the upper forties. Moreover, for perhaps the first time in history, the rise in the standard of living did not lead men and women to have more children. Slowly but perceptibly, the birth rate declined, from thirty-five births per thousand in the 1830s to thirty at the end of the century, and it continued downward thereafter.[132] The high rate of fertility that had contributed to the pauperization so salient earlier in the century had by century's end given way to a decline in childbearing that limited the growth of population and contributed to a rise in per capita consumption.[133] The same pattern occurred, with variations, almost everywhere that capitalist industrialization took hold.[134]

Thus, while Marx zoomed in on the undeniably horrific underside of capitalist development, many of the negative trends on which he had focused were beginning to turn around in the very years in which he was writing. His claim that capitalist industrialization was leading to physical degeneration is supported by the fact that the average height (one measurable indicator of physical well-being) did in fact decline from the 1830s into the 1860s, but after that it began to rise again.[135] The number of hours worked did indeed increase from the mid-eighteenth through the mid-nineteenth centuries. But then it began to fall, from sixty-five hours per week for the average full-time worker in 1856, down to fifty-six in 1873; the figure remained at that level for the rest of the century.[136] The workday was not only shorter; it was also less dangerous, thanks to government health and safety inspectors. That inspection system was in its infancy during the years when Marx wrote *Capital*, though as we have seen, it provided him with much of the information that he used so selectively.[137] These were the decades when a professional civil service capable of carrying out such government actions was being created,[138] which ultimately led to improved standards of health and safety in one industry after another.

The pressure for government measures to better the conditions of life for the working classes came in part from a sense of moral obligation on the part of portions of the wealthier and educated classes, not least from those inspired to social conscience by religion—a development beyond Marx's imagination.[139] The stimulus to reform came also from the growth of trade unions, which bargained on the shop floor for better pay and working conditions, and began to enter electoral politics. Marx encouraged the growth of labor unions as a vehicle through which to prepare the working class for the overthrow of capitalism. He failed to consider that their very success in improving the conditions of work and the standard of living would make revolution even less necessary or desirable. In late-nineteenth-century Germany, pressure from the organized working class, together with the influence of middle- and upper-class conscience, led to government insurance schemes that eased the threats posed by unemployment and illness.

The influence of Marx and Engels varied from one country to another, but almost everywhere their critique of capitalism had some resonance. It was strongest in their native Germany, where the Social Democratic Party regarded their ideas as its lodestone. In the early years of rapid industrialization, as men and women flocked to the city in search of work and made their homes in shabby dwellings, living in overcrowded neighborhoods lacking in the basic amenities of urban life, breathing in the polluted air of the factory, and working long hours for a pittance, the Marxist scenario of proletarian impoverishment seemed compelling to both workers and to some "bourgeois ideologists" moved by their plight. Yet by the turn of the century, in Germany as elsewhere, the organizational success of the labor movement, along with the rising standard of living of the workers, created a working class ever less inclined to revolution.

By the first decades of the twentieth century, Marxist intellectuals faced a dilemma. Should they accept the incipient reformism of the labor unions and their political representatives and abandon the hope of superseding capitalism? Or should they insist, like Lenin and Lukács, upon the primacy of the intellectuals, and build a party in which those whose superior insight into the desirable direction of history would channel the working class toward the revolutionary goal prescribed by Marx? Some intellectuals (especially those who came from stigmatized ethnic and religious minorities) were attracted by Marx's prospect of a communist future bereft of particularism. Others responded to Marx's critique of the effects of the division of labor, which saw specialization as stultifying. And then there were those who found the capitalist world cold and isolating, or who could not stomach the gap between the ethics of universal love they had been taught and the reality of self-interest upon which the market pivoted.

But Marx was not the only critic of the cultural constriction brought about by the spread of the market, nor was he the only intellectual to decry the reign of the philistines. Those themes were also central to the work of his younger English contemporary, Matthew Arnold, whose analysis took him in a very different direction.

CHAPTER EIGHT

MATTHEW ARNOLD:
WEANING THE PHILISTINES FROM
THE DRUG OF BUSINESS

Like Marx, Matthew Arnold (1822–1888) bridled at the prospect of a world turned "philistine," an epithet that both of them borrowed from Heinrich Heine, the German poet and cultural critic. For Arnold as for Marx, "philistinism" was a pejorative term for the mentality of the commercial and industrial middle classes, which both thinkers saw as increasingly giving the tone to government and society. But while they used the same term to describe the malady, they diverged in their diagnosis of its cause and the prescription for its cure. While Marx thought that religion was the opiate of the masses, diverting their minds from the discontents of capitalism, Arnold thought that business was an opiate, diverting the capitalists from religious and spiritual development. For Marx, the solution was to eliminate capitalism, the economic basis of philistine culture. Arnold, by contrast, regarded the economic achievements of capitalism as real enough, and never imagined that there was a viable economic alternative. What he feared was that the characteristic mentality of the commercial middle class was spilling over into the realms of culture and politics. His antidote was not the elimination of commerce but the improvement of the culture of the nation by intellectuals such as himself, acting through government, the press, and educational institutions. Arnold embodied and helped to shape a social role we might call "the critical but non-alienated intellectual."

Arnold's critique of middle-class philistinism has by now become so familiar that we are apt to underestimate its boldness. For he was writing at the zenith of belief in the cult of progress. The assumption that things were getting better materially was, as already noted, based in reality. At midcentury, Britain's industrial and financial hegemony was unrivaled, and the face of the land was being transformed by industrialization. Half the iron in the world was being produced in Britain.

Within a few decades, over five thousand miles of railway had been built, radically reducing travel time between the capital and the provinces, making it possible to go from London to Oxford in an hour—with consequences for both cities.

Signs of economic expansion and social dynamism were everywhere, with none more remarked upon than the Crystal Palace, a vast conservatory of glass and steel built in 1851 to house the Great Exhibition. Nearly a million feet of glass, suspended by a web of 3,300 columns and 2,300 girders, were assembled in a mere seventeen weeks, thanks to the industrial miracle of prefabrication. The exhibition and its Palace of Industry made progress visible and tangible. "The history of the world records no event comparable, in its promotion of human industry, with that of the Great Exhibition of the Works of Industry of all Nations in 1851," boasted Henry Cole, one of its leading sponsors. And in what he thought of as true British fashion, it was not a product of government or of coercion. "A great people invited all civilized nations to a festival, to bring into comparison the works of human skill. It was carried out by its own private means, was self-supporting and independent of taxes and employment of slaves, which great works had exacted in ancient days." The official head of the Great Exhibition was none other than Queen Victoria's consort, Prince Albert, whom Cole praised as "a prince of pre-eminent wisdom, of philosophic mind, sagacity, with power of generalship and great practical ability, [who] placed himself at the head of the enterprise, and led it to triumphant success." As one contemporary noted, the Crystal Palace reflected the age: "It is the aesthetic bloom of its practical character and of the practical tendency of the English nation."[1]

Arnold's vocation was to specify the limits of such practicality. To explain how he came to formulate his critique of philistinism, and his solutions to the problem of spiritual impoverishment amid material plenty that it posed, we must have a look at the milieu from which he sprang and the institutions that converged in his own person.

Life Among the Philistines and Hebraists

Born in 1822, Arnold was four years younger than Marx; he published his most important works of cultural criticism, *Culture and Anarchy*, in 1869, shortly after the publication of the first volume of *Capital*.[2]

Matthew's father, Thomas Arnold, was the headmaster of the Rugby School, a novel and remarkably influential educational institution intended to produce gentlemen capable of ruling the country in a Christian spirit. He was also a leading figure of the Broad Church, which sought to retain the established Church of England while making it as inclusive as possible. Matthew Arnold continued his father's commitments but in a more secularized fashion. He looked to men of letters to supply the spiritual guidance and moral encouragement that the priesthood was no longer capable of conveying.

In 1841 Matthew went up to Oxford, having won a scholarship to Balliol College by competitive examination, thus personifying the middle-class ideal of advancement through merit. Thomas Arnold was appointed professor of modern history at the university that same year, but he died shortly after taking up the appointment. The curriculum at Balliol consisted for the most part of the Greek and Latin classics of philosophy and literature, a storehouse from which Arnold (like Marx) would continue to draw. The Balliol connection was to be central not only to Arnold's career but to the larger intellectual project of reforming the ancient universities and enhancing their influence in the government and culture of the nation—in remaking Oxford in the image of Rugby, and remaking the philistine nation in turn.

The system of preferment that had brought the young and impecunious Edmund Burke to the attention of aristocratic politicians almost a century earlier functioned for Arnold as well. At age twenty-four, he became private secretary to a great Whig landowner and senior parliamentarian, Lord Lansdowne, who was just old enough to have heard Burke himself address Parliament. Lansdowne was also head of the Committee of the Council on Education.

Burke first established his reputation as a writer of prose, but it was as a poet that Arnold initially came to public attention. His poetic gifts would eventually lead to a professorship in 1857, when he was elected professor of poetry at Oxford, a position he held for a decade. His professorship only demanded three public lectures each year, commensurate with the pittance it paid. Poetry, even with a professorship attached, was not a profession from which a man could support a family. And so, spurred on by his desire to marry and the need to provide for his prospective offspring, Arnold at age twenty-eight accepted an appointment as one of Her Majesty's inspectors of schools—reluctantly, for fear that it would not allow him time for his own reading and writing. He would hold that job for the next thirty-five years. The work was indeed time-consuming, but Arnold's energy was prodigious. During the next three and a half decades, he produced a stream of essays and books, which when collected amounted to eleven stout volumes of prose, running the gamut from literary criticism to social and political analysis, including two book-length works on educational reform and three more on religious themes.[3]

Unlike Prussia, the England of Arnold's day had no state system of schools, and universal education remained elusive almost a century after Adam Smith had recommended it as an antidote to the negative effects of the market. Creation of a uniform and comprehensive school system on the continental model was stymied by an aristocratic tradition of antipathy toward the power of central government, together with an ongoing suspicion of state schools by non-Anglican Dissenters, who feared that state education would inculcate the tenets of the Church of England. Instead, schools were operated by churches and charities. But beginning in the 1840s, schools became eligible to receive a small government subsidy, in return for which the government sent its inspectors to monitor their quality. To satisfy religious sensibilities, there were separate inspectors for Anglican, Catholic, and Dissenting Protestant schools. Arnold's post took him to schools run by those Protestant groups that had rejected membership in the Church of England, known as Nonconformists or Dissenters.

To a remarkable degree, these Quakers, Presbyterians, Congregationalists, Unitarians, and Baptists formed the backbone of commercial and industrial leadership. The social structure of England was a sandwich, with Anglicans at the top (aristocracy and gentry) and bottom, and with Dissenters in the ever-growing middle. (Methodists, who had begun within the Church of England but were a separate denomination by Arnold's day, formed a layer socially just below the older Dissenting sects.) Excluded by virtue of their religion from government and from aristocratic patronage, from the great universities of Oxford and Cambridge, and from the army and navy, Dissenters went into trade and industry. Their style of life stressed laboring in one's vocation, practical education, sobriety, and high moral conduct.[4] Max Weber was not the first to note that the character traits inculcated by these descendants of the Puritans were conducive to economic advance. Because their experience had made them suspicious of government power, Dissenters formed a leading constituency of middle-class liberalism, and it was from their ranks that prominent liberal leaders, such as John Bright, sprang. Though the very top government posts remained largely in the hands of aristocrats like Lansdowne, by the 1850s this middle class increasingly set the tone of government policy. Below them on the social ladder were the working classes, which remained not only disenfranchised but often barely literate.

Arnold's job as inspector of schools brought him into daily contact with the educational institutions of the middle classes, visiting schools for children aged four to thirteen, primarily in booming industrializing areas of the nation, such as Birmingham. He was often appalled by what he saw. It was from his immersion in these strongholds of the middle classes that Arnold's critique of middle-class culture and politics evolved.

Arnold's Critique

The inspection of schools launched his first major work of social criticism, an essay entitled "Democracy," which first appeared as the preface to his published report of 1861, *The Popular Education of France*. The success of the middle classes in bringing about material advance and political liberty, he lamented, had led to a self-satisfaction that had itself become a barrier to improvement in any larger and higher sense. The middle class believed ardently in industry and in liberty of thought; what it lacked was "culture" and "ideas." "No one esteems them [the middle class] more than I do," he wrote, "but those who esteem them most, and who most believe in their capabilities, can render them no better service than by pointing out in what they underrate their deficiencies, and how their deficiencies, if unremedied, may impair their future."[5] As their influence increased, he feared that the commercial middle classes would "deteriorate" the country by "their low ideals and want of culture." Democracies characteristically define as their highest ideals those of the ordinary man. Echoing Aristotle, Arnold reminded his readers that "the difficulty for democracy is how to find and keep high ideals."[6] As Britain moved toward a broader, more democratic suffrage, Arnold feared that the working class would follow the middle classes in embracing a low and constricted conception of cultural aspiration.

Arnold, like Marx, was repelled by what the latter had called the "*Beschränktheit*" of bourgeois society. And like Marx, Arnold looked to Heine for a polemical term that would capture what Heine called the *ächt britische Beschränktheit* (the "genuine British narrowness"). That epithet was "philistinism," connoting the ethos of "a strong, dogged, unenlightened opponent of the chosen people, of the children of the light." "We have not the expression in English," Arnold noted drolly. "Perhaps we have not the word because we have so much of the thing. At Soli, I imagine, they did not talk of solecisms; and here, at the very headquarters of Goliath, nobody talks of Philistinism."[7]

His first public skirmish with the forces of philistinism came in 1862, and it occurred on his home ground, so to speak: schooling. Robert Lowe, a Liberal MP who was Arnold's political superior at the Education Office, had proposed a revision of the method of government funding for schools, based on "payment by results." The scheme was founded on the premise that "the duty of a State in public education is . . . to obtain the greatest possible quantity of reading, writing, and arithmetic for the greatest number."[8] Schools were to be funded based on the performance of their students in the "3 R's." Each school was to be visited annually by a school inspector, who was to quiz every student in English language and arithmetic. For every student who failed to appear or to answer questions successfully, a small sum would be deducted from the school's government funding. Lowe's reform was intended in part to cut costs, but above all to make school funding dependent on measurable results in the most basic and practical of skills, and to bring education into accord with his market-oriented principles by linking payment to performance.[9]

With a dose of bravery or brazenness, Arnold launched a public salvo against his political superior, in "The Twice-Revised Code," an essay that he published in a leading magazine and made certain was distributed to every member of Parliament. He attacked the narrow and mechanical conception of education behind Lowe's plan. The ability to read intelligently, he pointed out, came primarily not from narrowly tailored reading lessons, but from a more general cultivation, imbibed from the family or, failing that, from the school environment, which created the mental desire to read. The goal of the schools, therefore, should be "general intellectual cultivation," without which the skills of reading and writing would not develop.[10] The government sought to fund only the most rudimentary of educations instead of responding to "the strong desire of the lower classes to raise themselves."[11] Since many impoverished students would inevitably be absent when the annual test was administered, or would fail the test itself, he predicted that the net effect of the proposed reform would be to reduce the funding of schools for the poor. The education of the people, he concluded, was to be sacrificed to "the friends of economy at any price."[12] Arnold's argument was that market principles were inappropriate in this realm. In the end, Arnold won a partial victory over the philistines: the principle of payment for performance was enshrined in the new legislation, but it accounted for only a part of the government's grant to each school.[13]

Education, for Arnold, was not just the transmission of information or the learning of basic reading and computational skills: it was to be a civilizing agent.[14] Arnold frequently found himself inspecting schools in which students ingested mountains of facts and arithmetic but were bereft of analytic ability and utterly incapable of understanding sophisticated prose or poetry. They were taught not to reason but to cram.[15] Both before and especially after the adoption of "payment for performance," he criticized such education for being "far too little formative and humanizing . . . much in it, which its administrators point to as valuable *results,* is in truth mere machinery," unconcerned with cultivating taste and feeling.[16]

The "chosen people," to which the philistines were contrasted, were neither the Jews nor the Dissenters, whom Arnold referred to as "Hebraists" because of the strictness of their moral code. For Arnold, the "chosen people" were intellectuals like himself, those who strove for "culture" and practiced "criticism." He used these terms more or less interchangeably. In a widely read 1864 essay, "The Function of Criticism at the Present Time," he defined criticism as "a disinterested endeavor to learn and propagate the best that is known and thought in the world."[17] While Arnold greatly admired Edmund Burke as the man who had done more than any other to bring intellect to bear on British politics, he thought that the British had taken Burke's suspicion of rationalism too much to heart. They had made a stultifying dogma of Burke's perception that rational thought may overstep its bounds in attempting to realize ideals directly, and transformed his gospel of moderation into a generalized suspicion of ideas—and of intellectuals. As a result the British acted as if "practice is everything, a free play of the mind is nothing."[18] The practical, utilitarian mentality, which had been so useful in the creation of material wealth through market activity and industry, had, Arnold thought, become a barrier to any higher or nobler aspiration. The function of contemporary criticism was therefore "to keep man from a self-satisfaction which is retarding and vulgarising, to lead him towards perfection, by making his mind dwell upon what is excellent in itself, and the absolute beauty and fitness of things."[19]

And yet, Arnold suggested, the very accumulation of affluence might set the stage for higher aspiration, and the material comfort being created by capitalism might lead to a demand for intellectual substance:

> In spite of all that is said about the absorbing and brutalising influence of our passionate material progress, it seems to me indisputable that this progress is likely, though not certain, to lead in the end to an apparition [becoming visible] of intellectual life; and that man, after he has made himself perfectly comfortable and has not to determine what to do with himself next, may begin to remember that he has a mind, and that the mind may be made the source of great pleasure. I grant it is mainly the privilege of faith, at present, to discern this end to our railways, our business, and our for-tune-making; but we shall see if, here as elsewhere faith is not in the end the true prophet. Our ease, our travelling, and our unbounded liberty to hold just as hard and securely as we please to the practice to which our notions have given birth, all tend to beget an inclination to deal a little more freely with these notions themselves, to canvass them a little, to penetrate a little into their real nature.[20]

With the publication of this essay, Arnold broke through to a larger audience. His books were sold in railway bookstalls, his ideas debated in the pages of newspapers read by bankers and barristers, parliamen-tarians and businessmen.[21] The essay set off a critical battle in the major magazines of the day.

Arnold's next sally came in "My Countryman" (1866), an essay that aroused an even more irate response. Speaking in the voice of a foreign observer of English ways, he raised the question of what would bring about a life satisfying to the modern spirit, and tabulated

> the growth of a love of industry, trade, and wealth; the growth of a love of the things of the mind; and the growth of a love of beautiful things. Of these three factors of modern life, your middle class has no notion of any but one, the first. Their love of industry, trade, and wealth, is certainly prodi-gious. . . . But what notion have they of anything else? . . . Your middle class is educated, to begin with, in the worst schools of your country. . . . The fineness and capacity of a man's spirit is shown by his enjoyments; your middle class has an enjoyment in its business, we admit, and gets on well

in business, and makes money; but beyond that? Drugged with business, your middle class seems to have its sense blunted for any stimulus besides, except religion; it has a religion, narrow, unintelligent, repulsive. . . . Can any life be imagined more hideous, more dismal, more unenviable?[22]

Arnold's book *Culture and Anarchy: An Essay in Political and Social Criticism* grew out of a lecture entitled "Culture and Its Enemies," which he delivered at Oxford in June 1867 and published a month later in the *Cornhill Magazine*. It was a plea for attention to what Arnold called "culture" (and its bearers), which he contrasted to the market and to its middle-class devotees.

"Culture" for Arnold represented not so much a distinct body of knowledge as an attitude toward the world and the use of the mind in it. It was "a pursuit of our total perfection by means of getting to know, on all matters which most concern us, the best which has been thought and said in the world; and through this knowledge, turning a stream of fresh and free thought upon our stock notions and habits, which we now follow staunchly but mechanically, vainly imagining that there is a virtue in following them staunchly which makes up for the mischief of following them mechanically." It combined "the scientific passion" to know things as they really are with "the passion of doing good."[23]

It meant attention to one's cultural and mental development, to what Arnold called "inwardness," which he contrasted to "the mechanical and material civilisation we esteem." In a society characterized by the division of labor, culture was contrasted to specialization, "our intense energetic absorption in the particular pursuit we are following." And in a society in which competition loomed so large, culture meant the cultivation of sympathy and of "disinterestedness"—the impartial search for truth. Culture did not mean only self-development; it also had an altruistic element, demanding the pursuit of "*general* perfection, developing all parts of our society."[24] Culture, therefore, was "the endeavor to see things as they are, to draw towards a knowledge of the universal order which seems to be intended and aimed at in the world, and which it is a man's happiness to go along with or his misery to go counter to—to learn, in short, the will of God."[25] And intrinsic to the project of culture, at least as Arnold defined it, was its democratizing thrust, "to make the best that has been thought and known in the world current everywhere."[26]

Time and again, Arnold lamented that the culture of the British middle classes was focused on "machinery," by which he meant far more than mechanical devices.[27] "Machinery" connoted means of any sort. Arnold's complaint was that in a society in which means were increasing, men and women had lost sight of the ends that those means ought to serve. Indeed, they confused the agglomeration of means with the ends of life, and the increase of material wealth with moral improvement. They treated political liberty as a good in itself, instead of asking what purpose that liberty served. And because they identified progress with this "machinery," they were satisfied. (Like Marx, Arnold referred to the worship of means while losing sight of ends as a "fetish."[28]) Culture, by contrast, meant being subject to the self-dissatisfaction that comes from recognizing the gap between what is and what ought to be, a dissatisfaction that was the beginning of personal and collective betterment.

Arnold disparaged neither political freedom nor material affluence. He was grateful for England's political institutions, and nothing he wrote attacked the market as such. What he objected to were the assumptions that liberty was the last word in moral evaluation, and that the principles of free trade, industriousness, and self-interest, which fueled the market, ought to be applied to all other areas of life.

In Arnold's analysis, what too many Britons lacked was the sense that there might be more to collective life than liberty from government, the liberty "to do as one likes." In many ways, his arguments reformulated, in a less ponderous key, Hegel's distinction between choosing arbitrarily and choosing with good reasons. What was being lost in the self-congratulatory rhetoric of English liberty was the very notion that what was important was not just the *possibility* of choice, but what choice was actually made. Lost, too, was the aspiration to lead one's life rationally and reflectively.[29] The habits of mind of those who prided themselves on their dissent from the established church, Arnold argued, left the middle class ill equipped to become the establishment itself. The emphasis on individual freedom, together with the reflexes of dissent, had resulted in a principled antipathy to authority—not only the authority of institutions, but the authority of "right reason," the principle that there are good reasons for living one way rather than another.

Because the English had been taught to value liberty and self-reliance above all, Arnold contended, they gave too little thought and too small a role to the state. The very notion that the state might act in the general interest, rather than in the interest of the particular group that dominated it, was foreign to most Englishmen.[30] The result, Arnold claimed, was both dangerous and tragic.

Dangerous, because the only institution that could ultimately enforce order was losing its legitimacy. Until recently, Arnold maintained, the legitimacy of the government had been based upon deference to the aristocracy and monarchy. But now such deference was fading. Without respect for the state, lawlessness threatened. "As feudalism, with its ideas and habits of subordination dies out," he wrote, "we are in danger of drifting toward anarchy."[31] He cited as an omen a recent incident in which a London crowd, which had assembled in defiance of government order to demand extension of the suffrage to the working class, had torn down the railings and trampled the flower beds of Hyde Park. Troops were called out to aid the police, but they took no action, and for the next several days thousands of people milled about the park. Despite the rather minor property damage, this train of events evoked the specter of mob violence. To Arnold, it reflected "the deep-seated spiritual anarchy of the English people." He argued that the freedom so valued by liberals, the freedom to be left alone by government to do as one likes (what Americans mean when their response to criticism is "It's a free country"), had become an end in itself, and a barrier to thinking about the need for shared authority. He warned that without the development of a sense of shared authority, embodied in a state that was more than the tool of a particular class, the Hyde Park riots might be a harbinger of greater social disorder.

The underdeveloped British sense of a state capable of pursuing the general interest was tragic because it left unfulfilled the functions that could not be realized by the market or by voluntary activity. Foremost among these was the quantity and quality of education, which were dismal, largely because of suspicion of government and dependence on the market principles of supply and demand. Schooling for the poor was too brief, rarely extending beyond elementary school. Schooling for the middle classes did include secondary schools; the problem there, in Arnold's view, was the limited nature of the subjects taught, and the narrowness of mind such studies reflected and reproduced. Here the law of the market broke down, Arnold suggested:

> The mass of mankind know good butter from bad, and tainted meat from fresh, and the principle of supply and demand may, perhaps, be relied on to give us sound meat and butter. But the mass of mankind do not so well know what distinguishes good teaching and training from bad; they do not here know what they ought to demand, and therefore, the demand cannot be relied on to give us the right supply. Even if they knew what they ought to demand,

they have not sufficient means of testing whether or not this is really supplied to them. Securities, therefore, are needed.

That assurance of quality could be provided by state funding when combined with competent state inspection.[32]

What was needed, according to Arnold, was a stronger state, one based upon the idea of the public interest, and upon the assumption that people might at times act for the sake of the public interest rather than out of self-interest, be it individual self-interest or class self-interest. Yet the very idea of a "best self" that acted upon rational reflection and altruistic motivation was foreign to most of the British population, he asserted.[33]

In laying out his analysis, he divided the population into four groups, each dubbed with a satirical tag: the Barbarians, the Populace, the Philistines, and the Aliens. The Barbarians were the aristocrats, who possessed a certain style and serenity. But in a modern society, ideas mattered (here, too, a Hegelian echo), and British aristocrats were congenitally averse to ideas; indeed their serenity "appears to come from their never having had any ideas to trouble them."[34] As a result, their era of leadership was passing. The Populace comprised the working classes. Their material want and conditions of life left them excluded from "the best that had been thought and said," and hence prone to think of nonworking hours as little more than occasions for drink and "fun." Though in an era of inevitable democracy, power would increasingly flow to them, they were as of yet poorly positioned to exercise that power for the general good. Arnold feared that they would adopt the narrow horizons and mental habits of the middle classes.

The class that actually wielded power (here, too, Arnold agreed with Marx) was the middle class, which had risen as a result of commercialization and industrialization. It was on this class that Arnold concentrated his fire, because, for better or worse, he regarded it as dominant for the historical moment. It was the members of this class that he characterized as Philistines. They were "the people who believe most that our greatness and welfare are proved by our being very rich, and who most give their lives and thought to becoming rich." But, he asked rhetorically, in what did their riches consist?

> Consider these people, then, their way of life, their habits, their manners, the very tones of their voice; look at them attentively; observe the literature they read, the things which give them pleasure, the words which come forth out

of their mouths, the thoughts which make the furniture of
their minds; would any amount of wealth be worth having
with the condition that one was to become just like these
people by having it?[35]

Their religion, Arnold conceded, had made them capable of conquering their baser instincts and adhering to a level of personal morality of
which they were proud. But by Arnold's lights it had led to an exaggerated level of self-satisfaction.[36] He saw a common denominator behind
their religious and economic life, and that was the narrow-mindedness
with which they pursued both. Their twin goals were saving their
souls and making money. And their "narrow and mechanical" conception of their "religious business"—based on avoiding sin, and a literal-
ist understanding of the Bible and of Heaven and Hell—led in turn to a
"narrow and mechanical" conception of their "secular business."[37]

There was, Arnold suggested, an elective affinity between funda-
mentalism in religion and in economics. Liberals took their economic
dogmas and applied them mechanically. They worshipped free trade as
a fetish, as an end in itself, rather than asking how it was linked to personal happiness and national welfare.[38] While their policies had
brought about an increase in total population and in wealth, they
rarely paused to ask what wealth and population were for, or whether
more of each was always desirable. Their belief in the beneficent
effects of free trade and the growth of business made any form of government planning and intervention seem heretical.[39] Arnold suggested, by contrast, "that our social progress would be happier if there
were not so many of us so very poor, and in busying ourselves with
notions of in some way or other adjusting the poor man and business
one to the other, and not multiplying the one and the other mechanically and blindly . . ." "It turns out that our pursuit of free-trade, as of
so many other things, has been too mechanical," he wrote. "We fix
upon some object, which in this case is the production of wealth, and
the increase of manufactures, population, and commerce through free-
trade, as a kind of one thing needful, or end in itself; and then we pursue it staunchly and mechanically . . . not to see how it is related to the
whole intelligible law of things and to full human perfection, or to
treat it as the piece of machinery, of varying value as its relations to the
intelligible law of things vary, which it really is."[40]

The unreflective theology of the descendants of the Puritans also got
in the way of improving the quality of human life by conscious family
planning, Arnold asserted. The growing numbers of urban poor needed
to know more than biblical precepts for their ultimate salvation. They

needed to be told how to limit their family size "to give their moral life and growth a fair chance!" In place of the "unintelligent Hebraism" that keeps repeating that the man who has a great many children is happy, Arnold resolved to tell the poor that "a man's children are not truly *sent*, any more than the pictures upon his wall, or the horses in his stable are *sent*; and that to bring people into the world, when one cannot afford to keep them and oneself decently and not too precariously, or to bring more of them into the world than one can afford to keep . . . [is] by no means an accomplishment of the divine will or a fulfillment of Nature's simplest laws, but is just as wrong, just as contrary to reason and the will of God, as for a man to have horses, or carriages, or pictures, when he cannot afford them, or to have more of them than he can afford . . ."[41] Here, Arnold thought, a more calculated weighing of costs and benefits would be conducive to well-being.

If the aristocracy, the middle classes, and the working masses were ill fitted to guide the fortunes of the nation, who then was left? Arnold's answer lay with those he called Aliens. They came from every class, but they were aliens because they had transcended the mental boundaries of their classes of origin. He characterized them as those of every class who by nature have "a curiosity about their best self, with a bent for seeing things as they are, for disentangling themselves from machinery, for simply concerning themselves with reason and the will of God, and doing their best to make these prevail—for the pursuit, in a word, of perfection." The extent to which this "bent" would develop depended upon the encouragement it received. The aim of Aliens such as himself was to spread culture, in order to counter "the unchecked predominance of that class life which is the affirmation of our ordinary self," and to "disconcert mankind in their worship of machinery."[42]

The Roles of the Intellectual

Arnold's talk of criticism and of culture sounds airy and disembodied until we recognize that he was speaking on behalf of a group that was in part an existing reality, in part a project that he was working to bring into being. He was, to use an idiom quite foreign to him, an ideologist of the intellectuals, attempting to imbue them with collective self-consciousness and making universal claims on their behalf.

Arnold was part of an intellectual elite that was critical without being alienated from the powers that be. Though they were by no means affluent, they were welcome in the homes of at least some of the business elite. Arnold's whole plan was predicated on the assumption that a portion of the political and economic elites was open to the message he was preaching, and for this he had his own experience as a warrant. Arnold numbered among his friends Louisa de Rothschild, the wife of the head of the London branch of the great banking family, whom he first met in 1858, when he inspected a school on the family's estate. They struck up a friendship that lasted until the end of their days.[43] In his later years, Arnold was befriended by Andrew Carnegie, who had risen from a cottage in Dunfermline, Scotland, to become the steel lord of Pittsburgh and one of the richest men in the world. Carnegie was a true believer in the Arnoldian ideal of the civilizing effects of culture, and devoted much of his fortune to spreading it in the United States, subsidizing libraries throughout the republic. Nor was Arnold alienated from the world of politics: his brother-in-law was a Liberal MP, and Arnold himself knew both Disraeli and Gladstone.

In his easy movement between the worlds of thought and government, Arnold was characteristic of the small group of interlocking families who made up a sort of "intellectual aristocracy."[44] Since they read the same periodicals, belonged to the same clubs (above all, the Athenaeum), and often married one another's relatives, a relatively cohesive group was formed. While critical of the powers that be, they tried to modify what they criticized by working through the institutions of their society.

Unlike the earlier generation of Romantics, who had rejected bourgeois society and sought a historical alternative to it, and unlike the later generation of aesthetes, who sought to carve out a realm outside of bourgeois society, Arnold accepted the market and had a real if restrained appreciation of the virtues of the middle-class merchants, shopkeepers, and entrepreneurs who kept it humming.[45] For Arnold, as for many members of the Victorian intellectual aristocracy, the role of a cultured elite was to aid, elevate, and integrate society. They took their cue from Samuel Taylor Coleridge, who had written of the need to use the Church of England to create a "clerisy," men of culture who were to counter the negative effects of the capitalist ethos and create a shared sense of the authority of the state. Arnold secularized the notion even more.[46]

As we have seen, Hegel had similarly championed the "universal estate" of those imbued with *Bildung* and *Geist*. Arnold knew Hegel's work—some of it firsthand, some of it through Hegel's interpreters in

France[47]—and in a satirical self-portrait, Arnold identified himself as a proponent of *"Geist."*[48]

For Arnold, as for Hegel before him and Emile Durkheim after him, the intellectuals were obligated to articulate the rational basis of shared authority in order to provide the social cohesion once offered by common religious belief. Arnold, like Hegel, wanted men of culture to play a larger role in the bureaucracy, to use the state to preserve the commonweal by raising the economic level and security of the working class,[49] but, above all, to raise the cultural and spiritual level of the nation through the nexus of government, schools, universities, and magazines.

The goal of the university reformers of the 1850s and 1860s was to make the ancient institutions of Oxford and Cambridge into nurseries of what Coleridge had called the "clerisy" and Arnold "culture." That meant bringing Oxford and Cambridge into closer contact with the cultural and political currents of the day, and extricating them from their close connection to the Church of England. Until the 1850s, religious tests prevented Dissenters from studying at either university, and teaching at most colleges was restricted to clergymen of the Church of England, mostly men in religious orders bound by vows of celibacy. Because they taught all subjects, few taught any subject well, including theology. Excluded by religion and by vocational interests, the sons of the commercial classes were conspicuous by their absence.[50]

All of this changed in Arnold's day. Both universities developed fellowships open to merit, as determined by competitive examination. Acts of Parliament in 1854 and 1856 opened Oxford and Cambridge to those outside the Church of England. The ranks of the dons were no longer confined to the clergy. The range of subjects taught was expanded, greater specialization of teaching was encouraged, and research became a part of university life. The student body, which before 1870 had been composed for the most part of the sons of landowners and clergymen, came to be dominated by the offspring of the commercial and professional classes thereafter.[51]

The goal of the university reformers, especially at Oxford, was to nurture a spiritual clerisy, which would contribute to the cohesion of a society too dominated by what Thomas Carlyle had called the "cash nexus" (one of Marx and Engels' favorite phrases). The personification of university reform was Benjamin Jowett, who had been Arnold's tutor at Balliol College, and became professor of classics there. Like Coleridge, Jowett developed a spiritual and ideological ideal of the state as a force to counteract the fragmenting effects of commercial society, a view that he had imbibed from Plato and Hegel, and that he shared with Arnold.[52]

As Jowett and his fellow reformers conceived it, the role of college education was twofold. It was to bring about an expansion of horizons and flexibility of mind, by exposing students to what Arnold called "the best that has been thought and said in the world." In that sense, it was defined by its distance from specifically professional education.[53] The universities (or, at least, their colleges) were designed to counter the professional and practical orientation of the business middle class. A diet of classical learning was regarded as particularly well suited to nourishing future statesmen, civil servants, and professional men, and a knowledge of Greek was required for admission to Oxford or Cambridge until the First World War.[54] Those in search of direct preparation for commercial and industrial careers went elsewhere, to the newly founded municipal colleges. Yet the nonprofessional education at Oxbridge was supposed to have very practical value. For the broader horizons it opened and the habits of mind it inculcated were to render its products fit to govern Britain and the empire, and to contest the narrow and unimaginative conceptions of life characteristic of the business-oriented middle classes and the working classes who followed in their wake.

At the same time that he was reshaping Oxford, Jowett was deeply involved in transforming the civil service, opening its ranks, raising its standards, and broadening its purview. That transformation began with the Trevelyan-Northcote Commission of 1853–54, which aimed at reforming the civil service by abolishing patronage and replacing it with a system that based admission upon competitive examinations. The modifications introduced in the decades thereafter weighted the civil service exams to precisely the sort of literary and classical knowledge that Jowett and Arnold favored, and which was increasingly inculcated at the colleges of Oxford and Cambridge.[55] Thus a knowledge of Greek afforded a great advantage to those who took the competitive exams for entry into the civil service and even the royal military academy.[56]

Jowett established a close connection between his college and the civil service in London, beginning with the Education Office. Matthew Arnold was a forerunner and exemplar of that link. When Arnold took up his job as inspector of schools, his superior was his former tutor at Balliol; later, another old friend from Balliol assumed the task. They had found their way from Balliol to the Education Office by patronage, "the recruitment of public servants by private recommendation."[57]

Though patronage was soon to be disparaged as conflicting with merit, in Arnold's day it served as a rather efficient sifting mechanism. For Jowett, the civil service in general and the Education Department in particular provided an honorable vocational outlet for the graduates of his college. For London politicians such as Lord Lansdowne and his successors, Balliol provided a source of able men of broadly liberal political opinions and undogmatic religious convictions. In short, it served as an old boy network, of remarkably capable boys, a link that foreshadowed the more formalized entrance by merit later enshrined in the civil service reforms.[58] An impressive number of Arnold's friends and male relatives also pursued careers in the civil service. One brother, Edward Penrose Arnold, was also an inspector of schools; another, Thomas, served in the Colonial Office. Arnold's friend and fellow poet Arthur Hugh Clough served alongside him in the Education Office.

One of the state's most important roles, Arnold believed, was to foster education. Beyond the badly schooled children of the middle class lay the millions of children who received no formal education at all. Their parents would not send them to school unless the government enforced compulsory attendance, a policy that Arnold began to champion in 1853.[59] Arnold's longest book, *Schools and Universities on the Continent*, was intended to cast a fresh light on existing English conditions, in order to deflate his countrymen's assumptions about the adequacy of English education and the purported evils of state regulation of schools, not to mention compulsory education. He held up the German, Swiss, and French systems as models of national systems of education: they provided schooling for all, not only those with the wherewithal to pay, and elevated the education of teachers in order to improve the education of students.[60] He saw opposition to a state-regulated school system as a "pedantic application of certain maxims of political economy in the wrong place."[61] In England, he regretted, government policy was made without taking into account the opinion of those most knowledgeable about education. Here again, France and Germany provided an alternative—and, he thought, preferable—conception of how such matters might be handled.[62] Arnold's campaign for compulsory schooling under state auspices began to bear fruit in his own time. In 1870, the first Comprehensive Act was passed by the British Parliament. It required local school boards to provide elementary education; attendance was made compulsory a few years later.[63]

The main obstacles toward real progress, Arnold asserted time and time again, was the self-satisfaction engendered by material success, "our high opinion of our own energy and wealth." "This opinion is just," he continued, "but it is possible to rely on it too long, and to strain our energy and our wealth too hard. At any rate, our energy and our wealth will be more fruitful and safer, the more we add intelligence to them. . . ."[64] Intelligence, culture, and criticism: these were the master terms of Arnold's political vision of a democracy, led by a state authority guided by men of culture, recruited from all social classes and motivated by the desire for public service.

In addition to the universities and the civil service, Arnold had at his disposal a third forum for culture and criticism: the commercial journals of opinion.

That there was an interest in culture among the middle classes Arnold knew. To a far greater degree than the aristocracy or the working class, they read—though what they read left much to be desired. Arnold described it as "literature the absolute value of which it is almost impossible to rate too humbly, literature hardly a work of which will reach, or deserves to reach, the future."[65] The challenge was to take that middle class which Arnold admired for its industry and moral seriousness and to imbue it with "culture and intelligence," transforming it into a class "liberalised by an ampler culture, admitted to a wider sphere of thought, living by larger ideas, with its provincialism dissipated, its intolerance cured, its pettinesses purged away."[66]

Another role for the man of culture, as Arnold understood it, was therefore to make "the best that had been thought and said in the world" accessible to a nonprofessional audience. That required the ability to "humanise" knowledge, "to make it efficient outside the clique of the cultivated and learned" by taking the best ideas and laboring "to divest knowledge of all that was harsh, uncouth, difficult, abstract, professional, exclusive," thus bringing it "within the sphere of everyone's interest."[67] The great practitioner of that retailing of ideas was, of course, Voltaire, whom Arnold regarded as a model. One role of the critic, as Arnold understood it, was to open up the horizons of middle-class readers to the cultural and intellectual legacy of the past and to promising developments abroad. No wonder he devoted scores of review essays to acquainting the readers of Victorian journals with the great writers of ancient Greece, the Bible, and the Christian heritage, modern philosophers such as Spinoza, and the literary masters of modern France and Germany. At the same time, he explored issues of public policy and parliamentary contestation in a similarly accessible manner.

The intellectual as public critic seemed especially plausible in Arnold's day, in part because there was a distinct medium and palpable audience for his message. That audience was the readership of the mid-

Victorian journals, weekly and monthly, such as *Fraser's Magazine,*
The Saturday Review, The Fortnightly Review, The Quarterly Review,
Macmillan's Magazine, Cornhill Magazine, and the *Pall Mall Gazette.*
Many of the books that we now regard as the classics of Victorian
social and political thought first appeared as articles in these magazines, which also carried fiction as well as articles on history, literature, and politics.[68] With a circulation of about 10,000 to 20,000 each,
they had an overlapping readership, which made up the circle of "the
educated," above all the graduates of the universities and the public
schools (i.e., private schools).[69] In an age when the franchise was still
limited and before the domination of more specialized journals, writers like Arnold could publish, confident that anyone who really
counted in British society would be reached. To be read by an unspecialized audience, in turn, demanded the ability to write with wit and
grace, and to avoid the hermetic and the technical.

Unlike Marx, then, Arnold sought not to extirpate the philistines
but to convert them. The fact that so many read his essays and bought
his books, and now aspired to send their sons to Oxford and Cambridge
to be exposed to "the best that had been thought and said in the
world," made Arnold's hope plausible.

Arnold's notion of the intellectual as disinterested critic distinguished him from both Marx and Hegel. For Marx, the proper function
of the intellectual was to be a partisan on behalf of the proletariat, crit-
icizing bourgeois society for its fundamental, structural oppression.
For Hegel, the role of the intellectual was to stand above particular
group interests, and to bring to consciousness the ethical basis of modern, capitalist society, in the process creating standards by which to
guide politics and culture. Arnold's conception of "aliens" has obvious
affinities with this Hegelian image of the intellectual. But "disinterestedness" for Arnold had a rather different meaning. It implied the ability to free oneself from partisanship, to take a distanced enough view
to be able to criticize the side of the issue to which one had been committed, as circumstances required. "Living by ideas" he wrote, means
that "when one side of a question has long had your earnest support,
when all your feelings are engaged, when you hear all round you no
language but one, when your party talks this language like a steam-
engine and can imagine no other—still to be able to think, still to be
irresistibly carried, if so it be, by the current of thought to the opposite
side of the question . . ."[70] The role of intellectual, then, was to
embody and encourage that quality of mind that allowed individuals
to get some distance from their social, political, and economic milieu;
to reflect critically, and to be carried away by truth.

Arnold's hortatory essays warned his readers of the tendency of the culture of capitalism to promote the expansion of means while losing sight of ultimate ends. But it was the next generation of German intellectuals who would make that theme central to their understanding of the culture of capitalism. By the time of the First World War, a younger generation of intellectuals weaned on that understanding and despairing of converting the middle classes would seek far more radical solutions to those cultural dilemmas.

CHAPTER NINE

WEBER, SIMMEL, AND SOMBART: COMMUNITY, INDIVIDUALITY, AND RATIONALITY

Setting the Terms

"Just as the French have their theme, namely 'What was the great Revolution?' so our national destiny has given us our theme for a long time to come, namely 'What is capitalism?'"[1] Thus wrote Friedrich Naumann, the German pastor turned politician, in 1911. Perhaps never has capitalism received the level of intellectual attention and illumination as it did in Germany during the reign of Kaiser Wilhelm, in the two decades before the Great War. At the center of those debates were three academics: Max Weber (1864–1920), Georg Simmel (1858–1918), and Werner Sombart (1863–1941). All three came of age in the decades after Germany was unified in 1871. It was an era when German universities, research institutions, and museums—paid for by the state and by state-solicited donations from newly wealthy capitalists—were widely regarded as the best in the world, and when the prestige of professors within Germany was at its peak.[2] The debate focused on the question "Which human type is promoted by modern capitalism?"[3] That question not only dominated the social sciences, but was also at the center of the greatest novel of the era, Thomas Mann's *Buddenbrooks*.[4] (As with most novelists who treated the issue—Stendhal, Flaubert, and Zola all come to mind—Mann's answer was an unflattering one.) At least one leading industrialist, Walther Rathenau, felt compelled to weigh in on the controversy at book length.[5]

The book that set the terms for much of the debate was Ferdinand Tönnies' *Community and Society (Gemeinschaft und Gesellschaft)*, first published in 1887.[6] There were two fundamental forms of social life, he asserted. In community, individuals shared a basic solidarity.

They were united by an "organic will," by cultural assumptions so deeply shared that they became virtually second nature, leaving little room for conscious choice. His model of community was the family, but community according to Tönnies also existed in a more extended form when solidarity was based on shared membership in extensions of the family, such as the clan or the tribe. He saw community in its broadest form in the way of life of the guilds and villages championed a century earlier by Justus Möser.

If the model of community was the family and the guild, the model of society was the market, based upon self-interest, the exchange of commodities, and legal, contractual relations. In society the individual was faced with choice, most actions were motivated by rational calculation, and social peace was maintained by law. While Tönnies' distinction between community and society was intended to be objective, his presentation of it was in fact highly evaluative. "In community," he wrote, "people remain essentially united in spite of all separating factors, whereas in society they are essentially separated in spite of all uniting factors." His book presented a fundamentally pessimistic vision of historical development, depicting modern man as moving from the solidarity of shared aims and beliefs into a calculating society without shared ideals. Community was held together by common ends, society by common means.

Tönnies' description of modern society and of its central institution, the market, was heavily influenced by Marx, and though he regarded himself as a man of the left, his portrait was steeped in the prejudices of the new integral German nationalism of Paul de Lagarde.[7] These predilections are evident in his views on trade and on merchants. "Like every occupation, trade can be conducted in an honest and conscientious manner," Tönnies wrote. "However, the more purposefully and the larger the scale on which it is carried out, the more tricks and lies are introduced as effective means to gain high profits or cover losses. The will to enrich himself makes the merchant unscrupulous, egoistic, and self-willed, treating all human beings except his nearest friends as only means to his ends. He is the embodiment of *Gesellschaft*."[8]

Tönnies repackaged romantic anticapitalism at a time when Germany was once again being transformed by the market. *Community and Society* was to serve Weber and Simmel as both a conceptual stimulus and a foil.

Commercial Transformation

In the decades between its unification in 1871 and the outbreak of the First World War in 1914, Germany went from being a follower in the process of capitalist industrialization to a leader. While British industrial production doubled during the period, in Germany it increased six times over. The country was remade from a predominantly rural to an urban nation. The first wave of German industrialization, based on textiles and powered by steam, which Marx and Engels had witnessed in its infancy, was in full swing by the time Weber and Simmel were born, and by the turn of the century the country was immersed in the second wave of industrialization, based on the chemical and electric industries.[9] Companies such as Bayer, BASF, and Hoechst, in chemicals and pharmaceuticals, and Siemens and AEG, in electrical machinery, were world leaders.

Germany was also at the forefront of the development of the most characteristic feature of the twentieth century capitalist economy: the bureaucratic corporation. To stay competitive in the large market created by national unification and by participation in the international market, companies had to introduce new methods of mass production and distribution. They adopted new technologies that allowed them to reduce the cost of each unit produced by increasing the volume of production. The need to reduce costs and make use of new technologies led to an increase in the scale and scope of business. Sometimes companies in the same industry, such as coal, merged or formed cartels, in a process known as "horizontal integration." Other companies integrated "vertically" by buying up the sources of their raw materials.[10] Still others grew by diversification, producing a broader range of products based on the same technology (electrical appliances, for example), or drawn from the same raw materials (such as coal and its derivatives), or marketed through the same organizations.[11]

In the earlier stage of capitalist development, the family that owned the firm often managed it, so that sales, production, and distribution were often in the hands of brothers or cousins. But by the late nineteenth century, firms were developing on a scale that made such arrangements untenable. There was a gradual shift from owner-operated enterprises—in which families made long-range strategic decisions as well as day-to-day decisions about company performance—toward managed enterprises, in which such decisions were made by salaried managers. Take the case of Siemens, the German electrical appliance firm. In 1890, it employed over 3,000 people; by 1913, it employed 57,000.[12] There were too many decisions for the members of a single family, however large, to make. Day-to-day management of the firm increasingly fell into the hands of paid managers, who sat at the top of a hierarchy of salaried employees.

The division of labor, once evident primarily in production, now became characteristic of management as well. In order to coordinate the branches of the firm and assure that decisions made above would be carried out below, firms developed their own bureaucracies, based on formalized rules and a fixed division of functions and responsibilities. In the United States, large bureaucracies were first created in private business beginning in the 1870s, and only later in government. In Germany, the pattern was reversed: bureaucracy developed first in the army and in government administration, and private industry began building its bureaucracies by recruiting civil servants.[13] The expanding scale and scope of business and government required ever larger numbers of office workers, clerks, and managers. By the turn of the century, in the nations where capitalism was most advanced, these "white-collar" workers were the fastest growing segment of the workforce—although the urban, industrial, "blue-collar" workers whom Marxists called "the proletariat" were still the largest group in absolute numbers. The proportion of white-collar workers was particularly high in the expanding sectors of shipping, banking, and insurance, and in the newest form of retailing, the department store.[14] Even clear-eyed socialists, such as Eduard Bernstein, the leading "revisionist" theoretician of the Social Democrats, recognized the significance of this shift, which made Marx's image of a highly polarized society of capitalists and workers ever less plausible.[15]

The new scale of industry also required new legal forms of business organization. Industries such as railroads, mines, and steel works demanded more capital than any family could possibly amass. The traditional partnership—in which partners owned shares in a business and were personally liable for its losses—gave way to joint-stock companies, in which the shareholder's liability was legally limited to the extent of his investment. This newly created legal arrangement made it possible for many more people to participate in corporate ownership, and also expanded the pool of capital on which businesses could draw. A doctor or lawyer who had accumulated savings from his practice, for example, could buy shares, knowing that in the worst case, corporate bankruptcy, he would lose nothing more than his investment. Those shares were bought and sold on the stock exchange. Writing in 1894, Engels noted that, in the years since the publication of *Capital*, the stock exchange had become "the most pre-eminent representative of capitalist production as such."[16] The stock exchanges, together with commodity exchanges, became a lightning rod for popular discontent and stirred intellectual reflection.

Weber: Efficiency and Disenchantment

Max Weber, who came from a family of Calvinist entrepreneurs who sometimes turned to politics, is best known today for his study of the origins of modern capitalism, *The Protestant Ethic and the Spirit of Capitalism*, first published in 1906, and for his explorations of a wide range of sociological themes.[17] Less known, but essential for understanding his evaluation of the market, are his earlier essays on the stock and commodity exchanges, written shortly after Engels remarked on the stock exchange's centrality to capitalist production.

Weber's analysis and his policy prescriptions flowed from his political commitments. He was a liberal and a nationalist. He was a nationalist because he thought that in the modern world the nation-state was the broadest framework that could exert real power, but also because he felt that ultimately Germans ought to put the fate of their own society and culture above those of other peoples. In 1895, in his inaugural lecture upon assuming a professorship of political economy at the University of Freiburg, he scorned the assumption that the appropriate moral criterion for thinking about the economy was the well-being of the individuals within it.[18] On the contrary, he argued, the proper goal of the economy was the good of the German people (*Volk*), the pursuit of which would at times conflict with the interests of particular groups within society. Though Weber may have moderated his nationalism over time, he continued to believe that the economy should be viewed as a means to increase national power.

For most of the nineteenth century, liberals followed Adam Smith in arguing that one of the moral advantages of international trade was that it diminished international conflict and promoted cosmopolitan affinities. By the late nineteenth century, that was changing. Like most of his contemporaries in Germany and abroad in the age of imperialism, Weber viewed the relationship between nations through the lenses of social Darwinism.[19] His position was that nations competed with one another for power. Under modern conditions, the prerequisite of power was economic modernization, which was promoted, by and large, by participation in the world economy. But in order to compete successfully in the world economy, governments needed to encourage the development of a dynamic capitalism, and had to refrain from protecting less efficient producers who were harmed by foreign competition.[20]

Some of his political criticism was directed at those groups in German society, including Prussian Junkers and big industrialists, who sought to use their political influence to maintain their economic status by preventing competition from foreign goods.[21] But Weber also sought to combat the widespread suspicion of "big capital" among German workers, who, he thought, should recognize how much their welfare was tied to the development of a dynamic capitalist economy, which often required the concentrated resources of corporations.[22]

The liberal cast of Weber's nationalism was also evident in the way in which he treated the economic role of the Jews. They were conspicuously absent from his contemporary analysis. While liberal nationalism regarded all those within the borders of the nation as equal citizens, illiberal integral nationalists insisted that only those who shared a common past—religious, cultural, and biological—were truly part of the nation. In France, Germany, and much of eastern Europe, integral nationalism portrayed the peasant and the artisan as the heart of the nation and its culture.[23] The bêtes noires of integral nationalism were those who engaged in commerce, and above all the quintessence of commerce, the stock and commodity exchanges. Jews, who had long been involved in trade, were very active on these exchanges, and so it was but a small leap to identify the exchanges with the Jews.

Weber came to write about securities and commodity exchanges in the 1890s, at a time when they were at the cutting edge of world capitalist development and were under attack in Germany. In the course of the nineteenth century, the need of governments and of private companies for ever greater amounts of capital led to the expansion of markets for bonds. In the first half of the century, governments, which had until then borrowed only from large lenders, discovered that they could expand their borrowing if they could borrow from small creditors. They did so by floating bonds in small denominations. These bonds provided an annual dividend to their holders and were to be repaid at a given date in the future, when the bonds "matured." But their value depended upon the likelihood that the governments that issued the bonds could continue to pay dividends and ultimately redeem the bond at its face value. In the course of the century, exchanges were created at which such bonds could be traded; the bonds' value rose and fell with the relative stability of the governments that had issued them.

In the second half of the century, private companies required ever more capital to build railroads, mines, and factories. They too began to issue bonds as a way of borrowing money. To raise additional capital they sold ownership shares (stock) in their companies, and these shares too were traded on financial exchanges, which increased the availability of capital, while drawing in a wider range of people with small amounts of money to invest in the ownership of corporations. Thanks to the stock exchange, by the 1890s, as many as two million Germans (out of a population of some fifty million) owned shares.[24]

The existence of exchanges made stocks and bonds more desirable financial instruments, for the exchanges ensured that there would always be buyers and sellers for a stock or bond. The fact that stocks or bonds could always be converted into cash made them more attractive forms of investment, even if their price was higher than potential buyers hoped for or lower than potential sellers might desire. But who would buy shares or bonds of companies in decline? The answer was speculators, who aimed to profit from the gap between the supply and the demand for stocks and bonds. Speculators, then, were not parasites on the fundamental process of exchange; they were the grease that kept the exchange moving.

In the final decades of the century, commodity exchanges also emerged. In this financial sense, "commodities" are products (such as sugar or wheat or rye) made to standard specifications so that they are identical in quality and quantity. They can thus be exchanged without regard to origin. By the 1890s, Germany was becoming a worldwide center for the exchange of agricultural products: grain and flour in Berlin, coffee in Hamburg, cotton in Bremen, sugar in Magdeburg. On the commodity exchange one could buy or sell standardized quantities of such goods. More important yet was the trade in commodity *futures*. These were contracts to buy or sell a fixed quantity of some product at a set time in the future. They could be used by farmers and other producers to assure a known price for their products, helping to insulate them from vagaries in the market price of their goods and making it more likely that the producers would see a profit from their efforts. A farmer or estate owner who produced sugar, for example, could plant the cane in the spring and sell a sugar future for the next fall, so that he knew in the spring what he would get for his sugarcane once it was harvested in the autumn. A firm that processed and sold sugar could, in turn, buy fall sugar futures, which allowed it to know with greater certainty the price it would pay for sugarcane. On that basis it could calculate the price it would need to make a profit, and could inform wholesalers of the price they would pay for the processed sugar. For each of these economic actors, the use of commodity futures meant a reduction in financial risk.

As in the case of the stock exchange, that risk was taken on by those who neither produced nor consumed the goods themselves, but who bought and sold commodity futures because they hoped to profit from the movements of prices: the speculators. In the autumn, when the harvest was gathered, if the market price for sugarcane was higher than the price at which the grower had sold his sugar future, then the speculator who had bought a futures contract gained the difference. If, on the other hand, the market price of sugar had gone down, below the price at which the producer had sold his future, then the speculators had to make up the difference out of their pockets.

Commodity exchanges of this sort also promoted the growth of international trade by allowing for arbitrage, trading based on profiting from the differences in the price for the same good in two different exchanges. A trader in Germany who discovered that the cost of wheat on the Berlin futures market was more than the cost of the same wheat imported from South America or North America would sell wheat in Berlin, knowing he could import the wheat from the Americas if necessary. That in turn would drive down the price of wheat in Germany.[25] If the price of grain was lower in Berlin than in the Americas, the opposite could occur. In either case the overall effect was to even out prices across international markets.

During the 1890s, the exchanges in general—and commodity and currency exchanges in particular—came under massive public pressure across the globe, in Australia, the United States, Russia, and much of western Europe. The reason, paradoxically, was that the international trade in agricultural commodities was bringing down the price of food to consumers. German workers, for example, paid less for their bread, meat, and sugar because these goods could now be imported from Australia or from North or South America via steamship and railroad. As the supply of goods went up, their price went down. The price of wheat in 1894 was a third of what it had been in 1867. That benefited consumers, primarily those who lived in cities, and above all urban workers.

But that benefit often came at the expense of those in the countryside who grew the crops and raised the cattle. When the value of their products dropped, many went into debt, were threatened with forfeiture of their land, and saw a real decline in their standard of living.[26] Landowners, farmers, peasants, and agricultural workers complained that the commodity exchanges were destroying their livelihood. In Germany there were calls for greater government regulation of the exchanges, and, more radically, for prohibiting trade in commodity futures.

Widespread antagonism toward the exchanges existed among both the educated and the common folk. They suspected that the profits of trade were illicit and the activity of the merchant fundamentally unproductive, and such hostility escalated when the target was the exchanges. To outsiders, it seemed that speculators on the exchanges made enormous gains without adding anything of value: their gains seemed to come purely at the expense of others. Widely read tales told of once-solid citizens who had lost their family fortunes by "playing" the exchange, and the very vocabulary reflected the suspicion that the exchange was a veritable casino, and one in which the games were fixed to reward those with "inside" knowledge or the means to manipulate the market.[27] When prices on the stock or commodity exchanges dropped precipitously, politicians attacked the exchanges viciously. In 1879, the Prussian minister Albert von Maybach referred to them in parliament as a "poisoned tree which throws its ruinous shadow upon the life of the nation."[28] Nor were such condemnations confined to laymen: leading economists, such as Albert Schäffle and Adolph Wagner, decried "the unproductive and dishonorable gain from the exchanges."[29]

Stock bubbles are a perennial feature of capitalism. When stocks go up, even for good reason, more and more people are drawn into the market in search of profit, and begin to invest in companies of more dubious value. Germany experienced such a bubble in the boom years following unification. In the Gründerkrise (promoters' crisis) of 1873, a wave of speculation sent the price of stocks ever higher. That led unwary investors to buy shares in new companies floated on the most flimsy of bases. When the bubble burst, thousands of shareholders suffered huge losses. In the 1890s, when Weber entered the public debate about the exchanges, that fiasco was still fresh in the collective memory.[30]

Jews had been among the founders of the Berlin stock exchange, and Jews were overrepresented on the exchanges.[31] Antisemites characterized the exchanges as tools of Jewish domination. By the 1890s, antisemitism was not only the preserve of small, marginal parties: it was incorporated into the platform of the mainstream Conservative Party and expressed in new, powerful pressure groups with a mass following, such as the Agrarian League (*Bund der Landwirte*).³² The title of a pamphlet published by the Conservative Party in Saxony, the second-largest province in Germany, succinctly conveys the partisan message: *Die Konservativen im Kampfe gegen die Übermacht des Judentums und für die Erhaltung des Mittelstandes* (The Conservatives in Struggle Against Jewish Hegemony and for the Preservation of the Middle Class).³³

In response, the German government enacted a new exchange law in June 1896. It created a more constrictive legal framework for trading stocks and regulated the relationship between bankers who sold securities and their customers. The trade in commodity futures was to be prohibited entirely. Shortly thereafter, Max Weber—who only a few years earlier had become the first professor to lecture about exchanges at a German university—was appointed to a committee to advise the government on the implementing legislation.³⁴ It is against this background that he turned to writing about the stock and commodity exchanges for a wider public.

It was not only what Weber wrote but where he wrote it that added to the significance of these essays. For they appeared in the Göttingen Workers' Library, a series published by a Protestant labor movement formed to improve the education and condition of the working class and to draw workers away from the atheism of the Social Democrats. The editor of the series was Pastor Friedrich Naumann, founder of the movement, which had over 75,000 members. Naumann's organization called for greater regulation of the exchanges, and especially of the trade in foodstuffs.³⁵

While sympathetic to the aims of the organization and a supporter of the right of workers to form labor unions, Weber was skeptical of Naumann's economic acumen and of the economic wisdom of the workers who followed him. At the first convention of Naumann's National-Social Union (*Nationalsozialen Verein*), Weber spoke about the need to counteract the political power of large landowners and those big industrialists who tried to prevent the formation of labor unions. But he warned the workers that resentment of the economically powerful did not amount to an economic policy, and counseled that their interests lay in "bourgeois-capitalist development."³⁶ In a review of Naumann's essays published shortly thereafter, Weber called attention to the weaknesses of the pastor's economic prescription. Naumann favored the growth of large industrial firms as a lever of technological progress, but decried the concentration of capital. He therefore portrayed the Protestant industrialists Krupp and Stumm as exemplars of industrial progress, while holding up Rothschild—the paradigm of Jewish finance—as an example of those who earned income without working. This propensity of religious writers to regard the profits of trade as illicit, Weber remarked, was an antiquated legacy of the traditional prohibition of usury. He criticized Naumann's illogical conclusion that wages could be raised by lowering the rate of interest.[37] Weber thought Naumann's economic views an example of the woolly-mindedness of so much religiously inspired writing on economic matters. Weber set out to explain the realities of contemporary capitalism both to Naumann's working-class followers and to their clerical leader.

The workers' movement, Weber knew, tended to view the exchanges as "a conspiratorial club of treachery and lies, at the expense of those who work honorably." Such condemnations were evidence of "boundless superficiality," for, Weber contended, far from being an excrescence on the body of contemporary capitalism, the exchanges in fact were fundamental to its functioning.[38] They served the same purpose as a local market—providing a place where supply meets demand—but on a wider scale.[39] Given the fact that in a population of fifty million, there were two million holders of stock, it was foolish to think of the exchanges as serving only the interests of a few lazy coupon clippers.[40] Those outside the exchanges tended to focus on the quick fortunes made without work, but this was to confuse an incidental and marginal element of the exchanges with their essential function in creating market prices. The arguments for the market were arguments for the exchanges, and vice versa.

Written for workers, Weber's essays were a virtual primer on capitalism as a system of the transnational exchange of commodities upon which everyone in modern society depended. Much of Weber's account was given over to a straightforward explanation of the nature of the modern corporation as based on share owning, and to explaining how the exchanges actually operated. He focused on the role of commodity exchanges in improving the ability of buyers and sellers to diminish risk by providing secure prices for their commodities. From the point of view of the public at large, he pointed out, it was less important to shield investors from their own speculative urges than to protect the public against dramatic fluctuations of supply and of prices. Prohibiting futures trading in some commodity would only lead the market for it to move abroad; in the economic competition between nations, such a prohibition was a form of unilateral disarmament.[41] Weber's critique of the legislation banning commodity speculation proved astute, and within a few years the ban was lifted.

Throughout his career, Weber insisted that capitalism was the most efficient economic system possible under modern conditions. While he was ambivalent about its cultural effects, he devoted himself to dispelling the most frequent accusations against it. In *The Protestant Ethic and the Spirit of Capitalism*, which he published in midcareer, Weber took issue with those who identified capitalism with unscrupulous greed. The impulse of acquisition, he wrote, was not in itself a defining characteristic of capitalism. That desire exists at all times. "It should be taught in the kindergarten of cultural history that this naive idea of capitalism must be given up once and for all. *Unlimited greed for gain is not in the least identical with capitalism, and is still less its spirit*," Weber asserted,[42] for in fact "the universal reign of absolute unscrupulousness in the pursuit of selfish interests by the making of money has been a specific characteristic of precisely those countries whose bourgeois-capitalistic development . . . has remained backward." He dubbed the notion that modern capitalism is characterized by greater greed than other forms of life "the illusions of modern romanticists."[43]

From his early essays on the exchange to his final works, Weber insisted that capitalism was characterized by a higher level of rationality than any previous economic system had offered or than socialism could provide. The rational organization of legally free labor, rational bookkeeping, the rational organization of industry attuned to the market: for Weber, these were fundamental to capitalism.[44] But by "rationality" he did not mean some higher purpose in keeping with man's God-given or rationally ascertainable destiny. He meant rationality in an instrumental sense: the tendency to calculate as carefully as possible the most efficient means, and to implement them methodically in order to achieve control over nature, society, and the self. According to Weber, this instrumental rationality of capitalism was shared by other major institutions of the modern world. The modern state was characterized by bureaucratic administration of the rule of the law: laws were to be administered impersonally, so that their effects would be consistent, regardless of the particular bureaucrat administering the law or the particular characteristics of those to whom the law applied. The modern business corporation made use of the same bureaucratic means.[45] Modern science and technology were premised on observable rational calculation. The result was what Weber famously called the "disenchantment of the world"—the displacement of magic and mystery from more and more areas of life, and their replacement by the assumption that all things can, in principle, be explained by causal mechanisms and mastered by "technical means and calculations."[46]

As Weber used the term, "rationality" was a matter of matching means to ends. He did not mean that the ends themselves were reasonable from the point of view of some substantive purpose, value, or belief. The fact that method X was the most efficient means of getting from A to B did not mean that B was worth getting to. And indeed Weber sometimes suggested that capitalism did not make any larger sense, and that it created people who were so caught up in the pursuit of means that they lost sight of any substantive ends. It was not that people became more oriented to worldly pleasure or individual happiness. It was that they pursued economic means—money—at the *expense* of happiness or personal utility. Man becomes "dominated by the making of money, by acquisition as the ultimate purpose of life. Economic acquisition is no longer subordinated to man as the means for the satisfaction of his material needs."[47] Alongside capitalism and often intertwined with it was what Weber called vocationalism (*Berufsmenschentum*), the drive to excel in one's profession. Here too, Weber thought, calculating and methodical pursuit could often displace a sense of the ends worth pursuing.

Yet Weber insisted that, despite the limitations of capitalism, there was no desirable alternative to it. There was no going back to some bygone era, and as for socialism, it was likely to be inferior to capitalism in terms of productivity and vitality.[48] In his last years, before his death in June 1920, as the Bolshevik revolution in Russia and its abortive imitators in central Europe made the possibility of socialism more tangible, Weber turned his attention to the issue. Despite the hope of some intellectuals that socialism would provide a new sort of community, Weber suspected that it would preserve all the costs of capitalism without many of its advantages. The separation of the worker from the ownership of the means of production was not a problem that socialism could solve. Specialization was more productive, and technological development made it inevitable. Such separation would have to continue under socialism, even if the private factory owner was replaced by a state bureaucrat.[49] The discipline of factory life would be no less rigorous under socialism, he predicted, and the stultifying effects of bureaucracy would be worse than ever.[50] The Marxian vision of life beyond the division of labor was a fantasy. "Limitation to specialized work, with a renunciation of the Faustian universality of man which it involves, is a condition of any valuable work in the modern world," Weber stoically explained.[51]

Simmel: Money and Individuality

The theme of capitalism as the triumph of means over ends was elaborated by Weber's contemporary, Georg Simmel, who in 1900 published one of the most fertile works of reflection on capitalism and its cultural ramifications, *The Philosophy of Money*. In this and other works, Simmel explained how the development of the market economy made for new possibilities of individuality.

Like Weber, Simmel was an academic who ranged freely between philosophy, sociology, economics, history, and religion. Born near the commercial epicenter of Berlin in 1858, he lived in the capital until the age of fifty-six and experienced firsthand its development into a booming metropolis. In the years between Simmel's birth and the publication of his *Philosophy of Money*, Berlin's population grew from half a million to two million (and almost double that if its swelling suburbs were included). Simmel came from a family of Jewish merchants and traders, but both of his parents had converted to Christianity in their youth. While Simmel's parents raised him as a Protestant, in the manner of many such families, they continued to be regarded as Jewish by others, and he shared that consciousness to some degree. That Simmel's career was adversely affected by his Jewish origins is clear. When, in his initial attempt to acquire the postdoctoral degree needed to teach at a German university (*Habilitation*), a breach of decorum led his professors to fail him, one of them, Wilhelm Dilthey, received the following letter from his friend, the philosopher Count Paul Yorck von Wartenburg: "I congratulate you each time you manage to keep from the professoriate those routine, shallow, Jewish minds, who lack a true sense of intellectual responsibility, from a tribe without mental or physical roots."[52]

A religious outsider by familial origin but a religious insider by upbringing, a member of the upper middle class living at the cultural and commerical crossroads of German life, fluent in French and cosmopolitan in orientation, Simmel was keenly sensitive to the burgeoning possibilities of modern life. The circles of intellectuals, artists, and students in which he traveled brought him into contact with a plethora of movements in search of some new and all-encompassing way of life: socialism, feminism, vegetarianism, the youth movement, the student movement, and movements of religious renewal—Protestant, Jewish, and pagan.[53] The theme of multiple and sometimes conflicting options was to be central to his work.

These increasing options were not equally open to everyone, of course. But Simmel—by virtue of income, education, and the open-mindedness that comes from combining the roles of insider and outsider—was among those to whom new possibilities were most available.[54] At a time when other intellectuals like Ferdinand Tönnies or Werner Sombart were fixated on the decline of community, Simmel explored the possibilities created by greater social opportunities. While Marxists thought about modern individuals as bourgeois or proletarian, Simmel called attention to their role as consumers. While even Weber still thought about individuals primarily as members of a class or an occupational group, Simmel thought in terms of individuals whose identities were formed by belonging simultaneously to multiple cultural and social circles.[55]

If, from the perspective of the present, Simmel seems like the most modern of the turn-of-the-century thinkers (more modern, indeed, than Lukács and Freyer), it is because advanced capitalism has become ever more stamped by the forces upon which he fixed his gaze.[56] But before the relative advantages of that world could become clearer to a majority of Europeans, the continent would pass through tribulations brought about by movements seeking to recapture that sense of closed community and shared collective purpose which Simmel's world could not provide.

Simmel was an unorthodox academic who was able to transcend disciplinary and institutional boundaries. Despite the repeated efforts of Max Weber to get him a chair at a major university, it was only at age fifty-six that Simmel became a full professor, and then only in the provincial setting of Strasbourg. Within a short time of arriving there, he rued his move from Berlin; he died not long thereafter, in 1918. It was not antisemitism alone that accounts for his difficulties in the academy. It was also his failure to conform to the boundaries of academic disciplines. For Simmel wrote in several disciplines and in none. *The Philosophy of Money* began as an 1889 lecture entitled "The Psychology of Money," and ended as an amalgam of history, economics, sociology, social psychology, and cultural commentary. Not only did he address subjects outside of the purview of philosophy as then understood, from money to the nature of flirting, but he wrote without footnotes. The good graces and timely death of a well-to-do guardian had left him a sizable inheritance, which allowed Simmel to write and teach at the University of Berlin without a paid tenured professorship.[57] Financial independence made possible his intellectual independence.

Simmel's unorthodox mode of thought involved abstracting general patterns from the hurly-burly of everyday life, pointing to the connections between seemingly distant matters and finding structural parallels between disparate phenomena. In *The Philosophy of Money* he set out to explore the effect on the mind of living in a capitalist society. Rather than confining himself to a single line of analysis, Simmel attacked the problem from a variety of angles, providing both an appreciation and a critique.

Simmel drew attention to the psychological effects of living in an economy in which more and more areas of life could be measured in money. Such an economy created a mind-set that was more abstract, because the means of exchange themselves were becoming ever more abstract. Exchange had begun as barter, the very tangible giving of one thing for another. Later, in an early stage of a money economy, the means of exchange—gold, silver, or other precious metal—was itself of intrinsic value. In an advanced economy, money comprises pieces of metal or paper, the value of which is ultimately guaranteed only by the power of the central state: a mark is worth a mark, or a dollar a dollar, because the issuing government says so and has the ability to protect the economy against shocks that would destroy it. With the development of credit, money becomes more abstract still, little more than a bookkeeping notation.[58] (This process of the increasing abstraction of money would continue beyond Simmel's time, of course. By the 1960s, money existed in the form of plastic credit cards, by the 1980s as numbers on a computer screen.) Through constant exposure to an abstract means of exchange, individuals under capitalism are habituated to thinking about the world in a more abstract manner.

They also become more calculating and more used to weighing factors in making decisions. Where one is dependent on the market for almost everything, from food to entertainment to medicine, decisions about how to live become decisions about what to buy; choices about how to live better become choices of how much of one thing to trade off for another. Because each of these decisions requires calculations of more or less—if I pay more for item X, I'll have less left over for item Y—people in a money economy become acclimated to thinking in numerical terms. This numerical, calculating style of thought spills over into more and more personal decisions. Life becomes more cool and calculated, less impulsive and emotional.[59]

Life in a modern money economy, Simmel stressed, is characterized by ever greater distances between means and ends. Determining how to attain our ends is a matter of intellect: of calculation, weighing,

comparing the various possible means to reach our goals most efficiently. In primitive conditions, we eat by reaching out and picking the
fruit off the tree, by harvesting the grain we have grown, by bartering a
thing we have produced for another thing that we want. In a modern
capitalist economy we fulfill our desires more indirectly. To eat we
must buy our food. But to buy it we need money, and that money is
earned by working in an occupation. Becoming established in an occupation requires many steps, beginning with an education that itself
requires years of planning and calculation to acquire. Between the
desire to eat and the satisfaction of that desire are ever more steps, a
longer and longer series of means. Thus intellect, concerned with the
weighing of means, comes to play an ever greater role.

Building on his insight about the increasing importance of means in
capitalist society, Simmel offers an analysis of a phenomenon suggested by Voltaire almost two centuries earlier in his description of
how men of various religious faiths cooperate peacefully on the London exchange. Minds ever more oriented to the weighing of means,
Simmel tells us, become more tolerant, more conciliatory, because,
being focused on their own means, they are less concerned about the
ultimate ends of others. Spending less time thinking about ultimate
salvation or perfection and more on obtaining means, they become
more indifferent to the divergent ways in which others seek perfection
or salvation.[60]

While Simmel could at times echo the complaints of cultural pes-
simists and of cultural critics of capitalism, at his most creative he
upended their assumptions. Unlike Marx and Engels, who decried the
competitive process so central to capitalism as intrinsically evil, Simmel pointed out the integrative effects of competition. For competition
was not only a relationship between those who competed, it was a
struggle for the affection—or money—of a third party. To compete successfully, Simmel noted, the competitor must devote himself to discovering the desires of that third party. As a result, competition often
"achieves what usually only love can do: the divination of the innermost wishes of the other, even before he himself becomes aware of
them. Antagonistic tension with his competitor sharpens the businessman's sensitivity to the tendencies of the public, even to the point of
clairvoyance, regarding future changes in the public's tastes, fashions,
interests. . . ." And the competition for customers and consumers had
a highly democratic aspect as well. "Modern competition," Simmel
observed, "is often described as the fight of all against all, but at the

same time it is the fight of all *for* all." Thus, he concluded, competition forms "a web of a thousand social threads: through concentrating the consciousness on the will and feeling and thinking of fellowmen, through the adaptation of producers to consumers, through the discovery of ever more refined possibilities of gaining their favor and patronage."[61]

Thomas Carlyle—and, after him, Marx and Engels—might have scorned the "cash nexus," but Simmel explained that money tied modern society together in more positive ways. Like Voltaire before him (and Hayek after him), Simmel reminded his readers that money allowed for the cooperation of individuals who would otherwise have nothing to do with one another. The shareholders of a modern corporation join together with no common goal other than the making of profit: they cooperate without sharing all-encompassing goals. So too, Simmel pointed out, do those who contribute money to charities that serve people of various religious denominations; the possibility of donating money for limited but shared purposes made it possible to bypass theological differences.

In fact, Simmel suggested, the limited-liability corporation was a model for many characteristic forms of association under advanced capitalism, in which individuals cooperate for common but limited purposes. Unlike the guild, a "living community" that "included the entire person, socially, politically, and legally," modern life was based upon looser, more temporary associations, founded to pursue specific economic, cultural, or political interests, and demanding of the individual only a small part of himself, sometimes only a monetary contribution in the form of dues. As a result, the modern individual can belong to a greater range of groups, but groups that are looser and less encompassing. What Adam Smith had pointed out was becoming true to a greater degree than even he had imagined: individuals were increasingly interdependent, but ever less dependent on a single group or individual. Simmel concluded that "money establishes incomparably more connections among people than ever existed in the days of the feudal associations so beloved by romantics."[62] In contrast to earlier forms of association, modern groups allow for participation without absorption. They make it possible for the individual to develop a variety of interests and to become involved in a wider range of activities than would otherwise be possible, yet to do so without surrendering the totality of his time, income, or identity to any particular association, from the family to the state.[63] For Simmel, the eclipse of "community" was not a source of nostalgic lament: it presented new possibilities, along with potential pitfalls.

Unlike Marx, Simmel did not think that the net effect of capitalist development was to diminish individuality or eliminate any identity except that of class. On the contrary: one of Simmel's great interests was the way in which a developed money economy allows for the creation of new forms of individuality, as well as new conflicts *within* the individual.

It was with these concerns in mind that Simmel watched the emergence of the feminist movement at the turn of the century.[64] The rise of a movement for women's rights to property, higher education, professional equality, and political participation, he thought, could best be explained by the cultural dynamics created by capitalist development.[65] Middle-class women were being pushed out of the private realm of the household and into public realms by the psychological effects of market developments. New technologies that made housework less time-consuming, such as appliances, ready-made clothes, and other purchasable goods, made for less labor in the household, at least for those middle-class women who could afford them. Such women were left with time and energy that could no longer be fruitfully deployed in the home. The traditionally female domestic sphere of activity was being whittled away, while other spheres remained closed. The result was frustration, neuroses, a sense of wasted potential and of a stifling environment. This accounted for the rise of the women's movement, as such women demanded entrance into what had until then been the masculine realms of professional work, higher education, and politics. Simmel applauded these developments. He predicted that in the short run women would be forced to compete according to a set of rules created by men and for men, but that eventually the entrance of large numbers of women into work, commerce, and culture would have a transformative effect, infusing each of these realms with a more feminine sensibility.

Paradoxically, Simmel noted, women were developing their consciousness as women precisely at the time when they were demanding to be allowed to enter previously masculine realms and were becoming more like men. When middle-class women had been confined to the private realm of the home and family, their social roles were as distinct as possible from those of men. But since there had been only limited possibilities for associating with other women and since women had been focused on their husbands and children, the group with which they identified most was the family. The very notion of identifying as *women* was a product of the new circumstances created by recent developments of capitalism and its diminution of necessary labor in the household. Now, meeting together with other, similarly situated middle-class counterparts, these women developed a consciousness of themselves as women, with the shared collective goal of female emancipation.

Simmel explained the troubled relations between the women's movement and the labor movement in Germany by the different positions in which middle-class and working-class women found themselves. What they had in common was that "the sociological isolation of the woman, the consequence of her absorption in the home, is being superseded in both classes by her separation from the home." Working-class women had been driven out of the home and into the factory by economic need. There, labor took its toll on them physically and psychologically, so that what many desired most was the possibility of devoting more time to their familial roles as wife and mother. Thus, while for middle-class women moving into the world of paid labor seemed a blessing promising greater personal fulfillment, for working-class women it seemed a curse. Middle-class women wanted to get out of the house, working-class women to get back into it.[66] Yet in both cases, women were experiencing the tensions that came from identifying themselves both with their familial identity and as "women" with interests in common in the public realm.

For Simmel, that tension between the demands of multiple roles was not confined to women; it was characteristic of modern society.[67] His work began with the assumption that moral theory had often been led astray by its failure to examine the internal conflict of demands that arises from the complexity of social membership. Simmel thought that it was wrong to assume that individuals were faced with a clear hierarchy of moral demands at any given time. Because modern people belong to a number of social circles, each with its own demands, they live in a situation of ongoing internal conflict or tension between conflicting demands. Indeed, such conflicts are intrinsic to the modern personality: "The individual, who participates in a number of social circles and stands at their intersection, feels their contradictory pulls within himself."[68]

The very multiplicity of social circles to which one belongs allows for the development of individuality, Simmel asserted. Instead of having a single identity, as in earlier societies, the modern person has many sources of belonging, each of which exerts a weaker hold.[69] "Whereas earlier, individuality was determined primarily by belonging to a single group, it is now formed by the *combination* of the diverse groups to which the person belongs. . . . Someone may belong to various professional associations, at the same time as he belongs to a scientific society, is a reserve officer, plays a role in a civic association, and in addition has a social life that brings him into contact with diverse social strata." He or she may be more "prone to a certain solitariness (*Vereinsamung*), increasingly doing without those all-encompassing and familiar attachments (*Heimathlichkeit*) that offer both limitation and support. But the compensation is the creation of ever more circles and associations that provide support for every interest and inclination, " Simmel explained.[70]

The Dialectics of Means and Ends

To Simmel, money was an example, perhaps the quintessential example, of a larger pattern in the relationship between men and the objects they created. To meet its own needs, the human mind creates a variety of products. Over time, those products take on an existence independent of their original creators. From transient creations for immediate purposes, they become cultural objects, taking on a fixed and ongoing form. The creations that express man's sense of transcendence become religion; those created to control nature become technology. In time, efforts are made to develop and perfect these cultural creations: each becomes more and more ramified, forming a separate cultural "world," the understanding and mastery of which requires a human lifetime and more. There is, for example, a "world" of science—which comprises separate worlds of biology, physics, chemistry, etc., each of which in turn is broken into subworlds of its own. Alongside these worlds of science are worlds of religion, of the various arts, of sports, of the military, and so on. Each of these worlds (or cultural spheres) is internally differentiated, with only the most tenuous connection to the others. This pluralization of cultural spheres makes nonsense of the notion of a coherent "culture."

Simmel was interested in the effect on individuality of the proliferation of these cultural creations. On the positive side, he pointed out, the availability of a variety of cultural worlds allows us to enrich our individuality, through, for example, the availability of novels, the various genres of music, the many branches of science, philosophy, or religious culture. By assimilating some of each of these, we develop aspects of ourselves in ways that would be difficult if not impossible if these cultural forms were not readily available. But the cost of this was what Simmel called "the tragedy of culture": the frustrating recognition that there is so much we would like to know but cannot, that we will never have time or mental energy to master, the recognition that commitment to any one branch of culture comes at the expense of the possibility of using our time and energy in other ways. The different realms of culture compete with one another for our attention and resources. To decide in favor of one means giving up on others. The division of labor and the increasing complexity of modern life meant that amid an explosion of cultural products the individual had to become more specialized and one-sided.[71]

The money economy facilitates the creation of ever more cultural realms, ever more areas of potential interest, each increasingly complex. On the one hand, then, capitalism may increase individual frustration—as Rousseau had pointed out in his *Discourse on the Arts and Sciences*—as we become aware that there is so much that we might have, know, or do, which we will never have the time, energy, and perhaps money to accomplish. But on the other hand, the multiplication of cultural realms in which we participate allows individuality to develop, by allowing us to *select* the activities that best suit our personal particularity. The widely diverse culture facilitated by the growth of capitalism creates the possibility of personal refinement, distinctiveness, and introspection.

But that is only one possibility. The proliferation and availability of objects to buy will lead some people to become controlled by the pursuit of those objects, to a virtual worship of commodities. The outcome, Simmel concluded, depends not upon money but upon each person: the advanced capitalist economy creates possibilities for individual development, but also the danger of "unprecedented practical materialism."[72]

Like Hegel and Arnold before him, Simmel reminded his readers that the freedom created by the liberal capitalist state, while of great potential benefit, was not a good in and of itself. The liberal state eliminates old restrictions—on entering various professions, on owning property—and opens new possibilities. But unless the new freedom was filled by a sense of direction, it would lead to boredom, restlessness, and a lack of purpose. Those who defined themselves only by freedom from restraint easily fell victim to the illusion that vigor, stability, and purpose could be obtained through money or commodities. But money, since it is a means, cannot provide life with an end, and all too often the want that a newly obtained commodity was supposed to satisfy merely took on a new form.[73] The upshot was a never-ending round of joyless acquisition and consumption.

Money, Simmel reminded his readers, has no purpose of its own. It functions as an intermediary: we sell our goods or our labor in order to acquire money, and we acquire money in order to be able to buy something else. It is a moralistic commonplace that there are things that money can't buy, including satisfaction. It is one of Simmel's most striking insights, however, that owning money can actually be *more* satisfying than owning the things that money can buy. That is because money's worth surpasses the value of the objects for which it can be exchanged: money has a "surplus value," because the owner of money has the added satisfaction that comes from having a choice of all of the goods that his money *could* buy. Thus "the value of a given amount of money is equal to the value of any object for which it might be exchanged plus the value of free choice between innumerable other objects. . . ."[74]

Money, then, is a tool in the purest form. But, Simmel noticed, the improvement of tools does not merely result in the more efficient satisfaction of existing ends. New tools often provoke us to come up with new purposes for which the tools can be used. As Simmel put it, "Once a purpose has engendered the idea of means, the means may produce the conception of a purpose." Moreover, human psychology is such that what begins as a means may become an end in itself. Sometimes this is because the emotional value that we place on the goal is transferred to the means to obtain it. Once we begin developing new means or tools, developing them further takes on a certain fascination. Here again, means become ends in themselves.

The money economy thus intensified this dialectic of means and ends, for money provides an extreme example of the transformation of means into ends that occurs to some degree in every realm of human life.[75] People in such an economy have a tendency to get caught up in the pursuit of means, in the acquisition of money and the perfection of techniques. While devoting themselves to accumulation and the perfection of techniques, they tend to lose sight of ultimate purposes.

Like Weber, then, Simmel was ambivalent about the cultural effects of the spread of the market.[76] At times, he could sound Arnoldian in portraying contemporary society as the triumph of means over ends. Reflecting for a foreign audience on German developments in the past generation, Simmel wrote:

> The powers of the mind have been forced to serve the purposes of pecuniary gain in a manner previously unheard of in Germany, and, governed by extraordinarily active competi-

tion, national as well as international, to allow all other things to become subordinate to material interests. As the result of this, *technique* has become of late years the sole concern of most producers and consumers, and in a way that is most ominous for the inner and spiritual development of the nations. It is completely forgotten that *technique* is a mere means to an end, and its perfection is extolled as though it were one of the great objects of the human race; as though telegraphs and telephones were in themselves things of extraordinary value, despite the fact that what men say to each other by means of them is not at all wiser, nobler, or in any way more excellent than what they formerly entrusted to less rapid means of communication; as though the electric light raised man a stage nearer perfection, despite the fact that the objects more clearly seen by means of it are just as trivial, ugly, or unimportant as when looked at by the aid of petroleum.[77]

Yet despite such misgivings, Simmel pointed to the possibilities and opportunities offered by capitalist modernity.[78]

If the promise of modern capitalism was of greater and more complex individuality, the specter haunting it, for Simmel, was an ever-increasing number of possibilities, none of which seemed compelling. He highlighted the development of a new form of individualism promoted by the market economy, an individualism based on choice from among the many cultural spheres and social circles created by the market. The thrust of his analysis of capitalist modernity was of the proliferation of spheres of activity that did not fit together into a coherent whole, but that provided the individual with unprecedented opportunities for the development of his particularity. But Simmel could never quite free himself from the assumption—shared by the Christian and civic republican traditions and, in an attenuated form, by Hegel—that society *should* fit together into some larger whole that provided individuals with shared, ultimate purposes; that ultimately it should form a community. That assumption was expressed more emphatically by Werner Sombart.

Sombart: Blaming It on the Jews

If Weber and Simmel were ambivalent but predominantly positive about the prospects presented by capitalism, Werner Sombart viewed it with despair. Born in 1863, five years after Simmel and a year before Weber, Sombart was among the most renowned social scientists of his day; his works spanned the disciplines of history, economics, and sociology.[79] The term "capitalism" came into academic social science by way of his *Modern Capitalism* (*Der moderne Kapitalismus*), published in 1902, and his *Why Is There No Socialism in the United States?* (*Warum gibt es in den Vereinigten Staaten keinen Sozialismus?* [1906]) pointed to the significance of consumption and set off a debate that lasted for much of the century. Together with Weber, Sombart was on the editorial triumvirate of the Archive for Social Science and Social Policy (*Archiv für Sozialwissenschaft und Sozialpolitik*), the leading journal in its field. Sombart's books, written in an accessible and pointed style, reached far beyond the academy. But while Weber and Simmel wrote works that brought out the complexity of capitalism, weighing its costs and benefits and trying to rein in their own value preferences, Sombart's work became increasingly unrestrained, sensationalist, and shrill. According to him, capitalism meant the decline of all culture worthy of the name, and those most responsible for that decline were the Jews. Sombart forged a link between the romantic anticapitalism of *Community and Society* and the new antisemitism.

The first of Sombart's works to combine economic history with romantic anticapitalism was *Die deutsche Volkswirtschaft im neunzehnten Jahrhundert* (*The German Economy in the Nineteenth Century*), published in 1903. He portrayed the precapitalist economy of the artisan and peasant as "natural" and the modern capitalist economy as "artificial." Sombart shared the romantic prejudice that identified the archaic with the authentic. He treated the forms of life characteristic of the less modernized groups in the population as primordial, though they were in fact the product of earlier historical development. For Sombart, capitalism's dissolution of the traditional way of life of the *Volk* was leading to the "graveyard of culture." While capitalism marked a quantitative gain—he recognized that it was more productive and created a higher material standard of living—it meant a loss in the quality of life, robbing men of inner peace, of their relationship to nature, and of the faith of their fathers. It led to overvaluing the things of this world. (Like many romantic conservatives, Sombart was not religious, but he thought it a pity that others were not.) Capitalism, according to Sombart, destroyed the soul and led to the standardization or "massification" of cultural life.[80] Though he lived his entire life in major cities, Sombart saw nothing positive in the process of urbanization: he stigmatized city life as an artificial, inauthentic form of existence, producing what he dismissively dubbed "asphalt culture."

In the same book, Sombart began to draw attention to what was to become a leitmotif of his writing and lecturing for the next decade: the link between capitalism and the Jews. The Jewish mind was characterized by egoism, self-interest, and abstraction: precisely the qualities most suited for capitalism. His key witness for the elective affinity between capitalism and Jewish character was none other than Karl Marx, whose "On the Question of the Jews" he quoted approvingly: "What is the worldly basis of Jewdom? *Practical* need, *self-interest.* What is the worldly cult of the Jew? *Bargaining* (*Schacher*). What is his worldly god? *Money.*"[81] In 1911, six years after Max Weber published the essays that made up *The Protestant Ethic and the Spirit of Capitalism,* Sombart published his response, *The Jews and Economic Life* (*Die Juden und das Wirtschaftsleben*),[82] in which he sought to show that it was the Jews who had been crucial to the rise of modern capitalism, and that they had played so large a role in it because they were spiritually and culturally inclined to the rationalistic and calculative mentality so characteristic of capitalism. According to Sombart, it was the Jewish religion itself that predisposed Jews toward capitalism, for it was the religion of a rootless, nomadic "desert people," given to abstraction, a contractual conception of their relationship with God, and the numerical calculation of sin.[83] Jews were accustomed to living their lives teleologically, orienting their lives to a distant goal, Sombart speculated, taking a Simmelian line of analysis and giving it an antisemitic twist. They were therefore used to thinking of things as means to an end. Money, he noted, was a pure means. Therefore, Sombart concluded, Jews were particularly attentive to money, as the means par excellence.[84] According to Sombart, Jews were inclined less to the creative, entrepreneurial elements of capitalism and more to the calculative search for advantage characteristic of trade. And this calculating, means-weighing, abstract numerical mind fitted the Jew to be "the perfect stock-exchange speculator."[85] In his synthesis of Marx, Tönnies, and Simmel, Sombart portrayed the triumph of capitalism as the replacement of a concrete, particularist, Christian *Gemeinschaft* by an abstract, universalistic, judaized *Gesellschaft.*[86]

In a biting critique of Sombart's book, the liberal Catholic historian Lujo Brentano pointed out that even a simple reading of biblical sources would show that far from being nomadic, the Hebrews had spent only a few decades in the desert. Sombart's book was the antithesis of real scholarship, Brentano concluded, in that the author merely selected evidence to conform to his prejudices and predispositions.[87] Weber was no more gentle, writing to Sombart privately that in the book's section on the Jewish religion "almost every word is wrong."[88]

Sombart's identification of the Jews with the elements of capitalism that he most despised provided a scholarly patina for what was already one of the most frequent motifs of antisemites in Germany, as in Britain and France. The Jews, they claimed, were responsible for everything bad about capitalism and the modern world.[89] Leading German antisemitic authors in turn pillaged Sombart's work for evidence to buttress their cause. Theodor Fritsch, the author of *The Anti-Semitic Catechism*, who was later honored by the Nazis as their *Altmeister*, in 1913, published *Die Juden im Handel und das Geheimnis ihrer Erfolgen* (*The Jews in Commerce and the Secret of Their Success*), a book that criticized Sombart as too friendly to the Jews, but went on to paraphrase his arguments for hundreds of pages on end.[90]

The World War as Turning Point

The Wilhelmine era came to an end with the war that broke out in 1914. Though Weber, Simmel, and Sombart all supported it, indeed welcomed it, their reactions reflected their previous analyses of capitalism.

Like other intellectuals in Germany and elsewhere in Europe, Weber was awestruck by the display of national unity that greeted the outbreak of hostilities. Given the political fragmentation of the preceding decades, the apparent alacrity with which men of all classes marched off to war was unexpected, and Weber was thrilled at this display of self-sacrifice. "Whatever the outcome, this war is great and wonderful," he wrote to a friend in late August 1914, and a year later could still write that "it is a joy to live through what none of us had believed possible." Regretting that he was too old to fight on the front lines, he threw himself into war-related administration, running the military infirmary in Heidelberg, where he lived.[91] Weber thought the war unavoidable and necessary if Germany was to become a great power by holding its own against the power of England in the west and Russia in the east. Unlike more radical nationalists, Weber opposed the annexation of territory that Germany conquered early in the war. His opposition was grounded on considerations of realpolitik. Annexations, he believed, would leave Germany diplomatically isolated and poorly positioned for future international self-assertion.[92] While Weber's reaction reflected his long-standing nationalism, it was sobered by his skepticism about the political leadership provided by the Junker class and the emperor and by his deep-seated aversion to ideological fanaticism.

Simmel's reaction was more unexpected. His previous ambivalence about the cultural influence of capitalism seemed to vanish, replaced by a pessimistic portrait of prewar culture and society and a hopeful assessment of the effects of the war. It marked a spiritual turning point, he declared in November 1914, and Germany was "pregnant with great possibilities." In long eras of peace, Simmel observed, there is a tendency to confuse unessential aspects of life with essential goals, since there is no need to distinguish the unessential from the essential.[93] During the decades before the war, he now insisted, the burgeoning of cultural and technological means had led to the eclipse of a sense of broader purpose. The war, however, acted as a "unifying, simplifying, and concentrating force," in which even individual self-preservation—the usual end of life—was clearly subordinated to the higher goal of national self-preservation.[94] The war had thus brought a respite from the eclipse of ultimate goals by proximate means so characteristic of modern capitalist culture.

The war might also reverse the decline of a sense of community, Simmel told his audiences. In peacetime the means to which the individual devoted himself had no perceptible connection to the community as a whole. But in war the citizen feels the importance of his task for the entire community, an experience most intense for the soldier on the field of battle.[95] Simmel suggested that this sense of reconciliation of individual pursuits and communal purposes might be carried over into a postwar era. The wave of national unity experienced in the early war years was interpreted by Simmel and by many other intellectuals as the catalyst of a process that would transform the individualistic, economistic ethos of the prewar era into a new, more collectivist culture—a community.

Like Simmel, but with greater bombast and national chauvinism, Werner Sombart argued that the war had given back meaning and collective purpose to society. In his 1915 *Händler und Helden: Patriotis-*

che Besinnungen (*Traders and Heroes: Patriotic Reflections*), Sombart recast his disdain for the culture of capitalism into a "war of religion" between Germany and England. The Germans he romanticized as a nation of heroes; the English he scorned as a nation of traders and shop-keepers. The trader, he wrote, "regards the whole existence of man on earth as a sum of commercial transactions which everyone makes as favorably as possible for himself. . . . Within this conception of life, material values will thus be given an important place. . . . Economic and especially commercial activity will achieve honor and respect. Consequently, economic interest will . . . gradually subordinate the other aspects of life. Once the representatives of the economy have the upper hand in the country, they will easily transfer the attitudes of their profession to all sectors of life . . . until the trader's world view and practical commercialism finally join together in an inseparable unity, as is the case in England today."[96] Germany, too, had been headed down this road to ruin, Sombart argued, until "the miracle occurred" with the coming of the war, when the "ancient German hero's spirit" burst forth, recapturing virtues of courage, obedience, and self-sacrifice. (For good measure, he added "religiosity," combining a militarized version of civic republicanism with Christianity.)[97] Now the technical and economic growth "which previously seemed mean-ingless, have regained meaning and significance, which they derive from what is for us the highest value." That value was the German *Volk*, the "chosen people" of the twentieth century, who formed the "last dam against the slimy flood of commercialism."[98]

When the vehemence of Sombart's book met with widespread criti-cism in the press and alienated him from many of his colleagues, he blamed the book's poor reception on the Jews.[99]

The war experience was a watershed for the capitalist societies of cen-tral Europe, and for the interpretation of capitalism. Especially in Ger-many and Austria-Hungary, the Great War led to political polarization, as intellectuals abandoned the ambivalent liberalism of Weber and Simmel and moved toward political radicalisms of the left and right. The movement of the younger generation to the political extremes came in response not only to the war experience, but to the way in which leading intellectuals interpreted it. Georg Lukács and Hans Freyer were representative and particularly eloquent exponents of this radicalization, who sought not to reform capitalism but to transcend it.

CHAPTER TEN

LUKÁCS AND FREYER:
FROM THE QUEST FOR COMMUNITY TO THE TEMPTATIONS OF TOTALITY

The period from the First to the Second World War was the era of radical anticapitalism. While Max Weber and Georg Simmel were troubled liberals, their analyses of capitalism were developed into politically more radical directions by some of their students. Weber and Simmel were liberals in that they affirmed the market not only for its economic superiority, but also because it allowed for more individual freedom than any previous economic system or any imaginable alternative. They were German nationalists (Weber more emphatically than Simmel) at a time when liberalism and nationalism seemed compatible, indeed complementary. Yet they were troubled by the failure of capitalism to provide a sense of collective purpose or some transcendent sense of meaning. They flirted briefly with the notion that the Great War would itself transform into a cohesive whole the complex and fragmented culture to which advanced capitalism gave rise.

Georg Lukács and Hans Freyer were a generation younger than Weber and Simmel and deeply influenced by them. Lukács and Freyer provide examples of intellectuals whose analysis of the cultural effects of the market led them to reject liberalism altogether and, like so many European intellectuals, embrace totalitarian solutions to the cultural dilemmas created by capitalism. Lukács, born in 1885, embraced communism in 1918 and remained a loyal (though sometimes dissident) member of the Communist Party till his death in 1971. Freyer, born two years after Lukács, emerged from the First World War a theorist of the radical right and welcomed the rise of National Socialism. But his commitment to his radical choice was never as unequivocal as Lukács', and Freyer eventually became disillusioned with it, moving toward reconciliation with liberal capitalist democracy in the decades between the defeat of the Third Reich and his death in 1969. They were among the most articulate theoreticians of the radical critique of capitalism in interwar Europe. In this chapter we will explore their respective critiques, and try to explain why one responded by moving to the radical left, the other to the radical right.

From Intellectual to Revolutionary

Georg Lukács was born György Bernát Löwinger, into a Jewish family in Budapest, the capital of the Hungarian half of the Austro-Hungarian Empire. His family history reflects in an exaggerated way the peculiar combination of success, marginality, and genius that marked the fate of Hungarian Jewry. His mother, Adél Wertheimer, came from a family distinguished since at least the eighteenth century by its financial success and by its scholarship, Talmudic and secular. Raised in Vienna, she spoke German, the dominant language of the empire, which was the language of the Lukács home. Georg's father, József Löwinger, rose from obscurity to become one of the most prominent bankers in Hungary. Born the son of a quiltmaker in southern Hungary, he left school at the age of thirteen to work in a bank; by twenty-four he was manager of the Budapest branch of the Anglo-Austrian Bank; in 1906 he joined the Board of Directors of the Hungarian General Credit Bank, the most important credit institution in Hungary.[1]

The identification of Jewry with capitalism, which in much of Europe was a metaphor and elsewhere polemical hyperbole, was close to exactitude in Hungary. Hungary lacked an ethnically native commercial class, as was often the case in eastern Europe. Neither the Magyar nobility nor the peasantry was oriented to commerce, which they tended to regard as essentially immoral, degrading, or incompatible with the Magyar spirit.[2] In the course of the nineteenth century, as the Magyar aristocrats concluded that economic development was needed to build a modern nation, they permitted and even encouraged Jews with a background in trade to become active in the economy. An ethnic division of labor developed, an informal accommodation, in which the Magyar nobility dominated politics and government (with the aristocracy at the higher reaches and the gentry in lower, administrative posts), while Jews channeled their energies into the economic realm, promoting commerce, creating banks, and transforming the agricultural estates of the nobility into income-producing capitalist enterprises.

Perhaps nowhere in Europe—and certainly nowhere in central and eastern Europe—was the assimilation of Jews into the economy and culture so welcomed as in Hungary in the decades after 1867. That was the year of the *Ausgleich*, which bifurcated the Habsburg empire into Austrian and Hungarian halves, linked by a common legal system, armed forces, and emperor. Jews achieved more than legal equality: in the Hungarian half of the empire, their absorption was actively encouraged by the dominant Magyars, who were an ethnic minority in their own kingdom and saw the Jews as potential recruits who could add the weight of their numbers to the Hungarian side of the ethnic balance. By the turn of the century, Jews not only dominated Hungarian finance and commerce, but were highly visible in the free professions as well, comprising just under half of Hungary's doctors, lawyers, and journalists according to the census of 1910. Fin de siècle Budapest was booming. With a population of 800,000, it was the sixth largest city in Europe and the fastest growing. With over 200,000 Jewish inhabitants, Budapest had the largest Jewish community in Europe after Warsaw. In return for embracing the Hungarian language and the cause of the empire, Jews who prospered were offered titles of nobility and entrance into the upper levels of the civil service and even into government, though the price of admission often included conversion to Christianity.[3]

It was a price that more than a few were happy to pay, the Löwingers among them. In 1890, József Löwinger Magyarized his surname to Lukács. In 1901, in return for a considerable monetary sum, he was ennobled as "Szegedi Lukács" in Hungarian or "von Lukács" in German, the surname under which Georg published his early works. Georg converted to Lutheranism in 1907, not an unusual stepping stone for those of Jewish origin for whom Judaism meant little more than a barrier to full cultural assimilation. Since in his parents' household "no importance was attached even to the learning of Hebrew," Lukács later remembered, Jewish ceremonies and rituals were meaningless.[4] "My father, who otherwise never went to temple and certainly never prayed, once a year took me to some secret ceremony," Lukács' close friend, Béla Balázs, recalled: "There were men there whom I did not know and with whom my parents did not socialize. With white sheets on their shoulders, they wailed and beat their breasts. But what was really frightening for me was that my father too donned such a white sheet, which was edged with black stripes, and dressed like them, he joined and entered this alien and secret alliance. . . . I heard this was Yom Kippur and our most holy day of the year, because we are Jewish. Why are we Jewish? This I did not quite understand . . . [since] during the rest of the year no detail of our life gave me the sense that we were Jewish."[5] Lukács and Balázs thus resembled the Jew in Voltaire's description of the London exchange who recites Hebrew words without knowing their meaning. Not surprisingly, they embraced the universalism championed by Voltaire—and by Marx.

Young Lukács was a prodigy, reading the great works of European literature in several languages even as an adolescent. While Marx's father had insisted that his son pursue a practical career that would provide financial stability, the senior Lukács encouraged his son to follow his cultural star. Not only was the family's wealth sufficient to provide the son with an ongoing income, but among central European Jews by the turn of the century, it was common for well-to-do fathers to support the cultural interests of their gifted children. For cultural attainment was seen as a path not only to greater social status but to full acceptance by the larger world.[6] Mastery of the dominant culture of the west was the road to recognition. When, as a high school student, Georg became interested in contemporary theater, his father funded a theater company that Georg headed. Jószef Lukács funded not only Georg's university education in Hungary, but further studies in Berlin and Heidelberg, hoping that his son would obtain a university post as a philosopher. When Georg decided to found a new Hungarian journal of philosophy, many of the subscriptions were purchased by his father's business associates.

But if Lukács and his father shared the goal of cultural acquisition, culture had a very different significance for the two generations. For Lukács *père*, high culture, including philosophy, was the apex of integration into European bourgeois culture. For Lukács *fils*, the career of philosopher was a rejection of business, and the content of culture a critique of the bourgeois world of his parents.[7] To the young Lukács, his parents' life seemed bereft of meaning. His father's ethic of achievement was, to Georg, the pursuit of means without some higher purpose; the manners upon which his mother insisted were nothing more than empty conventions, against which he rebelled. When as a lad he read James Fenimore Cooper's *The Last of the Mohicans*, the message he took from it was that the losers in the process of historical development might be more noble than the winners. Reading *Tom Sawyer* and *Huckleberry Finn* confirmed his sense of the conflict between bourgeois respectability and personal authenticity.[8]

Nor did the aspiration of becoming Hungarian seem as plausible or desirable to Georg Lukács as to his parents' generation. For Lukács' father, coming to Budapest was a journey from the cultural periphery to the metropolis. To Georg, whose horizons stretched to Vienna, Berlin, Paris, and Florence, Budapest and Hungarian culture appeared provincial and limiting. In addition, Hungarian nationalism, like nationalism elsewhere in central and eastern Europe, was itself changing and becoming ever less welcoming of assimilating Jews like the Lukácses. The generation of the fathers embraced a Hungarian nationalism that was liberal, favorably disposed to capitalist development of the economy, and open to the assimilation of non-Magyars, including Jews. By the time Georg and his generation came of age after 1900, a new species of integralist and antisemitic Hungarian nationalism had made its presence felt. It drew its strength from those who had lost out in the process of capitalist modernization. Led by members of the gentry whose inefficient management of their estates had led to their takeover by Jews, the antisemitic movement included members of the landed aristocracy who resented the fact that economic and social dominance was slipping away from them and toward the new commercial bourgeoisie. The antisemitic movements drew their numbers from artisans threatened by factory production, from the landless peasantry, and from the Catholic lower clergy who opposed the secularization of marriage and divorce.[9] The very success of economic development began to lead to strains in the informal division of labor between Jews and Magyars. Jews moved beyond the economy into the civil service and into parliament, while Magyars turned to business careers and to the professions, bringing them into economic competition with Jews.[10] Under these conditions, Hungarian public debate after the turn of the century was increasingly preoccupied with what was known as "the Jewish problem."[11]

No wonder, then, that the themes of isolation and alienation loomed so large in the thought of Georg Lukács and the members of his circle in Budapest. As assimilated Jews they were almost completely estranged from their Jewish past. They were out of touch with the society and culture of the Hungarian countryside, where most of the population still lived in backward conditions. The Habsburg-oriented liberal identification of their parents seemed ever less plausible at a time when nationalism was beginning to define Jews as outside the national community.[12]

Though Georg Lukács came of age in Hungary, his intellectual orientation was to German philosophy and literature. He studied in Berlin with Simmel in 1906–7 and then again in 1909–10. In 1914 he moved to Heidelberg, became part of Weber's social circle, and hoped to pursue a professorial career. His writings were stamped by his encounter with German social thought. Marx's analysis of capital as the driving force of modern life,[13] Tönnies' depiction of the historical development from "community" to "society," and Weber's analysis of the intensification of instrumental rationality and the disenchantment of the world—these were guiding threads for Lukács' analysis of modernity. But his greatest intellectual debt was to Simmel.[14]

Lukács wrote three books before his turn to communism: a study of the development of modern drama (completed in 1909, published in Hungarian in 1912 and in part in German in 1914); *The Soul and the Forms*, a collection of essays on modern literature (which appeared in Hungarian in 1910 and in German in 1911); and *The Theory of the Novel* (written during the war and published in article form in 1916 and in book form in 1920). All of them interpreted works of art as reflections of the social processes Simmel had explored in *The Philosophy of Money* and in his essays.[15] Modern life, Lukács wrote, no longer formed a "totality," a unified culture in which everything was related to everything else and all expressed a common commitment.[16] While Simmel was ambivalent about modern society, Lukács was unequivocally critical of it. He valued modern literature insofar as it provided a fundamental critique of the age.[17] Permeating his three books was the theme that a meaningful life was impossible under modern conditions. Where Simmel found new possibilities for individuality, Lukács saw only alienation—a loosening of social ties, declining identification of the producer with his products, a technical rationalization of life that left ever less room for the expression of individual personality, and the eclipse of community.[18] In a phrase borrowed from the German philosopher Fichte, he characterized modern capitalist society as "an age of absolute sinfulness," in which men perceive their "self-made environment as a prison instead of a home."[19]

Until the war, Lukács was one of many intellectuals who lamented the purported spiritual emptiness and moral inadequacy of capitalism, a lament heard on the political left and right. But his writings did not point toward any solution, spiritual or political. It was the experience of the war itself, with its regimentation of society and mass slaughter, that gave him a sense of urgency, convincing him that the continuation of capitalism was not only spiritually painful but threatening to life and limb. And it was the Bolshevik revolution in Russia that led him from despair at capitalist civilization to the hope of a new beginning.

August 1914, as already noted, was welcomed by many German intellectuals, who like their counterparts elsewhere believed that their respective nations were fighting a defensive war. (Too often, historians of this phenomenon fail to distinguish between those intellectuals who were right about this, such as Emile Durkheim in France, and those German intellectuals who were all too credulous about their government's claims.) Unlike Weber, Simmel, and Sombart, Lukács hated the war from its very beginning. Lukács regarded the Habsburg empire as a senseless construct, in which a feudal aristocracy cooperated with a capitalist bourgeoisie at the expense of everyone else: he saw no sense in fighting a war to preserve it. Now the empire was to be salvaged with the aid of the strict but inhuman ethos of the militarized German empire. To preserve these two barriers to progress, men were called to arms, turning "each man into a murderer, a criminal, or a victim." To Lukács the war demonstrated the fundamental inhumanity of capitalism and of nationalism.[20] His vehement rejection of the war left him isolated in Heidelberg, creating a strain in his relationships with Weber and Simmel.[21]

As the war progressed, it brought hardship not only to the soldiers at the front, but to civilians on the home front. The citizens of Germany and Austria-Hungary suffered from the effects of the British blockade, which cut off the import of foodstuffs; their misery was exacerbated by a potato blight in 1917. By then, caloric intake for the average adult had dropped to one thousand calories a day, a third of its prewar level, leading to widespread malnutrition.[22] Faced by material deprivation at home and the prospect of yet more death at the front, workers struck against the government's further prosecution of the war. In Russia, the strain on the social fabric caused by the war led to the unraveling of the Romanov empire in March 1917 and then to the Bolshevik revolution of November 1917. For Lukács, the Bolshevik revolution seemed to offer the possibility of a new form of society beyond the horizon of capitalism and of the reformist, incremental policy of social democracy.[23]

In November 1918, the German empire and its Austro-Hungarian ally sued for peace. The German military leaders who in the course of the war had become the virtual rulers of their nation dumped political authority into the hands of liberal and social democratic politicians, leaving these civilians to bear the odium of defeat. Enraged by four years of seemingly senseless slaughter, workers and soldiers formed revolutionary councils in the major cities of central Europe—Vienna, Berlin, Hamburg, Munich, and Budapest—and demanded the abdication of the old ruling houses, a democratization of government, and, in some cases, socialism. In Germany, real power was temporarily shared between a provisional government, which comprised parliamentary representatives of the socialist and liberal parties, and the councils of workers and soldiers. The left confronted a political choice: between the direct rule of the councils, and representative, parliamentary democracy with universal suffrage. The Social Democrats favored parliamentary sovereignty and democratic elections. To their left were the Spartacists, who formed the new Communist Party, devoted to the sovereignty of the councils, the German equivalent of the Russian soviets. In the fateful months from November 1918 through the spring of 1919, the parliamentary democratic aspirations of the Social Democrats were challenged by attempts at revolution in Berlin and Munich. Ultimately the social democratic leaders chose to call upon elements of the old imperial army and the newly formed "free corps" militias to quash this threat from the radical left.

Munich, where Max Weber found himself at the war's end, experienced a series of short-lived revolutionary regimes. They were led by intellectuals, some of whom Weber knew but had failed to persuade of the folly of revolution. On November 7, 1918, Kurt Eisner, of the Independent Socialist Party (a left-wing splinter of the Social Democrats) proclaimed a Bavarian Republic. The disgust of the urban working class of Munich with the old regime allowed Eisner, a bearded, bohemian Jewish theater critic, to come to power in conservative, Catholic, rural, and antisemitic Bavaria. Massive unemployment and food shortages soon became the order of the day, as Eisner's new Bavarian Republic faced staggering problems of demobilization and the threat of government insolvency due to the unrealistic new social welfare policies it had adopted. When elections were held in January 1919, Eisner's party received a mere 2.5 percent of the vote, and while on his way to tender his resignation in February, he was assassinated by a young aristocrat. After a confused transitional period, on April 7 a new government made up in good part of leftist intellectuals of Jewish origin came to power in Munich and declared a socialist republic. A week later, this first Bavarian Socialist Republic was replaced by a more radical group affiliated with the Communist International, which proclaimed the Second Bavarian Socialist Republic. The Social Democrats, the largest party in the elected Bavarian parliament, looked to the government in Berlin for help in repressing the Communists. Troops were duly dispatched by the central government and joined by free corps from northern Bavaria. They marched into Munich in May, overturning the Bavarian soviet republic in a wave of terror.

From Budapest, Lukács watched the revolutions in Russia and Germany with growing fascination. In his writings and in debates with his circle of friends he turned from analyses of the alienation produced by capitalism to the ethics of its overthrow by violence. Late in 1918, he joined the small band of Hungarian Communists, becoming the editor

of the party's paper, the *Red News*. "To hell with bourgeois democracy!" its editorials proclaimed. "To hell with the parliamentary
republic and politics that discourage the masses from acting. To arms,
proletariat!"[24] Communists clashed violently with Social Democrats,
who supported parliamentary government and participated in the cabinet of the liberal prime minister, Mihály Károlyi. But when Károlyi
resigned in March 1919 rather than agree to the dismemberment of
Hungary by the victors of the First World War, he allowed power to fall
into the hands of a Communist-dominated coalition. The new government, headed by the Communist Béla Kun, proclaimed the dictatorship of the proletariat. This Hungarian Soviet Republic was to last for
133 days, until, weakened by inner disintegration, it succumbed to foreign troops.[25] Lukács, who was nominally the people's deputy commis-
sar of education, was in fact the soviet republic's dictator in matters
cultural.

The policy of the Hungarian Communist leadership was radical and
uncompromising, motivated by a hatred of capitalism and the desire to
destroy it as swiftly and thoroughly as possible.[26] Radical agitators
were dispatched to the countryside, where they ridiculed the institution of the family and threatened to turn churches into movie theaters.
More radical than Lenin, the Hungarian Communists nationalized all
estates over one hundred acres in size, rather than distributing land to
the peasants. Nationalized too were business establishments with over
ten employees, all apartments, all furniture "superfluous for everyday
life," gold, jewelry, and coin and stamp collections. The principles of
egalitarianism were strenuously applied. All wages were made uniform. All graves in Budapest were to be identical, and the sale of double
plots forbidden as an excess of capitalist individualism. Much of the
bourgeois press was first censored, then closed down.

Most Hungarian Jews, like their counterparts in Germany and elsewhere, were opposed to the Communist regime. Those who were religious opposed its atheism; those who owned property opposed its
socialism. Yet Communists of Jewish origin were highly visible,
because in a movement with a largely working-class constituency,
Jews tended to be more educated, more articulate, and thus more likely
to reach leadership positions. While Jews were very prominent in the
revolutions in Russia and Germany, in Hungary they were virtually
omnipresent: of forty-nine commissars, thirty-one were of Jewish origin.[27] Their actions reflected their principles of radical universalism.
The statues of Hungarian kings and national heroes were torn down,
the national anthem banned, and the display of the national colors
made a punishable offense. Nor did the revolutionaries forget their

antipathy to Jewish particularism: traditionalist Jews became targets of their campaigns of terror.

The regime's policies soon alienated most Hungarians. The uniformity of wages together with a government guarantee of employment led to a steep decline in labor discipline and productivity. Guided by an ideology antipathetic to the market, the regime attempted to set all prices, with little regard to production costs. Goods were soon scarce and prices on the black market highly inflated. Peasants chose to withhold agricultural goods rather than exchange them for currency with which they could buy little. Young revolutionary intellectuals, often of Jewish origin, were sent to the countryside to administer the newly collectivized agricultural estates. Their radicalism was exceeded only by their incompetence, which reinforced peasant antisemitism. Though the regime's antireligious campaign was in fact headed by a defrocked priest, the Hungarian Jesuits interpreted the revolution as in essence Jewish and anti-Christian. In Budapest as in the countryside, opposition to the regime, defense of the Church, and antisemitism went hand in hand.

The Kun regime fell in August 1919, overwhelmed by political and economic difficulties. It was ultimately crushed by Romanian troops acting with the encouragement of Hungarian opponents of the regime. When the Romanian forces withdrew from Budapest, they turned over power to the leader of the Hungarian counterrevolution, Admiral Horthy.[28] After the red terror of the revolution came the white terror of the counterrevolution, which was aimed not only at officials and sympathizers of the fallen red regime but at the Jewish community as such.[29] The Magyar ruling class, which before the war would not have tolerated such behavior, accepted the excesses of the white terror as a necessary reaction to the red terror which had preceded it. To avoid retribution at the hands of the counterrevolution, Lukács went into hiding for a few weeks until his father (who had been appalled at his son's revolutionary activities but did not disown him) arranged to have him smuggled out of Hungary and into Vienna.[30]

The Bolshevik revolution of 1917 and the abortive revolutions that followed it in Berlin, Munich, and Budapest influenced the way in which many people thought of the relationship between Jews, politics, and the economy. Until the nineteenth century, European antisemitism was predominantly religious in nature, grounded in the antipathy of the Christian churches to those who spurned the tidings of the gospels. With the development of capitalism in the nineteenth century, the focus of antisemitism changed. It was now the Jew as capitalist who was attacked as the destroyer and despoiler of traditional society. For this new political antisemitism of the late nineteenth century, it was the Rothschilds and Bleichröders who were the real *"rois de l'époque"* (kings of the age). The conspicuous role of men like Lukács in the revolutions of 1917–19—men who were no longer Jews in their own eyes, but who were Jews in the eyes of their opponents— gave antisemitism a new impetus. The Jew as revolutionary took his place alongside the Jew as deicide and the Jew as capitalist.

Among the books that spread the image of the Jew as communist revolutionary was *Quand Israël est roi (When Israel Rules)*, an eyewitness account of the Hungarian Soviet published in 1921 by Jean and Jérome Tharaud. The authors, long identified with the French radical right, portrayed the Hungarian revolution as a Jewish conspiracy, with some non-Jews thrown in as figureheads. The book described in lurid and somewhat fanciful detail the terror of the "Lenin Boys" (the red guard), the confiscation of wealth by the revolutionaries, and the replacement of Christian professors by young Jewish intellectuals. "A New Jerusalem was growing up on the banks of the Danube," the authors reported. "It emanated from Karl Marx' Jewish brain, and was built by Jews upon a foundation of very ancient ideas." The book sold 55,000 copies in France, went through scores of editions, and was translated into other languages, including English and German. The image of the Jew as Bolshevik became the center of the new mythos of the right. A clear-eyed analyst would have concluded that although Jews were conspicuously overrepresented in leadership positions, few Jews were Communists, and most Communists were not Jews. But Jewish Communists were viewed through a lens colored by previous antisemitic stereotypes of the Jew as the inevitable enemy of the Christian nations. To conclude that the Jewish revolutionary and the Jewish capitalist were actually partners working both sides of the street on their road to the conquest of Christian civilization required a skewed vision. Yet between the world wars, by refocusing on the activities of Lukács and his counterparts in Russia and Germany, the radical right managed to recast the Jewish question.[31]

Capitalism as a System of Illusion

It was the First World War that turned Georg Lukács toward Communism. Like other intellectuals drawn to Bolshevism, he was convinced by Lenin's argument that capitalism led to imperialist competition and to war.[32] But it was his reflections on the repeated failure of communist revolution beyond the borders of Russia that led Lukács to reformulate Marxist theory.[33] There had been abortive revolutions in Berlin, Munich, and Budapest in the course of 1919. In March 1921, the German Communists had once again called for insurrection, a call that met with little response from the German working class, most of which supported the Social Democratic Party. The trauma of the war had led Lukács and others like him to anticipate an apocalypse at war's end that would eliminate capitalism. Yet within a few years it seemed that at least the advanced capitalist societies were well on the way to containing the revolutionary threat and integrating the working class into parliamentary democracy.[34] It was in the shadow of these failed expectations that Lukács wrote a series of essays between 1919 and 1922; they were published in 1923 as *History and Class Consciousness*. Lukács not only updated Marx's analysis of "alienation" under capitalism, but also put forth an ingenious explanation of why the working class, defying Marx's expectations, had failed to revolt against capitalism.

What was most novel about Lukács' analysis was not the theme that capitalism led to alienation. That was already in Marx. Despite the weight sometimes given to the publication in the 1930s of the young Marx's "Paris Manuscripts" of 1844, that theme was so pervasive in Marx's work, early and late, published and unpublished, that the publication of the Paris manuscripts was not required to recover it. The theme that capitalism led to a sense of estrangement was pervasive in German social thought in the decades before the publication of *History and Class Consciousness* and in Lukács' earlier work. Somewhat more novel was Lukács' suggestion that the cultural dilemmas analyzed by Simmel and Weber could be overcome by socialism. That was counterintuitive if not downright irrational; as Weber himself stressed, socialism was likely to speed up and intensify the bureaucratization of the world. Lukács never responded to Weber's critique of socialism, nor to the criticisms of its economic plausibility put forth by other intellectuals in Vienna in the very years in which he was writing *History and Class Consciousness* (critiques that are taken up in subsequent chapters on Schumpeter and Hayek). Nor, for that matter, did Lukács appear to reflect at all on the fact that the attempts to implement socialism in the Soviet Union had been an abysmal failure, leading the Bolshevik regime to retreat to a partial restoration of private property and the market in 1921, in what was called the "New Economic Policy."[35] Lukács paid as little attention to the actual institutions of a socialist economy as Marx had two generations earlier. Like many other cultural critics, he was fundamentally uninterested in economics: he simply assumed that Marx's understanding of capitalism was correct, that the labor theory of value was the secret to decoding capitalist reality, and that socialism would work.

The most novel and most influential element of *History and Class Consciousness* was its explanation of why the proletariat had not embraced revolution, and why it would require the guidance of intellectuals, like Lukács himself, to bring about the end of capitalism.

Lukács began by taking up Marx's analysis of the condition of the worker under capitalism. The worker, as Marx argued and Lukács reiterated, lacked control of his own labor, was forced into one-sided specialization, and found all creativity eliminated from the work process. Marx had explored the physical toll taken by machine labor on the human body and its psychic toll on the human mind. Though the physical burden of labor under capitalism had not grown heavier, its psychic effects were even worse than in Marx's day, Lukács maintained. For with the coming of "Taylorism"—the ever more precise division and control of labor by means of "scientific time management," above all on the assembly line—the worker had even less control over the pace of work and ever less opportunity to exercise his mental faculties.[36] The effect of this, Lukács maintained, was precisely the process of mental dulling foretold so anxiously in *The Wealth of Nations*. But Lukács drew a conclusion that Marx had never suggested: that the mental dulling of the working-class mind caused by the nature of work under capitalism would prevent the working class from seeing its real interest and overthrowing capitalism itself. The problem, as Lukács conceived it, was not so much that capitalism made workers stupid. It was that working under capitalism engendered a passive attitude toward the world, making it impossible to imagine that the world could be transformed. Under advanced capitalism, Lukács wrote, the worker becomes "a mechanical part incorporated into a mechanical system. He finds that system already pre-existing and self-sufficient; it functions independently of him, and he has to conform to its laws whether he likes it or not. As labor is progressively rationalized and mechanized, the worker's lack of will is reinforced by the way in which his activity becomes less and less active, more and more *contemplative*. This contemplative stance is adopted toward what appears as a closed system—a mechanical process with its own fixed laws, unfolding independently of the individual's consciousness and uninfluenced by his human activity. . . ."[37] Thus the very process of work under capitalism tended to breed mental torpor in the working class. Workers suffered from what Lukács called "thingafication" (*Verdinglichung*, often translated as "reification"), the inability to see that the human relations created by capitalism were the results of particular historical conditions that could be changed by human will, rather than permanent, inevitable laws of nature to which men had to succumb.

Lukács also set out to explain why "meritorious and subtle . . . bourgeois thinkers" did not share his view of capitalism as bound for replacement by socialism in the present age of "the World Revolution."[38] His answer was that bourgeois intellectuals were rendered incapable of doing so by the very structure of bourgeois thought, which refused to accept that capitalism was doomed by its intrinsic contradictions. Since "the meaning of these tendencies is the abolition of capitalism," Lukács argued, "for the bourgeoisie to become conscious of them would be tantamount to suicide."[39] Marx had criticized the political economy of Smith and his successors as a form of intellectual self-defense of the property-owning capitalists, which made the laws of the capitalist market seem eternal and inevitable. Lukács now extended this critique of knowledge-as-ideology beyond economics, to philosophy and to the social sciences. According to Lukács, bourgeois (i.e., noncommunist) philosophy and social science suffered from its own form of "reification"; it too functioned to close off the possibility of imagining a society not organized along capitalist lines.[40] Simmel had explored the effects of the specialization of knowledge and culture due to the division of labor and cultural development. Lukács now insisted that this process of specialization and the fragmentation of knowledge was itself a form of bourgeois self-defense. For by compartmentalizing knowledge, it "destroys every image of the whole," and the ability to perceive the interconnection between the market and cultural discontents.[41] As a result, "a radical change of perspective is impossible" on the basis of bourgeois society and the knowledge it produces.[42] Only a fragmented perspective is available, which makes it impossible to imagine a radical transformation. The given "reified" world appears as the only possible world. Thus, "reification requires that a society should learn to satisfy all its needs in terms of commodity exchange."[43]

That is why, Lukács concluded, even so subtle a thinker as Weber had regarded capitalism as ineluctable. Simmel had thought that "the tragedy of culture" was built into the very nature of cultural development: cultivated individuals would feel frustrated by the gap between the exponential growth of culture and the inability of the individual to assimilate that culture. Not so, claimed Lukács: the tragedy of culture was merely a tragedy of *capitalist* culture, which presumably would be solved by the coming of socialism.[44]

Capitalism, then, is preserved by a massive system of illusion. The proletariat fails to revolt because it can't imagine that its problems are caused by a single force, capitalism, and can't imagine eliminating capitalism, as opposed to merely reforming it. Noncommunist philosophy and social science may explore many of the dilemmas caused by capitalism, Lukács asserted, but were incapable of conceiving of capitalism as a whole and of concluding that these dilemmas could be solved by supeseding capitalism. That conclusion was a product of wishful thinking, but Lukács treated it as the quintessence of historical reason.

Educator of the Revolution

At a time when most Marxists viewed their ideology as a materialist science, focused on economic processes caused by the development of capitalist production, Lukács emphasized the role of "consciousness," of the perception and interpretation of those processes.[45] For Lukács was steeped not only in Marx but in Hegel, a Hegel whom he read through Marxist lenses. From Hegel, Lukács adopted the concept of "totality," of explaining particulars in terms of ever-larger contexts, of finding coherence and connection in historical periods and assuming that there was a discernible purpose to the historical process itself. Yet Lukács' use of the concept of "totality" stood Hegel on his head. For while Hegel saw his work as reconciling men to history and their place in the present world, Lukács saw his role as weaning men from their passive acceptance of the present age, the age of capitalism. Only Marxism was "dialectical" in that it understood particular facts in light of the larger whole of which they were a part. In other words, Marxists alone knew the real direction of history and could interpret the present accordingly. "It is not the primacy of economic motives in historical explanation that constitutes the decisive difference between Marxism and bourgeois thought, but the point of view of totality," he wrote.[46] Marxists could understand the present from the perspective of the future "realm of freedom."[47] They knew that the present was a passing stage of alienation and fragmentation, which would be overcome in the communist future, in which social conflict would be abolished, and in which each individual would understand himself as part of a coherent whole with which he could identify. "Only the dialectical conception of totality can enable us to understand *reality as a social process...,*" Lukács insisted. "Only this conception dissolves the seeming objectivity of the social forms necessarily produced by the capitalist mode of production and enables us to see them as mere illusions which are no less illusionary for seeming to be necessary."[48] And because Marxist theorists could pierce the veil of illusion, they could transform the consciousness of the working class, awakening it from its passive stupor to its world-historical purpose.

Marxism or "historical materialism," Lukács insisted, could not be separated from the class struggle of the proletariat.[49] But neither was historical materialism "the inherent or natural possession of the proletariat as a class."[50] On the contrary, much of the working class had been led astray from its revolutionary role in the Marxist view of history toward an acceptance of capitalism. In the most audacious claim of *History and Class Consciousness,* Lukács insisted that the *true* consciousness of the workers as a class comprised the beliefs they *would* have if they were able to have the thoughts and feelings "objectively appropriate to their situation"—that is to say, the revolutionary consciousness assigned to them by Marx's theory. But this was demonstratively at odds with the nonrevolutionary sentiments of the workers themselves, what Lukács dubbed their "false consciousness."[51] The "real" class consciousness of the proletariat, therefore, bore little relationship to the *actual* beliefs of workers. The "view of the proletariat" was the view imputed to the proletariat by the Communist Party.[52] The proletariat's "real" interests and aspirations were therefore quite independent of the empirical desires and aspirations of the working class.

Here Lukács took up a line of analysis that Lenin had advanced two decades earlier in *What Is to Be Done?* (1902), and drove it to its logical conclusions.[53] Alarmed by the tendency of the labor unions and their leaders to become reformist participants in the existing system rather than revolutionaries, Lenin had insisted that workers by themselves would never bring about socialism. Capitalism would create discontent among the working class, but that discontent would not lead to revolution without a well-organized group of professional revolutionaries. While continuing to insist that Marxism was a determinist system, Lenin had turned Marxism in a more voluntarist direction, emphasizing the will and the skill of professional revolutionaries. Now Lukács explained in Marxist terms why the lenses of the workers were befogged by bourgeois ideology, and by the passive attitude they imbibed from their role in the economic system—all of which prevented the workers from clearly seeing the whole.[54]

For Lukács as for Lenin, another great barrier to the breakthrough of revolutionary class consciousness among the workers was the social democratic parties, which increasingly sought to participate in parliamentary democracy. Their errors stemmed from following the empirical desires of the working class, for better salaries, working conditions, and political participation. Their mistake was to accept "the actual, psychological state of consciousness of proletarians for the class consciousness of the proletariat"—in other words, to accept the views of actual workers for the "true" consciousness of the proletariat, despite the deeper knowledge offered by Marxist theory.[55] Following Lenin's lead, Lukács denounced as "opportunist" Social Democrats who tried to pursue the immediate, national, or professional interests of the workers—a great anathema in the lexicon of Leninist invective.[56]

Thus, although capitalism was in crisis, that crisis would only lead beyond capitalism to socialism once the consciousness of the proletariat had been effectively transformed by those whose knowledge of Marxist theory equipped them to see history as a totality.[57] Although the Communist Party was the "bearer of the class consciousness of the proletariat and the conscience of its historical vocation,"[58] this "educator himself must be educated."[59] Thus the position occupied by the state bureaucracy in Hegel's thought—as the "universal estate" vouchsafed with the general interest of society—was occupied in Lukács' scheme by the Communist Party. And into the place of Hegel's philosopher—who was to shape the consciousness of the new universal estate through his teaching—stepped the Marxist intellectual.

The Party as Community

For Lukács—and for many intellectuals who were later attracted to communism by similar motives and sometimes as a result of reading *History and Class Consciousness*—the Communist Party seemed to provide what capitalism could not: a cause to which one could devote one's whole life, rather than just part of oneself; a source of discipline worth accepting; and an all-encompassing community. In the name of ultimate freedom, according to Lukács, the individual must subordinate himself to the Party. "The *conscious* desire for the realm of freedom can only mean consciously taking the steps that will really lead to it," he declared. "And aware that in contemporary bourgeois society individual freedom can only be corrupting, because it is a case of privilege based on the unfreedom of others, this desire must entail the renunciation of individual freedom. It implies the conscious subordination of the self to that collective will that is destined to bring real freedom into being. . . . This conscious collective will is the Communist Party. . . . Only through discipline can the party be capable of putting the collective will into practice."[60]

Party activism also solved the problem of multiple, contending inner commitments that Simmel had diagnosed. "Really active participation in all events, real practical involvement of all the members of an organization can only be achieved by engaging the whole personality," Lukács claimed. "Only when action within a community becomes the central, personal concern of each and every individual participant can the split between rights and duties . . . and the fragmentation of the individual by the social forces that control him be overcome. . . ."[61]

For Lukács, the quest for community, which he thought capitalism unable to provide, was solved by the Communist Party, which promised not only purpose and discipline, but a special role for intellectuals who had mastered the culture of Marxism and hence could assume the role of spiritual guide that had been foreclosed to them in Hungary and Germany. The community they would help guide was to be a transnational, transethnic, universal community, in which Jewish origins were supposed to mean nothing. For Lukács, then, the Communist movement provided everything that capitalist society could not. Thomas Mann met Lukács in the early 1920s, after Lukács published a Marxist interpretation of Mann's *Buddenbrooks*. In *The Magic Mountain*, the novelist used Lukács as the model for one of his most memorable fictional creations, Leo Naphta, the Jew-turned-Jesuit prophet of communist community, the quintessential totalitarian intellectual.

The subsequent influence of *History and Class Consciousness* was not confined to intellectuals who tossed in their lot with the Communist Party, or even to those who looked to the working class as the social group that would provide the social dynamite with which to explode capitalism. Decades after Lukács published *History and Class Consciousness*, others would expand upon his conception of capitalist culture as smothering under an ideological haze the ability to imagine a postcapitalist future. They would seize upon his notion that it was up to those who knew the real possibilities of historical development to awaken the compliant from their passivity and stupor.

Freyer: Alienation and the Quest for Community

Hans Freyer was Lukács' ideological mirror twin. He shared with Lukács an alienation from bourgeois society, and he too was deeply influenced by Marx, Tönnies, Weber, and Simmel, as well as Hegel. Like Lukács, he thought capitalism bereft of community and of higher purpose, and sought a radical alternative to it. But while for Lukács that radical alternative took the form of universalist Communism, for Freyer it took the form of the particularist radical right in the shape of National Socialism. Yet he was neither a racist nor an antisemite. What he thought he saw in National Socialism—and what intellectuals elsewhere espied in other forms of fascism—was an escape from what they regarded as the moral dead end of capitalism.

In the disillusioned aftermath of the Third Reich, Hans Freyer described the sort of intellectual most vulnerable to the lure of totalitarian ideologies, and prone to espouse them. He was likely to be a man whose structure of thought preserved a good deal of the theological orientation of his ancestors, but who had himself become an apostate. "Thus," Freyer wrote, "his religious organs are highly developed, but have lost their function."[62] While his own father was a middle-level civil servant in the German state of Saxony, his grandfather came from generations of Lutheran pastors. Like Hegel, Freyer was originally destined for a theological career but found himself cut off from his theological moorings. Like Hegel, he sought a more secular guise in which he might embrace his destiny as a spiritual guide.

Freyer's main reference group during his university years was the youth movement, one of the most extraordinary phenomena of early-twentieth-century Germany. The *Jugendbewegung*, as its name implies, was a loose federation composed mostly of children of the educated middle class (*Bildungsbürgertum*). The members of the youth movement were disaffected by what they saw as the ascendancy of materialistic values and the prestige accorded to wealth in the culture of Wilhelmine Germany. They were critical of rote patriotism, swore off the hedonism and anti-intellectualism of the fraternities, and tried abstinence from tobacco, alcohol, and meat. Through nascent counterinstitutions they sought to minimize contact with the fraternity student, the bourgeois, and the bureaucrat. While their critique of

Wilhelmine Germany drew on diverse sources, their own predicament became the ultimate warrant for their indictment. They roamed the countryside to establish a relationship with nature, wrote poetry, sang folk songs, and experimented with reviving pagan customs such as the celebration of the solstice. Freyer shared their yearning for an intense emotional commitment to a community of purpose that they found lacking in contemporary Germany.

A few years after Lukács came to Berlin to study with Simmel, Freyer did the same. Exposure to the great German sociologists of the previous generation led Freyer to formulate in a more social scientific fashion the rather inchoate discontents of his comrades in the youth movement. The movement prided itself on its preparedness to commit itself to some spiritual principle, and to some larger whole. But to which principle and to what whole? Having rejected the culture and often the religion of their ancestors, they found themselves faced by multiple cultural choices, none of which seemed compelling. It was not the absence but the surfeit of freedom that seemed to threaten Freyer and his comrades.

When the war broke out in 1914, Freyer volunteered immediately and became a second lieutenant. He spent most of the next four years on the western front. Seriously wounded twice, he emerged a war hero. Freyer thrived as a junior officer and in later years looked back fondly on his years of command and camaraderie.

The experience of the Great War provided Freyer and part of his generation of the youth movement with an unanticipated solution to their dilemmas. The call to sacrifice on behalf of the *Volk* was greeted almost with relief by those who had chided their society for failing to provide a higher sense of purpose in which the individual might partake. In the widespread exhortation of the "community of the nation" (*Volksgemeinschaft*) during the war years, the youth movement heard the echo of its own call for community. Now it seemed that, for a time at least, the experience of collective concern that had been confined to its small conventicles was transposed to the national level. The experience of the "community of the trenches" was most intense for those who had long sought in vain for a larger community. For the common soldier, drawn from the peasantry or the working class, the war was a forced diversion from the pressing concerns of feeding and clothing one's family; the end of war would mean a return to the civilian communities of village, church, and party. But to Freyer and some of his comrades in the youth movement, the collective threat provided by war seemed the glue of a future national community. What the experience of belonging to the Communist Party provided for Lukács, the army experience provided for Freyer: the experience of subordination to a higher, collective purpose.

The Particularist Critique of the Market

The particularist critique of the effects of the market that Freyer developed after the war was a direct descendant of Justus Möser's analysis. But what Freyer championed was no longer the local particularity that Möser had lovingly defended. It was ethnic nationalism, which conceived of the *Volk* as the ultimate basis of identity. Part of the attraction of the term lay in its multiple connotations. It could be used as a synonym for the nation, in the sense of the entire citizenry of a country. Used in a populist sense, it referred to the common people. But by Freyer's day, the term also connoted a conception of the nation as based on common origin, common geography, and common history: "blood and soil." That was the sense in which it was used by *völkisch* nationalists. For most of them, membership in the *Volk* did not extend to Jews, who were viewed as racially other and as culturally alien, even when—indeed especially when—they moved into the mainstream of German culture.[63] Freyer did not share this antisemitic conception of the *Volk*, but in his writings for a popular audience, he used the language of blood and soil.

When Freyer returned to civilian life, he threw himself back into his studies, and in 1919 he published his *Habilitationsschrift*, the postdoctoral work required to teach at a German university.[64] Three years later, at the age of thirty-six, he was called to the chair of philosophy at the University of Kiel, and in 1925 he moved to the University of Leipzig to hold the first chair of sociology in Germany. During the 1920s he wrote a series of books and essays addressed to philosophers, political theorists, and sociologists, in which he laid out his critique of the cultural and political effects of capitalism.[65] He could couch his message in the conceptual language of the academy or in the more metaphorical and emotive language of *völkisch* nationalism.[66]

Freyer shared Möser's respect for the particular and unique in history and that delight in the multiplicity, variety, and diversity of culture articulated in the eighteenth century by Johann Gottfried Herder and later by the Romantics.[67] The Enlightenment's universalist, rationalist view of man and history, Freyer wrote, could not appreciate "the diversity of actual life" because it proceeded without regard for the intrinsic value of that which was foreign to it.[68] Freyer's view, like Hegel's, was historicist; he was convinced that all human communities, values, and indeed human nature itself are products of history and in a continuous process of change. But unlike Hegel, he no longer believed that history had a discernible direction or intrinsic purpose. Hegel's belief in universal moral norms derivable from reason was not shared by Freyer.

Freyer's particularist and historicist vision disparaged the possibility of discovering a universal ethical system based upon rational foundations.[69] The search for such an ethical system was a fool's errand, he insisted, for the human world comprises a multiplicity of traditions created by collectivities over time, each of which is ethically valid. The rationalist ideal, Freyer wrote, is to uproot all of these particular, historical traditions and replace them with a single ethic based on rational foundations and valid for all men. But this was a tragic error, since there is no "general humanity," and a morality freed from the accidents of birth is bound to be bloodless, trivial, unsatisfying. He maintained that meaning exists in history only in multiplicity. "History," he wrote, "thinks in plurals, and its teaching is that there is more than one solution for the human equation."[70] These "plurals" were the various distinct historical cultures, each of which was created and transmitted by a historical collectivity or *Volk*. The creation of a new appropriate ethic therefore required an affirmation of membership in a particular historical community and culture.[71]

Freyer linked personal meaning to collective purpose, which could only be based on collective particularity. Rationalist universalism, according to Freyer, dissolved all connection with a particular culture of the past that could add depth to the culture of the present, leaving no bounded collectivity toward which the individual could subordinate himself. Since there could be no meaningful culture without historical particularity, Freyer asserted that the individual ought to embrace the *Volk* into which he was born. The collective spirit or culture of one's nation, the *Volksgeist*, was to be affirmed not because of its superiority to other national cultures as judged by some universal, rational standard, but—since no such standard existed—because it was the historical basis of continuing particularity. Thus birth into a particular *Volk* was to be elevated into a consciously affirmed fate. A few years later Martin Heidegger would make many of the same points in his *Being and Time* (1927). Six years after that, Heidegger too would welcome the National Socialist assumption of power.[72]

Freyer's affirmation of collective particularity was based on the assumption that there existed a circumscribed collectivity that could be identified as the *Volk*, with a relatively homogeneous cultural tradition. It was a notion with a long pedigree in German intellectual history and with broad contemporary political resonance. But these premises could not survive systematic historical scrutiny, as Freyer was almost certainly aware, at some level at least. For one of his liberal teachers, the historian Walter Goetz, had published an extended critique of the notion that there existed some ongoing essence of the German *Volk*. He noted that contemporary Germans were a mixture of many races; he pointed to the ongoing importance of regional differences and religious divisions; and he stressed the continuing foreign influences on the development of German culture. Goetz emphasized the multiplicity of German culture and pointed out the conceptual confusions in notions of a unitary *Volk* or *Volksgeist*.[73] Another colleague, the philosopher Theodore Litt, explicitly rejected the notion of a metaphysical *Volksgeist* that was the historical *cause* of a collective culture.[74] Freyer's use of the concepts of *Volk* and *Volksgeist* was therefore based upon a selective forgetfulness, a tacit decision *not* to apply rational, critical scrutiny to these notions. Concerned with using collective particularity as a basis of social integration, Freyer left the origins and the content of the *Volksgeist* shrouded in mist.

A society that lacked a common collective purpose, Freyer believed, left the lives of its members bereft of meaning. It might leave them free to pursue their individual interests and vocations, but without some larger collective goal, the pursuit of individual choices would be arbitrary. Only a society devoted to the affirmation of its particularity could provide the individual with a sense of purpose. It was this perspective that lay at the heart of Freyer's critique of contemporary Germany in the 1920s. "We have a bad conscience in regard to our age," he wrote. "We feel ourselves to be unconfirmed, lacking in meaning, unfulfilled, not even obligated."[75] He abhorred "chaotic ages without any limits."[76] For Freyer an open society was a meaningless society. He saw capitalism as the prime agent behind that openness, and searched for a way in which society could be closed again.

Freyer took Simmel's reflections on capitalism and technology and considered their implications for the defense of cultural particularity. He adopted Simmel's notion that in advanced capitalism each realm of culture takes on a life of its own, but stressed that, as each realm develops according to its own logic, it loses its connection to a specific human group and to a specific historical culture. The various realms of culture no longer fit together into some meaningful totality, no longer provide a closed world of shared horizons for the *Volk*.

Freyer was more apprehensive than Simmel about the aimlessness of a capitalist society. For Freyer, individuals acquired a sense of meaning and purpose from the particular culture of the *Volk* of which they were a part. But the spread of the market—as Möser, Hegel, and Marx had recognized—had a universalist thrust. The search for new commodities to buy and to sell spread naturally across national borders, drawing individuals into relationships beyond the nation, and creating a taste for foreign goods and culture. Technology likewise knew no natural national boundaries. What the market economy and technology had in common was that both were transnational and transcultural, tending to break down national barriers and creating shared interests across borders. Like technology, the capitalist economy had an intrinsic tendency toward greater perfection, toward the development of better, more efficient means. Left to their intrinsic logic and without political control, the combination of capitalism and technology led to the dissolution of political and cultural barriers.[77] Given Freyer's premise that meaning arose only from cultural particularity, this prospect was tantamount to universal meaninglessness. Freyer's literary images conveyed his unexamined assumption that local and particular institutions are somehow more natural and authentic than those whose origins are more distant: the unguided spread of technology, he wrote, would lead to an artificial "crust" over the face of the earth, a "secondary system" without a historical or organic connection to any particular collective culture. All of humanity would eventually be absorbed into "a rationalized order of objective relations, an economic trading company."[78]

Yet Freyer contended that his prospect of a dawning age devoid of meaning was not an inexorable consequence of the development of technology. Technology might lack intrinsic meaning and purpose, but general purposelessness and an absence of "totality" threatened modern society not because it was dominated by technology but rather because it was dominated by capitalism. Until now, technology in modern Europe had developed hand in hand with capitalism, a system based upon the maximization of individual profit. It was capitalism, not technology, that was responsible for the loss of common goals in modern society. The challenge facing his contemporaries, Freyer believed, was to dissolve the connection between technology and capitalism. The political task at hand was the reintegration of technology into the "totality of life of the European nations."[79]

This required the re-creation of a collective purpose that would lift men out of their private concerns. That purpose was to reassert the power of the *Volk* and to create a state powerful enough to make Germany a player on the stage of world history, capable of defending its cultural particularity against the victors of the First World War and the system of international trade they had imposed.

War, the State, and the Preservation of Cultural Particularity

The preservation of the *Volk* would serve as the transcendent goal to which all aspects of culture, the economy, and technology were to be subordinated. The agency that would guarantee and control this subordination was the state. Under contemporary conditions, overcoming the internal pluralization of cultural life while maintaining the cultural particularity of the *Volk* required what Freyer and others on the Weimar right called a "total state." Freyer was thus led to a highly sophisticated justification for fascism, understood in a generic sense.

Preparation for war was a crucial element of Freyer's political philosophy, for only the transformation of consciousness facilitated by collective preparation for war could achieve the all-encompassing politicization of existence that was the ultimate goal of his political program. At the turn of the century, the American philosopher William James had sought a moral equivalent of war. Contrasting his own experience of the war with the years of cultural emptiness that succeeded it, Freyer concluded that no moral equivalent of war existed. His political theory of the 1920s testified to his belief that only actual war or the preparation for it could create the degree of consistent political commitment that he expected from the citizens of his state.

"War," he wrote, citing the dictum of Heraclitus, "is the father of all things, . . . if not in the literal sense then certainly for the thing of all things, the work of all works, that structure in which the creativity of *Geist* reaches its earthly goal, for the hardest, most objective and all-encompassing thing that can ever be created—for the state." Though an exceptional event in the life of the state, war actually revealed the state's historical quintessence. The war was not a horror to be forgotten as quickly as possible but rather a foretaste of the new age dawning.[80]

War for Freyer was the essence of politics. "The state as a state is constituted by war and is continuously reconstituted by the preparation for war," he wrote. Given the legitimate divergence between nations and the impossibility of reconciling their conflicting claims before some higher tribunal, Freyer expected that states would remain in a situation of open or latent war. A state that shunned the possibility of war would cease to be a sovereign actor on the stage of history and would be only the object of the action of others. The only alternative was constant preparedness for war. In this perspective, all foreign policy was based upon the latent or overt threat to fight other states; it was merely "the continuation of war by other means."[81]

Yet war was pivotal in an even more important sense. The constant need to prepare for war provides the intensity of emotional commitment that for Freyer is characteristic of politics, the constant reminder of the primacy of public over particular interests. Thus the state is created and maintained not by social contract but by the struggle against external threats. Lest these threats subside, the struggle slacken, and the degree of political commitment falter, Freyer provided a model of international relations that ensured that the external struggle of the state would continue in perpetuity. The state exists to assert the interests of the *Volk*, and to do so more effectively it must constantly attempt to expand its external range of control, to reorient its surrounding to its own needs. Imperialism, then, is the essence of the state: "It must conquer in order to be."[82]

Like Lukács' critique of social democracy in *History and Class Consciousness*, Freyer stressed that, left to themselves, natural or historical processes would never create a new totality. Though the *Volk* had a basis in language, history, and even nature, he considered these insufficient conditions for a collective political revival. It was only through a heightened *consciousness* of national particularity, through a will to act in common, that the *Volk* could become a politicized collectivity.[83] For Freyer as for Lukács, the burden of moving history forward fell upon those who, in Lukács' words, embodied "the point of view of totality"; or, as Freyer put it, "Only those who know the true direction of *Geist* have a right to historical action."[84] Only through a heightened perception of the need for such a totality could the masses be brought to revolution. One role of Freyer's writings, therefore, was to intensify the alienation from existing institutions felt by his countrymen, and to help them think systematically about an alternative to the democratic, capitalist welfare state of the Weimar Republic.

The alternative that Freyer foresaw was a state—far more powerful than what Hegel had envisioned—that would re-create a closed, self-sufficient, self-affirming community.[85] "This self-created world should completely, utterly, and objectively enclose a particular group; should so surround it that no alien influences can penetrate its realm."[86] Then all human pursuits would again acquire a sense of meaning, where "nothing is insignificant, and nothing is isolated."[87] The state would decide the relative weight that each human endeavor would have in "the whole."[88] Above all, the realms of technology and of the economy would be freed from the system based on the maximization of individual utility and reoriented instead to the purposes of the *Volk*.[89] The specific legal or institutional measures by which this was to be achieved were fundamentally unimportant and uninteresting to him.

Revolution from the Right?

In 1931 Freyer published *Revolution from the Right* (*Revolution von Rechts*), a pamphlet that attempted to influence the immediate political agenda. Though the National Socialist Party was never mentioned explicitly, the potential transformation of German politics presented by its electoral gains in September 1930 was the immediate impetus for the writing of the pamphlet.

Political instability and a sluggish economy had plagued the Weimar Republic long before both were exacerbated by the effects of the world depression. From 1919 through 1928, the average government cabinet lasted only fifteen months. Unemployment was higher than it had been before the war, and economic growth was laggard. High wage rates established by government commissions and the demands of the Weimar welfare state made for a lack of domestic capital formation, and began to scare off foreign investment, leading to a downturn of the German economy well before the stock market crash in New York.[90]

By the summer of 1929, the depression was unmistakable. Unemployment rose beyond 10 percent, inventories increased, and major corporations began to fail. In March 1930 came the dissolution of the Weimar Republic's last cabinet based upon a parliamentary majority. In September 1930, with almost three million Germans unemployed and welfare benefits cut by the government's deflationary policy, the most pivotal election in the history of the republic was held. The electoral strength of the National Socialists took a dramatic leap. From 0.8 million votes and twelve parliamentary seats in 1928, the Nazis gained

6.4 million votes and 107 parliamentary seats (out of a total of 577). With 18.3 percent of the popular vote, they became the second largest party in Germany, behind the Social Democrats. Support for the Communists—like the National Socialists, determined enemies of the democratic republic—rose from 3.3 to 4.6 million votes; with 77 deputies in parliament, their delegation was now the third largest. Fear of civil disorder and of the economic implications of the National Socialists' anticapitalist rhetoric led to the collapse of the foreign market for German treasury bills and a flight of domestic capital abroad, thereby exacerbating the country's economic ills.

It was under these circumstances that Freyer penned *Revolution from the Right*. His central proposition was that Germany faced a new political phenomenon, a movement that couldn't be explained by the existing socioeconomic categories that dominated the interpretation of contemporary politics. He dubbed that movement the "revolution from the right" and treated the electoral showing of the Nazis as a part of the phenomenon, without regarding Nazism as its final form or Hitler (who went conspicuously unmentioned) as its ultimate leader. It was the first modern movement capable of resisting co-optation into the system of liberal democratic capitalism, for welfare-state capitalism had demonstrated its ability to defuse challenges from the left.[91] Only a revolutionary movement of the nationalist right was capable of truly transforming that system.

Like Lukács, Freyer believed the greatest barrier to overcoming capitalism was the mentality or consciousness capitalism itself created. It was a utilitarian mentality of group self-interest, in which each class in civil society was motivated by the desire to get its share of the economic pie. Under such conditions, Freyer lamented, the state did not stand above the economy and could not serve the common interest. Instead, politics became a struggle to use the state to channel economic resources to one group or another. Adam Smith, of course, had already noted the attempt of each group in commercial society to use political influence for its own purposes, a problem manifested in his day primarily by the power of merchants. Hegel had envisioned the role of the civil service as countering the political pursuit of these particular interests. For Freyer, writing in an era of equal suffrage and parliamentary democracy, the problem was not so much that one class would use its political power at the expense of all others. It was that all classes would use their political power to pursue their own interests at the expense of the general good—the defense of the *Volk* from the influence of international capitalism.[92]

The promise of the new revolutionary movement of the right, in Freyer's analysis, lay in its rejection of economic interest as the primary motive of political action. Since the capitalist welfare state was capable of absorbing challenges based upon social and economic interests, only a movement that rejected such interests could offer a revolutionary challenge.[93] The revolution of the right was the revolution of those who did not define themselves by their social and economic interests, and hence could not be co-opted by the existing system. Unlike the left or the old right, it sought not to capture the state for its social benefit, but to liberate the state from its degraded condition as a forum for the pursuit of social interests.[94] Since capitalist society treated man as nothing but a producer and consumer, it had failed to provide the individual with a sense of belonging to a larger whole. It was this pent-up discontent with the inability of capitalism to provide a higher meaning or collective purpose to its members which Freyer saw as the real source of the new revolution of the right.[95]

To resist the capitalist welfare state, Freyer looked to the *Volk*. As he now used the term, it meant more than the product of nature and history. It designated all who refused to define themselves in terms of their social class and economic self-interest: it referred to a change in *consciousness*. In the discontent expressed in the Nazi vote, Freyer saw a mass political embodiment of the cultural critique of capitalism which he and like-minded intellectuals had enunciated, and the possibility at least of realizing the total state which he had long advocated.

The new state was to be "liberated" from the egoistical demands of social classes in order to engage in real history, namely the integration of the *Volk* for the sake of collective self-assertion and the acquisition of temporal power. The capitalist economy with its logic of production for profit was to be replaced by state socialism (*Staatssozialismus*).[96]

When the National Socialists came to power in Germany less than two years after the publication of *Revolution from the Right*, Hans Freyer was among the many intellectuals who not only supported the new regime but tried to shape it in their own image. He played a role in the "coordination" (*Gleichschaltung*) of the University of Leipzig and of the German Sociological Association, and set forth plans for the politicization of the university and the utilization of social research by the Nazi state. But he became increasingly disillusioned with the regime he had helped to bring about. In July 1944, a group of conspirators, many of whom had their origins in the same radical conservative circles as Freyer, failed in their attempt to assassinate Hitler. Had the coup succeeded, Freyer would have become minister of education, but he was peripheral enough to escape the Gestapo's brutal persecution of the conspirators. After the Second World War, a deradicalized Hans Freyer reoriented his social thought. He remained convinced of the inability of capitalism to provide meaning and purpose but now looked to institutions other than the nation and the state to provide that meaning, including the family, religious traditions, and professional identity.[97]

Lukács never experienced (or at least never admitted to) the same degree of disillusionment with his wager on Communism. Yet in 1956, when a group of reform-minded Communists briefly came to power in Stalinist Hungary, Lukács joined them. Had they succeeded, he too would have become minister of education, but the government was overthrown by Soviet tanks. Still, despite the fact that he lived in the Soviet Union during the height of Stalin's terror, that his first wife disappeared in the gulag, and that his stepson spent years in its camps, Lukács insisted to the end of his days that "the worst form of socialism was better to live in than the best form of capitalism."[98]

Lukács and Freyer were representative of intellectuals on the left and right who turned their backs on capitalism in interwar Europe. But capitalism was not without its defenders. One of the most brilliant of these, Joseph Schumpeter, set out to explain not only why capitalism might be worth keeping, but why intellectuals like Lukács and Freyer hated it so.

CHAPTER ELEVEN

SCHUMPETER:
INNOVATION AND RESENTMENT

The book for which Joseph Schumpeter is best known, *Capitalism, Socialism, and Democracy*, was published in 1942. Its author was a professor of economics at Harvard, where he had been a permanent member of the faculty since immigrating from Germany ten years earlier. Writing in the midst of the deepest depression the United States had ever known—a depression that had opened the door to Nazi domination in Germany and which many on the left saw as a validation of Marx's prediction of a final crisis of capitalism—Schumpeter made some startling claims. He argued that capitalism had been a great source of economic betterment for the mass of the population, and that despite the current depression there were excellent reasons to believe that it was capable of alleviating material want. Yet his paradoxical conclusion was that "capitalism is being killed by its achievements."[1] Much of the book's fascination lies in the deliberate irony of its explicit thesis: as Marx predicted, capitalism will be superseded by socialism, but that will occur not because capitalism is economically inadequate, but because it creates social and cultural forces that lead to its demise. The forces that have made capitalism the most creative and dynamic economic system in history are creating a social and psychological backlash that will bring it down.

Schumpeter believed that truly creative intellectuals have their major insights by the time they reach thirty. Whatever the general value of this proposition, he exemplified it. For the startling thesis of *Capitalism, Socialism, and Democracy*, published when Schumpeter was almost sixty, had been percolating in his work for more than three decades. Its origins can be found in his earliest works, published before the Great War. But it was the collapse of the Austro-Hungarian Empire and the subsequent failed wave of socialist revolution that led Schumpeter to develop the ironic style of presentation that is on full display in *Capitalism, Socialism, and Democracy*.

Creativity and Resentment in Schumpeter's Early Writings

Schumpeter was born in Moravia in 1883—the year of Marx's death—in what was then the Austro-Hungarian Empire. He was the scion of several generations of entrepreneurs.[2] His father died when Schumpeter was a boy, and his mother moved to Vienna, where she married an aristocratic army officer. She sent her only child to the most prestigious high school in the city, where he rubbed shoulders with the children of the empire's aristocracy and upper bourgeoisie. This background, together with the fact that as a Catholic by birth (though not by practice) he was part of the religious majority, made him at home in the upper reaches of Viennese society.

At the universities of Vienna and Berlin, Schumpeter studied history, sociology, economics, and law. In 1905–6 he participated in a seminar on Marx's economics led by an economist and former Austrian minister of finance, Eugen von Böhm-Bawerk, who had published a devastating critique of Marx's economic theory. Other participants included Otto Bauer and Rudolf Hilferding, who were to become leading political and intellectual figures in the Austrian and German Social Democratic Parties, and Ludwig von Mises, whose later analysis of the role of prices in a market economy would spur the neoliberal vision of Friedrich Hayek. Then Schumpeter made his way to the London School of Economics, where he studied ethnology and became interested in the work of the British eugenicists Francis Galton and Karl Pearson, who helped put the issue of explaining achievement on the agenda of the social sciences. After graduating with a law degree from the University of Vienna, Schumpeter moved to Cairo, where he became an associate of an Italian law firm, managed the money of an Egyptian princess, and made himself a fortune. In his spare time, he wrote a book on the nature of economic theory, which qualified him to teach at an Austrian university. In 1911, at the age of twenty-six, he was appointed to a professorship in Czernowitz, in Bukovina, an economic backwater four hundred miles east of Vienna with the second highest rate of illiteracy in the empire—a reminder of the geographical and cultural sweep of the Habsburg empire. By the time Schumpeter reached the magic age of thirty, he had published four books, at least three of which deserve the encomium "seminal." He also began to contribute to the *Archiv für Sozialwissenschaft und Sozialpolitik*, the most important social scientific journal in German-speaking Europe, then under Weber's editorship. In 1921, when the board of the journal was reorganized after Weber's death, Schumpeter became one of its three editors.[3]

One of the most striking features of European thought in the last decade of the nineteenth century and the first decades of the twentieth was a renewed emphasis on the significance of elites. The role of elites had been an important liberal theme through much of the nineteenth century, as liberals sought to create the legal conditions under which those of superior ability or creativity could rise and exert greater influence. To some thinkers, the spread of male suffrage in the last decades of the century seemed to threaten this process. Greater democracy led to the growth of new mass parties, preaching more egalitarian doctrines, most notably socialism. One response among intellectuals was to focus attention on the need for elites and for extraordinary individuals. Nietzsche might be assigned the role of godfather to the new wave of elite theorists, who borrowed heavily from his analysis of the psychology of *Ressentiment* in explaining contemporary socialism.[4]

Two of the most pervasive themes of Schumpeter's oeuvre are Nietzschean: the role of the superior few as a source of creativity, and the stultifying effects of the resentment of the many against the claims of the creative few. In his *Genealogy of Morality* (1887) and elsewhere, Nietzsche argued that the Christian morality of meekness and humility was best understood as a doctrine that provided psychological gratification to the weak and inferior, allowing them to feel morally superior to the strong, the vital, and the creative. The power of priests, Nietzsche thought, came from directing the resentment of the inferiors against their real superiors.

Schumpeter would make the theme of creative leadership central to his conception of capitalism, though he was not the first to do so. But he would develop the implications of creative leadership with greater subtlety than his predecessors and integrate it into existing economics. In the late nineteenth century, W. H. Mallock, a conservative British publicist, had written a string of books arguing that the material progress of the majority of men and women depended on a small talented elite. Economic advance was based on unequal contributions, Mallock argued, and these contributions had economic inequality as their legitimate reward. Inequality was therefore both inexorable and desirable, for it provided the incentive for the talented to apply their potential talents to actual economic improvement. Mallock first presented these views in his 1882 book, *Social Equality*, and developed them in *Aristocracy and Evolution* (1894). Schumpeter was an admirer of Mallock's work, describing him in later years as an analyst of merit "who was never recognized by the economic profession and seems to be entirely forgotten now, perhaps because he had the courage to tell unpopular truth."[5] Closer to home, the Viennese economist Friedrich von Wieser emphasized the importance of leadership as a fundamental category of social-scientific explanation in his lectures and in his books.[6] It would also become central to Weber's understanding of modern democratic politics.

From the very beginning of his career, Schumpeter thought of creativity, evolution, and superior individuals as central issues in social-scientific explanation, the implications of which he would explore in economics and then elsewhere.[7] The theme of creative elites is adumbrated in Schumpeter's first book, *The Nature and Major Principles of Political Economy* (1908), in explicitly Nietzschean terms.[8] After devoting the bulk of six hundred pages to explicating the stable and static elements of capitalism, he emphasizes that capitalism is in fact dynamic and calls for treating in a scientific fashion what was often referred to as "effort," or the "will to power" (*Wille zur Macht*) or the "will to domination" (*Heerenwillen*), in explaining that dynamism.[9]

The role of creative elites in the economic process was the subject of his second major work, *The Theory of Economic Development* (1911), in which he laid out his theory of entrepreneurship. He thought that Smith had been misled by overly egalitarian assumptions into underestimating the role of superior individuals.[10] Schumpeter argued that the laws of supply and demand, which had been the focus of economics since the time of Smith, missed what was most essential about capitalism: its dynamic transformation. Its source lay in the entrepreneur, a figure who had been rather neglected in nineteenth-century economic thought.[11]

Schumpeter distinguished the entrepreneur from the owner of capital, the inventor, and the manager—roles with which the entrepreneur was often confused. The function of the entrepreneur, Schumpeter thought, is to introduce economic innovation. That innovation took a variety of forms: introducing new commodities or qualitatively better versions of existing ones; finding new markets, new methods of production and distribution, or new sources of production for existing commodities; or introducing new forms of economic organization.[12] The role of the entrepreneur was to break out of the habitual routine of economic life, and this required a rare and extraordinary mental creativity and energy.[13] It required "the creative power and dominating force of a leader," as Schumpeter put it.[14] One form of innovation was to create large firms in an industry that had never known such organization, to bring about a more efficient utilization of the factors of production. That, Schumpeter noted, was a difficult task requiring special talents, since it had to overcome considerable social and political resistance.[15] Spectacular profits accrue to the innovator, who at first has a monopoly because of the novelty of his innovation. Eventually others imitate his innovation, competition erodes the initial large gains, and the result is a decline in profit and a return to the normal, static "circular flow" of economic life. The entrepreneur who successfully innovates stands to make large profits. "But he has also triumphed for others, blazed the trail and created a model for them which they can copy. They can and will follow him, first individuals and then whole crowds."[16] The pattern of boom and bust that makes up the business cycle, Schumpeter suggested, could be explained in good part by the introduction, imitation, and absorption of clusters of entrepreneurial innovations.

The entrepreneur not only fulfilled an economic function; he represented a psychological type. That psychology could not be explained by the scheme of motivations usually employed by economists, namely a hedonistic calculus of carefully maximized well-being. For the entrepreneur was more typically motivated by "the dream to found a private kingdom," often a transgenerational dynasty; the will to prove oneself superior to others, for which financial gains are "mainly valued as an index of success and as a symptom of victory"; and "the joy of creating, of getting things done, or simply of exercising one's energy and ingenuity."[17] It is precisely the nonutilitarian elements of capitalist activity that Schumpeter sought to recapture. As he later put it, when it comes to explaining capitalist development, "utilitarianism can only be described as a complete failure since its rationalistic conception of individual behavior and of social institutions was obviously and radically wrong."[18]

The process of innovation described in *The Theory of Economic Development* applied to other areas of life as well.[19] The distinction between leaders and followers, between those who essentially continue in the given way of doing things and those who devise new methods, held for every area of life, not just the economy.[20]

Some of the broader implications of Schumpeter's contentions for the social-scientific understanding of the role of elites were set out in his "Social Classes in an Ethnically Homogeneous Environment," an essay based on themes he explored in his teaching before the First

World War, though it was published later.[21] Schumpeter pointed to the role of aptitudes in determining class structure—both inherited aptitudes and those acquired through the possibilities offered by social position.[22] To some degree the particular aptitudes that led to upward social mobility depended upon the technological, economic, political, and cultural structure of society. But there was also, Schumpeter suggested, a "general capacity," which the psychologist Charles Spearman in a famous paper of 1904 had termed the "central factor." Schumpeter noted that it was distributed along a bell curve within an ethnically homogeneous environment, and distributed unevenly when there were sharp ethnic differences.[23]

Marxists were right to point to the significance of social class, Schumpeter wrote, but their understanding of how classes came about was flawed, and they downplayed the reality of mobility *between* classes. There was far greater mobility in and out of the modern bourgeoisie than was usually supposed, and that movement depended on the aptitude and behavior of individuals and families. For the capitalist bourgeoisie of nineteenth-century Europe, social mobility depended on competence: on saving, investing, and skill in the technical, commercial, and administrative leadership of family-owned enterprises. This was at odds with the Marxist assumption of the "automatism of accumulation," according to which the big get bigger and the small disappear. What Marxists (and not they alone) failed to notice was the fact of "automatic decline" under conditions of competitive capitalism. Without innovation, simply investing in tried and true methods leads to the decline of the family enterprise: "Mere husbanding of already existing resources, no matter how painstaking, is always characteristic of a declining position." Social mobility in the modern corporation also depended upon behavior and aptitude. While many of the same characteristics required by the entrepreneur were necessary for elevation into the new elite—qualities such as energy, intelligence, and vision—corporate leadership also demanded different qualities, such as the ability to manage men and to remain sharp through an endless round of meetings. The ongoing transformation of capitalism did not diminish the necessity of elites; it merely altered some of the characteristics required for ascent into the elite.

The second Nietzschean theme that runs through Schumpeter's work is that of *Ressentiment*: the psychological antipathy of the inferior many to the superior few, and the attempt of the resentful majority to devalue the achievements of the creative and successful.[24] As early as his *Theory of Economic Development* of 1911, Schumpeter portrayed antientrepreneurial sentiment as inherent in capitalist society. He argued that it was precisely the dynamism injected into capitalist society by the entrepreneur that made him an object of antipathy. For the *rise* of a new entrepreneur—and, with him, of new means of production and organization—necessarily meant the relative economic *decline* of those ensconced in the status quo. Farmers and artisans who lost out in the process of economic development decried the entrepreneur, while the descendants of those who had risen to the top in earlier stages of capitalist development disdained the innovator as a parvenu. This process of downward relative social mobility (*Deklassierung*), Schumpeter stressed, was an inevitable counterpart of the dynamic side of capitalism—what he would later call its "creative destruction."[25] Like Marx, Schumpeter argued that capitalism creates its own opposition. But according to Schumpeter, that opposition arose not because of material impoverishment but because of the psychological resentment created by entrepreneurial dynamism.

These assumptions lay behind Schumpeter's lifelong interest in explaining the appeal of socialism. He began his intellectual life at a time when the socialist parties of Austria and Germany were on the rise. Very early in his career he came to know the most distinguished socialist intellectuals of the age, and he maintained such contacts throughout his life. He was, therefore, well aware of the attraction of socialism not only to the working masses, but to the best and the brightest.

In attempting to account for the appeal of socialism, Schumpeter borrowed not only from Nietzsche but from the Italian political theorist Vilfredo Pareto.[26] A distinguished liberal economist, Pareto regarded socialism as economically irrational, and set out to explain why it was so attractive to both working-class masses and intellectuals. Pareto's 1901 essay "The Rise and Fall of Elites," conveys two themes to which Schumpeter would return time and time again: the inevitability of elites, and the importance of nonrational and nonlogical drives in explaining social action. Pareto suggested that the victory of socialism was "most probable and almost inevitable." Yet, he predicted, the doctrine would triumph, but the reality of elites would not change.[27] It was almost impossible to convince socialists of the fallacy of their doctrine, Pareto asserted, since they were enthusiasts of a substitute religion. In such circumstances, arguments are invented to justify actions that were arrived at before the facts were examined, motivated by nonrational drives.[28] These themes would recur in Schumpeter's writings.

The Birth of Irony from Catastrophe

The years of the First World War and its immediate aftermath were personally engrossing for Schumpeter, but a calamity for the institutions of the Habsburg Empire that he held dear. For the first and last time in his life, Schumpeter was drawn directly into government and politics.[29] During the war he traveled frequently to Vienna, dispatching memoranda on economic and political affairs to the emperor and to highly placed members of the aristocracy. Schumpeter opposed a customs union with the German Reich, Austria's military ally, because he thought it would strengthen ethnic German nationalism and corrode the multiethnic identity of the Habsburg empire. He recommended a more forceful pursuit of peace, and favored an assertive monarchy that would create a consensual basis for the empire through a more federative structure and end the favored status of Germans and Hungarians.[30]

For Schumpeter, as for others from his milieu, the collapse of the empire in 1918 was a shock; it meant the end of the world from which they drew their cultural breath. The class of educated, German-speaking Austrians to which he belonged were secular, committed to economic liberalism and the rule of law. Their cosmopolitanism took the form of attachment to a monarchy that served to integrate a polyglot empire.[31] At odds with the anticapitalist propensities of the aristocracy, the lower-middle-class Christian Socials, and the Social Democrats, as well as with the nationalist assertion of the Slavic minorities, this most economically and culturally modern sector of Habsburg society paradoxically looked to the "outdated" imperial house to protect its position and its modernizing project. To most of them it seemed that the empire, though "indefensible" in terms of modern doctrines of nationalism and of democratic self-determination, was in fact the most "rational" political structure for the region, in that it was best suited to the economic and cultural development of all the peoples within it. Indeed it was most useful, they would tacitly add, to the non-German minorities most in need of the economic development that only the empire could bring, and that was to prove woefully lacking in most of the successor states.[32] The notion that what seems rational to "enlightened" opinion might be profoundly mistaken was to become a frequent refrain of Schumpeter's subsequent work.[33]

The destruction of the empire was followed by the near victory of what seemed to Schumpeter another bad idea: socialism. As we have seen, a wave of revolutionary hopes and fears swept through central Europe in 1918 and 1919. Yet revolutionary socialist governments in Russia, Hungary, and Munich produced only negative economic results, and only in Russia did the revolutionary government survive beyond 1919. The most distinguished economic minds of German and Austrian socialism, such as Otto Bauer and Rudolf Hilferding, did not regard socialism as close at hand in 1917, and had given little thought to the actual blueprint for a socialist economy. But the radicalization of the working class in the closing year of the war stimulated practical plans for a postcapitalist economy. At the war's end, Vienna too was controlled by workers' and soldiers' councils. These were regarded with suspicion by the leaders of the socialist parties, who feared they would lead to a Bolshevik-style takeover. Radical workers, believing that socialization (collective ownership) would improve their economic situation, rioted to protest the lack of socialization of the economy. In April and June of 1919, Communist attempts to seize buildings in Vienna were put down by police action. Throughout 1919 and 1920 workers in Vienna, often at the initiative of the councils, engaged in violent protests, including looting shops and wrecking cafés in the *Innenstadt*. The Viennese middle class and its political spokesmen viewed these violent outbursts as the breakdown of civilization.[34]

With the collapse of the Romanov, Habsburg, and Hohenzollern empires, and with communist revolutions in progress in Russia, Budapest, and Munich, Schumpeter entered government service. First he served alongside Max Weber on a German government commission to consider nationalization of the German coal industry, a policy that both Weber and Schumpeter opposed. Then, in March of 1919, he became minister of finance in a new Austrian government that was composed of Social Democrats and (Catholic) Christian Socials. He lasted for six tumultuous months, until he was forced out. Some objected to his economic policy, which sought to stymie the socialization of industry favored by the Social Democrats. Both they and the Christian Socials resented his opposition to unification with Germany at a time when it was favored by both parties.[35]

The prospect that politicians would actually try to bring about socialism by either democratic or revolutionary means led Weber to pen his intellectual refutation of socialism, as we saw in Chapter 9.[36] Schumpeter's Viennese contemporary Ludwig von Mises, in one of the most prescient essays of the era, set out to prove by rational demonstration that socialism was economically unfeasible.[37] Schumpeter too remained a staunch though undogmatic advocate of market-oriented economic policies. But beginning with his 1918 essay "The Crisis of the Tax State," he adopted a different rhetorical strategy to stave off socialism. He became an ironist. When it suited his purposes, he could adopt the pose of the observer reflecting on the gap between the intentions of contemporary politicians and intellectuals and the consequences of their actions. The beneficent plans of these actors would lead to negative consequences that they did not intend, but that the wiser and ironic social-scientific observer could anticipate. And yet, Schumpeter suggested with a second ironic twist, his rational demonstration of the unintended negative consequences of such plans would not prevent the actors from trying to carry them out, since they were driven by nonrational motives.

Why adopt such a stance, which might appear to insult the reader? Schumpeter's irony was strategic: it tried to provoke the reader into self-recognition, and thus encourage him to open his mind to an otherwise unpalatable argument.[38] To be shown that one is headed for disaster yet told that one is powerless to decide otherwise may awaken one's will to defy this fate. Schumpeter felt that a direct and frontal onslaught against socialism would make little headway among intellectuals, either in postwar Vienna or later in New Deal America. Instead he offered a series of arguments about why socialism was undesirable under present circumstances. The time for socialism, he maintained, lay in the future; the time for capitalism was now. And, he explained, socialism would bring about few of the goals and expectations of the socialists themselves. Its viability could be purchased largely at the expense of its desirability.

Schumpeter's first highly ironic work, a long 1920 essay entitled "Socialist Possibilities Today," adumbrated many of the themes of his later and much better known *Capitalism, Socialism, and Democracy*.[39] Schumpeter began by reiterating the claims of economists since Smith. There was a need to restate certain obvious truths, he wrote, since most of the public understood little about how capitalism actually works. The goals of socializing the means of production and instituting conscious economic planning would not bring an end to "the anarchy of free competition," since the competitive market economy is not in fact anarchic. On the contrary, Schumpeter argued, "the combined effect of individual egoisms of economic subjects results in a whole, which from the point of view of the outside observer would give the impression of a conscious plan as much as does the economy of a socialist society guided by a central organ." Nor did the distinction between a socialist and a capitalist organization of the economy lie in the fact that one serves the public while the other serves only individual interests, for the profit motive that drives the production process in a competitive economy serves the interests of all as much as a socialist economy would, he asserted.⁴⁰

The popular understanding of socialism was no better. What most of the mass supporters of socialist parties had in mind, he asserted, was the confiscation and redistribution of consumer goods. "Socialization with a pleasant life and plentiful income—that childish ideal of enrichment through appropriation of existing wealth—is politically attractive, but it is nonsense," he wrote.⁴¹ For the result of such measures would be to bring economic life to a halt and to destroy "cultured private life."⁴² He charged that responsible socialists showed a failure of courage in refusing to acknowledge that socialization would lead to a regression of production and a worsening of the already dire economic circumstances of almost everyone. And if socialization were to be successful, it would require the imposition of an unprecedentedly strict level of discipline upon the working classes.

Nevertheless, he continued, capitalist economic development would in the long run lead in the direction of socialism. The competitive capitalist market destroys traditional, noneconomical forms of production, thus rationalizing the economy and performing the "necessary preliminary work for socialism." When the process proceeded far enough, he suggested, it would be possible to replace the "automatic" rationalization brought about by capitalism with a more planned economic policy. Over the long run, Schumpeter added, the classic functions of the entrepreneur would become less necessary and might be systematized into teachable methods. Then the social significance of the entrepreneur and of the capitalist would decline, and as their functions became less essential, they would slowly go the way of the aristocracy after the decline of knighthood. In addition, as familial ownership and operation of enterprises gave way to shareholding in which actual control was in the hands of paid managers, the sense of private property would weaken. Thus, Schumpeter suggested, the capitalist process itself leads to a more rationalized economy, even as it prepares the spirit for renunciation of the private ownership of the means of production.⁴³ Socialists ought therefore to welcome ongoing capitalist development.

Socialists had other reasons as well to promote capitalist development, he argued. They hoped to end the need for economic activity as the prime task of life. That would only become possible after the buildup of tremendous capital. But investment comes at the expense of present consumption, and socialist politicians would find it difficult to withhold present income from consumers in order to devote it to investment for the future. It was best therefore to begin socialism from a high level of economic production, which capitalism was more likely to bring. Because it would have difficulty creating savings and investment, socialism required demographic stagnancy. Here too capitalism was preparing the way, Schumpeter contended, by suppressing irrational impulses and bringing down the birthrate.[44]

Socialism would slow down economic development, Schumpeter explained, but that was consonant with its purpose of freeing human energies from economic purposes. But that prospect remained for the future. In the present, he concluded, socialization of the means of production would be disastrous, alienating the most productive citizens, bringing about a decline in the standard of living, and leading to social conflict. Therefore the current policy of any rational socialist must be to encourage the development of capitalism.[45]

Having presented his reasoned case in favor of continued capitalist development, Schumpeter added that "of course these arguments have no impact on the convinced socialist" because the socialist had "a mystical, religious, or substitute-religious, non-rational faith in socialism, which cannot be overcome by any argument, proof, or fact."[46] In arguing with socialists, only irony helps, he seemed to feel.

Schumpeter returned to these themes occasionally in his writings of the late 1920s, reiterating his belief in the economic ineffectiveness of socialism compared to capitalism.[47] But once again he affirmed that "[c]apitalism, while economically stable, and even gaining in stability, creates, by rationalizing the human mind, a mentality and style of life incompatible with its own fundamental conditions, motives and social institutions, and will be changed, although not by economic necessity and probably even at some sacrifice of economic welfare, into an order of things which it will be merely a matter of taste and terminology to call Socialism or not."[48]

From Prosperity to Depression

After his short stint as Austrian finance minister, Schumpeter became chairman of the board of a small bank. The position was more titular than real, and he could devote most of his time to his personal investments, purchased in part by money borrowed from his bank. These investments went sour in 1924, after hyperinflation in Germany and Austria led to a market crash that wiped out much of his fortune. He had to borrow from friends to repay the funds he had borrowed from his bank and spent much of the next decade repaying his debts.[49] Returning to the academy, he became a professor at the University of Bonn, and wrote frequently for the financial press. As an analyst of the economic problems of the Weimar Republic, he warned against excessive governmental entanglement in the economy and thought that excessive wage demands by unions had led to a lack of investment capital that retarded economic growth—an analysis echoed by recent historians.[50]

Schumpeter, who had spent a year as a visiting professor at Columbia University in 1913–14 and another at Harvard in 1927–28, expected the United States to be spared from these drags on capitalist expansion, and from the temptations of socialism.[51] In 1932 he left Germany to settle permanently in the United States, moving to the economics department at Harvard just in time to observe the Roosevelt administration's handling of the Great Depression.

In the United States the decades from the late nineteenth century through 1929 had been an era of enormous economic growth. Farmers in 1929 brought 50 percent more produce to market than at the beginning of the century, and the gains in agriculture were paltry compared to those of industry. Thanks to more efficient forms of industrial organization and to the introduction of electrically powered machinery on the factory floor, American industrial production quadrupled during the same period. The motor car, still a plaything of the rich at the turn of the century, was becoming part of the equipment of middle-class and even working-class life by 1929. The purchase of millions of automobiles each year was made possible by the falling costs of production brought about by technological and organizational innovation. A single Ford Model T took fourteen hours to assemble in 1913; by 1925 one was rolling off the assembly line at Henry Ford's plant in Highland Park, Illinois, every ten seconds. The wheels of mass consumption were oiled by two financial innovations: consumer credit (or buying "on installment") and mass advertising. While much of rural America remained mired in poverty, urban workers—many of them recent immigrants from Europe—could command a cornucopia of new products, including canned foods, washing machines, refrigerators, telephones, and radios.[52] The economy grew more slowly in western and central Europe than in the United States, but it grew nonetheless.

In the United States as in Germany, observers called attention to the growing scale of economic enterprise, and its concentration into ever larger units.[53] In the United States, "trustbusters" such as Louis Brandeis believed that bigness led to monopoly, or at least to oligopoly, in which a few firms dominated the market for some product. They thought they had learned from Adam Smith that monopoly was bad, though by "monopoly" Smith had clearly meant the granting of sole legal permission to manufacture or sell some product, not the domination of a market by a few companies. The task of government, as the trustbusters conceived it, was to break up concentrations of economic power to re-create a more competitive market. Other American observers, such as Charles Van Hise, author of *Concentration and Control: A Solution of the Trust Problem in the United States* (1912), who saw economic concentration as inevitable and desirable, believed in the need for a more active and powerful state to control such corporations through governmental regulatory bodies.[54]

The development of capitalism was transforming the family as well. Children, an economic boon for farming families who depended on child labor, were a greater burden to urban dwellers. As the costs of educating a child to prepare it for the world of urban work increased, and as parents aspired to upward social mobility for their children, couples desired fewer offspring. Radical advocates of birth control, such as Margaret Sanger, preached a gospel of female erotic liberation. More moderate, and with greater appeal to middle-class women, was her British counterpart, Marie Stopes, whose book, *Married Love or Love in Marriage,* first published in 1918 and often reprinted thereafter, proclaimed the desirability of female sexual satisfaction, within a more companionate idea of marriage. To a degree that seems remarkable to later generations, married couples limited their fertility by sexual abstinence and by coitus interruptus, as well as by abortion. But here, too, new commodities played a role, including improved condoms, spermicidal jelly and the Mensinga diaphragm, and the less effective but more accessible spermicidal douches. With, or more often without, artificial contraception, the birthrate declined in most countries of western Europe and the United States, first among upper- and middle-class women, and then increasingly among their working-class counterparts.[55] Cultural commentators, Schumpeter among them, speculated about the causes and consequences of the decline in fertility in the midst of rising incomes, often interpreting it as evidence of the rationalization of life, or cultural decline, or both.[56]

Then the great prosperity train came to a grinding, screeching halt and seemed to go over a cliff. Though commonly attributed to the crash of the New York Stock Exchange in October 1929, the Great Depression had deeper and more complex causes. A long-term decline in the prices of agricultural goods had radically reduced the buying power of farmers; disasters among central European banks had ramifications across the Atlantic; and an antiquated and unstable banking system in the United States led to bank failures, which in turn had a domino effect. Though the causes of the Depression were obscure, its effects were blatant. In Germany, unemployment shot upward with breathtaking speed, reaching three million at the beginning of 1930, 4,380,000 by the end of the year, and 5,615,000 at the end of 1931. Economic distress strained a political system that many Germans accepted only as long as it served their economic interests. The most radical opponents of democracy, the National Socialists and the Communists, saw their electoral fortunes blossom as the economy withered. When Schumpeter left for Harvard in late 1932, effective parliamentary democracy had been suspended for two years, and a more radical dictatorship of one sort or another was on the horizon. In the United States democracy had deeper roots, which allowed it to survive the squalls of the Depression. But there too the economic situation was dire: when Schumpeter arrived, over ten million people were out of work, almost a fifth of the workforce. In big cities like Chicago and Detroit, home to the hard-hit steel and automotive industries, almost half of the workforce was idle.[57] By 1933, when Franklin Delano Roosevelt became president, the gross national product had dropped to one-half its 1929 level, and one worker in four was unemployed.[58]

Analysts of very diverse political hues concluded that the era of dynamic capitalism was over and that the United States and other "mature economies" had entered into a period of long-term economic stagnation. Some argued that there were no new technologies in sight for consumers to buy. Others feared that natural resources were nearing exhaustion, or that slowing population growth translated into a lack of consumer demand.[59] Such assumptions lay behind Roosevelt's 1932 campaign address to the San Francisco Commonwealth Club, a speech that laid out the rationale for what became the New Deal.

> As long as we had free land; as long as population was growing by leaps and bounds; as long as our industrial plants were insufficient to supply our own need, society chose to give the ambitious man free play and unlimited reward provided only that he produced the economic plant so much desired. During this period of expansion, there was equal opportunity for all and the business of government was not to interfere but to assist in the development of industry.

[But now] our industrial plant is built; the problem just now is whether under existing conditions it is not overbuilt. Our last frontier has long since been reached . . .

Clearly, all this calls for a re-appraisal of values. A mere builder of more industrial plants, a creator of more railroad systems, an organizer of more corporations is as likely to be a danger as a help. The day of the great promoter or of the financial Titan . . . is over. Our task now is not discovery, or exploitation of natural resources, or necessarily producing more goods. It is the soberer, less dramatic business of administering resources and plants already in hand . . . of adjusting production to consumption. . . .[60]

Roosevelt's speech expressed the shared consensus of the "Brain Trust" of intellectuals associated with the New Deal, such as Rexford Tugwell, Lauchlin Currie, and Schumpeter's Harvard colleague, Alvin Hansen. They all agreed that the private sector, left to its own devices, would never be able to re-create the economic growth of earlier decades. Indeed, business could not even return the country to the level of prosperity of the 1920s.[61] They drew upon arguments developed by the British economist John Maynard Keynes in contending that without large-scale intervention by government, the level of unemployment was bound to remain at unacceptably high levels. By and large, the New Dealers set out to stabilize capitalist institutions. Some of their innovations, such as the Federal Deposit Insurance Corporation and the Securities and Exchange Commission, had that effect. But they also engaged in a series of more radical measures aimed at changing the basic rules of the competitive market.

At first, they tried to promote stability by limiting competition. The National Recovery Administration, initiated in 1933, for example, reflected a government policy of deliberate cartelization, creating agreements among all the businesses in a particular sector with the aim of keeping up prices and, it was hoped, raising employment and wages as well. Here was a policy at odds with the very concept of a competitive economy, which created winners and losers; instead the NRA attempted to keep all players in the game.[62] What it could not do was make American business more robust.

The failure of the New Deal to solve the problem of unemployment, and the ongoing misery in the country, gave rise to more radically anti-capitalist sentiments, both among demagogues and among some of the New Dealers themselves. In the industrial north, the Reverend Charles Edward Coughlin, a Roman Catholic priest based in suburban Detroit, developed a huge following using the new medium of radio. He preached against the Money Power ensconced in Wall Street, entwined with international bankers, its machinations orchestrated by a sinister Jewish directorate—a litany that drew upon *The Protocols of the Elders of Zion*, an antisemitic forgery embraced for a time by Henry Ford himself. After supporting Roosevelt in the election of 1932, and having proclaimed that "the New Deal is Christ's deal!" Coughlin turned on the president in the course of 1934 and formed his own National Union for Social Justice. In the South, the populist Huey Long also denounced Roosevelt for being in bed with the Money Power and big corporations. In 1934 he launched the "Share Our Wealth Society," devoted to making "every man a king" by seizing the fortunes of the rich through confiscation and taxation, and then redistributing the revenue to every American family.

Roosevelt dealt with the political threat posed by the anticapitalist demogogues by embracing some of their rhetoric and policy prescriptions. In his presidential campaign of 1936, Roosevelt declared himself in favor of the Wealth Tax Act.[63] He demanded "very high taxes" on large incomes (rising to 79 percent for the individual with the very highest income), stiffer inheritance taxes, and new taxes on corporate profits. He accompanied his soak-the-rich legislative agenda with a rhetorical palette to match. The rich were tyrants, "economic royalists," an "autocracy" seeking "power for themselves, enslavement for the public," he declared in his state of the union address of 1936.[64] When business responded with understandable hostility, Roosevelt upped the rhetorical ante. By the time the campaign ended, he was denouncing "organized money," and in a fiery speech to a mass audience in New York's Madison Square Garden, he identified his enemies as the practitioners of "business and financial monopoly, speculation, reckless banking, class antagonism, war profiteering."[65]

The New Deal did not "solve" the Depression, and certainly not its worst manifestation, unemployment. Even as the American economy recovered between 1933 and 1937, 14 percent of workers remained unemployed. Roosevelt won the election of 1936, but during 1937 the economy slumped once again—not least, as contemporary observers and subsequent historians have remarked, because Roosevelt's rhetoric and policies made businessmen reluctant to invest. The president's response was to unchain the dogs of anticapitalist vilification. His secretary of the interior, Harold Ickes, inveighed against the "Sixty Families" who supposedly controlled the American economy and who threatened to create "big-business Fascist America—an enslaved

America."[66] If there was one core belief shared by the diverse policy makers in the New Deal, it was a suspicion of businessmen in general and big business in particular.[67]

Schumpeter's Analysis of the Depression and New Deal

Schumpeter's first major literary response to the Depression in the United States came in his mammoth work, *Business Cycles: A Theoretical, Historical, and Statistical Analysis of the Capitalist Process*, published in 1939.[68] He sought to show that cyclical booms and busts were an inevitable part of the history and process of capitalist development, though he thought that the swings of the business cycle could be moderated as business cycles were better understood by corporations and by government. Toward the end of the book, Schumpeter offered his own analysis of the current depression and the chances for escaping from it.

At a time when many thought the drastic and protracted downturn of the economy vindicated Marx's prediction of the ultimate crisis of capitalism, Schumpeter offered a far less apocalyptic diagnosis. He maintained that the Depression in the United States had come about as a confluence of long-term and short-term cyclical factors. The recovery that had begun to occur in 1933 was due more to the "natural" effects of the business cycle than to government policy.[69] But that recovery had been slowed by government policies such as the National Industrial Recovery Act of 1933. Such measures, which sought to stabilize existing firms rather than allowing economically obsolete companies to decline, had the unintended result of weakening the dynamism of the market, in which innovation by some firms led inevitably to the disappearance of others.[70] Government attempts to raise wages, while not inevitably harmful, had under the cyclical conditions of the day produced an adverse effect on business expansion and on employment levels.[71]

The Keynesian analysis of the Depression held that contemporary capitalism suffered from a shrinking of opportunities for investment. Schumpeter concurred, but not for the reasons offered by the Keynesians. The problem, in his view, was that popular and governmental hostility to economic elites had led to a situation in which those who ought to have made the most significant innovative investments were discouraged from doing so. A combination of high income taxes and estate taxes on the highest-earning taxpayers and a special surtax on undistributed corporate profits, together with the general perception that those implementing policy in the New Deal were antipathetic to capitalism, led to a lack of new investment and innovation.[72] These measures struck at the largest firms and largest incomes. Yet "since economic 'progress' in this country is largely the result of work done within a number of concerns at no time much greater than 300 or 400," wrote Schumpeter, "any serious threat to the functioning of these will spread paralysis in the economic organism. . . ." The problem was exacerbated by the decline of available investment capital thanks to the high taxes levied on the wealthiest 30,000–40,000 taxpayers.[73]

Schumpeter was skeptical of the government's antitrust efforts. He defended large corporations, part of his lifelong justification of the creatively superior. He thought that the attack on "monopoly" during the New Deal was motivated by egalitarian resentment of the successful.[74] The firms often attacked as monopolies, he wrote, "increase the sphere of influence of the better . . . brains."[75] What those who criticized monopoly in the name of free competition failed to understand was that it was in the very nature of dynamic capitalism to produce high, "monopoly" profits for those who were the first to innovate successfully. But that superior position had to be defended against potential new innovations, so that large firms had to continue to innovate or face decline.

In America, too, antielitist resentment was killing the capitalist goose, creating "a situation in which neither capitalism nor its possible alternatives are workable." This was a result of a process that had concerned him for almost thirty years, the fact that "capitalism produces by its mere working a social atmosphere—a moral code, if the reader prefers—that is hostile to it, and this atmosphere, in turn, produces policies which do not allow it to function."[76] In the early 1930s, the shock of the Depression and the dominant *interpretation* of the Depression by intellectuals had led to a "radicalization of the public mind" in the United States, which in turn had resulted in policies that left capitalism in shackles. Feeling itself under attack, the "industrial bourgeoisie" responded by refraining from investment and innovation, creating a far weaker cyclical recovery than would otherwise have been the case.[77] The weakness of the economic recovery, in turn, seemed to vindicate those who believed that capitalism was a spent force.

Capitalism, Socialism, and Democracy

Under such circumstances Schumpeter brought together ideas that he had been exploring for several decades in *Capitalism, Socialism, and Democracy*.[78] He reiterated some of the arguments of *Business Cycles*, but now he presented them within a highly ironic framework. Why would a social scientist write a book in the ironic mode? Probably because he had reason to believe that a frontal intellectual attack on socialism would fall on deaf ears among the younger intellectuals he sought to influence. At Harvard, Schumpeter faced an audience of graduate students that, as one of them recalled, was "supersaturated with Keynes, Marx, and Veblen."[79] In *Capitalism, Socialism, and Democracy*, irony served as a wedge with which to pry open minds. That the days of capitalism were numbered, and that the capitalist era must now give way to socialism: these were assumptions widely held by intellectuals on both sides of the Atlantic.[80] Schumpeter's strategy of ostensible concurrence served as bait, leading leftist intellectuals who would never pick up or take seriously the work of a more overt defender of capitalism to bite into the book. Once he had them hooked, he presented an ironic evaluation of the prospects for capitalism and socialism that was more likely to get them to reconsider their assumptions.[81] As an ironic work, its overt contention is the opposite of its intended message. And the explicit thesis of *Capitalism, Socialism, and Democracy* is that capitalism will be superseded by socialism as Marx predicted, but not for the reasons he had predicted it. Capitalism would be done in not by its economic failures but in spite of its economic triumphs.

Probably because Schumpeter recognized that the Depression had made Marxism more attractive than ever, especially to intellectuals, he began his book with an inquiry into what made Marxism so appealing, and went on to anatomize Marx's achievements and failures. Though Marxism condemns religion as the opium of the masses, it is best understood as a religion itself, Schumpeter insisted, since it provides a plan of salvation and a vision of earthly paradise. The real source of Marx's success lay in "formulating with unsurpassed force that feeling of being thwarted and ill treated which is the auto-therapeutic attitude of the unsuccessful many."[82] Marx sneered at the "bourgeois nursery tale that some people rather than others became, and are still becoming every day, capitalists by superior intelligence and energy in working and saving." He was well advised to do so, Schumpeter wrote, "[f]or to call for a guffaw is no doubt an excellent method of disposing of an uncomfortable truth, as every politician knows to his profit." In fact, Schumpeter suggested, alluding to his earlier work, "Supernormal intelligence and energy account for industrial success and in particular for the *founding* of industrial positions in nine cases out of ten."[83] Marxism, in short, was the latest and most powerful vehicle for channeling the resentment of the weak and uncreative against the strong and creative.

Marxism was also attractive because it claimed to explain everything according to a few principles.[84] Take the Marxist explanation of imperialism as caused by the influence of big business or high finance on foreign policy: a highly plausible explanation, Schumpeter thought, to those with no firsthand knowledge of how the world actually works. In fact, he wrote, "The attitudes of capitalist groups toward the policy of their nations are predominantly adaptive rather than causative, today more than ever. Also, they hinge to an astonishing degree on short-run considerations equally remote from any deeply laid plans and from any definite 'objective' class interests. At this point Marxism degenerates into the formulation of popular superstitions." In a parallel guaranteed to stick in the minds (and perhaps the craws) of leftist readers, he disparaged this interpretation of imperialism as on a level with the explanation of modern history "on the hypothesis that there is somewhere a committee of supremely wise and malevolent Jews who behind the scenes control international or perhaps all politics."[85]

Such conceptual shortcomings were dissected, amidst frequent praise of Marx for asking the right questions. Yet Schumpeter concurred with him that capitalist evolution would destroy capitalist society. But that was not, as Marx had contended, because capitalism led to the immiseration of the working masses. On the contrary, Schumpeter argued, the record of capitalism was one of unprecedented economic growth, which had profited the working classes the most. "The capitalist achievement," he wrote, "does not typically consist in providing more silk stockings for queens but in bringing them within the reach of factory girls in return for steadily decreasing amounts of effort."[86]

Freed of the shackles placed upon it by New Dealers who either hated capitalism or failed to understand it, capitalism would continue to bring about economic growth and a rising standard of living, Schumpeter asserted. In short order, he disposed of then-popular arguments that capitalist growth was permanently stalled due to the vanishing of investment opportunities, the exhaustion of natural resources, or the inhibition of innovation by monopolies and oligopolies. The notion that investment opportunities and natural resources had vanished overlooked the fact that entrepreneurs create new frontiers and make "resources" out of materials once regarded as useless or as not worth retrieving, such as oil buried deep beneath the surface of the earth. "The conquest of the air may well be more important than the conquest of India was," he suggested.[87] Moreover, technological progress actually creates *more* raw materials, he argued, such as increasing quantities of foodstuffs.[88] The popular notion that technological possibilities had been exhausted because no major innovations were clearly in view missed the fact that under capitalism "technological possibilities are an uncharted sea"; there were possibilities that lay beyond the present horizon and would transform productivity as radically as had the coming of electricity since the turn of the century.[89] As for monopoly, the fact that a few large firms dominated an industry, though at odds with the notion of perfect competition, did not in itself harm consumers by stifling innovation. For even large firms dominant in their markets were often forced to innovate, not because some other firm would produce their product more cheaply but because someone might come along with a new product that would displace the old one entirely.

It was no accident, Schumpeter thought, that capitalism had been so productive in the past and had the prospect of increasing wealth in the future. For it appeals to, and helps create, a system of motives that is both simple and forceful. It rewards success with wealth and, no less important, holds up the threat of destitution to those who fail. Moreover, it attracts the brightest and most energetic into market-related activity: as capitalist values come to dominate, a large portion of those with "supernormal brains" move toward business, as opposed to military, governmental, cultural, or theological pursuits.[90]

Rewards in the capitalist economy, Schumpeter explained, do not correlate precisely with the "ability, energy and supernormal capacity for work" expended. An element of chance beyond the control of the individual intervenes. But ability and energy still count for a great deal, so that "the game is not like roulette, it is more like poker." But the system is all the more successful in attracting the energy and ability of the brightest because of the lure of making huge profits. Though these "spectacular prizes" will in fact go to very few, the prospect of earning them calls forth "the activity of that large majority of businessmen who receive in return very modest compensation or nothing or less than nothing, and yet do their utmost because they have the big prizes before their eyes and overrate their chances of doing equally well."

Similarly, the realization that failure will bring destitution "threatens or actually overtakes many an able man, thus whipping up *everyone,* again much more efficaciously than a more equal and more 'just' system of penalties would." Last but not least, business promotes the quest for success because "both business success and business failure are ideally precise. Neither can be talked away."

Not only did capitalism lure the able and energetic toward business, it kept them focused on economic activity. For precisely because business was characterized by the quest for innovation, those who had achieved success could never be certain that their firms or families would remain on top for more than a generation or two. Thus, Schumpeter argued in one of his most arresting images, capitalism "effectively chains the bourgeois stratum to its tasks" of economic productivity.[91]

But the benefits of capitalism were not only economic. Schumpeter argued that much of what is most characteristic about modernity could, at bottom, be attributed to the spread of capitalism, and to the patterns of thought that it promoted. That was the mentality of "rationalistic individualism": the tendency not to take things for granted, to try to use human reason to weigh advantages and disadvantages in order to calculate what was best for oneself. It was a mental spillover from the habits of mind that characterize market activity, the matter-of-fact, quantitative, numerical weighing of profit and loss.[92] It also led to a belief in the need to judge for oneself, based on conclusions derived from worldly experience, rather than from tradition or supernatural authority.[93] These habits of mind led in turn to modern trends such as the emancipation of women and the tendency toward pacifism.[94] Indeed the emphasis on individual worldly well-being, and the belief that society was malleable and poverty not an inevitable part of the human condition, led to the development of humanitarianism, a sense of duty inspired by "utilitarian ideas about the betterment of mankind." As a result, compared to precapitalist societies, "there was never so much personal freedom of mind and body for *all,* never so much readiness to bear with and even to finance the mortal enemies of the leading class, never so much active sympathy with real and faked sufferings, never so much readiness to accept burdens, as there is in modern capitalist society."[95] In short, capitalism was ultimately responsible for the growth of the good things valued by right-thinking people.

Schumpeter concluded his evaluation of capitalism with an exquisitely ironic paragraph:

I am not going to sum up as the reader presumably expects me to. That is to say, I am not going to invite him, before he decides to put his trust in an untried alternative advocated by untried men, to look once more at the impressive economic and still more impressive cultural achievement of the capitalist order and at the immense promise held out by both. I am not going to argue that that achievement and that promise are in themselves sufficient to support an argument for allowing the capitalist process to work on and, as it might easily be put, to lift poverty from the shoulders of mankind.[96]

Then Schumpeter turned to socialism. He began by arguing that a socialist economy was indeed plausible.[97] This contention—which was bound to raise the hackles of more orthodox (or less ironic) defenders of capitalism—was probably a rhetorical strategy intended to keep the socialistically inclined reader interested. But socialism was economically superior only to the capitalism fettered by anticapitalist resentment.[98] Socialism would achieve economic growth only to the extent that it co-opted those of superior intellectual ability, and rewarded them accordingly in terms of differential prestige. Thus the economic success of socialism could be purchased only at the cost of its egalitarian aspirations. Moreover, socialism was likely to bring about the increasing use of political force against workers, as the restraints on government were loosened with the elimination of private ownership of the means of production. "There is little reason to believe that this socialism will mean the advent of the civilization of which orthodox socialists dream," he concluded. "It is much more likely to present fascist features. That would be a strange answer to Marx's prayer. But history sometimes indulges in jokes of questionable taste."[99]

But capitalism might disappear despite its economic triumphs, because of social and, above all, cultural processes that capitalism itself sets into motion. About the cultural effects of capitalism he was genuinely ambivalent. For by promoting a rationalistic mind-set—the belief that each individual ought to submit institutions to a cost-benefit analysis—capitalism calls into question the political and economic institutions of society.[100] Although, as Schumpeter indicated, this "rationalism" often turns out to be wrong, the harm done to the authority of institutions is real enough. This was particularly dangerous, Schumpeter believed, because the argument in favor of capitalism was too difficult for many people to grasp, so that when most people stopped accepting it on faith, they would misjudge its real merits. In any case, the argument for capitalism was based on long-term collective interest, an argument with little appeal to those left unemployed by the process of "creative destruction" so central to capitalism, as entrepreneurial innovation led to the obsolescence of existing forms of production and those employed in them.

Echoing Edmund Burke and generations of subsequent conservatives, Schumpeter argued that capitalist society owed its stability to precapitalist sources, the power of which it tended to erode. In a line of analysis that seemed to reflect the experience of the Habsburg and Hohenzollern empires rather than the America of the New Deal, he suggested that the politically timid bourgeois class had been politically protected by a more forcefully minded nobility. With the definitive political decline of the nobility as a result of the First World War, the capitalist class was left politically exposed. The many small farmers, artisans, and shopkeepers who had existed alongside the class of merchants and manufacturers had once provided a reservoir of support for private property. Such people had property of their own and an emotional attachment to it. But the process of economic consolidation brought about by large corporations tended to eliminate this petty bourgeoisie, and with it any mass support for the private property rights upon which capitalism rested. The commitment to property once prevalent in a society of small enterprises was further weakened because the modern corporation replaced owner-managers with managerial employees who felt no strong attachment to property as such.[101]

The individualistic and utilitarian mentality promoted by capitalism was transforming family life, with dire implications for the future of capitalism. The bourgeois family was disintegrating, Schumpeter declared, and with it the motivation for entrepreneurial activity. For as men, and especially women, applied the criteria of individualistic cost-benefit analysis to the familial sphere, they concluded that they needed, and wanted, fewer children, or perhaps no children at all. The rationalistic analysis of costs and benefits seemed to indicate that the sacrifices entailed in bearing and raising children outweighed the pleasure they brought. To many potential parents, the relevant question seemed to be "Why should we stunt our ambitions and impoverish our lives in order to be insulted and looked down upon in our old age?" For Schumpeter, this was another case where seemingly "rational" judgments might well turn out to be wrong, because those who did the judging proceeded with less than adequate information. In this case, they might simply fail to appreciate the real value of becoming a parent, "the contribution made by parenthood to physical and moral health—to 'normality' as we might express it—particularly in the case of women." Such considerations, Schumpeter lamented, tend to escape "the rational searchlight of modern individuals who, in private as in public life, tend to focus attention on ascertainable details of immediate utilitarian relevance and to sneer at the idea of hidden necessities of human nature or of the social organism." This "decline of philoprogenitivity" meant the end of the quest for the sort of income that would found a transgenerational dynasty. Without the incentive to earn more than they could ever spend, potential entrepreneurs lacked the psychological motive to throw themselves into the quest for creative innovation, Schumpeter asserted. And with greater concern for themselves and less concern for their descendants, they lost the incentive to keep working once their own financial needs had been met.[102]

Capitalism might also lose its appeal, Schumpeter asserted, for reasons that Weber and Simmel, Lukács and Freyer had analyzed. The spread of rationalistic and means-oriented mentalities threatened "a wholesale destruction of meanings," leaving individuals without a sense of participation in some larger purpose. And capitalist activity, he thought, must appear mundane compared to more traditional forms of extraordinary human achievement. Making money was antiheroic. The stock exchange, in this sense, was no substitute for the Holy Grail.[103]

Capitalism, in short, would meet its doom because of the unintended effects of capitalist development, which sapped the social and cultural sources of capitalist support. Here Schumpeter revived the arguments of previous generations of conservatives. His analysis may have suffered from the characteristic conservative vice of mistaking change for decline and imagining that because certain motives, such as the desire to own private property, were once connected with particular historical institutions, they can only exist together with those institutions, rather than taking on new forms.

The Role of the Intellectuals

If capitalism creates its own gravediggers, Schumpeter suggested ironically, they are the class of intellectuals—those whom Marx called "ideologists" of bourgeois origin and Matthew Arnold the "aliens," the sort of person exemplified by Georg Lukács or Hans Freyer. Their power came from their role in shaping the minds of others. Through teaching, writing, and influencing governmental bureaucracy, they fashioned the cultural climate of their societies.

It was not that intellectuals *created* discontent with capitalism. Their significance came from their ability to crystallize and channel the otherwise diffuse disappointments and resentments that were intrinsic to the creative destruction wrought by capitalism. It was the intellectuals, in other words, who gave form to the grievances created by capitalism, transforming their significance by explaining that the solution lay in the overthrow of capitalism itself.[104] Trade unions, for example, were a typical attempt by actors in the capitalist game to cartelize in order to improve their own market opportunities. There was nothing intrinsically radical about them, Schumpeter asserted; most union members, left to their own devices, sought to raise their standard of living and become petit bourgeois. It was intellectuals— following Marx—who radicalized the trade unions and tried to transform them into vessels of anticapitalist struggle.[105] Intellectuals are the group "whose interest it is to work up and organize resentment, to nurse it, to voice it and to lead it."[106] As Nietzsche had traced Christianity to the will to power of priests who gained influence by channeling the resentment of slaves, Schumpeter saw socialism as the expression of intellectuals who channeled the discontents of capitalist society into a new pseudoreligion that allowed the unsuccessful to rationalize their fate.

By "intellectual," Schumpeter made clear, he did not mean all, or even most, of those with higher education. Rather he meant those "who wield the power of the spoken and the written word" without "direct responsibility for practical affairs." As a result they tended to lack "that first-hand knowledge of them which only actual experience can give"[107]—characteristics isolated over a century earlier by Justus Möser and repeated, with variations, by Edmund Burke and Alexis de Tocqueville.

The influence of those who formulated the written and spoken word increased with the spread of new means of communication: first with print in ever more affordable forms, and more recently with the rise of radio. It was there that "public opinion" was formulated. The rise of the intellectual class was therefore itself a product of capitalist development. And as capitalism increased disposable income and leisure time, more and more people would come under the influence of the new media and the intellectuals who provided their content. Along with journalism, another outpost of critical intellectuals was the teaching professions. The staff of political parties and the coteries that provided politicians with ideas and speeches were also drawn from the ranks of the intellectuals. The rise of a professional civil service based on educational attainment—the Hegelian-Arnoldian ideal—meant that government bureaucrats and policy makers came to share in the spirit and sensibilities of the intellectual class, from which they were increasingly recruited.[108]

But why should intellectuals be critical of capitalism? One reason, according to Schumpeter, was that criticism served the intellectual's self-interest, in that "his main chance of asserting himself lies in his actual or potential nuisance value," so that "the intellectual group . . . lives on criticism and its whole position depends on criticism that stings."[109] Antipathy to capitalism was also encouraged by the cyclical overproduction of educated men and women. The exaltation of the benefits of humanistic education by Arnold and others led to an ongoing expansion of university education, producing more broadly educated humanists than the economy could absorb. But the effect of a humanistic education, Schumpeter noted, was not necessarily benign: "The man who has gone through a college or university easily becomes psychically unemployable in manual occupations without necessarily acquiring employability in, say, professional work." University education, then, has the unanticipated effect of leaving many of its graduates unfit for work in the capitalist world, or fit only for work they consider beneath them, or at wages below their worth in their own eyes. Hence their sense that the system does not reward them adequately. "Discontent breeds resentment. And it often rationalizes itself into that social criticism which . . . is in any case the intellectual spectator's typical attitude toward men, classes and institutions especially in a rationalist and utilitarian civilization."[110] The upshot was an anticapitalist resentment, which lay behind the hostility of so many intellectuals toward capitalism and which made them virtually impervious to rational argument. "In a rationalist culture, their manifestations will in general be rationalized somehow. . . . [C]apitalism stands its trial before judges who have the sentence of death in their pockets. They are going to pass it, whatever the defense they may hear; the only success victorious defense can possibly produce is a change in the indictment."[111]

But why would the owners of the means of production not restrain or repress the criticism of capitalism and its institutions? In part,

Schumpeter answered, because they shared the critical, questioning attitude that was part of the utilitarian rationalism promoted by capitalism itself. In addition, though businessmen might sometimes wish to see the critical intellectuals crushed, the bourgeoisie on the whole was loath to allow government to do so, fearing that an attack on the means of expression would lead to an attack on other forms of property. By and large, Schumpeter judged, the bourgeoisie will rally to defend the intellectuals because it believes that "the freedom it disapproves cannot be crushed without also crushing the freedom it approves." Thus despite flurries of short-run resistance, the long-term trend was toward the removal of all restraints on criticism.[112]

The favorite pastime of the intellectuals was bourgeois bashing, a delegitimation of capitalist ideals that would, over time, take its toll, sapping the confidence of the capitalist class in the rightness of its way of life.[113] The intellectuals would remain so disposed, Schumpeter suggested, despite his arguments. "Utilitarian reason is in any case weak as a prime mover of group action," he wrote, echoing Nietzsche and Pareto. "In no case is it a match for the extra-rational determinants of conduct."

In the decades after the Second World War, the capitalist economies of western Europe and the United States did indeed continue the historical expansion that Schumpeter had predicted was possible. By the 1960s, poverty in the western world was diminishing markedly, while the "proletariat" in its traditional form was on the way to extinction, increasingly assimilated into the life patterns of the middle class.

As the world formed by capitalism changed, so did the terms of the indictment, an indictment best exemplified by the work of Herbert Marcuse, but foreshadowed by John Maynard Keynes.

CHAPTER TWELVE

FROM KEYNES TO MARCUSE: AFFLUENCE AND ITS DISCONTENTS

The Paradox of Keynes

John Maynard Keynes (1883–1945) is often regarded as the intellectual godfather of postwar welfare capitalism, and Herbert Marcuse as among its leading critics. Yet there are surprising affinities between them.

In the face of the deep and seemingly intractable Depression, Keynes offered a series of critiques of government policies of laissez-faire, culminating in his *General Theory of Employment, Interest, and Money* (1936). Taking aim at the conception of the economy as a self-regulating entity, which had come to be seen as the Smithian legacy, Keynes interpreted the Depression as a product of the mistaken assumption that the market would bring about full employment on its own. He provided an economic rationale for governments to try to actively combat unemployment by raising the level of government spending. In periods when private investment and consumption were too low, government would step in to stimulate economic activity. Government spending, Keynes argued, would put people to work; their spending would increase the demand for goods; that would create the prospect of higher profits, which would lead the holders of capital to invest more readily. Unemployment would vanish and economic growth resume.

Keynes became the most influential economist in the Western world from the 1930s through the 1970s. That was in part because he offered a seemingly scientific rationale for what politicians wanted to do, in part because he provided economists with a self-image combining the authority of technique with high moral purpose, and in part because he created an arsenal of economic concepts that proved indispensable even to those who disagreed with his particular policy prescriptions.

In many respects, John Maynard Keynes was the personification of the intellectual-as-civil-servant that Smith, Hegel, and Arnold had all aimed to create. The son of politically active academic parents, he studied mathematics and philosophy before turning to economics. He became the paragon of the university-trained, administrative elite, dividing his time between teaching economics at Cambridge and serving in a variety of economic posts in the civil service. He was also a man of artistic culture, who devoted a good deal of his time and money to financial support for the arts. He set his fine mind to saving Britain (and any other country that would listen) from the Depression's extended unemployment, which he feared would undermine support for liberal democracy, as it had in Germany.

Though he thought a good deal about the issue, Keynes did not write systematically about the moral, social, and cultural consequences of capitalism. What he said on these topics is too unsystematic and even self-contradictory to warrant discussion at chapter length. But it is worth casting a glance at his unsystematic remarks, not least because they show that a keen appreciation of the economic growth created by capitalism could coexist with the most extreme antipathy to the sources of that growth. What had been a bearable tension for Smith or Arnold became, for Keynes, a moral burden to be escaped as soon as possible.

If Keynes' head was in the mathematics and economics of Cambridge, his heart was in the London neighborhood of Bloomsbury, where his cultural sensibilities were shaped by his participation in its famed and flamboyant circle of artists, musicians, and writers. His vision of the good life was an ideal of aesthetic development and cultivated friendship, combined with public service. From the heights of Bloomsbury he looked down at the City of London.[1] From early on, he portrayed the price of economic progress as the cultural deformation of those he invidiously dubbed the "rentier bourgeoisie," who had sacrificed the "arts of enjoyment" to "compound interest."[2] In the *General Theory* he called for government policies that would so increase the availability of capital that it would fetch only the most minimal return, leading to "the euthanasia of the rentier."[3] If Keynes thus appeared as an Arnoldian in Smithian clothing, some of his deepest sentiments were closer to Marx and Engels.

These sentiments were on display in a startling and much-reprinted lecture first published in 1930 as "Economic Prospects for Our Grandchildren." Like Schumpeter, Keynes noted the remarkable past performance of capitalism as an engine of economic growth, and predicted that if war and internal instability could be avoided, its future performance could be as dramatic. Indeed, Keynes speculated that mankind was on its way to solving its "economic problem." Within a few generations, there would be enough to satisfy man's "absolute needs," though not the needs that "are relative in the sense that we feel them only if their satisfaction lifts us above, makes us feel superior to, our fellows."[4] A society was within sight in which the problem would be how to spend one's leisure time when there was so little necessary labor to be done.

Adam Smith portrayed market activity as motivated by the desire to improve one's place in the world. For Smith, such motives were not evil, though, as in the case of the ambitious poor man's son, they might not be conducive to the happiness of those most directly involved. Many of the subsequent thinkers we have examined were also led to reflect on the moral hazards or personal disappointments attendant upon too exclusive a pursuit of means, especially the ultimate means, money. Keynes' vision for the future reverted to an older language reflecting a more hostile sensibility:

> When the accumulation of wealth is no longer of high social importance, there will be great changes in the code of morals. We shall be able to rid ourselves of many of the pseudo-moral principles which have hag-ridden us for two hundred years, by which we have exalted some of the most distasteful of human qualities into the position of the highest virtues. We shall be able to afford to dare to assess the money-motive at its true value. The love of money as a possession—as distinguished from the love of money as a means to the enjoyments and realities of life—will be recognised for what it is, a somewhat disgusting morbidity, one of those semicriminal semi-pathological propensities which one hands over with a shudder to the specialists in mental disease.[5]

The problem for Keynes, as for the young Marx, was deferred gratification, what he called "purposiveness," which boiled down to being "more concerned with the remote future results of our actions than with their own quality or their immediate effects on our own environment." He disparaged this elevation of the future over the present as an attempt "to secure a spurious and delusive immortality."[6] In a rhetorical flourish worthy of Marx or Sombart, Keynes identified deferred gratification with the quest for immortality, with usury, and with the Jews.[7] "Perhaps it is not an accident that the race which did most to bring the promise of immortality into the heart and essence of our religions has also done the most for the principle of compound interest and particularly loves this most purposive of human institutions," he declared. In the more affluent future,

> I see us free . . . to return to some of the most sure and certain principles of religion and traditional virtue—that avarice is a vice, that the exaction of usury is a misdemeanour, and the love of money is detestable, that those walk most truly in the paths of virtue and sane wisdom who take least thought for tomorrow. We shall once more value ends above means and prefer the good to the useful. We shall honour those who can teach us how to pluck the hour and the day virtuously and well, the delightful people who are capable of taking direct enjoyment in things, the lilies of the field who toil not, neither do they spin.[8]

Such were the prospects two generations hence. Individualism would flourish, shorn of its unlovely, Jewish, features.[9] For the moment, however, the fundamental moral hypocrisy behind capitalist society would have to continue: "We must go on pretending that fair is foul and foul is fair; for foul is useful and fair is not. Avarice and usury and precaution must be our gods for a little longer still. For only they can lead us out of the tunnel of economic necessity into the daylight." In the meantime, it was people like his Bloomsbury companions who were the seed of a more cultivated future. "The strenuous purposeful money-makers may carry all of us along with them into the lap of economic abundance," he wrote, "but it will be those peoples, who can keep alive, and cultivate into a fuller perfection, the art of life itself and do not sell themselves for the means of life, who will be able to enjoy the abundance when it comes."[10]

A few years later, in the concluding chapter of his *General Theory*, Keynes was more restrained, reminding his readers that "there are valuable human activities which require the motive of money-making and the environment of private wealth-ownership for their full fruition," though he thought the motive of making money could function with the inducement of "much lower stakes" than at present.[11] Because Keynes was by no means consistent, it is difficult to know whether these more circumspect remarks in the *General Theory* were his considered views and "Economic Prospects for Our Grandchildren" merely a jeu d'esprit. His leading biographer, Robert Skidelsky, however, judges the more radical views as "the lines on which his mind instinctively, and habitually, ran, when not reined in by the requirements of formal treatment."[12]

Keynes' cultural antipathy to deferred gratification had a decided influence on his economic analysis and prescriptions.[13] At the turn of the century, Simmel had offered an analysis of why owning money could actually be more satisfying than owning the things that money can purchase. Money's worth surpasses the value of the objects for which it can be exchanged, he reflected, because the holder of money has the additional psychic satisfaction that comes from having a choice of all of the goods that his money can buy.[14] Keynes focused on this phenomenon, gave it a scientific name (the marginal propensity to save), connected it to the ancient condemnation of usury, and held it primarily responsible for the Great Depression. He maintained that the high level of interest rates was responsible for the ongoing depression. The problem was that the "liquidity preference" of holders of money (their preference for cash over investment) kept interest rates too high to provide full employment. He also believed that under present circumstances, thrift—the monetary embodiment of deferred gratification—was an antiquated virtue, indeed a counterproductive propensity, because it kept consumption too low. Together with the high propensity to save, it was now a barrier to sufficient investment, and thus to sufficient employment and to economic growth. Hence the "paradox of thrift": "In contemporary conditions the growth of wealth, so far from being dependent on the abstinence of the rich, as is commonly supposed, is more likely to be impeded by it."[15] Keynes therefore concluded that there was a need for "central controls to bring about an adjustment between the propensity to consume and the inducement to invest."[16]

Yet such "central controls" were not intended to socialize the economy. For Keynes was a liberal, who argued in favor of a large measure of individual liberty in economic life in terms that echoed John Stuart Mill and would be reasserted by Friedrich Hayek:

> Individualism, if it can be purged of its defects and its abuses, is the best safeguard of personal liberty in the sense that, compared with any other system, it greatly widens the field for the exercise of personal choice. It is also the best safeguard of the variety of life, which emerges precisely from this extended field of personal choice, and the loss of which is the greatest of all the losses of the homogeneous or

totalitarian state. For this variety preserves the traditions which embody the most secure and successful choices of former generations; it colors the present with the diversification of its fancy; and being the handmaid of experiment as well as of tradition and of fancy, it is the most powerful instrument to better the future.

Keynes defended the expansion of the role of government "as the only practicable means of avoiding the destruction of existing economic forms in their entirety and as the condition of the successful functioning of individual initiative."[17] His *General Theory* was an attack not so much on what Smith had actually written as on its reduction to the dogma of laissez-faire. Keynes set out to free the minds of economic policy makers from too rigid an adherence to the belief that the invisible hand of the market was the solution to every economic problem—a belief that Smith himself never held.

Like Smith, Keynes thought that government policy makers ought to listen to economists. But for Keynes, the government had to compensate for the errors created by avarice, usury, and a debased culture that made individuals too frugal and prone to defer gratification. Proper government management of the economy by technically adept economists would leave room for more men and women to engage themselves in more aesthetic and cultural pursuits. "The economic problem," he wrote, "should be a matter for specialists—like dentistry."[18]

That was for the short run. But he held out the hope that in the not-so-long run avarice would be not harnessed but extirpated, and that the restrictive demands of deferred cultural gratification would be made superfluous by economic growth. Within a few years, Herbert Marcuse would argue that that time had indeed come. The pairing of the two thinkers may seem remarkable or perverse. But in some respects Marcuse's ideas read like Keynes'—with the economics left out.

The New Affluence and the End of Ideology

Given a chance, both Schumpeter and Keynes predicted, capitalism could perform prodigious feats of productivity—though Schumpeter doubted it would get the opportunity. Yet in the two decades after

World War II, after some fits and starts, it did. And much as they had predicted, the economy grew, and with it the standard of living of the vast majority of the population of western Europe and the United States. In the United States, the renewal of growth began during the war itself and continued through the early 1970s. In western Europe, economic growth began in the late 1940s, and from then on it outpaced that of the United States. The most stunning growth was in West Germany: in the decade from 1950 to 1960 its economy expanded at an annual rate of 8.6 percent, which meant that its gross national product doubled in a decade. France and Italy did almost as well. In Britain the economy also grew rapidly, though less spectacularly than on the continent. A new affluence spread across western Europe. It was palpable in Britain by the mid-1950s, and by the 1960s it had reached Italy. Indeed, in western Europe the economy was growing so rapidly that by the 1960s only about 1.5 percent of workers were unemployed. In the advanced capitalist nations of western Europe and the United States, poverty—in the sense of absolute want of food, clothing, shelter, and education—was visible only on the margins of society.[19] By the late 1950s observers took to describing the United States as "the affluent society" (a phrase coined by the American liberal economist John Kenneth Galbraith in his 1958 book of that name), and the term could soon have been extended to the nations of western Europe as well.

What had been luxuries in the era before the Second World War now became necessities: refrigerators, clothes washers, telephones, and record players. Mass automobile ownership, which began in the United States in the 1920s, came to western Europe in the 1950s and 1960s, where automobile production grew from half a million in 1947 to over nine million annually in 1967.[20] The peoples of western Europe and the United States were better housed, better clothed, and better fed than ever before. For the first time in history "leisure" became a problem. Average citizens could live as only the wealthy had lived in their parents' day (except that the personal servants who had performed routine tasks in the homes of the wealthy were replaced by electrical appliances). The manufacturers and marketers of the ever-expanding range of consumer goods turned to the new disciplines of market research and applied psychology to enhance and focus demand.[21] As a former miner in Britain explained to an American journalist, "It's not so long ago since I saw people ill-nourished, ill-clad, their homes sparsely furnished. Now you see them well-dressed, well-fed. You go into their homes and they have decorations, pianos, carpets, radios, some of them are getting TV sets. It's all changed."[22]

A college education, still the preserve of an elite before the Second

World War, became available to ever larger numbers of men and women. In the United States, the G.I. Bill was a social landmark, the modern equivalent of free western land in the nineteenth century in spreading the range of economic opportunity. In western Europe, too, higher education exploded in the decades after the war. In France, for example, where there were fewer than 100,000 university students at the end of the war, the number of students had doubled by 1960, and reached 651,000 a decade later. Universities in West Germany, Italy, and Britain saw a similar rate of growth. Increasingly, a college education, once a luxury, was coming to be seen as a necessity.

During the Depression it had been widely asserted that capitalism had exhausted the technological possibilities for further expansion, or that the dearth of raw materials made a repeat of the economic growth of the past unlikely in the future. Schumpeter had dismissed both notions as shortsighted fallacies, and here again he was proved correct. The striking growth during the postwar decades was built on yet another revolution of industrial technology. A host of new materials known as "plastics," many first developed before or during the Second World War, were now applied to consumer products, transforming kitchens and then other rooms of the household. Nuclear fission provided a new source of power. The transistor gave a new portability first to the radio and then much else. There were new sources of entertainment as well: vinyl records, later tapes, and above all, television. New pharmaceuticals, such as the antibiotics beginning with penicillin, transformed health and lifted the fear of death from those with bacterial infections. Agriculture too was transformed, so that consumers needed to spend an ever smaller portion of their income on food. Between the middle of the century and its end, global food prices fell by half. The "green revolution"—the creation by plant breeding of new, hardier, and more nutritious varieties of rice, corn, and wheat—made it possible to feed many more mouths than could have been imagined earlier, especially in Asia, and for far less. Some of these gains in agricultural productivity occurred outside the market, through an international network of research institutions funded in good part by the legacy of the Rockefeller and Ford fortunes—perhaps the most dramatic example of the role of nonprofit institutions whose origins were in large profits.[23] What all of these technological innovations had in common was that they required fewer and fewer raw materials, the relative economic importance of which shrank, as Schumpeter had anticipated.

Behind the stunning increase in the standard of living was a set of international institutional arrangements drawn from the intellectual legacy of Adam Smith, who had done so much to explain the advantages of an international division of labor based on free trade. "In practice," notes the foremost Marxist historian of our age, Eric Hobsbawm, the "Golden Age" of postwar economic growth "was the era of free trade, free capital movements, and stable currencies . . ."[24] The American planners of the postwar order reacted against the economic protectionism that had preceded the war and helped contribute to its outbreak. They deliberately removed trade barriers in order to stimulate international trade, and urged their western European allies and dependents to lower tariff barriers as well. In the two decades after 1953, world trade in manufactured goods multiplied more than tenfold.

The economic golden age that created the affluent society was an age of the market—guided, goaded, and tapped by government. Almost everywhere in the capitalist world, governments took a larger role in trying to steer the economy. There was a great deal of rhetoric about economic planning, though most planning took the mild form, as in France, of government allocation of credit to selected industries. In some cases, influenced by Keynes, governments attempted to smooth out the business cycle by spending more when economic activity slackened in order to increase the level of demand in the economy and limit unemployment. Governments encouraged consultation and compromise between labor unions and the management of large corporations, either through formal institutions, as in Germany and France, or more informally, as in the United States. Governments went further than ever before in protecting individuals against the hazards of illness, unemployment, and old age, either through governmental insurance or, as in Germany, through contributory insurance funds. Directly or through tax incentives, governments subsidized the costs of housing and of raising children. Despite a short phase of nationalization immediately after the war—motivated occasionally by socialist ideology and more often by the pragmatic desire to keep failing industries from closing down—the 1950s were primarily an era of "neoliberalism." The market was treated as the engine of economic production, which produced the wealth that could then be partially redistributed by the welfare state.[25]

Under the political, military, and economic conditions created after the war largely by the United States, then, capitalism demonstrated an unanticipated resilience. It provided more things for more people, including profit for those with capital, even while much was being siphoned off in the form of taxes to pay for the expanding welfare state. Soon observers of the political scene began to notice a remarkable convergence between the major parties of the left and right in many western democracies.[26] That was in part because the old radical right was discredited by the experience of fascism, while the radical left— the Communists—were either outlawed (as in West Germany and the United States), were kept at arm's length by the dominant democratic coalitions (as in France and Italy), or failed to arouse much support under conditions of rising prosperity. Just as striking was the convergence in programs between the parties of the moderate right and the moderate left. The former dampened their antipathy to redistributive government; the latter abandoned the great pillar of socialist ideology, nationalization of the means of production, either explicitly, as in West Germany, or tacitly as in Britain, France, and Italy. (In the United States, socialism had never been the dominant political ideology of the left-of-center Democratic Party.) As early as 1955, observers of intellectual life in Europe and the United States took note of what seemed to be an "end of ideology."[27]

The success of welfare-state capitalism in diminishing the problems of poverty, squalor, mass unemployment, and systemic instability seemed to portend the end of the subversive role of the intellectuals described by Schumpeter. What such observers did not reckon with was the reaction of a younger generation of college students who had never known the scarcity of their parents' generation and took economic growth for granted. Schumpeter had observed that "capitalism stands its trial before judges who have the sentence of death in their pockets. They are going to pass it, whatever the defense they may hear; the only success victorious defense can possibly produce is a change in the indictment."[28] The most penetrating version of the new indictment came from a German philosopher who had come to the United States to escape Nazism, Herbert Marcuse (1898–1979). Marcuse reformulated Marx's cultural critique of capitalism, revived by Lukács, for a generation that came of age amidst unparalleled affluence and that was steeped in the Freudian economy of the self.

The European Roots of Marcuse's Thought

Marcuse was fifteen years younger than Schumpeter, thirteen years younger than Lukács, and eleven years younger than Freyer, so his formative experiences differed from theirs. He was born in Berlin in 1898, the son of a businessman who had begun in the textile trade and made substantial sums in real estate.[29] The family was Jewish, but its Judaism was much watered down: the Marcuses attended synagogue twice a year, and celebrated Christmas at home, though in a form that played down its Christian content. It was a family in which the real religion was high culture. As a teenager, Marcuse, like Freyer, joined the youth movement. He was conscripted into the army in 1916, served as a noncombatant, and, like Lukács, was radicalized by the war. At the age of twenty, he participated in one of the soldiers' councils created at the war's end, where he saw firsthand how nonrevolutionary the German working class really was. The question of why the working class failed to fulfill the historical role assigned it in Marxist theory would form the leitmotif of his mature works. But, unlike Lukács, Marcuse was forced to reformulate the question—and the answer—in light of two other seminal experiences: the rise of National Socialism and the resilience of capitalism in the decades of economic growth after the Second World War.

Marcuse spent the years of the Weimar Republic at the intersection of the left-wing and right-wing critiques of capitalism, personified by Georg Lukács and Martin Heidegger. The critical approach to literary history pioneered by Lukács in his early work, *Theory of the Novel*, was echoed by Marcuse in his doctoral dissertation of 1922 on the *Künstlerroman*, a genre of novels focused on the artist and his alienation from society.[30] Marcuse met Lukács and read *History and Class Consciousness*, which became the single most important influence on his own work.[31] To the end of his days he remained loyal to the Lukácsian tenet that it was up to those who knew the real possibilities of historical development to awaken the compliant from their passivity and stupor. Marcuse's own brief experience of the market came in the mid-1920s, when his father bought him a partnership in a Berlin rare-book dealership. But that experience was hardly representative: by his own account, he spent much of his time working on a bibliography of the works of Friedrich Schiller, the great German dramatist and critic whose *Letters on Aesthetic Education* had been a milestone in the critique of the emerging capitalist order.[32] Marcuse soon decided that market activity was not for him. He made his way to the University of Freiburg, where he studied with Heidegger, whose radical philosophical and cultural critique echoed many of the themes of Lukács and Freyer, but in a highly abstract vocabulary bereft of sociological or historical specifics. When Freyer published his major work of sociological theory, Marcuse welcomed it for bringing the Heideggerian theme of the necessity for "decision" (*Entscheidung*) into the study of sociology. Marcuse shared Freyer's premise that social analysis must be preceded by political commitment.[33] He remained a committed radical, publishing in the socialist press, though without joining either the Social Democratic Party, which he scorned for its nonrevolutionary reformism, or the Communist Party, which he disdained for its authoritarian, Stalinist organization. When the "Philosophical Manuscripts" of the young Marx were published in 1932, Marcuse was one of the first to call attention to their significance as prefiguring the themes of alienation so central to the work of Lukács and Heidegger.[34]

Marcuse had hoped to pursue a career as a professor of philosophy, and under Heidegger's direction he wrote a postdoctoral book (*Habilitationsschrift*) to qualify for a university post. By the time his study was finished in 1932, however, it was increasingly clear to him that the turn in the political climate toward the radical right made it highly unlikely that a Jewish leftist would be appointed at a German university. He looked instead to the Institute for Social Research in Frankfurt, a Marxist research institute established a decade earlier by the son of a Jewish entrepreneur who had made a fortune exporting beef from Argentina. The son, Felix Weil, a self-described "salon Bolshevik," became the patron of the intellectual left. He funded the publishing house that brought out Lukács' *History and Class Consciousness*, and then founded the Institute for Social Research, which was connected to the University of Frankfurt, where Weil's father was a major donor.[35]

By the time Marcuse joined the institute, its recently appointed head, Max Horkheimer, was convinced that National Socialism would soon come to power in Germany and thought it prudent to move the institute's endowment to Switzerland. To prepare for the possibility of flight abroad, Horkheimer opened a branch in Geneva and hired Marcuse to head it. Horkheimer put out feelers to the London School of Economics and to Columbia University in New York, hoping to link his institute to one of them, as it had been linked to the University of Frankfurt. When negotiations with the London School of Economics became serious, however, they were scuttled by the efforts of another central European émigré, Friedrich Hayek, a liberal for whom the Marxism of Horkheimer and company was anathema.[36] The authorities at Columbia University were more open-minded, or less knowledgeable, about the institute's political commitments.[37] And so, on the Fourth of July 1934, Marcuse arrived in New York City and immediately took out naturalization papers. Together with Horkheimer and a handful of other members of the institute, he moved into the institute's new headquarters near Columbia University.

The institute's refugee Marxist intellectuals now devoted themselves to documenting and understanding the nature of the new National Socialist regime in their native land. When America entered the war against Japan and Hitler in turn declared war on the United States, the American government found itself in need of experts on German affairs who could provide research and analysis of the Nazi enemy, and of the likely conditions that American soldiers would encounter when they reached German soil. Not surprisingly, a number of the members of the Institute for Social Research were recruited by the newly created American intelligence agency, the Office of Strategic Services. Herbert Marcuse was among them. His move into government service was prompted by the fact that the institute could no longer support him, its endowment having dwindled thanks to the investment acumen of its Marxist economist, Friedrich Pollock.[38]

It was taken for granted by most members of the institute that the "Third Reich" should be regarded as a German form of "fascism," and that fascism was to be understood as the form taken by monopolistic capitalism when the demands of the private enterprise economy were no longer compatible with a liberal polity.[39] But that left open the question of how such a regime actually garnered popular support.

Even before Hitler attained power, some members of the institute recognized that the rational, utilitarian theory of motivation, which most Marxists used to understand politics, was inadequate in explaining the failure of the working class to revolt. Indeed the institute's members concluded on the basis of their empirical surveys of working-class opinion in Germany before Hitler's rise to power that many workers were likely to be attracted to authoritarian movements such as Nazism. In search of some theory that might help illuminate the nonrational sources of behavior, a number of the institute's members began to look to the work of Sigmund Freud.[40] Marcuse and Horkheimer were interested not in the clinical application of Freudian ideas but in Freud's focus on irrational drives in motivating social and political action. It was this emphasis that colored Marcuse's interpretation of the Nazi regime, an interpretation that in turn shaped his analysis of postwar capitalist society.

At the time, most analysts of the National Socialist regime stressed its repressive nature—its use of force to keep individuals in line. Some psychoanalytically oriented observers, such as Wilhelm Reich, treated the regime as "repressive" in the Freudian sense as well, that is, as based upon the internal repression of instinctual drives. Marcuse, by contrast, was struck by the degree of voluntary, indeed enthusiastic, compliance with the regime by the German population. And he attributed that compliance in part to the regime's ability to unleash, rather than repress, basic drives. "The *abolition of highly sanctioned taboos* is one of the most daring enterprises of National Socialism in the field of mass domination," Marcuse claimed. "For paradoxical as it may seem, the liberty or license implied in this abolition serves to intensify the '*Gleichschaltung*' (integration) of individuals into the National Socialist system." He pointed out that the regime "has done away with discrimination against illegitimate mothers and children, encourages extra-marital relations between the sexes, introduced a new cult of nudity in art and entertainment, and dissolves the protective and educational function of the family." The satisfaction of sexual urges helped to explain the emotional attachment of so many Germans to a system that suppressed human potential.[41] Sexual life was "emancipated" or "liberalized" only so that the regime could more effectively use sexuality for its own purposes. The regime tried to control mating and breeding, and politicized the previously private realm of childbearing. "The political utilization of sex has transformed it from a sphere of protective privacy in which a recalcitrant freedom could endure to a sphere of acquiescent license," he noted.[42] It was not only sexual but aggressive drives that the regime channeled to its own purposes. "The regime, far from suppressing him, has emancipated the human individual in his most sinister instincts and aspects," Marcuse concluded. "The New Order has a very affirmative content: to organize the most aggressive and destructive form of imperialism which the modern age has ever seen."[43] That the release of instinctual drives could be made to serve repressive purposes was a lesson that Marcuse would later transfer to his explanation of the unexpected resilience of capitalism after the Second World War.

Marcuse spent the five years following the war in government service, moving from the OSS (which was disbanded and replaced by the CIA) into the State Department, where he became the leading analyst of central European affairs. As H. Stuart Hughes, a Harvard historian who worked with Marcuse at the OSS, rightly notes, it seems "deliciously incongruous that at the end of the 1940s, with an official purge of real or suspected leftists in full swing, the State Department's leading authority on Central Europe should have been a revolutionary socialist who hated the cold war and all its works."[44] Marcuse left his government job not because he was dismissed, but because he had long been eager to enter the academy and took the first opportunity that came along. After a few years on temporary research grants at Columbia University and Harvard, he joined the faculty of Brandeis University in 1954, where he taught in the History of Ideas program until 1965. His students there included a number of subsequent stars of the New Left, including the Yippie leader Abbie Hoffman and the Communist activist Angela Davis. After his retirement from Brandeis in 1965, he moved to the University of California at San Diego. In the years from 1964, when he published *One-Dimensional Man*, through 1969, when he published *An Essay on Liberation*, Marcuse was at the height of his international fame, which tracked the rise and fall of the New Left. By the time of his death in 1979, Marcuse's star had faded: paperback copies of his works filled the shelves of used-book stores, supply having overcome demand.

Redefining Oppression as Repression

Even as World War II was ending, Marcuse's mind was turning back to the question that had exercised Lukács as well as Marcuse's colleagues from the Institute for Social Research. In 1946, he informed Horkheimer that he was at work on a new book "centered on the problem of the 'revolution that never happened.' "[45] An unpublished document written a year later contains the seeds of the analysis, which would be fully expressed in *One-Dimensional Man*.[46] Already in 1947 Marcuse was struck by the fact that "the majority of the proletariat" of the western world was not revolutionary because it had been integrated into the political and economic system, just as it had been in the Third Reich; Marcuse even used the Nazi term *gleichschalten* to describe what was happening to the working class in the democratic, capitalist nations.[47] Among the reasons he offered for their seeming satisfaction was the share of the workers in the increasing productivity visible under contemporary capitalism.[48] In order to help bring about "the revolution that never happened," Marcuse therefore needed to explain to those increasingly satisfied with the system why they should be more dissatisfied. That was the purpose of Marcuse's book *Eros and Civilization*, published in 1955.

Subtitled "A Philosophical Inquiry into Freud," *Eros and Civilization* is a peculiar work. At a time when Marxism was suspect in the United States because of its linkage with Communism, Marcuse contrived to write a successor to *History and Class Consciousness* that did not mention Marx. Instead he recast the radical critique of capitalism into the psychoanalytic language favored by American cultural elites of the 1950s. Many American intellectuals, alienated from religion and disappointed by Marxism, then looked to Freud for answers to their personal dilemmas. As Philip Rieff (who was briefly Marcuse's colleague at Brandeis) put it in the most penetrating book on Freud and his cultural significance published during the decade, "The reform of institutions by which the liberal and radical mind hoped to achieve a true and lasting transformation of human society did not appear to bear up under the test of events. Of all the positions to which liberalism has retreated in the face of recalcitrant events, psycho-analysis is not only the most influential but also the most easily learned."[49] At the highest reaches of American academic life, political and cultural conflicts were played out in interpretations of Freud. Erich Fromm offered a socialist humanist Freud,[50] Lionel Trilling a disabused liberal Freud,[51] and Rieff a more conservative Freud.

Marcuse was quite uninterested in the empirical validity of Freud's thought or in psychoanalysis as technique. Rather he latched on to a few key Freudian ideas that had much older roots and used them to reformulate a radical critique of contemporary capitalism. Freud had democratized the Romantic idea of genius, of the creative individual with powerful inner urges demanding creative expression.[52] For Freud, these hidden urges could be found in all men. Marcuse, in turn, concluded that all men could experience that thrill of expressive creativity that the Romantics had regarded as the province of a select few. The grand theme of Marcuse's book was that contemporary capitalist society was unnecessarily "repressive." He used the term in a broad, nontechnical sense to designate "both conscious and unconscious, external and internal processes of restraint, constraint, and suppression."[53] He returned to the Schillerian theme of the suppression of human creativity by the capitalist division of labor, now restated in a Freudian vocabulary as the suppression of erotic possibilities.

For Freud, sexual drives were fundamental to human psychology. Much of his theory was concerned with their expression, direction, channeling, and repression. Freud maintained that civilization is founded on the "sublimation" of the sexual drive (libido), its redirection to other purposes. For Freud, as for Burke, civilization is founded on restraint and on the redirection of the passions. To the infant, Freud theorized, the entire body is a source of immediate pleasure. Much of the process of maturation is learning to delay and restrain immediate pleasure for the sake of more certain, enduring, and long-term satisfactions.[54]

Just as Marx insisted that bourgeois economists had reified the historical patterns created by the capitalist market into permanent laws, so, Marcuse argued, Freud had taken the historically created need for the repression and restraint of pleasure and made it seem eternal and unchangeable. Marcuse asserted that although some degree of instinctual repression was necessary for the perpetuation of the species and the preservation of civilization, under capitalism there was more repression of pleasure than was actually necessary. That excess of actual repression over necessary repression he dubbed "surplus repression," playing on the Marxist term "surplus value." Marcuse resurrected Marx's arguments that, in a capitalist society (what Marcuse called "an acquisitive and antagonistic society"), production "becomes the more alien the more specialized the division of labor becomes."[55] "For the duration of work, which occupies practically the entire existence of the mature individual, pleasure is 'suspended' and pain prevails."[56] But the potential for a more pleasurable existence was gestating in the womb of capitalism, and Marcuse hoped to be its midwife.

For Marcuse, the future predicted by Keynes was now at hand. The current level of technology, Marcuse asserted, made it possible to move beyond the conditions of scarcity that had made alienating toil so dominant a feature of existence. It was now possible for people to meet all their basic needs while doing very little unpleasant labor. Thanks to the rationalization and mechanization of work, there was less need for instinctual energy to be channeled into alienated labor, thus freeing such energy for "the attainment of objectives set by the free play of individual faculties."[57] If only men saw the light, they would realize that it was possible to live a more pleasurable life, in which work itself would be more creative and hence more fulfilling. Instead of their sexual energy being narrowly focused on "genital sexuality"—on heterosexual intercourse within the context of monogamy—their entire bodies would once again become objects of pleasure.[58]

At first blush, Marcuse's analysis and terminology sounded like an argument for better and more varied orgasms. (And this is the way he was read by some sixties radicals, especially in Germany, where his work was conflated with that of the Freudian-Marxist sex radical Wilhelm Reich.) But that was not what he had in mind. He advocated not a society of "sex maniacs," but one that would "*minimize* the manifestations of *mere* sexuality by integrating [erotic drives] into a far larger order, including the order of work."[59] The sexual drives would still be sublimated, Marcuse asserted, but not repressed, and the result of that sublimation would be "Eros," understood as pleasurable, creative activity. The division of labor would somehow be overcome through an "exchangeability of functions."[60] In place of work as toil, Marcuse evoked a future where "work is play." Instead of labor oriented to capitalist productivity, men and women would engage in more "contemplation."[61] Existence would bring more pleasure because work would allow for more creativity and more opportunity to pursue a variety of facets of the self. Marcuse repeated Schiller's lament that under contemporary conditions

> enjoyment is separated from labor, the means from the end, exertion from recompense. Everlastingly chained to a single little fragment of the Whole, man himself develops into nothing but a fragment; everlastingly in his ear the monotonous sound of the wheel that he turns, he never develops the harmony of his being, and instead of putting the stamp of humanity upon his own nature, he becomes nothing more than the imprint of his occupation, of his specialized knowledge.[62]

But now, Marcuse asserted, that fragmented, alienated condition could finally be relegated to the past. He invoked the cultural ideal that lay at the cradle of Marxism: the dilettante ideal of the multifaceted creative personality. Not more orgasms, but more *Bildung* (cultivation) was Marcuse's ideal, in which "the spiritual sphere becomes the 'direct' object of Eros and remains a libidinal object."[63] Under capitalism, erotic energy was forced into the narrow constraints of genital sexuality in order to leave the rest of the body available for unpleasurable toil.[64] In the socialist future Marcuse sought to evoke, erotic energy would extend beyond the monogamous family, helping to create real "community."[65]

Eros and Civilization, then, set out a new basis from which to criticize capitalism. Capitalism should be superseded not because it failed to "provide the goods" but because it provided them in a way that closed off the possibilities of a culturally richer form of existence that was already on the horizon. Marcuse's book gave men and women new reasons to revolt against the successful capitalist order of the "Golden Age" by calling into question its criteria of success.

Domination Through Sex and Affluence

But why were so few people radically dissatisfied with their lives under capitalism? Why did they remain oblivious to the new and better possibilities on the horizon beyond the bounds of the capitalist economy? Because, Marcuse answered, the minds of the masses were controlled by the forces of capitalist production through the mass media, which kept people "entertained" while excluding all truly subversive ideas.[66] More perniciously, their consciousness was controlled to make them focus on the choices between consumer goods, between innumerable gadgets, which, according to Marcuse, were all of the same sort. Minds so occupied were diverted from the real issue: the awareness that men could both work less and determine their own needs and satisfactions.[67] For Marcuse as for Lukács, it was not the empirical, known wishes and consciousness of men and women that was deemed decisive, but what they *ought* to be wishing and thinking. The fact that men and women *feel* happy is the worst symptom of the problem, for "happiness is not in the mere feeling of satisfaction but in the reality of freedom and satisfaction."[68] And since their work was not satisfying and their purposes were imposed upon them by the forces of the market, they could not be truly happy or satisfied—even if they *felt* happy and satisfied.

It was this line of analysis that Marcuse was to develop in his most famous and influential work, *One-Dimensional Man,* the book that set out to explain why the revolution that failed to happen in 1918 had still not occurred almost a century after Marx wrote *Capital.* It had not happened, Marcuse contended, because the affluent, capitalist welfare-state, liberal democracies were totalitarian, and their populations enslaved. But this was a totalitarianism without terror, and the slaves were so happy they were oblivious to their bondage. His purpose was to trace "a pattern of *one-dimensional thought and behavior,* in which ideas, aspirations, and objectives that, by their content, transcend the established universe of discourse and action are either repelled or reduced to terms of this universe."[69]

In characterizations such as "totalitarian" and "slavery," Marcuse was consciously engaged in rhetorically reversing the political connotation of key terms. "Totalitarian" was the designation commonly

used to describe Nazi Germany and the Soviet Union. Marcuse deliberately used the word to describe the societies of the United States and
western Europe in order to shock his readers, much as Burke had
shocked his enlightened readers by his defense of "prejudice." But like
Burke's defense of prejudice, this was no mere wordplay. Marcuse
really believed that the western democracies resembled Nazi Germany
in significant ways. In both cases, he thought, most people were
enslaved, in the sense that their lives were guided by subjectively felt
needs that were not really their own and that did not serve their real
interests. In Nazi Germany, those needs were inculcated by a panoply
of organizations from the Hitler Youth and the Nazi Women's League
to the Nazi Labor Front and the Ministry of Propaganda. Contemporary western society had none of these, but according to Marcuse it too
should be considered totalitarian "to the extent to which [the productive apparatus] determines not only the socially needed occupations,
skills, and attitudes, but also individual needs and aspirations."[70]
Because the felt needs of individuals sprang not from themselves but
from these external "vested interests," individuals were not truly free.
Just as effectively as in Nazi Germany, but with greater subtlety,
people were manipulated and indoctrinated, but to a way of life that
revolved around the production and consumption of commodities.[71]

Marcuse's purpose was to awaken the populace from the anestheti-
zation of consciousness by the forces of commerce. Contemporary capitalist society, he contended, "is repressive precisely to the degree to
which it promotes the satisfaction of needs which require continuing
the rat race of catching up with one's peers and . . . enjoying freedom
from using the brain." Marcuse returned time and time again with
unconcealed disgust to the intellectually stultifying nature of mass
culture under capitalism, describing it as a process of "stupification"
and "moronization."[72]

The function of what Marcuse called "critical theory" was to
judge—and condemn—existing society in light of what he took to be
its inherent but unused possibilities. If capitalism was in danger of
winning its competition with socialism by providing material comfort,
the task of the Marxist critic was to move the goalposts.[73] Thanks to
modern technology, the prospect existed of what Marcuse called "the
pacification of the struggle for existence," a way of life with less anxiety and less fear, in which society would provide for the ill, the infirm,
and the aged. Such a society would allow for "non-repressive sublimation," for the multifaceted human development he had described in
Eros and Civilization.[74] For Marcuse, as for Hans Freyer, the problem
was to divorce technology from capitalism.

A society of "non-repressive sublimation" required an alternative conception of needs, different from the wants that perpetuated the regime of competition and private property, of toil and surplus repression. Just as the distinction between false consciousness and true consciousness had been central to *History and Class Consciousness*, the distinction between false needs and true needs was the key to *One-Dimensional Man*. False needs were those that most men and women actually felt—because they had been brainwashed by capitalist institutions. True needs were the needs that men and women ought to feel and would feel if they heeded Marcuse's message of the better, happier, less repressed, and more cultured life that awaited them beyond the threshold of capitalism. In a regime of true needs, Marcuse explained, "economic freedom would mean freedom *from* the economy—from being controlled by economic forces and relationships; freedom from the daily struggle for existence, from earning a living . . ."[75] False needs, by contrast, were "those which are superimposed upon the individual by particular social interests in his repression: the needs which perpetuate toil, aggressiveness, misery, and injustice." The working class, like almost everyone else in contemporary capitalist society, was pacified by the "manipulation of needs by vested interests." Capitalist advertising (here Marcuse borrowed from a work by the investigative journalist Vance Packard, *The Hidden Persuaders*) not only inculcates new wants for new products, it creates an illusion of choice. The options were various "brands and gadgets." Echoing Hegel, he reminded his readers that "free choice among a wide variety of good and services does not signify freedom" if these come at the expense of toil and fear, that is "if they sustain alienation."[76]

In the eighteenth century, Rousseau asserted that civilization inflames passions without being able to fulfill them, leading to a sense of frustration. Hegel had reformulated this in his notion of "bad infinity," the empty feeling that results when consumer goods are chosen merely on the basis of the newly induced wants created by the market, rather than because they fit into a rational life plan. Lukács had picked up the theme, suggesting that capitalism creates ways of life that leave the individual unhappy, but prevents him from imagining an alternative. The novelty of Marcuse's analysis lay in his insistence that contemporary capitalism was pernicious because it *created* new needs and then *fulfilled* them, leaving individuals feeling happy and satisfied. The individual becomes a slave to his passions, but passions that are molded and directed by others who seek to profit from creating the needs for new commodities and inculcating them through the mass media, through advertising, and through the means of entertainment.[77]

One of the most effective ways in which men and women were kept happy and submissive, Marcuse thought, was through what he called "repressive desublimation." Unlike most societies of the past, contemporary capitalism did not demand asceticism. On the contrary, sexual freedom had become a market value. Sex was integrated into the workplace, into public relations, and of course into advertising. For Marcuse, this open recourse to direct sexual stimuli and sexual activity was part of the problem. The permissiveness of modern society had itself become a tool of mass control. It was gratifying. It was fun. It thus made men and women docile, distracting them from the possibilities of a richer life. The direct release of sexual energy offered immediate gratification without providing the deeper satisfactions of creative work and community, which the real development of Eros would bring. The direct expression of sexual energy removed the necessity for the redirection of sexual drives to other purposes, with great costs to man as a cultured being. "Sublimation demands a high degree of autonomy and comprehension," Marcuse noted. The desublimation characteristic of a sexualized capitalist society made self-direction and comprehension seem unnecessary, thus producing self-satisfied conformity.[78] The result, Marcuse concluded, was that sexuality reinforced the hold of the existing order.

From a Marxist point of view, Marcuse's most heretical proposition was that the working class had ceased to be a force capable of revolutionizing capitalist society. For by raising the standard of living of the great mass of the working population, by promising more and then delivering it, the capitalist system had defused revolutionary sentiment within the working class.[79] This "containment" of revolutionary possibilities, Marcuse emphasized, was due to a great extent to "the sheer *quantity* of goods, services, work, and recreation" available.[80] The development of the welfare state had also drawn the sting from the threat of revolution.[81] But the welfare state and its material benefits, Marcuse stressed, were only possible because of the *warfare* state: it was massive defense spending, he claimed, that stimulated the economy, providing high levels of employment and sustaining the standard of living. Marcuse contended that the image of the "enemy" in the Cold War—the Soviet Union and international Communism—was manufactured by capitalist interests. Indeed one of his most influential claims was that "the system" keeps men subjugated not only by creating false needs that it then satisfies, but also by creating false enemies abroad, which it uses to mobilize the population to support the system. The anti-Communism of the Cold War was interpreted by Marcuse as a social psychological mechanism for deflecting the attention of the population of the west from the possibility of liberation within their own society. (Earlier, however, Marcuse had offered another, more discouraging analysis of the effect of the Soviet experiment: "The fact that the first successful socialist revolution has not yet led to a freer and happier society has contributed immeasurably to reconciliation with capitalism and has objectively discredited the revolution. These developments have allowed the existing society to appear in a new light, and the existing society has understood how to use this to its advantage."[82] He repeated this line of analysis in abbreviated form in *One-Dimensional Man*, noting that "the tangible benefits of the system are considered worth defending—especially in view of the repelling force of present day communism which appears to be the historical alternative."[83])

The fundamental Marxist premise of a distinct working class at odds with a distinct capitalist class had become ever less plausible, Marcuse showed. Thanks to changes in the technology of production, physically harsh and brutal labor was gradually disappearing, thus disguising the enslavement of the human being to the machine.[84] Because of changes in the organization of production, the division between manual and nonmanual labor and between "workers" and "management" had become less distinct, so that all were increasingly part of administrative hierarchies, without clear dichotomies.[85] The old antagonistic relationship between labor and management was giving way to greater cooperation; in any case, the power of organized labor was weakened by "the declining portion of human labor power in the productive process."[86]

Marcuse then set out to explain why the more educated were also so disinclined to revolt against capitalism. Large stretches of *One-Dimensional Man* were devoted to updating the critique of ideology begun by Marx and continued by Lukács.

While high culture, like sexuality, had once provided an alternative to the market, it too had lost its ability to cultivate dissatisfaction with the capitalist status quo. Culture, like sexuality, had become more widely dispensed by the market, but in a manner that removed its critical sting. "Great bourgeois art" had once pointed to possibilities of beauty and happiness that transcended the realities of capitalist existence, and in doing so had intensified the longing to go beyond capitalism.[87] Much of high culture had "expressed a conscious, methodical alienation from the entire sphere of business and industry, and from its calculable and profitable order."[88] With the spread of higher education and new technologies such as records and paperback books, high culture was more widely disseminated than ever before. But the results,

Marcuse observed, were quite different from what Arnold had anticipated, for once high culture ceased to be the preserve of a minority,
it ceased to be a subversive force. As the works of the great thinkers
and artists of the past became objects of mass culture, the conflicts
between those works and the present status quo were flattened out and
lost. Through mass reproduction and consumption, great art was
absorbed into the culture of capitalism.[89] Indeed, Marcuse argued, the
very cultural pluralism of contemporary capitalism made ideas less
subversive: "Where the most contradictory works and truths peacefully co-exist," the result is harmony and "indifference."[90] That indifference is what Voltaire had aimed at two centuries earlier. Simmel
had registered its spread at the turn of the century. Now Marcuse
lamented it as a barrier to the buildup of discontent that might transcend capitalism itself.

Intellectuals from Arnold to Simmel and Weber had traced the
increasing dominance of means over ends in capitalist culture, and so
had Keynes. Marcuse's teacher, Martin Heidegger, had pursued this
line of analysis further in *Being and Time* (1927), claiming that the
technological attitude toward the world characteristic of modern man
had eclipsed the very awareness that there might be more to life. In
One-Dimensional Man Marcuse restated this lament in Marxist
terms. Technical reason, he claimed, had become the only form of
rationality admitted as valid. But it was purely instrumental reason,
dealing with the relation between means and ends. It could not call the
ends themselves into doubt. While instrumental reason portrayed
itself as neutral in respect of values, Marcuse wrote, the fact that it was
the only type of reasoning deemed legitimate kept the dominant values
of society from being called into question.[91]

Like *Capital* and *History and Class Consciousness, One-Dimensional Man* was about the inadequacies of capitalism, not about the
organizational mechanisms of the system that would replace it. Like
Marx and Lukács, Marcuse took it for granted that centralized control
over the economy would replace the market. "If the productive apparatus could be organized and directed toward the satisfaction of the vital
needs, its control might well be centralized; such control would not
prevent individual autonomy, but render it possible," Marcuse blithely
assured his readers.[92] He was fundamentally uninterested in economics, and wrote as if Weber or Hayek had never undermined these
assumptions, or as if the experience of the Soviet economy had never
called them into question. On the contrary, Marcuse assumed that
Soviet industrialization had proceeded "without waste and obsolescence, without the restrictions on productivity imposed by the inter-

ests of private profit."[93] But Marcuse hedged his bets about the purported productive superiority of socialism over capitalism by questioning the very desirability of greater productivity. Characterizing the capitalist societies of the west as "overdeveloped," he assured his readers that the future society he envisioned could function at a lower material standard of living, because men and women would no longer have their wants artificially raised by capitalist forces beyond their control.[94] He also envisioned a "reduction in the future population," which would alleviate the cramped conditions of the present. Population growth, he suggested, was irrational in terms of human happiness, but it was kept going by the needs of business for more customers and soldiers.[95]

One-Dimensional Man painted a pessimistic picture of a society so self-satisfied, a populace so steeped in controlled wants, and a culture so bereft of effective intellectual opposition that transformative change was impossible. Though the book's vision of an unrepressed future was attractive—if implausible—its vision of the present seemed unremittingly negative. "The critical theory of society possesses no concepts which could bridge the gap between the present and its future," he concluded, "holding no promise and showing no success, it remains negative."[96] But in its final pages, the book did hold out a thin ray of hope. Marcuse looked above all to those "who comprehend the given necessity as insufferable pain, and as unnecessary."[97] As with Lukács some forty years earlier, Marcuse in 1964 thought that socialist revolution depended on the spread of the *consciousness* of other possibilities among the intellectuals. He also looked to those *outside* the capitalist system of production and consumption, to "the substratum of the outcasts and outsiders, the exploited and persecuted of other races and other colors, the unemployed and the unemployable."[98] His hope seemed to lie in a coalition between radicalized intellectuals and those whom Marx had called the *Lumpenproletariat* (ragged proletariat), those beneath the working class. Precisely because they were marginalized by contemporary capitalism, they might still be capable of revolting against it.

When Marcuse published *One-Dimensional Man*, he had no good reason to believe that it would be more widely received than *Eros and Civilization*, which had made many of the same points a decade earlier. But the book became a veritable bible of the New Left in Germany, France, and the United States, and Marcuse became an icon. Like many icons, he was the object of genuflection more often than real contemplation. He was cited along with Marx and Mao by student rebels in Paris in 1968. He was fêted in Berlin and Frankfurt, and from Berkeley,

California, to Cambridge, Massachusetts. The leading intellectual lights of the German New Left produced a book of essays engaging with his thought, as did some of their less illustrious American counterparts.[99]

Marcuse responded by identifying the student New Left as one of the forces (together with the blacks of the ghettos and peasant communist movements such as the Viet Cong) that might indeed lead beyond capitalism. In his *Essay on Liberation,* he praised the young middle-class intelligentsia as bearers of a new consciousness and a "new sensibility" that combined Marxism with elements of surrealism to produce "total nonconformity."[100] He urged them to engage in "radical enlightenment" by developing the consciousness of the exploited and by incorporating "the critical analysis of contemporary societies" into the university curriculum.[101]

However unlikely, the notion that university students and the recently college educated might spearhead an anticapitalist revolt seemed more plausible in the late 1960s than ever before—or since. That was partly because of demography: the cohort that reached the age of university study in the mid to late 1960s was much larger than the cohort that had preceded it. In most western societies, fertility had begun to fall in the late nineteenth century and continued to do so throughout the twentieth century, declining especially sharply in the 1930s and early 1940s as a response to depression and war. The great exception was in the decade after the Second World War, when childbearing increased—especially in the United States, but in western Europe as well—in response to pent-up demand and to the prospects of the expanding economy. That huge bulge of a generation reached late adolescence in the mid-1960s, creating an unprecedented market for cultural products oriented to "youth" and increasing its generational consciousness. Even more important was the fact that an ever-higher portion of this oversized age cohort was going to college, thanks to the commitment of western governments to the expansion of higher education. For the first time there were so many students that they could be conceived as a mass social group.

Most students were not radicals, but it was the student radicals of the New Left who set the tone and increasingly the terms of debate of the era. Having come of age in the prosperity of the postwar era, they tended to take affluence for granted and to be more aware of the spiritual limits of affluence. In the United States, the war in Vietnam and the possibility of being drafted to fight there acted as an immediate and pressing stimulus for university students (males at least) to question the wisdom of their government. The widely shared perception among Europeans that the United States was fighting the war in Vietnam with technologically sophisticated brutality led to the questioning of both American motives and American technology, while the technologically primitive brutality of the Viet Cong and other communist movements in southeast Asia was often ignored or romanticized.

In his speeches to German students, Marcuse linked antifascism to anti-Americanism, suggesting that America, with its terroristic war in Vietnam, was the contemporary analogue of Nazism: both were cases in which monopoly capitalism had led to imperialistic violence.[102] It is instructive to compare Marcuse's views with those of his former colleague in the Institute for Social Research, Max Horkheimer. After the war, he had returned to West Germany and reestablished the institute, now shorn of its Marxism. Horkheimer remained committed to the critique of capitalist civilization, but also believed that the democratic capitalist welfare states of the west were infinitely superior to the totalitarian Communist societies of the eastern bloc. He became a great defender of the United States as the guarantor of West Germany's freedom in the face of the Communist threat. Now he was appalled to find his erstwhile collaborator, Marcuse, marching alongside radical student champions of the Viet Cong.[103] Writing to their mutual friend Friedrich Pollock, he complained that on the West German left, anti-Americanism "has largely taken on the function of antisemitism," an excuse for aggressive and mindless scapegoating.[104]

Marcuse's Legacy

The decline of Marcuse's reputation was as rapid as its rise. His fame paralleled the trajectory of the New Left: launched in 1964, reaching its zenith in 1968, and all but exhausted by 1973. The American withdrawal from Vietnam and the end of the draft in the United States took the wind out of the sails of student protest. When, after the fall of Saigon and its renaming as Ho Chi Minh City, hundreds of thousands of Vietnamese took to the sea in boats to escape their Communist conquerors, some opponents of the war came to have second thoughts about their glorification of the Viet Cong. At least as significantly, the wave of economic growth that had swollen in the postwar decades had begun to ebb, followed by an era of seemingly contracting possibilities. Earning a living became more of a challenge, overshadowing the discontents of consumption and uncreative labor.

Yet Marcuse's legacy outlived the 1960s, and his critique was incorporated into advanced capitalist societies in disparate and diffuse forms. As perhaps the most prominent intellectual associated with the New Left, Marcuse served as a role model for younger intellectuals, who, as they moved up the academic hierarchy, institutionalized his conception of the intellectual within the universities. Scholarship, in this understanding, was not about objectivity, still less about the belief that "the primary task of a useful teacher is to teach his students to recognize 'inconvenient' facts—that means facts that are inconvenient for their party opinions." Instead, many scholars in the humanities and social sciences came to believe "that all choices are political choices, that every intellectual interest serves some social end." "Disinterestedness," regarded as a virtue in the Arnoldian conception of the intellectual, was now treated as a mirage. "Scholars who believed that scholarship itself is an all-important vehicle for social reform became, starting in the mid-1970s, the most visible body of opinion within universities. . . ."[105] The model of the professor as critical intellectual, liberating his or her audience from one or another variety of false consciousness, became institutionalized in some academic disciplines, above all literary studies and sociology.[106] Three decades after the zenith of the New Left and the publication of Marcuse's *Essay on Liberation*, for example, the annual convention of the American Sociological Association was devoted to the theme of "Oppression, Domination, and Liberation"; it focused on racism as well as "other manifestations of social inequality such as class exploitation and oppression on the basis of gender, ethnicity, national origin, sexual preference, disability and age."[107] In some parts of the academic market, "critical theory" premised upon a vague but fundamental antipathy toward capitalism became a marketable commodity; a specialization in "critical theory" became a desideratum for academic posts in literature, sociology, and the burgeoning field of "cultural studies."

Nor was it in the academy alone that Marcuse's sensibility was integrated into advanced capitalist society. While Marcuse and the New Leftists who echoed him repeated the traditional socialist charge that capitalism created inequality, the core of their complaint was that capitalism compartmentalized the self, constrained it within rigid corporate hierarchies, and above all separated work from creativity, labor from play. While "critical theory" became a commodity on the academic market, its critique of work under capitalism was being incorporated into the education and culture of the business class. By the 1990s there was a stream of books for managers, counseling them "to abandon hierarchical and authoritarian traditions and facilitate (not manage) self-organizing work groups whose principal imperative is not work, but a form of creative play called the learning organization."[108] Much of this, to be sure, was merely the latest ripple of fashion in an ongoing sea of scientific management, using the latest psychological theory to try to improve work performance and ultimately the bottom line. But the values of self-expression and creativity in work had penetrated deeply not only to the managerial technicians, but to the owners of the means of production.

For the new, more meritocratic, more highly educated upper class that came of age in the decades after the publication of *One-Dimensional Man*, achievement was increasingly combined with creativity in work and multisided development. Greater status accrued to those whose mode of work expressed their creativity, especially in the growing sectors of information and entertainment.[109] Schumpeter had emphasized that the motivation of the entrepreneur was less that of hedonism than "the joy of creating, of getting things done, or simply of exercising one's energy and ingenuity."[110] Now those romantic and Nietzschean values were increasingly diffused beyond the narrow circle of the entrepreneurial elite, transforming capitalism even as they were co-opted by what Marcuse and his devotees would have called "the system."

But if Marcuse served to articulate the vague discontents that were increasingly felt by those who had prospered economically under welfare-state capitalist democracy, his work, unlike Keynes', was less than useless in providing tangible institutional solutions. For Marcuse was fundamentally uninterested in institutions, whether economic or political. Indeed, as one of his severest contemporary critics, Alasdair MacIntyre, pointed out, Marcuse's critique treated experience as nothing but a constraint on the imagination of future possibilities, thereby ignoring the fact that past experience had demonstrated that "certain combinations of states of affairs are possible and others are not."[111] *One-Dimensional Man* seemed to proceed on the assumption that the economic organization of the society Marcuse envisioned, one of self-expressive work without an extensive division of labor, would be based on a centralized "planning for the whole," and that this could easily be achieved using existing "technological rationality."[112] Despite Marcuse's assurance that such an economy would allow for "meaningful self-determination," the problem of who would do such planning and how they would reconcile different individual conceptions of the good simply never occurred to him. Nor, even when pressed by sympathetic interlocutors, did he have anything significant to say about the most basic question of political organization, namely how political institutions should deal with real differences of interests or values.[113] Marcuse proceeded as if these fundamental issues of modern political and economic life could simply be ignored. His contemporary, Friedrich Hayek, by contrast, put the issues of coordinating and reconciling the conflicting desires of individuals and groups at the center of his vision of the market, a vision that was to prove increasingly attractive in the final decades of the twentieth century.

CHAPTER THIRTEEN

FRIEDRICH HAYEK:
UNTIMELY LIBERAL

Friedrich August von Hayek was a year younger than Marcuse. He was born in 1899, in Vienna, when it was still the capital of the Austro-Hungarian Empire, and came of age intellectually in the highly antiliberal culture of Vienna of the 1920s and in the shadow of Communism and fascism. Though Hayek wrote his most systematic and comprehensive book, *The Constitution of Liberty*, while living in the United States and dedicated it "To the unknown civilization that is growing in America," his work grew out of his experiences in Europe.[1] "My mind," he noted, "has been shaped by a youth spent in my native Austria and by two decades of middle life in Great Britain. . . ."[2] He published his most seminal works from the mid-1930s to the 1970s, an era in which it was widely assumed that the expansion of the role of the state and of state expenditure was both desirable and inevitable. Just as Marcuse, after decades of laboring in the obscure corners of academe, found himself a mentor to the New Left of the 1960s, so Hayek emerged from intellectual marginality to become, along with his American comrade-in-arms, Milton Friedman, the most important influence on the neoliberalism that reappeared on the intellectual and political scene from the 1970s through the 1990s.

Hayek's was a conservative brand of liberalism, focused on individual liberty and the restriction of government, not, as with Keynes or most American liberals, on increasing equality. He first came to the attention of a broader public with the publication of *The Road to Serfdom* in 1944. Hayek defended a culture of individual achievement against an enemy he called "collectivism," which came in both left- and right-wing versions. On the left it took the form of social democracy, socialism, or, most radically, Communism; on the right it took the form of ethnic or nationalist particularism and, most radically, fascism and Nazism. In the eighteenth century, Adam Smith laid out a vision of international free trade as a deliberate alternative to the national chauvinism of his day. Hayek, too, would link the market to overcoming particularism and group self-interest, whether of the left or of the right. His work was an unremitting attack on attempts to use government power to protect some particular identity, whether based on race, class, religion, or ethnicity.

The Making of a Liberal

Hayek drew two enduring lessons from his Viennese milieu: that a modern liberal society must be bound together primarily by factors other than shared cultural commitments,[3] and that democracy could pose a threat to a liberal political order.

Young Hayek's interest in social science was kindled by his experience in the army of the Habsburg empire during the First World War, when he saw the empire destroyed by nationalism, which put the interests of ethnic particularity above those of the multiethnic state.[4] After his demobilization, Hayek studied law, psychology, and economics at the University of Vienna before focusing—provisionally, as it turned out—on economics. The teacher who influenced him most deeply at the university was Friedrich Freiherr von Wieser. Wieser, who had served as minister of commerce during the war, was a man of broad social scientific interests. A pioneer of marginal utility theory, Wieser maintained that economic commodities had no intrinsic, objective value. They acquired their value only through the market process, through the relationship of supply to the shifting demand created by the preferences of individual consumers. From 1921 to 1923, and then again after returning from a study visit to America in 1924, Hayek was employed by Ludwig von Mises. A contemporary of Schumpeter, and of Jewish origin, Mises was an economist who was developing a reputation for his incisive critiques of socialism and for his innovative analyses of market processes.

By his own testimony, Hayek learned more from Mises than from any other man.[5] But there was a tension, both intellectual and political, between Wieser, his first teacher, and Mises, his second. Mises represented an uncompromising and market-oriented liberalism, Wieser something quite different. Hayek's liberalism was a conscious choice, and an untimely one in interwar Vienna. It was by no means a self-evident consequence of Wieser's influence. For Wieser was in many respects illiberal. By the time Hayek came to study with him, Wieser was given not only to antisemitic sentiments but also to near-paranoid pronouncements about the domination of finance capitalists who had pushed the United States into the First World War against Austria.[6] Mises had come to despise him.[7] To appreciate the significance of Hayek's embrace of Mises' individualist, market-oriented liberalism, we must look at the politics and society of interwar Vienna.

Viennese Liberalism, the Jews, and the Defense of Creative Minorities

Hayek's liberalism was not a typical product of Vienna: like much of what has come to be considered "Viennese culture," it was produced *against* its Viennese environment.[8] Hayek was not Jewish, and he wrote relatively little about the Jews. But his liberalism was influenced by his close contacts with Jews in Vienna, at a time when many others of his class, including members of his own family and his leading academic teacher, favored attempts to exclude those of Jewish origin from economic, cultural, and political life. For Hayek, Jews were paradigmatic of the type of person whose talents led to economic progress, but whose success was resented by the mass of the population.

Hayek's origins were in the educated civil service class of the Austro-Hungarian Empire. His family was made up of academics and civil servants who had been ennobled by the monarch for their services. They were well placed. His maternal grandfather, Franz von Juraschek, was a professor of law and statistics who taught Schumpeter. His parents, while nominally Catholic, shared in the secularized, scientific-minded culture of the turn of the century.[9]

The Austrian liberals of the late Habsburg era sought to administer and maintain the coherence of an empire riven by divisions of nationality, class, and religion. They stood for a political order characterized by the rule of law, the protection of property, market exchange, and promotion by merit and achievement rather than by origin. The short-lived political dominance of the liberals was a product of the restricted franchise, which limited the vote to owners of substantial property. The influence of the liberals was eroded as the franchise was widened, culminating in the extension of the vote to all adult males in 1907. The electoral winners in the spread of democracy were in the first instance the antiliberal Christian Social Party, and later the antiliberal Social Democrats. In the last decade of the empire, with politics fragmented by ethnic and class rivalries, the government ended up ruling through imperial emergency decrees and negotiating parliamentary deals behind closed doors. The achievements of liberal constitutionalism were thus preserved not by democracy, but in spite of it.[10] The spread of democracy increased the influence of groups that sought to destroy the liberal political order in the name of class, religious, or ethnic interests. No wonder the Viennese liberals were suspicious of democracy. Their loyalty was focused on the emperor, who served to unify a culturally diverse empire.[11]

The liberal era in the Habsburg empire began in 1867, with the adoption of a new constitution that included an extensive bill of rights and the elimination of legal barriers based on religion, and ended in 1918. No group had benefited more from the liberal era than the Jews, nor was any group more closely identified with liberalism. We have seen (in chapter 10, on Lukács) that in the Hungarian half of the empire the Jews played a leading role in the modernization of the economy, and the spectacularly successful were elevated into the nobility. Their rise was only slightly less meteoric in the Austrian half of the empire. Previously excluded from the protected guild economy, after 1867 Jews found economic opportunities opened to them by liberal legislation that granted them legal equality with their Christian counterparts. These upwardly mobile Jews championed the bourgeois values of work, order, and achievement, in a city more accustomed to hedonism and *Schlamperei* (slovenly disorder).[12] They embraced the liberal values of education and individual self-development. Once the legal playing field had been leveled, they triumphed, and they came to be heavily overrepresented in the upper bourgeoisie. By the end of the empire, between a quarter and a third of students at the University of Vienna were Jewish.[13] Jews dominated the liberal professions of medicine and law. They owned many of the major Austrian banks as well as the most important newspaper in the country, the *Neue Freie Presse*.[14] By the late nineteenth century, Jewish writers pointed with pride to Jewish achievement in commerce and in the professions, made possible by the enactment of liberal principles of equality before the law regardless of religious or ethnic origin.[15]

Not only was the fate of the Jews tied to the fate of liberalism, the fate of liberalism became intertwined with the fate of the Jews. "The deep irony" of the late Habsburg empire into which Hayek was born, writes Ernst Gellner, one of its most penetrating analysts, was that "an authoritarian Empire, based on a medieval dynasty and tied to the heavily dogmatic ideology of the Counter-Reformation, in the end, under the stimulus of ethnic, chauvinistic centrifugal agitation, found its most eager defenders amongst individualist liberals, recruited in considerable part from an erstwhile pariah group and standing *outside* the faith with which the state was once so deeply identified. . . . But now the logic of the situation led [the house of Habsburg] to be the patron of a pluralistic and tolerant society." In the final decades of the Habsburg empire, one nationality after another turned its back on the empire, including, finally, the Austro-Germans, who adopted a national, indeed *völkisch*, identification as Germans. The last and most faithful supporters of the Habsburg regime turned out to be "the new men: the commercial, industrial, academic, professional merito-crats, interested in maintaining an open market in goods, men, ideas, and a universalistic open society." It was these newly arrived merito-crats, many of them of Jewish origin, who became the cadres of Aus-trian liberalism.[16]

The result was what Gellner has dubbed "pariah liberalism," a liber-alism formulated by cultural outsiders and antipathetic to the very notion of cultural insiderdom and outsiderdom. These liberals favored cultural openness and individualism over closed communities, ethnic or economic. In a culture where their roots were stigmatized, they stood for an abstract and universalistic individualism against the romantic communalism represented by both socialism and national-ism.[17]

The prospects for the postwar Austrian republic were never bright.[18] Vienna, a city of two million, had been the financial and administra-tive center of an empire of fifty million inhabitants. Now it became the capital of a small nation of six million. The industrial heartland that Vienna had served now lay across the border in Czechoslovakia. The policies of economic nationalism adopted by the other successor states of the Habsburg empire—Hungary, Romania, Yugoslavia, and Czecho-slovakia—destroyed the prewar division of labor and damaged the economy of the entire region.[19] Indeed industrial production in inter-war Austria never reached its prewar level.

If liberals had been embattled in the late Habsburg empire, in the new postwar republic they were vanquished, at least as a political force. The political culture of the Austrian Republic was fragmented into three political camps: the Catholic Christian Socials, the Marxist Social Democrats, and the *völkisch* German nationalists. The only common denominator among them was antipathy to liberalism. As a university student, Hayek belonged to the Democratic Party, a short-lived counterpart to the liberal German Democratic Party that Max Weber had helped to found in Germany after the war.[20] Tellingly, the Austrian party never got enough votes to be represented in parliament. The *Grossdeutsche Volkspartei*, the ethnic German nationalist party, had the support of non-Jewish civil servants, members of the free professions, and university students. It was this professional middle class that lost out most heavily in the great inflation of the early 1920s. Fearful of socialism and disoriented by the effects of the inflation that wiped out the inherited income which had ensured their social status, many blamed their fate on the Jews.[21] In the early 1930s, the Austrian Nazis, like their German counterparts, increasingly sucked up their support. In Vienna the Nazis eventually won the backing of the white-collar middle class, the civil servants, and non-Jewish professionals and intellectuals.[22]

What the Christian Socials, the Socialists, and the German nationalists had in common was their antipathy to liberalism in both the political and the economic sense. From different starting points, they all opposed liberal capitalism and the culture of individual rights and differential individual achievements that went with it. The German nationalists did so in the name of preserving the purity and dominance of the German *Volk* from ethnic interlopers. They demanded quotas that would limit the political, educational, and professional opportunities of Jews and Slavs.[23]

The most vehemently anticapitalist force in Austrian politics was the Social Democrats, who after 1918 controlled the municipal government of Vienna. With the Christian Socials dominant beyond Vienna and in the federal parliament, the Social Democrats resolved to use their municipal power to turn Vienna into a socialist island within a larger Christian Social sea. Opposed in principle to capitalism but unable to topple it by democratic means, they set out to move Vienna as far in the direction of socialism as circumstances would allow.

The economic ideology of the Christian Social Party was geared to protecting the livelihood of the peasants, artisans, and shopkeepers who formed the party's social base.[24] In the late nineteenth century, each of these groups had come to resent the forces of capitalist modernization that threatened their income and way of life. By the interwar years, they were strongly attracted to the vision of a postliberal, postcapitalist, postdemocratic society in which production and representation would be organized by "estates" or "corporations"—an attempt to re-create a social order like the one Justus Möser had defended a century and a half earlier. That ideology had been resuscitated at the end of the nineteenth century by Karl von Vogelsang, a noble Prussian convert to Catholicism who became a major ideological influence on the Austrian Christian Socials. The economic pronouncements of the Austrian Catholic bishops were drawn from the same source. In their Advent Pastoral Letter of 1925 they condemned "mammonistic capitalism" as the great evil of modern times and chastised the "financial powers [who are] able to rob the people of the earth, to impoverish them through charging excessive interest rates."[25] Christian Social corporatism called for the use of governmental power to maintain the economic status of the peasants, small shopkeepers, and artisans whose income was threatened by the forces of market competition.

In Vienna, the rhetoric of anticapitalism and antisemitism were often closely intertwined. The three major political groupings vied with one another to link capitalism and the Jews, always invidiously. Even the Social Democrats, who officially condemned antisemitism and had dubbed it "the socialism of fools," resorted to antisemitic imagery in the course of anticapitalist agitation.

The Christian Socials, for their part, drew on the most anti-Jewish traditions within Catholicism. The party had been developed by Karl Lueger on a program that included antisemitism and the protection of the Catholic lower middle class from Jewish competition.[26] In 1919, Ignaz Seipel, who would soon become the leader of the Christian Social Party and then chancellor, asserted that "the Jewish question" was not one of religious toleration. Echoing Sombart, he described it as a class conflict against mobile capital and the trader spirit (Händlergeist) that had come to permeate politics, the press, scholarship, literature, and art.[27]

But not only were the Christian Socials and the German nationalists antisemitic; so, often enough, was the propaganda of the Social Democrats, which was all the more remarkable because so many of their leaders were of Jewish origin. Though officially opposed to antisemitism, the party's newspaper, the Arbeiter Zeitung, portrayed "capitalists," "Schieber" ("profiteers" who sold goods on the black market), and "speculators" as having stereotypically Jewish hooked noses.[28] The message of such Social Democratic propaganda was that the antisemitism of the Christian Socials and German nationalists was mere hypocrisy—and that the Social Democrats were the real opponents of the "Jewish big-capitalists," "Jewish exploiters," and "rich Jews." To the Socialist Democrats these targets were objectionable not because they were Jewish but because they were capitalists. But such images and rhetoric only reinforced the invidious association of capitalism with Jews.[29]

The German nationalists wanted government to use its power to protect people of their ethnic background against competition from Slavs and especially from Jews. They treated "Jewry" as an ethnic designation, not only a religious one. There were similar movements throughout east-central Europe, where the stagnant economies of most of the successor states made the struggle for civil service and professional spoils all the more bitter. Such movements used cultural claims to seek economic protection for professionals and bureaucrats of the dominant ethnic group.[30]

The defenders of liberalism in Austria were few, and often of Jewish descent. That set them apart in the Vienna of the 1920s. Yet it was with these liberals of Jewish origin that Friedrich Hayek identified, despite the fact that he was neither Jewish nor of Jewish background. What did such an identification signify?

An example of the degree to which non-Jewish Austro-Germans of Hayek's class had moved from liberalism to *völkisch* nationalism is provided by Hayek's major professor at the University of Vienna, Friedrich von Wieser. During the empire, Wieser had inclined toward government paternalism and a conception of the state as a *Kulturstaat*, guarding and spreading German culture. His last book, published in 1926, was a conceptually fuzzy and long-winded work entitled *The Law of Power*. (As Schumpeter put it, Wieser lacked "the natural aptitude for turning out an effective argument.")[31] While his late work included some liberal themes—he treated modern history as the slow development toward a world in which force was replaced by milder forms of power—its thrust was increasingly illiberal. It is instructive to read the book's long excursus on "The Jews."

Jews had been prepared by their history for success in the modern world, Wieser wrote. By virtue of their religious heritage and historical experience, Jews had developed a talent for abstract thought, for incisive linguistic expression, and for calculation. As an oppressed minority they had had to learn to get along with people of all classes. They were also industrious. All of these qualities stood them in good stead. The modern capitalist economy and their legal emancipation had allowed the Jews with these cultural characteristics to dominate trade, industry, and the educated professions that gave the tone to public opinion.[32] That had led to what Wieser described as an understandable and healthy reaction among the "Aryans":

The stratum of Jews who have risen to power . . . form an ethnically united stratum of power, and seek to advance in closed ranks, similar to the way in which the Normans at one time inserted themselves into the body of the Saxons, even if the Jews have not been able to take over the entire apparatus of domination. No wonder, then, that the Aryans, for their part, unite in order to triumph in the struggle for power. They have every right to do so as individuals pursuing their personal interests, and are obligated to do so by their national consciousness (*Volksgefühl*) when they are convinced that the Jewish leadership is leading the *Volk* away from its heritage and history.[33]

Hayek identified with the Jewish liberals not because they were Jews but because they were liberals. But this meant that for Hayek the fate of the Jews was closely aligned with the fate of liberalism, and the fate of liberalism was inextricably intertwined with the fate of capitalism.

"The Vienna of the 1920s and 1930s is not intelligible without the Jewish problem," Hayek recalled. As defined by the antisemitic standards increasingly evident in the Viennese middle classes, "Jewishness" was a matter of origin, not of religion or self-affirmation. Converts from Judaism to Christianity and the offspring of mixed marriages were still liable to be viewed as Jewish by Jews and gentiles.[34] College fraternities (*Burschenschaften*) excluded those of Jewish origin, even if they had converted to Christianity. The German Student Association (*Deutsche Studentenschaft*) at the University of Vienna, which dominated campus politics, was nativist, demanding the exclusion of Jews and Slavs from the university, and campaigning for quotas (*numerus clausus*) on the number of Jewish students and faculty. These sympathies were shared by much of the faculty; in 1930, the rector of the university sponsored a law to limit the number of Jews at the university to their proportion of the population.[35] Among the leading lights of the university faculty was Othmar Spann, a professor of economics identified with the radical right, who kept a list of graduate students and faculty members who were to be refused promotion because of their Jewish origin or socialist leanings.[36] Hayek briefly attended Spann's seminar but was expelled for being too critical and thus "confusing" the other participants.[37]

In the race-conscious society of interwar Vienna, there were circles made up purely of Christians, others made up purely of Jews, and "a very large middle group in between the two, partly of baptized Jews, partly of Christians who had made friends with the Jews."[38] Though Hayek stemmed from the "purely Christian" group, he identified himself with the "middle group," and it was from their perspective that he viewed the world. In his memoirs, Hayek stressed that "it is difficult to overestimate how much I owe to the fact that, almost from the beginning of my university career, I became connected with a group of contemporaries who belonged to the best type of the Jewish intelligentsia of Vienna." More cosmopolitan than his own family, and retaining a commitment to liberal values, they were confronted by the obstacle of antisemitic discrimination.[39] When Hayek wrote of Viennese antisemitism those of Jewish origin, he knew of what he spoke. Though he tactfully refrained from mentioning it in his memoirs, his own father was president of the Vienna branch of the Society of German Physicians—where "German" denoted "Aryan."[40] And his younger brother, Heinrich, eventually joined the Nazi Party, in hopes, he claimed after the Second World War, of easing his path to a professorship.[41]

Although he was one of the most accomplished economic minds in Vienna, Hayek's mentor, Ludwig von Mises, was excluded from a university chair, partly because he was Jewish, but also because of his rigidly "classical liberal" views and his demonstrated inability to tolerate those he regarded as fools.[42] Denied a tenured teaching post, Mises instead became secretary of the Vienna Chamber of Commerce, a civil service position, which allowed him to conduct research and serve as an adviser to governments. He hired Hayek as his assistant in 1921, and in 1927, to create a suitable salary for the newly married Hayek, Mises established the private Institute for Business Cycle Research, funded in part by the Rockefeller Foundation, which was eager to encourage empirical social scientific research in Europe.[43] While the university became intellectually stultified, creative discussion went on in a myriad of extra-academic seminars and circles, in which younger intellectuals exchanged ideas and work in progress. The weekly seminar that met in Mises' office at the Chamber of Commerce was the center of advanced economic thought in interwar Vienna. Of the twenty-nine members of that seminar, twenty-three were of Jewish descent.[44]

As *The Vienna That's Not in the Baedeker*, a contemporary guidebook to the city, informed its readers, the question "Is he a Jew?" was ubiquitous in the Vienna of the 1920s; compared to it, all "other questions are of secondary importance." At issue was the explanation of achievement. "I advise you not to be too interesting or remarkable during your stay in Vienna," the guidebook noted; "otherwise people will try to make out that you are a Jew."[45] In Hayek's circles, too, the question of who was of Jewish origin was a subject of constant speculation. Hayek investigated his own family tree, but came up with no Jewish ancestors.[46]

For Hayek, there was a close link between anticapitalism and antisemitism, not least because the Jews embodied precisely those characteristics that were essential to capitalist progress. In his *Road to Serfdom*, he wrote:

> In Germany and Austria the Jew had come to be regarded as the representative of capitalism because a traditional dislike of large classes of the population for commercial pursuits had left these more readily accessible to a group that was practically excluded from the more highly esteemed occupations. It is the old story of the alien race's being admitted only to the less respected trades and then being hated still more for practicing them. The fact that German anti-Semitism and anti-capitalism spring from the same root is of great importance for the understanding of what has happened there, but this is rarely grasped by foreign observers. . . . That in Germany it was the Jew who became the enemy . . . [was the] result of the anticapitalist resentment on which the whole movement was based . . . [much like] the selection of the kulak in Russia.[47]

Without mentioning the Jews explicitly, he discussed their fate in *The Constitution of Liberty*:

> There can be little question that, from the point of view of society, the art of turning one's capacity to good account, the skill of discovering the most effective use of one's gift, is perhaps the most useful of all; but too much resourcefulness of this kind is not uncommonly frowned upon, and an advantage gained over those of equal general capacity by a more successful exploitation of concrete circumstances is regarded as unfair. In many societies an "aristocratic" tradition . . . that has often been developed by people whose privileges have freed them from the necessity of giving others what they want, represents it as nobler to wait until one's gifts are discovered by others, while only religious or ethnic minorities in a hard struggle to rise have deliberately cultivated this kind of resourcefulness (best described by the

German term *Findigkeit*)—and are generally disliked for
that reason. Yet there can be no doubt that the discovery of a
better use of things or of one's own capacities is one of the
greatest contributions that an individual can make in our
society to the welfare of his fellows and that it is by providing the maximum opportunity for this that a free society can
become so much more prosperous than others. The successful use of this entrepreneurial capacity (and, in discovering
the best use of our abilities, we are all entrepreneurs) is the
most highly rewarded activity in a free society, while whoever leaves to others the task of finding some useful means
of employing his capacities must be content with a smaller
reward.[48]

For Adam Smith, every man in a commercial society "becomes in
some measure a merchant," in that he lives by exchanging. For Hayek,
in a capitalist society everybody becomes in some measure an entrepreneur, on the lookout for the more effective use of resources.[49] But
not every group would be equal in its resourcefulness. A central theme
of Hayek's liberalism was the role of the innovative few in bringing
about historical advance. This notion had an impeccable liberal lineage. Indeed it was fundamental to John Stuart Mill's conception of historical progress.[50] As we have seen, by 1909 Schumpeter had developed
a similar theory, with a more Nietzschean vocabulary, to explain the
role of the entrepreneur. Wieser had made the same point in a number
of essays, some of which Hayek edited and published after Wieser's
death in 1926.[51] Mises restated the theme in his 1922 book, *Socialism*,
a work that Hayek described as a turning point in his own intellectual
development. "The great mass of people are incapable of realizing that
in economic life nothing is permanent except change," Mises wrote.
"To see and act in advance, to follow new ways, is always the concern
only of the few, the leaders. . . ."[52]

But the progress created by the resourceful few, while it brought
long-term benefits to society at large, came at the expense of some
established social groups. Hayek regarded fascism and Nazism as the
desperate attempt by social losers in the process of capitalist development to regain through force and ideological special pleading the
rewards denied them in the marketplace. In *The Road to Serfdom*,
Hayek would take issue with the notion, then popular among intellectuals, that National Socialism should be understood primarily as a
form of capitalist defense—precisely Marcuse's interpretation at the
time.[53] Hayek, by contrast, thought that fascism and Nazism repre-

sented a collectivism of the middle classes. Dispossessed by inflation, left outside the process of bargaining between industrial employers and the labor movement, and in decline, the "resentment of the lower middle class" led its members to embrace totalitarianism movements that promised to protect their position.[54] What socialism, fascism, and National Socialism shared, according to Hayek, was the notion that the state "should assign to each person his proper place in society." Fascism and Nazism were so successful "because they offered a theory, or *Weltanschauung,* which seemed to justify the privileges they promised to their supporters."[55] Schumpeter understood socialism as an expression of what Nietzsche called resentment; Hayek thought that the same social psychological process was evident in fascism.

Hayek's identification with political and economic liberalism was a choice of Mises over Wieser.[56] That choice was due in part to his Jewish circle of friends, in part to his observation of the effects of antimarket government policies in Vienna.

Rent Control and the Hazards of State Intervention

Hayek's skepticism of government attempts to control the market was reinforced by his experience of rent control in the 1920s. It was the subject of one of Hayek's most searching examinations during his years in Vienna, and one to which he would return thirty years later, in *The Constitution of Liberty.* Rent restriction, he wrote there, "has probably done more to restrict freedom and prosperity than any other measure, excepting only inflation. . . . [W]hoever has seen the progressive decay of housing conditions and the effects on the general manner of life of the people of Paris, of Vienna, or even of London, will appreciate the deadly effect that this one measure can have on the whole character of an economy—and even of a people."[57]

Rent control was one of the most economically far-reaching and politically contentious issues in interwar Vienna, leading to the brink of civil war. The city's housing problems predated the world war. Like most cities in eras of rapid urbanization, prewar Vienna had a perennial housing crisis. The solution of rent control arose during the First World War, as displaced persons flooded into Vienna from the east. The imperial government sought to prevent landlords from taking advantage of the increased demand for housing. It decreed a series of measures that made it difficult for landlords to evict existing renters or to increase their rents. The war ended, but not the restrictions on landlords.

In 1921 and 1922, a great wave of inflation devastated the value of the Austrian currency, which plummeted to 1/14,400 of its prewar value. The Social Democrats responded in 1922 with legislation that fixed rents at four times their prewar rate, meaning that tenants were paying almost nothing. A new law passed the next year allowed the raising of rents to cover part of the costs of maintenance, and set up an elaborate bureaucratic process to determine the relevant costs. Yet even these minor increases in rent were resented by the Viennese working class, which had become accustomed to living virtually rent-free. Such protection for tenants was instituted in many European cities during the war, but was maintained longer and in a more radical fashion in Vienna than elsewhere. Social Democratic leaders prided themselves on the role that rent control played in improving the well-being of the working class.[58]

Landlords, who were actually losing money after paying upkeep and taxes on their property, stopped maintaining their buildings. There was no economic incentive to construct new apartments, and since landlords could not use their buildings as collateral—what bank wanted to accept a money-losing building?—they could not raise the money for new construction. The result was an intensification of the prewar housing crisis. Matters were made worse by the fact that tenants, who had previously taken in subtenants to help pay the rent, now turned them out as rent became less of a burden. That diminished crowding within homes, but exacerbated the problem of finding a place to live. Travelers who approached Vienna by train in the 1920s would see rows of coaches bordering the tracks, coaches used as shelter by people unable to find a dwelling.[59]

In the election of 1923, the Christian Social leader, Ignaz Seipel, spoke out about the negative effects of rent control and the need to scale it back. The Social Democrats responded by running on a platform of tenant protection, and improved their showing. Having paralyzed the private construction of housing, the Social Democratic municipal government began building thousands of apartments with public funds. In 1928, the issue of rent control almost led to civil strife. When the Christian Social–dominated federal government proposed legal changes in the law that would have increased rents, the Social Democrats protested vehemently. The landlords, frustrated by years of de facto expropriation of their property, offered material and propaganda support to the right-wing paramilitary Home Guard (*Heimwehr*) in an attempt to change the balance of power and regain their property rights.[60]

Hayek turned to the issue in 1928.[61] He treated rent control as an example of a policy that offered obvious immediate benefits but with the sort of unintended negative consequences that economists ought to point out. The effects of the government's attempt to control rents reached well beyond the landlords and tenants most immediately affected, he insisted. Occupants of apartments in rent-controlled buildings, Hayek pointed out, held on to their apartments regardless of their size and suitability, since moving to another apartment, even a smaller one, would lead to a huge increase in rent. As a result the rental market lost its adaptability. Rather than moving out of a large apartment when their children left, for example, couples would retain apartments larger than what they really needed or wanted. Conversely, families with children found suitably sized apartments ever more difficult to obtain, so that they lived in smaller and more cramped conditions than would otherwise have been the case. Worse yet, rent control also led indirectly to unemployment. Employees who got a job offer outside Vienna would turn it down rather than move out of their cheap apartments. Those who lived in Vienna and got a job in a part of the city far from their existing homes could not afford to move closer to work. Instead they commuted long distances and paid ever greater transportation costs. Businesses in Vienna found it increasingly difficult to recruit good help from beyond the city because those workers could not find a place to live in the capital.

In addition to such negative effects on the labor market, rent control also affected the availability of capital, Hayek argued. A good deal of the capital for new business investment would ordinarily have come from the rent earned by landlords. Since that rent was no longer coming in, not only did landlords fail to invest in maintaining their buildings or in constructing new ones; they could no longer buy stocks, which choked off the capital needed for the economy to grow. In addition, Hayek calculated that the amount spent on public housing in Vienna—a sum derived from tax income—was equal to the value of all the shares on the Vienna stock exchange. For all these reasons, Hayek recommended that rent control be phased out.

Rent control might seem a narrow intervention in the capitalist market, but in fact it had a distorting effect on the entire economy. Hayek's analysis of rent control served to bring home the liberal point about the hazards of government intervention in the price-setting mechanisms of the market, even when such measures were well short of government ownership of the economy.

Socialism, Planning, and the Functions of the Market

Not long after presenting his findings on rent control to the leading conference of German-speaking social scientists, Hayek left Vienna—permanently, as it turned out. In 1931, at the age of thirty-two, he was invited to the London School of Economics by Lionel Robbins, a British economist heavily influenced by the Viennese economists, and soon thereafter Hayek was named to a professorship.[62] Hayek thus became the first of many members of the Mises seminar to abandon the sinking ship of the Austrian Republic for better prospects in western Europe or the United States. "The day of the capitalist system, the era of the capitalist-liberal economic order is past," declared the Christian Social chancellor, Engelbert Dollfuss, in March 1933. In 1934, the Christian Socials replaced the republic with an authoritarian regime. A new constitution (never implemented) replaced liberal democracy with a corporatist state, in which representation was to be based on economic estates. The Christian Socials were under increasing pressure from the more radical and *völkisch* right, and when Hitler marched his troops into Austria in 1938, the local response was sufficiently enthusiastic that he decided upon immediate annexation.

Hayek, who saw himself as a legatee of the British tradition of liberty, became a British citizen in 1936. But within a few years of his arrival in England, many leading intellectuals were concluding with Keynes that the Depression had revealed the limits of traditional liberalism; they were searching for an alternative. Intellectuals and politicians not only on the left but on the center right as well were attracted to the idea of planning, which came into vogue in the mid-1930s. Observers were impressed by the Soviet Five-Year Plans (without looking closely at their human and material costs) that seemed to be bringing Russia into the industrial age with impressive speed. They decided that the nations of the west would likewise benefit from government planning of the economy. In 1931 the fortnightly journal *Planning* began publication under the auspices of "Political and Economic Planning," a group of businessmen, professionals, and academics. The "Liberty and Democracy Leadership Group," which included National Labourites and centrist Conservatives such as Harold Macmillan, issued a manifesto in 1934 calling for leadership to develop "scientific schemes of a far-sighted and far-reaching order."[63]

Alarmed after his arrival in England by what he saw as the threat to economic rationality and political liberty inherent in such schemes, Hayek turned his attention to the issue. His interest in economics had been influenced by a very lively debate in the early 1920s on the economic viability of socialism.[64] A formative influence on his thought was Mises' 1920 essay, "Economic Calculation in the Socialist Commonwealth." Not long after arriving in England, Hayek publicized Mises' critique and expanded upon it in a 1935 volume, *Collectivist Economic Planning: Critical Studies on the Possibilities of Socialism.*[65] It was in the course of these debates that he elaborated his economic and then his political understanding of the market.

Until the Bolshevik revolution and the abortive revolutions of 1918, socialists had given little attention to the institutions of a postcapitalist economy. On the eve of the Bolshevik revolution, Lenin thought of the economy of socialism as if an entire country were part of a single firm. "The whole of society will have become a single factory, with equality of labor and pay," he wrote. To Lenin, economics was essentially a matter of administration, of "accounting and control," the methods for which "have been simplified by capitalism to the utmost and reduced to the extraordinarily simple operations—which any literate person can perform—of supervising and recording, knowledge of the four rules of arithmetic, and issuing appropriate receipts."[66] Since Lenin, like many Marxists, thought of money as the embodiment of exploitation if not the root of all evil, he and the Bolsheviks set out to entirely eliminate a money economy.[67] Socialists elsewhere—including Otto Neurath, a Viennese intellectual who served as minister of socialization in the short-lived Bavarian Socialist Republic—toyed with the notion that socialism meant the elimination of money as well as the market and their replacement by "calculation in kind."[68]

Mises argued that in an economy without private property and markets the efficient coordination of economic activity was simply impossible.[69] Prices in a market economy conveyed the relationship between the supply and effective demand for goods. Without prices set by free exchange, there was no effective way to plan, since planners could not decide on the relative efficiency of the many possible combinations of physical and human resources that could in theory produce the same product. Lenin, like many people without experience of entrepreneurial activity, fundamentally misunderstood the nature of economics, Mises wrote. It was not a question of routing discrete bits of information to meet given goals, as in bookkeeping or statistics.[70] Except in abstract models, change is inevitable in economic life, and this gives an element of uncertainty to all economic decisions. Nor were there standard units to be manipulated, as the labor theory of value implied.[71] Only money provides a common denominator for comparing the relative scarcity of goods. Only the market produced a way of evaluating the relative availability of the thousands of items in an advanced economy, in the form of price.[72] "Where there is no free market, there is no pricing mechanism," he argued, and without a pricing mechanism, there was no way of calculating the most efficient way of achieving any particular economic goal. "Socialism is the abolition of rational economy," Mises concluded.[73]

Without private property, socialism faced another insurmountable obstacle: the problem of initiative. Only private ownership could provide the self-interested incentives to innovate, to adapt to the ever changing conditions of economic life and to take advantage of them by finding out what to produce and the most efficient way to do so. The manager of a socialized enterprise, Mises asserted, would have neither the power to act on his own initiative, nor the incentive to innovate, nor the sense of responsibility that comes from knowing that he himself will bear the cost of wrong decisions.[74]

In presenting Mises' work to an English-speaking audience in 1935, Hayek pointed out that the Soviet economy exhibited the massive inefficiencies that Mises had predicted fifteen years earlier,[75] and called attention to the broader significance of the "socialist calculation debate" for the understanding of capitalism. In a capitalist economy, economic activity is coordinated, but in a manner that most people are unaware of. That is why Smith dubbed it "the invisible hand." The coordination of their purposes is unintended: it occurs through the coordinating mechanism of the market.[76] Thus the debate on socialism led Hayek to explore and explicate the functions served by the market in a capitalist society.

Smith portrayed the market as making possible the division of labor, thus increasing human productivity. Hayek now pointed out that the market permitted an ever greater division of knowledge in society, while at the same time it coordinated that knowledge through prices, a system of signals that convey information.[77] Knowledge of the availability of resources is widely dispersed in society. Market prices act as signals of where those resources could be put to their most valuable use; the profit motive serves as an incentive to bring one's knowledge to bear in the market. Those with knowledge of where to buy a commodity more cheaply or how to produce it at less expense can use that knowledge to make a larger profit.[78] The efficient use of resources depends on having particular knowledge at a particular time and a particular place, not on the aggregate statistics that might be available to a government planner.[79] It also depends on the ability to perceive opportunities that others miss and to know when to take advantage of them—the characteristics associated with the entrepreneur rather than with the bureaucrat.

In his subsequent work, Hayek expanded on the role of the market not only in conveying information, but also in producing new knowledge. He insisted that the abstract model of the market based on perfect competition for essentially similar services under conditions of complete information, a model then central to much of economics, was fundamentally misleading. For much of what happens in the market involves gaining somewhat better information about products or services that are not quite the same and require the experience of comparison. "Our inadequate knowledge of the available commodities or services is made up for by our experience with the persons or firms supplying them. . . . The function of competition is here precisely to teach us *who* will serve us well: which grocer or travel agency, which department store or hotel, which doctor or solicitor. . . ."[80]

As Hayek continued to explore the knowledge-generating role of the market, he concluded that the most valuable effect of competition is not that it shows the most efficient method of reaching some previously known aim, but that "its results are unpredictable and on the whole different from those which anyone has, or could have, deliberately aimed at."[81] The competitive market was not merely about exchanging information; it also served to create new knowledge about the potential use of resources. For discovering which goods are "valuable" to the other members of society and how much value is actually placed on them is not something that can be known with certainty in advance. It is based on guesswork, on conjecture or hypothesis, the truth or falsity of which can only be discovered through the process of market competition.[82] Capitalism, as Hayek conceived it, was fundamentally dynamic, and that dynamism was due to the discovery of new needs and new ways of fulfilling them by entrepreneurs possessed with "resourcefulness"—an analysis that owed a good deal to Schumpeter and jibed with that of Hegel.

That economic vibrancy created a social and cultural dynamic, demanding the adaptation of old ways of thinking and behaving. It was the dynamic and resourceful few who forced the less resourceful many to adapt, to rationalize their behavior by imitating the more successful.[83] This process was sometimes painful, Hayek knew, and bound to be resented by those who preferred to run in the well-wrought grooves of established ways of life. That was why they would try to prevent it. Competition creates an "impersonal compulsion" of its own, without government command, by forcing individuals to adapt or to forfeit their income.[84]

> Competition is . . . always a process in which a small number makes it necessary for larger numbers to do what they do not like, be it to work harder, to change habits, or to devote a degree of attention, continuous application, or regularity to their work which without competition would not be needed.[85]

But what was intrinsically desirable about working harder, with greater attention and application—a characterization that sounded awfully like Marx's and Marcuse's description of alienated labor? This was a question that Hayek never addressed.[86] Could the economy not be shaped by government to realize some higher conception of human purposes and possibilities?

It could not, Hayek insisted, because to do so would violate the other major function of the market in a liberal society. The market was a mechanism that coordinated not only dispersed economic *information*, but also diverse human *purposes*. Hayek first suggested this theme in his work of the late 1930s, articulated it more fully in *The Road to Serfdom* of 1944, and then developed it in his later writings.

Drawing upon Wieser's notion that market prices reflect not some objective quality or quantity but the subjective evaluations of individuals, Hayek argued that the market did not merely coordinate economic values, because, he insisted, *there is no such thing as "economic values."* He explained: "Economic considerations are merely those by which we reconcile and adjust our different purposes, none of which, in the last resort, are economic. . . ."[87] The market, therefore, was about more than economics.

It was also about more than "self-interest," at least as that term was ordinarily understood. The notion that market activity was based on self-interest, Hayek argued, was true enough, but highly distortive, suggesting both that all economic activity was motivated by selfishness and that only selfish goals required market activity for their fulfillment. We pursue our interests in the market, Hayek suggested, but (following Weber) he noted that "interests" are both ideal and material. Thus it was analytically fallacious to separate "self-interest" from "purposes," not because all purposes were ultimately selfish but because whether our conceptions of self-interest are egotistical or altruistic, they are pursued through the market. Those who want to earn money to raise their children, or to build a church to the greater glory of God, need to participate in the market as much as the fellow who earns money to acquire a flashy car that he hopes will attract women. The parent and the religious believer are acting on their interests no less than the would-be playboy; they merely have a different conception of their interests and purposes.

Hayek thought that Smith's definition of freedom was true but misleading. Smith had characterized liberty as a situation in which "every man, so long as he does not violate the laws of justice, [is] left perfectly free to pursue his own interests in his own way." The problem with Smith's definition, Hayek maintained, was that it inadvertently suggests "a connection of the argument for individual freedom with egotism and selfishness." Hayek thought it more accurate to define freedom as "a state in which each can use his knowledge for his purposes."[88] Where Voltaire had portrayed self-interest as an *alternative* to religious or ideological purposes, Hayek now suggested the two could not be distinguished, and that all were pursued through the market.

If all of life's purposes came into economic play, it followed that to try to plan "the economy" was to attempt to plan life as a whole. Since there was no economic realm distinct from politics, religion, and culture, there could be no discrete "economic planning" that left men otherwise free to pursue their own purposes. Hayek made the point emphatically in *The Road to Serfdom*, then returned to it in his subsequent works. "Economic control is not merely control of a sector of human life which can be separated from the rest; it is the control of the means for all our ends. And whoever has sole control of the means must also determine which ends are to be served, which values are to be rated higher and which lower—in short, what men should believe and strive for."[89]

For Hayek, modern capitalist society was characterized by the absence of "unity of purpose," except in times of national crises, such as war. In opposition to the vogue for planning in the 1930s, he argued that economic planning was possible only at the price of a liberal society and a democratic polity, for it would require a degree of social consensus about the precise and relative value of various goods that was impossible in a liberal society.[90] In a liberal society the state is *not* moral; it is "a piece of utilitarian machinery intended to help individuals in the fullest development of their individual personality."[91] Gone was any Hegelian or even Arnoldian notion of the state as having educative functions. The very idea was seen as discredited by Nazism and Communism.

"It is the great merit of a liberal society that it reduces the necessity of agreement to a minimum compatible with the diversity of individual opinions which will exist in a free society," Hayek argued. But democracy could only survive if its citizens accepted the fact that the shared consensus would have to remain limited, and that meant that the purposes for which government could be used were minimal as well. "The price we have to pay for a democratic system is the restriction of State action to those fields where agreement can be obtained," he wrote. While capitalism makes democracy possible, "if a democratic people comes under the sway of an anti-capitalistic creed, this means that democracy will inevitably destroy itself."[92]

This was the major theme of *The Road to Serfdom*. The book's polemical contention was that the very processes that led to the rise of Nazism in Germany were gaining strength in England. Politicians committed to central economic planning would inadvertently create an ever less efficient economy and an ever larger, more intrusive, and more arbitrary state that would seek to mold the tastes and values of its citizens to conform to the government's plan. Hayek contended that socialism, even when it was pursued with democratic intentions, tended toward governmental control over ever more spheres of life, leading toward totalitarianism.

Like Marx's and Engels' *Communist Manifesto*, Hayek's *The Road to Serfdom* summarized much of its author's earlier work. And just as Marx spent much of the rest of his life spelling out the assumptions and implications of his best-known book and publicizing them, so too did Hayek devote the rest of his life to deepening the analysis of *The Road to Serfdom* and bringing its message to intellectuals, politicians, and policy makers. His subsequent work was an attempt to draw out the implications of his understanding of the relationship between capitalism, liberty, and progress, and to apply them to the circumstances of the postwar world.

The Critique of "Social Justice" and the Hazards of the Welfare State

The publication of *The Road to Serfdom* brought Hayek a modicum of popular fame in Britain and in America, where an abridged version (edited by an ex-socialist, Max Eastman) appeared in the mass-circulation *Reader's Digest*. The book was embraced by some British Conservatives, and found even greater resonance among conservative opponents of the New Deal in the United States. Public acclaim, however, was purchased at the price of some academic respectability. Leftist academics were of course fiercely antipathetic to Hayek's argument. But even sympathizers felt that the links he suggested between British socialism and German National Socialism were forced and unfair, that his claims were exaggerated, and that he had crossed the boundary between social science and polemic.

After the war, Hayek visited Vienna and renewed his relationship with Helene Warhanek, a woman with whom he had been in love before he met his wife. They resolved to divorce their spouses and marry each other. Helene was spared the trouble: shortly thereafter, her husband died.[93] Hayek divorced his wife and married his old flame, an act that alienated many of his closest British friends and led Hayek to look for a post abroad. Whether because of the notoriety of *The Road to Serfdom* or because economists viewed his work on monetary theory as outdated, Hayek found it difficult to find a job at an economics department at a major American university.[94] After failed overtures to a number of institutions, the chairman of the University of Chicago's Committee on Social Thought worked out an unusual arrangement by which Hayek became professor of social and moral science there, his salary paid by a private American foundation, the Volker Charities Fund.[95]

Hayek taught at Chicago from 1950 to 1962, but his mind remained focused on Europe, where he returned frequently. He remained a British subject to the end of his days and regarded England as his homeland.[96] That he lived elsewhere was a matter of personal opportunities, not commitment. In 1962 he moved to the University of Freiburg in Germany, a center of the politically conservative brand of German economic liberalism known as "Ordo-Liberalism." His move was primarily motivated by the need for a job that would provide him with a guaranteed pension, since he was a man of limited means nearing the normal age of retirement in a job without retirement benefits. While Hayek spent the bulk of his remaining years in Germany and Austria, his greatest influence was in the English-speaking world. It was in English that he published his two most significant books of political thought, *The Constitution of Liberty* of 1960 and the trilogy *Law, Legislation, and Liberty*, published between 1973 and 1979.

The Constitution of Liberty and its successor aimed at a critical, though not entirely hostile, examination of what had come to be known as "the welfare state." Just as Marcuse's message was misinterpreted by disciples who thought that he stood for more and better orgasms, Hayek was often cited by advocates of laissez-faire and opponents of the welfare state. His position was actually more subtle and supple than such support might indicate.

Hayek's concern was the tensions between liberty and the welfare state. He defined liberty as the limitation of the coercive power of the state, such that "coercion of some [people] by others is reduced as much as is possible in society."[97] But Hayek was clear that liberty existed only when protected by the state, which enforced the rule of law, a set of rules that applied equally to all and that assured each individual "a known sphere of unimpeded action." These laws included "a right to privacy and secrecy, the conception that a man's house is his castle and nobody has a right even to take cognizance of his activities in it."[98] They also included the right to property, which Hayek regarded not as some eternal and unchanging essence, but as in need of redefinition in keeping with changing social needs.[99] "The rationale of securing to each individual a known range within which he can decide on his actions is to enable him to make the fullest use of his knowledge," Hayek reiterated.[100]

He approved of some of the goals of the welfare state, and regarded some of them as practicable. He acknowledged that "there are common needs that can be satisfied only by collective action," and asserted that as society grows richer, "that minimum of sustenance which the community has always provided for those not able to look after themselves, and which can be provided outside the market, will gradually rise, or that government may, usefully and without doing any harm, assist or even lead in such endeavors. There is little reason why the government should not also play some role, or even take the initiative, in such areas as social insurance and education," he noted.[101] Nor was he opposed in principle to government regulation of working conditions, buildings, and so on.[102] Hayek's criticism of proposals for the welfare state lay not so much with the aims as with the methods of government action.[103] He was suspicious above all of government monopolization of the provision of social, medical, or educational services, since that eliminated the competitive process by which new and possibly better means could be discovered. Hayek tried to show how social security (in the broad sense) could be provided in a manner that did as little damage as possible to individual freedom and to social innovation.[104] What he opposed was government measures that distorted the information system of the market by actually setting wages, rents, or the price of commodities to conform to some social ideal or political expedient. The result of that, Hayek thought, would be a less efficient economy as well as a less free society. Yet he believed that political and intellectual tendencies were moving in that direction.

By the late 1950s, the traditional socialist platform—the collective ownership of the means of production, the replacement of the profit motive, and the egalitarian redistribution of income—had been abandoned by almost all socialist parties in the west, in practice if not in theory.[105] For Hayek, the threat to liberty and progress no longer came from traditional socialism and proponents of comprehensive planning. It came from attempts to reshape capitalism to conform to one notion or another of "social justice," from group self-interest expressed through democratic politics, and from the pernicious interaction of the two.

Though the socialist ideal of equality had been largely abandoned as unfeasible, Hayek asserted, its place had been taken by another: the ideal of "social justice." The term was favored by those who, without deliberately setting out to destroy the market mechanism, thought it desirable "to manipulate the economy so that the distribution of incomes will be made to conform to their conception."[106] Hayek claimed that those who used the term didn't know what they were talking about, in two senses. First, the term had no clear and discernible meaning. Second, the notion that the economy could be structured to reflect some conception of "social justice" was based on a deep misapprehension about the nature of liberal capitalist society. The phrase had become the mantra of moralists. It had been incorporated into the official doctrine of the Roman Catholic Church, and was especially beloved by "the clergy of all Christian denominations, who, while increasingly losing their faith in a supernatural revelation, appear to have sought a refuge and consolation in a new 'social' religion which substitutes a temporal for a celestial promise of justice. . . ." Indeed, a commitment to "social justice" had become the recognized sign of the possession of a moral conscience. But, Hayek noted caustically, "the near-universal acceptance of a belief does not prove that it is valid or even meaningful, any more than the general belief in witches or ghosts proved the validity of these concepts." The concept had become "a quasi-religious superstition."[107]

Those who preached the need to restructure the market economy to conform to the standards of "social justice" rarely had a precise sense of what they actually meant by the term, Hayek charged. That is why it was so readily adopted and manipulated by self-interested groups. They claimed that their incomes were not commensurate with the standards of social justice, that government ought to intervene to raise their wages or the prices they received for their services or products, in order to protect their accustomed way of life or to create the standard of living to which they felt they were justly entitled.

Any such conception of social justice ran up against what Hayek regarded as an insurmountable barrier: social justice was impossible in a capitalist society—and that was a good thing. We have seen that a series of modern analysts of the cultural effects of the market and of the liberal state that sustains it had criticized these arrangements as the triumph of means over ends. Tönnies depicted modern man as moving from "community," characterized by the solidarity of shared aims and beliefs, into a calculating "society" without shared ideals. "Community" was held together by common ends, "society" by common means. Money has no purpose of its own, Simmel noted, but functions as an intermediary in the series of purposes. Hayek agreed with these analyses but gave them a wholly positive spin. Liberal capitalist institutions made it possible for men and women of very different persuasions to live together in peace, he argued. They could cooperate precisely because their dealings with one another were mediated by money and by shared basic rules, both of which were systems of means, not ends. Unwittingly echoing Matthew Arnold, Hayek characterized the liberal state and the capitalist economy as a piece of "utilitarian machinery," useful for and usable by those who disagreed with one another on how life ought to be lived.

Hayek argued that precisely because the liberal state and economy are not based on a shared, coherent vision of the common good, they cannot be used to reward individuals economically according to some common scale of values. There *was* no society-wide agreement on values. That did not mean that it was an immoral society in which individuals were without higher values and ultimate ends, only that the diverse individuals and groups within the larger society did not all share the same ends and values. Individuals and groups could use their own money for their own purposes, selfish or altruistic. What they could not do was insist that government impose their purposes on everyone else through the state or by having government set wages, rents, or prices. Borrowing a term from Adam Smith, Hayek referred to modern liberal society as a "Great Society," to highlight the fact that it brings together a large number of people with a wide range of purposes, who for the most part do not know one another. Justice does exist in a Great Society, but only in the sense of the protection of person, property, and contracts—what was traditionally known as "commutative justice" as opposed to "distributive justice." These rules of justice served primarily to allow individuals to pursue their self-interest as they saw it. He contrasted the abstract and impersonal nature of the rules of the Great Society with the particularistic and altruistic shared moral code of earlier "tribal society."[108]

For Hayek, the demand for "social justice" derives from conceptions of ethical obligation that made sense when confined to small, face-to-face groups, but that are now obsolete and indeed dangerous.[109] The Great Society did not pretend to reward individuals according to commonly shared standards of merit or virtue, for that would require a consensus of values that simply did not exist. The fact that the rock star was paid far more than the teacher was not because "society" regarded the former as more meritorious than the latter, but simply because of the relationship between supply and effective demand—because more people were willing to pay more for a ticket to see that particular rock star than for the salary of any given teacher.[110] Capitalism, Hayek asserted, does not reward merit in some moral sense, and he thought it dangerous for conservatives to argue as if it did.[111]

Coming to terms with the logic of a society coordinated more by the market than by common purposes presents a shock to many traditional moral sensibilities, Hayek recognized, since those sensibilities reflected the needs of an earlier stage of history, that of a "tribal society" connected by common ends. But those sensibilities were now archaic and even pernicious. For they failed to recognize that limiting political coercion to enforcing the rules of commutative justice was what made a Great Society possible.[112]

For Hayek, then, the market, together with the laws of the liberal state, makes pluralism possible, but only if groups (religious, ethnic, and economic) give up their attempt to use the power of the state to enforce their conceptions of justice or the good life. Smaller groups will continue to exist in such a society, Hayek asserted, but political power must not be used to enforce their rules. Membership in them will be voluntary, and individuals will be able to move between "groups into which they may be accepted if they submit to their rules."[113]

The problem of protecting the resourceful few, even if they were ethnic, religious, or cultural outsiders, was solved by minimizing the cultural and moral claims of the state, by discrediting the notion that the state existed to protect one group of cultural insiders. Hayek knew that this too was hard for most people to swallow. But the price of voluntary cooperation among ever larger groups of people was to limit the moral claims for assistance that had bound smaller groups together. Modern capitalist society was based on a revolution in consciousness, in which those outside one's family or cultural group—foreigners and strangers—were no longer treated as enemies, as beyond the bounds of moral obligation. But that also meant that the moral obligation toward others in society could not be as great as had been the case in the pre-capitalist past.[114]

Hayek also suggested that there were dangers inherent in trying to use government to bring about "equality of opportunity" for everyone. In truth, Hayek claimed, there is no substitute for intelligent parents or for an emotionally and culturally nurturing family. Those who did not come from such a family would be at a disadvantage, a disadvantage that could be eliminated only at the cost of ever more radical government attempts to control the environments in which children were raised. Moreover Hayek, like Burke and like Hegel, pointed out that one of the major motivations for most people to engage in market activity was to secure advantages to their children, by providing funds for housing, education, and other opportunities. To equalize the opportunities for children by penalizing those of "privileged" backgrounds or rewarding those of "disadvantaged" backgrounds was to remove the most fundamental incentive for people to work and exercise their ingenuity in the market.[115]

Adam Smith believed that the main obstacle to universal opulence through the competitive market came from groups who used their political power to pursue their self-interest in a way that circumvented the market mechanism. He pointed to merchants as a group who in his day were particularly well situated to do so, by virtue of their small numbers, urban location, and access to the ears of politicians. They made use of the distorted ideas of national interest that Smith dubbed "mercantilism" to argue in favor of political restrictions on trade that ultimately benefited the merchants themselves at the expense of the larger society. Almost two centuries later, Hayek saw a similar threat to the development of the market and of liberal society, from those best situated to exert political influence for particular purposes. But under the conditions of modern mass democracy, Hayek asserted, that threat came not primarily from merchants (who would always be a small numerical minority) but from other organized interests, especially labor unions. For labor unions had the numbers that counted as votes in a democracy, as well as the advantages that accrued to the well organized. Moreover, the very vagueness of the notion of social justice made it a flexible ideological tool with which to pursue their group self-interest.[116] And unions could make an emotional, irrational appeal to the yearning for solidarity that lurked unquenched and archaic in liberal capitalist society.[117]

Hayek noted the propensity of the progressive-minded not to treat unions as self-interested monopolies, but to assume that they were conducive to the public good simply because they had many members.[118] That, he thought, was a fallacy. Truly voluntary labor unions, Hayek thought, could play a valuable role in shaping the workplace. Like other groups in society, labor unions legitimately pursued their self-interest. But they presented a danger when they were able to use physical coercion (such as picket lines) or laws that granted them a monopoly to keep nonmembers from being employed. Like other successful monopolists, union members increased their own returns (in the form of wages). But that came at the cost of those outside the union who would only be able to get jobs that paid less well, Hayek argued.[119]

When unions pushed up the cost of wages beyond the point where it was profitable for companies to hire workers, they caused unemployment, as firms laid off workers or went bankrupt, and as it became unprofitable to form new businesses because labor costs were too high. "The present position of the unions cannot last," he predicted in 1960, "for they can function only in a market economy which they are doing their best to destroy."[120]

What Hayek found particularly worrisome was a growing consensus among western politicians that government had a responsibility to maintain full employment, a belief enshrined in the economic doctrine of Keynesianism. Governments committed to keeping down unemployment, Hayek noted, could only do so by increasing the supply of money and credit in the economy. That worked by causing inflation, which decreased the real value of the wages that unions had obtained, temporarily allowing businesses to regain profitability. By selling their products at higher prices while still paying workers at preinflated wages, businesses became profitable again, while the real wages of their employees declined. But that was only a temporary fix, since in order to catch up with inflation, everyone demanded higher wages. The effect was a wage-price spiral, in which the expectation of ongoing inflation led to ever higher wage demands and government injection of ever more money into the economy, resulting in ever higher inflation. That would create pressures on government to try to control the process by actually setting wages and then prices. Governments would thus back into what amounted to administration of the economy, distorting if not destroying the informational system of the market.[121] The danger was accelerating inflation, that is a currency which was constantly decreasing in value, but at an unpredictable rate. Since money was the unit in which market actors calculated how to act economically, the system of information was increasingly distorted, like a thermometer whose units changed as one tried to measure the temperature.[122]

Hayek was not opposed to democracy, but he thought that its virtues were overrated compared to those of the market and the liberal state, and that its greatest benefit came in allowing for a peaceful transition of power. He feared that unless institutional limits were placed on democratic legislatures, the existing structure of political and ideological incentives would lead one economic interest group after another to make demands upon democratically elected politicians in the name of social justice. The result would be a constant expansion of state intervention in the wage- and price-setting mechanisms of the economy, a steady rise in the state's share of national income, and a steady diminution of the freedom to engage in economic innovation. Democracy, in other words, could destroy liberalism—a recurrent fear among nineteenth-century liberals, which Hayek revived. Given the opportunity, most men and women would try to have government protect their existing way of life and sources of income from the "creative destruction" through which capitalism brought about new social and material possibilities. To decide economic questions by majority vote was therefore a recipe for stagnation.[123] In the long run, Hayek argued, liberal democracy would survive only if it put limits on the range of questions that could be decided through the political process.[124] "Is there really no other way for people to maintain a democratic government than by handing over unlimited power to a group of elected representatives whose decisions must be guided by the exigencies of a bargaining process in which they bribe a sufficient number of voters to support an organized group of themselves numerous enough to outvote the rest?" he asked rhetorically.[125]

Hayek's answer, in his late work of the 1970s, was to suggest constitutional mechanisms that would limit the ease with which politicians could pass legislation that promoted the interests of particular individuals or groups.[126] Given the centrality of money in the information system of the capitalist economy, and given the propensity of democratically elected governments to create inflation, Hayek also made the radical suggestion that money be denationalized. Take it out of the hands of government, he suggested, permit international competition of currencies, and people would choose to use the one that maintained its stability.[127]

To many readers, all of this must have seemed exaggerated and alarmist in 1960 or even in 1970, just as Burke's *Reflections on the Revolution in France* had in 1790. But within a decade Hayek's predictions were proving remarkably prescient. Politicians and policy makers devoted new attention to his writings. That was in part, as we will see, because the world seemed to be going in the direction Hayek had predicted. But it was also because Hayek's ideas had been taken up and disseminated by other intellectuals.

The Intellectuals—Again

Like so many other thinkers whose works we have explored, beginning with Voltaire, Hayek believed in the power of intellectuals, who exerted long-term influence over public opinion. Hayek distinguished between two levels of thinkers: the small number who were original, and the "intellectuals" proper, whom he defined as "secondhand dealers in ideas" or "experts in the technique of getting knowledge over." They took the ideas of original thinkers, filtered them, and presented them to a larger public: "It is their convictions and opinions which operate as the sieve through which all new conceptions must pass before they can reach the masses."[128] Ideas only became politically effective when intellectuals—at least *some* intellectuals—were convinced of their validity and passed on that conviction.

It was futile, Hayek thought, to expect that politicians would strike out in new directions beyond the horizon of public opinion, which intellectuals did so much to shape. "The successful politician owes his power to the fact that he moves within the accepted framework of thought, that he thinks and talks conventionally. It would be almost a contradiction in terms for a politician to be a leader in the field of ideas. His task in a democracy is to find out what the opinions held by the largest number are, not to give currency to new opinions which may become the majority view in some distant future."[129] While politics was the art of the possible, political philosophy was the art of making the seemingly impossible politically plausible.[130] The role of political philosophers like himself was to challenge majority opinion "by insisting on considerations which the majority do not wish to take into account, by holding up principles which they regard as inconvenient and irksome."[131]

Hayek believed that ideas first put forth in a systematic, abstract form trickled down to the level of political debate, often attaining influence a generation or more after they were first articulated.[132]

Schumpeter had insisted (tongue half in cheek) that the intellectuals who were the audience for his *Capitalism, Socialism, and Democracy* were so driven by nonrational resentments as to be impervious to arguments in favor of the market. Hayek, by contrast, eschewed irony. He tended toward the view that over time intellectuals could be swayed by the power of ideas.[133]

That was borne out by his own experience. In the decade after the publication of *The Road to Serfdom*, Hayek's work was sharply criticized by academics, even those who fundamentally shared his liberalism, for what they saw as his one-sided neglect of values other than those of freedom from government coercion.[134] But his books began to transform intellectual life. Writing in 1954, H. Stuart Hughes, a moderately left-wing historian at Harvard, asserted that "the publication ten years ago of F. A. Hayek's *The Road to Serfdom* was a major event in the intellectual history of the United States . . . it marked the beginning of that slow reorientation of sentiment—both in academic circles and among the general public—toward a more positive evaluation of the capitalist system which has marked the past decade."[135]

Because he believed in the power of ideas in a democracy—as mediated through intellectuals—Hayek devoted a good deal of energy to creating institutions beyond the academy to cultivate what he called his "classical liberal" perspective on the present. Shortly after publishing *The Road to Serfdom*, he founded an international organization of liberal-minded intellectuals for purposes of debate and mutual support. Dubbed the Mont Pélerin Society, after the Swiss resort where its members first gathered in 1947, the organization exerted influence not by pressing an agenda upon governments, but by generating and spreading neoliberal ideas. Its members, mostly economists, included Ludwig Erhard, who was most responsible for launching the West German economy on a market-based footing after the fall of Nazism. The Mont Pélerin Society also helped spawn national organizations more oriented to concrete influence on public policy.[136]

Hayek provided the inspiration and the intellectual basis for another institution, the "think tank," modeled after the British Fabian Society. The first of these, the Institute for Economic Affairs, was founded in London in 1957, where it conducted studies that took their orientation from the work of Hayek as well as that of Milton Friedman, his colleague at the University of Chicago. The IEA in turn helped spawn the Centre for Policy Studies, which was devoted to converting the Conservative party to a more Hayekian direction. It was headed by Keith Joseph; its vice chairman was Margaret Thatcher. In 1974, Thatcher became leader of the Conservative Party and put Joseph in charge of policy and research. The major themes of Joseph's speeches and pamphlets—the need for "wealth-creating entrepreneurs," the dangers of corporatism, the perils of inflationary policies—were popularizations of themes on which Hayek had been writing for decades.[137] Hayek's *Constitution of Liberty* "is what we believe," Thatcher told the party's research department.[138] In the United States, too, new think tanks were created to conduct research, formulate policy, and disseminate the Hayekian word.

But the rise of Hayek's intellectual stock was due not so much to the organization he founded or the think tanks that sought to spread his gospel. It was because by the 1970s his ominous hypotheses about the development of communism and of the western welfare state seemed increasingly to match the data. When the Swedish Nobel committee awarded him the prize for economics in 1974, it was a harbinger of greater recognition to come.

The Hayekian Moment

While the 1950s and 1960s had been years of economic growth and of expanding government services in most of western Europe and the United States, the 1970s were a decade of economic slowdown and stagnation. In the 1950s and 1960s, there was a tacit understanding between employers and labor organizations to keep labor demands within limits that did not destroy profits. Labor unions regularly obtained rising wages and employer-paid benefits for their members; they used their political clout to enlarge the welfare state. By the late 1960s, however, the center of gravity in most western polities had shifted toward the left. Labor shortages, combined with a more radicalized political culture, created an atmosphere that led to ever higher demands by labor unions, most strikingly in the United Kingdom. Wages went up more quickly than profits, limiting the availability of investment capital.[139] At the same time, taxes were increasing to pay for ever larger government expenditures on income maintenance, education, and health care.[140] The combination of slow economic growth and expectations of continuous increases in the provision of government welfare measures soon had their effects. Government's share of national income moved ever upward, and government budgetary deficits ballooned.

Inflation, which in western Europe had averaged only about 1 percent per annum in 1960 when Hayek warned of its dangers in *The Constitution of Liberty*, rose to 3.7 percent per annum during the years from 1961 to 1969, jumped to 6.4 percent in 1969 to 1973, and then shot up to over 10 percent per annum from 1973 to 1979.[141] As inflation crept upward, governments responded by one form or another of what the British Labour party called "incomes policy": politicians tried to set wages from industry to industry, either through legislation or through consultation with labor and business leaders. In the United States, a Republican president, Richard Nixon, reacted to galloping inflation with a governmentally mandated temporary freeze of wages and prices in 1971, and then again in 1973.[142] His British counterpart, Conservative prime minister Edward Heath, imposed a system of comprehensive controls on wages and dividends.[143] Nixon's successor, Gerald Ford, presided over an economy in which unemployment stood at 9.2 percent, higher than at any point since the end of the Second World War. Both inflation and unemployment got worse under his Democratic successor, Jimmy Carter.

What puzzled and alarmed informed observers was that the tools of Keynesian economic policy now seemed blunted. Governments since the war had fought unemployment by increasing government spending or by increasing the supply of money and credit in the economy to try to stimulate economic demand and thus create more jobs. This policy was known to be inflationary, but that hazard was seen as controllable: when inflation threatened to get out of hand, government could respond by decreasing the money supply, thus reducing inflation at the cost of greater unemployment. But by the second half of the 1970s, these instruments no longer served their purposes. Both unemployment and inflation increased, while economic growth came almost to a halt. This was stagnation and inflation, a combination that was dubbed "stagflation." In the countries of western Europe and North America that belonged to the Organization of Economic Cooperation and Development (the OECD), the combined statistics for unemployment and inflation were over 15 percent in the years from 1973 to 1979.[144] Public expenditures continued to rise, consuming an ever larger share of gross national product. In the late 1970s, government outlays in the OECD countries rose to 48.5 percent of the gross national income.[145] In Sweden, the paradigm of the welfare state, total public expenditure reached 66 percent of the gross domestic product in 1980.[146] All of this set the stage for a rebellion by taxpayers who balked at having so high a portion of their earnings taken out of their hands.

It was the economic crisis of the western welfare state that led policy intellectuals, then politicians, and finally voters to reconsider their premises and consider policies more in keeping with Hayek's strictures. The first breakthrough came in Great Britain, where the problems evident in other welfare states were most blatant. By the late 1970s, British governments seemed to have lost control of public spending, inflation was rampant (as high as 24 percent per annum), and economic growth was low. Substantial government revenue was poured into preserving the jobs of workers in the declining steel and mining industries, which had been nationalized after the war to keep open plants and mines that were no longer profitable. When, in 1974, the Conservative government sought to resist the coal miners' demands for higher wages, the miners went on strike, plunging the nation into nighttime darkness. The strike brought down the Conservative government of Edward Heath. In the winter of 1978–79, a Labour government came close to declaring a state of emergency in response to a series of strikes by public-sector unions that left garbage piling up in the streets, hospital services curtailed, and—thanks to a strike by gravediggers—the dead unburied. Picketing in support of striking truck drivers brought the flow of all but essential goods to a halt.[147] In response to this "winter of discontent," voters turned to the new Conservative leader, Margaret Thatcher, whose party triumphed in the elections of 1979. She named Keith Joseph, her associate at the Hayekian Centre for Policy Studies, to her cabinet as secretary of state for industry.

Together, they reoriented government economic policy. New legislation limited the power of trade unions by curbing the rights of picketers and holding national union organizations financially responsible for actions taken by each union local. Thatcher rejected the Keynesian policies that had led to inflation. Government no longer increased the supply of money in an effort to induce economic activity, and it accepted unemployment as a necessary if short-term evil. Her administration sold off government-owned businesses, diminished direct government intervention in the economy, encouraged entrepreneurship, and reduced income taxes.[148] Thatcher was reelected in 1983 and 1987. By the time she left office in 1990, she had presided over the structural transformation of the economy. The greatest triumph of "Thatcherism" was in so transforming the British political landscape that many of her policies and some of her rhetoric were copied by the Labour Party under Tony Blair.

While one Hayekian-oriented head of government was transforming the British economy, another was attempting similar reforms in the United States. For Hayek, together with Mises, was the economist most cited by Ronald Reagan.[149] Of his seventy-six economic advisers during his 1980 U.S. presidential campaign, twenty-two were members of the Mont Pélerin Society.[150] Like Thatcher, Reagan worked to reduce the power of trade unions. One of his first acts was to replace the members of the striking air traffic controllers union. He too encouraged entrepreneurship, reduced taxes, and cut back on government regulation. Like Thatcher, Reagan was prepared to tolerate substantial unemployment as a way of breaking out of the wage-price spiral that Hayek had analyzed.

In launching the Uruguay Round of the international General Agreement on Tariffs and Trade in 1986, Thatcher and Reagan pursued Smithian policies of reducing tariffs to encourage international trade. These policies were continued and intensified by their Labourite and Democratic successors. Domestic deregulation and the need to compete with foreign producers induced a new dynamism into each national economy, as corporations were forced to revamp their practices in order to compete with foreign producers. In sectors such as steel and automobile production, corporations were forced to abandon the cozy arrangements between a few large firms and their unions, which allowed both to exploit their semimonopolistic position.[151] In the United States as in Britain, the greatest triumph of Hayek's ideas came in the transformation of the parties of the left toward the positions identified with Thatcher and Reagan.

The Thatcher and Reagan administrations represent one "Hayekian moment," which began in the world of think tanks in the 1970s and influenced government policy in the 1980s. But another Hayekian moment was occurring elsewhere in Europe, in what had been the Soviet bloc.

If the travails of the capitalist welfare state seemed to bear out Hayek's predictions in *The Constitution of Liberty*, the economic fate of the Soviet Union and its eastern European satellites seemed to confirm the critique of socialist economic planning put forth by Mises and Hayek. It would be a simplification, but by no means a distortion, to say that the Communist system foundered on the rocks of information and incentive.[152] Its abject inferiority to the market economies of western Europe was disguised in part by contrived statistics, but above all by the fact that these statistics revealed little about the quality, suitability, durability, and availability of the goods produced by the planned economies of the eastern bloc. Economic growth in Communist regimes came largely from increasing the inputs of land, labor, and capital, rather than from more efficient use of resources. As early as the 1960s this strategy was breaking down, as the limits of adding land and people to the economy, and of deferring consumption to provide capital, were reached. The Communist economies stagnated in the 1970s, and by the 1980s were actually shrinking. From the late 1950s through the 1980s, Eastern European regimes experimented with a series of attempted reforms, each of which was intended to decentralize decision making and create a semblance of market prices. But without private ownership of the means of production, the incentives were lacking for the managers of factories or socialist "firms" to meet consumer needs, to produce efficiently, or to innovate.[153]

It was the intractability of the problem of socialist production, together with a repugnance at the lack of liberty in Communist regimes, that led intellectuals in eastern Europe to Hayek. While university students in the west were being taught the "critical theory" of Marcuse and the Frankfurt School, intellectuals in Communist eastern Europe discovered that for them the really critical theory was Hayek's. His work was widely circulated and read in Poland.[154] In Czechoslovakia Václav Klaus, an economist in the Communist regime, was entrusted with the task of reading the work of Hayek and Milton Friedman in order to "know the enemy." Klaus became convinced that his "enemies" were right, and he became an advocate of their ideas within the Communist regime. After the fall of the Berlin Wall, he emerged as minister of finance in the new liberal government of Czechoslovakia, then, after the separation from Slovakia in 1992, as prime minister of the new Czech Republic. As prime minister, Klaus presided over the liberalization of the economy, including selling off nationalized industries and creation of a convertible currency.[155] The results were a great (though temporarily painful) leap forward into the international capitalist economy. Other governments in the former Soviet bloc made similar attempts, with varying degrees of success.

When Friedrich Hayek died in 1992, many nations seemed to be moving in a Hayekian direction in other respects as well. Though no nation adopted his blueprint for reducing the economic power of democratically elected legislatures, that influence was attenuated in other ways. In the United States, attempts to change the constitutional rules by passing a constitutional amendment mandating a balanced budget failed. But Congress and the president agreed on a balanced budget plan, which (if adhered to) would set limits to the spending power of the legislature. In western Europe, countries that aspired to join the European Currency Union were required to limit their budget deficits to 3 percent of GDP—another way of creating rules that limited the power of elected legislatures to spend. Democratic influence on the currency was also curtailed. In the United States this took the form of a consensus that the Federal Reserve Board use its independence to fight inflation. Several Latin American nations, beginning with Argentina, officially adopted the American dollar as legal tender, another way of removing control from democratically elected politicians. In Europe, the adoption of the euro as a unified currency also worked toward diminishing the economic power of elected legislatures. In all of these instances, democratic legislatures tied their own hands, to keep themselves from pursuing the temptations of greater government spending and inflation.

All in all, the 1980s and 1990s were a Hayekian moment, when his once untimely liberalism came to be seen as timely. The intensification of market competition, internationally and within each nation, created a more innovative and dynamic brand of capitalism. That in turn gave rise to a new chorus of the laments that, as we have seen, have recurred since the eighteenth century. Community was breaking down; traditional ways of life were being destroyed; identities were thrown into question; solidarity was being undermined, egoism unleashed, wealth made conspicuous amid new inequality; philistinism was triumphant. Yet it also led new groups and nations into the circle of wealth; expanded the peaceable relations of exchange among nations; and created new cultural combinations and, as Simmel had noted, new possibilities for individual development.

The Tensions and Limits of Hayek's Thought

Like many thinkers who formulate their views primarily in response to some looming foe, Hayek's work had a tendency to one-sidedness and exaggeration. There were also tensions that arose from trying to incorporate disparate intellectual traditions into his work.

He asserted that the notion that society as a whole could be shaped to conform to some desired set of values betrayed a misunderstanding of the nature of capitalist society, which was an example of what he called a "spontaneous order." By that he meant two things (which he tended to conflate, but which are actually distinct). He called the market order "spontaneous" because it coordinated human purposes by appealing to existing motives of self-interest, rather than trying to coordinate activity through deliberate planning.[156] By a "spontaneous" order Hayek also meant that the market order had not come about in a planned, deliberate fashion to conform to a set of ideals. It had developed "spontaneously" over time, through a process of trial and error, and had been retained because it was found to be useful to a wide range of individuals. In that sense, it had developed—and was still developing—by a process of cultural evolution.[157] It was a set of institutions that were "artificial" in the sense of having been created by man. But that did not mean that those institutions had either been created intentionally or could be reconfigured to conform to any ideal. He passed over the fact that in most places the market had been deliberately introduced, often by rulers seeking to increase the wealth of the nation and the revenue of the state.

In his explorations of "spontaneous order," Hayek picked up a theme from Adam Ferguson, David Hume, and Adam Smith, but gave it a far more conservative turn than it had had for the Scots whom he annexed to his intellectual family tree.[158] A conservative undercurrent already present in Hayek's articles of the 1930s became more pronounced in his later work,[159] as he increasingly stressed that the major institutions he sought to conserve—the free market and the legal structure that made it possible—were the product not of rational deliberation but of the unintended results of human action. Though Hayek clearly thought that the market order had increased human well-being, he was wary of judging it by any specific criterion. Taken to the extreme to which Hayek sometimes took it, his emphasis on our inability to fully comprehend the market order amounted to a counsel of acceptance and resignation.[160] Hayek offered a cultural evolutionary scheme to explain the development of the institutions of the market and the rule of law, suggesting that they were adopted over time because they provided more adequately for changing human needs.[161] But like many evolutionary thinkers, he seemed to regard the survival of institutions as itself proof of their fitness and superiority. It sometimes seems that for Hayek, evolutionary development becomes an end in itself, a purposeless movement that we have no reason to embrace.[162]

In the last decades of his life, Hayek's tone became more conservative in another sense as well. A secularist, he came to regard religious traditions as usefully conveying modes of behavior that were necessary complements to the institutions of the market and the rule of law, even if they were untrue or mythical.[163] But this growing rhetorical warmth toward traditions seemed to be in tension with his emphasis on the progressive role of social and economic innovators, who set the example to be emulated by others. Another dilemma overlooked by Hayek was that the tradition of the modern west that he defended acted as a solvent on those older, traditional ways of life he dubbed "tribal."[164] How far can earlier traditions be reshaped, one might ask, before they lose the positive functions that Hayek ascribed to them? All of this is to say that Hayek never fully reconciled his dynamic Smithian-Schumpeterian side with his conservative side. But then neither did Burke. Indeed, it remains a tension for all conservative defenders of capitalism, including conservative liberals like Hayek.

Hayek's weaknesses as a thinker come from his propensity to exaggerate the scope of his very real insights. His was the crystal-clear vision of the one-eyed man. His antipathy to the notion that government exists to protect any particular culture—a legacy of Viennese pariah liberalism—led him to ignore the need for a shared ethos, however limited—what Hegel had called *Sittlichkeit*. The experiences of illiberal Vienna, and then of Communism and Nazism, made it difficult for Hayek to think systematically about the role of a moral consensus for the proper functioning of market institutions. It was not that he failed to appreciate the role of shared traditions: it was that he could never reconcile that awareness with his broader, individualist social theory. His well-founded suspicion of the protection of particular interests through the romanticization of community led him to underrate the value of a sense of social solidarity, however loose. The self-sacrifice necessary for national self-defense against hostile powers lay beyond his theoretical horizon, though he often favored a hawkish position, first against the Third Reich and later against the Soviet Union and then against the Argentineans during the Falkland Islands conflict.[165] His fierce opposition to governmental coercion led him to define liberty as freedom from government power, but he overlooked the coercion felt by the employee constrained by the private power of his employer, and the possibility that such private coercion might usefully be restrained by the power of government.[166]

Sometimes Hayek's tendency to exaggerate his own insights led to self-contradiction. His emphasis on the limits of human knowledge—the extent of our ignorance—led him to a distrust of all rational institutional design. But this was at odds with his own suggestions for institutional reform based upon a rational analysis of the malfunctions of contemporary democratic institutions.[167]

Hayek's opposition to the use of government to enshrine any single culture led him to deny that there could be any shared cultural standards for the sake of which the market might be restrained. As a result, he had no way to evaluate the negative effects of the market or to suggest a principled reason to try to remedy them. Here he proved far more one-sided than his revered predecessor, Adam Smith. Burke's admonition—"The effect of liberty to individuals is, that they may do what they please: We ought to see what it will please them to do, before we risk congratulations"—never seems to have occurred to Hayek. The Arnoldian ideal of the disinterested intellectual willing to criticize one side and then the other in order to create balance and counteract the one-sidedness that led toward fanaticism: that too was as alien to Hayek as it had been to Marcuse. If it was partisanship that led Hayek to push forward intellectually to new insights, it was also partisanship that kept him from a balanced and rounded philosophy.

Perhaps a familiarity with "the best that has been thought and said" about the market will aid us in attaining a more disinterested and informed perspective. Such a perspective might well begin with Hayek's insights. But it would by no means end with them.

CONCLUSION

The Centrality of the Market

What this book has demonstrated, above all else, is the centrality of its theme for modern intellectual history. The question of the market—of its moral significance, of its social, political, cultural, and economic ramifications—has been at the focus of modern European thought. Its importance is not confined to those conventionally regarded as economists, such as Smith, Schumpeter, or Hayek. Nor is it possible to understand many of the burning concerns of thinkers such as Burke, Hegel, and Arnold without attention to what the market represented for them.

Much of the story we have told falls outside the boundaries of modern academic disciplines and their respective histories. Contemporary economics focuses on issues of efficiency in allocation, political science on the institutions of governmental power, political theory on questions of justice, sociology on social groups as defined by interactions outside the market. Some division of intellectual labor is of course productive, and the conceptual lenses that each discipline brings to bear may genuinely help us see an aspect of reality that would otherwise remain undetected. Yet those concerned with the moral implications and ramifications of the market—as any self-critical person in modern society ought to be—get a very skewed picture when they view it through only one of these lenses. Seeing the market with the added perspectives offered by the thinkers treated here provides us with a richer and more rounded view.

The Roles of Intellectuals

At various times and places, intellectuals have imagined a range of roles for themselves in a capitalist order. One, of course, is as opponents of capitalism, and as guides to its overthrow. But that has been only one imagined role, and by no means the most frequent or significant. One myth that this book should put to rest is that intellectuals are all anticapitalist, a myth given wide currency by Schumpeter. Like many social myths, it contains a grain of truth—but no more than that. To be sure, intellectuals on the left such as Marx, Lukács, and Marcuse really *were* fundamentally anticapitalist; so were those on the right, such as Sombart and Freyer. But it would be absurd to regard those who favored the market—such as Voltaire, Smith, Burke, Hegel, Arnold, Weber, Simmel, Schumpeter, Keynes, or Hayek—as anything but intellectuals. They are, on the contrary, among the most distinguished figures in modern European thought. At some times and places, antipathy to capitalism *has* been considered the mark of the intellectual, but that was out of ignorance of "the best that has been thought and said in the world," not because of it. Intellectuals have regarded their role within a capitalist order in a variety of ways: as advisers to legislators, attempting to maximize the potential advantages and minimize the inherent pitfalls of the market; as philosophers bringing the implicit moral assumptions of capitalism into consciousness; as critics, engaging in the ongoing and perhaps Sisyphean battle to improve tastes and preferences.

To say that many great intellectuals were far from fundamentally antipathetic to capitalism does not mean, of course, that they were its uncritical boosters. Of those listed above, only Hayek comes close to this characterization, and that one-sidedness is a mark of his embattled, ideological posture. Just as seeing a thing's faults does not necessarily give reason to destroy it, seeing its benefits is not a reason for overlooking those faults and, if possible, trying to mitigate them.

Analytic Tensions

The intellectuals' analysis of the market presents us not with a single moral but with a series of tensions. Thinkers of insight and intelligence have put forth plausible but conflicting claims about the market. One is reminded of the joke about two men who come to a rabbi to resolve their dispute. The rabbi listens to the first claimant, and remarks, "You're right." Then he hears the side of the second disputant, and declares, "You're also right." "But they can't both be right!" an onlooker comments. To which the rabbi responds, "You're right too."

On certain key issues, Smith and Marx, or Marcuse and Hayek, cannot both be right. Sometimes their views are indeed contradictory. But at other times they are merely in tension. Indeed, as we will see, there are some ongoing tensions in the analyses even of those who accept the market as a good thing. And those tensions may simply reflect the reality they purport to describe. Some tensions can be fatal contradictions, while others are productive. Time and again in the history of capitalism, one finds productive if painful tensions mistaken for fatal contradictions.

Self-Interest and Its Limits

Despite the divergences among the intellectuals we have examined, there are some broad areas of consensus.

The first concerns the productivity of capitalism. All analysts, from Voltaire through Hayek, have commented upon the increase in productivity that capitalism has brought about. For most, this has been one of the most telling points in its favor. For conservative defenders of pre-market regimes, like Möser, the superior productivity of capitalism was its most threatening aspect. Precisely because it made things more cheaply, it was likely to undermine the viability of existing forms of production and distribution, and the way of life that went with them. Marx and Engels were also struck by the fantastic productive power of capitalism. "The bourgeoisie," they wrote in *The Communist Manifesto*, "has been the first to show what man's activity can bring about. It has accomplished wonders far surpassing Egyptian pyramids, Roman aqueducts, and Gothic cathedrals." But they nevertheless insisted that since the market was "anarchic," socialism would maintain the productivity of capitalism without its distributional inequalities and its moral blemishes. Weber, Mises, Schumpeter, and Hayek explained in theory why socialism would be less productive; the history of communist states proved it in practice.

From time to time, critics asserted that the creative powers of the market were at an end: that there were no more opportunities left to exploit, that the technological frontier had been reached, that natural resources were running out. A popular claim in the 1930s, it was repeated by the Club of Rome in its 1972 report, "The Limits to Growth." This, as Schumpeter indicated, was a mirage. The notion that natural resources represent an objective limit on capitalism proved false, because the history of capitalism, as Schumpeter observed, is of finding new ways to make use of formerly insignificant resources. That was the case with coal during the first industrial revolution, petroleum during the second, and, during the third, uranium for atomic power and sand for silicon chips. We may well be at the beginning of the fourth wave of capitalist industrial innovation, the biotechnology revolution. In each case, the history of capitalism involves the discovery of new uses for substances previously of negligible worth.

Virtually every analyst has traced the greater productivity of capitalism, in whole or in part, to its ability to mobilize those self-interested propensities that have variously been termed greed (Marx), avarice (Burke, Keynes), or self-interest. Hayek focused on the market as conveying information, and as facilitating the creation of new knowledge. But he, too, believed that it was self-interest that made the market effective in fulfilling these functions.

Yet, if virtually all analysts have traced the greater productivity of capitalism to its ability to harness self-interest, even those who have been well-disposed toward the market have agreed that the pursuit of self-interest does not inevitably or automatically lead to socially desirable outcomes. Above all, they have agreed on the importance of the rule of law, enforced by the state, in preserving individuals from the depredations of others who, motivated by the desire for gain and unconstrained by law, would be eager to dominate them. For Adam Smith as for Hegel, the decline of serfdom brought about by the spread of market relations and the power of the state was morally significant for placing a limit on personal domination. Smith, as we have seen, reserved his greatest outrage for New World slavery, in which the absence of legal constraint allowed for the triumph of those he termed "the refuse of the jails of Europe." For Burke, the new men of the East India Company were able to wreak havoc on Indian civilization because they were unconstrained by law, as well as by inherited moral codes. Hayek, who loathed communism and fascism for their suppression of individual liberty, devoted the second half of his life to specifying the conditions under which the rule of law could be maintained. For all his suspicion of government power, he never imagined that without government meaningful freedom was possible in an advanced society.

In addition to an awareness of the indispensability of the rule of law if a market society was to be a civilized society, many of the thinkers we have examined have also looked to government, in part at least, to *counteract* the unintended but anticipatable negative effects of the market. Smith's eloquent analysis of the negative effects of the division of labor, and the disaster that would result unless steps were taken to counteract it, was but the first of these. Subsequent thinkers have insisted on a role for government in supplementing the market, whether it is providing public goods such as infrastructure, museums, and defense against foreign enemies, mitigating unemployment, assisting in provision for the poor, or expanding educational opportunity.

The Necessity of Countermarket Institutions

Those intellectuals favorably disposed toward capitalism have tended to emphasize the need for countermarket institutions. Since Adam Smith, most, though not all, have maintained that the market itself tends to provide institutional incentives for the development of some desirable character traits required for its own functioning, such as industriousness, frugality, the deferral of gratification, and honesty. (The actual attainment of wealth might provide incentives for laziness, prodigality, and reckless behavior. But those who developed such vices would be more than offset by others still striving to make their fortune.) That, as we have seen, was among the moral arguments in favor of the market, from Smith on, though Marx, Keynes, and Marcuse held frugality and deferred gratification against the market as overly repressive suspensions of the joy of life.

The notion that sociopolitical orders require dispositions or virtues not cultivated by their dominant institutions is at least as old as
Aristotle. In keeping with this tradition of thought, those who were
favorably disposed toward the market emphasized the need for counterinstitutions. Time and again, they asserted or implied that the dispositions, character traits, virtues, and experiences promoted by the
market were insufficient for human flourishing.[1] Market relations
were almost by definition contractual relations, entered into for self-
interested motives and capable of being dissolved when self-interest
was at an end. But there was more to life—or, more precisely, they
believed there *should* be more to life—than contractual relations. That
included relations of friendship and of love, with their accompanying
altruism, in which individual interest was subordinated to that of others. The family was the most frequent site of such relations, a point
stressed especially by Hegel, but also important for Smith, Burke, and
others.

The Family

For many, the family was the most important extra-market institution,
which transformed self-interest into something quite different. "The
power of perpetuating our property in our families is one of the most
valuable and interesting circumstances belonging to it, and that which
tends the most to the perpetuation of society itself," Burke wrote, "It
grafts benevolence even upon avarice."[2] Hegel pointed out that earning
a living in the marketplace is one of the most important ways in which
the love and deep obligation of family life is expressed. Schumpeter
saw the drive to found a transgenerational familial fortune as an important spur to entrepreneurial activity, and Hayek pointed to the desire
to provide opportunities for one's children as central to many life decisions in a capitalist society.

The State

Another counterinstitution was the state. To be sure, many analysts,
from Smith through Hayek, have emphasized that self-seeking behavior occurs in the political realm as well as in the market, indeed that
such self-seeking can become a major barrier to the market's effective
functioning. But precisely because the state was both indispensable for
the very existence of the market, yet threatened by organized interests,
intellectual analysts thought it necessary to cultivate a real commitment to the public good among at least part of the population. That is

why Smith's *Theory of Moral Sentiments* reserves its highest praise for legislators and generals, rather than for prudent men of business. Hegel and Arnold championed the role of a publicly minded civil service, and Keynes was the embodiment of that ideal. The trick was (and is) to have legislators and civil servants who are public-minded and yet capable of resisting the pressures to expand government endlessly, a temptation built into the reward structure of representative democracy, and into the natural propensity of civil servants to expand the purview of their power and control. That is why, in addition to institutional limits on government power, intellectuals from Smith to Hayek have written works to cultivate the desire among potential legislators and civil servants to be public-minded, while limiting government power.

Radicals opposed to capitalism have sometimes assumed that its elimination would bring about human liberation. Marx, therefore, had no theory of the future role of the state under socialism, nor did Lukács or Marcuse. Such institutions, which lay between the individual and humanity at large, were not seen as having ongoing significance.

The Nation

Some of the intellectuals we have examined regarded a concern for the nation—whether conceived as a distinct ethnic or cultural or political entity—as another counterweight to the market, an object of allegiance and duties beyond self-interest. For Hegel and for others, the nation was a necessary mediation, an intermediate point of identification between the individual and humanity in general. Weber defended participation in the world capitalist market as a necessary prerequisite of national power. Sombart conceived of the *Volk* as the antithesis of the market, and Freyer thought that only a total state could counteract the threat posed by capitalism to the cultural integrity of the nation, but not all nationalists or defenders of ethnic particularity have been so radical. Many, like Hegel or Weber, have viewed national identity as a complement to the market, and as a further basis of identification with the indispensable institution of the state.[3]

Cultural Institutions

Intellectuals have also suggested a variety of cultural institutions that would develop sensibilities, tastes, and traits not fostered by the market. For Burke, the Church played such a role, and Arnold, among others, thought that it still might. Arnold, like Hegel and many subsequent thinkers, also looked to the universities as a source of cul-

tural ideals and commitments different from those most readily promoted by the market. And, beginning with Voltaire, they tried to use
the world of journalism—the market of ideas—as a forum for what
Arnold called "criticism," the use of "the best which has been thought
and said in the world" to turn "a stream of fresh and free thought upon
our stock notions and habits."

Professional Associations

A number of thinkers maintained that meaning and direction could
also be provided by professional associations, such as unions and professional societies. While Hegel, for example, was pleased to consign
the closed, hereditary guilds to the past, he valued the guilds' integrative role and hoped to retain them in a more open version. Emile
Durkheim and a host of Catholic and fascist thinkers looked to such
professional associations as providing a desirable focus of identity and
solidarity, as have champions of the labor movement on both sides of
the Atlantic.[4]

Yet, though many thinkers have thought such mediating institutions important, liberals of various stripes from Smith on have been
suspicious of them as distinct sources of power. They have feared the
power that such institutions have over individuals. That is why
Hayek, for example, regarded such associations as desirable only so
long as they were voluntary. Liberals have been especially suspicious
of such associations when they are allowed to pursue political power,
fearing that they will use the power of the state to distort the market in
order to serve particular interests: what economists now term "rent-
seeking."

Choices Devoid of Meaning

The importance of such counterinstitutions was connected to perhaps
the most consistent worry of intellectuals: that the market (sometimes
in tandem with other forces in modern society, such as science and
technology) would lead to a life filled with choices but devoid of meaning.[5] There were several ongoing sources of concern. Hegel, as we have
seen, revived the Aristotelian theme of *pleonexia*, the danger that
arises from the open-ended desire for acquisition without limit or

reflective purpose. For Aristotle, *pleonexia* was a psychological disposition most often associated with merchants. In a commercial society,
where, as Smith wrote, "every man becomes in some measure a merchant," the hazards posed by unbounded acquisitiveness might be
institutionally limited, but never vanquished. Hegel warned of the
dangers of "negative infinity." His fear was that individuals might
become mere playthings of the want-creating machine that was the
market. Without a firm mooring in institutions like the family or the
professional association, and unguided by cultural frameworks that
provided an independent notion of appropriate wants, the individual
might be attracted to one commodity after another, in an endless
round of joyless consumption. Like Hegel, Arnold was critical of the
liberal belief that "doing as one likes" was the highest maxim, since it
tended to obscure the question of which things were worth doing—or
buying, or working for. Simmel explicated the related theme of the
danger of the triumph of means over ends, the notion that people
would become so caught up in the quest for means that they would
lose a sense of what those means were for, a danger inherent in that
quintessential means, money. Marcuse, more radically, saw the market as little more than a machine for want manipulation, at the
expense of real happiness.

Other than Rousseau, Möser, or Marcuse, none of the other thinkers
regarded the growth of new needs as itself pernicious. Voltaire pointed
out the developing, historical nature of needs and the enjoyment that
came from them, and most Enlightenment thinkers, including Smith,
welcomed new wants that arose from the refinement of tastes. What
all were concerned about, each in his own way, was that the growth of
new commodities, new wants, new means, and new choices would be
unsatisfying if it did not fit into some larger scheme, reflectively chosen by individuals and linked to their institutional attachments. Those
intellectuals who saw no possibility of such meaningful lives under
capitalism often opted, like Lukács and Freyer, for totalitarian alternatives.

Fear of Spillover

A recurrent theme, at least since Burke, has been the fear of spillover:
the notion that values and orientations that were appropriate in the

market would spill over to other forms of human association. Burke, like Hegel and then Arnold, warned against viewing the state as just another contractual relationship. There were also concerns that the sort of ongoing calculation of costs and benefits seen as characteristic of the market would spill over into marriage, destabilizing it and, as Schumpeter thought, diminishing progenitivity, as prospective parents calculated their utilities (not always wisely) and decided that children were not among them. For Marx, of course, it was axiomatic that the relations of domination and exploitation most visible in the market and the factory were equally present in the family, and that the state too was merely "the executive committee of the ruling class."

For at least two hundred years, then, from Möser and Burke down to Jürgen Habermas in our own day, intellectuals have repeatedly expressed concern that the modes of thought and action characteristic of the market would permeate all human relations.[6] The result, they warned, would be the impoverishment or disabling of the very institutions on which human flourishing depends.

Are There "Market Values"?

Yet in apparent contradiction to this venerable line of analysis, Friedrich Hayek made the provocative but no less plausible suggestion that there *are* no market values. Individuals act in the market to fulfill a variety of purposes, and try to get what the market offers—money— not because they lack nonmonetary goals, but because money provides a means to attain their varied goals. In this understanding of the situation, individuals bring to the market purposes generated in nonmarket institutions. Of course, as so many of the thinkers we have examined have explained, the capitalist market itself constantly produces new products and services, some of which come to be perceived as new needs. These products and services may be at odds with or complementary to purposes and attachments created elsewhere. The desire to provide education for one's offspring, for example, may be translated into the purchase of books, tutors, or computers, or into parental time devoted to education, depending on what the market has to offer.

It turns out, then, that the term "market values," which is often used as if it denoted something specific, covers a range of very different phenomena. Some analysts, no doubt, use it as a synonym for the desire for social status through material acquisition, which Smith described as one of the prime motives of market activity. Others use it to mean the more careful and calculating weighing of advantages and disadvantages that Weber called "rationalization" and Schumpeter "the utilitarian mentality." For still others, it is a synonym for professional advance, whether for purposes of social status or because, as Weber emphasized, professional identity is one of the most characteristic forms of modern identity. Though critics from Marx through Marcuse have condemned capitalist society for not providing an outlet for creative energies, the expression of creativity has long been another major motive to market activity, as Schumpeter pointed out, and may be increasing in importance.

As theorists from Voltaire through Hegel and on to our day have emphasized, much of what we regard as culture and cultivation, beginning with the scissors we use to trim our nails, comes to us through the market. To be cultured and cultivated is to have tastes that more often than not require the market for their fulfillment, whether for compact discs with which to experience the music of past and present, books to read the best that has been thought and said, or ecotourism to experience the wonders of nature.

The market, in short, *creates* needs and wants, even as it *reflects* needs and wants created elsewhere. (In the language of contemporary economics, preferences are endogenous to the market as well as exogenous.) What is striking is the ability of the capitalist market to co-opt and incorporate a remarkable range of preferences, trends, tastes, and identities. In Nazi Germany, Coca-Cola advertisements featured a storm trooper coming home thirsty from a rally and reaching for his Coke. Conversely, in the late 1960s, "Mao jackets" were briefly a hot commodity in the west. From sports cars to spirituality, from dashikis to communion wafers, from skullcaps to pornography—where there is demand, the market creates supply.

The problem is not the prudent calculation of costs and benefits—it is too constrained or misinformed a conception of costs and benefits. The challenge for the individual is to choose among the possibilities offered by the market in a reflective manner, so that they form part of some larger plan of life. The alternative is to become what Hegel saw as a possibility and Marcuse as a reality: a reactive slave to the manipulation of one's desires by those without an interest in one's well-being. The ability to produce individuals capable of making reflective choices and sticking to them may reflect the strength of those nonmarket or extra-market institutions, which seek to educate us, to mold our preferences to some more satisfying conception of what it means to be a worthy person than simply having more of what marketers succeed in making most alluring.

Are There Nonmarket Institutions?

Yet, as both Smith and Marx would have agreed, in many ways it is a fallacy to think of the family, the state, universities, and other "nonmarket" institutions as separate from the world of commerce. For the market reaches into each of those institutions. The process is hardly novel: Möser complained about the peddler invading the home and creating a taste among peasant women for the consumption of new commodities. The coming of print, radio, television, and the Internet have all intensified the reach of the market into the home, and perhaps into the self. The most intimate decisions about reproduction are influenced, in part, by the perceived costs (including opportunity costs) of bearing and raising children. If the family is sufficiently permeated by the market, its members lose that sense of subordinating their individual interests to the interests of the family, which analysts have seen as constitutive of familial relations.[7] Education, too, is sought with at least one eye on what it will bring in the marketplace. And the state, as we have seen, is intertwined with the market, not least because, as Smith suggested and Hayek explored, virtually every group seeks to make use of its political power in its own economic self-interest.

Another tension, then. If nonmarket institutions are indispensable for human flourishing in capitalist society, they are at the same time constantly being transformed by the market. The shape of the family changes, as fertility declines and as women move into the world of paid labor. Professional associations and labor unions are forced to respond to new products, new markets, and new forms of production that may destroy their economic basis. Voluntary organizations rise and decline with the perceived value of leisure time. The very dynamism of capitalism appears to be constantly threatening and undermining such institutions, and sometimes at least that perception is quite accurate.

Often enough, however, old institutions are reshaped by the market rather than destroyed by it. That has arguably been the case with the family. Or the decline of old institutions is followed by the rise of new ones, as guilds gave way to labor unions and professional associations. But, as Simmel pointed out, the general tendency seems to be for attachment to all-encompassing forms of association to be replaced by individual participation in many organizations, each of which exerts a looser hold on the self. Still, at each point in history, it seems unimaginable to some that new institutions will replace the old, or that new institutions may be more satisfying than those they replace. The lyrics of the lament have changed from Möser's defense of the guilds and their political role to Pierre Bourdieu's defense of contemporary French unions and their political clout.[8] But the tune remains familiar.

Community and Individuality

What should we make of the recurrent claim that capitalism destroys community? If community is defined as an all-encompassing form of association, then the claim is certainly true, as very disparate analysts from Möser to Marx to Simmel and Hayek would have agreed. But this process has its compensations, which its critics tend to overlook. Hayek pointed to the fact that the looser form of social organization he called "the Great Society" allowed people of very different orientations to live with one another, cooperate on a limited basis, and hence profit from their differences. The attempt to conceive of such a society as if its members made up a single, extended family, a larger version of the Greek polis, a traditional village, or a community of faith is bound to run aground on the shoals of a more complex reality.

Simmel pointed out that the development of capitalism creates more complex forms of individuality, since individuals can pursue a wider range of unconnected interests and belong to multiple associations without being defined (or swallowed up) by any one. Those associations often create linkages across borders, which means, for example, that two chamber music enthusiasts, one in Peoria, the other in Pretoria, may have more in common with one another than each has with his more immediate neighbors. Under such circumstances, individual identity arises from the set of one's interests and associations, a set different, in theory at least, for each individual and valued precisely because it is voluntarily chosen. As the contemporary philosopher John Gray has put it:

> We are none of us defined by membership in a single community or form of moral life. We are . . . heirs of many dis-

tinct, sometimes conflicting, intellectual and moral traditions. . . . The complexity and contradictions of our cultural
inheritance give to our identities an aspect of complexity
and even of plurality which is not accidental, but essential
to them. For us, at any rate, the power to conceive of ourselves in different ways, to harbour dissonant projects and
perspectives, to inform our thoughts and lives with divergent categories and concepts, is integral to our identity as
reflective beings.[9]

Such an identity carries the danger of degenerating into a series of
noncommitting choices, leading to the unsatisfying "negative infinity" that Hegel warned about. Or, conversely, the attempt to avoid the
logic of choice and contingency that the market facilitates may evoke
an opposite result, as individuals choose to define themselves according to a single attribute or interest (sex, race, religion, nationality, etc.),
and to declare that others must do so as well.

Pluralism and Diversity

Though capitalism is sometimes blamed for racism, sexism, and chauvinism, the most sophisticated analysts (whether of the left or the
right) have noted that the market tends to break down barriers between
groups. It creates incentives for members of various groups to reach out
to one another, whether as potential employers, employees, or customers. As Simmel noted, capitalist competition creates inducements
for empathy, and thus "achieves what usually only love can do: the
divination of the innermost wishes of the other, even before he himself
becomes aware of them."[10]

The market appears as a threat to particular cultures, because it
makes elements of foreign cultures available and even attractive. In
the eighteenth century it was British-made goods; today those goods
are most often American. But such cultural exchange is usually a two-
way street. Elements of various cultures, transformed into salable
commodities, are transported around the world. One can live in the
suburbs of Boston, drive to work in a Japanese car, eat Thai food, listen
to classical music written by Austrians and played by Korean virtuosi,
visit an acupuncturist, call a customer-service line answered in the

Philippines—it's the American way of life. If one begins with the dubious assumption that cultures should be integrated wholes, then this syncretism—or the synthesis made by each individual drawing upon the multiple possibilities presented by the market—may appear inauthentic or decadent. But for most people, the historical record is likely to bear out the thesis of Libanius of Antioch that commerce allows men to enjoy the widely scattered fruits of the earth, an idea revived by Voltaire in his defense of luxury and by Adam Smith in his description of the far-flung sources of the poor man's coat.

Yet here too there is a tension. For a world in which the same commodities were sold everywhere would be a world with far less diversity of cultures and societies. That is not necessarily a bad thing. The assumption that every culture and society is equally precious and ought to survive unrefined by the challenge of other cultural and social practices is an article of faith difficult to justify rationally. Nevertheless, a world in which local, regional, ethnic, and national coloration was eliminated would be poorer. To protect cultures from international competition was one of the goals of fascism, articulated by intellectuals like Hans Freyer. Its costs were greater than its benefits, not only because of its suppression of human liberty but because it was an attempt at collective delimitation that was based on treating the fluid reality of collective life as if it were a stable and coherent whole. (At the turn of the twenty-first century, new integralist movements beyond Europe, especially in the Islamic world, proclaimed similar goals of using state power to restore the imagined purity of their purportedly more valuable cultures and to protect them from the influence of the capitalist west.) Other states and regions have tried, more modestly and more effectively, to use law to protect commodities and ways of life that they regard as intrinsic to their national identity from the forces of market competition. The French, for example, tax themselves (and their fellow members of the European Union) to subsidize French farmers to produce "typically" French products like Camembert cheese and to maintain the scenic glory of the rural landscape.[11] Recently, some left-wing intellectuals, such as Jürgen Habermas, have argued that the welfare state has become so defining a characteristic of European identity that it should be preserved from the threats posed by international competition.[12] Different nations will no doubt continue to decide on a variety of trade-offs between the market and the state.[13]

Capitalism and Equality

Few have argued for capitalism primarily on the grounds that it increases equality—certainly none of the authors discussed in this book. Those who cared most about equality, from Rousseau on, have tended to be the most antipathetic to capitalism. Though capitalism often diminishes the significance of old sources of inequality based on birth, the argument by supporters of the market, at least since Smith, is not that it creates less inequality, but that it makes inequality more useful to society at large, and above all to the vast majority of the populace who profit from the availability of cheaper goods produced for the mass market. Cultures that favor equality in poverty over greater but unequally distributed affluence tend to be less market-oriented. There is some evidence that, historically, societies in the early stages of capitalist industrialization went through a period of increasing inequality, followed by a stage of greater equality.[14] Some of that pattern, as we have seen, can be explained in terms of demographic developments. Population growth that arose from improvements brought about in part by the spread of the market created new people faster than new jobs. The subsequent decline of inequality may therefore have been linked to the decline in fertility that eventually set in. (This process of "demographic transition," which took several generations in nineteenth-century Europe, has occurred much more quickly in many contemporary industrializing nations.) That pattern of increased inequality followed by a tendency toward equality may well repeat itself with each new wave of capitalist innovation.

Yet Schumpeter and Hayek draw our attention to another side of the issue of capitalism and inequality, one that remains unfashionable, even taboo. That is the extent to which economic growth may depend on the unequal contributions of the innovative, the gifted, the creative, and the entrepreneurial—qualities only partially captured by the language of "human capital" in which such matters tend to be discussed by economists. In democratic societies (or perhaps in academic precincts obsessed by the quest for equality) the argument that collective prosperity depends on allowing scope for the most driven or talented is likely to be understated.

Is Capitalism Good for People?

Is capitalism good for people? Here one must ask, "Compared to what?" Smith and Hegel thought it much preferable to the relations of direct domination that preceded it. A good deal of the history of the nineteenth and twentieth century is the search for viable alternatives to capitalism, most notably the various forms of communism and fascism. The popularity of capitalism, as Marcuse recognized, increased in part as these alternatives were tried and discredited. But that was not the whole answer, of course. Over time, the "universal opulence" that for Smith was the potential benefit of commercial society became increasingly palpable. The increase of material means and the multiplication of opportunities may or may not have made people better or happier (though there are good arguments for each of these), but it certainly made them better off. The material promise of *The Wealth of Nations* has been largely redeemed in the west, and its ongoing if uneven spread to the nonwestern world is in many respects the great story of our time. Despite an ongoing flurry of popular tracts purporting to show that international capitalism makes people poorer, the proposition will not bear much empirical scrutiny, and the quest of most nations in what was once the Communist bloc or the Third World is to join the international capitalist economy.[15]

"Abundance is the mother of the arts," wrote Voltaire in *The Worldling*, and the argument that material prosperity was the prerequisite for the development of higher civilization was repeated by virtually every advocate of economic growth. Thinkers such as Arnold and Keynes, not to mention Marcuse, wondered whether prosperity was wasted on the bourgeois philistines, and on the culture of means they created. It is to the credit of capitalism that so much of the debate in the more advanced capitalist nations has shifted over time from the question of how to liberate people from poverty to the question of what to do with prosperity. Here contemporary analysts and critics can draw on what is by now a long tradition of asking what economic growth is for, and whether it might be more adequately measured in terms other than gross national product, a question posed over a century ago by Arnold and recently revived by Amartya Sen.[16]

The notion that capitalist prosperity destroys the institutional foundations that created it is a theme almost as old as capitalism itself.

Every new revolution in consumption is greeted with the same warnings of impending doom. In the eighteenth century, John Wesley warned that "[r]eligion must necessarily produce both industry and frugality, and these cannot but produce riches. But as riches increase, so will pride, anger, and love of the world in all its branches."[17] Schumpeter revived the theme of the crumbling foundations in the middle of the twentieth century, a theme repeated with new variations by Daniel Bell in *The Cultural Contradictions of Capitalism* (1976) and revived most recently by Pierre Bourdieu, who argues that capitalism destroys the institutional legacy of the past that helps to stabilize the present. One inference of our survey is surely that if capitalism tends to undermine existing sources of morality, authority, trust, and cohesion, it also seems to allow for the creation of new ones. In this area, too, to focus on destruction without an eye to creation is to be myopic.

Capitalism and the Jews

The identification of capitalism with the Jews, as we have seen, sometimes had an element of plausibility in parts of modern Europe, though more often one of exaggeration. While that identification could be seen as positive (in the case of Hayek, for example), more often it served to delegitimate capitalism by identifying it with a long-stigmatized religious minority. Indeed, it was often a vehicle for expressing discontent with capitalist modernity itself. At the end of the twentieth century, that linkage seemed in decline, at least in the western world. That was not only because the deepening awareness of the Holocaust led (temporarily at least) to a diminution in antisemitism in much of the western world, but also because of the growing awareness that capitalism was the only game in town, and a game from which most could hope to profit. Yet, to the surprise of many, at the dawn of the twenty-first century, the negative identification of capitalism with the Jews seemed to migrate to portions of the Islamic world. When in the summer of 1997 Malaysia's prime minister, Mohammed Mahathir, went on a tirade and accused the Jews (including one Jew in particular, the hedge-fund manager George Soros) of conspiring to wreck Malaysia's economy, he provided a distant echo of what had once been an ongoing theme in European life.[18] Four years later, the attack on the World Trade Center was followed in parts of the Islamic world by a wave of rhetoric identifying Jews with the evils of international capitalism. Resentment against the success of the liberal, capitalist west, and revulsion toward the more open model of society it represented once more found in the Jews a useful personification of the processes seen as most threatening.

In general, acceptance of the market, popular and intellectual, seems to go hand in hand with a decline in antisemitism, together with other exclusionary ideologies. For, as Hayek pointed out, a capitalist society is one in which the polarity between ethnic, religious, or racial "insiders" and "outsiders" becomes ever more difficult to define and defend. The notion of offering favorable treatment to insiders becomes less acceptable. The cost of diminishing identification with an in-group will be seen by some as a decline of solidarity, by others as a healthy expansion of the bounds of association. The more different the butcher, baker, and brewer appear to us, the more we appeal to their self-interest rather than to their identification with our own interests. But the more we regard the ethnicity, race, religion, or nationality of the butcher, baker, and brewer as irrelevant to our self-interest, the more likely we are to include them within the circle of our commercial intercourse.

Vital Tensions

One might say that in the capitalist era, the older tension between this world and the next have been replaced (or, for some, overlaid) with a new set of inner-worldly tensions. The tensions between choices and purpose, between cultivating individuality while preserving the sense of attachment that gives life meaning, between independence and solidarity, between collective particularity and cosmopolitan interests, between productivity and equality—these are the characteristic tensions of the capitalist epoch, tensions with which we will continue to live. They will be experienced differently by different individuals and societies, and resolved with greater or lesser success in an endless variety of ways. An awareness of how these tensions came about and why they are intrinsic to the human condition in a market society—an awareness that draws upon the best that has been thought and said in the past—may lead us to greater criticism or greater reconciliation. But in either case, it provides a richer conceptual road map of where we have been, where we are, and where we might go.

NOTES

INTRODUCTION

1. Jürgen Habermas, *Legitimationsprobleme im Spätkapitalismus* (Frankfurt, 1973), translated by Thomas McCarthy as *Legitimation Crisis* (Boston, 1975); Daniel Bell, *The Cultural Contradictions of Capitalism* (New York, 1976); Irving Kristol, *Two Cheers for Capitalism* (New York, 1978); Christopher Lasch, *The Culture of Narcissism: American Life in an Age of Diminishing Expectations* (New York, 1979); Alasdair MacIntyre, *After Virtue* (Notre Dame, Ind., 1981).
2. Hans Freyer, *Die Bewertung der Wirtschaft im philosophischen Denken des 19. Jahrhunderts* (Leipzig, 1921); Raymond Williams, *Culture and Society, 1780–1950* (New York, 1958), and *Keywords: A Vocabulary of Culture and Society* (New York, 1976).
3. See Jerry Z. Muller, "Capitalism: The Wave of the Future," *Commentary* (December 1988), pp. 21–6.
4. Michael Oakeshott, review of Q.R.D. Skinner, *The Foundations of Modern Political Thought*, in *The Historical Journal*, vol. 23, no. 2 (1980), pp. 449–53, at p. 451.
5. For a thoughtful exploration of these issues, see Dominick LaCapra, "Rethinking Intellectual History and Reading Texts," in Dominick LaCapra and Steven Kaplan (eds.) *Modern European Intellectual History* (Ithaca, N.Y., 1982), pp. 47–85. Also the exchanges between Quentin Skinner and his critics, collected in James Tully (ed.), *Meaning and Context: Quentin Skinner and His Critics* (Princeton, N.J., 1988).
6. As noted by Steven Lukes, "The Singular and the Plural: On the Distinctive Liberalism of Isaiah Berlin," *Social Research*, vol. 61, no. 3 (fall 1994), pp. 686–717, at p. 692.
7. Karl Polanyi, *The Great Transformation* (Boston, 1957), pp. 42, 69–70, a book that, despite serious flaws and exaggerations, makes this particular point well.

CHAPTER ONE
HISTORICAL BACKDROP

1. Thomassin, *Traité du Négoce et de l'Usure* (1697), pp. 96 ff, quoted in Bernard Groethuysen, *The Bourgeois: Catholicism vs. Capitalism in Eighteenth-Century France* (New York, 1968), pp. 191–2.
2. Charles Davenant, "Essay upon the Probable Methods of Making a People Gainers in the Balance of Trade" (1699), in *Works*, vol. 2, p. 275; quoted in J. G. A. Pocock, *The Machiavellian Moment* (Princeton, N.J., 1975), p. 443.
3. For an evocation and analysis of the ethos of the Greek city-states, see Paul Rahe, *Republics Ancient and Modern: Classical Republicanism and the American Revolution* (Chapel Hill, N.C., 1992), book 1.

4. Plato, *Republic*, 550.
5. See Richard Mulgan, "Liberty in Ancient Greece," in Zbigniew Pelczynski and John Gray (eds.), *Conceptions of Liberty in Political Philosophy* (London, 1984), pp. 7–26, esp. pp. 8–10; Joseph Schumpeter, *History of Economic Analysis* (New York, 1954), p. 60.
6. Aristotle, *Politics*, ed. Carnes Lord (Chicago, 1994), book 1, chapter 9, and book 7, chapter 9. See also Thomas L. Lewis, "Acquisition and Anxiety: Aristotle's Case Against the Market," *Canadian Journal of Economics*, vol. 11, no. 1, pp. 69–90; and Rahe, *Republics*, pp. 57 ff and esp. 88 ff.
7. See S. C. Humphreys, *Anthropology and the Greeks* (London, 1976), pp. 139–50; and Rahe, *Republics*, chapter 3, "The Political Economy of Hellas."
8. See Rahe, *Republics*, pp. 72 ff.
9. Paul Millett, *Lending and Borrowing in Ancient Athens* (Cambridge, 1991), pp. 206–7, 218–21.
10. Aristotle, *Politics*, book 1, chapter 9; and the useful discussion in David Harris Sacks, "The Greed of Judas: Avarice, Monopoly, and the Moral Economy in England, ca. 1350–ca. 1600," *Journal of Medieval and Early Modern Studies*, vol. 28, no. 2 (spring 1998), pp. 263–307.
11. Aristotle, *Politics*, book 1, chapter 10.
12. See John W. Baldwin, *The Medieval Theories of the Just Price: Romanists, Canonists, and Theologians in the Twelfth and Thirteenth Centuries* (Philadelphia, 1959), pp. 12–16. For a brief but instructive comparison of rabbinic Jewish and Christian attitudes toward commerce and economic matters, see Derek J. Penslar, *Shylock's Children: Economics and Jewish Identity in Modern Europe* (Berkeley, Calif., 2001), pp. 52 ff.
13. Quoted in Raymond de Roover, "The Scholastic Attitude Toward Trade and Entrepreneurship," *Explorations in Entrepreneurial History*, second series, vol. 1, no. 1 (fall 1963), pp. 76–87, at p. 76.
14. John Gilchrist, *The Church and Economic Activity in the Middle Ages* (New York, 1969), pp. 52–3; Baldwin, *Medieval Theories*, p. 35.
15. Gratian, *Decretum*, pt. 1, dist. 88, cap. 11.
16. Lester K. Little, *Religious Poverty and the Profit Economy in Medieval Europe* (Ithaca, N.Y., 1978), p. 53.
17. Quoted in Jacob Viner, *Religious Thought and Economic Society* (Durham, N.C., 1978), pp. 35–6.
18. Viner, *Religious Thought*, pp. 37–8. On Libanius of Antioch and his influence see also Jacob Viner, *The Role of Providence in the Social Order* (Princeton, N.J., 1972), pp. 36–7. On the revival of Libanius' doctrine by Grotius, see Douglas A. Irwin, *Against the Tide: An Intellectual History of Free Trade* (Princeton, N.J., 1996), pp. 15–7.
19. Baldwin, *Medieval Theories*, p. 8.
20. See the insightful summary and analysis in Ernst Troeltsch, *Die Soziallehren der christlichen Kirchen und Gruppen* (Tübingen, 1922), volume 1 of his *Gesammelte Schriften* (reprinted 1965), pp. 334–48.
21. See Schumpeter, *History of Economic Analysis*, pp. 91–4; de Roover, "Scholastic Attitude," pp. 76–9; John F. McGovern, "The Rise of New Economic Attitudes—Economic Humanism, Economic Nationalism—During the Later Middle Ages and the Renaissance, A.D. 1200–1500," *Traditio*, vol. 26 (1970), pp. 217–54, at p. 230; Little, *Religious Poverty*, pp. 176 ff.; Julius Kirshner, "Raymond de Roover on Scholastic Economic Thought," in Julius Kirshner (ed.), *Business, Banking, and Economic Thought in Late Medieval and Early Modern Europe* (Chicago, 1974), p. 19. Kirshner's introductory essay provides a useful review of the scholarship on scholastic economic thought and a balanced critique of de Roover's work.

22. De Roover, "Scholastic Attitude," passim; McGovern, "Rise of New Economic Attitudes," p. 230; R. H. Tawney, *Religion and the Rise of Capitalism* (London, 1926), pp. 30 ff; Little, *Religious Poverty*, p. 181, exaggerates the extent of their embrace of commerce.

23. See Alasdair MacIntyre, *Whose Justice? Which Rationality?* (Notre Dame, Ind., 1988), p. 157.

24. MacIntyre, *Whose Justice?*, 162, 199, citing Aquinas, *Summa*, IIa–IIae, pp. 61–6.

25. De Roover, "Scholastic Attitude," p. 80.

26. On avarice as the root of the cardinal sins in Aquinas' *Summa Theologica*, see Morton Bloomfield, *The Seven Deadly Sins* (East Lansing, Mich., 1952), pp. 87–8.

27. Cited in de Roover, "Scholastic Attitude," p. 80; see also Viner, *Religious Thought*, pp. 35–8; and Schumpeter, *History of Economic Analysis*, pp. 60, 92, 99.

28. For examples, see Simon Schama, *The Embarrassment of Riches: An Interpretation of Dutch Culture in the Golden Age* (New York, 1987), pp. 329 ff; J. H. Hexter, "The Historical Method of Christopher Hill," in his *On Historians* (Cambridge, Mass., 1986), pp. 234–6.

29. Quoted in Stephen Innes, *Creating the Commonwealth: The Economic Culture of Puritan New England* (New York, 1995), p. 26.

30. Quoted by Max Weber, *The Protestant Ethic and the Spirit of Capitalism* (New York, 1958), p. 175 from Southey, *Life of Wesley* (2nd U.S. ed., vol. 2, p. 308).

31. Benjamin Nelson, *The Idea of Usury: From Tribal Brotherhood to Universal Otherhood*, 2nd ed. (Chicago, 1969), chapter 1.

32. Baldwin, *Medieval Theories*, pp. 33–7.

33. See Tawney, *Religion*, pp. 36–7, for examples drawn from medieval England; Dante, *Inferno*, cantos XI, XVII.

34. Little, *Religious Poverty*, pp. 178–80. On the Church's changing conception of usury in this period, see also Jacques Le Goff, *Your Money or Your Life: Economy and Religion in the Middle Ages* (New York, 1988).

35. On the casuistry of usury in eighteenth-century France, see Emma Rothschild, *Economic Sentiments: Adam Smith, Condorcet, and the Enlightenment* (Cambridge, Mass., 2001), p. 42.

36. Kirshner, *Business, Banking, and Economic Thought*, pp. 27–9; de Roover, "Money Theory prior to Adam Smith: A Revision," in Kirshner, *Business, Banking, and Economic Thought*, pp. 317–20.

37. See Robert S. Lopez, *The Commercial Revolution of the Middle Ages, 950–1350* (New York, 1976), chapters 2 and 3; and on the broader picture, R. W. Southern, *Western Society and the Church in the Middle Ages* (Harmondsworth, England, 1970), pp. 34–44.

38. Quoted in Hans-Jörg Gilomen, "Wucher und Wirtschaft im Mittelalter," *Historische Zeitschrift*, vol. 250, no. 2 (1990), pp. 265–301, at p. 265; this article provides a useful overview of recent historical literature on the gap between the theological condemnation of moneylending and its actual practice.

39. Salo W. Baron, *A Social and Religious History of the Jews*, 18 volumes to date (New York and Philadelphia, 1952–), vol. 4, p. 203, and vol. 9, p. 50; Le Goff, *Your Money*, pp. 9–10. For a useful overview of medieval Christian theological opinion on Jewish moneylending, see Léon Poliakov, *Jewish Bankers and the Holy See from the Thirteenth to the Seventeenth Century* (London, 1977), pp. 13–35. The question of whether Jews were permitted to engage in usury was disputed within the Church, on which see Gilomen, "Wucher und Wirtschaft im Mittelalter."

40. Little, *Religious Poverty*, pp. 34, 53.

41. Baron, *History of the Jews*, vol. 11, p. 144; Joshua Trachtenberg, *The Devil and the Jews* (New Haven, Conn., 1943), p. 193.

42. Baron, *History of the Jews*, vol. 4, pp. 120–1; Little, *Religious Poverty*, p. 56.

43. Little, *Religious Poverty*, p. 57.
44. Trachtenberg, *Devil and the Jews*, p. 191; and R. Po-chia Hsia, "The Usurious Jew: Economic Structure and Religious Representations in Anti-Semitic Discourse," pp. 161–76, in R. Po-chia Hsia and Hartmut Lehmann (eds.), *In and Out of the Ghetto: Jewish-Gentile Relations in Late Medieval and Early Modern Germany* (Cambridge, England, 1995), pp. 165 ff.
45. Baron, *History of the Jews*, vol. 4, pp. 150–6, 170–4, 223 ff.
46. Baron, *History of the Jews*, vol. 4, pp. 202–7; vol. 9, pp. 50 ff.
47. Fernand Braudel, *The Wheels of Commerce*, (New York, 1982), pp. 559–63; Charles P. Kindelberger, *A Financial History of Western Europe*, (London, 1984), pp. 41–3; R. H. Helmholz, "Usury and the Medieval English Church Courts," *Speculum* vol. 61/2 (1986), pp. 364–80; *Encyclical Letter of Our Holy Father by Divine Providence Pope Leo XIII on the Condition of Labor*, in Oswald von Nell-Breuning, S.J., *Reorganization of Social Economy: The Social Encyclical Developed and Explained* (New York, 1936), p. 367; Herbert Lüthy, "Lending at Interest or the Competence of Theology in Economic Matters," pp. 71–104, in Herbert Lüthy, *From Calvin to Rousseau: Tradition and Modernity from the Reformation to the French Revolution* (New York, 1970); John T. Noonan, Jr., *The Scholastic Analysis of Usury* (Cambridge, Mass., 1957), p. 382. Noonan's work provides the most detailed and precise treatment of the subject, and takes it up to the 1950s.
48. Tawney, *Religion*, pp. 92–5.
49. Lüthy, "Lending," pp. 74–9; Tawney, *Religion*, pp. 102–19.
50. Schama, *Embarrassment*, pp. 337, 330.
51. Helmholz, "Usury," p. 380; Kindelberger, *Financial History*, p. 41.
52. See Trachtenberg, *Devil and the Jews*, pp. 191–2; see also Steven E. Aschheim, " 'The Jew Within': The Myth of 'Judaization' in Germany," in his *Culture and Catastrophe* (New York, 1996), pp. 45–68.
53. For examples of the charge of usury against Calvinists, Puritans, and Presbyterians, see Tawney, *Religion*, pp. 209, 232–3, 252.
54. Cited in Werner Sombart, *The Jews and Modern Capitalism* (New Brunswick, N.J., 1982), pp. 250–1.
55. Tawney, *Religion*, pp. 152–3; Jean-Christophe Agnew, *Worlds Apart: The Market and the Theater in Anglo-American Thought, 1550–1750* (Cambridge, 1986), p. 121.
56. James Harrington, *Oceana*, p. 159, quoted in Steve Pincus, "Neither Machiavellian Moment nor Possessive Individualism: Commercial Society and the Defenders of the English Commonwealth," *American Historical Review* (June 1998), pp. 705–36.
57. See above all book 1 of Paul A. Rahe, *Republics*; also Stephen Holmes, *Benjamin Constant and the Making of Modern Liberalism* (New Haven, Conn., 1984), pp. 1, 179.
58. MacIntyre, *Whose Justice?* p. 163.
59. This brief summation of the civic tradition is drawn from Jeff A. Weintraub, "Virtue, Community, and the Sociology of Liberty: The Notion of Republican Virtue and Its Impact on Modern Western Social Thought" (Ph.D. diss., Berkeley, Calif., 1979), chapter 1; and the succinct account in J. G. A. Pocock, "Cambridge Paradigms and Scotch Philosophers," pp. 235–52, 235–6, and John Robertson, "The Scottish Enlightenment at the Limits of the Civic Tradition," pp. 137–178, 138–40, both in Istvan Hont and Michael Ignatieff (eds.), *Wealth and Virtue: The Shaping of Political Economy in the Scottish Enlightenment* (Cambridge, 1983); and Forrest McDonald, *Novus Ordo Seclorum: The Intellectual Origins of the Constitution* (Lawrence, Kans., 1985), pp. 70–1.
60. On the image of Sparta, see Elizabeth Rawson, *The Spartan Tradition in European Thought* (Oxford, England, 1969), esp. pp. 5–8. On the reality of the Spartan regime, insofar as it can be reconstructed, see Rahe, *Republics*, chapter 5.
61. James Harrington, *Oceana*, p. 295, quoted in Pincus, p. 717.

62. On England see Pincus, "Neither Machiavellian Moment nor Possessive Individual-ism," pp. 705–36, esp. pp. 720–4; and David Harris Sacks, "The Greed of Judas," pp. 263–307, especially the conclusion. On Holland, see especially a work first published in Dutch in 1662, John de Witt [Pieter de la Court], *The True Interest and Political Maxims of the Republic of Holland*, published in English translation in London, 1746, and reprinted New York, 1972; on the De la Courts see Eco Haitsma Mulier, "The Language of Seventeenth-Century Republicanism in the United Provinces," in Anthony Pagden (ed.), *The Languages of Political Theory in Early-Modern Europe* (Cambridge, 1987), pp. 179–95. On the often favorable view of commerce among Flo-rentine civic humanists, see Mark Jurdjevic, "Virtue, Commerce, and the Enduring Florentine Republican Moment: Reintegrating Italy into the Atlantic Republican Debate," *Journal of the History of Ideas*, vol. 62, no. 4 (2001), pp. 721–43, an impor-tant critique of J. G. A. Pocock's *The Machiavellian Moment* (Princeton, N.J., 1975) and the literature to which it has given rise.

63. See Pocock, *The Machiavellian Moment*.

64. Baldwin, *Medieval Theories*, p. 17.

65. J. H. Hexter, "Republic, Virtue, Liberty, and the Political Universe of J. G. A. Pocock," in his *On Historians* (Cambridge, Mass., 1979), pp. 255–303, at 294–303; Pocock, "Cambridge Paradigms," pp. 240–50.

66. On the normative role of theology versus the practical role of civil law in medieval Europe, see Baldwin, *Medieval Theories*, pp. 59–63.

67. See J. G. A. Pocock, "Virtues, Rights, and Manners: A Model for Historians of Politi-cal Thought," in Pocock, *Virtue, Commerce, and History* (Cambridge, 1985), pp. 43–5.

68. For a concise overview of the problems that the struggles of the sixteenth and seven-teenth centuries posed for political theorists, see F. J. C. Hearnshaw, "Introductory: The Social and Political Problems of the Sixteenth and Seventeenth Centuries," in F. J. C. Hearnshaw (ed.), *The Social and Political Ideas of Some Great Thinkers of the Sixteenth and Seventeenth Centuries* (New York, 1967), pp. 9–41.

69. Though the work of Leo Strauss was attacked in Quentin Skinner's manifesto of "contextualist" intellectual history, "Meaning and Understanding in the History of Ideas," *History and Theory*, vol. 8 (1969), pp. 3–53, Skinner has recently rediscovered Strauss' key insight on seventeenth-century thought: the denial of aristocratic and religious conceptions of the good life as the basis of political association. Compare, for example, Leo Strauss, *Spinoza's Critique of Religion* (New York, 1965; reprinted Chicago, 1997 [German original, 1930]), chapter 4, "Thomas Hobbes"; Leo Strauss, *The Political Philosophy of Hobbes* (Oxford, 1936), and Leo Strauss, *Natural Right and History*, chapter on Hobbes and Locke, with Quentin Skinner, *Reason and Rhetoric in the Philosophy of Hobbes* (Cambridge, 1996), pp. 284–93 ("The Attack on the *Vir Civilis*") and pp. 316–26 ("The Science of Virtue and Vice").

70. On this theme see, among others, Pierre Manent, *An Intellectual History of Liberal-ism* (Princeton, N.J., 1995; French original 1987).

71. Richard Tuck, "The 'Modern' Theory of Natural Law," in Anthony Pagden (ed.), *The Languages of Political Theory in Early-Modern Europe* (Cambridge, 1987), pp. 99–119; p. 114–9.

72. Grotius, *The Rights of War and Peace*, p. 64, quoted in Tuck, "The 'Modern' Theory of Natural Law," p. 117.

73. See the discussion of Grotius and his influence in Richard F. Teichgraeber III, *"Free Trade" and Moral Philosophy: Rethinking the Sources of Adam Smith's Wealth of Nations* (Durham, N.C., 1986), p. 177.

74. On the relationship between the thought of Grotius and Hobbes, see Richard Tuck, *Philosophy and Government, 1572–1651* (Cambridge, 1993). For an insistence upon Hobbes's radical originality, see Perez Zagorin, "Hobbes Without Grotius," *History of Political Thought*, vol. 21, no. 1 (spring 2000), pp. 16–40.

75. Hobbes, *Leviathan*, books 3 and 4, esp. chapter 38.
76. See the discussion of "courage" in *Leviathan*, chapter 6, and the deflation of glory and command in chapter 11, and the insightful discussion in Strauss, *The Political Philosophy of Hobbes*, pp. 113-6.
77. *Leviathan*, ed. Richard Tuck (Cambridge, 1991), chapter 46, pp. 470-1.
78. *Leviathan*, chapter 30, p. 231.
79. *Leviathan*, chapter 6, p. 42.
80. *Leviathan*, chapter 9, pp. 70-3.
81. *Leviathan*, chapter 16, p. 111.
82. Skinner, *Reason and Rhetoric*, pp. 163 ff. Despite Skinner's illuminating discussion of the place of paradiastole in the rhetoric of Hobbes' day, he fails to note how often Hobbes himself makes positive use of the technique.
83. On Mandeville see M. M. Goldsmith, *Private Vices, Public Benefits: Bernard Mandeville's Social and Political Thought* (Cambridge, 1985), and the valuable article by Russell Nieli, "Commercial Society and Christian Virtue: The Mandeville-Law Dispute," *Review of Politics*, vol. 51, no. 4 (fall 1989), pp. 581-611; on his influence, see E. J. Hundert, *The Enlightenment's Fable: Bernard Mandeville and the Discovery of Society* (Cambridge, 1994).

CHAPTER TWO
VOLTAIRE

1. See Jeremy Popkin, "Recent West German Work on the French Revolution," *Journal of Modern History*, vol. 59 (December 1987), pp. 737-50, at p. 749.

   Among the most useful overviews of Voltaire's life and thought are Peter Gay, *Voltaire's Politics: The Poet as Realist* (New York, 1964); Theodore Besterman, *Voltaire*, 3rd ed., (Chicago, 1976); Haydn Mason, *Voltaire: A Biography* (Baltimore, 1981); and a biography that supersedes earlier treatments, René Pomeau, *D'Arouet à Voltaire* (Oxford, 1985), the first volume of the now completed five-volume *Voltaire et son temps* (Oxford, 1985-1994). The admiration of these authors for their subject, however, leads them to underrate his faults of mind and character. The chapter on Voltaire in Maurice Cranston, *Philosophers and Pamphleteers: Political Theorists of the Enlightenment* (Oxford, 1986), provides a concise introduction.
2. See Keith Michael Baker, "On the Problem of the Ideological Origins of the French Revolution," in Dominick LaCapra and Steven Kaplan (eds.), *Modern European Intellectual History* (Ithaca, N.Y., 1982), pp. 197-219, at p. 217.
3. Quoted in C. B. A. Behrens, *Society, Government, and the Enlightenment: The Experiences of Eighteenth-Century France and Prussia* (New York, 1985), p. 153. The actual term "intellectual" arose in France during the Dreyfus Affair, with the publication of the Dreyfusard "Manifesto of the Intellectuals" in 1898. See Dietz Bering, *Die Intellektuellen* (Frankfurt, 1978), p. 38.
4. Voltaire to d'Alembert, 1765, quoted in Peter Gay, *Voltaire's Politics*, p. 34.
5. B. Faujas de Saint Fond, *A Journey Through England and Scotland to the Hebrides in 1784*, 2 vols. (Glasgow, 1907), vol. 2, pp. 245-6.
6. Burke, writing early in 1790 to an unknown correspondent, in Harvey C. Mansfield, Jr. (ed.), *Selected Letters of Edmund Burke* (Chicago, 1984), p. 268.
7. For an overview of the transition from patronage to the market, see Priscilla P. Clark, *Literary France: The Making of a Culture* (Berkeley, 1987), pp. 39-52. On the development of publishing in eighteenth-century France, see the works of Robert Darnton, *The Business of Enlightenment: A Publishing History of the* Encyclopédie, *1775-1800* (Cambridge, Mass., 1979) and *The Literary Underground of the Old Regime* (Cambridge, Mass., 1982).
8. A useful summary of these new cultural institutions, which have been the subjects of much recent research, is provided by Isser Woloch, *Eighteenth-Century Europe:*

Tradition and Progress, 1715–1789 (New York, 1982), pp. 183–97. See also the acute comments on the transformation of discourse into a commodity in J. G. A. Pocock, "Transformations in British Political Thought," *Political Science* (July 1988), pp. 160–78, at p. 174–8. For an excellent overview of the social basis of the French Enlightenment, see Hans Ulrich Gumbrecht, Rolf Reichardt, and Thomas Schleich, "Für eine Sozialgeschichte der Französischen Aufklärung," in Gumbrecht et al., *Sozialgeschichte der Aufklärung in Frankreich. Teil I* (Munich, 1981), pp. 3–54.

9. Keith Michael Baker, "Politics and Public Opinion Under the Old Regime: Some Reflections," in Jack R. Censer and Jeremy D. Popkin (eds.), *Press and Politics in Prerevolutionary France* (Berkeley, Calif., 1988), pp. 204–46, at pp. 208–14 and 230–1. On the origins and development of "public opinion" and the "public sphere," see Jürgen Habermas, *Strukturwandel der Öffentlichkeit* (Darmstadt, 1962), translated as *The Structural Transformation of the Public Sphere* (Cambridge, Mass., 1982), and Ernst Manheim, *Aufklärung und öffentliche Meinung: Studien zur Soziologie der Öffentlichkeit im 18. Jahrhundert* (Munich, 1979).

10. The notion that it was his altercation with Rohan that led Voltaire to flee to England is corrected in Pomeau, *D'Arouet à Voltaire*, pp. 201–2.

11. Quentin Skinner, *The Foundations of Modern Political Thought*, 2 vols. (Cambridge, 1978), vol. 2, p. 250.

12. Skinner, *Foundations*, vol. 2, pp. 241–54, 352.

13. Quoted in Besterman, *Voltaire*, p. 125.

14. André Michel Rousseau, *L'Angleterre et Voltaire*, 3 vols. continuously paginated (Oxford, 1976), *Studies on Voltaire and the Eighteenth Century*, vol. 145–7, pp. 109–11. On Fawkener see also Pomeau, *D'Arouet à Voltaire*, pp. 215–7.

15. The book was first published in London as *Letters Concerning the English Nation*, and much of the text appears to have been written in English by Voltaire himself. A French version was published in London in 1734, though the title page gave Basel as the place of publication to throw off the censors. See Harcourt Brown, "The composition of the *Letters Concerning the English Nation*," in W. H. Barber et al. (eds.), *The Age of Enlightenment: Studies Presented to Theodore Besterman* (Edinburgh, 1967), pp. 15–34. There is an outstanding critical edition published by the Société des Textes Français Modernes, edited and with commentary by Gustave Lanson, revised and updated by André M. Rousseau: Voltaire, *Lettres Philosophiques* (Paris, 1964). A useful recent discussion of the book's contents and composition is Dennis Fletcher, *Voltaire: Lettres Philosophiques* (London, 1986).

Quotations in English are drawn for the most part from the translation by Leonard Tancock in the Penguin Classics edition, Voltaire, *Letters on England* (New York, 1980).

16. On the strategy of using self-interest as a check on ideological zealotry in modern liberal thought, see Stephen Holmes, *Benjamin Constant and the Making of Modern Liberalism* (New Haven, Conn., 1984), pp. 252 ff. On the older argument that interest might be used to restrain ambition and the quest for political power, see Albert O. Hirschman, *The Passions and the Interests: Political Arguments for Capitalism Before its Triumph* (Princeton, N.J., 1976), part 1.

17. *Spectator*, no. 69, May 19, 1711; the French edition of 1722 is cited in Lanson (ed.), *Lettres Philosophiques* p. 76, n11.

18. Letter of Oct. 7, 1722, to Marquise de Bernieres, D128, p. 138, in *The Complete Works of Voltaire* (*Oeuvres complètes de Voltaire*), ed. Theodore Besterman, vol. 85 (Geneva, 1968).

19. Theodore Besterman (ed.), *Voltaire's Notebooks*, 2 vols. (Geneva, 1952). The quotation is on p. 43, the previous one on p. 31.

20. Andrew Marvell, "The Character of Holland," in *Poetical Works* (Boston, 1857), pp. 171–7, quoted in Simon Schama, *The Embarrassment of Riches: An Interpretation*

of Dutch Culture in the Golden Age (New York, 1987), p. 267. The poem was first published in 1651 and often reprinted thereafter.

21. P. G. M. Dickson, *The Financial Revolution in England: A Study in the Development of Public Credit, 1688–1756* (London, 1967), p. 514; Paul Mantoux, *The Industrial Revolution in the Eighteenth Century* (Chicago, 1983), p. 98.

22. Douglass C. North and Robert Paul Thomas, *The Rise of the Western World: A New Economic History* (Cambridge, 1973), p. 153.

23. Jacques Donvez, *De quoi vivait Voltaire?* (Paris, 1949), p. 62.

24. Carolyn Webber and Aaron Wildavsky, *A History of Taxation and Expenditure in the Western World* (New York, 1986), chapter 5; Fernand Braudel, *The Wheels of Commerce* (New York, 1982), pp. 521 ff; Charles P. Kindelberger, *A Financial History of Western Europe* (London, 1984), pp. 151–3.

25. Dickson, *Financial Revolution*, p. 514; Ranald C. Michie, *The London Stock Exchange: A History* (Oxford, 1999).

26. See John Brewer, *The Sinews of Power: War, Money, and the English State, 1688–1783* (New York, 1989), chapter 4.

27. On the limited role of such colonial profits in providing the capital for the industrial revolution, see Patrick O'Brien, "European Economic Development: The Contribution of the Periphery," *Economic History Review,* 2nd series, vol. 35, no. 1 (February, 1982), pp. 1–18.

28. For indications of Voltaire's involvement in currency speculation in 1722, see Donvez, *De quoi,* p. 22

29. Mantoux, *Industrial Revolution,* p. 96.

30. Dickson, *Financial Revolution,* pp. 17 ff.

31. Dickson, *Financial Revolution,* p. 495

32. Dickson, *Financial Revolution,* p. 514

33. Dickson, *Financial Revolution,* p. 156

34. See J. G. A. Pocock, *The Machiavellian Moment: Florentine Political Thought and the Atlantic Republican Tradition* (Princeton, N.J., 1975), pp. 446–61, 467–75.

35. Dickson, *Financial Revolution,* p. 515

36. Gedalia Yogev, *Diamonds and Coral: Anglo-Dutch Jews and Eighteenth Century Trade* (New York, 1978), pp. 17–21, 55; Addison is quoted on p. 21. Harold Pollins, *Economic History of the Jews in England* (Rutherford, 1982), pp. 54–60.

37. Yogev, *Diamonds,* pp. 50, 58; Dickson, *Financial Revolution,* pp. 263, 278–9, 498.

38. The letter to Thieriot is in Theodore Besterman (ed.), *Voltaire's Correspondence* (Geneva, 1953), vol. 2, pp. 36–9. The best account is now in Pomeau, *D'Arouet,* pp. 201–2, 212, 220; on the Mendes da Costa family and its relationship with Voltaire, see Norma Perry, "La chute d'une famille séfardie: les Mendes da Costa de Londres," *Dix-huitieme siècle,* vol. 13 (1981), pp. 11–25.

39. Letter to Lord Hailes, quoted in Rousseau, *L'Angleterre et Voltaire,* pp. 688–9n.

40. This analysis draws upon the brilliant stylistic analysis in Erich Auerbach, *Mimesis: The Representation of Reality in Western Literature* (Princeton, N.J., 1953), pp. 401 ff. But Auerbach's contention that Voltaire wants to demonstrate "the blessings of productive work" rather misses the point of setting the scene at the exchange rather than the harbor.

41. Much later, in his *Examen important de milord Bolingbroke* (1767), Voltaire wrote: "Today, in Rome, in London, in Paris, in all the great cities . . . All have but one god. Christians, Jews, and all the others worship him with the same ardor: that is money." Voltaire, *Oeuvres complètes,* L. Moland (ed.) (Paris, 1879), vol. 26, p. 306.

42. On the theme of the merchant as hero in English poetry and drama in the first half of the eighteenth century, see John McVeagh, *Tradefull Merchants: The Portrayal of the Capitalist in Literature* (London, 1981), chapter 3, and, more briefly, Neil McKendrick, "'Gentlemen and Players' Revisited: The Gentlemanly Ideal, the Business Ideal, and the Professional Ideal in English Literary Culture," in Neil

McKendrick and R. B. Outhwaite (eds.), *Business Life and Public Policy* (Cambridge, 1986), pp. 98–136, at pp. 108–10.

For subsequent attempts by the French *philosophes* to raise the status of the merchant, see the articles by Joncourt, D'Alembert, and Diderot in the *Encyclopédie*, cited in John Lough, *The Encyclopédie* (New York, 1971), pp. 357–9.

43. For Voltaire's subsequent development of this theme, see his article "Gens de lettres" in the *Encyclopédie*, and the discussion in Robert Darnton, "Philosophers Trim the Tree of Knowledge," in Robert Darnton, *The Great Cat Massacre and Other Episodes in French Cultural History* (New York, 1984), pp. 205–8. On the development of the "man of letters" as a self-conscious group ideal in eighteenth-century France, especially as expressed in literature, see Paul Bénichou, *Le sacre de l'écrivain, 1750–1830: Essai sur l'avènement d'un pouvoir spirituel laique dans la France moderne* (Paris, 1973), pp. 25–36.

44. On the role of the *Lettres philosophiques* in spreading Locke's reputation on the continent, see Jonathan I. Israel, *Radical Enlightenment: Philosophy and the Making of Modernity* (New York, 2001), p. 527.

45. Quoted in Besterman, *Voltaire*, p. 167.

46. Rousseau, *L'Angleterre et Voltaire*, pp. 137–8, 153–5.

47. For other instances see Pomeau, *D'Arouet à Voltaire*, p. 146; Donvez, *De quoi*, p. 83.

48. This account is based on Donvez, *De quoi*, pp. 39–55; Pomeau, *D'Arouet à Voltaire*, pp. 259 ff. On the role of lotteries in eighteenth-century Europe and the moralist critque of the institution, see Lorraine Daston, *Classical Probability in the Enlightenment* (Princeton, N.J., 1988), pp. 141–63.

49. Donvez, *De quoi*, pp. 71–4.

50. See Ernst Labrousse et al., *Histoire économique et sociale de la France*, vol. 2, (Paris, 1970), pp. 503–9; Werner Sombart, *Luxury and Capitalism* (1913; reprint, Ann Arbor, Mich., 1967), p. 127; Fernand Braudel, *Capitalism and Material Life, 1400–1800* (New York, 1973), pp. 156–91, 236–9.

51. Donvez, *De quoi*, pp. 57–69.

52. For acute observations on the recurrent suspicion of new wealth, see Albert O. Hirshman, *Shifting Involvements: Private Interest and Public Action* (Princeton, N.J., 1982), chapter 3.

Among the most useful examinations of the notion of "luxury" in eighteenth-century thought are Ellen Ross, "The Debate on Luxury in Eighteenth-Century France: A Study of the Language of Opposition to Change" (unpub. Ph.D. diss., University of Chicago, 1975); Simeon M. Wade Jr., "The Idea of Luxury in Eighteenth-Century England," (unpub. Ph.D. diss., Harvard University, 1968); John Sekora, *Luxury: The Concept in Western Thought, Eden to Smollett* (Baltimore, 1977); and André Morize, *L'Apologie du Luxe au XVIIIe Siècle et "Le Mondain" de Voltaire: Étude critique sur "Le Mondain" et ses Sources* (1909; reprint, Geneva, 1970). Line references to "Le Mondain" and "Défense de Mondain" are to this edition.

53. Sekora, *Luxury*, pp. 39–44.

54. M. M. Goldsmith, "Liberty, Luxury, and the Pursuit of Happiness," in Anthony Pagden (ed.), *The Languages of Political Theory in Early-Modern Europe* (Cambridge, 1987), pp. 225–52, at p. 236; M. M. Goldsmith, *Private Vices, Public Benefits: Bernard Mandeville's Social and Political Thought* (Cambridge, 1985), p. 26.

55. David Hume, *An Enquiry Concerning the Principles of Morals* (1751), ed. J. B. Schneewind (Indianapolis, Ind., 1983), pp. 73–4; Voltaire, *Philosophical Dictionary*, article "Virtue."

56. Voltaire, *Philosophical Dictionary*, article "Morality"; Voltaire, *Philosophie de l'histoire* (1740), quoted in Lucien Febvre, "*Civilization*: Evolution of a Word and a Group of Ideas," in Peter Burke (ed.), *A New Kind of History: From the Writings of Febvre* (New York, 1973), p. 229.

57. Febvre, "*Civilization*," pp. 219–57.

58. "Mondain," line 14.
59. "Mondain," lines 46–59.
60. "Mondain," lines 40 ff; "Défense," lines 73 ff.
61. Voltaire, "Observations sur Mm. Jean Lass" (1738), in Moland ed., *Oeuvres complètes*, vol. 20, p. 363, quoted in Ross, *Debate*, p. 64.
62. *Philosophical Dictionary* (Gay translation), article "Luxury."
63. "Défense," lines 55–72. For contemporary eighteenth-century variations of this argument, see Sombart, *Luxury and Capitalism*, pp. 113–5.
64. "Mondain," lines 19–24.
65. "Défense," lines 99–111.
66. "Défense," lines 35–45; this translation is from Besterman, *Voltaire*, p. 244 n. 4.
67. Donvez, *De quoi*, pp. 131–40. On the institution of lifelong annuities and the chicanery to which it could lead, see Kindelberger, *Financial History*, pp. 217–8.
68. Donvez, *De quoi*, p. 175.
69. D104, April 1722, in *Complete Works of Voltaire*, vol. 85, pp. 116–7. Voltaire appears to have brokered the privilege of collecting the salt tax, for which service he earned a commission from the newly formed company: Pomeau, *D'Arouet à Voltaire*, pp. 146–7.
70. Theodore Schieder, *Friedrich der Große: Ein Königtum der Widersprüche* (Frankfurt am Main, 1983), pp. 285, 442.
71. See Schieder, *Friedrich*, pp. 303–7, 458; for a similar conclusion, see Charles Morazé, "Finance et Despotisme: Essai sur les Despostes éclairés," *Annales: Économies, Sociétés, Civilisations*, vol. 3, no. 3 (1948), pp. 279–96.
72. On the *philosophes'* tactical support of expanded monarchial sovereignty, see Cranston, *Philosophers and Pamphleteers*, pp. 1–6, 49–50; Gay, *Voltaire's Politics*, chapters 3, 4, 7; Holmes, *Benjamin Constant*, pp. 9, 67–8; Leonard Krieger, *Kings and Philosophers, 1689–1789* (New York, 1970), pp. 189–204; Leonard Krieger, *An Essay on the Theory of Enlightened Despotism* (Chicago, 1975).
73. The account that follows is based largely on the analysis of the relevant documents offered by Wilhelm Mangold in his *Voltaires Rechtsstreit mit dem königlichen Schutzjuden Hirschel 1751: Prozeßakten des königlich Preußischen Hausarchivs* (Berlin, 1905), pp. i–xxxiii, as well as on the accompanying documents.
74. The classic study is Selma Stern, *The Court Jew* (Philadelphia, 1950). See also Jonathan Israel, *European Jewry in the Age of Mercantilism, 1550–1750*, 2nd ed. (Oxford, 1989), chapter 6.
75. D4359, quoted in Mason, *Voltaire*, p. 60.
76. Voltaire to Darget, Feb. 20, 1751; D4389, *Complete Works of Voltaire* (Geneva, 1971), pp. 124–5.
77. D5714, March 10, 1754, quoted in Besterman, *Voltaire*, p. 350.
78. D104, *Correspondence*, vol. 1, pp. 146–7. For the context see Pomeau, *D'Arouet à Voltaire*, pp. 148–9. For a similar characterization of Jews in the New World written by Voltaire in 1773, see *Correspondence*, vol. 86, p. 166.
79. The most thorough examination of Voltaire's portrait of the Jews in his published works is Hanna Emmrich, *Das Judentum bei Voltaire* (Breslau, 1930). On the question of Voltaire's antisemitism, see Peter Gay, "Voltaire's Anti-Semitism," in his *The Party of Humanity* (New York, 1971), pp. 97–108; and Arthur Hertzberg, *The French Enlightenment and the Jews* (New York, 1968), esp. pp. 280–308. Gay takes note of Voltaire's frequent references to the Jews as unscrupulous and usurious, but pays little attention to it in explaining Voltaire's antisemitism, which he regards primarily as a residue of popular prejudice. Hertzberg pays greater attention to Voltaire's negative economic characterization of the Jews, but explains it primarily as a response to his sour financial dealings with da Costa and Hirschel.

80. Voltaire, *La Bible enfin expliquée* (1776), *Oeuvres complètes*, vol. 30, quoted in Emmerich, *Judentum*, p. 142.

81. *Philosophical Dictionary*, Besterman translation, p. 144. For additional references to the ancient Hebrews as usurers, see the articles on "États, Gouvernements" and "Des Loix," section 1, pp. 193, 281.

82. *Essai sur les moeurs, Oeuvres complètes*, vol. 12, p. 159.

83. Emmerich, *Judentum*, pp. 139, 249 ff.

84. See the still valuable article by Isaac Eisenstein Barzilay, "The Jew in the Literature of the Enlightenment," *Jewish Social Studies*, vol. 18, no. 4 (October 1956), pp. 243–61.

85. Emmerich, *Judentum*, p. 257; Hertzberg, *French Enlightenment*, pp. 279–80, 299 ff, 312–3. On the cosmopolitan ideal in the Enlightenment see Thomas J. Schlereth, *The Cosmopolitan Ideal in Enlightenment Thought* (London, 1977), and Gerd van den Heuvel, "Cosmopolite, Cosmopoli(ti)sme," in Rolf Reichardt et al., *Handbuch politisch-sozialer Grundbegriffe in Frankreich, 1680–1820* (Munich, 1986), vol. 6, pp. 41–7; and Tzetvan Todorov, *On Human Diversity: Nationalism, Racism, and Exoticism in French Thought* (Cambridge, Mass., 1993).

86. Adam Smith, *The Theory of Moral Sentiments*, ed. A. L. Macfie and D. D. Raphael (Indianapolis, Ind., 1982), VI. i. 10, pp. 214–5.

CHAPTER THREE
ADAM SMITH

1. Voltaire, *Oeuvres complètes*, ed. Beaumarchais, 70 vols. (Kehl, 1784–89), 21:1.71, quoted in Deidre Dawson, "Is Sympathy So Surprising? Adam Smith and French Fictions of Sympathy," *Eighteenth-Century Life*, vol. 15, nos. 1 and 2 (1991), pp. 147–62, at p. 147. This chapter draws on Jerry Z. Muller, *Adam Smith in His Time and Ours: Designing the Decent Society* (Princeton, N.J., 1995), though with changes in emphasis and interpretation.

2. For a useful survey of English writings on this theme, see Milton L. Myers, *The Soul of Modern Economic Man: Ideas of Self-Interest, Thomas Hobbes to Adam Smith* (Chicago, 1983); for foreign sources see Muller, *Adam Smith*, pp. 48–54.

3. Josiah Tucker, *The Elements of Commerce and Theory of Taxes* (1755), quoted in T. W. Hutchison, *Before Adam Smith: The Emergence of Political Economy, 1662–1776* (Oxford, 1988), p. 230.

4. Adam Smith, *An Inquiry into the Nature and Causes of the Wealth of Nations*, ed. R. H. Campbell and A. S. Skinner, 2 vols. (The Glasgow Edition of the Works of Adam Smith, Oxford, 1976; cited hereafter as *WN*.) Introduction, 1, p. 428. The standard biography is now Ian Simpson Ross, *The Life of Adam Smith* (Oxford, 1995). Still invaluable for its treatment of Smith's thought and personality is the study by his student, Dugald Stewart, "Account of the Life and Writings of Adam Smith, L.L.D.," first published in 1794 and reprinted in Adam Smith, *Essays on Philosophical Subjects*, edited by W. P. D. Wightman and J. C. Bryce (Oxford, 1980).

5. See Leo Strauss, "On Classical Political Philosophy," in Thomas Pangle (ed.), *The Rebirth of Classical Political Rationalism: An Introduction to the Thought of Leo Strauss* (Chicago, 1989), pp. 49–62, at p. 54.

6. See Quentin Skinner, *The Foundations of Modern Political Thought*, vol. 1, *The Renaissance* (Cambridge, 1978), pp. 213 ff.

7. On the links between education, patronage, and government service in the Scotland of Smith's day, see Robert Wuthnow, *Communities of Discourse: Ideology and Social Structure in the Reformation, the Enlightenment, and European Socialism* (Cambridge, Mass., 1989), pp. 254–64, which summarizes a great deal of recent research on the topic.

8. Lewis Namier and John Brooke, *Charles Townshend* (London, 1964), p. 34.
9. See, for example, Sir Grey Cooper to Smith, Nov. 7, 1777, in *The Correspondence of Adam Smith*, ed. E. C. Mossner and L. S. Ross (Oxford, 1977), pp. 227–8.
10. John Rae, *Life of Adam Smith* (1895; reprint, New York, 1965), p. 437.
11. Duncan Forbes, "Scientific Whiggism: Adam Smith and John Millar," *Cambridge Journal*, vol. 7 (1953–54).
12. *WN*, V.ii.k, p. 870.
13. For an analytic portrait of Britain's development into a market economy from the sixteenth to the mid eighteenth centuries, see Keith Wrightson, *Earthly Necessities: Economic Lives in Early Modern Britain* (New Haven, Conn., 2000).
14. Paul Langford, *A Polite and Commercial People: England, 1727–1783* (Oxford, 1989), pp. 174–6; R. P. Thomas and D. N. McCloskey, "Overseas Trade and Empire, 1700–1860," in Roderick Floud and Donald McCloskey (eds.), *Economic History of Britain Since 1700*, vol. 1 (Cambridge, 1981), p. 93; and Ralph Davis, "The Rise of Protection in England, 1689–1786," *Economic History Review*, 2nd ser. (1966), pp. 306–17, pp. 313–4.
15. D. E. C. Eversley, "The Home Market and Economic Growth in England, 1750–1780," in E. L. Jones and G. E. Mingay (eds.), *Land, Labour, and Population in the Industrial Revolution* (London, 1967), p. 255. See more generally the excellent survey by Daniel Baugh, "Poverty, Protestantism, and Political Economy: English Attitudes Toward the Poor, 1660–1800," in Stephen B. Baxter (ed.), *England's Rise to Greatness, 1660–1763* (Berkeley, Calif., 1983), pp. 63–108, at pp. 81–90.
16. Langford, *Polite*, p. 150, and Neil McKendrick, "Introduction," in Neil McKendrick, John Brewer, and J. H. Plumb, *The Birth of a Consumer Society: The Commercialization of Eighteenth-Century England* (Bloomington, Ind., 1982), pp. 9 ff.
17. Neil McKendrick, "Commercialization and the Economy," in McKendrick, Brewer, and Plumb, *Birth of a Consumer Society*, p. 23.
18. Neil McKendrick, "Home Demand and Economic Growth: A New View of the Role of Women and Children in the Industrial Revolution," in Neil McKendrick (ed.), *Historical Perspectives: Studies in English Thought and Society* (London, 1974); Jan de Vries, "The Industrial Revolution and the Industrious Revolution," *Journal of Economic History*, vol. 54, no. 2 (June, 1994), pp. 249–70.
19. McKendrick, "Commercialization and the Economy," pp. 28–9.
20. Neil McKendrick, "Introduction," pp. 1–2; Langford, *Polite*, pp. 67 ff.
21. See Nathan Rosenberg, "Adam Smith on Profits—Paradox Lost and Regained," in Andrew S. Skinner and Thomas Wilson (eds.), *Essays on Adam Smith* (Oxford, 1975), pp. 377–89, at pp. 388–9.
22. W. A. Cole, "Factors in Demand 1700–80," in Floud and McCloskey (eds.), *Economic History of Britain*, p. 58; David S. Landes, *The Unbound Prometheus: Technological Change and Industrial Development in Western Europe, from 1750 to the Present* (Cambridge, 1969), pp. 58–9.
23. For examples, see Istvan Hont and Michael Ignatieff, "Needs and Justice in the 'Wealth of Nations,'" in Istvan Hont and Michael Ignatieff (eds.), *Wealth and Virtue: The Shaping of Political Economy in the Scottish Enlightenment* (Cambridge, 1983), p. 5; and Langford, *Polite*, p. 150.
24. Baugh, "Poverty," pp. 85–6. See also the discussion in Rosenberg, "Adam Smith on Profits," pp. 378–9.
25. *WN*, I.viii.35–42, pp. 95–9.
26. Stewart, "Account," p. 310. On this theme see also Duncan Forbes, "Sceptical Whiggism, Commerce, and Liberty," in Skinner and Wilson (eds.), *Essays on Adam Smith*, pp. 179–201. On the upward evaluation of "ordinary life" in early modern thought, see Charles Taylor, *Sources of the Self* (Cambridge, Mass., 1989), pp. 211–8; on the transformation of Christian charity into practical benevolence, pp. 84–5, 258, 281.
27. *WN*, I.i.11, p. 22–4.

28. "It is the great multiplication of the productions of all the different arts, in consequence of the division of labour, which occasions, in a well-governed society, that
universal opulence which extends itself to the lowest ranks of the people," *WN*,
I.i.19, p. 22.

29. *WN*, I.i.5, p. 17; on the importance of the development of machinery in bringing
about greater productivity see also *WN*, II 3–4, p. 277.

30. *WN*, I.iii.1, p. 31.

31. *WN*, I.ii.1–2, pp. 25–6.

32. *WN*, I.iv.1, p. 37.

33. *WN*, I.ii.4–5, pp. 28–30.

34. *WN*, I.ii.2, p. 27.

35. Adam Smith, *The Theory of Moral Sentiments*, ed. A. L. Macfie and D. D. Raphael
(The Glasgow Edition of the Works and Correspondence of Adam Smith, Oxford,
1976; rep. Indianapolis, Ind., 1982; cited hereafter as *TMS*). VI.ii.intro.2, p. 218;
VII.ii.3.18, p. 305.

36. *WN*, II.iii.28, p. 341.

37. *WN*, I.vii.1–6, pp. 72–3.

38. *WN*, I.vii.; I.x.a.1, p. 116.

39. *WN*, I.vii.15, p. 75.

40. *WN*, I viii 36, p. 96.

41. *TMS*, IV.2.6, p. 189.

42. *WN*, IV ii. 4, p. 454; *WN*, IV.ii.9, p. 456.

43. *WN*, IV.ii.10, p. 456.

44. This has been recognized by Nathan Rosenberg, "Some Institutional Aspects of the
Wealth of Nations," *Journal of Political Economy*, vol. 18, no. 6 (1960), pp. 557–70;
George Stigler, "Smith's Travels on the Ship of State," in Skinner and Wilson (eds.),
Essays on Adam Smith, pp. 237–46; and Lionel Robbins, *The Theory of Economic
Policy in English Classical Political Economy* (London, 1953), p. 56.

45. *WN*, V.i.e., p. 755.

46. *WN*, IV.ii.43, pp. 471–2

47. *WN*, I.x.c.61, pp. 157–8.

48. *WN*, I.viii.11–13, pp. 83–5.

49. *WN*, I.vii.26–7, pp. 78–9.

50. *WN*, I.vii.28, p. 79; I.x.c.3–17, pp. 135–40.

51. Stigler, "Smith's Travels," includes a useful chart of Smith's account of such
attempts on pp. 248–9.

52. *WN*, I.x.c.27, p. 145.

53. *WN*, I.x.c.18–24, pp. 141–4.

54. *WN*, IV.ii.43, p. 471.

55. *WN*, I.x.c.25, p. 144.

56. *WN*, IV.ii.21, p. 462.

57. *WN*, IV.ii.1, p. 452.

58. *WN*, IV.ii.2–3, p. 453.

59. See Charles Wilson, "Trade, Society, and the State," in *The Cambridge Economic
History of Europe*, vol. 4 (Cambridge, 1967), pp. 487–575, pp. 573–4. On mercantilist
thought and the history of the use of the term, see Jacob Viner, "Economic Thought:
Mercantilist Thought," in the *International Encyclopedia of the Social Sciences*.

60. *TMS*, VI.ii.2.3, p. 229.

61. *WN*, iii.c.9–11, pp. 493–5.

62. *WN*, IV.iii.c, esp. pp. 60–6, pp. 612–7, and *WN*, V.iii, 92, pp. 946–7.

63. *WN*, IV.i.33, pp. 448–9.

64. *WN*, IV.vii.c.91–108, pp. 631–41.

65. On the early modern notion that commerce makes men more "gentle," see Albert O.
Hirschman, *The Passions and the Interests: Political Arguments for Capitalism*

Before its Triumph (Princeton, N.J., 1977), passim, and esp. pp. 56–66; and Albert O. Hirshman, *Rival Views of Market Society and Other Recent Essays* (New York, 1986), pp. 106–9.

66. *TMS*, VII.ii.3.15–16, p. 304.

67. *WN*, I.iv.1, p. 37.

68. *WN*, I.x.c.31, p. 146.

69. On the distinction between virtue and propriety, see *TMS*, I.i.5. pp. 6–7.

70. *TMS*, VI.I, pp. 212–7.

71. *TMS*, I.iii.2.1, p. 50.

72. *TMS*, I.iii.3.1, p. 62.

73. *TMS*, I.iii.3.5, p. 63.

74. *TMS*, I.iii.3.6, p. 63.

75. On this point see Allan Silver, "Friendship in Commercial Society: Eighteenth-Century Social Theory and Modern Sociology," *American Journal of Sociology*, vol. 95, no. 6 (1990), pp. 1474–504, esp. p. 1493.

76. *TMS*, V.2.9, pp. 206–7.

77. *WN*, III.ii.10, p. 388. See also *WN*. I.vii.41, pp. 98–9.

78. *TMS*, IV.i.8–9, pp. 181–3; for similar comments on the psychic costs of wealth, see *TMS*, I.iii.2.1, p. 51.

79. *TMS*, IV.2.6–8, pp. 189–90; similarly III.5.8, pp. 166–7 and VI.i.1–14, pp. 212–6.

80. Adam Smith, *Lectures on Jurisprudence*, ed. R. L. Meek, D. D. Raphael, and P. G. Stein (The Glasgow Edition of the Works and Correspondence of Adam Smith, Oxford, 1978; rep. Indianapolis, Indiana, 1982), p. 239.

81. *WN*, V.i.g.24, pp. 802–3.

82. *WN*, IV.v.b.44, p. 540.

83. *WN*, V.i.a.14, p. 697.

84. *WN*, I.i.19, p. 22.

85. *WN*, V.i.f.50, p. 782.

86. Adam Smith, *Lectures on Rhetoric and Belles Lettres*, ed. J. C. Bryce (The Glasgow Edition of the Works and Correspondence of Adam Smith, Oxford, 1983; rep. Indianapolis, Indiana, 1985), p. 62.

87. See Jacob Viner, "Man's Economic Status," in his *Essays on the Intellectual History of Economics*, ed. Douglas Irwin (Princeton, N.J., 1991), pp. 286–7, on the attitude of the British upper classes toward popular schooling; for the quote from Voltaire, see p. 283.

88. On the economic incentives for child labor, see McKendrick, "Home Demand and Economic Growth," and de Vries, "The Industrial Revolution and the Industrious Revolution," pp. 249–70.

89. Smith, *Lectures on Jurisprudence*, pp. 539–40.

90. *WN*, V.i.f.54, p. 785.

91. *TMS*, VI.iii.13, p. 242.

92. *TMS*, VI.1.13, p. 216.

93. *TMS*, VI.1.14, p. 216.

94. For a brilliant evocation of the origins and recurrent laments of this criticism, see Allan Bloom, "Commerce and 'Culture,'" in his *Giants and Dwarfs: Essays, 1960–1990* (New York, 1990), pp. 277–94.

95. *TMS*, I.iii.2, p. 62.

96. Daniel Gordon, "On the Supposed Obsolescence of the French Enlightenment," in Daniel Gordon (ed.), *Postmodernism and the Enlightenment: New Perspectives in Eighteenth-Century French Intellectual History* (New York, 2001), pp. 201–21, at p. 204.

97. The best commentary on *The Theory of Moral Sentiments* is Charles L. Griswold, Jr., *Adam Smith and the Virtues of Enlightenment* (Cambridge, 1999). For my under-

standing of Smith's book I am also indebted to discussions with Nicholas Philippson and Samuel Fleishhacker.

98. *WN*, IV.ii.39, p. 468.

99. Walter Bagehot, "Adam Smith as a Person" (1876), reprinted in *The Works of Walter Bagehot*, 5 vols., vol. 3, (Hartford, Conn., 1889), pp. 269–306, at p. 303.

CHAPTER FOUR
JUSTUS MÖSER

1. All references to Möser's work are cited from the standard modern edition, *Justus Mösers Sämtliche Werke. Historisch-kritische Ausgabe in 14 Bänden* (Gerhard Stalling Verlag, Oldenburg/Berlin, 1943–1990). Henceforth cited as *SW*. All translations are my own. Perhaps the best portrait of Möser's thought is in Klaus Epstein, *The Genesis of German Conservatism* (Princeton, N.J., 1966), chapter 6; though like Karl Mannheim before him (in Karl Mannheim, *Conservatism: A Contribution to the Sociology of Knowledge*, ed. David Kettler, Volker Meja, and Nico Stehr [London, 1987]), Epstein tends to underrate Möser's dissatisfaction with the status quo in Osnabrück. On those aspects of Möser's thought relating to guilds, see Mack Walker, *German Home Towns: Community, State, and General Estate, 1648–1871* (Ithaca, N.Y., 1971), a book of great value in its conceptualization of the town and its dissolution under the pressures of the state and the capitalist economy. Jonathan Knudsen, *Justus Möser and the German Enlightenment* (Cambridge, 1986), is an invaluable source on Möser's social, economic, and political environment, as well as on his thought. An important source on Möser's economic milieu is Joachim Runge, *Justus Mösers Gewerbetheorie und Gewerbepolitik im Fürstbistum Osnabrück in der zweiten Hälfte des 18. Jahrhunderts* (Berlin, 1966). For an overview of Möser's political thought, see Frederick C. Beiser, *Enlightenment, Revolution, and Romanticism: The Genesis of Modern German Political Thought, 1790–1800* (Cambridge, Mass., 1992), pp. 288–302.

2. Voltaire, Introduction to chapter 2 of *Siècle de Louis XIV*.

3. In Voltaire's *Dictionnaire philosophique*, "Des Loix, section 1," quoted in Justus Möser, "Der jetzige Hang zu allgemeinen Gesetzen und Verordnungen ist der gemeinen Freiheit gefährlich" (1772), in *SW* 5, pp. 22–7, at p. 22.

4. Mack Walker, "Rights and Functions: The Social Categories of Eighteenth-Century German Jurists and Cameralists," *Journal of Modern History* 50 (June 1978), pp. 234–51, at p. 243. See also the sketch of Justi's thought in Walker, *German Home Towns*, pp. 161 ff.

5. Johann Gottlob Justi, *Die Grundfeste zu der Macht und Glückseligkeit der Staaten* (Königsberg, 1760), vol. I, pp. 555–8, 636, quoted in Walker, *German Home Towns*, p. 169.

6. On the rise of this conception of governmental activity, see Marc Raeff, *The Well-Ordered Police State: Social and Institututional Change Through Law in the Germanies and Russia, 1600–1800* (New Haven, Conn., 1983), chapter 1, esp. pp. 39–42; and David F. Lindenfeld, *The Practical Imagination: The German Sciences of the State in the Nineteenth Century* (Chicago, 1997), chapter 1.

7. Justus Möser, "Der jetzige Hang," pp. 22–7, at pp. 23–4.

8. On this theme see Otto Brunner, *Land und Herrschaft*, 5th ed. (Vienna, 1965), pp. 111–20. For a description of the control exercised by the Prussian noble over those under him see Robert M. Berdahl, *The Politics of the Prussian Nobility: The Development of a Conservative Ideology, 1770–1848* (Princeton, N.J., 1988), chapters 2–3.

9. In Möser's day, the term "patriotism" was often used in this sense, to denote a commitment to the commonweal, defined in local terms. See Rudolf Vierhaus, " 'Patriotismus'—Begriff und Realität einer moralisch-politischen Haltung," in his

Deutschland im 18. Jahrhundert: Politische Verfassung, soziales Gefüge, geistige Bewegungen (Göttingen, 1987), pp. 96–109, esp. pp. 97, 100.

10. *SW*, vol. 5, p. 22.

11. Möser, "Die Vorteile einer allgemeinen Landesuniforme, deklamiert von einem Bürger," *SW*, vol. 5: 58–66, atp. 64; and "Über die zu unsern Zeiten verminderte Schande der Huren und Hurkinder," *SW*, vol. 5: pp. 142–5, at p. 142. For an English translation of the latter essay, see Jerry Z. Muller (ed.), *Conservatism: An Anthology of Social and Political Thought from David Hume to the Present* (Princeton, N.J., 1997), pp. 70–3.

12. Muller, *Conservatism*, pp. 14–7.

13. The following description of Osnabrück in Möser's day is drawn largely from Knudsen, *Justus Möser*, chapters 2–5.

14. See Fernand Braudel, *The Wheels of Commerce* (New York, 1982), pp. 81–93.

15. Runge, *Justus Mösers Gewerbetheorie*, p. 45.

16. For an excellent analysis of this distinction, see Peter Berger, Brigitte Berger, and Hansfried Kellner, *The Homeless Mind: Modernization and Consciousness* (New York, 1973), pp. 83–96. On the concept of honor see also Friedrich Zunkel, "Ehre," in Otto Brunner and Werner Conze (eds.), *Geschichtliche Grundbegriffe*, 2 (Stuttgart, 1975). pp. 1–63; and Hans Reiner, *Die Ehre: Sichtung einer abendländischen Lebens- und Sittlichkeitsform* (Darmstadt, 1956).

17. A translation of the text of the document forms the appendix of Walker, *German Home Towns*, here p. 440.

18. Walker, *German Home Towns*, p. 91.

19. Möser, "Haben die Verfasser des Reichsabschiedes von 1731 wohl getan, dass sie viele Leute ehrlich gemacht haben, die es nicht waren?" *SW*, pp. 4, 240–44; Möser, "Über die zu unsern Zeiten verminderte Schande."

20. Möser, "Gedanken über den westfälischen Leibeigentum," *SW*, vol. 6, pp. 224–49, p. 227.

21. Möser, "Was ist bei Verwandelung der bisherigen Erbesbesetzung mit Leibeignen in eine freie Erbpacht zu beachten?" *SW*, vol. 7, pp. 263–73.

22. See, for example, Möser, "Nichts ist schädlicher als die überhandnehmende Ausheurung der Bauerhöfe," *SW* 6, pp. 238–55, and Knudsen, *Justus Möser*, pp. 136–7.

23. Knudsen, *Justus Möser*, p. 117; Möser, "Vorschlag zu einer Zettelbank," *SW*, vol. 5, pp. 278–81.

24. Knudsen, *Justus Möser*, pp. 50–1.

25. On the centrality of this question in eighteenth-century economic policy see Steven L. Kaplan, *Bread, Politics, and Political Economy in the Reign of Louis XV*, 2 vols. (The Hague, 1976).

26. Möser, "Vorschlag, wie die Teurung des Korns am besten auszuweichen," *SW*, vol. 5, pp. 27–35; in a similar vein, see "Den Verkauf der Frucht auf dem Halme ist eher zu begünstigen als einzuschränken," *SW*, vol. 5, pp. 103–6.

27. Möser's proto-romanticism is emphasized by Friedrich Meinecke, *Historism: The Rise of a New Historical Outlook* (New York, 1972), pp. 276 ff.

28. Möser, "Gedanken," pp. 15–28, and "Von dem Verfall des Handwerks in kleinen Städten," *SW*, vol. 4, pp. 155–77.

29. Braudel, *Wheels*, pp. 297–349.

30. See for example Möser, "Ein sichers Mittel, das gar zu häufige Koffeetrinken abzuschaffen," *SW*, vol. 6, pp. 146–7.

31. On the mercantilist fight against the consumption of coffee and tea, see Henri Brunschwig, *Enlightenment and Romanticism in Eighteenth-Century Prussia* (Chicago, 1974), pp. 75–7.

32. Möser, "Der notwendige Unterscheid zwischen dem Kaufmann und Krämer," *SW*, vol. 5, pp. 150–4.

33. Möser, "Die Vorteile einer allgemeinen Landesuniforme, deklamiert von einem Bürger," *SW*, vol. 5, pp. 58–66, at 61.

34. For explorations of this theme, see Christopher J. Berry, *The Idea of Luxury* (Cambridge, 1994), and Albert O. Hirschman, *Shifting Involvements: Private Interest and Public Action* (Princeton, N.J., 1982), pp. 46–62.

35. Möser, "Klage wider die Packenträger," *SW*, vol. 4, pp. 185–8, at p. 187.

36. On peddlers, see Braudel, *Wheels*, pp. 75 ff.

37. Möser, "Klage," p. 188.

38. Möser, "Noch etwas gegen die Packen oder Bundträger," *SW*, vol. 8, pp. 113–9, at p. 117.

39. Möser, "Noch etwas," p. 117.

40. Möser, "Klage," p. 188. For similar complaints about the invasion of domestic space by hawkers and itinerant salesmen almost two centuries later and a continent away, see Timothy Burke, *Lifebuoy Men, Lux Women: Commodification, Consumption, and Cleanliness in Modern Zimbabwe* (Durham, N.C., 1996), pp. 70–1.

41. Möser, "Das *Pro* und *Contra* der Wochenmärkte," *SW*, vol. 5, pp. 218–1.

42. Möser, "Urteil über die Packenträger," *SW*, vol. 4, pp. 194–7.

43. This was a central theme of Möser's multivolume *Osnabrückische Geschichte*, his Germanic version of "the ancient constitution" explored in its French and British versions in J. G. A. Pocock, *The Ancient Constitution and the Feudal Law* (Cambridge, 1957, 1987), chapters 1 and 2.

44. Möser, "Der Bauerhof als eine Aktie betrachtet," *SW*, vol. 6, pp. 255–70.

45. Möser, "Von dem Einflusse der Bevölkerung durch Nebenwohner auf die Gesetzgebung," *SW*, vol. 5, pp. 11–22.

46. On the creation of a mass population outside of the traditional social and political structure, see generally Peter Kriedte, *Peasants, Landlords, and Merchant Capital: Europe and the World Economy, 1500–1800* (Cambridge, 1983), pp. 148 ff; on the alarm it created among policy makers in central Europe, see James van Horn Melton, *Absolutism and the Eighteenth-Century Origins of Compulsory Schooling in Prussia and Austria* (Cambridge, 1988), chapters 5–6, esp. pp. 119, 123 ff.

47. Runge, *Justus Mösers Gewerbetheorie*, p. 23.

48. For illuminating general descriptions of dispersed manufacture, see Max Weber, *General Economic History* (New Brunswick, N.J., 1981), pp. 158–61; David S. Landes, *The Unbound Prometheus: Technological Change and Industrial Development in Western Europe from 1750 to the Present* (Cambridge, 1969), pp. 44–5; Braudel, *Wheels*, pp. 287 ff.

49. Möser, "Die Frage: Ist es gut, dass die Untertanen jährlich nach Holland gehen? wird bejahet," *SW*, vol. 4, pp. 84–97.

50. Möser, "Die Frage: Ist es gut"; see also Knudsen, *Justus Möser*, chapter 5. Möser's claims regarding a causal link between rural manufacture and population growth corresponds closely to the model posited by Hans Medick in Peter Kriedte, Hans Medick, and Jürgen Schlumbohm, *Industrialization Before Industrialization: Rural Industry in the Genesis of Capitalism* (Cambridge, 1981), pp. 54 ff. The generalizability and empirical validity of the processes described by Medick have been called into question by Hans Linde, "Proto-Industrialisierung: Zur Justierung eines neuen Leitbegriffs der sozialgeschichtlichen Forschung," *Geschichte und Gesellschaft*, vol. 6 (1980), pp. 103–24, and by Eckart Schremmer, "Industrialisierung vor der Industrialisierung: Anmerkungen zu einem Konzept der Proto-Industrialisierung," *Geschichte und Gesellschaft* 6 (1980), pp. 420–48. The pattern that Möser describes appears to have been widespread in northwestern Europe; it does account for the increase in population in some areas, though some areas without cottage industry also grew in population, indicating that the spread of rural industry cannot be used as a general explanation of the eighteenth-century rise in population. For a skeptical view of the literature on proto-industrialization, see the informative review article

by Rab Houston and K. D. M. Snell, "Proto-industrialization? Cottage Industry, Social Change, and Industrial Revolution," *Historical Journal*, vol. 27, no. 2 (1984), pp. 473–92.
51. Möser, "Ist es gut," p. 94.
52. Möser, "Vorschlag, wie die gar zu starke Bevölkerung im Stifte einzuschränken," *SW*, vol. 8, pp. 299–300.
53. Möser, "Von dem Einflusse," pp. 20–1.
54. Möser, "Etwas zur Verbesserung der Armenanstalten," *SW*, vol. 4, pp. 68–73.
55. Möser, "Vorschlag," pp. 299–300.
56. Möser, "Die moralischen Vorteile der Landplagen," *SW*, vol. 5, pp. 37–40.
57. On this aspect of Möser's thought, see Martin Greiffenhagen, *Das Dilemma des Konservatismus in Deutschland*, 2nd ed. (Munich, 1977), pp. 51–61.
58. Möser, "Die Vorteile einer allgemeinen Landesuniforme, deklamiert von einem Bürger," pp. 58–66.
59. Möser, "Vorteile," p. 59.
60. Möser, "Von dem Verfall des Handwerks in kleinen Städten," *SW*, vol. 4, pp. 155–77, 168–9.
61. Möser, "Vorteile," pp. 65–6.

CHAPTER FIVE
EDMUND BURKE

1. On the recurrent predispositions, arguments, substantive themes, and metaphors of conservative thought, see the introduction to Jerry Z. Muller (ed.), *Conservatism: An Anthology of Social and Political Thought from David Hume to the Present* (Princeton N.J., 1997).
   Among the best and most up-to-date discussions of Burke's conservatism are Iain Hampsher-Monk, "Introduction," to Iain Hampsher-Monk (ed.), *The Political Philosophy of Edmund Burke* (New York, 1987), pp. 1–43; and the same author's chapter on Burke in his *A History of Modern Political Thought* (Oxford, 1992). A penetrating analysis of Burke's political writings is provided by David Bromwich in the introduction to the volume of Burke's speeches and letters, *On Empire, Liberty, and Reform*, ed. David Bromwich (New Haven, Conn., 2000).
2. On English society and government in the period, see Paul Langford, *A Polite and Commercial People: England 1727–1783* (Oxford, 1989). Despite some overstatement, C. B. Macpherson is fundamentally correct in asserting that the traditional order that Burke cherished "was not simply any hierarchical order but a capitalist one." C. B. Macpherson, *Burke* (Oxford, 1980), p. 61.
3. The most up-to-date works on Burke's life, from which I have drawn, are Stanley Ayling, *Edmund Burke: His Life and Opinions* (London, 1988), and Conor Cruise O'Brien, *The Great Melody: A Thematic Biography of Edmund Burke* (Chicago, 1992).
4. For a description of the "Club" or "Academy of Belles Lettres" founded by Burke and his friends at Trinity College, see Arthur P. I. Samuels and Arthur Warren Samuels, *The Early Life, Correspondence and Writings of the Rt. Hon. Edmund Burke LL.D.* (Cambridge, 1923), pp. 203–4.
5. See *The Reformer* of February 18, 1747/8, reproduced in Samuels, *Early Life*, pp. 306–7, 287–98.
6. Burke, *A Philosophical Enquiry into the Origin of Our Ideas of the Sublime and Beautiful*, ed. James T. Boulton (Notre Dame, Ind., 1968), p. 53.
7. Quoted in Ayling, *Edmund Burke*, p. 20.
8. On Burke's role in the Rockingham Whigs in this period, see Paul Langford, "Introduction," to Paul Langford (ed.), *The Writings and Speeches of Edmund Burke*, volume 2, *Party, Parliament, and the American Crisis, 1766–1774* (Oxford, 1981).

9. H. V. F. Somerset, *A Note-Book of Edmund Burke* (Cambridge, 1957), p. 82.

10. Burke, *Thoughts on the Causes of the Present Discontents*, in *The Works of the Right Honorable Edmund Burke*, 6th ed. (Boston, 1880), p. 529. For a searching analysis, see Harvey C. Mansfield, Jr., *Statesmanship and Party Government: A Study of Burke and Bolingbroke* (Chicago, 1965).

11. *Thoughts*, p. 530; italics added.

12. *Thoughts*, p. 533; italics in original.

13. *Thoughts*, p. 530.

14. *Thoughts*, pp. 534–5.

15. Carl B. Cone, *Burke and the Nature of Politics: The Age of the French Revolution* (Lexington, Ky., 1964), pp. 146–8. The surviving correspondence between Burke and Smith indicates a relationship of mutual esteem and warmth. See *The Correspondence of Adam Smith*, ed. E. C. Mossner and I. S. Ross (Oxford, 1977).

16. Burke, "Speech at the Conclusion of the Poll in Bristol, November 3, 1774," in Burke, *On Empire, Liberty and Reform* ed. Bromwich, pp. 48–58, p. 55.

17. See Langford, "Introduction," p. 19.

18. See Langford, "Introduction," pp. 4–7.

19. Quoted in Ayling, *Edmund Burke*, p. 27.

20. See Geoffrey Carnall, "Burke as Modern Cicero," in Geoffrey Carnall and Colin Nicholson (eds.), *The Impeachment of Warren Hastings: Papers from a Bicentenary Commemoration* (Edinburgh, 1989).

21. The extent of Burke's ongoing involvement in the *Annual Review* after his entry into Parliament remains uncertain. See Carl B. Cone, *Burke and the Nature of Politics*, pp. 112–3, 121–2.

22. See Langford, "Introduction," p. 18, remarking on Burke's "Short Account of a Late Short Administration"; John Brewer, "Rockingham, Burke, and Whig Political Argument," *Historical Journal*, vol. 18, no. 1 (1975), pp. 188–201; and Rocco L. Capraro, "Typographic Politics: The Impact of Printing on the Political Life of Eighteenth-Century England, 1714–1772" (unpub. Ph.D. diss, Washington University, 1984).

23. Paul Langford, *A Polite and Commercial People: England, 1727–1783* (Oxford, 1989), p. 720.

24. Langford, *Polite*, pp. 706–9; Christopher Reid, *Edmund Burke and the Practice of Political Writing* (New York, 1986), p. 216.

25. See Christopher Reid, *Edmund Burke*, pp. 95–136, for an analysis of this process.

26. See the editorial notes of P. J. Marshall, in P. J. Marshall (ed.), *The Writings and Speeches of Edmund Burke*, vol. 5 (Oxford, 1981), pp. 479–80.

27. J. A. W. Gunn, "Public Spirit to Public Opinion," in his *Beyond Liberty and Property: The Process of Self-Recognition in Eighteenth-Century Political Thought* (Kingston, 1983), pp. 281–9; and "The Fourth Estate," in the same volume, p. 91.

28. Keith Michael Baker, "Public Opinion as Political Invention," in his *Inventing the French Revolution* (Cambridge, 1990), pp. 187–8.

29. The distinction between "public opinion" and "published opinion" is drawn from Arnold Gehlen, especially his essays "Die öffentliche Meinung" and "Die Öffentlichkeit und ihr Gegenteil," in Arnold Gehlen, *Einblicke* (Arnold Gehlen Gesamtausgabe, vol. 7), ed. Karl-Siegbert Rehberg (Frankfurt am Main, 1978).

30. Burke, "Thoughts on French Affairs," in *The Writings and Speeches of Edmund Burke*, ed. L. G. Mitchell, vol. 8 (Oxford, 1989), p. 346.

31. Burke, "Thoughts on French Affairs," p. 348.

32. Burke, "Second Letter on a Regicide Peace," *Writings and Speeches*, vol. 9, p. 295.

33. Somerset, *A Note-Book of Edmund Burke*, p. 83.

34. Somerset, *A Note-Book of Edmund Burke*, p. 93.

35. Somerset, *A Note-Book of Edmund Burke*, p. 90.

36. Somerset, *A Note-Book of Edmund Burke*, p. 91.

37. Edmund Burke, *A Vindication of Natural Society*, in Ian Harris (ed.), *Burke: Pre-Revolutionary Writings* (Cambridge, 1993), pp. 10–11.

38. Burke, *Vindication*, pp. 8–10.

39. Lucy Sutherland, "Edmund Burke and the First Rockingham Ministry," in her *Politics and Finance in the Eighteenth Century*, ed. Aubrey Newman (London, 1984), p. 318; see also Burke, "A Short Account of a Late Short Administration" (1766), in *The Works of the Right Honorable Edmund Burke*, 6th ed. (Boston, 1880), vol. 1, pp. 265–8.

40. Lucy Sutherland, "The City of London in Eighteenth-Century Politics," in Sutherland, *Politics and Finance in the Eighteenth Century*, pp. 59–60.

41. Langford, *Polite*, pp. 706–10.

42. *The Reformer*, March 10, 1747/8, reprinted in Samuels, *Early Life*, p. 314.

43. Burke, "Letter to a Noble Lord," in *Writings and Speeches*, vol. 9, pp. 159–60.

44. R. H. Campbell and A. S. Skinner, *Adam Smith* (New York, 1982), pp. 204–5.

45. Burke, "Tract on the Popery Laws," in Ian Harris (ed.), *Burke: Pre-Revolutionary Writings* (Cambridge, 1993), p. 96.

46. Burke, "Third Letter on a Regicide Peace" (1797), in *Writings and Speeches*, vol. 9, pp. 347–48.

47. Letter to Span, 1778, in *The Works of the Right Honorable Edmund Burke*, 6th ed. (Boston, 1880), vol. 2, pp. 249–58.

48. Letter to Harford, Cowles and Co., May 2, 1778, in *The Correspondence of Edmund Burke*, vol. 3, ed. George G. Guttridge (Cambridge, 1961), p. 442. The letter, together with the letter to Span cited above, was published jointly as *Two Letters from Mr Burke to Gentlemen in the City of Bristol*. Both may be found in Bromwich (ed.) *Edmund Burke*.

49. On Burke's parliamentary efforts on behalf of freer trade for Ireland, see Carl B. Cone, *Burke and the Nature of Politics*, pp. 336 ff; and R. B. McDowell's "Introduction" to part 2 of *The Writings and Speeches of Edmund Burke*, vol. 9 (Oxford, 1991), pp. 399 ff.

50. See the note by R. B. McDowell in R. B. McDowell (ed.), *The Writings and Speeches of Edmund Burke*, vol. 9 (Oxford, 1991), p. 130.

51. See the note by R. B. McDowell cited in note 50, above, p. 123.

52. On the background to "Thoughts and Details on Scarcity," see Thomas Horne, *Property Rights and Poverty: Political Argument in Britain, 1605–1834*, p. 162.

53. Now available in R. B. McDowell (ed.), *The Writings and Speeches of Edmund Burke*, vol. 9 (Oxford, 1991), pp. 119–45.

54. "Thoughts and Details," in *Writings and Speeches*, vol. 9, pp. 120–1.

55. Both judgments tend to be confirmed by recent historiography. For evidence of greater work, see Jan de Vries, "Between Purchasing Power and the World of Goods," in John Brewer and Roy Porter (eds.), *Consumption and the World of Goods* (London, 1993), pp. 85–132, and his "The Industrial Revolution and the Industrious Revolution," *Journal of Economic History*, vol. 54, no. 2 (June 1994), pp. 249–70. For evidence that real wages had indeed increased over the period in question, see the works cited in McDowell's note to p. 122 of "Thoughts and Details."

56. Adam Smith, *The Wealth of Nations*, ed. R. H. Campbell and A. S. Skinner (Oxford, 1976) IV.ii.10, p. 456.

57. "Thoughts and Details," pp. 129–33.

58. "Thoughts and Details," p. 123.

59. "Thoughts and Details," pp.126–7.

60. "Thoughts and Details," p. 133

61. "Thoughts and Details," p. 121.

62. "Thoughts and Details," p. 129.

63. "Thoughts and Details," p. 137.

64. Burke, *Reflections on the Revolution in France,* in *Writings and Speeches,* vol. 8, p. 209. The divergences in this regard between Smith and Burke are presented (and perhaps exaggerated) by Donald Winch, "The Burke-Smith Problem and Late Eighteenth-Century Political and Economic Thought," *The Historical Journal,* vol. 28, no. 1 (1985), pp. 231–47.

65. "Thoughts and Details," p. 125.

66. Dixon Wecter, *Edmund Burke and His Kinsmen: A Study of the Statesman's Financial Integrity and Private Relationships,* University of Colorado Studies, series B, Studies in the Humanities. vol. 1, no. 1 (Boulder, 1939), pp. 24–7. On Burke's finances, in addition to Wecter, I have relied on Lucy Sutherland (with John A. Woods), "The East India Speculations of William Burke," in Sutherland, *Politics and Finance,* pp. 327–60; and Ayling, *Edmund Burke.*

67. On the history of the EIC in this period I have relied primarily on P. J. Marshall, "Introduction," in his *Problems of Empire: Britain and India* (London, 1968), pp. 18–9; and C. A. Bayly, *Indian Society and the Making of the British Empire* (Cambridge, 1990), pp. 47–55.

68. For the details, see Lucy Sutherland, *The East India Company in Eighteenth-Century Politics* (Oxford, 1952), pp. 188–9.

69. Such is the judgment of the best modern historians of the incident; see Wecter, *Edmund Burke and His Kinsmen,* p. 95, and Sutherland, "East India Speculations," p. 331.

70. Langford, *Polite,* p. 372.

71. Langford, *Polite,* p. 533.

72. Langford, *Polite,* p. 374.

73. Sutherland, *East India Company,* p. 193 and passim.

74. "Ninth Report of the Select Committee, June 25, 1783," in P. J. Marshall (ed.), *The Writings and Speeches of Edmund Burke,* vol. 5, *India: Madras and Bengal, 1774–1785* (Oxford, 1981), p. 202.

75. "Ninth Report," p. 226.

76. "Ninth Report," p. 232.

77. "Ninth Report," p. 242.

78. "Ninth Report," p. 223.

79. "Ninth Report," pp. 227, 236.

80. "Speech on Fox's India Bill," p. 443, in P. G. Marshall (ed.), *Writings and Speeches,* vol. 5, p. 443.

81. The information in this paragraph is drawn from "Appendix C: Paul Benfield" in P. J. Marshall (ed.), *Writings and Speeches,* vol. 5.

82 *Writings and Speeches,* vol. 5, pp. 125–132; and see the account in O'Brien, *Great Melody,* pp. 307–8.

83. Sutherland, *East India Company,* pp. 398–400.

84. "Speech on Fox's India Bill," pp. 437–40.

85. See the account in O'Brien, *Great Melody,* pp. 335–6.

86. See James Raven, *Judging New Wealth: Popular Publishing and Responses to Commerce in England, 1750–1800* (Oxford, 1992), pp. 221–48.

87. P. J. Marshall editorial notes in Marshall (ed.), *Writings and Speeches,* vol. 5, pp. 478–80; and Carl B. Cone, *Burke and the Nature of Politics,* pp. 165–7.

88. "Speech on the Nabob of Arcot's Debts," Marshall (ed.), *Writings and Speeches,* vol. 5, pp. 516 ff.

89. "Speech on the Nabob of Arcot's Debts," p. 518.

90. "Speech on the Nabob of Arcot's Debts," p. 493.

91. "Speech on the Nabob of Arcot's Debts," p. 496; similarly, "Speech on Fox's India Bill," p. 407.

92. "Speech on the Nabob of Arcot's Debts," p. 486.

93. "Speech on the Nabob of Arcot's Debts," p. 544.
94. See note by McDowell, in *Writings and Speeches*, vol. 9, p. 552.
95. On the low priority of India reform among the Rockingham Whigs, see Sutherland, *East India Company*, p. 382.
96. O'Brien, *Great Melody*, p. 304. This work contains the fullest account of Burke's campaign against the EIC and its agents.

    Burke's campaign on behalf of the Indian population—a campaign from which neither he nor his country stood to gain in any but a moral sense—demonstrates the limits of an entirely utilitarian approach to his thought. "We have obligations to mankind at large, which are not in consequence of any special voluntary pact," he wrote in his "Appeal from the New to the Old Whigs" of 1791. "They arise from the relation of man to man, and the relations of man to God, which relations are not a matter of choice." (In *Further Reflections on the Revolution in France: Edmund Burke*, ed. Daniel E. Ritchie [Indianapolis, Ind., 1992], p. 160.) In this sense, natural law was a fundamental if diffuse element of Burke's thought.
97. "Speech on Fox's India Bill," pp. 389-90.
98. "Speech on Fox's India Bill," p. 402.
99. On avarice as the root of the cardinal sins in Aquinas' *Summa Theologica*, see Morton Bloomfield, *The Seven Deadly Sins* (East Lansing, Mich., 1952), pp. 87-8.
100. "Speech on the Nabob of Arcot's Debts," pp.532, 536. For similar images, see p. 543.
101. Burke, *Reflections*, p. 293.
102. Florin Aftalion, *The French Revolution: An Economic Interpretation* (Cambridge, 1990), pp. 57-8.
103. *Moniteur*, vol. 2, p. 54 (Oct. 13, 1789). See also Louis Bergeron, "National Properties," in François Furet and Mona Ozouf (eds.), *A Critical Dictionary of the French Revolution* (Cambridge, Mass., 1989), p. 512.
104. On Burke's sources of information during the writing of his "Reflections," see F. P. Lock, *Burke's Reflections on the Revolution in France* (London, 1985), pp. 44-5.

    Such considerations are entirely absent in Burke's initial analysis of the revolution, found in his "Letter to Charles-Jean-François Depont" of November 1789. J. G. A. Pocock, whose important article, "The Political Economy of Burke's Analysis of the French Revolution" (in his *Virtue, Commerce, and History* [Cambridge, 1985], pp. 193-212), places great emphasis on the fact that Burke's argument reflects a long-standing British debate on the political effects of public debt, overlooks the extent to which Burke borrowed his analysis from participants in the French debate.
105. *Reflections*, p. 157.
106. *Reflections*, pp. 94-5.
107. *Reflections*, p. 201.
108. *Reflections*, p. 238.
109. *Reflections*, p. 242.
110. *Reflections*, p. 154. For other references to "money-jobbers, usurers, and Jews," see *Reflections*, pp. 99-100. In his "Letter to a Member of the National Assembly" (1791), the expropriation of Church lands and their use to back the *assignats* is said "to gorge the whole gang of usurers, pedlars, and itinerant Jew-discounters at the corners of streets." (In *Writings and Speeches*, vol. 8, p. 304). Clearly Burke is drawing upon the traditional linkage between Jews as moneylenders and as normative outsiders, discussed in chapter 1 above.
111. "Third Letter on a Regicide Peace," pp. 346 ff.
112. *Reflections*, pp. 160-1. In the *Reflections on the Revolution of France*, Burke conjectured that in France men of finance regarded the landed nobility with rancor because the newly rich resented the disdain with which they were viewed by the nobility, and were prevented from joining it (*Reflections*, p. 159). But as he became

more immersed in French affairs, he gave less weight to this explanation. ("Thoughts on French Affairs" [1791], in *Writings and Speeches*, vol. 8, pp. 346–7.)

113. *Reflections*, p. 160.
114. *Reflections*, p. 162.
115. *Reflections*, p. 197.
116. *Reflections*, p. 102.
117. *Reflections*, pp. 213, 218, 268–272. See on this process Keith Michael Baker, "Inventing the French Revolution," in his *Inventing the French Revolution: Essays on French Political Culture in the Eighteenth Century* (Cambridge, 1990).
118. *Reflections*, pp. 258–69.
119. *Reflections*, pp. 112, 129–30.
120. *Reflections*, pp. 128–9.
121. For a useful explication of Burke's conservatism, see Iain Hampsher-Monk's "Introduction" to his *The Political Philosophy of Edmund Burke*; as well as the chapter on Burke in his *A History of Modern Political Thought*.
122. *Reflections*, pp. 110–1.
123. See Jerry Z. Muller, *Adam Smith in His Time and Ours: Designing the Decent Society* (Princeton, N.J.), 1995, pp. 93–112.
124. See Muller, *Adam Smith*, pp. 113–30.
125. See on this theme J. G. A. Pocock, "The Political Economy of Burke's Analysis of the French Revolution" and "Virtues, Rights, and Manners: A Model for Historians of Political Thought," in Pocock, *Virtue, Commerce, and History*.
126. *Reflections*, p. 129.
127. On the Enlightenment metaphor of the "naked truth" see Hans Blumenberg, "Paradigmen zu einer Metaphorologie, " *Archiv für Begriffsgeschichte*, vol. 6 (1960), pp. 7–142, at pp. 49–54; and Jean Strarobinski, *Jean-Jacques Rousseau: Transparency and Obstruction* (Chicago, 1988).
128. There is a good analysis of this imagery in Lock, *Burke's Reflections*, pp. 127–8.
129. *Reflections*, p. 127.
130. On Burke's earlier use of such imagery in his speeches on India, see Isaac Kramnick, *The Rage of Edmund Burke: Portrait of an Ambivalent Conservative* (New York, 1977), pp. 134–42.
131. *Reflections*, pp. 128–9.
132. *Reflections*, p. 130.
133. *Reflections*, p. 141. The quote from Cicero in Burke's footnote is particularly revealing in this regard.
134. *Reflections*, p. 130.
135. *Reflections*, p. 130.
136. *Reflections*, p. 290. On Burke's movement from a libertarian position on church/state issues toward a greater emphasis on the social and political role of the established church, see J. C. D. Clark, *English Society, 1688–1832* (Cambridge, 1985), pp. 247–58.
137. "Second Letter on a Regicide Peace" (1796), in *Writings and Speeches*, vol. 9, p. 291–2.
138. This point is also made by Christopher Reid, *Edmund Burke and the Practice of Political Writing* (New York, 1986), pp. 222–3.
139. *Reflections*, p. 214.
140. "Letter to a Noble Lord" (1796), in *Writings and Speeches*, vol. 9, p. 176. See similarly "Appeal from the New to the Old Whigs" (1791), in Daniel R. Ritchie (ed.), *Edmund Burke: Further Reflections on the Revolution in France* (Indianapolis, Ind., 1992), p. 182.
141. "Letter to a Noble Lord," pp.176–7.
142. "Second Letter on a Regicide Peace," p. 289. Plaidoyers were the legal pleas presented by defense lawyers, such as Robespierre.

143. *Reflections*, p. 147.
144. "Appeal," p. 160.
145. "Appeal," pp. 160–1.
146. On Arnold, see chapter 8 below.

CHAPTER SIX
HEGEL

1. Those lectures have been published and are available in an English translation as *Lectures on Natural Right and Political Science: The First Philosophy of Right—Heidelberg 1817–1818 and Additions from the Lectures of 1818–1819 (Transcribed by Peter Wannenmann)*, translated by J. Michael Stewart and Peter C. Hodgson (Berkeley, 1995).

2. On the background of the student notes, see the introduction by Karl-Heinz Ilting to volume 1 of Hegel, *Vorlesungen über Rechtsphilosophie, 1818–1831*, ed. Karl-Heinz Ilting (Stuttgart, 1974), pp. 111 ff. For a brief and thoughtful discussion of the student notes and their uses, see Mark Tunick, *Hegel's Political Philosophy: Interpreting the Practice of Legal Punishment* (Princeton, N.J., 1992), pp. 5–12. The most useful for my purposes have been Hegel, *Vorlesungen über Rechtsphilosophie, 1818–1831. Band 3: Philosophie des Rechts nach der Vorlesungnachschrift von H. G. Hotho 1822/23*, ed. Karl-Heinz Ilting (Stuttgart, 1974), cited hereafter as "Hotho"; and Hegel, *Vorlesungen über Rechtsphilosophie 1818–1831. Band 4, Philosophie des Rechts nach der Vorlesungsnachschrift K. G. von Griesheims, 1824–1825*, ed. Karl-Heinz Ilting (Stuttgart, 1974), cited hereafter as "Griesheim." The recent English translation by H. B. Nesbit, edited by Allen Wood, *Elements of the Philosophy of Right* (Cambridge, 1991), includes only those portions of the lecture notes excerpted by Hegel's student Eduard Gans in his edition of 1833.

    In citing, I have referred to the paragraph numbers of the *Philosophie des Rechts* (*PR*), which are the same in all German and English editions. When citing from the published lecture notes, I have referred to the paragraph numbers and to the page numbers in the volumes edited by Ilting.

3. Hegel is often said to have asserted that the modern state is "the march of God in the world." What he actually wrote (*PR* 258A) is *"Es ist der Gang Gottes in der Welt, daß der Staat ist,"* best translated as "It is the way of God in the world that there should be a state." Rather than identifying the state with God, Hegel means that the state actualizes certain potentialities for human freedom that are inherent in man as created by God but that require the historical development of the modern state for their realization.

4. Another red herring in understanding Hegel's interpretation of capitalism comes from the practice of seeing it through the lens of the dialectic between *Herr* and *Knecht* (master and slave) set out in Hegel's *Phenomenology* (1807), as in the famous interpretation by Alexandre Kojève in his *Introduction à la lecture de Hegel* (Paris, 1947). For the *Phenomenology* reflects a relatively early point in Hegel's interpretation of the modern world, a stage of his intellectual development at which he had not yet assimilated into his thought the work of the political economists, which he came to see as central to understanding the nature of modern society and its philosophical import. As Joachim Ritter notes, "In the *Philosophy of Right* civil society has finally become the centerpoint; all political, legal, and spiritual problems of the age are referred to it as the epochal upheaval determining all, whose theory supersedes the consideration of the political revolution . . ." Joachim Ritter, "Hegel and the French Revolution" (1956) in Joachim Ritter, *Hegel and the French Revolution: Essays on The Philosophy of Right*, trans. Richard Dien Winfield (Cambridge, Mass., 1982), p. 68.

5. As noted by George A. Kelly, "Hegel and 'the Neutral State,'" in *Hegel's Retreat from Eleusis* (Princeton, N.J., 1978), p. 137.
6. *PR* 182A.
7. *PR* 75.
8. *PR* 15A.
9. Michael O. Hardimon, *Hegel's Social Philosophy: The Project of Reconciliation* (Cambridge, 1994). Several other recent works of scholarship have illuminated this side of Hegel's thought, namely Steven B. Smith, *Hegel's Critique of Liberalism* (Chicago, 1989); Tunick, *Hegel's Political Philosophy*; Allen W. Wood, *Hegel's Ethical Thought* (Cambridge, 1990); and Terry Pinkard, *Hegel's* Phenomenology: *The Sociality of Reason* (Cambridge, 1994). For an explicit statement of this intention, see *PR*, Preface, *Grundlinien der Philosophie des Rechts: G.W.H. Hegel: Werke in 20 Bd.* (Frankfurt am Main, 1986), pp. 26–7; Hegel, *Elements of the Philosophy of Right*, ed. Allen W. Wood (Cambridge, 1991), p. 22.
10. There is a good analysis of this element of Rousseau's work in Bernard Yack, *The Longing for Total Revolution: Philosophic Sources of Social Discontent from Rousseau to Marx and Nietzsche* (Princeton, N.J., 1986), chapters 1 and 2.
11. Rousseau, *Of the Social Contract*, book 1, chapter 7 and note thereto, in *The Social Contract and Other Later Political Writings*, edited and translated by Victor Gourevitch (Cambridge, 1997), pp. 50–1.
12. Adam Ferguson, *An Essay on the History of Civil Society* (New Brunswick, N.J., 1980), p. 54.
13. Ferguson, *Essay on the History of Civil Society*, p. 58
14. Ferguson, *Essay on the History of Civil Society*, pp. 180–3.
15. M. H. Abrams, *Natural Supernaturalism: Tradition and Revolution in Romantic Literature* (New York, 1971), pp. 211–2; for the influence of Ferguson on Schiller, and the differences in their emphases, see Fania Oz-Salzberger, *Translating the Enlightenment: Scottish Civic Discourse in Eighteenth-Century Germany* (Oxford, 1995). There is an excellent analysis of Schiller's critique in Yack, *Longing*, chapter 4.
16. Friedrich Schiller, *On the Aesthetic Education of Mankind in a Series of Letters*, edited and translated by Elizabeth M. Wilkinson and L. A. Willoughby (Oxford, 1967), pp. 32–5. This useful edition has the German text with facing English translation.
17. Quoted in Elie Kedourie, *Hegel and Marx* (Oxford, 1996), p. 57.
18. On the theme of compensating for the one-sidedness created by the division of labor in the thought of Fichte during the 1790s, see Theodore Ziolkowski, *German Romanticism and Its Institutions* (Princeton, N.J., 1990), pp. 242–5.
19. Cf. Kedourie, *Hegel and Marx* , p. 32.
20. For recent works of scholarship that illuminate the historical and institutional side of Hegel's thought see the works cited in note 9 above, as well as Donald R. Kelley, *The Human Measure: Social Thought in the Western Legal Tradition* (Cambridge, Mass., 1990), p. 253.
21. Hegel, *Vorlesungen über die Philosophie der Geschichte*; English translation by Leo Rauch, *Introduction to the Philosophy of History* (Indianapolis, Ind., 1988), pp. 21–2.
22. At the end of the Preface to the *PR*, Hegel calls this *"Eigensinn,"* which is mistranslated by Nesbit as "obstinacy." What Hegel clearly means to convey by the term is that modern individuals demand that institutions make sense to them. This point is discussed by Kenneth Westphal, "The Basic Context and Structure of Hegel's *Philosophy of Right*," in *The Cambridge Companion to Hegel*, ed. Frederick C. Beiser (Cambridge, 1993), pp. 234–69, at p. 237; by Pinkard, *Hegel's Phenomenology*, p. 272; as well as by Hardimon, *Hegel's Social Philosophy*, passim.
23. There is an excellent treatment of Hegel's family background and its self-conception in John Edward Toews, *Hegelianism: The path Toward Dialectical Humanism, 1805–1841* (Cambridge, 1980), pp. 13 ff; for additional detail, Horst Althaus, *Hegel*

und die heroischen Jahre der Philosophie (Munich, 1992), p. 23. Previous biographies of Hegel are now superseded by Terry Pinkard, *Hegel: A Biography* (Cambridge, 2000), which appeared after this chapter was written, but presents a compatible interpretation.

24. Toews, *Hegelianism*, p. 21. See also Hans Erich Bödecker, "Die 'gebildeten Stände' im späten 18. und frühen 19. Jahrhunder: Zugehörigkeit und Abgrenzungen. Mentalitäten und Handlungspotentiale," in Jürgen Kocka (ed.), *Bildungbürgertum im 19. Jahrhundert. Teil IV: Politscher Einfluß und gesellschaftliche Formation* (1989), pp. 21–52.

25. Bödecker, "Die 'gebildeten Stände,' " pp. 23–4.

26. See James J. Sheehan, *German History, 1770–1866* (Oxford, 1989), pp. 143–58; and Mack Walker, *German Home Towns: Community, State, and General Estate, 1648–1871* (Ithaca, N.Y., 1971), passim.

27. Sheehan, *German History*, pp. 195–6.

28. Mack Walker, "Rights and Functions: The Social Categories of Eighteenth-Century German Jurists and Cameralists," *Journal of Modern History*, vol. 50, (June 1978), pp. 234–51; and David F. Lindenfeld, *The Practical Imagination: The German Sciences of State in the Nineteenth Century* (Chicago, 1997), chapters 1 and 2. On the permeation of Smith's *Wealth of Nations* into the university curriculum, especially at Königsberg, see Norbert Waszek, *The Scottish Enlightenment and Hegel's Account of "Civil Society"* (Dordrecht, 1988), p. 75.

29. Walker, *German Home Towns*.

30. On Württemberg, Toews, *Hegelianism*, p. 17.

31. Quoted in Sheehan, *German History*, p. 305.

32. Sheehan, *German History*, p. 428.

33. Sheehan, *German History*, pp. 305 ff; Thomas Nipperdey, *Deutsche Geschichte 1800–1866: Bürgerwelt und starker Staat* (6. durchgesehene Auflage, Munich, 1993), pp. 31–49; Hans-Ulrich Wehler, *Deutsche Gesellschaftsgeschichte, Erster Band, 1700–1815* (Munich, 1987), pp. 397 ff. On Hardenberg's commitment to economic liberalization, see especially Reinhart Koselleck, *Preußen zwischen Reform und Revolution: Allgemeines Landrecht, Verwaltung und soziale Bewegung von 1791 bis 1848*, 2nd ed. (Stuttgart, 1975), pp. 318 ff, and Barbara Vogel, *Allgemeine Gewerbefreiheit. Die Reformpolitik des preussischen Staatskanzlers Hardenberg, 1810–20* (Göttingen, 1983).

34. Theodore Ziolkowski, *German Romanticism*, p. 290.

35. Robert M. Berdahl, *The Politics of the Prussian Nobility: The Development of a Conservative Ideology, 1770–1848* (Princeton, N.J., 1988), pp. 164–76.

36. Carl Ludwig von Haller, *Restauration der Staatswissenschaft: oder Theorie des natürlich-geselligen Zustands der Chimäre des künstlich-bürgerlichen entgegengesetzt*, 6 vols., 1816–1834.

37. See the discussion in Warren Breckman, *Marx, The Young Hegelians, and the Origins of Radical Social Theory* (Cambridge, 1999), pp. 68–70; Berdahl, *Politics of the Prussian Nobility*, pp. 56, 158–9.

38. On Altenstein and his negotiations with Hegel, see *Hegel: The Letters*, translated by Clark Butler and Christiane Seiler with a commentary by Clark Butler (Bloomington, Ind., 1984), pp. 377 ff.

39. See Toews, *Hegelianism*, pp. 60 ff.; and Toews, "Transformations of Heglianism, 1805–1846," in *The Cambridge Companion to Hegel*, p. 384.

40. This is the upshot of Hegel's discussion of the French Revolution in the chapter of his *Phenomenologie des Geistes* on "Absolute Freedom and Terror." For an extended discussion see Charles Taylor, *Hegel* (Cambridge, 1975), chapter 15; for a summary, *PR 5, PR 29*.

41. *PR, 341–60*; and more generally the famous introduction to the *Vorlesungen über die Philosophie der Geschichte*; a good English translation is Leo Rauch, *Introduction to*

the Philosophy of History. And see Allen W. Wood, "Editor's Introduction" to Hegel, *Elements of the Philosophy of Right*, ed. Wood (Cambridge, 1991).

42. *PR* 151.

43. "Die Thätigkeit des Selbsterwerbs durch Verstand und Fleiss, und die Rechtschaffenheit in diesem Verkehr und Gebrauch des Vermögens, die Sittlichkeit in der bürgerlichen Gesellschaft." §552 of "Der objecktive Geist. Aus der Berliner Enzykopädie, zweite und dritte Auflage (1827 und 1830)" in Hegel, *Vorlesungen über Rechtsphilosophie, 1818–1831*, ed. Ilting, vol. 4 (1973), p. 889. On Hegel's critique of Catholicism, see also Kelly, "Hegel and 'the Neutral State,'" pp. 110–53.

44. Hegel, "Der objecktive Geist," p. 891.

45. See Toews, *Hegelianism*, chapters 2 and 3; and Gerald N. Izenberg, *Impossible Individuality: Romanticism, Revolution, and the Origins of Modern Selfhood, 1787–1802* (Princeton, N.J., 1992).

46. *PR* 5.

47. *PR*, Preface, p. 12.

48. See Jerry Z. Muller, *Adam Smith in His Time and Ours: Designing the Decent Society* (Princeton, N.J., 1995).

49. There are some useful observations about this aspect of Hegel's thought in Wood, *Hegel's Ethical Thought*, pp. 33–4.

50. Griesheim, p. 408. In these respects, Hegel's thought is highly Aristotelian. See Jonathan Lear, *Aristotle: The Desire to Understand* (Cambridge, 1988), pp. 160–74.

51. Wood, *Hegel's Ethical Thought*, p. 210; *PR* 132R.

52. *PR* 147

53. *PR* 144

54. *PR* 149.

55. *PR* 150.

56. *PR* 152.

57. Steven B. Smith, "At the Crossroads: Hegel and the Ethics of *bürgerliche Gesellschaft*," *Laval théologique et philosophique*, vol. 51, no. 2 (June 1995), pp. 345–62, at pp. 353–4. See *PR* 260, *PR* 185, and *PR* 186, especially as expanded in Griesheim, p. 481.

58. *PR* 157.

59. *PR* 188.

60. See Muller, *Adam Smith in His Time and Ours*, p. 187.

61. See Smith, "At the Crossroads," p. 355; also Mark Tunick, "Are There Natural Rights?—Hegel's Break with Kant," in Ardis B. Collins (ed.), *Hegel on the Modern World* (Albany, N.Y., 1995), pp. 219–36.

62. Part 1 of *PR*, which deals with these matters, is entitled "Abstract Right." Burke had made a similar point in *Reflections on the Revolution in France*; see the excerpts in Jerry Z. Muller (ed.), *Conservatism: An Anthology of Social and Political Thought from David Hume to the Present* (Princeton, N.J., 1997), pp. 98–9.

63. *PR* 185 Zusatz (Addition H).

64. *PR* 33 Zusatz (Addition H) and 41 Zusatz (Addition H).

65. *PR* 154.

66. *PR* 124. Nisbet translation, Hegel's italics.

67. *PR* 44.

68. *PR* 189, and the additional remarks in Griesheim, p. 487.

69. Hegel mentions all three in *PR* 189. He restates the major theses of *The Wealth of Nations* in *PR* 198–9. For the timing and influence of Hegel's reading of Smith's *Wealth of Nations* see Waszek, *Scottish Enlightenment*, especially chapter 4.

70. This point is well made in Raymond Plant, "Economic and Social Integration in Hegel's Political Philosophy," in Lawrence S. Stepelevich, *Selected Essays on G.W.F. Hegel* (Atlantic Highlands, N.J., 1993), pp. 76–103, at p. 89.

71. *PR* 192 and additions.

72. *PR* 190–7, and the more extended discussions in Hotho, p. 596; and Griesheim, p. 493.
73. Griesheim, p. 490.
74. *Journal des Luxus und der Moden*, vol. 3 (1788), as quoted in Hans Erich Bödecker, "Die 'gebildeten Stände,'" p. 35.
75. *PR* 191, and Hotho, pp. 593–4. Hegel here is following the lead of Say.
76. Ilting, vol. 2, p. 643; Hotho, p. 596.
77. *PR* 244 and Griesheim, p. 614.
78. *PR* 207. For more on this theme see Wood, *Hegel's Ethical Thought*, pp. 243–6.
79. There is a good discussion of this in Waszek, *Scottish Enlightenment*, pp. 161–70.
80. *PR* 207, and additional comments in Hotho, p. 636, and Griesheim, pp. 524–5, as well as the comments on *PR* 187 in Griesheim, p. 482.
81. See also the discussion in Wood, *Hegel's Ethical Thought,*, pp. 216–7.
82. *PR* 206.
83. *PR* 206; and Griesheim, pp. 521–2.
84. *PR* 162.
85. On this see Tunick, *Hegel's Political Philosophy*, pp. 55–64.
86. *PR* 185, and the expansions in Griesheim, pp. 475–7. Hegel notes Rousseau's anticipation of this line of analysis.
87. *PR* 250–5; and Griesheim pp. 617–27. See also G. Heiman, "The Sources and Significance of Hegel's Corporate Doctrine," in Z. A. Pelczynski (ed.), *Hegel's Political Philosophy: Problems and Perspectives* (Cambridge, 1971), pp. 111–35. At the end of the century, Emile Durkheim would put forward a similarly corporatist solution to the problem identified by Hegel and dubbed "anomie" by Durkheim. See especially his preface to the second edition (1902) of his *De la division du travail social*, "Quelques Remarques sur les Groupements professionnels," available in English in Durkheim, *The Division of Labor in Society*, translated by W. D. Halls (New York, 1997), pp. xxxi–lix. For a useful secondary discussion see Dominick LaCapra, *Emile Durkheim: Sociologist and Philosopher* (Chicago, 1972), pp. 211–24. For similar themes in other twentieth-century thinkers, see Thomas L. Haskell, "Professionalism Versus Capitalism: R. H. Tawney, Emile Durkheim, and C. S. Peirce on the Disinterestedness of Professional Communities," in Haskell (ed.), *The Authority of Experts* (Bloomington, Ind., 1984), pp. 189–225.
88. Griesheim, pp. 622–7.
89. Comments on *PR* 243 in Griesheim, p. 608.
90. *PR* 243; 246.
91. *PR* 243.
92. *PR* 244, and Griesheim addition.
93. *PR* 224, and comments in Griesheim, pp. 608–9.
94. As several recent commentators have noted, Hegel's description of the "Pöbel" is close to what is now termed the "underclass."
95. Griesheim, p. 611–2.
96. *PR* 248.
97. *PR* 239.
98. *PR* 236.
99. Griesheim, p. 587.
100. Griesheim, p. 415.
101. Hotho, pp. 557–8.
102. *PR* 163.
103. *PR* 159.
104. *PR* 163.
105. *PR*161 and the additions in Griesheim, pp. 428–9.
106. Hegel, *Lectures on Natural Right and Political Science*, p. 150.
107. *PR* 169–70, and the additional comments in Griesheim, p. 450

108. Griesheim, p. 450.

109. *PR* 178, *PR* 180, and the comments in Griesheim, pp. 557–8.

110. There is an excellent discussion of these matters in Shlomo Avineri, *Hegel's Theory of the Modern State* (Cambridge, 1972), chapters 9 and 10.

111. *PR* 302, and Zusatz (Addition).

112. *PR* 258, *PR* 323–4.

113. *PR* 268.

114. *PR* 302.

115. *PR* 314–5. See Z. A. Pelczynski, "Political Community and Individual Freedom in Hegel's Philosophy of State," in Z. A. Pelczynski (ed.), *The State and Civil Society: Studies in Hegel's Political Thought* (Cambridge, 1984), pp. 55–76.

116. PR 291.

117. PR 294.

118. *PR* 294.

119. See Lindenfeld, op. cit.

120. *PR* 296.

121. Nipperdey, *Deutsche Geschichte*, p. 528.

122. Eric Voegelin, "On Hegel—A Study in Sorcery," *Studium Generale,* vol. 24 (1971), pp. 335–68, p. 338.

CHAPTER SEVEN

KARL MARX

1. Leszek Kolakowski, *Main Currents of Marxism,* (3 vols.), vol. 1, *The Founders* (New York, 1978), p. 181.

2. For biographical information, I have depended most on David McLellan, *Karl Marx: His Life and Thought* (New York, 1973), and have also made use of Auguste Cornu, *Karl Marx und Friedrich Engels: Leben und Werk,* 3 vols. (Berlin, 1954), which entombs a large body of facts in a Communist conceptual sarcophagus. I have also profited from some of the interpretations offered in Jerrold Seigel, *Marx's Fate: The Shape of a Life* (Princeton, N.J., 1978). Frank E. Manuel, *A Requiem for Karl Marx* (Cambridge, Mass., 1995), is a fine psychological portrait, flawed by the author's utter indifference to economics or social history.

   Unless noted, all references to the writings of Marx and Engels are from *Karl Marx/Friedrich Engels Gesamtausgabe* (Berlin, 1972–) published by the Institut für Marxismus-Leninismus of the Soviet Communist Party and the Institut für Marxismus-Leninismus of the Socialist Unity Party of Germany. Citations are to *MEGA* sections, volumes, and page numbers. Though some of the translations are my own, wherever possible I have indicated page numbers in well-known English translations as well.

3. Cornu, *Karl Marx,* vol. 1, p. 53.

4. Cornu, *Karl Marx,* p. 54, 63n.

5. See Jacob Katz, *From Prejudice to Destruction: Anti-Semitism, 1700–1933* (Cambridge, Mass., 1980), p. 171.

6. On the development of this new style of life, see Hans Erich Bödecker, "Die 'gebildeten Stände' im späten 18. und frühen 19. Jahrhundert: Zugehörigkeit und Abgrenzungen. Mentalitäten und Handlungspotentiale," in Jürgen Kocka (ed.), *Bildungsbürgertum im 19. Jahrhundert. Teil IV: Politscher Einfluß und gesellschaftliche Formation* (1989), pp. 21–52, at pp. 36–41.

7. McLellan, *Karl Marx,* p. 15.

8. McLellan, *Karl Marx,* pp. 18–23.

9. Quoted in McLellan, *Karl Marx,* p. 33.

10. Marx to Engels, April 30, 1868, quoted in Manuel, *Requiem,* p. 101.

11. Seigel, *Marx's Fate,* p. 63.

12. Quoted in McLellan, *Karl Marx*, p. 105.
13. Marx's inability to complete his projects is stressed in Seigel, *Marx's Fate*.
14. On the antimodernist impulse in Marx, see John Gray, "The Politics of Cultural Diversity," in John Gray, *Post-Liberalism: Studies in Political Thought* (London, 1993), p. 256.
15. McLellan, *Karl Marx*, p. 42–8.
16. Hans-Ulrich Wehler, *Deutsche Gesellschaftsgeschichte, 2 Band, 1815–1845/49* (Munich, 1987), p. 266.
17. Werner Conze, "Proletariat, Pöbel, Pauperismus," in Otto Brunner, Werner Conze, and Reinhart Kosellek (eds.), *Geschichtliche Grundbegriffe*, vol. 5, pp. 27–68, pp. 40, 42.
18. Quoted in Wehler, II, p. 267. On conservative critiques of market-oriented liberal policies as leading to the creation of a proletariat, see Werner Conze, "From 'Pöbel' to 'Proletariat': The Socio-Historical Preconditions of Socialism in Germany" (German original, 1954), in Georg Iggers (ed.), *The Social History of Politics* (Leamington Spa, U.K., 1985), pp. 49–80, at pp. 58 ff.
19. Wehler, II, p. 289.
20. Wehler, II, p. 244; David Blackbourn, *The Long Nineteenth Century: A History of Germany, 1780–1918* (New York, 1997), pp. 116–7.
21. Wehler, II, pp. 247–57.
22. Jonathan Sperber, *The European Revolutions, 1848–1851* (Cambridge, 1994), pp. 23–4.
23. Sperber, *European Revolutions*, p. 23.
24. Wehler, II, p. 21; and Charles Tilly, "Demographic Origins of the European Proletariat," in Charles Tilly, *Roads from Past to Future* (Lanham, Md., 1997), pp. 293–383, at p. 335.
25. Wehler, II, pp. 284–9.
26. Engels, "Briefe aus dem Wuppertal," in *MEGA* I, 3, pp. 32–51, at pp. 34–6.
27. Engels, "Briefe aus dem Wuppertal," in *MEGA* I, 3, p. 51.
28. Sperber, *European Revolutions*, pp. 105–7.
29. Wehler, II, p. 280.
30. Sperber, *European Revolutions*, p. 83.
31. Hegel, *Philosophy of Right*, paragraph 261.
32. Sperber, *European Revolutions*, p. 41.
33. Marx, "Debatten über das Holzdiebstahls-Gesetz," *MEGA* I, 1, p. 224.
34. Marx, "Debatten über das Holzdiebstahls-Gesetz," *MEGA* I, 1, p. 230. Marx so loved this image that he used it again in *Kapital: Kritik der politischen Ökonomie Erster Band, Hamburg, 1872*, chapter 8, "Der Arbeitstag," *MEGA* II, 6, p. 289; Karl Marx, *Capital: A Critique of Political Economy*, trans. Ben Fowkes (London, 1976), p. 400.
35. Karl Marx, "Bemerkungen über die neueste preußische Zensurinstruktion. Von einim Rheinländer," February 1842; "Debatten über Preßfreiheit und Publikation der Landständischen Verhandlungen" (May 5, 1842), and the subsequent articles on press censorship in *MEGA* I, 1, pp. 99 ff.
36. Marx, *Critique of Hegel's Philosophy of Right*, ed. Joseph O'Malley (Cambridge, 1972), p. 71.
37. John C. Calhoun, *Exposition and Protest* (1828), quoted in Richard Hofstadter, *The American Political Tradition* (New York, 1948), p. 81.
38. Conze, "Proletariat, Pöbel, Pauperismus," pp. 48–56.
39. Norman Levine, "The German Historical School of Law and the Origins of Historical Materialism," *Journal of the History of Ideas*, vol. 48 (1987), pp. 431–50, p. 443; and McLellan, Karl Marx, pp. 107–7.
40. David McLellan, *Friedrich Engels* (New York, 1977), p. 22; on the work's importance in Marx's development, see also Terrell Carver, *Marx and Engels: The Intellectual Relationship* (Bloomington, Ind., 1983), pp. 32, 36–8. Marx characterized it as one of

the major influences on his thought in his preface to his "Economic-Philosophic Manuscripts" of 1844, *MEGA* I, 2, p. 326.

41. Friedrich Engels, "Outlines of a Critique of Political Economy," in *Karl Marx–Friedrich Engels Collected Works*, vol. 3 (Moscow, 1975), pp. 418–43, p. 418; "Umrisse zu einer Kritik der Nationalökonomie," in *MEGA* I, 3, pp. 467–94, at p. 467.

42. Engels, "Outlines," p. 423; "Umrisse," p. 474.

43. Engels, "Outlines," p. 432; "Umrisse," p. 483.

44. Engels, "Outlines," p. 423; "Umrisse," p. 475.

45. Engels, "Outlines," p. 430; "Umrisse," p. 481.

46. Engels, "Outlines," pp. 434–5; "Umrisse," p. 485.

47. Engels, "News from Prussia" *The Northern Star*, June 29, 1844, reprinted in *Karl Marx–Friedrich Engels Collected Works*, vol. 3 (Moscow, 1975), pp. 530–1.

48. Engels, "Outlines," p.441; "Umrisse," p. 491.

49. Engels, "Outlines," p. 434; "Umrisse," p. 484.

50. Engels, "Outlines," p. 435; "Umrisse," p. 485.

51. Stefi Jersch-Wenzel, "Legal Status and Emancipation," in Michael Meyer (ed.), *German-Jewish History in Modern Times*, vol. 2 (New York, 1997), p. 31.

52. Hegel, *Philosophy of Right*, paragraph 270.

53. Jersch-Wenzel, "Legal Status and Emancipation," p. 41; and the very useful discussion in Jacob Katz, *From Prejudice to Destruction* (Cambridge, Mass., 1986), chapter 12, "The German Liberals' Image of the Jew."

54. Raphael Gross, *Carl Schmitt und die Juden* (Frankfurt, 2000), pp. 202–44. On Bauer's later anti-Jewish writings see Katz, *From Prejudice to Destruction*, pp. 214–8.

55. On the identification of Jews with egoism in German culture of the 1830s, see Paul Lawrence Rose, *Revolutionary Antisemitism in Germany from Kant to Wagner* (Princeton, N.J., 1990), part 4.

56. Bruno Bauer, *Die Judenfrage* (Braunschweig, 1843), translated by Helen Lederer as *The Jewish Problem* (Cincinnati, 1958), and excerpted in Lawrence S. Stepelevich, *The Young Hegelians: An Anthology* (Cambridge, 1983); and Bruno Bauer, "Die Fähigkeit der heutigen Juden und Christen frei zu werden," in Georg Herwegh (ed.), *Einundzwanzig Bogen aus der Schweiz* (Zürich, 1843), pp. 56–71.

57. Marx, "Zur Judenfrage," *MEGA* I, 2, pp. 141–69, at p. 147. With alterations, I have used the translation by Lloyd D. Easton and Kurt H. Guddat, now in Lawrence H. Simon, *Karl Marx: Selected Writings* (Indianapolis, Ind., 1994).

58. Marx, "Zur Judenfrage," p. 149.

59. Marx, "Zur Judenfrage," p. 158.

60. *Oxford English Dictionary*, s.v. "huckster."

61. James F. Harris, *The People Speak! Anti-Semitism and Emancipation in Nineteenth Century Bavaria* (Ann Arbor, Mich., 1994), p. 24. On the propensity of Jews for "Schacher," see Friedrich Buchholz, *Moses und Jesus: Ueber das intellektuelle und moralische Verhaeltnis der Juden und Christen* (Berlin, 1803), discussed in Steven E. Aschheim, " 'The Jew Within': The Myth of 'Judaization' in Germany," in his *Culture and Catastrophe* (New York, 1996), pp. 45–68, at p. 48.

62. Friedrich Kluge, *Etymologisches Wörterbuch der deutschen Sprache*, 17. Auflage (Berlin, 1957), s.v. "*schachern*."

63. On Jewish peddlers and petty traders, see Jersch-Wenzel, "Legal Status and Emancipation," pp. 69–71, 80.

64. Engels, "Umrisse zu einer Kritik der Nationalökonomie," in *MEGA* I, 3, p. 480, my translation.

65. Marx, "Zur Judenfrage," pp. 164–5.

66. "[I]n der jetzigen Gesellschaft finden wir das Wesen des heutigen Juden . . . nicht nur als Beschränktheit des Juden, sondern als die jüdische Beschränktheit der Gesellschaft." Marx, "Zur Judenfrage," p. 169.

67. Marx, "Zur Judenfrage," p. 167.
68. Marx, "Zur Judenfrage," p. 168.
69. Marx, "Zur Judenfrage," p. 166.
70. See on this topic Aschheim, "The Myth of 'Judaization' in Germany."
71. "Ein Briefwechsel von 1843," in *MEGA* I, 2, p. 479, translation in *Marx-Engels Collected Works* (New York, 1975), vol. 3, p. 141.
72. Marx, "Zur Kritik der Hegelschen Rechtsphilosophie: Einleitung," in *MEGA* I, 2, pp. 170–83, at p. 180. English translation in Karl Marx, *Critique of Hegel's "Philosophy of Right,"* ed. O'Malley, p. 140.
73. Marx, "Zur Kritik," p. 182; *Critique,* p. 142.
74. Marx, "Zur Kritik," pp. 181–3; *Critique,* pp. 140–2. For an excellent discussion of the proletariat in Marx's thought, see Kolakowski, *Main Currents,* vol. 1, p. 180.
75. Friedrich Engels, "Lage der arbeitenden Klasse in England," in *Marx-Engels-Werke* (Berlin, 1970), vol. 2, pp. 486–7. My translation.
76. "[D]ie Aufgabe sei, das *Judentum der bürgerlichen Gesellschaft,* die Unmenschlichkeit der heutigen Lebenspraxis, die im *Geldsystem* ihre Spitze erhält, aufzuheben." Karl Marx, Friedrich Engels, "Die Heilige Familie," in *Historisch-kritische Gesamtausgabe* (Berlin, 1932), I, 3, p. 284. Italics in original.
77. Marx, "Theorien über den Mehrwert," in *Marx-Engels Werke* (Berlin, 1965), vol. 26, part 1, p. 364. "Nur war Mandeville natürlich unendlich kühner und ehrlicher als die philisterhafen Apologeten der bürgerlichen Gesellschaft."
78. Ibid., part III, p. 525.
79. Marx, "Comments on James Mill," 1844, in *Marx-Engels Collected Works* vol. 3, (Moscow, 1975), pp. 211–28; pp. 219–20, *MEGA* IV, 2, pp. 219–20.
80. On the romantic origins of Marx's conception of man, see Manuel, p. 175; and M. A. Abrams, *Natural Supernaturalism* (New York, 1971), pp. 313–4 and passim. On multifacetedness as central to his ideal, see S. S. Prawer, *Karl Marx and World Literature* (Oxford, 1976), p. 107–14; John E. Toews, "Introduction" to Toews (ed.), *The Communist Manifesto* (Boston, 1999), pp. 32–5.
81. Adam Müller, "Die heutige Wissenschaft der Nationalökonomie kurz und fasslich dargestellt," *Ausgewälte Abhandlungen,* ed. J. Baxa (Jena, 1921), p. 46; quoted in Shlomo Avineri, *The Political and Social Thought of Karl Marx* (Cambridge, 1968), pp. 55–6.
82. Marx and Engels, "Die deutsche Ideologie," in Karl Marx/Friedrich Engels, *Werke* (Berlin, 1962), vol. 3, p. 33; Marx and Engels, *The German Ideology* in David McLellan (ed.), *Karl Marx: Selected Writings,* p. 169; translation slightly altered.
83. Marx, "Critique of the Gotha Program" (written 1875, first published in 1891), in Robert C. Tucker (ed.), *The Marx-Engels Reader,* 2nd ed. (New York, 1978), p. 531.
84. "We have shown that the worker sinks to the level of a commodity, the most miserable commodity; that the misery of the worker is inversely proportional to the power and volume of his production; that the necessary result of competition is the accumulation of capital in a few hands and thus the recreation of monopoly in a more frightful form; and finally that . . . the entire society must disintegrate into two classes of *proprietors* and propertyless *workers.*" Marx, *Ökonomisch-philosophische Manuskripte, Heft 1, MEGA* I, 2, p. 363.
85. Marx, *Ökonomisch-philosophische Manuskripte, Heft 1,* p. 365.
86. *Ökonomisch-philosophische Manuskripte, Heft 1, MEGA* I, 2, p. 421.
87. Manuel, *Requiem,* p. 24, On de Brosses' work, see Frank E. Manuel, *The Eighteenth Century Confronts the Gods* (Cambridge, Mass., 1959), pp. 184–209. Kant also used "fetishism" to characterize the Catholic mass, see Immauel Kant, *Religion Within the Limits of Reason* (New York, 1960), book 4, part 2, section 3.
88. *Kapital, Mega* II, 6, p. 103; *Capital,* p. 165.

89. On the background to the *Communist Manifesto*, see *The Communist Manifesto by Karl Marx and Friedrich Engels*, edited with related documents and an introduction by John E. Toews (Boston, 1999).

90. Manuel, *Requiem*, p. 171.

91. *Kapital*, MEGA II, 6, pp. 465–6; *Capital*, pp. 617–18.

92. "Manifest der Kommunistischen Partei," in *Marx-Engels Werke* (Berlin, 1969), vol. 4, p. 465; my translation.

93. "[E]in Teil der Bourgeoisideologen, welcher zum theoretischen Verständnis der ganzen geschichtlichen Bewegung sich hinaufgearbeitet haben." Marx and Engels, "Manifest der Kommunistischen Partei," p. 472.

94. On the Romantic element in Marx's conception of politics and law, see Blandine Kriegel, *Sovereigns and Despots: A Case for the State* (Princeton, N.J., 1997; translated from the Second French edition of 1989), pp. 133–43.

95. "Der Kapitalist weiß, daß alle Waaren, wie lumpig sie immer aussehn oder wie schlecht sie immer riechen mögen, im Glauben und in der Wahrheit Geld, innerlich vernschnittne Juden sind, und zudem wunderthätige Mittel, um aus Geld mehr Geld zu machen." *Kapital*, MEGA II, 6, p. 172, my translation. Cf. *Capital*, vol. 1, trans. Ben Fowkes, p. 256.

96. "Je grösser der menschliche Antheil an eine Waare, um so grösser der Gewinn des todten Capitals." (*MEGA* I, 2, pp. 199 and 341.)

97. Marx, "Wage-Labour and Capital," in McLellan (ed.), *Karl Marx: Selected Writings*, pp. 250, 266, original in Marx and Engels, *Werke*, 41 vol. (Berlin, 1956 ff), 6, pp. 397 ff.

98. *Capital* (Fowkes translation), p. 342, translation modified; MEGA II, 6, pp. 239–40.

99. "Den Trieb nach Verlängerung des Arbeitstages, den Wehrwolfheißhunger für Mehrarbeit," *MEGA* II, 6, p. 249.

100. *Capital* (Fowkes translation), p. 346, translation modified; MEGA II, 6, p. 243.

101. *Capital*, p. 425; *MEGA* II, 6, pp. 309–10.

102. On Marx's attachment to the labor theory of value for reasons fundamentally noneconomic, and the resulting analytic inadequacy, see Joseph Schumpeter, *Capitalism, Socialism, and Democracy* (New York, 1950), pp. 22–8.

103. Adam Smith, *An Inquiry into the Nature and Causes of the Wealth of Nations*, ed. R. H. Campbell and A. S. Skinner, 2 vols. (The Glasgow Edition of the Works of Adam Smith, Oxford, 1976), II.ii. See the analysis of Andrew Skinner, *A System of Social Science*, pp. 364 ff, and especially Joseph Schumpeter, *History of Economic Analysis* (New York, 1954), pp. 590 ff.

104. Mark Blaug, *Economic Theory in Retrospect*, 4th edition (Cambridge, 1985), pp. 92–3.

105. Schumpeter, *History of Economic Analysis*, p. 648. For a similar conclusion see Samuel Hollander, "Sraffa and the Interpretation of Ricardo: The Marxian Dimension," *History of Political Economy*, vol. 32, no. 2 (2000), pp. 187–232.

106. Schumpeter, *History*, p. 599, 486–7; and Anthony Brewer, "A Minor Post-Ricardian? Marx as an Economist," *History of Political Economy*, vol. 27, no. 1 (1995), pp. 111–45, at p. 116.

107. Marx, *The Poverty of Philosophy* (New York, 1963), pp. 49, 43, quoted in Siegel, *Marx's Fate* p. 296.

108. Blaug, *Economic Theory*, p. 242.

109. *Kapital*, MEGA II, 6, p. 433; *Capital*, p. 578.

110. *Kapital*, MEGA II, 6, p. 433; *Capital*, vol. 1, p. 578; and *Capital*, vol. 3, passim.

111. *Kapital*, MEGA II, 6, pp. 463, 410 ff; *Capital*, pp. 614, 548 ff.

112. *Kapital*, MEGA II, 6, pp. 410 ff; *Capital*, pp. 548 ff.

113. *Kapital*, MEGA II, 6, pp. 411, 416; *Capital*, pp. 549, 557.

114. *Kapital*, MEGA II, 6, pp. 384 ff; *Capital*, pp. 517 ff.

115. *Kapital, MEGA* II, 6, pp. 249 ff; *Capital*, pp. 353 ff.

116. *Kapital, MEGA* II, 6, p. 250; *Capital*, p. 355.

117. *Kapital, MEGA* II, 6, p. 254; *Capital*, p. 358.

118. As Mark Blaug, *Economic Theory*, p. 271, quite rightly notes, "the statistical and historical data in *Capital* is used, not to test the conclusions of theory, but to build up a graphic picture of capitalist society. . . . By virtue of its style of presentation, however, it has a powerful effect upon the reader. The suggestion is that the conditions depicted are a necessary product of capitalism, generated by the peculiar nature of that system, and that similar conditions will be found wherever such a system is in force."

119. The figure is from Asa Briggs, *The Making of Modern England, 1783–1867: The Age of Improvement* (New York, 1965), p. 403.

120. K. Theodore Hoppen, *The Mid-Victorian Generation, 1846–1886* (Oxford, 1998), p. 82.

121. *Kapital, MEGA* II, 6, p. 682; *Capital*, p. 929.

122. *Kapital, MEGA* II, 6, pp. 467–8; *Capital*, pp. 620–1.

123. Marx, *Das Kapital*, Hamburg, 1872 edition, in *MEGA* II, 6, p. 106, my translation; *Capital*, vol. 1, trans. Ben Fowkes, p. 168.

124. See E. K. Hunt and Mary Glick, "Transformation Problem," in *The New Palgrave*.

125. See the editors' introduction to Karl Marx, *Das Kapital: Kritik der politschen Ökonomie, Erster Band, Hamburg 1872, MEGA* II, vol. 6 (Berlin, 1987), p. 20.

126. Shalom Groll and Ze'ev Orzech, "Technical Progress and Values in Marx's Theory of the Decline in the Rate of Profit: An Exegetical Approach," *History of Political Economy*, vol. 19, no. 4 (1987), pp. 591–613; and the same authors' "From Marx to the Okishio Theorem: A Genealogy," *History of Political Economy*, vol. 21, no. 2 (1989), pp. 253–72.

127. Engels in *Neue Zeit*, 1895 ("Supplement and Addendum" to *Capital*, vol. 3, trans. David Fernbach [London, 1981]), p. 1045.

128. The contemporary responses are discussed in Eugen von Böhm-Bawerk, *Karl Marx and the Close of His System*, trans. Paul Sweezy (New York, 1949; German original 1896), pp. 31–2.

129. See on this Blaug, *Economic Theory*, p. 250, and Seigel, *Marx's Fate*, p. 344.

130. See the chart in Hoppen, *Mid-Victorian Generation*, p. 278.

131. Hoppen, *Mid-Victorian Generation*, p. 78.

132. Hoppen, *Mid-Victorian Generation*, pp. 86–7.

133. On Marx's inattention to demography, see William Petersen, "Marxism and the Population Question: Theory and Practice," in Michael S. Teitelbaum and Jay M. Winter (eds.), *Population and Resources in Western Intellectual Traditions* (Cambridge, 1988), pp. 77–101.

134. For an overview see Susan Cott Watkins, "The Fertility Transition: Europe and the Third World Compared," *Sociological Forum*, vol. 2, no. 4 (1987), pp. 645–71.

135. Hoppen, *Mid-Victorian Generation*, p. 89.

136. Hoppen, *Mid-Victorian Generation*, pp. 81–2.

137. Hoppen, *Mid-Victorian Generation*, pp. 95, 109.

138. On the civil service innovations of 1855 and 1870 see Gillian Sutherland, *Studies in the Growth of Nineteenth-Century Government* (London, 1972); Hoppen, *Mid-Victorian Generation*, pp. 111–2; and the following chapter on Matthew Arnold.

139. Peter Marsh, "Conscience and Conduct of Government in Nineteenth-Century Britain," in Peter Marsh (ed.), *The Conscience of the Victorian State* (Syracuse, N.Y., 1979).

CHAPTER EIGHT
MATTHEW ARNOLD

1. Asa Briggs, *Victorian People: A Reassessment of Persons and Themes, 1851–1867*, rev. ed. (Chicago, 1970), pp. 16, 35–43, and Asa Briggs, *The Making of Modern England, 1783–1867: The Age of Improvement* (New York, 1965), pp. 395–8.

2. Unless otherwise noted, biographical information on Arnold is drawn from Park Honan, *Matthew Arnold: A Life* (Cambridge, Mass., 1983). Other particularly valuable studies of Arnold include Stefan Collini, *Arnold* (New York, 1988), and Lionel Trilling, *Matthew Arnold* (New York, 1939).

3. R. H. Super (ed.), *The Complete Prose Works of Matthew Arnold* (Ann Arbor, Mich., 1960–1977), a wonderful scholarly edition to which all references apply unless otherwise noted. Henceforth *CPW*.

4. Harold Perkin, *The Origins of Modern English Society, 1780–1880* (Toronto, 1969), pp. 34–6, 71–2, 351–3.

5. Arnold, "Democracy," in *CPW*, vol. 2, pp. 23–4.

6. Aristotle's enduring influence on Arnold is noted by J. Dover Wilson, "Matthew Arnold and the Educationists," in F. J. C. Hearnshaw (ed.), *The Social and Political Ideas of Some Representative Thinkers of the Victorian Age* (New York, 1933), pp. 165–93, at p. 169.

7. Matthew Arnold, "Heinrich Heine," *Cornhill Magazine* (August 1863), reprinted in *CPW*, vol. 3, pp. 111–2.

8. Quoted in Matthew Arnold, "The Twice-Revised Code" (1862), in *CPW*, vol. 2, pp. 214–5.

9. Honan, *Matthew Arnold*, pp. 318–9; R. H. Super notes to "The Twice-Revised Code," in *CPW*, vol. 2, p. 349.

10. Arnold, "The Twice-Revised Code," pp. 223–4.

11. Arnold, "The Twice-Revised Code," p. 226.

12. Arnold, "The Twice-Revised Code," p. 243.

13. Arnold, "The Code Out of Danger" (1862), in *CPW*, vol. 2, pp. 247–51.

14. Chris Baldick, *The Social Mission of English Criticism, 1848–1932* (Oxford, 1983), p. 34.

15. Fred G. Walcott, *The Origins of Culture and Anarchy: Matthew Arnold and Popular Education in England* (Toronto, 1970), pp. 7–8.

16. Arnold, "Special Report on Certain Points Connected with Elementary Education in Germany, Switzerland, and France" (1886), in *CPW*, vol. 11, pp. 1, 28.

17. Arnold, "The Function of Criticism at the Present Time," in *CPW*, vol. 3, p. 283.

18. Arnold, "The Function of Criticism at the Present Time," p. 268.

19. Arnold, "The Function of Criticism at the Present Time," p. 271.

20. "The Function of Criticism at the Present Time," p. 269; similarly, *Culture and Anarchy: An Essay in Political and Social Criticism* (henceforth cited as *CA*), *CPW*, vol. 5, pp. 104–5.

21. Honan, *Matthew Arnold*, p. 329.

22. Arnold, "My Countryman," incorporated into *Friendship's Garland* and reprinted in *CPW*, vol. 5, p. 19.

23. *CA*, p. 92.

24. The book was, in that sense, typical of the "culture of altruism" so characteristic of Victorian intellectual life, on which see Stefan Collini, *Public Moralists: Political Thought and Intellectual Life in Britain, 1850–1930* (Oxford, 1991), chapter 2.

25. *CA*, p. 92.

26. *CA*, p. 113.

27. *CA*, p. 96.
28. *CA*, p. 189.
29. *CA*, "Doing As One Likes," passim.
30. *CA*, p. 117.
31. *CA*, p. 118.
32. Arnold, "A French Eton" (1864), in *CPW*, pp. 282-3.
33. *CA*, pp. 134-5.
34. *CA*, p. 125.
35. *CA*, pp. 97-8.
36. *CA*, pp. 101-2.
37. *CA*, pp. 186-7.
38. *CA*, p. 209.
39. *CA*, p. 212.
40. *CA*, pp. 211-3.
41. *CA*, pp. 218-9.
42. *CA*, p. 146.
43. On their relationship, see Ruth apRoberts, *Arnold and God* (Berkeley, 1983), pp. 165-70.
44. N. G. Annan, "The Intellectual Aristocracy," in J. H. Plumb (ed.), *Studies in Social History* (London, 1955), pp. 241-97; T. W. Heyck, *The Transformation of Intellectual Life in Victorian England* (Chicago, 1982), p. 36; and most broadly Collini, *Public Moralists*, chapter 1.
45. Heyck, pp. 190-3, makes a similar point.
46. Ben Knights, *The Idea of the Clerisy in the Nineteenth Century* (Cambridge, 1978), and Stephen Prickett, " 'Hebrew' Versus 'Hellene' as a Principle of Literary Criticism," in G. W. Clarke (ed.), *Recovering Hellenism; The Hellenic Inheritance and the English Imagination* (Cambridge, 1988), pp. 137-160.
47. Honan, *Matthew Arnold*, pp. 95-6.
48. See his satirical self-portrait as a proponent of "Geist" in *Friendship's Garland*, a collection of essays written between "The Function of Criticism at the Present Time" and *Culture and Anarchy*, in *CPW*, vol. 5, pp. 37 ff.
49. See Arnold's essay "Democracy" (1861), in *CPW*, vol. 2.
50. Heyck, pp. 157 ff; and Christopher Harvie, "Reform and Expansion, 1854-1871," in M. G. Brock and M. C. Curthoys (eds.), *History of the University of Oxford*, vol. 6, *The Nineteenth Century, Part 1* (Oxford, 1997).
51 R. D. Anderson, *Universities and Elites in Britain Since 1800* (Cambridge, 1995), pp. 48-9; Heyck, op. cit.; Sheldon Rothblatt, *Revolution of the Dons: Cambridge and Society in Victorian England* (New York, 1968); and Christopher Harvie, *The Lights of Liberalism: University Liberals and the Challenge of Democracy, 1860-1886* (London, 1976).
52. Frank M. Turner, *The Greek Heritage in Victorian Britain* (New Haven, Conn., 1981), pp. 427-30.
53. See, for example, John Stuart Mill's 1867 "Inaugural Address at St. Andrews" and the analyis thereof, in Rothblatt, *Revolution of the Dons*, pp. 248 ff.
54. Turner, *Greek Heritage*, p. 5
55. Roy Lowe, "English Elite Education in the Late Nineteenth and Early Twentieth Centuries," in Werner Conze and Jürgen Kocka (eds.), *Bildungsbürgertum im 19. Jahrhundert, Teil I* (Frankfurt, 1985), pp. 147-62, at p. 151; R. D. Anderson, *Universities and Elites*, p. 9; Hans-Eberhard Mueller, *Bureaucracy, Education, and Monopoly: Civil Service Reforms in Prussia and England* (Berkeley, 1984), pp. 191-2.
56. Turner, *Greek Heritage*, p. 5.
57. The quote is from Samuel Finer, quoted in Richard Johnson, "Administrators in Education Before 1870: Patronage, Social Position and Role," in Gillian Sutherland (ed.),

Studies in the Growth of Nineteenth-Century Government (London, 1972), pp. 110–38, at p. 115.

58. Richard Johnson, "Administrators in Education," pp. 118–21.
59. Walcott, *Origins of Culture and Anarchy*, p. 27.
60. Arnold, "Special Report on Certain Points Connected with Elementary Education in Germany, Switzerland, and France" (1886), in *CPW*, vol. 11.
61. Arnold, "Education and the State," *Pall Mall Gazette*, Dec. 11, 1865; reprinted in *CPW*, vol. 4, pp. 1–4.
62. See especially the 1868 "Preface" to *Schools and Universities on the Continent* in *CPW*, vol. 4, pp. 15–30.
63. Walcott, *Origins of Culture and Anarchy*, p. xiii.
64. Arnold, 1868 "Preface" to *Schools and Universities on the Continent*, p. 30.
65. "A French Eton," *CPW*, vol. 2, p. 316.
66. "A French Eton," p. 322.
67. *CA*, p. 113; "The Bishop and the Philosopher" (1862), *CPW*, vol. 3, p. 41.
68. Collini, *Public Moralists*, pp. 51–4.
69. Heyck, *Transformation*, p. 33; Collini, *Public Moralists*, pp. 52–3.
70. Matthew Arnold, "The Function of Criticism at the Present Time," in *CW*, vol. 1, p. 267.

CHAPTER NINE
WEBER, SIMMEL, AND SOMBART

1. Friedrich Naumann, "Kulturgeschichte und Kapitalismus," *Neue Rundschau*, XXII (1911), pp. 1337–48, at p. 1340, quoted in Friedrich Lenger, *Werner Sombart, 1863–1941: Eine Biographie* (Munich, 1994), p. 219.
2. On state support for research and the role of state-solicited private donations, see Bernhard vom Brocke, "Der Kaiser-Wilhelm Gesellschaft im Kaiserreich," in Rudolf Vierhaus and Berhard vom Brocke (eds.), *Forschung im Spannungsfeld von Politik und Gesellschaft: Geschichte und Struktur der Kaiser-Wilhelm-/Max-Planck-Gesellschaft* (Stuttgart, 1990).
3. Wilhelm Hennis, *Max Weber: Essays in Reconstruction* (London, 1988), p. 59.
4. On which see Wolf Lepenies, *Between Literature and Science: The Rise of Sociology* (Cambridge, 1988), esp. chapter 13.
5. On Rathenau and his critique of contemporary German capitalism see Hartmut Pogge von Strandmann (ed.), *Walther Rathenau: Industrialist, Banker, Intellectual, and Politician* (Oxford, 1985), and Hans Dieter Hellige (ed.), *Walther Rathenau, Maximilian Harden: Briefwechsel, 1897–1920* (Munich, 1983). For an essay-length portrait, see Fritz Stern, "Walther Rathenau and the Vision of Modernity," in Fritz Stern, *Einstein's German World* (Princeton, N.J., 1999).
6. See the informed chapter on Tönnies in Harry Liebersohn, *Fate and Utopia in German Sociology, 1870–1923* (Cambridge, Mass., 1988); still useful is Arthur Mitzman, *Sociology and Estrangement: Three Sociologists of Imperial Germany* (New York, 1973).
7. See Liebersohn, *Fate and Utopia*, pp. 36–7.
8. Ferdinand Tönnies, *Community and Society*, trans. and ed. Charles L. Loomis (New York, 1963; German original 1887), p. 165.
9. Thomas Nipperdey, *Deutsche Geschichte: 1866–1918. Erster Band: Arbeitswelt und Bürgergeist* (Munich, 1990), pp. 268–78; David Blackbourn, *The Long Nineteenth Century: A History of Germany, 1780–1918* (New York, 1998), chapter 7, provides a useful overview.
10. On the rise of the modern corporation, see the seminal works by Alfred D. Chandler, Jr., *The Visible Hand: The Managerial Revolution in American Business*

(Cambridge, Mass., 1977), and *Scale and Scope: The Dynamics of Industrial Capitalism* (Cambridge, Mass., 1990), which extends the story to Germany and Japan.

11. Jürgen Kocka, "Big Business and the Rise of Managerial Capitalism: Germany in International Comparison," in Jürgen Kocka, *Industrial Culture and Bourgeois Society: Business, Labor, and Bureaucracy in Modern Germany* (New York, 1999) pp. 156–73, at p. 165; and Alfred D. Chandler, Jr., "*Fin de Siècle:* Industrial Transformation," in Mikulas Teich and Roy Porter (eds.), *Fin de Siècle and Its Legacy* (Cambridge, 1990), pp. 28–41.

12. Jürgen Kocka, "Family and Bureaucracy in German Industrial Management, 1850–1914: Siemens in Comparative Perspective," pp. 26–50, in his *Industrial Culture and Bourgeois Society*, p. 36.

13. Kocka, "Family and Bureaucracy," pp. 26–50, and "Big Business and the Rise of Managerial Capitalism," in his *Industrial Culture and Bourgeois Society*.

14. Blackbourn, *The Long Nineteenth Century*, p. 324.

15. In Eduard Bernstein, *The Assumptions of Socialism and the Tasks of Social Democracy* (Die Voraussetzungen des Sozialismus und die Aufgaben der Sozialdemokratie [1901]).

16. Friedrich Engels, "Supplement and Addendum to Volume 3 of *Capital*," in Karl Marx, *Capital: Volume 3*, trans. David Fernbach (London, 1981), p. 1045.

17. On Weber's family background, see Guenther Roth, "Weber and the Would-Be Englishman: Anglophilia and Family History," in Hartmut Lehmann and Guenther Roth (eds.), *Weber's Protestant Ethic: Origins, Evidence, Contexts* (Cambridge, 1993), pp. 83–120.

18. Max Weber, "Der Nationalstaat und die Volkswirtschaftspolitik" (1895), in Wolfgang J. Mommsen, (ed.), *Max Weber Gesamtausgabe*, I, 4, 2. Halbband (Tübingen, 1993), pp. 543–74, at p. 558. In English translation, "The Nation State and Economic Policy" (1895), the essay appears in Peter Lassman and Ronald Speirs (eds.), *Weber: Political Writings* (Cambridge, 1994), pp. 1–28.

19. For some of his most social Darwinist statements, see Weber, "Der Nationalstaat und die Volkswirtschaftspolitik,"pp.558–60. On imperialist social Darwinism as a phenomenon in Germany and in almost all other major nations in the late nineteenth century, see Heinz Gollwitzer, *Europe in the Age of Imperialism, 1880–1914* (New York, 1969).

20. Wolfgang J. Mommsen, *Max Weber and German Politics* (Chicago, 1984), pp. 72–3. For a time, Weber thought that peaceful competition for markets would be followed by a violent struggle between great powers.

21. Mommsen, *Max Weber and German Politics*, pp. 91 ff; on the groups arrayed against a dynamic capitalist economy, see also Max Weber, "Capitalism and Rural Society in Germany" (1906), in Hans Gerth and C. Wright Mills (eds.), *From Max Weber* (New York, 1946), pp.363–85.

22. See, for example, Weber, "Die bürgerliche Entwicklung Deutschlands" (1897), in Wolfgang J. Mommsen (ed.), *Max Weber Gesamtausgabe*, I, 4, 2. Halbband, pp. 810–8, at p. 816.

23. On France, see Herman Lebovics, *True France: The Wars over Cultural Identity, 1900–1945* (Ithaca, N.Y., 1992), chapter 1; on Germany, George L. Mosse, *The Crisis of German Ideology* (New York, 1981).

24. Knut Borchardt, "Einleitung," to Borchardt and Cornelia Meyer-Stoll, *Max Weber Gesamtausgabe*, I/5, Halbbd.1 (Tubingen, 1999), pp. 1–114, at p. 45. The estimate was made by the leading economist, Gustav Schmoller.

25. Knut Borchardt, "Einleitung," pp. 1–17.

26. Borchardt, "Einleitung," pp. 25 ff, and Eric Hobsbawm, *The Age of Empire, 1875–1914* (New York, 1987), pp. 36–46.

27. Borchardt, "Einleitung," pp. 26 ff.

28. Quoted in Borchardt, "Einleitung," p. 27.

29. Schäffle, quoted in Borchardt, "Einleitung," p. 41.

30. Borchardt, "Einleitung," p. 36.

31. On the role of Jews, see Werner E. Mosse, *Jews in the German Economy: The German-Jewish Economic Elite, 1820–1935* (Oxford, 1987), pp. 380 ff.

32. See the classic study by Peter Pulzer, *The Rise of Political Anti-Semitism in Germany and Austria* (Oxford, 1964; rev. ed. Cambridge, Mass., 1988).

33. Cited in James Retallack, "Conservatives and Antisemites in Baden and Saxony," *German History* (1999), vol. 17, no. 4, pp. 507–26, p. 516 n28.

34. Borchardt, "Einleitung," p. 86.

35. Editors' introduction to Weber, "Die Börse: I. Zweck und äußere Organisation der Börsen," pp. 127–33 in Borchardt (ed.), *Max Weber Gesamtausgabe*, I, 5, Halbband I.

36. "Diskussionsbeitrag in der Debatte über das allgemeine Programm des Nationalsozialen Vereins," in Wolfgang J. Mommsen (ed.), *Max Weber Gesamtausgabe*, I, 4, 2. Halbband (Tübingen, 1993), pp. 620–1.

37. Max Weber, "[Rezension von:] Was heißt Christlich-Sozial? Gesammelte Aufsätze von Fr Naumann" (1894), reprinted in Mommsen (ed.), *Max Weber Gesamtausgabe*, I, 4, pp. 350–61, at pp. 354–5.

38. Max Weber, "Die Börse: I," reprinted in Knut Borchardt (ed.), *Max Weber Gesamtausgabe*, I, 5, 1, pp. 135–74, and "Die Börse: II," reprinted in *Max Weber Gesamtausgabe*, I, 5, 2. Halbband (Tübingen, 2000) pp. 630–55.

39. "Börse: I," pp. 139–40.

40. Ibid, pp. 148–9.

41. Weber, "Die Börse: II," pp. 651–5.

42. Max Weber, "Vorbermerkung," in *Gesammelte Aufsätze zur Religionssoziologie I* (Tübingen, 1988), p. 4; Max Weber, *The Protestant Ethic and the Spirit of Capitalism*, trans. Talcott Parsons (New York, 1958), p. 17.

43. Weber, "Die protestantische Ethik und der Geist des Kapitalismus," in *Gesammelte Aufsätze*, p. 41; translation from Weber, *Protestant Ethic*, p. 56.

44. *The Protestant Ethic and the Spirit of Capitalism*, p. 21. Later, Weber coined the term "Zweckrationalität" (instrumental rationality) to describe this. Max Weber, *Economy and Society*, ed. Guenther Roth and Claus Wittich, 2 vols. (Berkeley, 1978), Max Weber, *Wirtschaft und Gesellschaft*, 4th ed. (Tübingen, 1956), p. 43. As Lawrence Scaff rightly notes, it was this conception of modernity that connected Weber's early and late studies; in Lawrence A. Scaff, *Fleeing the Iron Cage: Culture, Politics, and Modernity in the Thought of Max Weber* (Berkeley, 1989), p. 33. A useful exploration of the varied meanings of rationality in Weber's work is Rogers Brubaker, *The Limits of Rationality: An Essay on the Social and Moral Thought of Max Weber* (London, 1984).

45. Weber, *Economy and Society*, ed. Guenther Roth and Claus Wittich (Berkeley, 1978), pp. 956–1005.

46. Max Weber, "Science as a Vocation," in Gerth and Mills (eds.), *From Max Weber*, p. 139; *Gesammelte Aufsätze zur Wissenschaftslehre* (Tübingen, 1922), p. 449.

47. *The Protestant Ethic and the Spirit of Capitalism*, p. 53.

48. Wolfgang J. Mommsen has repeatedly explored this theme in Weber's writing and career. See especially his essays "The Alternative to Marx: Dynamic Capitalism instead of Bureaucratic Socialism," in Wolfgang J. Mommsen, *The Age of Bureaucracy: Perspectives on the Political Sociology of Max Weber* (New York 1974), pp. 47–71; and "Capitalism and Socialism: Weber's Dialogue with Marx," in Wolfgang J. Mommsen, *The Political and Social Theory of Max Weber* (Chicago, 1989), pp. 53–73.

49. "Der Sozialismus" (1918), in Max Weber, *Gesammelte Aufsätze zur Soziologie und Sozialpolitik*, pp. 492–518, at pp. 498–9. This essay was originally delivered as a lecture to Austro-Hungarian officers in Vienna, where Weber was a visiting professor, to aid in combatting the threat of socialist revolution. See the "Editorischer Bericht" to

"Der Sozialismus," in *Max Weber Gesamtausgabe*, I, 15, ed. Wolfgang J. Mommsen (Tübingen, 1984), pp. 597–8.

50. "Der Sozialismus" (1918), pp. 508–16.

51. *The Protestant Ethic and the Spirit of Capitalism*, p. 180.

52. *Briefwechsel zwishen Wilhelm Dilthey und dem Graf Paul Yorck v. Wartenburg* (Halle, 1923), p. 254, quoted and placed into context in Klaus Christian Köhnke, *Der junge Simmel in Theoriebeziehungen und sozialen Bewegungen* (Frankfurt, 1996), p. 116.

53. On these see Köhnke, *Der junge Simmel*, part 3.

54. This is the topic of one of Simmel's best-known essays, "The Stranger," in *The Sociology of Georg Simmel*, ed. and trans. Kurt H. Wolff (New York, 1964), pp. 402–8; original in Georg Simmel, *Soziologie* (Leipzig, 1908; 3rd ed. 1923), pp. 509–12.

55. Cf. Paul Nolte, *Die Ordnung der deutschen Gesellschaft: Selbstentwurf und Selbstbeschreibung im 20. Jahrhundert* (Munich, 2000), p. 56.

56. On Simmel's ongoing relevance, see Klaus Lichtblau, *Georg Simmel* (Frankfurt, 1997), p. 14. This book is perhaps the best available exploration of Simmel's work.

57. Köhnke, *Der junge Simmel*, p. 172.

58. Georg Simmel, *Philosophie des Geldes* (*Georg Simmel Gesamtausgabe*), vol. 6 (Frankfurt, 1989), cited hereafter as *PdG*; Georg Simmel, *The Philosophy of Money*, 2nd ed., ed. David Frisby (New York, 1990), cited hereafter as *PM*.

59. *PdG*, pp. 612–6; *PM*, pp. 443–6. For an earlier formulation, Georg Simmel, "Das Geld in der modernen Kultur" (1896), in Heinz-Jürgen Dahme and Otthein Rammstedt (eds.), *Georg Simmel: Schriften zur Soziologie* (Frankfurt, 1983), pp. 78–94, at pp. 90–1, translated as "Money in Modern Culture," in David Frisby and Mike Featherstone (eds.), *Simmel on Culture* (London, 1997), pp. 243–55, at pp. 252–3.

60. *PdG*, pp. 595–6; *PM*, p. 432.

61. "Soziologie der Konkurrenz," in Dahme and Rammstedt (eds.), *Georg Simmel*, p. 177; Georg Simmel, "Conflict," in *Conflict and the Web of Group Affiliations*, trans. Kurt H. Wolff and Reinhard Bendix (New York, 1955), pp. 61–2.

62. Simmel, "Das Geld in der modernen Kultur," pp. 80–2; "Money and Modern Culture," pp. 244–6.

63. *PM*, pp. 342–4.

64. On the women's movement, see Ute Frevert, *Women in German History: From Bourgeois Emancipation to Sexual Liberation* (New York, 1989), pp. 113–30.

65. This paragraph and the two that follow draw upon a number of works by Simmel that overlap in content, beginning with "Der Frauenkongress und die Sozialdemokratie,"*Die Zukunft*, vol. 17 (1896), pp. 80–4, now in Heinz-Jürgen Dahme and Klaus Christian Köhnke (eds.), *Georg Simmel: Schriften zur Philosophie und Soziologie der Geschlechter* (Frankfurt, 1985), pp. 133–8; translated as "The Women's Congress and Social Democracy," in Frisby and Featherstone, *Simmel on Culture*, pp. 270–4; then Simmel, "Tendencies in German Life and Thought Since 1870," *The International Monthly* (1905), vol. 5, reprinted in David Frisby (ed.), *Georg Simmel: Critical Assessments*, 3 vols. (New York, 1994), vol. 1, pp. 5–27, at pp. 16–20; *PdG*, p. 644, and *PM*, p. 464; and most fully in "Die Kreuzung socialer Kreise," in Simmel, *Soziologie*, 3rd ed. (Munich, 1923; 1st ed., 1908), pp. 335–8, translated by Reinhard Bendix as "The Web of Group-Affiliations" in Georg Simmel, *Conflict and the Web of Group-Affiliations* (New York, 1955), pp. 179–84.

66. Simmel, "Tendencies" and "Der Frauenkongress und die Sozial-demokratie."

67. There is an excellent discussion of this element of Simmel's thought in Lichtblau, *Georg Simmel*, pp. 31–8.

68. "Das Individuum, das an mehreren solcher Kreise theil hat, gleichsam in ihrem Schnittpunkt steht, wird den Gegensatz ihrer Richtungen in sich fühlen." *Georg Simmel Gesamtausgabe* (Frankfurt, 1989; hereafter cited as *GSG*) 4, 354, quoted in Köhnke, *Der junge Simmel*, p. 324.

69. *PM*, pp. 342–4.

70. *GSG* 4, 380; Köhnke, *Der junge Simmel*, pp. 327–8. On the origin of Simmel's analytic interest in the way in which social formations affect individual identity in the German tradition of social psychology (*Völkerspsychologie*), see Köhnke, *Der junge Simmel*, pp. 337 ff.

71. Georg Simmel, "Der Begriff und die Tragödie der Kultur," in Simmel, *Philosphische Kultur* (Leipzig, 1911), trans. Mark Ritter and David Frisby as "The Concept and Tragedy of Culture," in David Frisby and Mike Featherstone (eds.), *Simmel on Culture* (London, 1977); *PdG*, pp. 591–616; *PM*, pp. 446–70.

72. *PdG*, pp. 651–4; *PM*, pp. 468–70.

73. *PdG*, pp. 552–6; *PM*, pp. 400–4.

74. *PM*, pp. 212–3.

75. *PM*, pp. 228–32, 481–3.

76. These ambivalences are explored in Gianfranco Poggi, *Money and the Modern Mind: Georg Simmel's Philosophy of Money* (Berkeley, 1993), a useful guide through some of the themes of Simmel's book.

77. Georg Simmel, "Tendencies in German Life and Thought since 1870," p. 6; similarly *PM*, p. 482.

78. A point rightly made by Poggi, *Money and the Modern Mind*, p. 54.

79. For information on Sombart I have relied largely on the very thorough biography by Friedrich Lenger, *Werner Sombart, 1863–1941: Eine Biographie* (Munich, 1994).

80. Quoted in Lenger, *Werner Sombart*, pp. 137–40.

81. Werner Sombart, *Die deutsche Volkswirtschaft* (1903), p. 129, quoted in Lenger, *Werner Sombart*, p. 189.

82. Werner Sombart, *Die Juden und das Wirtschaftsleben* (Munich, 1911), translated by Mordechai Epstein as *The Jews and Modern Capitalism* (1913; reprinted New Brunswick, N.J., 1982).

83. Sombart, *Die Juden und das Wirtschaftsleben*, pp. 242–9, 403–27; *The Jews and Modern Capitalism*, pp. 213–21, 323–44.

84. Sombart, *Die Juden*, p. 330; *The Jews and Modern Capitalism*, p. 275.

85. For the distinction between the entrepreneur and the trader, and the Jews' greater fitness for the latter role, see Sombart, *Die Juden und das Wirtschaftsleben*, pp. 189–97, 332–3; *The Jews and Modern Capitalism*, pp. 160–8, 227–8.

86. This last formulation is adapted from the useful chapter on Sombart in Jeffrey Herf, *Reactionary Modernism: Technology, Culture, and Politics in Weimar and the Third Reich* (Cambridge, 1984), p. 136.

87. Lujo Brentano, *Der Wirtschaftende Mensch in der Geschichte: Gesammelte Reden und Aufsätze* (Leipzig, 1923), "Judentum und Kapitalismus," pp. 426–90. See also the excursus on "Handel, Puritanismus, Judentum und Kapitalismus," in Brentano, *Die Anfänge des modernen Kapitalismus* (Munich, 1916; first published 1913).

88. Quoted in Lenger, *Werner Sombart*, p. 448, n43. Weber's work on "the Protestant ethic and the spirit of capitalism" may have been stimulated by his dissatisfaction with Sombart's earlier treatment of the subject, on which see Hartmut Lehmann, "The Rise of Capitalism: Weber Versus Sombart," in Hartmut Lehmann and Guenther Roth, *Weber's Protestant Ethic: Origins, Evidence, Contexts* (Cambridge, 1993), pp. 195–210, at p. 198.

89. The antisemitic identification of Jews with plutocratic capitalism was by no means confined to Germany. For British cases see Jay P. Corrin, *G. K. Chesterton and Hilaire Belloc: The Battle Against Modernity* (Athens, Ohio, 1981), and with caution, Bryan Cheyette, *Constructions of "The Jew" in English Literature and Society* (Cambridge, 1993), chapter 5.

90. Lenger, *Werner Sombart*, p. 210 and 452, n108. On Fritsch as the *Altmeister* of National Socialism, see George L. Mosse, *The Crisis of German Ideology: Intellectual Origins of the Third Reich* (New York, 1964), p. 112. On the reception of

Sombart's work by Jews, see Lenger and Derek J. Penslar, *Shylock's Children* (Berkeley, 2001), chapter 4.

91. Letter of August 28, 1914, quoted in Mommsen, *Max Weber and German Politics*, pp. 190–1.

92. Mommsen, *Max Weber and German Politics*, pp. 192–4.

93. Georg Simmel, "Deutschlands innere Wandlung" (November 1914), and "Die Krisis der Kultur" (January 1916), both in his *Der Krieg und die geistigen Entscheidungen* (Munich, 1917), p. 59.

94. Simmel, *Der Krieg*, p. 64.

95. Simmel, *Der Krieg*, pp. 11-2, 61.

96. Werner Sombart, *Händler und Helden: Patriotische Besinnungen* (Munich, 1915), pp. 64, 14, quoted in Fritz Ringer, *The Decline of the German Mandarins: The German Academic Community, 1890–1933* (Cambridge, Mass., 1969), pp. 184–5. There is also a useful discussion in Lenger, *Werner Sombart*, pp. 245–52, and in Hermann Lübbe, *Politische Philosophie in Deutschland* (Munich, 1974), pp. 210–4.

97. Sombart, *Händler und Helden*, p. 65, quoted in Ringer, *Decline of the German Mandarins*, pp. 187–8.

98. Sombart, *Händler und Helden*, pp. 125, 143. Quoted in Lenger, *Werner Sombart*, pp. 247–8.

99. Lenger, *Sombart*, pp. 250–1.

CHAPTER TEN
LUKÁCS AND FREYER

1. For biographical information on Lukács, his family, and his context, I have drawn on his autobiographical reminiscences in Georg Lukács, *Gelebtes Denken*, ed. István Eörsi (Frankfurt, 1981), as well as the English version, *Record of a Life: An Autobiographical Sketch* (London, 1983); Lee Congdon, *The Young Lukács* (Chapel Hill, N.C., 1983); Arpad Kadarkay, *Georg Lukács: Life, Thought, and Politics* (Cambridge, Mass., 1991), which though analytically weak provides additional biographical detail; and Mary Gluck, *Georg Lukács and His Generation, 1900–1918* (Cambridge, Mass., 1985), which is particularly strong on the Hungarian context and intergenerational dynamics of Lukács and his circle. On Lukács' father, see also William O. McCagg, Jr., *Jewish Nobles and Geniuses in Modern Hungary* (Boulder, Colo., 1972), p. 106.

2. For a brilliant evocation of this anticapitalist sensibility, set in neighboring Bukovina, see Gregor von Rezzori, *Memoiren eines Antisemiten* (Munich, 1979), translated as *Memoirs of an Anti-semite* (New York, 1985).

3. Michael K. Silber, "A Jewish Minority in a Backward Economy: An Introduction," in Michael K. Silber, *Jews in the Hungarian Economy, 1760–1945* (Jerusalem, 1992), pp. 3–22, provides an excellent and succinct overview of the role of the Jews in the economy and society of Hungary. The theme is also explored in Gluck, *Georg Lukács and His Generation*, and at greater length in McCagg, *Jewish Nobles and Geniuses*, and McCagg, *A History of Habsburg Jews, 1670–1918* (Bloomington, Ind., 1989), chapters 8 and 11.

4. Lukács, *Record of a Life*, pp. 144–5. On turn-of-the-century Budapest in general, there is an exemplary overview by John Lukács, *Budapest 1900: A Historical Portrait of a City and Its Culture* (New York, 1988).

5. Béla Balázs, *Almodó ifjuság* (Dreams of Youth) (Budapest, 1976), pp. 84–5, quoted in Gluck, *Georg Lukács and His Generation*, p. 70.

6. On this pattern as characteristic of Lukács' generation, see Gluck, *Georg Lukács and His Generation*, p. 78; as a general pattern among German Jews, see Hannah Arendt, "Introduction," to Walter Benjamin, *Illuminations* (London, 1970), pp. 26–7. On the affinity of central European Jews for high culture, see George L. Mosse, *German Jews*

Beyond Judaism (Cincinnati, 1985). Though most intense among central European Jews, it was by no means confined to them. For other examples see Carl E. Schorske, "The Transformation of the Garden," in Carl E. Schorske, *Fin-de-Siècle Vienna: Politics and Culture* (New York, 1980).

7. Gluck, *Georg Lukács and His Generation*, p. 79.

8. Lukács, *Gelebtes Denken*, pp. 242–3; *Record of a Life*, p. 146.

9. Gluck, *Georg Lukács and His Generation*, pp. 55–7; John Lukács, *Budapest 1900*, pp. 108–36, 187–96.

10. Silber, "A Jewish Minority," p. 21.

11. Gluck, *Georg Lukács and His Generation*, 57–62; John Lukács, *Budapest 1900*, p. 89–91.

12. Gluck, *Georg Lukács and His Generation*, 8–9, 23–5.

13. See especially Georg von Lukács, "Zur Soziologie des modernen Dramas," *Archiv für Sozialwissenschaft und Sozialpolitik*, vol. 38 (1914), pp. 303–45, 662–706, and the analysis in Andrew Arato and Paul Breines, *The Young Lukács and the Origins of Western Marxism* (New York, 1979), pp. 15 ff.

14. Georg von Lukács, "Zum Wesen und zur Methode der Kultursoziologie," *Archiv für Sozialwissenschaft und Sozialpolitik*, vol. 39 (1915), pp. 216–22, cites *Gemeinschaft und Gesellschaft* and *Die Philosophie des Geldes* as the most significant works for the sociology of culture. On the influence of Simmel's *Philosophy of Money* on Lukács, see David Frisby, "Introduction to the Translation," in Georg Simmel, *The Philosophy of Money* (London, 1990), pp. 15–21.

15. See the "Curriculum Vitae," which Lukács submitted to the University of Heidelberg in May 1918, first published in *Text+Kritik*, No. 39/40 (1973), p. 5, and in translation in Judith Marcus and Zoltán Tar (eds.), *Georg Lukács: Selected Correspondence, 1902–1920* (New York, 1986), pp. 284–8.

16. This recurrent theme in Lukács' work is expressed in his essay of 1913, "Aesthetic Culture," in the Hungarian volume of the same name, discussed in György Márkus, "Life and Soul: The Young Lukács and the Problem of Culture," in Agnes Heller (ed.), *Lukács Reappraised* (New York, 1983), pp. 1–26.

17. Lukács, *Gelebtes Denken*, p. 75; *Record*, pp. 48–9.

18. After reading some of Lukács' early book on modern drama, Simmel wrote to Lukács that the spiritual effects of modern processes were more ambiguous than one would be led to believe by Lukács' interpretation, so that it was "plausible to arrive at opposite conclusions from the same presuppositions." Letter of Simmel to Lukács, July 22, 1909, in Marcus and Tar (eds.), *Georg Lukács: Selected Correspondence, 1902–1920*, p. 93. Though many commentators have noted the influence of Simmel on Lukács, some have tended to assimilate Simmel's views to Lukács' more pessimistic analysis. See for instance Kurt Lenk, "Das tragische Bewußtsein in der deutschen Soziologie," *Kölner Zeitschrift für Soziologie und Sozialpsychologie*, vol. 16, no. 2 (1964), pp. 257–87, and similarly Congdon, *The Young Lukács*, p. 25. Michael Löwy, *Georg Lukács—From Romanticism to Bolshevism* (London, 1979), p. 96, rightly notes that Lukács objected to Simmel's reconciliation with capitalist society.

19. Georg Lukács, *Theory of the Novel* (Cambridge, Mass., 1971), p. 64, quoted in Martin Jay, *Marxism and Totality: The Adventures of a Concept from Lukács to Habermas* (Berkeley, 1984), p. 95.

20. Lukács, *Gelebtes Denken*, pp. 254–5; *Record of a Life*, pp. 153–4; see also Löwy, *Georg Lukács*, p. 111–2.

21. Lukács, *Gelebtes Denken*, p. 257; *Record of a Life*, p. 156; and Kadarkay, *Georg Lukács*, pp. 156–8.

22. For a good account of the social effect of the war, see Roger Chickering, *Imperial Germany and the Great War, 1914–1918* (Cambridge, 1998).

23. See Löwy, *Georg Lukács*, p. 123.

24. Quoted in Kadarkay, *Georg Lukács*, p. 208.
25. On the Hungarian Soviet dictatorship, see Rudolf L. Tökés, *Béla Kun and the Hungarian Soviet Republic* (New York, 1967). On Lukács' role, see Kadarkay, *Georg Lukács*, chapter 9, and Congdon, *The Young Lukács*, chapter 6.
26. Lukács, *Gelebtes Denken*, p. 96; *Record of a Life*, p. 60.
27. Kadarkay, *Georg Lukács*, p. 212, gives a slightly different figure, but the proportions are the same.
28. On which see Thomas Sakmyster, *Hungary's Admiral on Horseback: Miklos Horthy, 1918–1944* (Boulder, Colo., 1994).
29. See Andrew Janos, *The Politics of Backwardness in Hungary, 1825–1945* (Princeton, N.J., 1982), pp. 201–6.
30. Kadarkay, *Georg Lukács*, pp. 237–8.
31. See, on this topic, Jerry Z. Muller, "Communism, Anti-Semitism, and the Jews," *Commentary* (August 1988), pp. 28–39; as well as the essays by Ivan T. Berend in Randolph L. Braham and Attila Pok (eds.), *The Holocaust in Hungary Fifty Years Later* (New York, 1997). On the centrality of the theme in Hitler's speeches and worldview, see Ian Kershaw, *Hitler, 1889–1936: Hubris* (New York, 1999), pp. 23–4. On the permeation of this theme into American military intelligence, see Joseph Bendersky, *The "Jewish Threat": Anti-Semitic Politics of the U.S. Army* (New York, 2000).
32. See François Furet, *The Passing of an Illusion: The Idea of Communism in the Twentieth Century* (Chicago, 2000), chapters 2 and 3.
33. A classic and still valuable analysis of the fundamental dynamics of Communist strategy and ideology in the period following the failure of the revolution to spread beyond Russia is Franz Borkenau, *World Communism* (1939; reprint Ann Arbor, Mich., 1962), chapter 9.
34. Charles S. Maier, *Recasting Bourgeois Europe: Stabilization in France, Germany, and Italy in the Decade After World War I* (Princeton, N.J., 1975).
35. On the NEP see Martin Malia, *The Soviet Tragedy: A History of Socialism in Russia, 1917–1991* (New York, 1994), chapter 5.
36. Georg Lukács, *History and Class Consciousness: Studies in Marxist Dialectics* trans. Rodney Livingstone (Cambridge, Mass., 1971), hereafter cited as *HCC*, pp. 88–9; Georg Lukács, *Geschichte und Klassenbewußtsein*, hereafter cited as *GK*, following the pagination in Georg Lukács, *Werke* (Neuwied, 1962), Band II, pp. 262–3; I have altered the translation occasionally. On Taylorism and European-bred sciences of work during this period, see Anson Rabinbach, *The Human Motor: Energy, Fatigue and the Origins of Modernity* (New York, 1990), chapters 9 and 10.
37. *HCC*, p. 89; *GK*, pp. 263–4.
38. *HCC*, p. 157; *GK*, p. 340.
39. *HCC*, pp. 181, 54; *GK*, pp. 367, 227.
40. *HCC*, p. 7; *GK*, p. 178.
41. *HCC*, p. 103, *GK*, p. 279.
42. *HCC*, pp. 109–10; *GK*, p. 286.
43. *HCC*, p. 91; *GK*, p. 265.
44. *HCC*, p. 95; *GK*, p. 272.
45. Antonio Gramsci (1891–1937) was to present a similar line of Marxist analysis in the late 1920s and 1930s. But he wrote in prison in Fascist Italy, and his writings were published posthumously only after the Second World War. For an overview of his thought, see Leszek Kolakowski, *Main Currents of Marxism. Volume 3, The Breakdown* (New York, 1978), chapter 6.
46. *HCC*, p. 27; *GK*, p. 199.
47. *HCC*, p. 69; *GK*, pp. 244–5.
48. *HCC*, p. 13; *GK*, p. 186.
49. *HCC*, pp. 20–1; *GK*, p. 194.

50. *HCC*, p. 21; *GK*, p. 195.
51. *HCC*, p. 51–3; *GK*, p. 223–5.
52. This point is brought out in the excellent analysis by in Leszek Kolakowski, *Main Currents of Marxism*, vol. 3, chapter 7.
53. See Kolakowski, *Main Currents of Marxism*, vol. 3; George Lichtheim, *Lukács* (London, 1970), pp. 50–1; and Bernard Yack, *The Longing for Total Revolution* (Princeton, N.J., 1986), pp. 286 ff.
54. *HCC*, p. 76 ; *GK*, p. 252.
55. *HCC*, p. 74 ; *GK*, p. 249.
56. *HCC*, p. 75, *GK*, pp. 250–1.
57. *HCC*, pp. 79–80; *GK*, p. 253.
58. *HCC*, p. 41, *GK*, p. 212.
59. *HCC*, p. 208, *GK*, p. 397.
60. *HCC*, pp. 315–6; *GK*, pp. 493–4.
61. *HCC*, p. 319; *GK*, pp. 496–7.
62. Hans Freyer, *Theorie des gegenwärtigen Zeitalters* (Stuttgart, 1955), p. 127. The description and analysis of Freyer and his work is drawn primarily from Jerry Z. Muller, *The Other God That Failed: Hans Freyer and the Deradicalization of German Conservatism* (Princeton, N.J., 1987), to which the reader is referred for further bibliography and further detail. Of more recent work on Freyer, most useful for purposes of this chapter is the analysis in Rolf Peter Sieferle, *Die Konservative Revolution: Fünf biographische Skizzen* (Frankfurt, 1995), pp. 164–97.
63. Two classic works on the history of *völkisch* nationalism are Fritz Stern, *The Politics of Cultural Despair: A Study in the Rise of the Germanic Ideology* (Berkeley, 1961), and George L. Mosse, *The Crisis of German Ideology* (New York, 1964).
64. Hans Freyer, *Die Bewertung der Wirtschaft im philosophischen Denken des 19. Jahrhunderts* (Leipzig, 1921).
65. Hans Freyer, *Theorie des objektiven Geistes: Eine Einleitung in die Kulturphilosophie* (Leipzig, 1923), translated from the second German edition of 1928 by Steven Grosby as *Theory of Objective Mind: An Introduction to the Philosophy of Culture* (Athens, Ohio, 1998); "Zur Philosophie der Technik," *Blätter für deutsche Philosophie*, vol. 3 (1929–30), pp. 192–201; *Der Staat* (Leipzig, 1926); Hans Freyer, *Soziologie als Wirklichkeitwissenschaft* (Leipzig, 1930); *Einleitung in die Soziologie* (Leipzig, 1931).
66. Hans Freyer, *Antäus: Grundlegung einer Ethik des bewußten Lebens* (Jena, 1918), and *Prometheus: Ideen zur Philosophie der Kultur* (Jena, 1923).
67. On the tradition of German historicism, see Friedrich Meinecke, *Die Enstehung des Historismus* (Berlin, 1936); Hans-Georg Gadamer, *Truth and Method* (New York, 1982), pp. 153–203; Georg G. Iggers, *The German Conception of History* (rev. ed., Middleton, Conn., 1983), chapter 1, passim. On Herder see the classic essay by Isaiah Berlin, "Herder and the Enlightenment," in Berlin, *Vico and Herder: Two Studies in the History of Ideas* (New York, 1976).
68. Johannes (Hans) Freyer, *Geschichte der Geschichte der Philosophie im achtzehnten Jahrhundert*, in *Beiträge zur Kultur- und Universalgeschichte*, gen. ed. Karl Lamprecht, vol. 16 (Leipzig, 1912), pp. 150–1, 42.
69. Freyer, *Antäus*, pp. 90 ff.
70. Freyer, *Prometheus*, p. 78.
71. Freyer, *Prometheus*, pp. 80, 82.
72. Martin Heidegger, *Sein und Zeit* (1927; 9th ed., Tübingen, 1963), pp. 382–7.
73. Walter Goetz, *Das Wesen der deutschen Kultur* (Darmstadt, 1919), p. 3.
74. Theodore Litt, *Individuum und Gemeinschaft*, 3rd ed. (Leipzig, 1926), p. 382.
75. Freyer, *Prometheus*, p. 107.
76. Freyer, *Prometheus*, p. 57.
77. Freyer, *Der Staat*, pp. 174–5.

78. Freyer, *Prometheus*, pp. 55–6.
79. Freyer, "Zur Philosophie der Technik," p. 201; similarly, the conclusion of *Die Bewertung der Wirtschaft*. On the attitude of Freyer and other intellectuals of the Weimar right toward technology, see Jeffrey Herf, *Reactionary Modernism: Technology, Culture, and Politics in Weimar and the Third Reich* (Cambridge, 1984).
80. Freyer, *Der Staat*, pp. 140–3.
81. Freyer, *Der Staat*, pp. 142–3.
82. Freyer, *Der Staat*, pp. 144–9.
83. Freyer, *Der Staat*, pp. 112, 145.
84. Freyer, *Der Staat*, pp. 37–8.
85. Freyer, *Theorie*, pp. 90–1; Freyer, *Prometheus*, pp. 4–5.
86. Freyer, *Der Staat*, p. 99.
87. Freyer, *Prometheus*, p. 4.
88. Freyer, *Der Staat*, p. 105.
89. Freyer, *Der Staat*, pp. 128, 175.
90. Harold James, "Economic Reasons for the Collapse of the Weimar Republic," in Ian Kershaw (ed.), *Weimar: Why Did German Democracy Fail?* (New York, 1990), pp. 30–57; and Knut Borchardt, "Constraint and Room for Manoeuvre in the Great Depression of the Early Thirties: Toward a Revision of the Received Historical Picture" and "Economic Causes of the Collapse of the Weimar Republic," both in Kurt Borchardt, *Perspectives on Modern German Economic History and Policy* (Cambridge, 1991), pp. 143–83.
91. Hans Freyer, *Revolution von rechts* (Jena, 1931), pp. 26–33.
92. Freyer, *Revolution*, pp. 23, 58–60. Freyer was here following the analysis of his friend, Carl Schmitt. See Jerry Z. Muller, "Carl Schmitt, Hans Freyer, and the Radical Conservative Critique of Liberal Democracy in the Weimar Republic," *History of Political Thought* 12, no. 4 (Winter 1991), pp. 695–715.
93. Freyer, *Revolution*, pp. 43–4, 69.
94. Freyer, *Revolution*, pp. 54–5, 61.
95. Freyer, *Revolution*, pp. 47–9.
96. Freyer, *Revolution*, pp. 64–72.
97. On Freyer's career and thought from 1933 until his death see Muller, *The Other God That Failed*, chapters 6 through 10.
98. Interview with *New Left Review*, originally published in 1971 and quoted here from the reprint in Lukács, *Record of a Life*, p. 181.

CHAPTER ELEVEN
SCHUMPETER

1. Preface to Joseph A. Schumpeter, *Capitalism, Socialism, and Democracy*, 1st ed. (New York, 1942), pp. ix–x. Henceforth cited as *CSD*.
2. I have profited from recent biographical studies by Richard Swedberg, *Schumpeter: A Biography* (Princeton, N.J., 1991); Robert Loring Allen, *Opening Doors: The Life and Work of Joseph Schumpeter*, 2 vols. (New Brunswick, N.J.; 1991); and Wolfgang F. Stolper, *Joseph Alois Schumpeter: The Public Life of a Private Man* (Princeton, N.J., 1994).
3. Regis A. Factor, *Guide to the* Archiv für Sozialwissenschaft und Sozialpolitik *Group, 1904–1933: A History and Comprehensive Bibliography* (New York, 1988).
4. Schumpeter regarded Carlyle's emphasis on the heroic personality as closer to his own economic sociology than utilitarian approaches to economics: Joseph Schumpeter, *History of Economic Analysis* (New York, 1954), pp. 409–11. For speculation on the possible influence of Henri Bergson and Gabriel Tarde on Schumpeter's conception of the process of capitalist development, see Fritz Redlich, "Unternehmer-

forschung und Weltanschauung," *Kyklos*, vol. 8 (1955), pp. 277-300; and Enrico Santarelli and Enzo Pesciarelli, "The Emergence of a Vision: The Development of Schumpeter's Theory of Entrepreneurship," *History of Political Economy*, vol. 22, no. 4 (1990), pp. 677-96.

5. Schumpeter, *History*, p. 789 n13.

6. Friedrich von Wieser, *Recht und Macht* (1910), and his contribution, "Theorie der gesellschaftlichen Wirtschaft," to Max Weber's *Grundriß der Sozialökonomik* (1914), cited by Jürgen Osterhammel, "Joseph A. Schumpeter und das Nicht-ökonomische in der Ökonomie," *Kölner Zeitschrift für Soziologie und Sozialpsychologie*, vol. 39, no.1 (1987), pp. 40-58, at pp. 52-3.

7. As his essay on social classes makes clear, Schumpeter appears to have paid attention to British developments in ethnology, eugenics, and the study of the family, all of which he thought useful but in need of critical assimilation by those "who know the relevance of what these disciplines have to offer." "Die sozialen Klassen im ethnisch homogen Milieu," *Archiv für Sozialwissenschaft und Sozialpolitik*, vol. 57 (1927), pp. 1-67; translation, "Social Classes in an Ethnically Homogeneous Environment," now in Joseph A. Schumpeter, *The Economics and Sociology of Capitalism*, ed. Richard Swedberg (Princeton, N.J., 1991), pp. 231-2.

8. For an excellent and succinct overview of Nietzsche's thought, see the chapter "Friedrich Nietzsche" by Werner J. Dannhauser, in Leo Strauss and Joseph Cropsey (eds.), *History of Political Thought* (Chicago, 1963, and subsequent editions). Henning Ottmann (ed.), *Nietzsche-Handbuch* (Stuttgart, 2000), is an invaluable guide to scholarship on Nietzsche.

9. Joseph A. Schumpeter, *Das Wesen und der Hauptinhalt der Nationalökonomie* (Leipzig, 1908), pp. 615, 618.

10. For the negative effects on economic analysis of ignoring elites, see Schumpeter's comments on Adam Smith in *History of Economic Analysis*, p. 186: "A judiciously diluted Rousseauism is also evident in the equalitarian tendency of his economic sociology. Human beings seemed to him to be much alike by nature, all reacting in the same simple ways to very simple stimuli, differences being due mainly to different training and different environments. This is very important considering A. Smith's influence upon nineteenth-century economics. His work was the channel through which eighteenth-century ideas about human nature reached economists."

11. On the neglect of the entrepreneur in economic theory, see Redlich, "Unternehmerforschung und Weltanschauung"; and for more recent literature on the subject, Israel M. Kirzner, *Discovery and the Capitalist Process* (Chicago, 1985), chapter 1. On the attention devoted to entrepreneurs and their functions among German-language economic theorists in the nineteenth century, see Erich Streissler, "The Influence of German and Austrian Economics on Joseph A. Schumpeter," in Yuichi Shionoya and Mark Perlman (eds.), *Schumpeter in the History of Ideas* (Ann Arbor, Mich., 1994), pp. 13-38, esp. pp. 15-22, 34-5. For a useful overview, Mark Blaug, "The Concept of Entrepreneurship in the History of Economics," in Blaug, *Not Only an Economist* (Cheltenham, England, 1997), pp. 95-113.

12. Joseph A. Schumpeter, *The Theory of Economic Development* (New Brunswick, N.J., 1983), p. 66. This translation of the second German edition (1926) of Schumpeter's book first appeared in 1934.

13. Schumpeter, *Theory*, p. 86.

14. Joseph A. Schumpeter, "[D]er Schöpferkraft und Herrschgewalt des Führers," in *Theorie der wirtschaftlichen Entwicklung* (Leipzig, 1912; first published Vienna, June 1911) (hereafter cited as *TWE*), p. 304. The phrase appears in the English translation of 1934 as "the creative power of a leader." Schumpeter, *Theory*, p. 147.

15. *TWE*, p. 285; *Theory*, p. 133.

16. Schumpeter, *Theory*, p. 133.
17. Schumpeter, *Theory*, pp. 92–3. Schumpeter's emphasis on the degree to which ratio-nalist economic models cannot account for the behavior of the entrepreneur is dis-cussed in Nathan Rosenberg, "Joseph Schumpeter: Radical Economist," in Yuichi Sihionoyo and Mark Perlman (eds.), *Schumpeter in the History of Ideas* (Ann Arbor, Mich., 1994).
18. Schumpeter, *History*, p. 409.
19. *TWE*, pp. 542–6. In the preface to the English translation of 1934, Schumpeter refers to "the theory of cultural evolution, which in important points presents striking analogies with the economic theory of this book." *Theory*, p. lxiii.
20. *TWE*, pp. 542–5.
21. Although this essay was first published in 1927, its genesis lies in the decade before the First World War. It grew, Schumpeter tells us in a prefatory note, from lectures he delivered at the University of Czernowitz in 1910–11, and then in a course he offered three years later while a visiting professor at Columbia University in New York.
22. Schumpeter, "Social Classes," p. 274.
23. Schumpeter, "Social Classes," pp. 276–7. Schumpeter thought that Spearman's book *Abilities of Man* (1927) should be required reading for all economists, along with William Stern's *Differentielle Psychologie* (1911): Schumpeter, *History*, pp. 796–7n.
24. A frequent theme in Nietzsche's work, the locus classicus is *On the Genealogy of Morality*.
25. *TWE*, pp. 534 ff.
26. See Schumpeter's essay on Pareto in Joseph A. Schumpeter, *Ten Great Economists from Marx to Keynes* (New York, 1951).
27. Vilfredo Pareto, *The Rise and Fall of Elites: An Application of Theoretical Sociology* (New Brunswick, N.J., 1991; Italian original published in 1901), pp. 39–40.
28. Pareto, *Rise and Fall*, p. 50.
29. Such activities were in keeping with the tradition of Viennese professors of econom-ics, who frequently served in high governmental posts. See William Johnston, *The Austrian Mind: An Intellectual and Social History, 1848–1938* (Berkeley, 1972), pp. 48 and 70, and chapter 4.
30. See the letters of Schumpeter to Graf Otto Harrach, a member of the Austrian House of Lords, written from 1916 to 1918, in Joseph A. Schumpeter, *Politische Reden*, ed. Christian Seidl and Wolfgang F. Stolper (Tübingen, 1992), pp. 359–76.
31. See Barbara Jelavich, *Modern Austria: Empire and Republic, 1800–1986* (Cambridge, 1987), pp. 144–5; Paul Silverman, "Law and Economics in Interwar Vienna: Kelsen, Mises, and the Regeneration of Austrian Liberalism" (Ph.D. diss., University of Chicago, 1984), introduction and chapter 1; and Malachi H. Hacohen, *Karl Popper: The Formative Years, 1902–1945* (Cambridge, 2000).
32. An analysis affirmed retroactively by Frederick Hertz, *The Economic Problems of the Danubian States: A Study of Economic Nationalism* (1947; reprint New York, 1970). For a recent reaffirmation of this analysis, see John W. Mason, *The Dis-solution of the Austro-Hungarian Empire, 1867–1918*, 2nd ed. (London, 1997), chapter 4.
33. As Schumpeter put it in *Capitalism, Socialism, and Democracy*, "The rationalist attitude may go to work with information and technique so inadequate that actions—and especially a general surgical propensity—induced by it may, to an observer of a later period, appear to be, even from a purely intellectual standpoint, inferior to the actions and anti-surgical propensities associated with attitudes that at the time most people felt inclined to attribute to a low I.Q." (p. 122). As Schumpeter notes, this insight goes back at least as far as the conservative critique of the Enlight-enment.
34. Helmut Gruber, *Red Vienna: Experiment in Working-Class Culture, 1919–1934* (New York, 1991), pp. 18–20. Jelavich, *Modern Austria*, pp. 164–5. See also Rudolf

Gerlich, *Die gescheiterte Alternative. Sozialisierung in Österreich nach dem Ersten Weltkrieg* (Vienna, 1980), p. 99.

35. Christian Seidl, "The Bauer-Schumpeter Controversy on Socialization," *History of Economic Ideas* vol. 2, (1994), pp. 41–69, at p. 69. Schumpeter seems also to have worked behind the scenes to prevent the socialization of the Alpine-Montan Corporation, the largest iron producer in Austria and the linchpin of the government's socialization program. Haberler quite rightly notes that as minister of finance, Schumpeter worked against socialization and other radical economic measures. Gottfried Haberler, "Joseph Alois Schumpeter 1883–1950," *Quarterly Journal of Economics*, vol. 64 (August 1950), reprinted in John Cunningham Wood (ed.), *J. A. Schumpeter: Critical Assessments*, 4 vols. (London, 1991), vol. 1, p. 93.

36. See for example "Der Sozialismus" (1918), in Max Weber, *Gesammelte Aufsätze zur Soziologie und Sozialpolitik* (Türbingen, 1924), pp. 492–518, and Weber's posthumously published *Economy and Society*, ed. Guenther Roth and Claus Wittich (Berkeley, 1978), pp. 82–113.

37. Many of the major documents in the subsequent "socialist calculation debate" are collected in Friedrich A. Hayek (ed.), *Collectivist Economic Planning* (London, 1935). For a discussion of the debate, see David Ramsey Steele, *From Marx to Mises: Post-Capitalist Society and the Challenge of Economic Calculation* (La Salle, Ill., 1992), and chapter 13 below.

38. Peter L. Berger, *Redeeming Laughter: The Comic Dimension of Human Experience* (New York, 1997), p. 41.

39. Joseph Schumpeter, "Sozialistische Möglichkeiten von heute," *Archiv für Sozialwissenschaft und Sozialpolitik*, vol. 48 (1920–21), pp. 305–60. Reprinted in his *Aufsätze zur ökonomischen Theorie* (Türbingen, 1952). Page references are to the original publication. Schumpeter's recurrent argument that "the time for socialism was in the future, the time for capitalism was now" goes back even earlier, to his 1918 "Crisis of the Tax State," now in Joseph A. Schumpeter, *Economics and Sociology of Capitalism*, pp. 130–31.

40. Schumpeter, "Sozialistische Möglichkeiten," pp. 310–1.

41. Schumpeter, "Sozialistische Möglichkeiten," p. 308.

42. Schumpeter, "Sozialistische Möglichkeiten," p. 336.

43. Schumpeter, "Sozialistische Möglichkeiten," pp. 312–9.

44. Schumpeter, "Sozialistische Möglichkeiten," p. 323.

45. Schumpeter, "Sozialistische Möglichkeiten," pp. 343–6.

46. Schumpeter, "Sozialistische Möglichkeiten," pp. 348–9.

47. "Unternehmerfunktion und Arbeiterinteresse," in Joseph A. Schumpeter, *Aufsätze zur Wirtschaftspolitik*, ed. and introduced by Wolfgang F. Stolper and Christian Seidl (Tübingen, 1985).

48. Joseph Schumpeter, "The Instability of Capitalism," published in the *Economic Journal* 38 (1928), pp. 361–86; reprinted in Joseph A. Schumpeter, *Essays on Entrepreneurs, Innovations, Business Cycles, and the Evolution of Capitalism*, ed. Richard V. Clemence (New Brunswick, N.J., 1989).

49. The details of this phase of Schumpeter's life remain unclear. The information available is presented in Stolper, *Joseph Alois Schumpeter*, chapter 21.

50. See the articles collected in Joseph A. Schumpeter, *Aufsätze zur Wirtschaftspolitik*, and pp. 36–43 of the introduction; as well as Joseph A. Schumpeter, *Business Cycles: A Theoretical, Historical, and Statistical Analysis of the Capitalist Process* (New York, 1939), 2 vols. continuously paginated, pp. 714–6. More recent historians of the Weimar economy, such as Knut Borchardt and Harold James, have reached similar conclusions.

51. Schumpeter, *Business Cycles*, pp. 708–10.

52. David M. Kennedy, *Freedom from Fear: The American People in Depression and War, 1929–1945* (New York, 1999), pp. 20–3.

53. Rudolf Hilferding, *Das Finanzkapital* (Vienna, 1910); see also the discussion on Simmel and Weber in chapter 9. Adolf Berle and Gardiner Means, *The Modern Corporation and Private Property* (New York, 1932).

54. Kennedy, *Freedom from Fear*, pp. 120–1.

55. On changes in fertility and contraception, see Eugen Weber, *Peasants into Frenchmen: The Modernization of Rural France, 1870–1914* (Stanford, Cal., 1976), chapter 11; Simon Szreter, *Fertility, Class, and Gender in Britain, 1860–1940* (Cambridge, 1996); Ute Frevert, *Women in German History: From Bourgeois Emancipation to Sexual Liberation* (New York, 1989; German original 1986), pp. 186 ff; John Gillis, Louise A. Tilly, and David Levine (eds.), *The European Experience of Declining Fertility, 1850–1970* (Cambridge, Mass., 1992); Janet Farrell Brodie, *Contraception and Abortion in Nineteenth-Century America* (Ithaca, N.Y., 1994); on Mensinga and the diaphragm, see Paul Weindling, *Health, Race, and German Politics Between National Unification and Nazism, 1870–1945* (Cambridge, 1989), p. 264; Kennedy, *Freedom from Fear*, p. 28. On the marketing of spermicidal douches, see Andrea Tone, "Contraceptive Consumers: Gender and the Political Economy of Birth Control in the 1930s," *Journal of Social History*, vol. 29, no. 3 (June 1996), pp. 485–506.

56. For the debate in England, see Szreter, *Fertility, Class, and Gender in Britain*, and Richard Solway, *Demography and Degeneration: Eugenics and the Declining Birthrate in Twentieth-Century Britain* (Chapel Hill, N.C., 1995); for the contours of German debates, see Weindling, *Health, Race, and German Politics*, pp. 241–69, and Atina Grossman, *Reforming Sex* (New York, 1995).

57. Kennedy, *Freedom from Fear*, pp. 86–7.

58. Kennedy, *Freedom from Fear*, p. 163.

59. Kennedy, *Freedom from Fear*, pp. 122–3. The left-Keynesian English economist Joan Robinson wrote in 1937 that an era of technological advance comparable to the nineteenth century was "scarcely to be hoped for": Joan Robinson, *Introduction to the Theory of Employment* (New York, 1937), quoted in John A. Garraty, *The Great Depression* (New York, 1986), p. 135. For Keynes' stagnationist views, see Robert Skidelsky, *John Maynard Keynes*, vol. 2, *The Economist as Saviour, 1920–1937* (London, 1992), pp. 608–9.

60. Quoted in Kennedy, *Freedom from Fear*, p. 373.

61. Kennedy, *Freedom from Fear*, pp. 374–5. On Hansen see also Theodore Rosenof, *Economics in the Long Run: New Deal Theorists and Their Legacies, 1933–1993* (Chapel Hill, N.C., 1997), chapter 5.

62. Kennedy, *Freedom from Fear*, p. 151.

63. Kennedy, *Freedom from Fear*, pp. 227–42, 276.

64. Kennedy, *Freedom from Fear*, pp. 275–80.

65. Kennedy, *Freedom from Fear*, p. 282.

66. Kennedy, *Freedom from Fear*, p. 352.

67. Kennedy, *Freedom from Fear*, p. 353.

68. Schumpeter, *Business Cycles*, hereafter cited as *BC*.

69. *BC*, pp. 995–6, 1026.

70. *BC*, pp. 992–3.

71. *BC*, pp. 994–5.

72. *BC*, pp. 1039–41. Kennedy, *Freedom from Fear*, pp. 284, 351, and 376, comes to this conclusion.

73. *BC*, pp. 1044, 1039.

74. *BC*, p. 1044. He reiterated in the preface to the second edition of *Capitalism, Socialism, and Democracy* that he believed that *"most* of the current talk about monopoly . . . is nothing but radical ideology and has no foundation in fact" (p. x).

75. *CSD*, p. 101. As Neil McInnes has noted, Schumpeter destroyed the logical foundations of antitrust doctrine, but it refused to fall over: Neil McInnes, "Wrong for Supe-

rior Reasons," *The National Interest* (Spring 1995), pp. 85–97, at p. 94; this is a very intelligent review of the reception of *CSD* in the decades since its publication.

76. *BC*, p. 1038; see the more extended analysis in chapter 14, B, C.

77. *BC*, pp. 1046–50.

78. Schumpeter mentions most of the major themes of *Capitalism, Socialism, and Democracy* in his review of Werner Sombart's *Moderner Kapitalismus*, as key themes in the era of high capitalism that deserve systematic discussion but are not adequately explored by Sombart. Schumpeter, "Sombarts Dritter Band," *Schmollers Jahrbuch*, vol. 51, no. 3 (1927), pp. 349–69; reprinted in Bernhard vom Brocke (ed.), *Sombarts "Moderner Kapitalismus": Materialien zur Kritik und Rezeption* (Munich, 1987), pp. 196–219; esp. p. 207.

79. D. M. Wright, "Schumpeter and Keynes," *Weltwirtschaftliches Archiv*, vol. 65 (1950), pp. 195–6, reprinted in Wood (ed.), *J. A. Schumpeter: Critical Assessments*, vol. 1, pp. 26–36, at p. 36; McInnes, "Wrong for Superior Reasons."

80. As Schumpeter noted in the preface to *CSD*, 1st ed., pp. ix–x.

81. On the whole, the reviewers who shared Schumpeter's Viennese background were the most likely to catch the book's ironic drift. Fritz Machlup, reviewing the book in the *American Economic Review*, termed its style "humorous-ironic rococo." In his extensive summary, he hit upon virtually every major point of the book and noted "the firm impression that Schumpeter dislikes socialism, nay, despises it. I read this between the lines only . . .": Fritz Machlup, "Capitalism and Its Future Appraised by Two Liberal Economists," *American Economic Review*, vol. 33 (1943), pp. 301–20, at p. 302. Similarly Haberler, "Joseph Alois Schumpeter," p. 84.

82. *CSD*, p. 6.

83. *CSD*, p. 16.

84. *CSD*, pp. 46–7.

85. *CSD*, p. 55.

86. *CSD*, p. 67.

87. *CSD*, p. 117.

88. *CSD*, p. 116.

89. *CSD*, pp. 117–8.

90. *CSD*, pp. 124–5.

91. *CSD*, pp. 73–4.

92. *CSD*, pp. 123–4.

93. *CSD*, p. 127.

94. *CSD*, p. 127.

95. *CSD*, pp. 126–7.

96. *CSD*, p. 129.

97. *CSD*, p. 172.

98. *CSD*, pp. 201, 198.

99. *CSD*, p. 375.

100. *CSD*, p. 127. By "rationalism," Schumpeter means much the same as what Michael Oakeshott was to call "rationalism in politics" and Friedrich Hayek "constructivism."

101. An argument that Schumpeter had put forth in his article "Unternehmer," *Handwörterbuch der Staatswissenschaften*, 4th ed. (Jena, 1928), vol. 8, pp. 476–87.

102. *CSD*, pp. 157–62, For Schumpeter's views on demographic trends, see also his lecture "The Falling Birth Rate," part of his 1941 Lowell Lectures, in Schumpeter, *The Economics and Sociology of Capitalism*, ed. Swedberg, pp. 372–80.

103. *CSD*, pp. 127–9.

104. *CSD*, pp. 153–5.

105. *CSD*, pp. 154, 311 n4.

106. *CSD*, p. 145.

107. *CSD*, p. 147.
108. *CSD*, pp. 154-5.
109. *CSD*, pp. 147, 151.
110. *CSD*, p. 153.
111. *CSD*, p. 144.
112. *CSD*, pp. 150-1.
113. *CSD*, p. 156.

CHAPTER TWELVE
FROM KEYNES TO MARCUSE

1. Robert Skidelsky, *John Maynard Keynes*, volume 2, *The Economist as Saviour, 1920-1937* (London, 1992), p. 237.
2. Keynes, *The Economic Consequences of the Peace* (New York, 1920), quoted in Skidelsky, *John Maynard Keynes*, volume 2, p. 234.
3. John Maynard Keynes, *The General Theory of Employment, Interest, and Money* (1936), in *The Collected Writings of John Maynard Keynes* (London, 1973), p. 376.
4. Keynes, *General Theory*, p. 365-6.
5. Keynes, *General Theory*, p. 369.
6. Keynes, *General Theory*, p. 370.
7. On Keynes' views on Jews, see Skidelsky, *John Maynard Keynes*, volume 2, pp. 238-9.
8. Keynes, *General Theory*, pp. 371-2.
9. Skidelsky, *John Maynard Keynes*, vol. 2, p. 236.
10. Skidelsky, *John Maynard Keynes*, vol. 2, p. 368
11. Skidelsky, *John Maynard Keynes*, vol. 2, p. 374.
12. Skidelsky, *John Maynard Keynes*, vol. 2, p. 237.
13. Skidelsky, *John Maynard Keynes*, vol. 2, p. 238
14. Georg Simmel, *The Philosophy of Money*, 2nd ed., ed. David Frisby (New York, 1990), pp. 212-13.
15. Keynes, *General Theory*, p. 373. See also Robert Skidelsky, "Keynes," in D. D. Raphael, Donald Winch, and Robert Skidelsky, *Three Great Economists* (Oxford, 1997), p. 315.
16. Keynes, *General Theory*, p. 379.
17. Keynes, *General Theory*, p. 380.
18. John Maynard Keynes, "Economic Possibilities for Our Grandchildren" (1930), in his *Essays in Persuasion* (New York, 1932), p. 373.
19. Eric Hobsbawm, *The Age of Extremes: A History of the World, 1914-1991* (New York, 1994), pp. 257 ff, provides a concise overview of the economy and society of the west during this period.
20. Mark Mazower, *Dark Continent: Europe's Twentieth Century* (New York, 1999), p. 305.
21. Mazower, *Dark Continent*, p. 304.
22. Mazower, *Dark Continent*, p. 307.
23. Robert Evenson, *The Green Revolution* (forthcoming).
24. Hobsbawm, *Age of Extremes*, p. 275.
25. Mazower credits postwar planning for a good deal of growth; Hobsbawm, *Age of Extremes*, pp. 272-3, is rightly skeptical. On planning in postwar France, see Richard F. Kuisel, *Capitalism and the State in Modern France* (Cambridge, 1981), chapters 8 and 9; and Peter Hall, *Governing the Economy: The Politics of State Intervention in Britain and France* (Oxford, 1986), chapters 6 and 7. On the relationship between politics and economics in the 1950s and 1960s see also A. J. Nicholls, *The Bonn Republic: West German Democracy, 1945-1990* (London, 1997), chapter 5.

26. Otto Kirchheimer, "The Waning Opposition in Parliamentary Regimes," *Social Research*, vol. 24 (Summer, 1957), pp. 127–56.
27. The term was introduced in Edward Shils, "The End of Ideology?" *Encounter*, vol. 5 (November 1955), pp. 52–8, and obtained wider currency with the publication of Daniel Bell's collection of essays, *The End of Ideology: On the Exhaustion of Political Ideas in the Fifties* (New York, 1960; rev. ed. 1962).
28. Joseph Schumpeter, *Capitalism, Socialism, and Democracy,* 1st ed. (New York, 1942), p. 144.
29. Information about Marcuse's biography and intellectual development is drawn from Barry Katz, *Herbert Marcuse and the Art of Liberation: An Intellectual Biography* (London, 1982), and from Douglas Kellner, *Herbert Marcuse and the Crisis of Marxism* (Berkeley, Calif., 1984). A critical biography, making use of material in the Marcuse archives and in the recently published correspondence of Max Horkheimer, remains a desideratum of intellectual history. On Marcuse's relationship to the Frankfurt Institute for Social Research, Martin Jay, *The Dialectical Imagination: A History of the Frankfurt School and the Institute of Historical Research, 1923–1950* (Boston, 1973), remains an illuminating introduction; Rolf Wiggershaus, *The Frankfurt School: Its History, Theories, and Political Significance* (Cambridge, Mass., 1994; German original, *Die Frankfurter Schule* [Munich, 1986]), brings the story forward in time and adds additional detail; Clemens, Albrecht, et al., *Die intellektuelle Gründung der Bundesrepublik: Eine Wirkungsgeschicthe der Frankfurter Schule* (Frankfurt, 1999), draws on additional material and provides a more critical perspective.
30. Katz, *Herbert Marcuse*, pp. 46 ff.
31. Jürgen Habermas, "Gespräch mit Herbert Marcuse" (1977), in Jürgen Habermas, *Philosophisch-politische Profile* (Frankfurt, 1981), p. 268.
32. See chapter 6 of this volume.
33. Herbert Marcuse, "Zur Auseinandersetzung mit Hans Freyers 'Soziologie als Wirklichkeitswissenschaft,'" *Philosophische Hefte*, vol. 3 (1931), pp. 83–91.
34. "Neue Quellen zur Grundlegung des historischen Materialismus," *Die Gesellschaft* (Berlin, 1932), vol. 9, part 2, pp. 136–74, translated as "The Foundations of Historical Materialism," in Herbert Marcuse, *Studies in Critical Philosophy* (Boston, 1973).
35. Wiggershaus, *The Frankfurt School*, pp. 12–3.
36. On this episode see Lionel Robbins, *Autobiography of an Economist* (London 1971), p. 139, and Stephen Kresge and Leif Wenar (eds.), *Hayek on Hayek: An Autobiographical Dialogue* (Chicago, 1994), p. 85; as well as Wiggershaus, *The Frankfurt School*, p. 110.
37. Wiggershaus, *The Frankfurt School*, pp. 145–6.
38. Wiggershaus, *The Frankfurt School*, pp. 249–50, 261–5, 298 ff. On Marcuse's service in the Office of War Information and then in the OSS see Douglas Kellner, "Introduction," in Herbert Marcuse, *Technology, War, and Fascism: Collected Papers of Herbert Marcuse, Vol. 1* (London, 1998), pp. 15 ff, and Barry Katz, *Foreign Intelligence: Research and Analysis in the Office of Strategic Services 1942–1945* (Cambridge, Mass., 1989).
39. For one of Marcuse's earliest statements of this thesis, see his "Der Kampf gegen den Liberalismus in der totalitären Staatsauffassung," *Zeitschrift für Sozialforschung,* vol. 3, no. 1 (1934), pp. 161–95; translated as "The Struggle Against Liberalism in the Totalitarian View of the State," in Herbert Marcuse, *Negations: Essays in Critical Theory* (Boston, 1968), pp. 3–42.
40. See on this Jay, *Dialectical Imagination,* chapters 3 and 4, and Wiggershaus, *The Frankfurt School,* chapter 3.
41. Herbert Marcuse, "State and Individual under National Socialism" (1942), first published in Marcuse, *Technology, War, and Fascism*, pp. 67–92, at p. 84.
42. Marcuse, "State and Individual," pp. 85–6.

43. Marcuse, "State and Individual," p. 92.

44. H. Stuart Hughes, *The Sea Change: The Migration of Social Thought, 1930–1965* (New York, 1975), p. 175.

45. Marcuse letter to Horkheimer, April 6, 1946, published in translation in Marcuse, *Technology, War, and Fascism*, pp. 250–1.

46. Herbert Marcuse, "33 Theses" (1947), published in translation in *Technology, War, and Fascism*, pp. 215–27.

47. Marcuse, "33 Theses," pp. 226–7.

48. Marcuse, "33 Theses," p. 221.

49. Philip Rieff, *Freud: The Mind of the Moralist* (Chicago, 1959; 3rd ed., 1979, with a new epilogue), p. 220.

50. Erich Fromm, *The Sane Society* (New York, 1955).

51. Lionel Trilling, "Freud and Literature," in Trilling, *The Liberal Imagination* (New York, 1950), and *Freud and the Crisis of Our Culture* (Boston, 1955).

52. Rieff, *Freud*, pp. 34–5.

53. Herbert Marcuse, *Eros and Civilization: A Philosophical Inquiry into Freud* (Boston, 1955) (hereafter cited as *EC*), p. 8

54. *EC*, pp. 12–3.

55. *EC*, pp. 35–45.

56. *EC*, p. 36.

57. *EC*, pp. 92–3.

58. *EC*, pp. 129–31, 201.

59. *EC*, pp. 201–2.

60. *EC*, p. 152.

61. *EC*, pp.171, 195.

62. Friedrich Schiller, *On the Aesthetic Education of Mankind in a Series of Letters* edited and translated by Elizabeth M. Wilkinson and L. A. Willoughby (Oxford, 1967), pp. 32–5. Quoted by Marcuse in a slightly different translation in *EC*, p. 186.

63. *EC*, pp. 208–11.

64. *EC*, p. 48.

65. *EC*, pp. 223–4.

66. *EC*, p. 104.

67. *EC*, p. 100.

68. *EC*, p. 102.

69. Herbert Marcuse, *One-Dimensional Man: Studies in the Ideology of Advanced Industrial Society* (Boston, 1964, hereafter cited as *ODM*), p. 12.

70. *ODM*, p. xiv.

71. *ODM*, pp. 11–12.

72. *ODM*, pp. 7, 42.

73. *ODM*, pp. x–xi.

74. *ODM*, pp. 232–4.

75. *ODM*, pp. 4–5.

76. *ODM*, pp. 7–8. For Marcuse's interpretation of Hegel, see his *Reason and Revolution: Hegel and the Rise of Social Theory* (New York, 1941).

77. See the analysis in Michael Walzer, "Herbert Marcuse's America," in his *The Company of Critics* (New York, 1988), pp. 170–90.

78. *ODM*, pp. 73–6. For a similar analysis, see Allan Bloom, *The Closing of the American Mind* (New York, 1987), pp. 132–7.

79. *ODM*, pp. xiv, 23.

80. *ODM*, p. 242.

81. *ODM*, p. 49.

82. Marcuse, "33 Theses," p. 221.

83. *ODM*, p. 145. For Marcuse's view of the Soviet Union, see his *Soviet Marxism: A Critical Analysis* (New York, 1958).

84. *ODM*, pp. 24–7.

85. *ODM*, pp. 28–31.

86. *ODM*, pp. 32–8.

87. Herbert Marcuse, "The Affirmative Character of Culture" (1937), in Marcuse, *Negations*, pp. 98–9.

88. *ODM*, p. 59.

89. *ODM*, pp. 59–64.

90. *ODM*, p. 61.

91. *ODM*, pp. 144–69.

92. *ODM*, p. 2.

93. *ODM*, p. 39.

94. *ODM*, pp. 151–7.

95. *ODM*, pp. 242–3.

96. *ODM*, p. 257.

97. *ODM*, p. 222.

98. *ODM*, p. 256.

99. Jürgen Habermas (ed.), *Antworten auf Herbert Marcuse* (Frankfurt, 1968); Paul Breines (ed.), *Critical Interruptions: New Left Perspectives on Herbert Marcuse* (New York, 1970).

100. Herbert Marcuse, *An Essay on Liberation* (Boston, 1969), pp. 51, 21, 33.

101. Marcuse, *Essay on Liberation*, pp. 57, 61.

102. Albrecht, et al., *Die intellektuelle Gründung*, p. 346.

103. See the letter of Adorno to Marcuse of May 5, 1969, quoting Horkheimer, in Marcuse/Adorno, "Correspondence on the German Student Movement," edited and introduced by Esther Leslie, *New Left Review*, no. 233 (January–February 1999), p. 127.

104. *Horkheimer Gesammelte Schriften*, vol. 14, p. 444, quoted in Albrecht, et al., *Die intellektuelle Gründung*, p. 323.

105. David Bromwich, "Scholarship as Social Action," in Alvin Kernan (ed.), *What's Happened to the Humanities?* (Princeton, N.J., 1997), pp. 220–44;. See also Peter Novick, *That Noble Dream: The "Objectivity Question" and the American Historical Profession* (Cambridge, 1988), pp. 427 ff.

106. Bromwich, "Scholarship as Social Action," pp. 220–44.

107. Walter Goodman, "Sociologists to the Barricades," *New York Times*, August 19, 2000, p. 17; and the title essay of Irving Louis Horowitz, *The Decomposition of Sociology* (New York, 1994). For the application of *One-Dimensional Man's* model of ideological criticism to literary theory, see the influential work of Terry Eagleton, sometime professor of literature at Oxford, *Literary Theory* (London and Minneapolis, 1983), esp. pp. 195–6; as well as Edward W. Said, *Representations of the Intellectual* (New York, 1994).

108. Mary Britton King, "Make Love, Not Work: New Management Theory and the Social Self," *Radical History Review*, no. 76 (Winter 2000), pp. 15–24, at p. 18.

109. See the insightful exploration in "comic sociology" by David Brooks, *Bobos in Paradise: The New Upper Class and How They Got There* (New York, 2000), pp. 48–51, 103–17, and passim.

110. Joseph Schumpeter, *The Theory of Economic Development* (New Brunswick, N.J., 1983), pp. 92–3. This translation of the second German edition (1926) of Schumpeter's book first appeared in 1934.

111. Alasdair MacIntyre, *Herbert Marcuse: An Exposition and a Polemic* (New York, 1970), p. 40.

112. *ODM*, p. 251.

113. See Marcuse's 1977 interview with Jürgen Habermas and Heinz Lubasz, in Jürgen Habermas, "Gespräch mit Herbert Marcuse" (1977), in Habermas, *Philosophisch-politische Profile*, pp. 287, 290, 295.

CHAPTER THIRTEEN
FRIEDRICH HAYEK

1. Hayek's major works are abbreviated as follows:
   Road = *The Road to Serfdom* (Chicago, 1944; reprinted with a new preface 1976).
   CL = *The Constitution of Liberty* (Chicago, 1960).
   LLL, 1 = *Law, Legislation, and Liberty*, volume 1, *Rules and Order* (Chicago, 1973).
   LLL, 2 = *Law, Legislation, and Liberty*, volume 2, *The Mirage of Social Justice* (Chicago, 1976).
   LLL, 3 = *Law, Legislation, and Liberty*, volume 3, *The Political Order of a Free People* (Chicago, 1979).
   Hayek on Hayek = *Hayek on Hayek: An Autobiographical Dialogue*, ed. Stephen Kresge and Leif Wenar (Chicago, 1994).
2. *CL*, p. vi.
3. In this respect he shared a good deal with the "imagined cosmopolitan community" of his friend, Karl Popper. The phrase comes from Malachi H. Hacohen, *Karl Popper: The Formative Years, 1902–1945* (Cambridge, 2000), p. 308.
4. *Hayek on Hayek*, p. 48.
5. *Hayek on Hayek*, p. 68.
6. See Wieser's 1901 rectoral address at the University of Prague, "Ueber die gesellschaftlichen Gewalten" (1901), reprinted in Friedrich von Wieser, *Gesammelte Abhandlungen* (Tübingen, 1929), ed. Friedrich A. von Hayek, p. 375; and Friedrich Freiherr von Wieser, *Das Gesetz der Macht* (Vienna, 1926), pp. 486–97 (there is an English translation by W. E. Kuhn, edited by Warren J. Samuels: *The Law of Power* [Lincoln, Neb., 1983]); and Erich Streissler, "The Austrian School of Economics," p. 35, and Streissler, "Arma Virumque Cano: Friedrich von Wieser, the Bard as Economist" (1985), reprinted in Stephen Littlechild (ed.), *Austrian Economics*, 3 vols. (Aldershot, 1990), vol. 1, pp. 72–95, at p. 75.
7. Erich Streissler, "Arma Virumque Cano," vol. 1, pp. 72–95, at p. 85.
8. I have borrowed this formulation from Steven Beller, *Vienna and the Jews: A Cultural History* (Cambridge, 1989), p. 187. My discussion of the role of the Jews in Viennese culture and politics owes a great deal to Beller's insightful book.
9. Their secularism was reflected in the consternation they felt when young Friedrich was pressured to attend mass at his *Gymnasium*: *Hayek on Hayek*, pp.40–1.
10. Hacohen, *Karl Popper*, p. 39.
11. See Barbara Jelavich, *Modern Austria: Empire and Republic, 1800–1986*, (Cambridge, 1987), pp. 144–5; Paul Silverman, "Law and Economics in Interwar Vienna: Kelsen, Mises, and the Regeneration of Austrian Liberalism" (Ph.D. diss., University of Chicago, 1984), introduction and chapter 1; and Malachi Hacohen, "Karl Popper, Jewish Identity, and 'Central European Culture,' " *Journal of Modern History*, vol. 71, no. 1 (March 1999), pp. 105–49. For an evocation of this milieu see the autobiographical reflections of Friedrich Hayek in *Hayek on Hayek*, pp. 37 ff.
12. Beller, *Vienna and the Jews*, p. 183.
13. Beller, *Vienna and the Jews*, p. 34.
14. See Marsha Rosenblitt, *The Jews of Vienna, 1867–1914* (Albany, N.Y., 1983), chapters 2 and 3; and Beller, *Vienna and the Jews*, passim.
15. Derek J. Penslar, *Shylock's Children: Economics and Jewish Identity in Modern Europe* (Berkeley, 2001), chapter 4.
16. Ernest Gellner, *Language and Solitude: Wittgenstein, Malinowski, and the Habsburg Dilemma* (Cambridge, 1998), pp. 12, 85, 11.
17. Gellner, *Language and Solitude*, p. 35.

18. For an overview see Fritz Weber, "Hauptprobleme der wirtschaftlichen und sozialen Entwicklung Österreichs in der Zwischenkriegzeit," in Franz Kadrnoska (ed.), *Aufbruch und Untergang: Österreichsche Kultur zwischen 1918 und 1938* (Vienna, 1981), pp. 593–621.

19. Frederick Hertz, *The Economic Problems of the Danubian States: A Study of Economic Nationalism* (1947; rep. New York, 1970).

20. *Hayek on Hayek*, p. 53. Hayek also belonged to a liberal democratic student association, the Demokratische Hochschüler Vereinigung. Hans Jörg Hennecke, *Friedrich August von Hayek: Die Tradition der Freiheit* (Düsseldorf, 2000), p. 42.

21. Hacohen, *Karl Popper*, p. 294.

22. Hacohen, *Karl Popper*, pp. 296–7.

23. Adam Wandruszka, "Deutschliberale and deutschnationale Strömungen," in Norbert Leser (ed.), *Das geistige Leben Wiens* (Vienna, 1981), pp. 28–33.

24. On the Christian Socials and their electoral constituencies see John Boyer, *Political Radicalism in Late Imperial Vienna: Origins of the Christian Social Movement, 1848–1897* (Chicago, 1981), and John Boyer, *Culture and Political Crisis in Vienna: Christian Socialism in Power, 1897–1918* (Chicago, 1995).

25. Quoted in Alfred Diament, *Austrian Catholics and the Social Question, 1918–1933* (Gainesville, Fla., 1959), p. 23.

26. Boyer, *Political Radicalism in Late Imperial Vienna*. On Christian Social antisemitism see also Beller, pp. 193–201.

27. Quoted in Anton Staudinger, "Christlichsoziale Judenpolitik in der Gründungsphase der österreichischen Republik," *Jahrbuch für Zeitgeschichte 1978* (Vienna, 1979), pp. 11–48, at p. 17. On antisemitism of the Christian Socials after 1918, see Peter Pulzer, *The Rise of Political Anti-Semitism in Germany and Austria*, rev. ed. (Cambridge, Mass., 1988), pp. 309–12.

28. *Arbeiterwille*, July 14, 1920, p. 1, "Die Christlichsozialen und die Bauernbündler für die jüdischen Börsianer," quoted in Dieter A. Binder, "Der 'reiche Jude': Zur sozialdemokratischen Kapitalismuskritik und zu deren antisemitischen Feindbildern in der Ersten Republik," *Geschichte und Gegenwart*, no. 1 (1985), pp. 43–53, at p. 51.

29. Binder, "Der 'reiche Jude,'" passim, and Helmut Gruber, *Red Vienna: Experiment in Working-Class Culture, 1919–1934* (New York, 1991), pp. 26–7, and the works cited in p. 195, n74.

30. See Andrew C. Janos, *The Politics of Backwardness in Hungary, 1825–1945* (Princeton, N.J., 1982).

31. Wieser, *Das Gesetz der Macht*. Schumpeter, *History of Economic Analysis*, p. 848.

32. Wieser, *Das Gesetz der Macht*, pp. 368–9.

33. Wieser, *Das Gesetz der Macht*, pp. 373–4.

34. Beller, *Vienna and the Jews*, p. 12.

35. See Erika Weinzierl, "Hochschulleben und Hochschulpolitik zwischen den Kriegen," in Norbert Leser (ed.) *Das geistige Leben Wiens* (Vienna, 1981), pp. 72–85, and her "Historical Commentary on the Period," *The Collected Works of Eric Voegelin*, vol. 4, *The Authoritarian State* (Columbia, Mo. 1999), pp. 11–2; and Brigitte L. Fenz, *"Deutscher Abstammung und Muttersprache": Österreichische Hochschulpolitik in der Ersten Republik* (Vienna, 1990).

36. Earlene Craver, "The Emigration of the Austrian Economists," *History of Political Economy*, vol. 18, no. 1 (1986), pp. 1–32, at p. 7.

37. *Hayek on Hayek*, p. 54.

38. *Hayek on Hayek*,, p. 59.

39. *Hayek on Hayek*, pp. 57–59.

40. Hennecke, *Friedrich August von Hayek*, p. 33.

41. Hennecke, *Friedrich August von Hayek*, p. 203.

42. Craver, "Emigration," p. 5. For later examples of Mises' fanaticism, see Hennecke, *Friedrich August von Hayek*, p. 223.

43. Craver, "Emigration," p. 19.

44. Beller, *Vienna and the Jews*, p. 20.

45. T. W. MacCallum, *The Vienna That's Not in the Baedeker* (Munich, 1929), translated from the original German book written by Ludwig Hirschfeld, *Was nicht im Baedeker steht: Wien und Budapest* (Munich, 1927), pp. 54–5.

46. *Hayek on Hayek*, pp. 61–2. The name Hajek was indeed often a Jewish name, formed from the Hebrew "Hayim," combined with the German ending expressing affection. Dietz Bering, *The Stigma of Names: Antisemitism in German Daily Life, 1812–1933* (Ann Arbor, Mich., 1992), p. 284.

47. *Road*, pp. 140, 139.

48. *CL*, p. 81.

49. *CL*, p. 80.

50. John Stuart Mill, *On Liberty*, ed. Gertrude Himmelfarb (New York, 1974), pp. 129, 131.

51. See the essays "Ueber die gesellschaftlichen Gewalten" (1901) and "Arma virumque cano" (1907), in which Nietzsche is treated (together with Tolstoy) as "a central figure of our age"; both are reprinted in Friedrich von Wieser, *Gesammelte Abhandlungen* (Tübingen, 1929), ed. Friedrich A. von Hayek. See also Wieser, *Theorie der gesellschaftlichen Wirtschaft* (Tübingen, 1914), and Wieser, *Das Gesetz der Macht*.

52. Ludwig von Mises, *Die Gemeinwirtschaft: Untersuchungen über den Sozialismus* (Jena, 1922), p. 202; translated by J. Kahane as *Socialism: An Economic and Sociological Analysis* (Indianapolis, Ind., 1981), p. 188. The original wording reads "stets nur Sache der wenigen, der Führer.." For the book's impact on Hayek, see his "Foreword" to the English-language edition of 1981.

53. *Road*, p. 6.

54. *Road*, pp. 4–5, 116–7, 209.

55. *Road*, p. 118.

56. In a 1963 lecture, "The Economics of the 1920s as Seen from Vienna," published in Peter G. Klein (ed.) *The Fortunes of Liberalism: The Collected Works of F. A. Hayek*, vol. 4 (Chicago, 1992), pp. 19–39, at pp. 27–9, Hayek noted that Wieser and his generation of Austrian economists were far from the classical liberalism embraced by Mises.

57. *CL*, p. 343.

58. Charles A. Gulick, *Austria from Habsburg to Hitler*, vol. 1, *Labor's Workshop of Democracy*, 2 vols., (Berkeley, 1948), pp. 439–45, offers a thorough account, which interprets the Social Democrats' policies in the most favorable light possible.

59. Gulick, *Austria from Habsburg to Hitler*, vol. 1, p. 448n.

60. Gulick, *Austria from Habsburg to Hitler*, vol. 1, pp. 492–3.

61. In Hayek, *Das Mieterschutzproblem. Nationalökonomische Betrachtungen. Vortrag gehalten in der Nationalökonomischen Gesellschaft in Wien am 18 Dezember, 1928, Bibliothek für Volkswirtschaft und Politik*, no. 2 (Vienna, 1929). The piece was republished with minor changes as Friedrich von Hayek, "Wirkungen der Mietzinsbeschränkungen," *Schriften des Vereins für Sozialpolitik*, vol. 182 (1931), pp. 253–70. An English translation of the 1929 version was published as "Austria: The Repercussions of Rent Restrictions," in Hayek et al., *Verdict on Rent Control* (London, 1972).

62. Lionel Robbins, *The Autobiography of an Economist* (London, 1971).

63. Arthur Marwick, "Middle Opinion in the Thirties: Planning, Progress and Political 'Agreement,'" *English Historical Review* (April 1964), pp. 285–98.

64. *Hayek on Hayek*, p. 66.

65. F. A. von Hayek, *Collectivist Economic Planning: Critical Studies on the Possibilities of Socialism* (London, 1935). See also his criticism of planning in his inaugural

address, "The Trend of Economic Thinking" (1933), reprinted in *The Collected Works of F. A. Hayek*, vol. 3 (Chicago, 1991), pp. 17–34, at pp. 32–4.

66. V. I. Lenin, *State and Revolution* (1917), in Lenin, *Collected Works* (Moscow, 1960), vol. 25, pp. 478–9, quoted in David Ramsay Steele, *From Marx to Mises: Post-Capitalist Society and the Challenge of Economic Calculation* (La Salle, Ill., 1992), pp. 68–9.

67. See Steele, *From Marx to Mises*, pp. 69 ff; Martin Malia, *The Soviet Tragedy: A History of Socialism in Russia, 1917–1991* (New York, 1994), chapter 4.

68. Steele, *From Marx to Mises*, pp. 124 ff.

69. On the historical precursors of Mises' critique of socialism , see Richard M. Ebeling, "Economic Calculation Under Socialism: Ludwig von Mises and His Predecessors," pp. 56–101, in Jeffrey M. Herbener, *The Meaning of Ludwig von Mises* (Norwell, Mass., 1993). On some Austrian socialist contributions to the debate over economic calculation under socialism in the 1920s, see Günther K. Chaloupek, "The Austrian Debate on Economic Calculation in a Socialist Economy," *History of Political Economy*, vol. 22, no. 4 (1990), pp. 671–5. On the debate and its significance, see Karen I. Vaughn, "Economic Calculation under Socialism: The Austrian Contribution," *Economic Inquiry*, vol. 18 (October 1980), pp. 535–54, reprinted in *Austrian Economics*, vol. 3, pp. 332–51; Bruce Caldwell, "Hayek and Socialism," *Journal of Economic Literature*, vol. 35 (December 1997), pp. 1856–90. The most useful discussion of the place of the debate over socialism in the development of Hayek's political thought is Jeremy Shearmur, *Hayek and After: Hayekian Liberalism as a Research Programme* (London, 1996), chapter 2.

70. Ludwig von Mises, "Economic Calculation in the Socialist Commonwealth" (1920), in Hayek (ed.), *Collectivist Economic Planning*, p. 126.

71. Mises, "Economic Calculation," p. 96, 116.

72. Erich Streissler, "The Intellectual and Political Impact of the Austrian School of Economics," *History of European Ideas*, vol. 9, no. 2 (1988), pp. 191–204, reprinted in *Austrian Economics*, vol. 1, pp. 24–37, at p. 28. Page references refer to the reprint edition.

73. Mises, "Economic Calculation," pp. 97–111.

74. Mises, "Economic Calculation," pp. 121–2.

75. Hayek, "The Present State of the Debate," in *Collectivist Economic Planning*, pp. 203–6.

76. Hayek, "The Nature and History of the Problem," in *Collectivist Economic Planning*, pp. 7–8.

77. Hayek, "Economics and Knowledge," first published in 1937 and reprinted in Hayek, *Individualism and Economic Order* (Chicago, 1948), p. 50.

78. "Economics and Knowledge," and "The Uses of Knowledge in Society," first published in 1945 in the *American Economic Review*, vol. 35, no. 4, pp. 519–30 and reprinted in Chiaki Nishiyama and Kurt R. Leube (eds.), *The Essence of Hayek* (Stanford, Calif., 1984).

79. Hayek, "The Uses of Knowledge."

80. "The Meaning of Competition" (1946), in Hayek, *Individualism and Economic Order* (Chicago, 1948), p. 97.

81. Hayek, "Competition as a Discovery Procedure," in *New Studies in Philosophy, Politics, and the History of Ideas* (Chicago, 1978), p. 180; also reprinted in *The Essence of Hayek*. See also the earlier "The Meaning of Competition" (1946), in Hayek, *Individualism and Economic Order* (Chicago, 1948).

82. Hayek, "The Meaning of Competition," (1946), in Hayek, *Individualism and Economic Order* (Chicago, 1948), and "Competition as a Discovery Procedure," in *New Studies in Philosophy, Politics, and the History of Ideas* (Chicago, 1978), also reprinted in *The Essence of Hayek*.

83. *LLL*, 3, p. 75.

84. Hayek, "Competition as a Discovery Procedure," p. 189.
85. *LLL*, 3, pp. 76–7.
86. As Yvon Quinious has noted, in this respect Hayek's work can be seen as the "veritable theorization of indifference toward human happiness." Yvon Quinious, "Hayek, les Limites d'un Défi," *Actuel Marx*, no. 1 (1989), p. 83, quoted in Alain de Benoist, "Hayek: A Critique," *Telos*, no. 110 (Winter 1998), pp. 71–104, at p. 85. This is a thoughtful if not always fair article.
87. *CL*, p. 35.
88. *LLL*, 1, pp. 56–7.
89. *Road*, p. 92; repeated with slight variation in *LLL*, I, pp. 186–7.
90. Friedrich Hayek, "Freedom and the Economic System," *Contemporary Review*, April 1938, pp. 434–42, reprinted in Bruce Caldwell (ed.), *Socialism and War: The Collected Works of F. A. Hayek*, vol. 10 (Chicago, 1997), to which page numbers refer; p. 183. Similarly, *Road*, p. 58.
91. *Road*, p. 77.
92. Hayek, "Freedom and the Economic System," pp. 184–5. Repeated with slightly different phrasing in *Road*, p. 69.
93. Hennecke, *Friedrich August von Hayek*, p. 230.
94. For a claim that it was the latter motive that kept Hayek out of the economics department at Chicago, see Alan Ebenstein, *Friedrich Hayek: A Biography* (New York, 2001), p. 174.
95. John U. Nef, *Search for Meaning: The Autobiography of a Nonconformist* (Washington, D.C., 1973), pp. 237–8; John Raybould, *Hayek: A Commemorative Album* (London, 1998), p. 67; *Hayek on Hayek*, pp. 125–8, 143.
96. Hennecke, *Friedrich August von Hayek*, p. 329.
97. *CL*, p. 11.
98. *CL*, pp. 141–2.
99. *Road*, pp. 36–39; *LLL*, I, pp. 108–9.
100. *CL*, p. 156.
101. *CL*, pp. 257–8. Similarly, *Road*, pp. 120–1; *LLL*, 3, pp. 41, 44, 61–2.
102. *CL*, pp. 220 ff.
103. *CL*, pp. 257–8.
104. *CL*, pp. 257–9.
105. *CL*, pp. 253–6. Among the significant milestones in this process were the German Social Democratic Party's Bad Godesberg platform of 1958 and C. A. R. Crossland's *The Future of Socialism* (London, 1956).
106. *CL*, p. 256.
107. *LLL*, 2, p. 66.
108. *LLL*, p. 3. The term "Great Society," in the sense in which Hayek uses it, seems to be taken from Adam Smith, *The Wealth of Nations*, I, viii, 57. Hayek's use of the term "tribal society" is adopted from his friend Karl Popper's *The Open Society and Its Enemies*, 2 vols. (Princeton, 1966; first published in 1945), vol. 1, pp. 173 ff.
109. *LLL*, 2, pp. 111, 133–4.
110. *LLL*, 2, p. 76.
111. *CL*, pp. 94–5; *LLL*, 2, p. 70.
112. *LLL*, 2, p. 88–90.
113. *LLL*, 2, pp. 148–9.
114. *LLL*, 2, pp. 88–9.
115. *CL*, pp. 89–92; *LLL*, 2, pp. 84–5.
116. *CL*, p. 282.
117. *CL*, p. 266; *LLL*, 2, p. 67.
118. *CL*, p. 266; *LLL*, 3, p. 90.
119. *CL*, p. 270; *LLL*, 3, p. 144.

120. *CL*, p. 283.
121. *CL*, pp. 270, 280–2; see also *LLL*, 3, p. 94.
122. *CL*, pp. 331–2.
123. *CL*, pp. 50–1.
124. *CL*, pp. 106, 115.
125. *LLL*, 3, pp. 4–5.
126. *LLL*, 3, pp. 106ff.
127. Hayek, *The Denationalization of Money* (London, 1976). Hayek's pamphlet on the denationalization of money was written "while I was working on my main book," i.e., at the same time as *LLL: Hayek on Hayek*, p. 150.
128. Hayek, "The Intellectuals and Socialism" (1949), reprinted in Bruce Caldwell (ed.), *The Collected Works of F. A. Hayek*, vol. 10, *Socialism and War* (Chicago, 1997), pp. 229–37, 222, 224, 225.
129. *CL*, p. 112.
130. *CL*, p. 114.
131. *CL*, p. 115.
132. Hayek, "The Intellectuals and Socialism," pp. 229–37; Hayek, *CL*, pp. 112 ff.
133. *Hayek on Hayek*, p. 155. Mises had held a similar view, see Mises, *Socialism*, pp. 460–1.
134. See for example the critical reviews of *The Constitution of Liberty* written by Lionel Robbins, "Hayek on Liberty," *Economica* (February 1961), pp. 66–81; by Jacob Viner, "Hayek on Freedom and Coercion," *Southern Economic Journal*, vol. 27 (January 1961), pp. 230–6; by F. H. Knight, "Laissez Faire: Pro and Con," *Journal of Political Economy*, vol. 75 (October 1967), pp. 782–95 (all reprinted in J. C. Wood and Ronald N. Woods (eds.), *Friedrich A. Hayek: Critical Assessments*, vol. 2 [London, 1991]); and Raymond Aron, "La Définition libérale de la Liberté" (1961), in his *Études politiques* (Paris, 1972), reprinted in Pierre Manent (ed.) *Les Libéraux*, 2 vols., vol. 2 (Paris, 1986), pp. 467–88.
135. Quoted in Neil McInnes, "The Road Not Taken: Hayek's Slippery Slope to Serfdom," *The National Interest* (Spring 1998), pp. 56–66, at p. 59.
136. R. M. Hartwell, *A History of the Mont Pélerin Society* (Indianapolis, Ind., 1995); *Hayek on Hayek*, p. 133.
137. Daniel Yergin and Joseph Stanislaw, *The Commanding Heights: The Battle Between Government and the Marketplace That Is Remaking the Modern World* (New York, 1998), pp. 98–101; see also R. Cockett, *Thinking the Unthinkable: Think-Tanks and the Economic Counter-Revolution, 1931–1983* (London, 1994), and Dennis Kavanagh, *Thatcherism and British Politics: The End of Consensus?* (New York, 1987).
138. Yergin and Stanislaw, *Commanding Heights*, p. 106.
139. Samuel Brittan, *The Economic Consequences of Democracy* (London, 1977), pp. 142–6, and A. Glynn and R. Sutcliffe, *British Capitalism* (London, 1973).
140. Eric Hobsbawm, *The Age of Extremes: A History of the World, 1914–1991* (New York, 1995), pp. 282–5.
141. Mark Mazower, *Dark Continent: Europe's Twentieth Century* (New York, 1999), p. 329.
142. Yergin and Stanislaw, *Commanding Heights*, p. 62.
143. Yergin and Stanislaw, *Commanding Heights*, p. 96.
144. Robert Skidelsky, *The Road from Serfdom: The Economic and Political Consequences of the End of Communism* (New York, 1995), p. 93.
145. Skidelsky, *Road from Serfdom*, p. 93.
146. Yergin and Stanislaw, *Commanding Heights*, p. 92; and Hartwell, *A History of the Mont Pélerin Society*, p. 199.
147. Yergin and Stanislaw, *Commanding Heights*, p. 104.
148. Yergin and Stanislaw, *Commanding Heights*, pp. 112–3.

149. See Rowland Evans and Robert Novak, *The Reagan Revolution* (New York, 1981), p. 229; and Martin Anderson, *Revolution* (New York, 1988), p. 164.
150. Martin Anderson, *The Power of Ideas in the Making of Economic Policy* (Palo Alto, Calif., 1987), quoted in Hartwell, *A History of the Mount Pélerin Society.*
151. For some suggestive comments on this phenomenon, see David Frum, *How We Got Here* (New York, 2000), pp. 328 ff.
152. On which see János Kornai, *The Socialist System: The Political Economy of Communism* (Princeton, N.J., 1992), pp. 127–30, who declares (p. 476) that "[l]ooking back after fifty years one can conclude that Hayek was right on every point in the debate."
153. See Charles S. Maier, *Dissolution: The Crisis of Communism and the End of East Germany* (Princeton, N.J., 1997), pp. 83–96; Skidelsky, *The Road from Serfdom*, pp. 104–8; on the failure of the socialist economies to innovate, see Hobsbawm, *The Age of Extremes*, chapter 13.
154. See Andrzej Walicki, "Liberalism in Poland," *Critical Review*, vol. 2, no. 2 (Winter, 1988), and Timothy Garton Ash, *Magic Lantern: The Revolution of '89* (New York, 1990).
155. Yergin and Stanislaw, *Commanding Heights*, pp. 270–1.
156. *ILL*, I, pp. 39–46.
157. *CL*, chapter 4.
158. See on this Hennecke, *Friedrich August von Hayek*, p. 386, and Emma Rothschild, *Economic Sentiments: Adam Smith, Condorcet, and the Enlightenment* (Cambridge, Mass., 2001), pp. 146–53.
159. On the conservative element of Hayek's thought, see Chadran Kukathas, *Hayek and Modern Liberalism* (Oxford, 1989), pp. 174 ff.
160. This point has been made by many of Hayek's critics, including Alain de Benoist, "Hayek: A Critique," p. 90; and Richard Epstein, "Hayekian Socialism," *Maryland Law Review*, vol. 58 (1999), pp. 271 ff.
161. *CL*, chapter 4; and *LLL*, 3, p. 155 ff. Hayek's utilitarianism has been characterized as "*indirect or system utilitarian*, inasmuch as the proper role of utility is not prescriptive or practical but rather that of a standard of evaluation for the assessment of whole systems of rules or practices." John Gray, *Hayek on Liberty*, 2nd. ed. (Oxford, 1986), p. 59.
162. Jeffrey Friedman, "Hayek's Political Philosophy and Economics," *Critical Review*, vol. 11, no. 1 (1997), pp. 1–10, at pp. 6–7.
163. See for example *CL*, pp. 61 ff; and Hayek, *The Fatal Conceit* (Chicago, 1988), pp. 135–40. I have not made much use of this volume because how much of it was actually written by Hayek and how much by his editor, W. W. Bartley III, remains an open question among scholars.
164. A point made by de Benoist, "Hayek: A Critique," p. 92. For similar criticisms by James Buchanan and Stefan Böhm, see Hennecke, *Friedrich August von Hayek*, p. 374.
165. Hennecke, *Friedrich August von Hayek*, pp. 346–7.
166. The last two criticisms stem from Aron, "La Définition libérale de la Liberté."
167. This point has been made by a number of commentators, including Andrew Gamble, *Hayek: The Iron Cage of Liberty* (Boulder, Colo., 1996), p. 106; Kukathas, *Hayek and Modern Liberalism* p. 189; and Ronald Kley, *Hayek's Social and Political Thought* (Oxford, 1994), pp. 169 ff.

CONCLUSION

1. For a recent restatement of this theme, see Amartya Sen, "Social Choice and Individual Behavior," in his *Development as Freedom* (New York, 1999), pp. 249–81.

2. Edmund Burke, "Reflections on the Revolution in France," in *The Writings and Speeches of Edmund Burke*, vol. 8 (Oxford, 1989), p. 102.

3. See Bernard Yack, "The Myth of the Civic Nation," *Critical Review*, vol. 10, no. 2 (spring 1996), pp. 193–211.

4. On the purported virtues of such solidarity, see Norman Birnbaum, *After Progress: European Socialism and American Social Reform in the Twentieth Century* (New York, 2001).

5. For a more recent reiteration of this theme, see Ralf Dahrendorf, *Life Chances* (Chicago, 1979).

6. See especially Jürgen Habermas, *Legitimation Crisis* (Boston, 1975; German original Frankfurt, 1973), parts 1 and 2; and Jürgen Habermas, *Theory of Communicative Action*, vol. 2; *Lifeworld and System: A Critique of Functionalist Reason* (Boston, 1987; German original 1981).

7. Jan de Vries, "The Industrial Revolution and the Industrious Revolution," *Journal of Economic History*, vol. 54, no. 2 (June 1994), pp. 249–70, at p. 265.

8. Pierre Bourdieu, "Neo-liberalism, the Utopia of Unlimited Exploitation," in his *Acts of Resistance: Against the Tyranny of the Market* (New York, 1998), pp. 94–105.

9. John Gray, "The Politics of Cultural Diversity," in Gray, *Post-Liberalism: Studies in Political Thought* (London, 1993), pp. 262–3.

10. Georg Simmel, "Conflict" in *Conflict and the Web of Group Affiliations*, trans. Kurt H. Wolff and Reinhard Bendix (New York, 1955), pp. 61–2.

11. Thomas L. Friedman, *The Lexus and the Olive Tree: Understanding Globalization*, expanded edition (New York, 2000), pp. 298 ff.

12. Jürgen Habermas, "Warum braucht Europa eine Verfassung? Nur als politsches Gemeinwesen kann der Kontinent seine in Gefahr geratene Kultur und Lebensform verteidigen," *Die Zeit*, June 28, 2001, p. 7.

13. For a thoughtful overview of contemporary arguments in favor of the market and the welfare state, see Wolfgang Streeck, "Wohlfahrstaat und Markt als moralische Einrichtungen: Ein Kommentar," in Karl Ulrich Mayer (ed.), *Die Beste aller Welten? Marktliberalismus versus Wohlfahrstaat* (Frankfurt, 2001), pp. 135–67.

14. A theory first presented by Simon Kuznets in "Economic Growth and Income Inequality," *American Economic Review*, vol. 45 (1955), pp. 1–28; the thrust of his argument has been verified by Peter H. Lindert and Jeffrey G. Williamson, "Growth, Equalilty, and History," *Explorations in Economic History*, vol. 22 (1985), pp. 341–77.

15. One such work, which spent a year on the French best-seller lists and sold over a million copies, was Viviane Forrester, *L'horreur Économique* (Paris, 1996); for a critique see Alain Minc, *La mondialisation heureuse* (Paris, 1997). On the resilience of anti-capitalism in French political culture, see Philippe Maniére, *L'Aveuglement français* (Paris, 1998). For a wide-ranging and thoughtful account of "globalization," see Friedman, *The Lexus and the Olive Tree*.

16. Amartya Sen, "Poverty as Capability Deprivation," in his *Development as Freedom* (New York, 1999), pp. 87–110.

17. Quoted by Max Weber, *The Protestant Ethic and the Spirit of Capitalism*, p. 175, from Southey, *Life of Wesley* (2nd U.S., vol. 2, p. 308).

18. See Friedman, *The Lexus and the Olive Tree*, p. 245, and Michael T. Kaufman, *Soros: The Life and Times of a Messianic Billionaire* (New York, 2002), pp. 299–301.

ACKNOWLEDGMENTS

A number of scholars graciously agreed to read and comment upon individual chapters of this book or on more extensive portions of the manuscript. For their help, I am grateful to Yehoshua Arieli, Steven Beller, Peter Boettke, David Bromwich, John Patrick Diggins, Daniel Gordon, Jeffrey Herf, Mark Lilla, James van Horn Melton, Robert Schneider, Fritz Stern, Mack Walker, Elise Kimerling Wirtschafter, and Michael Zöller. Stephen Whitfield not only read the entire manuscript but helped sharpen the prose on virtually every page, an act of scholarly friendship for which I am particularly appreciative. Eli Muller read much of the manuscript and provided sound editorial advice. Steven Aschheim, Peter L. Berger, Peter Berkowitz, David Landes, Rainer Lepsius, Virgil Nemoianu, Melvin Richter, James Sheehan, and Noam Zion have provided encouragement over the course of this project. I treasure the ongoing advice, encouragement, and friendship of Peter Dougherty of Princeton University Press. My friend Eliot Cohen has provided a sounding board and a source of intellectual inspiration on a wide range of subjects. Larry Poos introduced me to demographic history; I thank him for that and for his promotion of research as chairman of the department of history at Catholic University. My colleagues in the department have provided an environment supportive of intellectual inquiry, and allowed me to combine teaching and research in a manner fructifying for both. After almost three decades, I remain grateful to Gerald Izenberg for inspiring me to go into the intellectual history business.

Funding for research on this project has come from the Catholic University of America, the Lynde and Harry Bradley Foundation, and the John M. Olin Foundation. A major revision of the manuscript took place in the lovely surroundings of the Rockefeller Foundation's Study Center in Bellagio, Italy, during the summer of 2001, where I profited from the advice of Philippe Manière, Manuel Pastor, Peter Schuck, and Alan Taylor.

I thank Carol Brown Janeway of Alfred A. Knopf for having taken on this project, and for guiding it from manuscript to book and from my mind to the market. I am also grateful to her colleagues at Knopf, especially Stephanie

Koven Katz, and the book's production editor, Kathleen Fridella. I am indebted to Susanna Sturgis for her highly competent copyediting of the manuscript.

This book is dedicated to my children: Eli, Sara, and Seffy. One motive for writing it was to offer them some guidance on making their way in a capitalist world. One advantage of having taken so long to complete it is that they are now old enough to read it. Not only have they been what economists call "durable consumption goods," providing me with more enduring pleasure than money can buy; in the final stages of completing this book they also served as factors of production. I thank our friend Roy Pinchot for contributing to their moral and intellectual capital by guiding them into the proper perplexities. I remain indebted to my grandmother, my parents, and my siblings, and particularly to my brother Michael for his minding of *tachles* while I thought about *schmonzes*. My wife, Sharon, was not only my partner in producing those to whom this work is dedicated, she was also the first reader and editor of virtually every chapter of the book. I am grateful to her for all that, and for much besides.

I benefited from opportunities to present my work at the History Department Colloquium of the Catholic University of America, the European History Seminar of the Johns Hopkins University, the German History Seminar at Georgetown University, the Center for Public Choice and the Kaplan Seminar on Political Economy at George Mason University, the European History Seminar of the University of Maryland, the Washington Area German History Seminar, the first convention of the Historical Society at Boston University, and the conference on "Pluralism and Relativism," organized by João Carlos Espada at Arrábida, Portugal. I am grateful to those who invited me, and to those who provided suggestions and criticism on each occasion.

This project has been long in gestation, and I have drawn ideas and patches of text from my previous books and from a number of articles, not always with direct acknowledgment. Here I have followed the dictim of Rabbi Meir of Vilna (quoted [and created] by Peter L. Berger in his book, *Redeeming Laughter*), "If an author cannot borrow from himself, from whom can he borrow?" I have borrowed in particular from "Communism, Anti-Semitism, and the Jews," *Commentary* (August 1988), pp. 28–39; "Justus Möser and the Conservative Critique of Early Modern Capitalism," *Central European History* 23: 2/3 (June/Sept., 1990), pp. 153–78; "Capitalism, Socialism, and Irony: Understanding Schumpeter in Context," *Critical Review: An Interdisciplinary Journal of Politics and Society* 13: 3/4 (1999) pp. 239–68; and "Pluralism and the Market," *Society* 37: 5 (July/August 2000), pp. 47–54.

INDEX

A NOTE ABOUT THE AUTHOR

Jerry Z. Muller is Professor of History at the Catholic University of America in Washington, D.C. He is the author of *The Other God That Failed: Hans Freyer and the Deradicalization of German Conservatism; Adam Smith in His Time and Ours: Designing the Decent Society;* and *Conservatism: An Anthology of Social and Political Thought from David Hume to the Present.*

A NOTE ON THE TYPE

The text of this book was composed in Trump Mediæval. Designed by Professor
Georg Trump (1896–1985) in the mid-1950s, Trump Mediæval was cut and cast by
the C. E. Weber Type Foundry of Stuttgart, Germany. The roman letter forms are
based on classical prototypes, but Professor Trump has imbued them with his own
unmistakable style. The italic letter forms, unlike those of so many other typefaces,
are closely related to their roman counterparts. The result is a truly contemporary
type, notable for both its legibility and its versatility.

Composed by Stratford Publishing Services, Inc., Brattleboro, Vermont

Printed and bound by Berryville Graphics, Berryville, Virginia

Designed by Iris Weinstein